THE
SECRET UNIVERSE
OF
NAMES

ROY FEINSON

Assisted by KB Imle

Overlook Duckwoth
New York • Woodstock • London

First published in the United States in 2004 by
Overlook Duckworth, Peter Mayer Publishers, Inc.
Woodstock, New York, and London

WOODSTOCK:
One Overlook Drive
Woodstock, NY 12498
www.overlookpress.com
[for individual orders, bulk and special sales, contact our Woodstock office]

NEW YORK:
141 Wooster Street
New York, NY 10012

LONDON:
90-93 Cowcross Street
London EC1M 6BF
inquires@duckworth-publishers.co.uk
www.ducknet.co.uk

∞ The paper used in this book meets the requirements for paper
permanence as described in the ANSI Z39.48-1992 standard.

Cataloging-in-Publication Data is available from the Library of Congress

Manufactured in the United States of America
FIRST EDITION
ISBN 1-58567-594-6 (US)
ISBN 0-7156-3337-6 (UK)
1 3 5 7 9 8 6 4 2

For
Sidney Feinson
1921–2003

Acknowledgments

They say that every person knows roughly two hundred people well enough to comment on their personalities. This book required such a wide range of experience in human behavior that it needed the cumulative insights of the following people. In first-name popularity order, they are:

David Feldman, John Nelson, Jonathan Cullen, Melissa Laituri, Christina Payne, Robert Brocke, Mark Norman, Nancy McConnell, Maria Nelson, Dennis Barton, Susan Clemens, Joe Mozdzen, Pam James, Philippa Strelitz, Hilary Feldman, Bonnie Smith, Leigh-Ann Watson, Joanne Karney, Marcia Feinson, Vicki Holland, and Lenka Bolkova and Henning Visser.

A particular thank-you goes to the researchers and assistant writers of the biographies in this book: Grace Kwon and Sophie Armondo. Their input and support was invaluable.

This book could not have been written were it not for the tireless work of KB Imle, who battened down the hatches and came through when it counted. Her writing skill and patience were just what the captain ordered.

Special gratitude goes to Peter "The Literary Lion" Miller and Peter Mayer of The Overlook Press for their patience and much-welcomed guidance as well as to my persnickety editor, Caroline Trefler.

Finally to Grace Kwon, whose support and encouragement in the long winter of this book kept the sun shining: Thank you for everything.

Preface

The debate over the neuro-mechanics of language has become increasingly argumentative ever since the Linguistic Society of Paris banned all discussion of the origins of language in 1866 in an attempt to calm the intellectual storm over the issue. When Charles Darwin joined the fray by suggesting that human speech might have evolved from animal cries and snorting, critics were quick to dismiss his hypothesis by dubbing it the "bow-wow" theory. Darwin promptly withdrew from the discussion.

In the 1980s the debate took a dramatic turn when Noam Chomsky, a leading linguist, proposed that children are born with specific skills which enable them to learn language.

Recently, the debate swung in favor of the Darwinian argument when prominent psycholinguist Philip Lieberman argued that human language, although significantly more sophisticated than animal communication, is not fundamentally different from other forms of animal communication. In his book *Human Language and the Reptilian Brain* (Harvard University Press), Lieberman makes the case that there is simply no language instinct and that language is yet another device to enhance survival and reproduction.

This book does not deal with general theories about the structure of sentences and grammar and is not a contender in the language debate per se. Neither is it a treatise on etymology (the origin of words), which tracks the journey of words through various cultures from the perspective of a linguist. Instead, it proposes the idea that words evolve into our language and culture because the very sounds in these words evoke a particular emotional resonance in humans. And that in addition, the very pronunciation of these sounds requires a specific distortion of the speaker's face, which reinforces the emotion-response of the listener. Since these visceral reactions stem from deeply imbedded reptilian hardwiring of the human brain, this book further suggests that reactions to these sounds in our own names can affect our self-image and the expectations others have of us.

These issues are explored and postulated as a theory that helps explain some peculiarities regarding the matter of our names:

- Why are people whose names begin with the letter **J** 250% more likely to become millionaires compared to people with names beginning with the letter **N**?
- Why are **I** people becoming doctors at four times the rate of **O** names?
- Why do the **Keith**s of the business world statistically outperform the **Nigel**s by almost 300%?
- Why do the **John**s, **Peter**s, **Katherine**s and **Janine**s of the world consistently earn more money than the **Cody**s, **Austin**s, **Alexis**' and **Brittany**s?
- Why does the corporate world spend tens of millions each year to develop names for their products?
- What mechanisms explain why the name **Emma** evokes stronger romantic feelings than the name **Kate**?
- Can names influence our behavior and affect our self-image?

- How would your life improve if you were to change your name?
- Why do the anagrams of names possess such an uncanny ability to describe their subjects?
- What are the unseen forces in our names that affect our destiny, and how can we harness them to ensure our children's success?

To answer these questions, I conducted a study using the initial letters of sixty-three million American first names and compared them to professional lists of successful people in a variety of fields. The results of this study, which are detailed in Chapter 5, suggest that there is indeed a link between our names and society's expectations. I am not suggesting that people with the same names will share exactly the same personality characteristics, but this book does conclude with an informal analysis of personality traits for each name, taking into account its component letters and sounds. The personal experiences of a number of people were used to confirm or deny these general characteristics in order to corroborate their accuracy and authenticity.

Naming our children or even choosing our own names gives us the opportunity to make a statement that will persist for the rest of our lives. *The Secret Universe of Names* provides a basis for understanding how that choice impacts our lives and the impressions it will leave on our family, coworkers, and peers.

Introduction

Even before meeting a new person, every one of us tends to form an image of that person based solely on his or her name. More often than not, we're surprised at how accurate our suppositions are. Although we might dismiss these incidents as being coincidence, we cannot overlook the possibility that we are responding to powerful mechanisms buried in our names.

Why for example, does the name **Blake** evoke an image of a strong and confident man, while the name **Lance** creates visions of suave sophistication? Why is it that the name **Cedric** imbues its owner with a sense of timidity and reserve, while **Hannah** manages to project softness and femininity?

The popularity of baby-naming books attests to our cultural obsession with trying to give our children names that will give them a heads-up in life. A group calling themselves Kabalarian Philosophers, using principles drawn from the ancient Hebrew scripts of the Kabala, believes that the forces in our names can be discerned from the numerical formula of the letters in each name. This mathematical principle is supposed to embody the "nine basic forces of conscious intelligence" that hold sway over our fate.

The subliminal power of names certainly doesn't go unnoticed by corporate America, which spends millions of dollars a year creating sparkling new brand names for their latest products. In 1972 Esso Oil Corporation spent more than $100 million dollars to change its name to Exxon. We can intuitively understand why. The mysterious connotations of the xx in Exxon evoke a more ruggedly masculine quality than the high-pitched sound of Esso.

The Name Lab is a San Franciscan company that specializes in the creation of artificial names designed to instill confidence in the products of their clients. They were responsible for naming Compaq, the world's first portable computer company, as well as Acura, the precisely engineered luxury car. Using a process they call constructional linguistics, small semantic elements like acura from accurate and excel from excellent are combined into symbolic names to evoke the properties of the product.

In contrast to the inordinate care taken by corporations in selecting product names, most parents devote an average of less than four hours to selecting a name for their baby, relying on either some archaic definition, the name of a relative, or a character from popular literature. Many celebrities change their names to evoke a more glamorous, exotic, dramatic, or comedic image while the rest of us plod through life bearing the burden of our often-insipid names. Since our names last for life, it's critical that we understand their impact on our psyches and the perceptions others have of us based solely on our names.

If you have any doubt that your name can have a substantial effect on your life, consider the study conducted by researchers from the University of Chicago and MIT. According to Professor of Economics Marianne Bertrand, the results of the study show substantial job discrimination based solely on one's first name. Using "white" first names on five thousand resumes sent in response to want ads, they compared the call-back percentage to those mailed out with "black" first names. The white names included, **Jill**, **Emily**, **Anne**, **Neil**,

Brett and **Greg**, while some of the black names were **Ebony**, **Rasheed**, **Tamika**, **Aisha**, **Kareem** and **Tyrone**. The startling results showed that "white" names had a 50% higher frequency of responses from prospective employers.

There is, however, a more prosaic and "human" explanation for these effects that lies in the power of names to manipulate people's emotions, and ignoring these effects could be a potentially costly mistake for our children's future.

But choosing a anme is not always so black and white. Ignoring the ability of our names to manipulate people's emotions could be a potentially costly mistake for our children's future.

What's Really In a Name?

What's in a name?
That which we call a rose by any other name would smell as sweet.
So Romeo would, were he not Romeo called,
Retain that dear perfection which he owes.

In this lover's lament from Shakespeare's *Romeo and Juliet*, a lovelorn Juliet speculates how Romeo's personality might be altered if he were to change his name. Although Juliet argues that Romeo's essence would be unaffected by his a new name, Shakespeare was clearly aware of the profound impact that his characters' names would leave on his audiences' imagination.

In his quest to find a name to embody his teenage hero's lusty passions, and likely sensing that subliminal cues in names can stimulate our senses, Shakespeare mutated the word *romance* to create Romeo. A slow-motion replay of the name's pronunciation reveals the following effects.

R-o-m-e-o

As the initial letter of the color red, the universal color of sexual arousal, the **R** radiates carnality as it rolls off the tongue in a rough simulation of a contented cat, a lover's call to arms, and the promise of dark passions. It is the classic full-bodied, red-blooded letter full of sexual tension and sensuality embodied in the words ravish, racy, rapture, reproductive, relish, randy and ravage.

r-O-m-e-o

The very pronunciation of the letter **O** forms the mouth into an expression of surprise and sexual ecstasy, and

explains why the **O** is associated with sudden emotional surges as in ooh, orgasm, oo-la-la, oh-oh, oops and ouch. This facial cue is so powerful that even chimpanzees recognize this expression. Hooting an ooo ooo sound when excited or aroused, their mouths likewise form the shape of an **O**.

r-o-M-e-o

The melodiously mellow hum of the letter **M** begins the second syllable, evoking feelings of motherly warmth and tenderness. The physical cues spawned by its pronunciation evoke the image of a light kiss as the lips are softly pursed together. Its moderating influence accounts for its appearance in the word mother of almost every language on earth: mutter in German, mer in Vietnamese, imma in Sanskrit and Hebrew, matka in Polish, and mama in Zulu. Perhaps this is the reason why infants make an umm sound when they communicate their need for mother's milk and why chimpanzees smack their lips with an mmm sound when signifying approval.

r-o-m-E-o

When pronounced even silently, the letter **E** forces the face into a shape that is universally recognizable as a wry smile (as in "say cheese"). As we shall see in upcoming chapters, these facial expressions can have powerful effects on the emotions of the listener, which explains the emotional elements embedded in the words egads, eroticism, excitement, erogenous, ecstasy, earnest, eek, envy, exuberance, expressive and empathetic.

So when the letters of **R-O-M-E-O** are combined into this single name, their subconscious cues are powerful and persuasive. It's no coincidence that we think of Romeo and Juliet as lovelorn sweethearts. For when we examine the vowel pattern in the word lovelorn, we find that the same sequence of vowels (o-e-o) appears in the word Romeo! These identical vowel patterns are also found in the sexually charged words bordello, whoredom, womenfolk and Bolero, Ravel's sensual musical opus popularized by the movie 10.

It was with this instinctive understanding of the power of emotionally loaded letters that Shakespeare created the name that has become synonymous with a vigorously potent lover.

The inherent effects of how letters in a name can define an individual's personality is not limited to masters of literature. Consider the more contemporary example of The Simpsons, the longest-running television show still in production. When series creator Matt Groening designed the characters for this dysfunctional but sympathetic family, he carefully—perhaps unconsciously—selected names for his four-fingered family members that would herald their personality traits.

Homer, the hapless yet happy-go-lucky patriarch, sports a name comprised entirely of gently flowing letters without the sharp edges of explosive bilabials. The almost-whispered letter **H** is the defining letter of home, hearth, hope and heart, and when it is combined with the letter **M** (the symbol of motherly tenderness), it creates words suffused with the unambiguous down-home qualities of homely, home, hombre and homily. That's

why no matter how extreme or impulsive his behavior, the audience can be confident that Homer will quickly snap back into his munificent role.

And then there's Marge, the patient and long-suffering homemaker. Her name studiously begins with the classic letter of maternal warmth, emphasizing her unbreakable bond to her brood. But there's an edgy side to her name too, revealed by the gruff letter **G**, which is the letter of grumpy, growl, grab, grapple, gruel and glum. However, it's significant that the **G** in Marge is the softly pronounced version of the letter, which displays fewer of the snappish implications of the "hard" **G**. These qualities are strongly reflected in the benevolent themes of words like genuflect, genial, genuine and gentility.

Bart's hyperactive personality couldn't be more aptly telegraphed by his name. Not only is it an anagram of brat, but the name also begins with the bilabial letter **B** and ends with the fricative letter **T**, which requires the speaker respectively to make an explosive sound with his lips and sharp contact with his or her tongue against the palette. The **BR** combination of letters imparts an unmistakable sense of intense activity that we find in the words bright, brilliant, brash, brave, breezy and brusque, while the letter **T**, triumphantly tooting the name's termination, is associated with the sharp-witted spirit of tang, talent, turmoil, tweak and tallyho.

Like Homer, Lisa—the erudite, music-loving environmentalist of the family—has a name with no hard edges. The letter **L** imparts a gentle lilt to the name's pronunciation, which is why it is the standard bearer of life, liberty, love and learning. It is also the letter of musical expression as seen in words like lullaby, lyrical, Lorelei, and la-la-la. Finally, the softly sensual letter S hints at her as-yet-unrealized sexuality.

Baby Maggie is Marge's name in miniature. Since words that end with the high-pitched -ie sound are invariably associated with youth and innocence (baby, bootie, doggy and kitty), Groening simply appended the infantilizing sound to the end of her name to symbolize her terminal infancy.

LETTER POWER

Illustrations of the powerful effects of letters in words proliferate in literature. Notice how Tennyson's alliteration of the letter **M**, in "The Princess," resonates with our yearning for the maternal embrace:

> *Sweeter thy voice, but every sound is sweet;*
> *Myriads of rivulets hurrying thro' the lawn,*
> *The moan of doves in immemorial elms,*
> *And murmuring of innumerable bees.*

While, to infuse his poem "A Red, Red Rose" with its romantic textures, Robert Burns completely avoided the discordant tones of the initial letters **B, K**, **D, C** and **G**, and opted instead for softly sensual **R**s, **M**s, **L**s, and **O**s.

> *O my Luve's like a red, red rose*
> *That's newly sprung in June;*
> *O my Luve's like the melodie*
> *That's sweetly played in tune.*

Whether or not these techniques are conscious manifestations of their authors, subliminal attempts to influence our emotions crop up frequently in literature, pop culture and advertising. As noted by Herbert Barry, a psychologist from the University of Pittsburgh, Jane Austen communicated the personalities of her characters through her choice of names. When she wished to paint her characters as egotistical or foolish she ended their first names in an **E**, as in Jane Bennet, George Wicham, Lady Catherine, Marianne Dashwood, Catherine Morland and Anne Elliott. But when the letter was used to begin people's names, as in the name of her brother Edward, they were usually wise and altruistic: Elizabeth Bennet, Elinor Dashwood, Edward Ferrars, Eleanor Tilney, Edmund Bertram and Emma Woodhouse.

NAMES: INSIDE & OUT

An anagram is created by rearranging the letters of one word to form another word, using each letter only once. These new words have an uncanny ability to reflect the characteristics of their subjects by communicating emotional content through the letters of the original name. Although it's tempting to attribute many of these extraordinary anagrams to supernatural forces, there is a far more prosaic explanation in the context of letter-sounds. Words are simply an amalgamation of letters, and since each letter of the alphabet has a particular emotional resonance, it doesn't seem to matter in what order these letters are arranged. The overall gist remains surprisingly unchanged.

This effect can be seen in **Axl Rose**'s stage name, which complements the sneering sexuality of his rocker image in the anagram **oral sex**. For that matter, steely-eyed **Clint Eastwood**'s name also summarizes his remarkable career with the anagram: **old west action**. **James Taylor** croons confidently behind his anagram of **oral majesty**, and the droopy eyes of blues maestro **Eric Clapton** might be explained through the single-worded anagram: **narcoleptic**. If Mia Farrow had done her homework, she might have known in advance that **Woody Allen** was a **lewd loony**.

This phenomenon of how letters alone are able to influence the meaning of words explains why so many everyday words retain their meanings when their letters are rearranged: **evil is vile**, we are **silent** when we **listen**, and a **mother-in-law** is a **Hitler woman**. **Striptease** is an anagram of **tit, ass, peer**; we become enraged when **angered**; **death** is **hated**; a **dormitory** is a **dirty room**; an **elegant man** is a **gentleman** and **eleven plus two** is equal to **twelve plus one**.

Perhaps a subtle manipulation of the public by the corporate world is evidenced in the subliminal messages found in the name of **Crest Toothpaste**—an anagram of **apt tooth secrets**—and **Pepsi Cola**, which converts into **social pep**. Consider, too, the powerful subconscious advertising embedded in the anagram of **Apple Macintosh—laptop machines**; and **Western Union**, which translates into **no wire unsent**; or **Yale University** which is an anagram of **entirely USA ivy**.

Even the media seems to be trying to influence us with subtle messages. **Newsweek magazine** is an anagram of **We Eke Amazing News**, and **Ted Koppel** is happily still the man behind the **Inlighten** anagram for **Nightline**.

If we are to take these notions seriously, we could believe that **Charles Manson** was predisposed to be a persuasive manslayer because his name is an anagram of **slasher conman**. In politics we find **Ronald Wilson Reagan** to be an anagram of a **long-insane warlord**, the anagram of **George Bush** is **he bugs Gore**. And in a rare example of an anagram that also happens to be a pun, **Tipper Gore** is revealed to be an **ego tripper**. Are members of the **pro-life** group revealing their true intention to overturn the Supreme Court's ruling on abortion in their anagram **flip Roe**?

So it's not hard to understand why parents might choose **Abby** as the name for their **baby**, but might think twice before naming their son **Mervin** (**vermin**) or their daughter **Lana** or **Kristen** (**anal** and **stinker**). One might expect baby **Cameron** to **romance** his way to success, but is little **Irving** doomed to remain a **virgin**?

The Universal Language 2

Language is such an integral component of the human experience that even when we have no one to listen, we talk to our pets, our plants and ourselves. So how and why did language evolve? There is little argument over *why* it developed—language simply imparts users an enormous competitive benefit over groups that do not have any other one. An advantage like this would enable a particular culture to overwhelm and usurp the resources of another culture that doesn't possess one, in turn propelling the evolution of even more sophisticated languages. The question of *how* language evolved, on the other hand, is still under fierce debate.

One thing, however, is clear. Humans exhibit an autonomous response to sounds from the moment they're born. Millions of years before language evolved, humans and other animals were using grunts and primal sounds to communicate their emotions. Over time, the process of evolution has hardwired our reactions to these sounds, with profound effects and implications for how we respond to words and names today.

Inside the skull of virtually every vertebrate on earth we find a relatively small mass of neural fibers known as the medulla oblongata, also known as the reptilian brain. This primitive structure is responsible for basic survival functions in all animals—fight, flight, hunger, sex and fear. Because it appeared relatively early on in the evolution of life, we share its effects with crocodiles, frogs, lions and probably with dinosaurs as well.

It is ground-zero to our instincts and a hallmark of all complex biological beings.

Around the time of the dinosaurs, another section of brain matter began to evolve in an inconsequential group of animals known as mammals. What we now call the cerebellum, also called the mammalian brain, is regarded as the seat of emotions. It gives us additional survival skills and imparts the ability to feel emotions of tenderness, anger, anxiety, sadness and adoration. It also enables us to be social and drives our desire to communicate and understand the roles of dominance and submission, selfishness and altruism. This is where we differ from reptiles and amphibians, but what we have in common with other mammals.

The third part of the brain, the cerebral cortex, is where conscious rational thought occurs. And it is here that man's brain exhibits the only significant departure from the norm for all animals. Within the cortex reside specialized areas with the ability for self-reflection, facial recognition and highly advanced cognitive thought. Our cerebral cortex is so advanced, in fact, that it's capable of overriding the two other parts of our brain. It is the mark of our humanity. But if we simply bask in its glory and ignore the influence of our reptilian and mammalian brains, we're in danger of overlooking some very subtle but important survival techniques.

On its most basic level, our reptilian brain is hardwired to produce adrenaline in the presence of unexpected sounds. Yell "BOO" to the person sitting next to you and you will see this reflex in action. But it's not simply the volume of the sound that produces this effect—it's the way the sound of the word stands in contrast to background sounds. Our brains are tuned to notice differences in the environment, which is why a flashing light is so much more visible than a static one, and why a cat is more likely to chase after a running mouse than a stationary one.

Most mammals respond to a hiss in a similar fashion. Our reptilian brains short-circuit our cognitive-thinking processes and we find ourselves instinctively on the alert for a possible snake. That's why a cat's hiss is so effective at scaring off potential attackers. But as we shall see, there is a wide range of sounds—some obvious, some subtle—to which we are also programmed to respond.

To illustrate what a crucial role this mammalian predisposition plays in understanding the meaning of sounds, consider the prairie dog. Prairie dogs spend their lives in constant communication with each other using a spoken language surpassed only by our own. Living communally in massive coteries numbering up to 100 million individuals, they even display the components of rudimentary sentence construction. For example, when an alarm call is sounded to describe an approaching man, the noun for man is modified by an additional sound when the man is carrying a gun. The alarm then describes a gun-man or hunter. By combining "adjectives" with "nouns," prairie dogs have a vocabulary that approaches some two hundred words and phrases.

Elephants have evolved a sophisticated long-distance form of communication that originates from low frequency rumbles in their stomachs. These long-wavelength sounds, which carry over enormous distances, can be transmitted through the ground and "heard" by sensitive organelles in the elephants' feet. While this language doesn't display the sophistication of other species', it's clear that information about the fundamental four Fs of survival (food, flight, fight and sex) can be readily transmitted from herd to herd.

Cats, on the other hand, have discovered an even more efficient form of communication—silence. Many theories as to why cats purr have been postulated; ranging from the sound being an expression of contentment, or that purring helps to strengthen bones (at twenty-seven to forty-four hertz, it might be similar to ultrasound). But to really understand this clever device, consider what happens when a cat stops purring. A clowder of cats lying contentedly under a tree purrs softly to signal that all is well. But if one of the cats spots a rabbit strolling by and wants to alert the group to the rabbit's presence, it simply stops purring. The sudden silence instantly alerts the other cats that something is afoot. This clever device avoids sudden movements or noise that might scare off the prey. Every cat then stops purring and the hunt begins. In short, by maintaining a low-energy purr at times of rest, the absence of sound becomes a significant communication device. Human beings react in a similar fashion when we perceive a sudden eerie silence.

THE LANGUAGE COMPETITION

Scientists agree that early hominids (protohumans) lived in small groups of individuals dominated by one or two alpha males. These groups divided resource-gathering duties, shared in providing a common defense and provided a stable structure for reproduction. But troop size was necessarily limited in number because dominant males could only keep control over fifty individuals or so before social instabilities would spin off new factions and spawn additional territories. In small groups of individuals, there was no evolutionary pressure to form sophisticated language. With the exception of the growling, shrieking, and hooting that we find in primates today, there's no reason to suspect that hominids had the brain pathways capable of the complex syntax necessary for true language.

However, as these protohuman groups slowly established themselves as the dominant predator on the African veldt, they soon found themselves in competition for resources with rival groups of hominids. Small skirmishes and territorial contests were inevitable, which meant that evolutionary pressure was coming primarily from intraspecies competition. At this point, something dramatic occurred in man's history. Even though a group of fifty individuals was more than sufficient to ward off attacks by saber-toothed tigers, leopards and lions, with the emergence of his fellow man as his chief predator, there was a powerful reason to increase one's group size. Groups with larger populations had an enormous advantage in a clash with a smaller group. However, since large groups of individuals were inherently unstable, something had to change. And the most obvious lever of change was the evolution of effective communication, allowing warfare and group defense to be coordinated on a large scale.

It was undoubtedly at this point that the first simple words were formed. These words were by necessity concise and easy to pronounce, and probably associated with actions and objects on the order of "throw stones," "stop here," "look out," "go home" and "get sticks." We can see the residual effects of these early attempts at word and sentence development in our own language today. Most verbs associated with immediate action tend to be single-syllable words loaded with one or more explosive "stop-consonants": kick, go, jump, sit, look, kill, stab, run, push, beat, break, cut, etc. The terse structure of these words still echoes in the human brain, which responds far more readily to a cry of "Duck!" than it does to "lower your head!"

Early man accumulated these words and benefited from the subsequent improvements in his social organization. The group could now communicate and collaborate to ostracize an unwanted individual or overthrow an overly aggressive leader. Under such pressures, individuals would have to conform to the expectations of the group, and the alpha male was forced to substitute his brute aggression with a more cooperative form of

leadership. Groups that improved their internal communication flourished and dominated groups that failed to do so. To put it another way, if you couldn't communicate efficiently, your resources were usurped, your females kidnapped and your genetic lineage destroyed. Due to this strong evolutionary pressure, group sizes began to increase, from nomadic tribes of two hundred, to small settlements of five hundred, to towns of thousands, and ultimately to cities and states of millions of people. And with the emergence of these larger populations came the need for an even more efficient form of communication: writing and an alphabet.

ALPHABET SOUP

Knowledge proved to be power. As societies became increasingly complex and languages more sophisticated, power became concentrated in the hands of those who commanded the most information, spurring the next great leap over the communication divide: the invention of writing, which facilitated the transfer of knowledge among allies and between generations.

Three basic strategies of writing emerged. The first idea was to use logograms in which one symbol represented one word. While this is the basic idea of the Chinese writing system, some remnants of this logographic technique still persist in modern English in the use of symbols (%, $ and @) and numerals.

The second strategy employs a system in which each syllable is allocated a sign. The word barber, therefore, would require two distinct symbols. Although this somewhat awkward system requires many convoluted techniques to implement, some examples persist, like the Kana system used by the Japanese today for foreign words.

The third system of writing, which employs an alphabet, seems quite simple. But developing a system like this (and convincing everyone to agree on it) was a major human achievement. It can be traced back to Egyptian hieroglyphs, which used symbols to represent the twenty-four Egyptian consonants. But it was the Semites, around 4,000 years ago, who took the step of discarding all logograms, relying solely on their alphabet to spell words. Most alphabets today consist of a manageable twenty to thirty letters, representing the bulk of sounds that can be made by the human vocal system. Any sounds (called phonemes) not directly represented can easily be created by two letter combinations like -sh and -th.

The modern English alphabet is a study in theft. In the fourth century AD, Bishop Ulfilas created the first Germanic language alphabet with characters pilfered from the Greek, Roman and Runic alphabets. Even now our alphabet undergoes periodic changes as the need arises, as attested to by the recent additions of the W and the V, which arrived less than a thousand years ago.

THE EMERGENCE OF ENGLISH

Modern languages are complex and dynamic living entities whose form is the culmination of thousands of years of evolution in which words and sounds quietly competed in a fierce Darwinian struggle for survival. As words were absorbed into the vocabulary, others were relegated to extinction and fossilization until, after countless cycles of crossbreeding, a language came to embody the cultures of the people that contributed to its development.

As troops of early man spilled out of lush African forests into a Europe emerging from an ice age, fierce competition for resources in the bleak environment made the development of sophisticated languages even more vital. The history of European languages is the by-product of myriad European wars executed by fierce gangs of Viking, Greek, Roman, Gallic and Germanic warriors. Over time, the languages of the conquerors

congealed with those of the defeated, before coalescing on a trivial island in the North Atlantic known today as the British Isles.

As noted in the comprehensive work, *The Story of English* (Robert McCrum, William Mccran, Robert McNeil, Viking, 1997), English has emerged from its obscure roots to become the most widely used language in human history; it is spoken as either a primary or secondary language by over one billion people.

BRAVE NEW WORDS

We can often deduce at what point a particular word entered our language purely by evaluating the word's simplicity. Think about domain names on the Internet. When we see a website called Books.com, Buy.com or Frames.com, we know that these sites must have been reserved fairly early in the creation of the Internet in comparison to sites with names like Buybookshere.com or ExclamationMall.com. As previously discussed, words associated with fundamental survival needs tend to be short and simple (cow, dog, head, face, ear, eye, nose, toe, stone) while more conceptual words, which arrived much later, were naturally more intricate and complex (family, redemption, atmosphere, regardless, inconsequential).

This concept also affects the way people perceive our names. Names that are short, abrupt and simple, tend to signify no-nonsense, down-to-earth, active individuals, while longer multi-syllabled names evoke complex and imaginative personalities. Consider the example of Percival. Its indulgent three-syllabled complexity requires extra work simply to pronounce and suggests a self-important individual. The more succinct rendering of Percy, on the other hand, connotes a far more practical and unpretentious fellow. Since this individual could elect to use either version, the one he chooses says a great deal about who he is as a person.

Like all living things, languages must adapt to keep pace with a changing environment. A flexible vocabulary is an indication of a robust civilization, and one can, in fact, take the pulse of a culture's economic growth by measuring the frequency with which new words are incorporated to its language. Driven by technology and teenage slang, American English adds hundreds of new words each year. We not only invent new words, like fax, e-trade, shockjock, transgender and phat, we also find new meanings for old words, like spam (junk e-mail), boot (start a computer) and fly (very agreeable).

In an effort to establish how people actually make up words, researcher Margaret Manus asked a group of people from different language backgrounds to invent words to describe specific actions. One group was asked to invent a word that depicted the act of "scraping the black stuff off overdone toast." Interestingly, even though many of the respondents created words using the **S**, **K** and **R** sounds from the original word scrape, the letter **P** was not chosen with any more frequency than the letter appears in English in general. This shows how effective the **SKR** combination is in setting our teeth on edge with words like screech, scream, scrawl, scruff and scratch. Asked to create a word for the spikes on a hairbrush, the sharp toned letter **B** occurred in almost 60% of these words, while the soft letters **H**, **S** and **V** failed to be chosen even once.

Of course, it's much easier to steal words than to invent new ones. That's why we readily adopt words from other cultures such as sushi, kamikaze and karaoke from Japan, or orange and pepper from the Orient, and chutzpah and schlep from Yiddish. This carefree approach to adding new words to its lexicon mirrors the American attitude that change is good and that anything is possible. The same cannot be said for Britain, the birthplace of English, where there is often strong resistance to such change. In fact, English as spoken by the English is a topic of concern taken up even by Parliament, where there is a feeling that the mother tongue is being destroyed by the uncouth Americans.

LANGUAGE AS A REFLECTION OF CULTURE

If a name can convey the personality of an individual, it's arguable that a language can communicate the personality of a culture.

Germanic languages for example, consist largely of sharp, precise guttural tones, which perhaps unfairly stereotype Germans as a rigid, authority-fearing, regulation-infatuated people. In the United States, however, where individual expression and free thinking is worshipped, it's not surprising that we find casual speech, loose phrasing and slang the order of the day.

French, on the other hand, with its universally pleasing, smoothly flowing (if somewhat nasal) syntax, reflects a people in love with the delicate pleasures of life and love. This is, after all, the country that perfected the rules of chivalry and courtly love, and established the world's first restaurants.

Neighboring Italy sports a full-blooded romance language crammed with passionate rolling Rs and emotive vowel sounds, which aptly mirrors the passions of this hot-blooded Mediterranean culture. The British upper classes clearly reveal their aspiration for status in their heavily affected "Queen's English." This overly exaggerated accent is a relatively recent fabrication, stemming from the encroachment on their status by the newly moneyed middle classes during the Industrial Revolution.

THE NEED FOR WORDS

In the quest to uncover the roots of English words, etymologists and linguistic anthropologists focus on the fragments of Greek and Latin words that partially account for our vocabulary. And while it's interesting to know from whence these words emerged, all this research misses the real question. Instead of asking where our words came from, we must first understand why we retain certain words and discard others. Sometimes we choose words simply because we're tickled by their sound and structure, for words like tranquil, defrocked and quartz do have an indefinable aesthetic quality. (Occasionally we do make mistakes though; like the foreign couple who named their daughter after the most beautiful English word they'd ever heard: Diarrhea). Nonetheless, each of us subconsciously casts a vote for a word's existence simply by using it in our speech and writing.

We usually retain words that resonate with our primal past. Early man used hand gestures, facial expressions, grunts, gasps, murmurs and bellows to communicate emotional states, and although we'll never know precisely what these sounds were, they likely would have included threat noises (hiss, grr, tsk tsk), warning sounds (psst, shh), expressions of love (mmm, ooh, aah), violence (boo, bang, break) and surprise (ooh, eek, oops, eep). Although there are cultural variations—in Mandarin Chinese, dogs say wang instead of woof, and cats grr instead of purr—there are still significant structures common to every language on earth

At the core of every language are the building blocks called phonemes—letters or groups of letters that form the twenty or so basic sounds that create all words. Because all these sounds are generated from the rather restricted set of larynx, chest, mouth and tongue structures that all humans share, they do not vary significantly from language to language. But when used in combination with each other, these simple sounds can create an infinite number of words that we can use to communicate the complex ideas that define our species. These fundamental sounds did not evolve arbitrarily. They arose from the guttural grunts and primal screams of our hominid ancestors and were shaped by millions of years of trial and error on the competitive African plains. Through the process of natural selection, their evolutionary imprint has become deeply embedded in our brains, affecting our responses to words and, consequently, our reactions to our names.

FACIAL CUES

Facial expressions are almost certainly the most primitive form of language and are universal throughout every culture on the planet. The ability to interpret facial contortions depicting happiness (smile), sadness (frown), anxiety (puckered brow), anger (frown and puckered brow), and surprise (wide open mouth) is deeply ingrained in the mammalian brain. Not only do infants communicate their emotional states through these techniques, but humans are also able to read the emotive states of other social carnivores (dogs, ferrets, and chimpanzees, for example) through their facial signals. Interestingly enough, even congenitally blind people make faces to express their mood, proving that these facial distortions are part of a powerfully ingrained heritage.

The ability to interpret these facial distortions is so important to the survival of social animals that it provides an important clue into the origins of language. It's very evident that word pronunciation has a marked effect on the expressions of the face. Try saying cheese without a slight smile, or ow without forming your mouth in a circle. Given this, it's possible that language evolved as an extension of facial cues. But, while facial expressions of pain are sufficient to alert a small group of nearby individuals to the presence of danger, it is not a particularly effective means of communication when the group size is larger. Instead of simply making a face of pain, emitting a sound that communicates that pain would signal the danger to a larger number of people. These sounds would not be arbitrary, but formed from sounds that utilized the same facial expressions that represent the emotion being communicated.

Thus, sounds of pain and surprise, made with an

open-mouthed expression of pain, would logically contain a high proportion of vowel sounds, since vowels are the only letters that can be formed with an open mouth. This is why ooh, aah, ow, oops, eek, yow are such universal expressions of quick surprise.

As we shall see, humans, as preeminently social animals, usurped a wide range of these sounds to convey their wide spectrum of emotional states. These were the sounds that came to form the building blocks of our now richly diverse languages.

How Sounds Affect Our Mood

THE SCREAM

There is nothing more riveting than a scream of terror. Like fingernails on a chalkboard, it has the power to reach into our reptilian brain, trigger an adrenaline rush and a feeling of unshakable unease. Nevertheless, even though a scream is the most basic word in our vocabulary and understood by every mammal on earth, there are screams and there are screams.

Women shriek with fear; men bellow. This isn't to say that men are incapable of screaming, but the purpose of the female fear response is usually different from that of the male response. The primary intention of the female scream is to alert others of potential danger and to elicit the help of nearby people. But the problem with making such a loud noise is that it might alert predators that can take advantage of the individual's distress as well as potential rescuers. A scream must, therefore, alert only those close enough to help before quickly dissipating into the air. Because high-frequency sounds are absorbed by the air far more readily than low-frequency sounds, the high-pitched female scream is perfect for summoning help without signaling other predators. In contrast to the female, when a man expresses fear, it's usually with a low-pitched terror-bellow designed to intimidate the source of the danger and discourage other predators. The deeper the tone, the more effective the threat, since such resonance can only be effected by a large chest cavity.

We find similar behavior in canines. When a dog defends its territory, its bark is low and threatening, but if it becomes injured and cannot stand its ground, it changes its tune to a high-pitched yelp. English words convey these masculine and feminine qualities by their use of low- or high-frequency letters; male responses are booming, bellowing, blustering, brandishing, breast-beating, brazen, brawny and brutish, while females squeal, scream, screech, shriek, squawk, squeak and scurry.

THE SOOTHING

The gentle tones of the shh sound have the opposite effect of a scream, and millions of years of mammalian evolution has also hardwired our responses to its high pitch. Mothers universally use some form of it to hush crying babies and comfort restless children, so it's no wonder that the shh sound has percolated into our language to become synonymous with all things soft and retiring: shy, shun, shrug, shroud, shame, shrink and shrivel. It even has a similar effect when it appears at the ends of words, as in hush, mush, plush, slush, blush and diminish.

The soothing aspects of the high-pitched shh sound explain why it occurs five times more commonly in female names as male names. Notice how the traditional meanings of these names reflect its feminizing quality: Shasa (precious water), Shaquille (pretty), Shauna (merciful God), Sheena (gracious), Sheera (song), Sheri (beloved), Sherise (grace) and Shifra (beautiful), the name of the Hebrew midwife who refused the order of Pharaoh to kill newborn Jewish males.

When high-pitched sounds occur at the end of names, they have a feminizing effect. In a study conducted in 1992 by Dr. Albert Mehrabian of the University of California, Los Angeles, in which respondents listed the names they felt inferred femininity, over 70% of the top twenty most highly rated names ended with a high-frequency sound including Bunny, Barbie, Fifi, Missy, Susie, Katie, Didi, Melody, Crissy, Daisy and Honey.

SOUNDS OF THE HUNT

A number of our communication techniques evolved from the endeavors of our prehistoric ancestors as cooperative hunter-gatherers. We can see contemporary remnants and examples of these words as in the speech of the Namibian !Kung bushmen of Southwest Africa, whose language is substantially comprised of high-frequency clicks made by contact with the side, top, and bottom of the tongue against the palate.

What is significant about these sounds is that their high-frequency tones have the unique property of being loud when one is close to the speaker but then dropping off rapidly as the distance from the source increases. This makes such sounds ideal for communicating in the presence of prey.

Although English has no click sounds in its lexicon, it does employ similar techniques as in high-pitched warning sounds like psst, shh, and shush—perfect for alerting nearby allies without revealing one's position.

SOUNDS OF THE FEMME

In primitive societies, the consensus is that the female of the species played only a minor role in protecting the group from prey animals and roving bands of competitors. They therefore had little use for the low-frequency sounds that accompany aggressive male behavior. Instead of the large voice boxes (Adam's apples) found

in their male counterparts, the female vocal system is designed to generate the high-frequency tones that we find so universally soothing. In fact, when mothers speak to their children, they accentuate the high frequencies in their words and speak in a kind of motherese that differs in pitch from speech used in conversation with adults. Mothers also end many of their words with a rising pitch—even when not asking a question—and use this technique to diminutize many words: cat becomes kitty; blanket, blankie; dog, doggy; mother, mommy; and father, daddy. Children's names are also converted through this process, with John becoming Johnny, Dan becoming Danny, and so on. The French version is -ette, resulting in Paulette, Juliette, Yvette, Annette, Lynette, while in Ireland the -in suffix denotes the diminution seen in the names: Benjamin, Colin, Darrin and Devin.

Although expressed differently in each language, this process of diminutizing words is used by cultures across the world and plays a significant role in establishing the mother-child bond. Since motherese is used on children who are too young to actually understand the actual words, it is clear that mothers are communicating the feeling of comfort and reassurance through the use of these higher-pitched tones. The next section demonstrates how we retain these responses as adults, and how these sounds affect our psychological reactions to names.

LETTERS OF MOOD

Consider the effect of words containing the letter M. The mm sound evokes feelings of maternal warmth as in mother's milk, mollify, summer and mammary. Evidence that our response to the M sound is innate and cross-cultural comes from the fact that the word mother is dominated by the letter M in virtually every language on earth: mater (Latin), mere (French), madre (Spanish), mer (Vietnamese), mãe (Portuguese), mama (Zulu), imma in Sanskrit and Hebrew, matka in Polish. It is also the initial letter of the archetypal mother image Madonna (the Virgin Mary).

The strong psychological effects of the M have not been ignored by the entertainment industry, where names are routinely chosen to maximize feminine affection. Norma Jean Baker changed her name to Marilyn Monroe to enhance the mammalian aspects of her personality and became a feminine icon. The little trick seemed to have worked for a number of famous women: Mary Tyler Moore, Marla Maples, Marsha Mason, Marlee Matlin, Maid Marian, Melissa Manchester and even the gender-erratic Marilyn Manson.

But what's good for the goose isn't always good for the gander: it was only when Marion Michael Morrison shed the maternal mantle of his MMM initials and adopted the manly moniker of John Wayne that his star rose and never dimmed.

LETTERS OF EXPRESSION (THE VOWELS)

Humans had evolved a sophisticated system of facial expressions and hand signals millions of years before the development of language. Although largely replaced today by the spoken word, these cues are still an important means of expressing emotion. Anyone who travels to a foreign country where they're unable to speak the local language will find little difficulty in communicating their basic needs with hand and facial gestures alone. Because these signals are genetically hardwired into our brains, people from every culture instinctively recognize a smile, a frown or a look of anger. It's also not uncommon for people to supplement the spoken word with facial signals, as when they convert a statement to a question by raising their eyebrows, or change a remark into the negative by shaking their heads.

The defining characteristic of the vowels A, E, I, O, U, and occasionally Y, is that, when pronounced, the speaker's tongue doesn't make physical contact with the lips or palate. Instead, he modifies the shape of his mouth to alter the airflow from the lungs, and by reshaping his face, he unconsciously communicates the emotional state embedded in the very words he is pronouncing.

This is why people who are surprised say oops, ow, ooh, oh-oh and oy veh, and why the universal method of getting people to appear happy in photographs is to have them say cheese. It also explains the high percentage of vowels in words that convey the basic emotions of anger (aargh), happiness (yay, yeah), surprise (ooh), playfulness (yee-ha), excitement (whee), disgust (ugh, yuck), fear (eek) and pain (ow, uh, ouch).

WORDS OF WARNING

Anyone who has had a close encounter with a snarling dog has probably found himself or herself fixated on the surprisingly large canine teeth exposed by the drawing back of the dog's upper lip. The white teeth are starkly contrasted against the black shadows of the mouth cavity and accentuated by a threatening low-frequency growl. This signal of warning is universal and is even employed by humans themselves when scolding a dog with their own version of a snarl: "bad dog!" The explosive low-frequency B sound is a powerful attention-getter, and when combined with the letter A, it forces our mouths open and retracts our upper lip to expose our own (somewhat stunted) canines. Even the sharply pronounced letter D at the end reinforces the terse quality of the aggressive signal. It's not surprising that dogs are able to get the message without actually understanding the word itself.

Because of the powerfully aggressive qualities of these letters, the baleful ba sound has become synonymous with aggressive words expressing threats: We bark orders, badger opponents, bash enemies, batter our eggs, bang drums, banish our fears and fear the bastard barbarians. And from the instinctive reaction to the grr of a growling dog, we find the gr- phoneme conveying a cautionary tone, in the words grouch, grizzly, gruff, grate, grave and grind. In case you're wondering how this applies to the commonly used gr word great, consider that the original meaning of the word great in Old English was coarse, and in later years, the word was used to describe something powerful and fearsome, as in "Arthur was a great King." Only recently has the word been corrupted into "I'm great at math."

As already mentioned, all animals exhibit a universally instinctive response to the sound of hissing; a genetic memory of the dangers posed by a snake preparing to strike. This explains why so many English words that begin with an ss sound remind us of a sly snake: sinister, slinky, sinewy, sloppy, slick, slimy, slippery and serpentine. Even the written letter S is snakelike in form, and as the biblical symbol for temptation, it initializes the words sexual, sylph, sensuous, sinful, sassy and soulful.

LETTERS OF INTIMIDATION

We instinctively choose soft, high-frequency sounds when reassuring those around us. Conversely, we use loud, low-frequency sounds when we choose to make our presence felt. Strong consonants like B and D are pronounced with explosive, low-pitched sounds, and because they are able to travel longer distances without losing their impact, are ideal for communicating warning or threat cries.

Like the booming of a big bass drum, a large chest produces low-frequency sounds far more efficiently than a small one. Gorillas make use of this principle by beating on their chests to advertise their physical

size—the deeper the resonance, the larger the chest and therefore the more menacing the threat. Since it's impossible to intimidate an opponent by squeaking high-pitched words, most intimidating words begin with explosive, low-frequency letters, like boo, beat, bellow, boom, bang, bam, batter, break and bonk. The letter D, similar but not quite as aggressive as the letter B, initializes words like damn, despise, defend, dare and drag.

Police officers are trained to use their voices as an intimidation tool and can often break up fights just by barking orders. The words they choose are crisp and deeply resonant, and rely on instinctive human responses to particular sounds that have evolved over millions of years: stop!, halt!, back up! and get down! Formed from the tongue's hard contact with the palate or the forceful expulsion of air from the lips, the B, hard C, and hard G, D, K, P and T conspire to create words like kick, strike, beat, bite, cut, poke, punch, gun, conk, crash, kill and crack.

Although English, by virtue of its multi-faceted heritage, is a wonderful language to illustrate the psychological effects of letters, not all languages use the same conventions to differentiate between threatening and reassuring words. There are, however, significant parallels. The Indonesian word for father is bapak; its masculine letters in stark contrast to the inherently feminine word for woman, wanita. In the same language, the aggressive B also forms the roots of the words dangerous (berbahaya) and bad (buruk), while the word for lovely is the soft indah. In Polish, the word for kick is kopa, and the term for stab is the sharp zaklu.

In an illustration of how low-pitched sounds can be used for intimidation, primate researcher Jane Goodall recounted an incident she observed with a low-ranking male chimpanzee named Mike, while studying chimpanzee communities in Tanzania. Mike had begun using empty four-gallon kerosene cans to assist in his struggle for dominance within the group:

All at once Mike calmly walked over to our tent and took hold of an empty kerosene can by the handle. Then he picked up a second can and, walking upright, returned to the place where he had been sitting. Armed with his two cans Mike stared toward the other males. After a few minutes he began to rock from side to side. At first the movement was almost imperceptible, but Hugo and I were watching him closely. Gradually he rocked more vigorously, his hair slowly began to stand erect, and then, softly at first, he started a series of pant-hoots. As he called, Mike got to his feet and suddenly he was off, charging toward the group of males, hitting the two cans ahead of him. The cans, together with Mike's crescendo of hooting, made the most appalling racket: no wonder the erstwhile peaceful males rushed out of the way.

With his clever use of cans to supplement his aggressive hooting, Mike succeeded in achieving top-ranking status in the group. The Xhosa people of South Africa have a the word for kerosene can: iqoqoqo—where each q is pronounced with an explosive click made by the tip of the tongue snapping down from the palate—an imitation of the low-frequency sound produced by banging an empty can.

HOW LETTERS AFFECT WORD MEANINGS

Because our modern human brains have retained programming from our hunter-gatherer origins, each letter or sound in our alphabet corresponds roughly to a particular emotional trigger. Notice how the violent tone of the following words completely disappears when the belligerent initial B is replaced by the mild-mannered M:

- bellow ➔ mellow
- belted ➔ melted

- break ➔ make
- biff ➔ miff
- bite ➔ mite
- boo ➔ moo
- bend ➔ mend
- boss ➔ moss
- buck ➔ muck
- bear ➔ mare

A similar calming effect is observed when we substitute the flighty fl- for the bellicose bl- phoneme:

- blow ➔ flow
- bluster ➔ fluster
- blaming ➔ flaming
- blare ➔ flare
- blight ➔ flight

The nuance of letters can be subtle. Although the D is also a low-frequency, explosively pronounced letter like the letter B, it tends to convey the *consequences* of violence rather than the act itself (doom, death, danger, dark, damage, die and demise). The languid L on the other hand has the effect of soothing the words it initializes. Notice how the meanings of words shift when their initial letters are substituted with the B, D and L:

- Boom (danger)
   Doom (the consequence thereof)
      Loom (impending danger)
- Bark (a warning)
   Dark
      Lark (fun and happy)
- Bad
   Dad (authoritarian but benign)
      Lad (unthreatening)

Not surprisingly, our psychological responses to sounds result in some very predictable letter combinations in the English language, which infect groups of words with common meanings wherever they occur.

Consider the words sneeze, snort, sniffle, snot, snore, snarl, snuff, snigger, snicker and snout. Each of these words pertains to the human nose and is responsible for creating the sn- sound. The influence of this sn-phoneme extends even to words that have only an oblique reference to the human nose, as when one looks down it: sneer, snub, snippy, snide, snob, snipe and snooty. Predictably, there is little demand to have a name associated with this nasal sound, which is why the only name currently used by a celebrity in the U.S. beginning with this phoneme belongs to rapper Snoop Dog.

In similar fashion, the slimy influence of the sl-phoneme is evident in the phrase "the slippery slope was slathered in a slick slime."

The effect of phonemes can be surprisingly powerful. From the flap of a bird's wings comes the instinctive reaction to all things connected with flight and the flamboyant nature of birds: fly, flee, flirtatious, flaming, flowery, flushed, flashy and flaunt.

Consider these additional examples:

ASH CRASH: gnash, trash, smash, bash, dash, lash, mash, quash, thrash

BL BLUSTER: blowhard, blurt, blunt, blunder, bluff, bloody, blast, bloated

BR BRIGHT: breezy, brisk, brilliant, breathe, brusque, brash

CL CLUMSY: clunk, clump, clang, clap, clip, clank, clash, clatter, clamor

CR CRANKY: crabby, crass, cracked, cry, crash, crook, criminal, crypt, crafty, crazy

FR FRANTIC: frazzle, fray, freaky, frenetic, frenzy, frisky, frivolous, frothy, frolic

GL GLEAM: glossy, glamorous, glass, glaze, glitter, glib, glimmer, glint, glow

GR GRUMBLE: grouch, grizzly, gruff, grinch, grave, grind, grunt, grimace, grieve, growl

OB OBJECTIONABLE: obnoxious, obtrusive, obstreperous, obstinate

PL PLEASANT: playful, platonic, plush, platitude, placid, placate, plentiful, platitude

PR PRIZED: present, priceless, praise, pretty, pride, prime, princely, prince

SL SLIPPERY: slide, slick, slimy, slink, slither, slobber, slop, slush, sludge, sly, sludge

SM SMOOCH: smile, smoky, smirk, smolder, smooth, smut

SP SPLASHY: splatter, spew, spit, splash, sparkle, splat, splutter, spout

SPR SPRY: spring, spruce, spirit, spree, sprightly, sprite, sprint, sprinkle

SQU SQUABBLE: squawk, squeak, squall, squalor, squash, squeal, squelch

STR STRENGTH: straight, strive, strain, stress, stretch, strict, strident, structure

SW SWINDLER: swagger, swine, swipe, swinger, swoop, swear, sweaty

TW TWIST: twirl, tweak, twine, twinge

WH WHAT: when, which, why, who, whom, whether, while

WR WRONGED: wrath, wreak, wreckage, wretched, wry, wrestle

Sticks and Stones May BreakMy Bones

4

WHAT OUR NAMES SAY

Parents looking for a name to mirror their ambitious aspirations for their daughter might consider the name Kate, which bespeaks intensity and decisiveness. Beginning with an explosive K and followed quickly by an equally sharp T, the name forms the anagram teak—one of the hardest woods found in nature—and aptly reflects the unyielding timbre of her parents' aspirations. These same parents would be unlikely to consider a softly curved name like Mallory or Mary. Presumably this is what Shakespeare had in mind when he penned this verse from *The Tempest*.

> *The master, the swabber, the boatswain and I,*
> *The gunner, and his mate,*
> *Loved Mall, Meg, and Marian and Margery,*
> *But none of us cared for Kate;*

When Jimmy Carter made his successful bid for the presidency in 1976, there was some controversy surrounding the use of the first name Jimmy on the ballot rather than his legal name James. Feeling that the more approachable Jimmy was better aligned with his "man of the people" image, his campaign staff recommended its use. The strategy worked and encouraged William Clinton to use the same technique when campaigning under his nickname, Bill, in 1992. While not reducing the amount of syllables, adding a diminutizing I, Y or IE at the end of a name (Andrew to Andy, Randall to Randy, or Fred to Freddy) imparts a distinct air of approachability and submissiveness, albeit with a corresponding loss of dignity.

How we choose our nicknames reveals much about how we wish to be perceived. In general, when an individual shortens his or her name, there is a subconscious tendency to keep a lower profile. When a Christopher introduces himself as Chris, or an Elizabeth as Liz, they are demonstrating an unconscious respect for the other person by offering a reduced-syllable version of their name that is easier and quicker to pronounce. Also, because our words are necessarily short and sharply pronounced in times of stress, there tends to be a sense of urgency surrounding people with short, sharp names. Conversely, when we're relaxed, we tend to lengthen the vowel sounds, as in: free, jamboree, jubilee, spree, whoopee, whee, yippee, and glee. This is why the name Bob is more likely to be associated with an impulsive personality than the more delicate Sally.

Humans seem to have an innate response to these mechanisms, which explains why so many aspiring actors and singers readily change their given names. Notice how the new names are so much more reflective of the actors' styles. They are either more complex in construction like Sigourney from Susan, or sharper in pronunciation as in Rock from Roy.

- **Red Buttons** was originally **Aaron Chwatt**. The **RD** root in the new name fitted his comedic style perfectly: rude, ruddy, ridiculous, radiant, randy and random.

- **Bette Davis** started out as **Ruth Davis**, opting for the sharper **BT** combination of bright, bitch, bitter and best.

- The former **Roy Scherer** became **Rock Hudson** after his agent came up with an amalgamation of the Hudson River and the

Rock of Gibraltar. This masculine name helped conceal his homosexuality until his death in 1985.

🐎 Originally **Susan Weaver**, **Sigourney Weaver** picked out her complex three-syllabled name from a character in The Great Gatsby.

🐎 **Oprah** was actually a typo. Her parents intended to use the biblical name **Orpah**, but the nurse misunderstood and her name became Oprah.

🐎 **Luke Perry** was originally **Coy Luther Perry**, but he preferred the cutting resonance of the name of his favorite movie character, Cool Hand Luke.

🐎 Born **Frank Cooper**, **Gary Cooper**'s agent suggested naming himself after the agent's hometown: Gary, Indiana.

🐎 Comedian **Sinbad** was born **David Adkins**, but chose the name Sinbad—an amalgam of sin and bad— "because the mythical Sinbad didn't have the strength of Hercules, but he could outwit anyone."

🐎 **Gene Simmons** from Kiss, followed everyone's advice in renouncing his given name: **Chaim Witz**.

🐎 **Björk Gudmundsdottir** wisely opted simply for **Björk**.

PICKING A PERSONA

Every person uses a particular set of personality characteristics to best function in society. Subject to the vagaries of our DNA and environments growing up, each of us unconsciously tests our various talents to discover what works best. Some people find that it's better to use their brains, others their charm or agility, while some find that deception works best. Since our names play an important role in how people perceive us (and

how we perceive ourselves), is it possible that our names can give us a clue to which personality traits are best for us?

Consider the names traditionally associated with the following attributes:

Strength, power and physical ability. People who make their living through their physical prowess tend to be rugged and direct. Capable with their hands, they make their living as blue-collar workers, professional sports player, and police officers. It's not difficult to imagine that early names describing these hunters and warriors contained the low-pitched and explosive sounds of the letters B, G, T, K, and C. These were the brutes that did the trapping, killing, breaking, grabbing, bashing, bonking, tearing, destroying, and stabbing. Their names, albeit in primitive grunts, might well have reflected these roles. Perhaps the residue of these sounds accounts for the high percentage of these "power" letters found in names that are overwhelmingly perceived to be masculine: Butch, Conan, Buck, Duke, Bill, Kurt, Jake, Chuck, Jock, Kirk, Scott, Troy, and Dick.

Adorability and maternal roles. Babies of every animal species share common features that adults find irresistible: their heads are disproportionately large and their facial features are inversely small. These alluring qualities of innocence and youth play powerfully on the human psyche, which is why people are drawn to the cry of a cute baby or compelled to come to the aid of a damsel in distress.

A great many people in our society make their living by being adorable in some way, and names play a particularly important role in communicating their charms. This explains the high-pitched tones common to members of the world's oldest profession—Bambi, Dolly, Fifi, Barbi, etc.—and why actors, singers, dancers and sometimes politicians benefit from having cute-sounding names: Britney Spears, Betty Page, Betty White, Sally Fields, Amy Irving, Judy Garland and

Audrey Hepburn. Other popular names that clearly demonstrate this adorability effect include Bunny, Missy, Susie, Katie, Didi, Melody, Chrissy, Daisy and Honey.

Guile and intelligence are qualities found in the leaders, toolmakers and intellectuals of society. Their professions encompass jobs that require mental rather than physical attributes: teachers, writers, journalists, politicians, intellectuals, computer programmers, accountants, etc. This is why people whose names begin with the letters of learning and wisdom—J, L, W and D—have an almost 40% higher chance of becoming millionaires than those who don't.

The Influence of Letters

5

HOW NAMES COMPARTALIZE OUR PERSONALITIES

Many psychologists and social researchers acknowledge that there are predictable categories for personality types. While disagreement exists as to how many "personality categories" there are, it seems clear that various forces tend to "clump" human behavior, and that by understanding these forces, we can better understand ourselves. Books on the subject include: *The Wisdom of the Enneagram* (Don Richard Riso and Ross Hudson, Bantam, 1999), which uses the ancient symbol of the enneagram as a basis for defining nine distinct personality types; *What Color is your Personality* (Carol Ritberger, Hay House, 2000), which associates personality types with colors; and The Animal in You (St. Martin's Griffin, 1998), which proposes that we subconsciously adopt the characteristics of one of forty-five animal species. In addition, psychologists use the widely popular Myers-Briggs personality test to categorize human personalities.

It is reasonable, then, to suspect that the sounds within our names might also account for the clustering of our personality characteristics. This is not to say that every person with the same name will exhibit the identical behavior patterns, it's simply a recognition that people with particular sounds in their names will on average behave in a roughly predictable way.

FEEDBACK

How do the letters and sounds in our names influence which road we take in our lives? How could the mere spelling of our names compete with the powerful personality-shaping forces of our teachers, parents, friends and genes? The answer lies in the scientific principle of feedback.

We're all familiar with the high-pitched feedback squeal produced by a singer's microphone during a stage performance. The whine is created when sounds from onstage speakers are picked up by the microphone and then played back over the speakers. The amplified sound is then fed back into the microphone causing an ever-increasing feedback loop that spins rapidly out of control. The initial sound that sparked this deafening clamor might have been barely perceptible, but the feedback loop was able to magnify the noise to a deafening level. Feedback loops are responsible for weather, animal migrations, war and even life itself, and they also explain why our personalities are so deeply affected by our names. As we unconsciously prejudge people based on the sounds of their names, our responses subtly interact with the person's self-image, in turn affecting their responses in a classic feedback loop.

To illustrate how this process works with regard to our names, consider this hypothetical example of identical twin brothers. Imagine that the two boys look like each other and have the same IQ and ambitions. The only difference is that one is named Dirk and the other Timmy. Dirk was named after the leading man in a film the parents had seen on their first date. The hero was ruggedly masculine, as reflected in the name's strong, sharp letters (Dirk is also the Finnish word for dagger). Timmy was named after a sensitive character in a book they were both reading.

Throughout childhood, each boy received positive feedback when his behavior matched his parents' expectations. This was the beginning of a feedback loop in which Dirk, with his strong name, discovered that he was being treated by his peers with marginally more respect than Timmy, when it came to social activities like sports and dating. Imperceptibly at first, Dirk's self-esteem began to improve in these areas. As he strove for additional reinforcement, he was rewarded with even more respect and soon the feedback loop was in full swing. Timmy, on the other hand, was being rewarded by parents and peers whenever he behaved in a sensitive and communicative fashion. Timmy found it more rewarding to become the sensitive child his parents had hoped for, and soon the personalities of the two brothers began to diverge and eventually came to resemble their parents' original aspirations for them.

THE STUDY

In 1990, the U.S. Census Bureau made an unprecedented move and released the names of sixty-three million Americans. The Bureau, however, with its extraordinary sensitivity to the privacy of its respondents, stripped the names of addresses and phone numbers, and separated first names from surnames, making it impossible to capture an individual with a truly unique name in the sample.

By cross-referencing the initial letters of the sixty-three million individuals with the first letters in the names of eighteen thousand successful people in business, arts, medicine, politics and professional sports, I undertook to establish whether or not patterns of success or failure could be determined based solely on names. The frequency of all twenty-six initial letters in the general population was compared to the frequency of those letters found in various professional lists (see tables below).

Although this was an informal analysis, there were many fascinating discoveries. For example, based on the percentage of millionaires in the population, people whose names began with a J were almost three times more likely to become millionaires than names beginning with an N, while I people are becoming doctors at four times the rate of O names. People whose names contained the gentle sh- phoneme were twice as likely to become famous entertainers, while those names beginning with a bright Br- are five times more likely to become millionaires than those beginning with the sly Sl-.

Other interesting patterns began to emerge as well. In general, people whose first names begin with the strongly pronounced letters (B, T, J, C, K, D etc.) proved to be highly successful in professional sports, whereas those with names containing gently pronounced initials (H, S, M, N, V, W and L) consistently failed to make their mark in athletics.

In politics, letters of leadership and strength (J, D, T, B, P, G and L) were consistently found at the top, while the arts were dominated by names with the self-assured letters of I, A, E and J.

While there are a variety of possible sociological and demographic reasons for these unexpected results, the fact remains that the sounds of the letters in our name seem to have a significant impact.

The following table shows the letters with the highest frequency of success in their respective categories:

MOST LIKELY TO SUCCEED

SPORTS A B D E I J K O R T

MONEY A D E F G J L P R W

ARTS A D E I J K N P T V

MEDICAL A D E G I J N P R U

POLITICS B D E G J L P R T V

LEAST LIKELY TO SUCCEED

SPORTS F G H L M N P S V W

MONEY B C H K M N O S T V

ARTS B C F G H L M O S W

MEDICAL B C F H K L O T V W

POLITICS A C F H K M O S U W

SOURCE DATA

SPORTS	MONEY	ARTS	MEDICAL	POLITICS
2,110 records:	*780 records:*	*5,058 records:*	*64,13 records:*	*2.484 records:*
■ Major League Baseball players 1990–1998	■ *Forbes* 400 most wealthy	■ Acadamy Award winners (all categories)	■ First names of doctors in Ohio	■ Current and previous members of Congress
■ Listing of Topps™ baseball, football and basketball cards.	■ *St. Louis Dispatch* Top Executive Pay	■ List of 1000 most popular celebrities	■ First names of doctors in Indiana	■ Members of political organizations
■ NBA first round draft choices 1980–1998		■ Encyclopedoc references of artists and writers		
■ Baseball Hall of Fame, Cooperstown				
■ Football Hall of Fame, Canton, Ohio				

On Considering a Name

6

We have seen how the initial letter of our names can have a significant effect on the outcome of our lives. But in the struggle to select appropriate names for our children, we should bear in mind that there are other forces conspiring to influence our destinies as well. For example, not only is the name Grace affected by letter G, but it also falls under the influence of the growling combination of the G and R, and the sensual S sound of the terminating C.

Parents interested in having their children grow up to dominate their peer groups should gravitate toward names featuring a high percentage of the power letters—A, B, D, J, K, P and W—and avoid the more passive letters—E, F, H, L, M, O and Y. Those looking for names that indicate high levels of emotional intelligence, should use names containing A, E, F, H, I, L, M, N, O, P, R, U and V. Names dominated by vowels tend to display higher levels of feeling and passion.

Those interested in the wealth potential of their children are advised to choose names featuring A, D, E, F, G, L, J, R and W, and stay away from B, C, H, K, M, N, O, T and V. Names that advertise accessibility and friendship are likely to contain C, E, F, G, H, L, M, O, R, S, U, V and X, while names that suggest sensuality and charm will contain a high proportion of C, E, L, O, R, S, V, and W.

The following pages detail the personality types of over seven thousand names. They have been broken down into almost four hundred categories with each class representing the most significant sound groupings. The personality analyses were developed from the personal experiences of hundreds of people, countless hours of discussion and application of the success ratings on the preceding charts. You might notice that some letters are organized under the sound they make, rather than the actual letters. For example, the name Alicia is listed under ALS because the pronunciation of the C is very different from the name Alec, which is listed under ALK.

Each of the name groupings was given a series of ratings: Charisma, Career Success, Love & Friendship and Power. These ratings were calculated from the source data in Table III and overlaid with the emotional impact of the names' constituent letters. The initial letter of each name carries a higher weight in these measurements, but each key letter within the name affects its overall score.

The Charisma rating is a measure of how well the individual functions in social situations. It is also an indication of popularity and personal charm.

The Power score measures the assertiveness of the individual. Power names (featuring Bs, Ds, Ks and Ts) are more likely to command attention than names that have a high percentage of passive Hs, Ls, Ms and Fs.

The Love & Friendship score is an indication of how accessible the individual is to using their corporeal charms to garner resources. Names with a high proportion of sexually resonant letters (Vs, Rs, Ss, Es and Fs) are far more alluring than the brusque sounds of the Bs, Gs, Ks and Ps.

The Career Success rating is based on the source data from the table on page xxxvi and is a measure of how well the individual functions in the workplace. It is also an indication of how much money the individual might expect to earn.

In the name categories that follow, the vowels do not appear in the name groupings unless they happen to be the initial letter of a name. Vowels are certainly not without their influence, but since every name contains at least one vowel, their effects are usually overshadowed by the stronger consonants.

The Imperious

Adam was but human—this explains it all.
He did not want the apple for the apple's sake,
he wanted it only because it was forbidden.
The mistake was in not forbidding the serpent;
then he would have eaten the serpent.

—*Pudd'nhead Wilson,*
Mark Twain

As the first letter of both the Hebrew and Roman alphabets, the letter *A,* as pronounced in *father,* is the *only* sound common to every language on earth. This letter is the alpha male of the alphabet, and its *aristocratic* tendencies are apparent in the words *Adam, autocratic, ascendant, arrogant and absolute,* and with the exception of Europe, the *A* is the first and last letter of all the continents: *America, Asia, Australia, Africa* and *Antarctica.* It is also the initial letter of *Ankhankh,* the ancient Egyptian looped cross that symbolizes life, and *Aries,* the Greek god of war and the first sign of the Zodiac. ■ The letter *A*'s power to affect public attitudes is illustrated by the different ways it is pronounced between England and the United States. During the industrial revolution that swept England in the nineteenth century, the British aristocracy, sensing an erosion of their social status by the emerging middle class, gradually assumed a mode of speech to emphasize their superior status. Instead of saying, *I can't plant the grass,* they affected an accent which even today distinguishes the English upper classes from all other English speakers; *I cahn't plahnt the grahss.* ■ Additionally, schoolchildren whose names begin with an *A* are familiar with the special feeling that comes from being the first in alphabetical roll calls. Although being singled out in this way can have a positive effect on the child's self-image, it can also breed resentment in their peers. The superior attitude of *A* people is aptly expressed in the traditional meaning of the names *Andrew* (manly), *Alison* (of noble birth), *Audrey* (noble strength) and *Abraham* (father of a multitude). ■ The authoritarian elements of the letter *A* might explain why fully 10% of U.S. Presidents and Vice Presidents had an *A-* name—twice the frequency found in the general population. *A* people are also consistently found on top of the lists of medicine, arts, sports and making money. ■

THE INSIGHTFUL

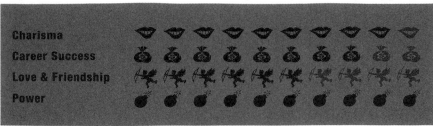

ab

Pragmatic Wise Altruistic
Curt Absent-minded All-knowing

Charisma	😗😗😗😗😗😗😗😗😗😗
Career Success	💰💰💰💰💰💰💰💰💰💰
Love & Friendship	🏹🏹🏹🏹🏹🏹🏹🏹🏹🏹
Power	💣💣💣💣💣💣💣💣💣💣

When the *arrogant* and *autocratic* letter *A* teams up with the *belligerent, boisterous B* to form the *AB* phoneme, it evokes the unmistakable connotation of *abruptness* that we find in words like *abduct, abort, abolish, abominable, abandon, abhor* and *abuse*. So although these names suggest individuals with little patience or empathy, this is less true of those who choose to use the diminutive version of their name, such as *Abby* and *Abbey*. This is because the addition of the letter *Y* at the end of names invariably softens their aggressive qualities—as when people soften their speech by ending words with high-frequency tones (*cat* becomes *kitty, dog* becomes *doggy*, and *blanket* becomes *blankie*).

Names that incorporate the *lyrical, laughing, laid-back* letter *L*—as in *Abel, Abigail* and *Abril*—are imbued with an air of genteel diplomacy. The *ABL* letter combination is so influential, in fact, that the word "able" has come to be the very definition of a capable and talented individual. At one time, a quarter of the world's population bore the name *Abel*, until dispatched by a man who fittingly bore the harsh mark of *Cain*.

Strong and confident—if not a little intolerant on occasion—these people radiate a serious and earnest air with an inclination toward simplicity and order.

Abe
Abby
Abdul
Abdiel
Abdullah
Abigail
Abril
Abel

People are drawn to *AB* individuals for their down-home goodness and strong, unyielding spirits, but are sometimes put off by their pedantic method of communication. No matter what you say about the *AB* personality, you'll have to concede that they're not the most exciting conversationalists. Erudite and insightful they may be, but a barrel of monkeys they're not.

Hardships in the *AB*'s busy life are met head-on and with a ready laugh and dry sense of humor. While their uncommon emotional strength tends to elevate them from the crowd, these are reluctant leaders who prefer to operate in the background. *AB*s perform at their best in careers requiring a high level of emotional toughness, such as teaching, journalism, medicine and politics.

If you're involved in close personal relationships with any *AB*s, it's best to stay on their good side, for although *AB*s can be playful at times, too much pressure will provoke a side of them that's as stubborn as a redwood. As parents, *AB*s run the home with ruthless efficiency, demanding obedience and discipline from their children. Still, this drill-sergeant attitude will be tempered with a large and loving heart, and an *AB*'s family will never have to guess where her affections lie.

Abigail van Buren Everyone knows Dear Abby. Born Pauline Esther Friedman, Abigail Van Buren began her career when she contacted the editor of the *San Francisco Chronicle* claiming that she could write a better advice column than the one currently appearing in the paper. Her style caught on, and Abby became an icon of American culture. ■ Defining her style of compassionate confrontation, Abby tackled difficult subjects including issues of child abuse and teen sex, and also founded Operation Dear Abby, which provided letters of support to millions of American servicemen. ■ Abby was born only seventeen minutes apart from her twin, Esther Pauline, and the girls shared many of the same interests. Her twin sister later made her own mark as an advice columnist, writing under the name Ann Landers.

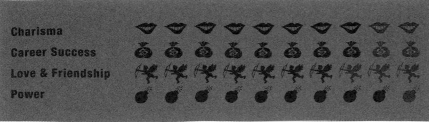

Charisma										
Career Success										
Love & Friendship										
Power										

Visionary Leadership Moral authority
Abrasive Stodgy Unyielding

Now here are some names for the ages, and a quick dissection of their components reveals why they have had such an impact on Western civilization. The initial letter *A* is full of *arrogant* self-confidence, and because it is followed by the no-nonsense power of the *bravely belligerent* letter *B*, sets the stage for an individual who is unlikely to be swayed by anything other than his own beliefs. The name *Abraham*, in fact, has no fewer than three *As*—more than any other name in the English language—and resonates with *absolute assurance*. It is significant that the second syllable of this root begins with the *BR* phoneme . . . the embodiment of all things *bright, brilliant, brave, breezy* and *brawny.*

All these influences explain why these names resound with courageous intelligence and yet evoke a sensitive spirit who relies on higher powers for guidance. And it's true that *ABR*s are often deeply spiritual individuals who seem guided by an external beacon. Close associates will treasure their dependable friendship, but *ABR*s sometimes struggle to convey their innermost feelings. It's not that they can't find the words, it's just that they seem unable to connect with their own ever-changing emotional states. So *ABR*s

Abner
Abraham
Abram
Aubrey

remain a bit of a mystery, as much to others as they are to themselves.

The flip side to the *ABR*'s morally directed personality is a shrewd and astute businessperson, and *ABR*s are not above using a little leverage to achieve their goals. So although their leadership can be inspiring, their willingness to bend the rules can make them ruthless competitors. But rest assured; *ABR*s' morally centered value systems would never allow them to actually hurt anyone, even if it meant the loss of a particular business deal.

The same solidness exhibited in their professional lives is evident in the *ABR*'s relationships, although it's sometimes accompanied by a proclivity for stuffiness and conservatism. And while one would accuse them of being compliant, their honesty and willingness to work with others prove to be great assets in their personal lives.

It's in the role of parent that *ABR*s truly come into their own: These are individuals who place the well-being of their families above all else. The *ABR*'s children will be raised with strong family values and will rarely challenge their parents' authority: partly out of respect and partly out of fear of being subjected to one of their moralizing lectures.

Abraham Lincoln "Honest Abe," like Winston Churchill and Rudy Giuliani, was the right man for the wrong times. He saw his country through a brutal civil war, put an end to slavery and reunited the country. ■ As President, he helped transform the newly formed Republican Party into a formidable organization, and although he was fundamentally uneducated, he proved to be a talented writer and orator. His death at the hands of John Wilkes Booth is remembered as sharply as the assassination of John F. Kennedy. ■ The clearest indication of his philosophy is the quote inscribed on the Lincoln Memorial: "With malice toward none; with charity for all; with firmness in the right, as God gives us to see the right, let us strive on to finish the work we are in; to bind up the nation's wounds."

ad

Charisma	👄	👄	👄	👄	👄	👄	👄	👄	👄	👄
Career Success	💰	💰	💰	💰	💰	💰	💰	💰	💰	
Love & Friendship										
Power										

Clearheaded Strong-willed Imposing
Impatient Overpowering Preoccupied

The letter *A* is the archetypal symbol of *authority* and *arrogance,* and the letter *D* is usually associated with the *darker* aspects of *demanding discipline.* So when these two letters come together, they evoke the shadowy and calculating elements found in the words *addictive, adjudicator, adultery, admonish* and *adversity.* Accordingly, you can expect *AD* personalities to take charge in group activities and decisions: Nothing annoys them more than having to wait for others to make up their minds. These are people who can walk into a meeting, usurp the floor and instantly imprint their goals onto the agenda.

Many people find getting close to an *AD* personality to be a daunting experience. But for those who manage to cut through the foreboding surface of their moody landscapes, the reward will be an unmatched level of loyalty and devotion. *AD*s respect dependability and persistence in their friends, and as long as they believe that you have their best interests at heart, they'll permit you to drink from their deep emotional wells. And while it's true that *AD*s are prone to the occasional bout of withdrawal and moodiness, this antagonism is largely confined to themselves, and serious arguments are surprisingly rare.

Adena
Adia
Addison
Adonis
Ahmed
Aidan
Audie
Aida

*AD*s' sharp minds and on-the-fly learning abilities allow them to blend chameleonlike into an assortment of careers and professions. Unfortunately, their dogged sense of purpose often ends up generating hurt feelings and ruffled tempers, but they're too impatient to sit around and worry about people's feelings. They're out there getting the job done while the committee is still deciding what kind of coffee to serve at the next meeting.

*AD*s are not the world's best listeners, and a conversation with one of them can prove to be as frustrating as a defective Rubik's Cube. And with their habit of interpreting constructive criticism as declarations of disloyalty, they tend to discourage otherwise healthy dialogue in their relationships.

When it comes to matters of intimacy, the strong-minded *AD* is a risky mate for anyone lacking a hefty sense of purpose, and non-assertive partners will usually end up wearing a permanent set of footprints on their backs. But pure force is never the antidote for an *AD* power play, and without a healthy dose of patience and flexibility, the union will almost certainly degenerate into a mere contest of wills.

Ada Lovelace Ada Lovelace was arguably the world's first computer programmer. The daughter of Lady Noel Byron, who was briefly married to Lord Byron, Ada was educated in mathematics, astronomy and philosophy and attended lectures by Charles Babbage. Babbage was the father of the "analytical engine," which is widely recognized to be the precursor of modern computers. ■ Ada wrote software for the "analytical engine," but due to its enormous expense, it was never built. To raise money for the machine, Ada tried gambling on horse races but became mired in debt and addicted to morphine. This led the great mathematician Augustus De Morgan to conclude that mathematics was too much of a strain for mere women. ■ Her heritage was secured when the modern programming language Ada was named in her honor.

Charisma	
Career Success	
Love & Friendship	
Power	

Because the *autocratic* letter *A* and the *dominant* letter *D* are both deeply influenced by the elements of power and discipline, it's not surprising that the *AD* phoneme forms the root of the words *addictive, adjudicator, adultery, admonish* and *adversity*. And while these controlling qualities define (in large part) the *ADL*'s character, their personalities are also significantly modulated by the calming elements of the letter *L*—the symbol of *love, learning, laughter* and *life*.

These are well-rounded, fleet-of-mind individuals with active imaginations and lifestyles. So if you're going to befriend an *ADL,* bear in mind that they are easily bored by routine and will be constantly looking for ways to challenge their intellects. Since they are very much in tune with their own emotional needs, it's not unusual to find *ADLs* switching careers, homes, partners and lifestyles with extraordinarily little consideration. These personality types are remarkably unafraid of failure; regarding it as simply a new learning experience. If anything, they have to resist their tendencies toward becoming overly preachy, especially when others hesitate to follow their impulsive leaps into the unknown.

The *ADLs*' lusty approach to life can sometimes blind them to the consequences of their actions, which,

Adela
Adele
Adelia
Adelina
Adeline
Adalberto
Adelaide
Adella
Aditya
Aldolfo
Adolph
Adriel
Adelle

if left unchecked, will often get them into hot water. They don't mean any harm, but they do have a chronic (and sometimes comical) case of foot-in-mouth disease. Fortunately, having a flexible personality also gives them the ability to simultaneously extricate the shoelaces from their teeth and make amends to the person they've just offended. Misunderstandings aside, the *ADL*'s friends will readily put up with a little embarrassment here and there in exchange for the boundless goodwill these affable people offer.

ADLs enter their intimate relationships with abandon, and once the two of you have bonded, you'll discover that this free spirit will give you plenty of room to explore your own desires. As lovers, they're perfectly in tune with their partners' needs and rarely lose sight of their own goals. But don't be disappointed if your *ADL* lover isn't the kind who sets off fireworks every night; they tend to be a little conservative when it comes to matters of carnality and wouldn't want you to think they're being overly aggressive.

While it may take an *ADL* a lifetime to decide to settle down, when the altar finally looms, the relationship will almost certainly glow with the same brightness that illuminates the *ADL*'s life.

Adelaide Hall Born on October 20, 1901, in Brooklyn, New York, Adelaide Hall's career began on Broadway in 1921. On stage, she worked with Bill "Bojangles" Robinson, Josephine Baker, Louis Armstrong, Lena Horne, and Cab Calloway, and recorded with such jazz luminaries as Duke Ellington, Fats Waller, and Art Tatum.■ Adelaide moved to London in 1938 to appear in Drury Lane and soon became one of Britain's best-loved entertainers. She was the first black star to be given a long-term contract with the BBC, which resulted in her own radio series. She also became an exclusive Decca recording artist, cutting over 70 discs for the label, many of which were released during WWII. It's fair to say she was heard almost everywhere: on radio airwaves, in night clubs, in movies, and on the stage. She died on November 7, 1993, in England.

Charisma	👄	👄	👄	👄	👄	👄	👄	👄	👄	👄
Career Success	💰	💰	💰	💰	💰	💰	💰	💰	💰	💰
Love & Friendship	🦅	🦅	🦅	🦅	🦅	🦅	🦅	🦅	🦅	🦅
Power	💣	💣	💣	💣	💣	💣	💣	💣	💣	💣

**Positive Self-assured Steadfast
Arrogant Possessive Overly Moral**

In the beginning, there was *Adam.* So it's hardly surprising to find this original alpha male's name to be dominated by the self-assured *AD* letter combination. The letter *A* is more than simply the first letter of the Greek, Roman and Hebrew alphabet. It is *arrogant, absolutist, able* and *artful*, and when joined with the *defiantly dominant* letter *D*, reflects the competence and self-*assuredness* found in the words: *admiration, adoration, adult, adaptable, adequate, adulation* and *adept.*

But the *ADM* root is also significantly influenced by the *maternal* and *mellow* letter *M,* which infuses it with a *moderate* and feminine touch; evoking images of a powerful, authoritative man who regularly phones his mother. But even the original Batman, Adam West, admits that *ADMs* are not perfect ("I'm not Superman, you know") and must guard against their tendency to view themselves as the center of the universe. This egocentric attitude explains why *ADMs*, while having little problem with getting respect, often struggle to find true love and even self-love. Their biggest challenges are in overcoming their need for outside approval and finding their worth from within.

Adam
Adama
Adamson

Not ones to avoid hard work, *ADMs* are drawn to careers that satisfy their need for social status: particularly in the medical fields, military, law, crime fighting and politics. But because power and influence remain their greatest aphrodisiacs, their true calling is in the management and motivation of people.

ADMs are drawn to situations that have the potential for excitement and passion, and perhaps because of this, are incorrigible flirts. But all too often, their choice of partners is based purely on physical attraction and their long-term relationships suffer from the lack of deeper connections. And when it comes to breaking off bad relationships, *ADMs* are second to none in the art of procrastination. They are so afraid of being viewed as the bad guy that they will usually muddle on in the hope that their partner breaks things off first.

On the positive side, the *ADM's* ability to maintain his sense of humor in the face of adversity allows him to take on emotionally risky relationships that others wouldn't even dream of. No matter how badly things turn out, the *ADM* will simply shrug off his mistakes and have a good laugh at his own expense.

Adam West In a classic case of how a name change can fundamentally alter the course of one's life, Willie West Anderson from Walla Walla, Washington, changed his name to Adam West and landed a role in the memorable 1959 drama with Paul Newman, *The Philadelphians*. ■ Adam's biggest break came via the 1966 TV series *Batman*, in which he was cast in the title role. His all-American square-jawed looks cemented him as the quintessential caped crusader and embodied the ADM qualities of forthright dependability tinged with a disdain for evil. ■ Unfortunately, Adam did such a fine job in playing the caped crusader that he found himself typecast and unable to get the kind of roles needed to sustain his career. ■ In the end Adam was reduced to making guest appearances at county fairs and rodeos.

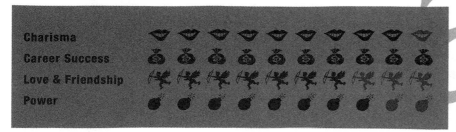

Charisma										
Career Success										
Love & Friendship										
Power										

Charismatic Sexy Admirable
Superior Complacent Unrealistic

Because the *authoritarian* letter *A* and the *dominant* letter *D* are both deeply influenced by the elements of power and discipline, it's not surprising to find them forming the roots of the austere words: *addictive, adjudicator, adultery, admonish* and *adversity.* But in the *ADR* names, the conservative aspects of the *AD* combination are nicely offset by the *robust, ribald, raunchy, racy* and *romantic* resonance of the letter *R,* suggesting people whose quiet inner strength is in perfect balance with a naturally flirtatious charm. Of particular interest is the name *Audrey,* whose traditional meaning is *noble strength.* Its inherent rhythms echo with the evocative and high-spirited *-ry* phoneme of *fairy, merry, spry, glory, cheery* and *brewery.*

With their dual natures of conscientiousness and casualness, the charming *ADR*s have the unique ability to be both the life of the party and the designated driver at the same time. Perceptive and sharp, they rely on their abilities to influence people's emotions (instead of their intellects) to win converts to their cause.

Like all *A* people, *ADR*s must guard against their egos becoming the driving force in their lives, for once they get a taste for being in the spotlight, they have a hard time retreating into the shadows. *ADR*s' intuitive understanding of how the universe works makes them

Adra
Adrian
Adria
Adrianna
Adrienne
Audrey
Audra

among the first people to whom others turn for guidance. But it's not their insight alone that draws people into their sphere; it's that critical/sympathetic combination, which makes others feel that they're getting honest advice for their money.

The *ADR*s' strong work ethic goads them to excel, particularly in the fields of arts and entertainment. And while success may seem to come easily to them, it's probably because they consider work to be nothing more than a means to an end. Life is for living, not working, so whether performing on stage or just animatedly telling jokes, it's done with passion and enthusiasm. Perhaps they would do well to leave things alone on occasion, especially at those times when silence speaks more effectively than eloquence.

If you're in love with an *ADR,* there's something you should know: They have an annoying habit of allowing platonic friends to distract them from their primary relationships, which often proves frustrating to long-term partners. You'll have to contend with being just another of a large network of friends and ex-lovers, all of whom care about them much as you do. But if you're not the jealous type, your relationship should prove to be enduring, satisfying . . . and always interesting.

Audrey Hepburn Audrey Hepburn's life was an illustration in how a name change can pave the way for a successful public career. Born with the mouthful, Edda van Heemstra Hepburn-Ruston, she adopted the timeless moniker Audrey to amplify her grace and confidence. ■ Arguably the most classically featured ingénue in cinematic history, her most memorable role proved to be the cockney Eliza Doolittle in *My Fair Lady*, in which Marni Nixon dubbed her singing voice. When she played the role of Holly Golightly in *Breakfast at Tiffanys*, the blonde streak in her hair initiated the first major Hollywood hairstyle craze. ■ With two Oscars under her belt, Audrey never left the public eye, and served as a UNICEF ambassador before passing away at her home in Tolochenaz, Switzerland, in 1993.

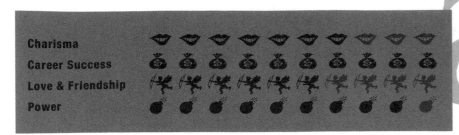

Charisma										
Career Success										
Love & Friendship										
Power										

ag

Dependable Ethical Composed
Morally Superior Moody Difficult

In the Germanic languages, the sound *Ag* or *Ach,* is used as an expression of distaste, and because the *AG* phoneme produces an altogether disagreeable sound, these names must overcome the prejudice of words like: *agony, against, aghast, aargh* and *agnostic.* The names *Agnes* and *Agnus* have the additional influence of the nasally dominated *NS* phoneme (associated with the words *nausea, nose, nasty* and *nostril), and with this double dose of awkward phonemes, it's easy to understand why these names have largely fallen out of favor in modern times.

The traditional Greek meaning of *Agnes* is *pure* and *chaste,* and in the Middle Ages, the name was often given to young girls to remind them of their obedience to God. This resulted in the canonization of no less than three Saint Agneses: *Agnes of Poitiers, Agnes of Montepulciano* and one of the church's most popular saints, *Agnes, Virgin Martyr of Rome.* Because of her insistence on sticking to her Christian vows of chastity, she was sent to a brothel as punishment. Unfortunately, her purity and inviolability had such an adverse affect on the brothel's clientele that she was eventually sentenced to death. With true *AG* toughness, she went to her execution more cheerfully than others go to their weddings.

But *AG* people have their upbeat sides too. They

Agatha
Agnes
Agustin
Agustina
Augustine
Augustus
Augusta
August

are generally highly organized people with punctuality and precision as built-in features of their personalities, both at work and at play. But having a strong work ethic comes with the expectation that friends and co-workers will be able to match the AG's high level of performance. And since *AGs* are not shy about reprimanding sloppy behavior, they often develop a reputation for being boorish and morally superior.

If you have a job opening requiring decisiveness and leadership, an *AG* individual could well be your best bet. With their strong personalities and quirky appeal, *AGs* excel in careers that give them the freedom to make up rules as they go, for with typical *A*-personality astuteness and alacrity, *AGs* are able to anticipate events ten moves ahead. Whether this is a sign of their distaste for being caught by surprise, or symptomatic of their control issues, it proves an effective instrument in both their professional and their personal lives.

When it comes to matters of intimacy, *AGs'* fixation for self-preservation often prevents them from exploring relationships that could be potentially fulfilling. Still, as any mate of an *AG* will tell you, their extraordinary loyalty and dogged determination to succeed makes them eminently desirable parents and partners.

Agnes Moorehead It's fairly evident that Agnes Moorehead's name was not a stage name. It's unlikely that one would willingly hog-tie themselves with such an unfortunate moniker. ■ The acerbic thespian enchanted us as Endora, Samantha's mother on the long-running TV hit *Bewitched*, and proved to be a prolific actress with over sixty films to her credit. Most people don't remember that she also won four Academy Award nominations for her film work which included, *Citizen Kane, Show Boat, Pollyanna* and *The Lost Moment*. ■ Agnes's first love was radio, where she appeared in *March of Time, Cavalcade of America* and *Mayor of the Town*. Her comedic talents were on par with the best in the business, and her showcases included the *Fred Allen, Phil Baker, Bob Hope* and *Jack Benny* shows.

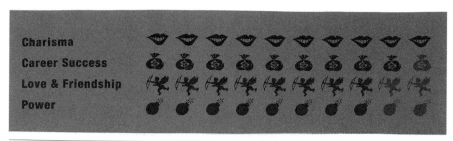

Charisma	👄 👄 👄 👄 👄 👄 👄 👄 👄 👄
Career Success	💰 💰 💰 💰 💰 💰 💰 💰 💰
Love & Friendship	🏹 🏹 🏹 🏹 🏹 🏹 🏹 🏹 🏹 🏹
Power	💣 💣 💣 💣 💣 💣 💣 💣 💣 💣

**Self-assured Friendly Intense
Proud Over-talkative Unaware**

The incisive letter *A* dominates the *AL* names and imbues them with all the qualities of an *aristocratic* and *authoritarian* essence. And like most names beginning with the letter *A*, *AL* names are associated with individuals who have healthy egos and a strong, no-nonsense approach to life. But the appearance of the lyrical letter *L* (*learning, life, love, liberty* and *laughter*) rescues these names from hyper-egotism, suggesting people who are *altruistic, alert, alive* and even a little bit *aloof.*

The dual themes of strength and *joie de vivre* dominate the *ALs'* lives. They are the types who steal the thunder at parties with their smart and jocular styles, but when lost in their passion for story-telling, *ALs* often lose track of their audiences' needs. After the first hour of listening to the *AL's* life story, even the most determined listeners will tire. But if they have a *real* flaw, it's their tendency to take on more than they can handle. Still, they are nothing if not enthusiastic in their approach to life, and whether it's in the workplace or in their personal lives, these go-getters will overcome problems with twice the energy and half the hassle of their counterparts.

Al
Aldo
Aleta
Aliya
Alia
Alijah
Aliza
Alla
Allie
Alta
Althea
Axel
Ayla
Ali

ALs are surprisingly thin-skinned, and harsh words affect them more than they are willing to admit. So expect to be occasionally surprised by a temperamental snarl here and there, especially when you inadvertently penetrate their shell of self-confidence. There's a profoundly sensitive soul under that blustery surface that needs a great deal of nurturing, and only once it's been revealed will you discover the *AL's* true potential for connectedness and caring.

In the workplace, *ALs'* tactful political skills allow them to take charge of situations without steamrolling others in the process. Diplomacy, expressiveness and sincerity may well be marks of the *AL's* leadership style, but for all their apparent geniality, they also exhibit the aloofness common to names beginning with the autocratic letter *A*.

ALs place a high priority on sharing and honest communication when it comes to matters of the heart. Consequently, you can expect your *AL* mate to be both affectionate and loyal . . . even if he or she is sometimes going to be a little pushy. Romance from such quarters will be a high-energy affair but a treat for anyone who loves to be loved without limits.

Al Franken Al Franken is a cerebral writer, producer and actor, who made his mark on the baby-boom generation with his caustic and intelligent blend of humor. ■ Although his primary claim to fame was as a writer and producer for *Saturday Night Live*, his true love has always been political satire. ■ Al reveled in pushing the envelope as a commentator for *SNL*'s "Weekend Update" and would receive thousands of letters from outraged viewers. In a particularly provocative piece on the supposed indestructibility of cockroaches, Al decapitated, skewered and set fire to a number of the insects on live TV. ■ In 2003, Fox News played right into Al's hands when they sued him for using the phrase "fair and balanced" as part of the title of his new book.

Charisma	👄👄👄👄👄👄👄👄👄👄
Career Success	💰💰💰💰💰💰💰💰💰💰
Love & Friendship	🐦🐦🐦🐦🐦🐦🐦🐦🐦🐦
Power	💣💣💣💣💣💣💣💣💣💣

Philospical Altruistic Bright
Aloof Demanding Troubled

It's easy to find the altruism and wisdom inherent in the *ALBRT* root. For when the self-confident *A* combines with the *learned, life-loving* letter *L*, it becomes associated with words like *alert, altruism, alive, alluring, all right* and *almighty.* The second part of these names, the *BRT* phoneme, is instantly recognizable as the essence of *bright, bratty* and *brilliant.*

All told, *ALBRT* names evoke an image of a serious, inwardly reflecting individual who willingly shoulders the burden of achieving great things in his life. And although *ALBRT*s are typically described as being alert and bright, the thing that truly defines their personalities is their intensity. Because they take life so seriously, *ALBRT*s must be careful about allowing their relentless passion for work to flower into full-fledged workaholism. Money is rarely their goal: it's the promise of discovery that keeps their shoulders to the wheel.

Their flair for unraveling problems would make them outstanding counselors and people-managers, and they should also consider psychology, psychiatry and medicine, to challenge their sharply inquisitive minds. But be prepared for the *ALBRT*'s blunt and sometimes scathing response to your opinions. It's not that these people are boorish by any means, it's just

Albert
Alberta
Alberto

that they cling to an unshakable belief that the world works in an orderly way that can be predicted and controlled.

If you ever want to impress an *ALBRT,* present him or her with a clearly thought-out logical argument; there's nothing they love more than a challenging debate. While they will gladly converse about any issue you choose, they are particularly interested in philosophy and nature, which perhaps explains why the breathtakingly scenic Alberta, Canada, was named for *Princess Louise Alberta* (Queen Victoria's daughter), after she fell in love with her mother's territory.

*ALBRT*s are usually described as being perfunctory mates with few fireworks but plenty of dependable breadwinning. And while it's true that with their tendency to lose themselves in the pursuit of knowledge *ALBRT*s are prone to becoming disconnected from their important relationships, they're usually the first to admit these shortcomings and will disarm their partners with genuinely humble self-appraisals.

Once they've convinced someone that they really love them, *ALBRT*s can get away with their unique brand of straightforward criticism, which makes a real difference to the people in their lives.

Albert Einstein Albert Einstein became an overnight celebrity when, after a solar eclipse in 1919, experiments confirmed his prediction that light rays from distant stars would be deflected by the sun's gravity. ■ Universally recognized as the archetypal scientist, he has also come to be regarded as one of the great humanists of our time. ■ Albert was never a great student, failing his entrance examination to the Swiss Institute of Technology in Zurich. And math? Hated it! ■ His famous correspondence with Sigmund Freud about man's inherent love of war foreshadowed his dismay at the development of the atom bomb, and in 1933, after Adolf Hitler became chancellor of Germany, Albert renounced his German citizenship and immigrated to America, where he took a position at Princeton University in New Jersey.

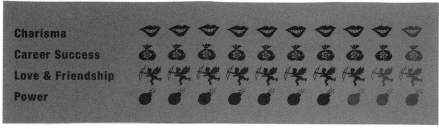

THE FEISTY
alf

Charisma	🙂🙂🙂🙂🙂🙂🙂🙂🙂🙂
Career Success	💰💰💰💰💰💰💰💰💰💰
Love & Friendship	🐉🐉🐉🐉🐉🐉🐉🐉🐉🐉
Power	💣💣💣💣💣💣💣💣💣💣

Frank Outgoing Irrepressible
Moody Unpredictable Chaotic

The *ALF* name root has a distinguished lineage of strong leadership from *Alfred the Great*, arguably the greatest King in the history of England, to *Alfred Nobel*, the creator of the Nobel Prize and the inventor of dynamite. This is hardly surprising when one considers the forces at work in this complex name root. For when the self-*assured* letter *A* combines with the *learned* and *loving* letter *L*, it becomes indelibly associated with the qualities found in the words *alert, altruism, alive, alluring, all right* and *almighty*.

In the spirit of complexity, there is also the matter of the prominent letter *F* in these names. This *free-spirited* letter sets the tone for the words like *fun, freedom, fairy, fancy* and *fine,* and when all these influences are put together, you have a serious individual with an irresistibly charming mischievous streak whose energy infects everyone around him or her. It is important to note that when an individual uses the long form of his name, rather than an acceptable contraction (e.g. *Alfred* instead of *Al),* he or she is actually demanding that others work harder to pronounce their names. Because these people see themselves as worthy of this extra effort, it reinforces the association of *ALF* people having exceptionally strong egos.

Alf
Alfie
Alford
Alfonzo
Alfreda
Alphonse
Alfredia
Alfredo
Alfred

Physically, sexually and intellectually, there's nothing the *ALF* won't try at least twice. With their mouthy and argumentative styles, they even have reputations for instigating conflict. It's as if they derive a secret pleasure from stirring things up while maintaining their innocence. And even though everyone has a bad day now and then, when *ALF*s are in a nasty mood, their impish spirits often take on a more malevolent quality . . . often resulting in hurt feelings and bruised egos.

The mate of an *ALF* would do well to watch out for these antagonistic tendencies, but shouldn't be distracted from the fun that can be had with this adventurous, adaptable personality. They are terrific sprinters in their relationships—lively and loads of fun over short distances—but it's the long haul that often proves to be their downfall. Still, a stoic and loving mate can do wonders for extending the longevity of the relationship.

*ALF*s are cautious about introducing children into their lives. It's not that they wouldn't love to have miniaturized versions of themselves running around, mind you, it's just that they're sensible enough to give the matter the careful consideration that such a big commitment deserves.

Alfred Nobel Few people in history can claim the kind of legacy achieved by Alfred Nobel. The Swedish chemist, inventor and philanthropist first made his mark as the inventor of dynamite. ■ His dynamic personality was typical of the charge-ahead mindset of the A names, and his masterstroke was his decision to endow the bulk of his estate for annual prizes to those who had most benefited mankind. The Nobel Prize is the highest honor that researchers in physics, chemistry, medicine, literature or peace can attain. ■ If it seems incongruous that the inventor of such a destructive material would bequeath a peace prize, it should be remembered that his invention was not the explosive itself, but simply the means with which to stabilize it.

alk

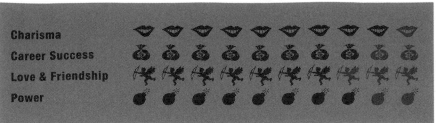

Charisma										
Career Success										
Love & Friendship										
Power										

Responsive Attentive Appreciative
Workaholic Preoccupied All-knowing

In the *ALK* name root, the *autocratic* letter *A* loses some of its *arrogance* when paired with the *laughing, lilting* letter *L* and the *crisply concise* letter *C (or letter K)*. The overall effect of these names is therefore one of supreme self-confidence tempered by an ability to laugh; even in the face of embarrassment. In fact, there's no such thing as embarrassment in the *ALK*'s life—why would anyone deign to laugh at *him* when the joke is really on everyone else? With his unmatched confidence and dazzling smile, he really believes that anything's possible and usually manages to prove it.

    Alec
    Alek

As goofy as the *ALK* can be at times, life is hardly all fun and games. He has a decidedly serious side and a book-knowledge that would shame a city library. You could say he's a student of life—in the way he carefully analyzes every little event and nuance that goes on around him—and is deeply interested in discerning the motivations of others. So don't be surprised to find your *ALK* friend watching you attentively, even coolly, as you go through the ups and downs of your daily life. His is not the softest shoulder on which to cry when your girlfriend runs off with your personal trainer, but if anyone can restore your sense of humor, it's going to be him.

Though the *ALK* isn't necessarily career-driven, he does manage to find success—or perhaps it finds him—in almost all his endeavors. This might be partly due to his stubborn refusal to give up when the going gets rough, but more than likely it has to do with his extraordinary range of talents. He is a jack of all trades who seems to specialize in everything.

Perhaps his analytical approach to life is responsible for holding the *ALK* back in his tangles with romance. It's not that women aren't drawn to him, mind you—he practically has to sweep them off the doorstep every time he leaves the house—but he just doesn't seem to get the finer points of romance. And his trademark smile isn't always enough to rescue him after some well-intended but flippant remark. Still, it must be said that because his confidence is unshakable (and eminently attractive), he's likely to simply brush off his shirtsleeves before moving on to the next lucky victim.

Eventually his instincts will kick in long enough to help him play the sensitive-man role so yearned for in the dating world. And once it does, the *ALK* will make a suave lover, a best friend, and a fine sparring partner on the road to the happily-ever-after.

Alec Baldwin There was a time when teenage girls would complete the phrase: as cute as a . . . with Baldwin. And while time has marched on, the Baldwin brothers certainly made their artistic and political mark—and none more so than big brother Alec. ■ Having changed his name from Alexander to the more sharply pronounced Alec, his film debut was an inauspicious role in a forgettable movie starring Dr. Ruth Westheimer. ■ A much-publicized marriage to Academy Award–winning actress Kim Basinger produced a daughter before Basinger filed for divorce in 2001. ■ Alec gained notoriety during the contested Presidential election of 2000 when he reportedly said that if George W. Bush was elected, he would leave the country. He later chose to stay, claiming that Bush wasn't elected, just selected.

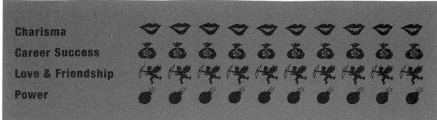

Charisma
Career Success
Love & Friendship
Power

Lively Vigorous Compassionate
Adamant Controlling Calculating

The *ALN* root is borne by over a million people in the United States, which is hardly surprising when one considers the positive influence of the key letters in this root. When the self-*assured* letter *A* combines with the *lively, life-loving* letter *L* to create the *AL* phoneme, it connotes all the dynamism and energy found in the words *alert, altruism, alive, alluring, all right* and *almighty*. However, the addition of the pessimistic letter *N* (as in *no, never, not, nyet, nada, nein, nothing, naught* and *nowhere*) adds a distinct element of conservative standoffishness that becomes more prominent as you get to know these people better. But all things considered, there's enough dynamism in the *ALN* letter group to create words like *talent, affluent, unfailing, gallant, galvanize, adrenalin* and *valiant*.

If you need a point person for a school pep rally, contact your local *ALN;* their vitality will infuse energy into any group without them dominating the situation. But although *ALN*s have an uncommon ability to mingle, there's something naggingly aloof about their social interactions. For no matter how caught up in a conversation they may seem, there's always the feeling that they might withdraw their involvement at any moment. This ability to detach themselves extends to their relationships as well,

Alan
Alana
Alden
Aleen
Alanis
Alejandro
Aileen
Alena
Alene
Alina
Aline
Allen

where *ALN*s often hold their lovers at arm's length as a way of easily extricating themselves when the situation gets too intimate.

Somehow *ALN*s manage to project an air of relaxed intensity. They certainly aren't excitable types and are able to accomplish great things while maintaining relatively low stress levels. Perhaps this is partly due to the subtle control that *ALN*s exercise over their friends and coworkers, but it likely has something to do with the tight discipline that *ALN*s maintain over their own lives. This seemingly laid-back attitude might sometimes be mistaken for weakness, but those who watch *ALN*s at work quickly grasp the fact that these are uncommonly persistent people.

*ALN*s usually take on traditional roles in their relationships. The male *ALN* dutifully brings home the bacon, while his female counterpart assumes her role as mistress of the house without protest. As can be expected from these conservatives-at-heart, their marriages are stable, their children well-disciplined and their friends carefully chosen. *ALN*s would be advised to occasionally loosen the self-imposed controls on their lives and indulge instead in the rewards of simplicity and disorder.

Alanis Morrisette Who better to play God than the empathetic, quirky Alanis Morrisette? Some fans even claimed she was being typecast when she appeared in the movie *Dogma* in 1999 as the Supreme Being. Isn't it ironic? ■ The Ottawa-born Alanis began writing songs at the age of nine and made an early impact on the local music scene where she was affectionately referred to as Canada's answer to the 1980s American pop star Tiffany. ■ Her quirky on-stage persona and the introspective lyrics of her first major album, *Jagged Little Pill*, made it one of the best-selling albums of all time. It currently holds the record for best-selling album by a solo artist. ■ "I have mixed emotions about getting awards. I don't feel I'm better than any other female artist. I'm just different. Everything we're all doing is valid."

Charisma	💋💋💋💋💋💋💋💋💋💋
Career Success	💰💰💰💰💰💰💰💰💰💰
Love & Friendship	💘💘💘💘💘💘💘💘💘
Power	💣💣💣💣💣💣💣💣💣💣

**Creative Sharp Attentive
Bossy Blunt Self-conscious**

Over three million people in the United States have names that begin with the letters *AL,* and it's easy to understand why. For when the self-*assured* letter *A* combines with the *lusty, lively* and *loving* qualities of the *L,* it creates the vibrant phoneme associated with the words *alert, altruism, alive, alluring, all right* and *almighty*. The addition of the *softly sensual* and *sexy S* sounds at the end of these names confers on these people their trademark air of feminine sexuality.

Even though *ALS*s have the native toughness common to most *A* names, these are not names designed for the rough and tumble of politics or leadership. The distinctly thoughtful and gentle qualities in their names make it much more likely to find them in creative and artistic fields, particularly in areas of dance and acting.

Although *ALS*s tend to elicit admiration from other people with their deliberately spunky and self-confident approach to life, no one would ever accuse them of being self-absorbed or disinterested in others. On the contrary, they can be downright annoying in their pursuit of information regarding the intimate details of people's lives. Nosey? Let's just say that they consider it their *duty* to know everything about everyone.

Alice
Alecia
Aleshia
Alesia
Ainsley
Alessandra
Allison
Alonzo
Alica
Alicia
Alisa
Alise
Alyse

The *ALS*'s belief that knowledge is power means that they hate being out of touch with what's going on in the world. Their love for listening to the news (or is it gossip?) comes in handy in their careers, which usually include a combination of creative challenges and people-management. It's the creative side of the *ALS* personality that usually brings them the most attention, so whether it's writing, performing or just messing about on their computers, self-expression is ultimately the reason that they get out of bed in the morning.

It's not easy to pin these elusive creatures down when it comes to matters of romance. While some might think that this is because *ALS*s are overly picky when it comes to dating, it's probably more of a reflection of the *ALS*s' unwillingness to commit themselves to long-term arrangements without minutely dissecting all the pros and cons.

Married to an *ALS*? They'll probably be your best friends, your biggest fans, and your most persistent annoyances all rolled into one. But this dynamic and affectionate package will be a boon to any family, and no one could ever ask for a more intently solicitous friend, lover and parent.

Alicia Silverstone With a bad girl on-screen persona that is said to be the mirror image of her off-screen personality, Alicia Silverstone has been responsible for the impure thoughts of millions of teen boys. ■ When filming *The Crush* at the age of fifteen, it was necessary for her to become legally emancipated in order to work the long hours demanded by the film's shooting schedule. The demure actress turned down the nude scene in the movie, requesting that a body double be used instead. She also turned down the movie *The Babysitter* until the screenwriters removed all nudity from the script. ■ For all her movie achievements, Alicia is still best remembered for her appearance in three Aerosmith videos, a career move that still needles her: "I hate people who call me 'that Aerosmith chick,'" she says.

THE INVENTIVE alx

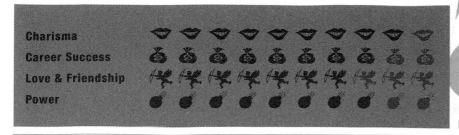

Charisma										
Career Success										
Love & Friendship										
Power										

**Individualistic Complex Unique
Restless Eccentric Escapist**

Over three million people in the United States have names that begin with the letters *AL*. This is hardly surprising when one considers the effect of the *authoritarian* letter *A*'s union with the *lively* and *loving* letter *L,* which creates the dynamism inherent in the words *alert, altruism, alive, alluring, all right* and *almighty.* Even so, *ALX* names number fewer than 200,000 in the United States, which is probably a reflection of parents' reluctance to incorporate the mysterious and misunderstood letter *X* in their children's names. When they do, however, the *X* colors these names with its distinct sense of non-conformity, and these children tend to take paths in life that express a love for the unusual.

Laid back? No doubt about it. The *LX* letter combination is found in words like *deluxe, luxury, relax* and *flexible*—all of which go a long way in describing these people's penchant for comfort and material wealth. These are *complex* people, too. In fact, the names *Alexander* and *Alexandria* are among the longest names in the English language, and their convoluted personalities reflect the intricate structure of their names.

*ALX*s are larger-than-life, enthusiastic individuals

Alex
Alexa
Alexander
Alexandra
Alexandria
Alexandro
Alexia
Alexis
Alix

whose charisma often proves irresistible. Yet although everyone seems to agree that *ALX*s are warm-hearted, they also have a tendency toward arrogance, which—if not reined in—can prevent them from being fully appreciated.

But for sheer originality and strength of character, *ALX* people are hard to beat. Nothing is without significance to the *ALX*. Their creative tendencies direct these individuals to uncharted modes of self-expression, which is why they are often noted for their odd hobbies and compulsion for the dramatic. Whether it's sculpture, design or computer programming, everything the *ALX* does will be influenced by his or her signature flair.

A relationship with an *ALX* will probably also prove to be an unconventional encounter. Without being militant, they are very much non-traditionalists when it comes to their love lives and will structure their personal affairs accordingly. On the upside, the *ALX*'s liberal attitude toward love and relationships often includes a refreshing approach to sexuality, to which partners are often surprised to find themselves becoming addicted.

Alexander Graham Bell It's always interesting when people go by both their first and middle names; particularly when one's first name is as complex as Alexander. There are, in fact, no fewer than six syllables in the man's name, suggesting a superiority complex or, at the very least, a very strong self-image. ■ Bell's invention, the telephone, came through his work with deaf children. After experimenting with a human ear, a tympanum, and magnets, he realized that an electric current could be made to change intensity as precisely as air density varies during sound production. ■ According to Bell's journal entry, the first words spoken through the telephone were to his assistant, Thomas Watson: "Mr. Watson— come here—I want to see you." ■ To this day, no one knows where Bell obtained the ear on which he experimented.

15

am

Charisma	👄 👄 👄 👄 👄 👄 👄 👄 👄 👄
Career Success	💰 💰 💰 💰 💰 💰 💰 💰 💰 💰
Love & Friendship	🦅 🦅 🦅 🦅 🦅 🦅 🦅 🦅 🦅 🦅
Power	💣 💣 💣 💣 💣 💣 💣 💣 💣 💣

Effervescent Nurturing Self-aware
Indecisive Self-doubting Impulsive

While most names beginning with the letter *A* tend to signify someone with *authority* and self-confidence, the letter *M* is the symbol for all things *motherly*, *maternal* and *mellow*. It's not surprising, then, that people whose names feature the *A* and *M* in close proximity to each other are often described as being *amiable, amenable, amusing, amazing* and *amorous*.

But *AM*s are no Casanovas or femmes fatales. For although their names resonate a mouth-watering sensuality, they lack the raw carnality of names beginning with the letters *R, V* and *S*. This may explain why *AM*s tend to play the ingénues rather than the sexual bombshells in Hollywood.

There are few dark corners in the *AM* personality, and although they're prone to making unwise emotional investments (making choices with their hearts instead of their heads), they are usually forthcoming about their expectations of their partners and themselves. When one has the *AM*'s level of sensitivity, emotional ups and downs are to be expected, and *AM*s are going to be at their best when paired with a partner able to keep them on an even keel. They *need* that stability and reassurance, for though they give the impression of being in complete control,

Amy
Aimee
Akeem
Amani
Amara
Amari
Annamarie
America
Amaya
Amina
Amira
Amya
Amos
Amir

there's often a person struggling with feelings of inferiority and self-doubt just under the surface. Cautious about introducing people into their lives, it can take many years for new acquaintances to gain the *AM*'s trust, which explains their insistence on maintaining so much private space in their new relationships.

*AM*s are more loyal and family-oriented than most, but because of their enormous creative intelligence, they tend to neglect the other aspects of their development . . . with education and reading taking a back seat to having fun. This isn't to say that *AM*s, bright as they are, aren't going to succeed in school; it's just that they often find it difficult saying "no" to social invitations.

Those out to find romance should definitely knock on the *AM*'s door. But you may not want to open that door right away unless you think you can handle *AM*s' reluctance to emotionally liberate themselves from ex-lovers. From the *AM*'s perspective, it doesn't make sense to sever ties with a person with whom they had a healthy and rewarding relationship, and only with the prospect of a *truly* committed relationship will they reluctantly throw away all the old photos and dedicate themselves entirely to one partner.

Amy Irving Amy Irving was a classic screen beauty when she made her acting debut in Stephen King's *Carrie*; and as the only survivor of the gym fire, went on to star in the unfortunate sequel, *Carrie 2*. Still, Amy's poise and grace led her to receive an Oscar nomination for her role in *Yentl* with Barbra Streisand. ■ Amy had a son during her four-year marriage to Steven Spielberg, before the couple divorced in 1989. Her divorce may have had something to do with the fact that Spielberg fathered a daughter with Kate Capshaw—of Indiana Jones fame—while they were still together. ■ The following year, a record divorce settlement left Amy $40,000,000 to help soothe her pride, and in 1990 she married Brazilian director Bruno Baretto.

ambr

Charisma	👄	👄	👄	👄	👄	👄	👄	👄	👄	👄
Career Success	💰	💰	💰	💰	💰	💰	💰	💰	💰	
Love & Friendship	🦅	🦅	🦅	🦅	🦅	🦅	🦅	🦅	🦅	
Power	💣	💣	💣	💣	💣	💣	💣			

**Strong Effervescent Nimble
Dawdling Overconfident Unheeding**

It's easy to understand why the parents of a young baby might choose to name her after the exquisite qualities found in fossilized tree sap: its radiant translucence and resilience against the depredation of time makes it a highly prized jewel. It's also no coincidence that these same qualities are conveyed through the letters in the name *Amber*. When the self-assurance of the letter *A* combines with the steadfastly maternal letter *M*, it embodies the reliable strength found in the words *amazing, ambassador, amulet, ample, amigo* and *ambrosia* (the food of the Gods). Then there's the matter of the *BR* suffix, shining through in the form of *brilliant, bright, brisk, breezy, breathy, bracing* and *brusque*. All told, an *AMBR* personality is singularly refreshing—a person to be appreciated like a cool glass of water. In fact, many people report that being around an *AMBR* is so invigorating that they were able to achieve things they think might have been impossible without his or her inspiration.

*AMBR*s tend to get tripped up, though, when it comes to their own decision-making. One of the weaknesses that comes with the strength of the *A* names is the arrogant assumption that they can single-handedly master any situation. As a result, many *AMBR*s charge

Amber
Ambrose

headlong into situations—careers, relationships and business deals—often leaving them floundering. And being the bold outgoing types that they are, they often turn to the wrong people for help and drive themselves even deeper into trouble. Still, even when they do make those impulsive leaps, *AMBR*s invariably land on their feet. They have the instinctive ability to make friends no matter where they go, which more than compensates for their sometimes-unsound judgments.

Their flighty tendencies often prevent *AMBR*s from settling into careers and relationships until relatively late in their lives—there are so many things and people to enjoy that they can't imagine choosing just one. And while this brand of free-spiritedness might get on other peoples' nerves when they're trying to pin her down, she isn't going to let it bother her too much. She'll make up her mind when she's good and ready.

When an *AMBR does* decide to settle down, it'll be because they are ready to raise a family and not because they are hopelessly in love. Even though their children will be doted upon, *AMBR*s will fiercely protect their own independence and make sure that they never lose their beaming spirit.

Amber Benson One of the stars of UPN's long-running series, *Buffy the Vampire Slayer*, Amber Benson was in her teens when she became involved in productions at her local community center. Her reviews were so positive that she signed up for acting lessons and asked her family to move to Los Angeles. ■ Turning pro, Amber's specialty—playing the "best friend" —landed her parts in the movies *The Crush* with Alicia Silverstone, and *Bye Bye Love* with Eliza Dusku. ■ It was as Tara, her recurring role in *Buffy*, that Amber made the most impact. Starring Sarah Michelle Gellar, the cult show is the only UPN TV show to appear on the list of the top one hundred TV series of all time.

Charisma	👄 👄 👄 👄 👄 👄 👄 👄 👄 👄
Career Success	💰 💰 💰 💰 💰 💰 💰 💰 💰 💰
Love & Friendship	🦁 🦁 🦁 🦁 🦁 🦁 🦁 🦁 🦁
Power	💣 💣 💣 💣 💣 💣 💣 💣 💣 💣

**Decisive Insightful Energetic
Restless Uncompromising Insecure**

Most names beginning with the letter *A* suggest a personality of *authority, arrogance* and *absolutism.* And when combined with the maternal and motherly letter *M,* these names take on the air of benign power found in the words: *amazing, ambassador, amulet, ample, amigo* and *ambrosia.* Because these reassuring characteristics are amplified by the *dominant* qualities of the *dapper, dignified* letter *D,* we expect the *AMD*s of this world to be defined by gentility and an adamant refusal to be pushed around. Those whose names also contain the letter *R* (*Armond, Armindo* and *Armondo*), are blessed with the lusty passions of this letter of *romance, raciness, randiness* and *robustness.*

Seldom aggressive and always tactful, *AMD* people are those behind-the-scenes individuals who prefer to facilitate rather than direct. Their natural sociability lends itself well to dealing with people in all kinds of situations, but *AMD*s are better designed to achieve success in their business lives than in their personal lives. Articulate, ambitious and commanding, they're characterized by a kind of dizzy energy, which—while allowing them to stay focused on their work—makes them vulnerable to losing sight of their goals.

Amado
Amanda
Armanda
Armand
Armando

Although *AMD*s are more likely to follow their heads than their hearts, they have an instinctive empathy for the emotional needs of others, which explains why so many people are drawn to the *AMD*'s intense nature. When you enter their inner circle, there's a sense of coming in from the cold, but like most people whose names begin with the letter *A*, this warmth can burn with resentment when disloyalty is suspected.

*AMD*s are industrious and efficient in their business lives, but have a tendency toward rigidity under stress. This lack of flexibility might cost them in their careers, but with their extraordinary abilities to overcome obstacles, new doors open as quickly as *AMD*s slam them shut. A low-key work environment would go a long way in easing their tension, but *AMD*s will have none of this: they are irresistibly drawn toward high-stress pursuits like journalism, medicine, management and finance.

Because *AMD*s' enthusiastic approach to their relationships is awkwardly coupled with some deep (and well-hidden) insecurities, the *AMD*'s mate will have to be particularly perceptive and even-tempered if the union is going to have a chance of surviving into old age.

Armand Hammer You're not alone if you always thought Armand Hammer was the manufacturer of the popular baking soda refrigerator deodorizer. The name actually belongs to an immensely wealthy industrialist, art collector and philanthropist, who was the son of a Russian immigrant and Communist Party member. Armand went on to make his first few million dollars running his father's pharmaceutical business. ■ After he bought the near-bankrupt Occidental Petroleum in 1956 and turned it into a billion-dollar conglomerate, he used his influence to promote U.S.-Soviet relations throughout the Cold War. ■ In fostering cultural and commercial exchanges with the Soviet Union, Armand became one of a handful of Americans trusted by both the Soviet and U.S. governments to represent the U.S. State Department in times of crises.

Charisma	👄	👄	👄	👄	👄	👄	👄	👄	👄	👄
Career Success	💰	💰	💰	💰	💰	💰	💰	💰	💰	💰
Love & Friendship	🦅	🦅	🦅	🦅	🦅	🦅	🦅	🦅	🦅	🦅
Power	💣	💣	💣	💣	💣	💣	💣	💣	💣	💣

**Resilient Intuitive Explorative
Repressed Moody Bossy**

As the letter of *arrogance, autocrats* and *absolutes*, the letter *A* suggests an air of superiority and dominance in the names in which it appears. So when this self-*assured* letter combines with the *maternal, motherly* and *mellow M* to form the *AM* phoneme, it reflects the benign power found in the words *amazing, ambassador, amulet, ample, amigo* and *ambrosia*. The appearance of the letter *L* (the symbol of *life, love, laughter* and *learning*) is responsible for suffusing these names with their erudite and bookish qualities: suggesting personalities that are superbly equipped to handle all aspects of human interactions.

Alma
Amalia
Amela
Amelia
Amal

This strong sense of self-awareness often leads *AML*s down untrodden paths, and whether they find themselves in the fields of psychology or business, or in personal relationships, they are explorers at heart who feel compelled to try out new approaches. This is what makes them such competent people-managers—they're always seeing things from the other point of view, chasing down the big picture, and sharing their visions. Unless you're made of stone, it's impossible not to feel inspired with an *AML* in your orbit.

The *AML*'s fundamental belief that the world works in an orderly way makes her the first person that others turn to for guidance. But it's not only her insight that draws people in; it's that critical/sympathetic combination that makes others feel that they're getting honest advice for their money. And once she's convinced someone that she really cares about them, she can get away with volunteering honest and straightforward criticism that can make a real difference. Her flair for pinning down problems would make her an outstanding counselor and caretaker, and she should consider psychology, psychiatry or medicine to challenge her sharp, inquisitive mind.

The downside of being an insightful, dynamic adventure-seeker is the corresponding loneliness when she can't find anyone able to keep up with her, or when she feels that no one understands her. When this occurs, it's not unusual for an *AML* to withdraw and run the risk of becoming isolated and depressed.

The *AML* needs someone to balance her moods and bring her back to reality from time to time, and she functions best when paired with a mate who is her psychological opposite: relaxed, upbeat and not overly analytical. Oddly enough, *AML*s often find their niche in motherhood, which transforms these somewhat changeable maidens into contented matriarchs.

Amelia Earhart It must have taken a great deal of resolve for a young woman in the 1920s to even think about becoming a pilot. But after being enthralled by flight at an air show in Long Beach California, Amelia Earhart purchased her first plane and became the first woman to cross the Atlantic—albeit as a passenger. Her subsequent solo flight over the Atlantic set a world record for speed. ■ In 1937 she set off to be the first woman to circumnavigate the world, but after flying over 22,000 miles, vanished into thin air. ■ Although no trace of her plane was found, rumors swirled that she had been captured by the Japanese and was living with a fisherman on an island in the Pacific. No definitive evidence ever surfaced.

an

Charisma	👄	👄	👄	👄	👄	👄	👄	👄	👄	👄	👄
Career Success	💰	💰	💰	💰	💰	💰	💰	💰	💰	💰	
Love & Friendship	💘	💘	💘	💘	💘	💘	💘	💘	💘		
Power	💣	💣	💣	💣	💣	💣	💣	💣	💣	💣	

Because the letter *A* tends to be associated with all that is *autocratic, authoritative* and *arrogant*, and the letter *N* is the letter of *no, never, not, nowhere, nothing, naught, nyet* and *nada,* the somewhat nasal *AN* names evoke an interesting meld of self-confidence and pessimism. These properties can be seen in many words that begin with the *AN* root, (*anger, antagonize, anxious, anti, anguish* and *annoy*) and perhaps accounts for the fickle tendencies of the *AN*'s emotional baseline. Those who use the lighthearted and youthful *Y* at the end of their names (*Annie, Ansley, Anaya and Anya*) offset this negativity by signaling a somewhat more approachable personality.

Even if these names exude a nobility and refinement reminiscent of English gentry, *AN*s are anything but Victorian. On the contrary, they are almost invariably passionate and even positively heady. It's their unique combination of the sensual and the divine that makes them so irresistible to the opposite sex, and *AN*s are not unaware of these charms—nor afraid to use them. This is why *AN*s are typically confident and extroverted, and why they pull so few punches in their relationships. Strong without being abrasive, if you're ever down on your luck and in need of an encouraging word, you should call on one of your

Ann
Anais
Anika
Anissa
Anna
Annalise
Aniya
Annie
Annika
Annmarie
Ansley
Anya
Austin
Ayana

AN friends. They will almost always have something positive to say, and while this may not put money in your wallet, they have a way of making you feel a little richer.

These are not names designed for hard-core business success. The independent *AN* personality prefers playing in the limelight (show business in particular), wherein they can indulge their playful and sensual charisma. Still, they always retain that cool inner distance and resent the familiarity of strangers. Their bonding instincts are satisfied through relationships with just a few close friends, although there's usually a troupe of casual acquaintances demanding their attentions.

Problems arise when an *AN* gives in to the creeping ennui of everyday life. They are people who need constant stimulation, and in their worst moods can become quite cranky and pessimistic, forcing partners to drag them out of their rut. And although these articulate and intelligent creatures can express their *ideas* clearly, they struggle to do the same with their emotions. Consequently, loved ones must tread softly in the realm of conflict lest the *AN*s shut their feelings in, and them out. But once you've garnered an *AN*'s trust, you'll be blessed with a partner who'll stop at nothing to make you happy.

Anne Heche Few actresses have attracted as much controversy in their ten-year careers as Anne Heche. What catapulted this otherwise journeyman actress to celebrity was the revelation that she was dating Ellen DeGeneres. ■ Anne's career had already survived some poor decisions (like appearing in the film *Girls in Prison*), and then her relationship with Ellen unfairly marked her as a gay actress. Even though she struggled to land romantic roles, she did do quite well playing opposite Harrison Ford in *Six Days Seven Nights*. ■ Her widely publicized breakdown after her separation from Ellen further hurt her chances at choice roles, but true to the Hollywood axiom of "any publicity is good publicity," she was soon back in the public eye with her best-selling memoir, *Call Me Crazy*.

Charisma	👄	👄	👄	👄	👄	👄	👄	👄	👄	👄
Career Success	💰	💰	💰	💰	💰	💰	💰	💰	💰	💰
Love & Friendship										
Power										

Humorous Pleasing Good-natured
Sentimental Bungling Imperceptive

When the *authoritarian* letter *A* and the *negative* letter *N* (*no, never, not, nyet, nein, nada, nothing, naught and nowhere*) come together at the beginning of a word, they create a level of tension manifested in words like *anger, antagonize, anxious, anti, anguish* and *annoy*. Fortunately, the *BL* phoneme gives these names a distinct sense of the wild, untamable spirit found in the words *blustery, blizzard, blowing, blaze* and *bloom*.

Consequently, *ANBL* personalities have an inherent duality . . . almost as if they're a mighty boss woman and a wild child rolled into one. These women are comfortable revealing their submissiveness, knowing full well that compliance comes from strength and not capitulation. But if they feel that their generosity is being taken for granted, they'll readily turn the tables and display their authoritarian sides. These displays of power are mostly short-lived, however, and *ANBLs* are quick to offer a conciliatory joke or a familial intimacy to salve any bruised egos.

These qualities make the *ANBLs* solid workmates and desirable partners when it comes to those sensitive jobs that call for someone responsible and dependable to grease the wheels. This is why *ANBLs* are so sought-after in journalism and broadcasting fields; they possess the serious-but-not-deadly demeanor so prevalent on newscasts like CNN. But *ANBLs* don't believe in limiting their experiences—there are too many other avenues for their inquiring minds. Their sense of adventure may lead them abroad or simply be expressed through their compulsive reading.

The *ANBL* lover tends to be deeply devoted to her mate, giving her a stable platform on which she can express her deepest secrets. But the downside of depending so heavily on her partner for companionship is a tendency to exclude all her other relationships. As a consequence, she has nowhere to turn when problems arise in her primary relationship.

If you're married to an *ANBL*, you'll enjoy the freedom afforded by being with someone who values her autonomy and encourages the same in her partner: your Monday-night football ritual is perfectly fine by her as long as she gets her weekly Saturday shopping spree. A word to the wise, however: don't make any changes to the routine (either yours or hers) without first consulting her. She isn't the sort who enjoys surprises, and any tinkering with her daily life is sure to generate conflict and provoke one of her sullen moods.

Annabella
Annabel

Annabel Lee It was many and many a year ago, / In a kingdom by the sea, / That a maiden there lived whom you may know / By the name of Annabel Lee; / And this maiden she lived with no other thought / Than to love and be loved by me. ■ The angels, not half so happy in heaven, / Went envying her and me. / Yes! That was the reason (as all men know, / In this kingdom by the sea) / That the wind came out of the cloud by night, / Chilling and killing my Annabel Lee. ■ For the moon never beams without bringing me dreams / Of the beautiful Annabel Lee; / And so, all the night-tide, I lie down by the side / Of my darling—my darling—my life and my bride, / In the sepulchre there by the sea, / In her tomb by the sounding sea. —Edgar Allan Poe

and

Charisma										
Career Success										
Love & Friendship										
Power										

Strong Introspective Aware
Conspiratorial Phobic Calculating

The combination of the authoritarian letter *A* and the negative letter *N* sets up a level of tension that manifests itself in many pessimistic forms (*anger, antagonize, anxious, anti, anguish* and *annoy*) and it's this friction that creates the inherent conflict in the *AND* personalities. The *dark* qualities of the letter *D* (*death, destruction, doom, damnation* and *despotism*) don't do much to mitigate the problem, and even those whose names incorporate the letter *R* (*Andrea, Andre, Andrew*) are affected by the *dr*amatic effects of the *DR* phoneme found in the words *druid, dragon, drek, drum, dream, drastic* and *dread*.

Consequently, many *AND*s choose to soften their names by using the diminutive form(*Andy* and *Andie*)—suggesting a person somewhat uncomfortable with the inherent arrogance of their names. The diminutizing effect of the *Y* and *IE* at the end of a name has its roots in childhood, when parents unconsciously soften their speech by appending words with high-frequency tones (*cat* becomes *kitty, dog* becomes *doggy,* and *blanket* becomes *blankie*).

Since these names are influenced by some of the darker aspects of the human condition, *AND*s tend to struggle with occasional bouts of cynicism that color their outlooks and permeate their relationships. But

Anders
Anderson
Andre
Andrea
Andreas
Andres
Andrew
Andy

although these are individuals who prefer to see the glass as being half empty, *AND*s consider themselves to be realists (rather than pessimists) who are simply being candid about the state of the world. While this may translate as a tendency to stomp on the flower of hope when it blooms, *AND*s feel that it's their duty to tell the truth. If nothing else, you'll never be in doubt as to where they stand. These are unquestionably strong individuals who are not going to be swayed by criticism.

As an extension of their serious natures, *AND*s have a tendency to parent those around them and bring all the elements of a big brother or sister into their relationships. While this might prove tedious to some, it will prove attractive to those who need honest criticism in their lives. And *this* is where the *AND* personality shines. When they feel appreciated, there is nothing they wouldn't do for a friend.

Life with *AND*s may be comfortable and predictable, but expect it to be punctuated by periodic bursts of high maintenance. Still, their saving grace is rooted in their exceptional communication skills, and because they will always talk things out before losing their tempers, you can count on family life flowing along relatively smoothly.

Andrew Jackson Old Hickory was a self-made man who went on to become the seventh President of the United States. The Southern politician married the same woman on two separate occasions after he discovered that she had not been legally divorced the first time. ■ A general of the Tennessee militia during the 1812 War, Andrew had proved to be a major pain to the British, routing them at the Battle of New Orleans. ■ After losing a close race to John Adams in 1824, Andrew won the Presidency in 1828. As a two-term President, he walked a tightrope between the issues of slavery and states' rights, and continued his merciless relocation of Indians. ■ Ultimately, Jackson's legacy was in giving the new Democratic Party its image of champion of the common man.

ang

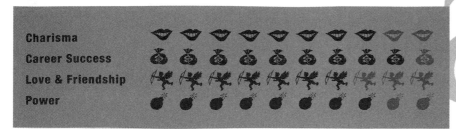

Charisma	💋	💋	💋	💋	💋	💋	💋	💋	💋	💋
Career Success	💰	💰	💰	💰	💰	💰	💰	💰	💰	
Love & Friendship	👼	👼	👼	👼	👼	👼	👼	👼		
Power	💣	💣	💣	💣	💣	💣	💣	💣		

**Complex Warn Spiritual
Dark Volatile Impulsive**

With its superficial connection to the word *angel*, the *ANG* root seems to promise a personality brimming with virtue and innocence. But on closer examination, we find that when the *authoritarian* letter *A* and the *negative* letter *N* (*no, nothing, nyet, nein, never, nowhere, naught*) appear at the beginning of names, it sets up the level of tension found in the words *anger, antagonize, anxious, anti, anguish* and *annoyance*. Fortunately, the letter *G* in these names is the softly pronounced version—as in *genial, gentle* and *generous*—and mitigates some of the *AN*'s bite. Names that incorporate the *GL* phoneme (*Angela, Angelina*) have the added advantage of being associated with the lighter side of life, as seen in the words *gleam, glitter, glitzy, glamorous, glint, glimmer* and *glow.*

In an attempt to further soften the implications of the darker aspects of the *AN* phoneme, many women use the feminizing *Angie* version of this root. It's always significant when individuals choose to end their names with this diminutizing sound, because the addition of the letter *Y* at the end of a name softens its aggressive qualities, as parents do when they end words with high-frequency tones (*cat* becomes *kitty*, *dog* becomes *doggy*, and *blanket* becomes *blankie*).

Angel
Angela
Angelica
Angelina
Angelique
Angelita
Angelo
Angie
Anjali
Anjelica

It's true that *ANG* personalities exhibit many of the qualities associated with angels: they are mysterious and ethereal, but also slightly dangerous. So it's good to be on your guard with an *ANG* around, because you never know when their sunny dispositions are going to cloud over and cast a chill over the encounter. *ANGs* usually don't mean any harm, but since their moods seem to change faster than they can handle, it leaves them unprepared for the impact of their emotions. And although *ANGs*' gifts may not lie in the area of empathetic friendship, they have their own particular ways of showing they care. Once you've been adopted into an *ANG*'s tight circle of friends, you'll never want for someone to watch your back.

To successfully partner an *ANG*, you'll need a blend of patience, imagination and independence. Although the *ANG* personality craves the kind of intimacy that comes from being attached at the hip, they also require plenty of room in which to experiment and are certainly not the stay-at-home types. So don't expect the traditional family routine of backrubs and breakfast in bed. You're far more likely to be treated to a wild ride of unexpected affection and unconventional bonding rituals.

Angelina Jolie Like her contemporary Liv Tyler, box-office queen Angelina Jolie can thank her father for her preternaturally pouty lips. ■ Born to Academy Award winning actor John Voight and French actress Marcheline Bertrand, Angelina chose to use her middle name instead of her real surname so as not to ride on the coattails of her famous father. ■ Her marriage to Academy Award–winning Billy Bob Thornton—who has a habit of tattooing himself with the name of every woman he falls in love with—was one of the most talked-about unions in Hollywood. After having three previous tattoos covered up, he was convinced that his mushroom-shaped Angie would stay. "She's my soul mate," he said. ■ Angelina and Billy Bob were divorced in 2003.

Charisma	👄	👄	👄	👄	👄	👄	👄	👄	👄	👄	
Career Success	💰	💰	💰	💰	💰	💰	💰	💰	💰	💰	
Love & Friendship											
Power											

**Focused Dependable Punctual
Smug Unheeding Self-important**

Whenever the *authoritarian* letter *A* and the *negative* letter *N* are combined at the beginning of a name, they set up the feeling of *anxiety* found in the words *anger, antagonize, anti, anguish* and *annoy.* The sharpness of the terminating letter *T* don't help matters either, for it's from the *ANT* phoneme that we get the words *anthrax, distant, vacant, adamant, errant* and *defiant,* as well as the negative *anti-* prefix: *antichrist, antisocial* and *antithesis.* Luckily, the name *Anthony,* these effects are largely offset by the spiritually uplifting *TH* phoneme, from which we get *thoughtful, theological, thankful, thorough, thespian* and *theater.*

Until you get to know *ANTs* quite intimately, expect them to project an aura of holier-than-thou or standoffishness; *ANTs* feel a responsibility to keep their friends (and society in general) on the straight and narrow. Nothing pleases them quite so much as spotting someone in need of advice, and *ANTs* will feel quite free to wag their fingers in the face of these unfortunates. Because this habit doesn't win them many friends, *ANTs* often find themselves alienated without ever understanding why.

Although there's a bit of the class nerd in every *ANT,* they somehow manage to come across as being classy and quasi-sophisticated. Thereafter, to success-

Anita
Anastasia
Annette
Anthony
Antoinette
Antonia
Antonio
Anton
Antony

fully converse with one of these brighter-than-average individuals, one needs to be well versed in everything from contemporary politics to the current alignment of the planets . . . and be prepared for a scholarly discussion on the topic to boot.

While *ANTs* experience a certain amount of internal angst, it's tempered by their thoughtful and analytical approach to life, and despite their touchiness, they are desirable employees to have around when a structured, no-nonsense environment is called for. They're the ideal administrative assistants, always checking clocks, marking calendars, and never running late for appointments. You could expect the *ANT* to take twelve pages of notes on a half-hour meeting and then make copies for everyone. It's interesting that their namesake is a small, dynamic, hardworking insect that can carry ten times its own body weight.

The *ANT's* home life is a well-ordered affair, with family members easily adapting to their place in the scheme of things. *ANTs* are anything but clingy, and although their authoritative side will occasionally flex its muscles, their firm and clearheaded parenting style will give their children the restraint and confidence for which they'll be grateful in later years.

Anastasia Romanova No name haunts the Russian conscience more than Anastasia, the youngest daughter of Tsar Nicholas II of Russia. Anastasia perished when the Romanov family was brutally executed by the Bolsheviks in 1918. ■ The family was imprisoned in Siberia after being taken prisoner during the Russian Revolution. One night they were roused from their sleep and ordered to the basement, where soldiers opened fire at point-blank range. The Tsar and his wife died quickly, but their teenage daughters did not. Jewels sewn inside their clothes deflected the fire until bayonets silenced their screams. ■ There were rumors that Anastasia survived the killings and a woman named Anna Manahan, amongst others, claimed to be Anastasia until DNA evidence disproved her claim.

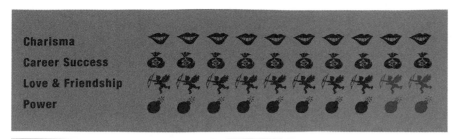

Charisma		
Career Success		
Love & Friendship		
Power		

Considerate Down-to-earth Versatile
Distracted Proud Flighty

The *AR* name root suggests a personality that takes itself rather seriously, and perhaps the influence of the drawn-out *aah* sound must take credit for this brand of confidence. After all, this sound is the key component of words like *father, awe, arbiter, archangel, aristocracy, Armageddon* and *arrogance*. The *autocratic A* and *royal, red-blooded* letter *R* renders them the kings and queens of whatever domain they inhabit, and they wear their autonomy with haughty grace. These individuals walk with their heads held high and their steps carefully measured.

But lest you feel intimidated in the *AR*s' presence, there's a trick you can use to gain their eternal affections: they're suckers for expensive gifts and wild nights on the town. Oh, and nothing pleases *AR*s more than finding someone who agrees with their opinion. When stroked, coddled and spoiled, *AR*s will return the favor tenfold, so if you've done your homework on the *AR* ego, you can expect them to behave with consideration, thoughtfulness and loyalty.

With all this jaunty self-confidence, *AR*s tend to ignore criticism that comes their way. It's not that they're particularly arrogant (in fact *AR*s can be quite approachable), it's simply that they're quite certain that they're a little better than everyone else. But they're more than willing to forgive an indiscretion committed

Areli
Araceli
Arden
Ari
Aria
Aric
Ariel
Artis
Arturo
Art
Artie
Aurelio
Aurora
Arjun

by a critic; after all, anyone (except an *AR*) can have a bad day.

In the working world, the *AR*'s combination of aggression and sensitivity goes a long way in furthering their choice of career, which often involves management or money-handling of some kind. People respond positively to their warm, direct (if sometimes pushy) leadership styles, but as long as the *AR*s are running the show, they'll be as happy as clams at high tide. The arts have a strong pull on the *AR*s, though it might be said that their enthusiasm is stronger than their ability. Still, a trifling thing such as lack of talent would never prevent *AR*s from doing exactly what they wanted, and you'll often find them practicing hard on their latest artistic or musical endeavors. It's usually through determination—rather than aptitude—that they manage to leave their mark in the creative fields, and they fulfill the adage about practice making perfect to an impressive degree.

When it comes to their intimate relationships, *AR*s tend to have so many irons in the fire that it's hard to get their attentions. So if you're expecting an attentive listener, you may want to look elsewhere. It's not that *AR*s don't care about your problems; it's just that they have a lot on their minds and aren't particularly skilled at multitasking.

Art Garfunkel When only fifteen, Art Garfunkel teamed up with school chum Paul Simon to form the band they called Tom and Jerry. In 1958 their song "Hey Schoolgirl" made an appearance on the charts and Simon and Garfunkel made their first appearance on *American Bandstand*. ■ The two disbanded after Simon pulled out, but reemerged in 1964, when "Sounds of Silence" hit number-one. ■ Although Art was somewhat overshadowed by Simon's musical skills, his ersatz hippie style was indispensable to the duo's success in winning five Grammy Awards in 1969 for their soundtrack to *The Graduate*. ■ After parting with Simon in 1971, Art tried his hand at acting, and garnered kudos for his role in the classic Joseph Heller film, *Catch 22*.

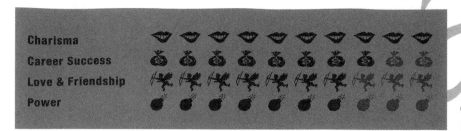

Charisma	😗 😗 😗 😗 😗 😗 😗 😗 😗 😗
Career Success	💰 💰 💰 💰 💰 💰 💰 💰 💰 💰
Love & Friendship	🐉 🐉 🐉 🐉 🐉 🐉 🐉 🐉 🐉 🐉
Power	💣 💣 💣 💣 💣 💣 💣 💣 💣 💣

Gregarious Affable Humorous
Loud Conservative Unaware

If the name *Archie* reminds you of someone who doesn't take himself all that seriously, it's not necessarily a consequence of reading too many comic books (even if the comic book *Archie*'s name was carefully chosen *because* it reflected his blithe, happy-go-lucky personality). The name *Archibald,* on the other hand—like most three-syllable names—reeks of self-consciousness and pretentiousness. When the name is contracted into *Archie,* it has the same diminutizing effect we see when *boots* become *booties, dolls* become *dollies* and *cats* become *kitties.*

Although the *ARCH* names are rich with the sense of self-*assuredness* that comes from the authoritarian letter *A,* they are redeemed by the addition of the benign qualities of the *CH* phoneme: *cheeky, cheery, childlike, chirpy, chummy, cherubic* and *church.* The result is a nonthreatening, rather earthy name that suggests a man whose goal in life is to be universally liked.

You know the guy at your favorite bar who always buys a round for the crowd? He's a quintessential *ARCH,* whose warm affability extends to everyone he encounters. He's no comedian, but don't try telling *him* that because no one laughs louder at his own jokes than

Archibald
Archy

he does. Beware of being lulled into thinking he's just a teddy bear, though, for true to his authoritarian nature, he will sometimes express his single-mindedness with closed fists instead of open arms. But in the end, the *ARCH*'s generous spirit will *always* get the better of him, and such forceful displays are usually followed by apologies or another round of drinks.

*ARCH*s have a mysterious way of ending up at the top of any profession in which they compete. This might be anything from management to retail sales to rocket science, where even though you'd never get the impression that they're working particularly hard, they rarely fail to leave their mark. They're not particularly driven or pushy; they just seem to know which buttons to push to get what they want. If there's any secret to their success, it would be that they are so often underestimated by their competitors.

If the altruistic *ARCH* personality has shortcomings, it's that his enthusiasm can sometimes run away with him and create situations in which he finds himself out of his depth. But generally, his straightforward approach colors all aspects of his life. His politics are simple, his work ethic strong and his family closely held.

Archibald Cox When prosecutor Archibald Cox was fired by President Nixon in the "Saturday Night Massacre," Archibald became a household name. ■ The distinguished public servant was the special prosecutor in charge of investigating President Nixon's Watergate role, when he was summarily dismissed by the President for refusing to withdraw his demand that the White House turn over the Nixon tapes. ■ Something of a legal conservative, he found the whole business of pursuing a case against a sitting President to be personally distasteful, but Cox proved to be a man who put his principles above all else. ■ Unlike many people with the name Archibald, Cox refused to shorten his name to Archie for fear of undermining his dignity. Perhaps only a self-possessed Archibald could have taken on the President and won.

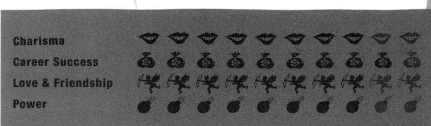

Charisma										
Career Success										
Love & Friendship										
Power										

Strong Tasteful Imaginative Cutting Fixed Haughty

Names beginning with the letter *A* usually bring with them an impression of a healthy ego, and this suggestion of self-esteem is reinforced when the *A* combines with the letter *R*. The mouth is forced open when the *AR* phoneme is pronounced (as when saying *aah)*, and one's teeth are revealed in a distinctive warning signal. Perhaps that is why the *AR* sound occurs so commonly in words demanding respect and deference: *father, arbiter, archangel, aristocracy, Armageddon* and *arrogance*. This somewhat snooty sound is hardly mitigated by the fact that the letter *N* is the archetypal symbol of *negativity,* as in *no, not, never, nyet, nein, nothing, nada* and *naught*. In an effort to soften these dictatorial elements, a significant percentage of *ARNs* add the letter *Y* (or *IE*) to the end of their names, giving them a considerably less threatening tone.

Though subtlety may not be one of their strong points, *ARNs* manage to exude a sense of refinement and innate dignity (which sometimes flares into conceit) even as young children. But if there's one thing an *ARN* personality can't abide, it's the idea that they're not getting their due recognition, and the *ARN's* associates must know which buttons to push in order to keep them happy. With a strong sense of responsibility propelled by an unmatched self-confidence, it's not unusual to find *ARNs* in political arenas,

Aaron
Ariana
Arianne
Arlen
Arlena
Arlene
Arnie
Arnold
Armani
Arnoldo
Arnulfo

as small-business owners, or simply running the lives of their friends and family.

Their propensity for emotionalism furnishes the *ARN* with an extraordinary charm, which is a good thing, because these expressive people spend a good portion of their lives unraveling the knots their impulsive hearts create. And even if you've found yourself on the wrong side of one of an *ARN's* emotional outbursts, you'll find it hard to resist his or her earnest apologies. but once you've reconciled, you'll quickly be able to bask in the glow of this enthusiastic and loving spirit.

ARNs are not ones for playing games when it comes to the important issue of love, and have limited patience for partners who refuse to pull their weight in the courting ritual. When *ARNs* enter into new partnerships, they usually do so with a strong vision of how they expect the relationship to unfold. Unfortunately, because *ARNs* are not particularly communicative about these expectations, relationships often splutter and burp before establishing their smooth tracks. This penchant for complicated relationships makes the *ARN* a stirring if somewhat exasperating mate, but with patience and a little massaging of their egos, *ARNs* will prove to be loyal and committed lovers.

Arnold Schwarzenegger One day there'll be a movie about a man who arrives in a strange country with only the barest of English skills, establishing himself as one of highest-grossing stars in Hollywood history, and finally becoming governor of California. ■ As is typical of ARN personalities, few people have a higher opinion of Arnold than Arnold himself. ■ The star of some of Hollywood's biggest-grossing movies casually describes his heart surgery: "I had to have two surgeries because the first one didn't work—I made the mistake to get up the next morning and go on the Lifecycle three hours after I woke up. The valve blew out again, and they had to go back and put another one in. I learned quickly after that to wait a little longer."

arth

Charisma	💋	💋	💋	💋	💋	💋	💋	💋	💋	💋
Career Success	💰	💰	💰	💰	💰	💰	💰	💰	💰	
Love & Friendship	🕊	🕊	🕊	🕊	🕊	🕊	🕊	🕊	🕊	🕊
Power	💣	💣	💣	💣	💣	💣	💣	💣	💣	💣

Tough Fatherly Leader
Intolerant Impatient Demanding

Notice how your teeth are revealed when you pronounce the name *Arthur*. This subtle signal serves as a subliminal warning to your audience and might explain why the *AR* word pattern so commonly occurs in deference-demanding words like *archangel, father, arbiter, aristocracy, Armageddon* and *arrogance*. The *TH* phoneme—traditionally associated with the benevolent aspects of *theology, thankfulness, thoughtful, hearth, health, father* and *mother*—compounds these names' paternal qualities and might explain why the name *Arthur* was chosen for the mythical first king of England.

Aretha
Arthur

*ARTH*s exhibit the self-assurance typical of people with *A* names and tend to be rather formal and detached individuals, like patient fathers presiding over their brood. Because they have the ability to inspire respect without a hint of intimidation, people instinctively tend to trust them, and *ARTH*s do their best to live up to these expectations.

There's no challenging *ARTH*s' status in their social groups, and as long as their "subjects" defer to their dignified authority, peace will reign in their little kingdoms. Yet the *ARTH*'s motive is not to dominate, but rather to foster an environment of learning and growth in others. From their perspectives, competent people create a better world for them to live in.

When choosing careers, the *ARTH*'s goal is to find positions that might allow him to work on his own—or at least control his own output. The *ARTH*'s work ethic is legendary, and even though they aren't driven purely by financial rewards, they almost always derive a great deal of their self-worth from their professional lives. *ARTH*s who take an entrepreneurial route in their professional lives will certainly inspire respect and loyalty in their workers, but make no mistake, working for an *ARTH* will whip even the most reticent employee into shape.

*ARTH*s often assume that they know everything about love and romance, and regard themselves as better lovers than their abilities justify. Those married to *ARTH*s have probably experienced their dominating influences (which can prove annoying to autonomous partners and downright intimidating to the meek), and explains why *ARTH*s instinctively gravitate to those who appreciate take-charge personalities and find comfort in these dovetailed unions.

Arthur Ashe Arthur Ashe's last name was taken from the name of Samuel Ashe, an early North Carolina governor who once owned Arthur's family as slaves. ■ In the sixties, it was difficult for a young black man to penetrate the elitist world of tennis, but not only did Arthur become the first black man to win a Wimbledon singles title, he eventually ranked number-one in the world. ■ His protests against apartheid in South Africa made him a controversial but respected figure. During a visit to South Africa in 1971, he was granted "honorary white" status, enabling him to eat at white restaurants. He became an inspiration to the local black community, who gave him the Zulu name Sipho, meaning "gift from God." ■ Arthur died of complications from AIDS in 1993.

ash

Charisma	👄👄👄👄👄👄👄👄👄
Career Success	💰💰💰💰💰💰💰💰💰
Love & Friendship	👼👼👼👼👼👼👼👼👼
Power	💣💣💣💣💣💣💣💣💣

Charming Moral Attractive
Escapist Obsessive Unrealistic

The demure hooks in the letter structure of the *ASH* names are easily identifiable and might explain why these were some of the most popular girls' names in the 1990s. The self-confident aspects of the initial letter *A* merge nicely with the high-frequency qualities of the *sh* sounds, which is often used as a baby-soothing mechanism by mothers. Many of these names (*Ashley, Ashlyn, Ashli*) are terminated by the *lyrical* tones of the *LY* phoneme, which is commonly associated with infantile words like *woolly, softly, lolly, golly* and *dolly*.

ASH people are natural comforters, and there's something oddly soothing about the way they communicate. Perhaps this is why aggressive type-A people tend to be so attracted to these gentle and introspective souls, who have an inherent talent for soothing the savage beast. But not all is sugar and spice when it comes to *ASH* personalities; like all names beginning with the letter *A*, there is an overriding sense of *absolute audaciousness*. ASH personalities consciously cultivate their sensual charms to wring every advantage for their careers and relationships. Not to suggest that this is a manipulation, mind you: they're simply taking stock of their assets and investing them where they're likely to generate the most interest.

Aisha
Ashanti
Asher
Ashley
Ashlyn
Ashton

More than most, *ASH*s shouldn't be judged by a first encounter. Their straightforward self-confidence is the mark of an extrovert (rather than an egotist), and this readily becomes apparent as the relationship deepens. They are deeply sensitive individuals who love a good laugh even when it's at their own expense.

When it comes to romantic entanglements, *ASH*s often prove to be serial monogamists who choose quality over quantity in their partners. And did we mention that the *ASH*s have a coarse side? They can curse like Teamsters and flaunt tempers to match—as anyone who's tried to control them has discovered. *ASH*s instinctively understand the concept of loyalty and are often surprised to discover that not every partner views life in the same way. When this happens, no reconciliation is possible, and the *ASH*s will climb onto their moral high horse and gallop off in pursuit of better pastures.

But once you've married an *ASH,* you'll encounter a deeply involved lover who depends heavily upon you for comfort and companionship. This can be a heavy burden to bear if you're the independent type who needs a lot of space, but you're likely to get back even more from the *ASH* in terms of love, reassurance and support.

Ashley Judd Being the daughter of a famous mother didn't help Ashley Judd to get started in Hollywood. In fact, when her mother Naomi and sister Wynonna were touring as the country-singing duo The Judds, it was Ashley who cleaned the trailer for ten dollars an hour. ■ It's easy to see how Ashley's demure features and passionate delivery made her a star, but it wasn't just her natural beauty—it was her iron-fist-in-a-velvet-glove routine. ■ Ashley made her big-screen breakthrough with the independent film *Ruby in Paradise*, which went on to win the Sundance Film Festival's Grand Prize, but although her films have consistently created big money at the box office, they almost always receive mixed reviews. Still, her asking fee is up from ten dollars an hour to a reported four million dollars per movie.

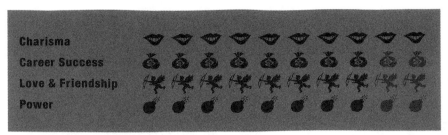

Charisma
Career Success
Love & Friendship
Power

Something magical happens when the aristocratic letter *A* teams up with the *vital, virile, voluptuous* letter *V.* The combination implies the uncommon strength and spunk found in the words *anvil, activist, advisor, avuncular, achieve* and *avalanche,* and there's really no danger that *AV* personalities will be perceived as stagnant or boring. And true to their incisive *A-* name personas, *AVs* are always on the lookout for opportunities to flaunt the plumage of their vital personalities. Some of these fine peacocks tone down their pride when choosing to end their names with the high-pitched *Y* or *IE* note (*Alvie* or *Alvy*), but they surrender some of their dignity for this more laid-back impression.

However they choose to present themselves, *AVs* are always pushing new boundaries and sating their appetite for the unusual. Nothing is off-limits to these people, and in many ways *AVs* are classic explorers: they are usually the first to try the new Ethiopian restaurant down the street or take that exotic overseas vacation.

AVs love working with their hands and bodies, and are perhaps the most expert among the *A* names at turning their hobbies into careers. Carpentry, design, dancing, creative writing and music are all possible avenues for the *AVs* to turn a little profit, and a significantly high percentage of *AVs* end up as small-business owners and entrepreneurs.

AVs believe communication to be the secret of a successful relationship and feel quite free to point out their mate's shortcomings. While it's true that some *AVs* can go a little overboard in this regard, no one would ever accuse them of having a mean bone in their bodies. Insensitive? Yes. But always with the best interests of their partner at heart. It doesn't hurt to have a steady stream of jokes attractively coupled to a charismatic, self-assured personality.

Most people can't resist an *AV* once they've turned on the charm. But friendly and approachable as they are, people still comment on the elusiveness of *AVs* when it comes to love, marriage and baby carriages. In fact, one may want to retract *elusive* and go straight to *averse* or downright *repelled*. It's not that they don't love love, mind you (for these are true sensualists who adore the *idea* of romance); it's just that they're not the settling-down types. They'd rather leave the mysteries of marriage and procreation to those with nothing better to do.

Alivia
Alvaro
Alvie
Alvin
Alvina
Alvis
Ava
Avery
Avis

Alvin Ailey Tap-dancing is not the easiest path to success for a young black man from the L.A. ghetto, but when you're blessed with the passion and spirit of an ALV personality, you might want to take your chances. ■ Alvin Ailey went on to establish the Alvin Ailey American Dance Theater, which subsequently become one of the most popular dance troupes in the United States. ■ Alvin's work as a pioneering choreographer was conducted in the face of crippling depression and an eventual mental breakdown. Still, he managed to forge collaborations with the likes of Duke Ellington, The Joffrey Ballet and the New York Metropolitan Opera. ■ Alvin died at the age of 58 in 1989, and his theater remains a successful and enduring legacy of his passion for dance.

Most Popular Girl's Names

Barbara
Betty
Brenda
Beverly
Bonny
Bertha
Beatrice
Bernie
Brittany
Beth

Most Popular Boy's Names

Brian
Benjamin
Bruce
Brandon
Billy
Bobby
Bryan
Bradley
Barry
Bernard

Like leviathans afloat
Lay their bulwarks on the brine,
While the sign of battle flew
On the lofty British line.

—THOMAS CAMPBELL,
The Battle of the Baltic

The Brash, Unyielding

The Phoenician symbol for the *B* was originally named *Beth*, meaning house. After the Greeks incorporated it into their alphabet and modified its shape to resemble the modern *B,* it was renamed *Beta.* ■ Like the beating of a big bass drum, the letter *B*'s powerful tones are associated with all things *booming* and *belligerent.* This low-frequency sound is designed carry long distances through the air and has an unmistakable intimidation effect. Pronounced with an aggressive explosion of air from both lips, this bilabial letter initializes the words *boastful, blustery, bawdy, beat, break, beastly, burly, bickering, blunt, battling, brutish, bullying* and *brave.* The more *B*s appearing in a word, the darker its tone: *Beelzebub, bomb, boo-boo, barbarian* and *backbreaking.* If the letter *B* were an animal, it would be a *bucking bronco,* a *badger,* a *bull* or a *bear.* ■ The *B* is also the first word of the Old Testament in Hebrew: *Bereishit* (in the beginning). And when used as the initial letter of modern first names, its commanding power imbues its owners with its brawny spirit, as seen in the traditional meanings of the names *Bernard* (bold as a bear), *Brock* (badger), *Burton* (fortress), *Brant* (strong one) and *Bridget* (strength). ■ *B* people are typically more assertive than most and exhibit a distinct lack of fear when it comes to their career choices. Their reliance on brawn, rather than brains, explains why they have a high chance of success in the hurly-burly of politics and professional sports, but tend to struggle in the arts and medical fields. ■

THE IMPUDENT b

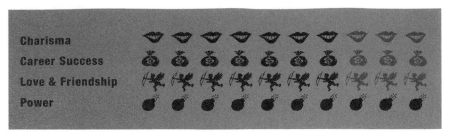

Charisma										
Career Success										
Love & Friendship										
Power										

Street-smart Strong Self-assured Intolerant Overdramatic Closed

The letter *B*'s *brassy* tones often herald a brazen, brash and belligerent personality. And when it is the only consonant in a name, it's not surprising that we find a heightened sense of self-confidence and bellicose hard-headedness. The feminine name *Bea*, luckily modulated by the happy-go-lucky sounds of the letter E, forces a slight smile in the speaker as the word is pronounced. But the same cannot be said for the *Bo* and *Beau* names, which exhibit the same churlish sounds found in the words *boar*, *boast*, *bogie*, *bold* and *bomb*. Indeed, the downside of having such a powerful name is a tendency to lack flexibility, and once in control of a situation, *B* individuals are unlikely to relinquish their power and consider someone else's point of view. Still, there's something beguilingly attractive about the *B*'s single-mindedness, and even at their bellicose best, their childlike charm still twinkles through.

While you'd never accuse *B* people of being overly sensitive, their stubborn lack of sentimentality does serve a purpose in society. Who else would take care of the nasty details like writing traffic tickets and working at the DMV? Perhaps this is why so many *B* people find

Bea
Beau
Bo

satisfaction in doing police and fire-prevention work. Playing the hero is just too irresistible to these daring, excitement-prone personalities, and besides, they're good at it. So what if they're a little on the blunt side with nonexistent bedside manners?

B's aren't the sort to do anything halfway, and they span the spectrum from ultra-success to ultra-failure. And with their huge emotional energy reserves, failure doesn't seem to faze them; it's more likely to be viewed as just another growth opportunity.

Clearly, if you want to date or mate with a *B* personality, you'll have to brush up on your flattery skills. You don't even have to work hard at it; just pay them the first compliment that comes to mind and they'll lap it up.

The *Bs*' say-it-like-it-is social style is put to excellent use when they're parents; *Bs* love the feeling of being surrounded by adoring children, who will return the favor by being responsible and dependable to a fault. Since it would never occur to *Bs* to neglect their marital duties, you can be pretty sure that your *B* mate will be in the relationship for life, unless of course, you decide to neglect your side of the bargain.

Bo Jackson Millions of Americans have undergone hip-replacement surgery, but only one of them has a hip fastened together by polyethylene and cobalt chrome, and has the distinction of being one of the greatest athletes in history. ■ Bo Jackson became a bona fide sports hero in the mid eighties when he played in two professional sports at the same time: summer baseball for the Kansas City Royals and winter football for the Los Angeles Raiders. And Bo was no journeyman player, either, scoring 141 career home runs and providing a key ingredient to the Raiders' attack. ■ His strong association to the key 18–25-year-old demographic made him irresistible to the advertising industry, and Bo became pitchman for Nike in its memorable *Bo Knows* campaign.

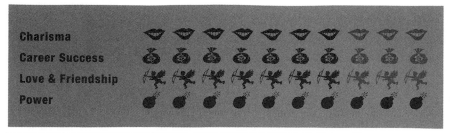

Charisma										
Career Success										
Love & Friendship										
Power										

Strong Spontaneous Capable
Awkward Dogmatic Thin-skinned

The letter *B* is the icon of all things *brash*, *brazen* and *belligerent*, and its *bass* tones imbue words and names with an unmistakable air of aggression and assertion. So when names come to be dominated by two *Bs*, they run the risk of becoming caricatures of themselves. The vigorous effects of the double *B* can be plainly seen in the words *boob*, *bomb*, *barbarous*, *babble*, *baboon* and *boo-boo*. Fortunately, those named *Bob* have the option of using the more elegant Robert, while others can modify their names to end with the diminutive Y or IE, as in *Barbie*, *Bobby* or *Bebe*, which moderates some of the double *B's* aggressive connotations.

Because of the antagonistic triggers imbedded in their names, *BBs* must continually be on guard against the prejudices of others, which perhaps partly explains why they live up to their reputation for hotheadedness. In addition to their impulsiveness, many *BB's* are accident-prone and will have their fair share of physical and emotional bumps and bruises.

But before we relegate them to the "bumbling misfit" category, it would be fair to consider their many virtues as well. For example, the *BBs'* boldly candid (if unconventional) views on life are a breath of fresh air

Baby
Bambi
Barb
Barbie
Bebe
Bibi
Bob
Bobbi
Bobby
Bubba

and certainly grist for some great conversation. And if nothing else, it's inspiring to watch *BBs* rise to their feet after taking a tumble with a practiced what-me-worry air.

With a talent for working with their hands, *BBs* dominate the workplace as builders, cooks and small business owners, preferring the freedom of working for themselves, or at least in unsupervised positions. If you've ever employed a *BB*, you'll be familiar with their hardheaded insistence on doing things their own way, and you'll have appreciated their aptitude for creative problem-solving. Most *BBs* learned the stick-to-itiveness—which characterizes their adult lives—when they were children. They also learned to listen to their internal voices and override their intellectual conclusions.

When it comes to relationships, *BBs* tend to barrel into their lovers' lives with the finesse of hippopotami, and the entire courtship often consists of little more than a dozen roses and a bottle of supermarket champagne. While this headlong approach may scare off some potential partners, certain people are very attracted to this devil-may-care style of wooing, and if the relationship is given a chance to stabilize, it invariably proves to be dedicated and enduring.

Bob Crane *Hogan's Heroes* was a hugely successful TV show for CBS in the seventies and made Bob Crane a household name. ■ The show enjoyed a six-year run, during which time Bob was nominated for two Emmy Awards. Even after CBS executives nixed the show, they tried capitalizing on Bob's popularity with *The Bob Crane Show* in 1975, but miserable ratings doomed the show after a few episodes. ■ Only death could have made a bigger star out of Bob Crane, and his unsolved murder in 1978 revealed the darker side of his personality. As it turned out, when the TV cameras were turned off, Bob was performing sex acts with hundreds of women and recording his exploits on videotape. ■ Said Bob: "I don't drink. I don't smoke. Two out of three ain't bad."

Charisma	💋	💋	💋	💋	💋	💋	💋	💋	💋	💋	💋
Career Success	💰	💰	💰	💰	💰	💰	💰	💰	💰	💰	
Love & Friendship											
Power	💣	💣	💣	💣	💣	💣	💣	💣	💣	💣	

**Interested Engaging Talented
Exaggerating Intolerant Restless**

When the *bossy, brash* tones of the letter *B* combine with the *dark* and *domineering* shadows of the letter *D,* they *denote brooding* individuals who run the risk of taking themselves too seriously. We see the *BD* combination's gloomy effects in words like *bad, abduct, subdue, obdurate, bedlam* and *abdicate.* But those who choose to end their names with the high-pitched Y or IE sound (as in *Buddy*), circumvent some of these darker aspects and are typically more jovial individuals. In general, however, *BDs* are the types who focus on the half-empty glass.

This is not to suggest that *BDs* spend their spare time moping around and looking for the worst in everything. But they do have the philosophy that if one pays attention to the bad and the ugly in life, then the good will take care of itself. You might not want these qualities in your psychologist, but you'll certainly appreciate the value of this approach if you've visited your stockbroker recently.

When it comes to career decisions, *BDs* tend to choose jobs in which they will be creatively challenged and have a clear path to the top. They are ambitious, are quick learners and prove eager to share their knowledge

Bud
Belinda
Boyd
Buddy

with co-workers. But like all alpha males and females, they have a tendency to take control of projects without even realizing that they are doing so. And given their ability to stamp their personalities onto everything they do, this often proves intimidating to the timid who are advised to give them a wide berth.

The same admonition holds true for those embroiled in a BD romance, and unless you're prepared to frequently challenge the *BD's* take-charge attitude, you'll find yourself playing second fiddle in the relationship. But it's nothing personal, *BDs* are just used to having things go their own way. So, if you want to give yourself a migraine by butting heads with the *BDs'* powerful personas, go ahead. You'll certainly get no quarrel from the *BDs*, who are always up for opportunities to test their intellectual wrestling skills.

These strong silent types can be tough to figure out at first. But for all their aloof dignity, there's also a little bit of a goofball just under the surface, and when given enough time for the relationship to settle into its rhythms, partners will encounter an upbeat and impeccably loyal side to these otherwise serious individuals.

Buddy Holly Considered to be one of the founding fathers of rock 'n' roll, Buddy Holly was first signed to Decca Records after opening for Bill Haley and the Comets. Buddy next formed a band he called The Crickets and hit big with "That'll Be the Day," "Maybe Baby," "Oh Boy" and "Peggy Sue." ■ The Crickets' entry into the rhythm and blues realm initially caused them to be mistaken for a black group and booked at the Apollo Theater where they were booed by the audience. Two days later, they had standing ovations, and Buddy had the musical world at his feet. ■ The music died in 1959 when a plane carrying Buddy, Ritchie Valens and the Big Bopper crashed, killing everyone on board. The incident inspired Don McLean to write the poignant ballad "American Pie."

Charisma	💋	💋	💋	💋	💋	💋	💋	💋	💋	💋
Career Success	💰	💰	💰	💰	💰	💰	💰	💰	💰	💰
Love & Friendship	🏹	🏹	🏹	🏹	🏹	🏹	🏹	🏹	🏹	🏹
Power	💣	💣	💣	💣	💣	💣	💣	💣	💣	💣

Enthusiastic Dedicated Hardworking Tempestuous Petty Condescending

It's a gamble to couple the *brashly bold* letter *B* with the *flighty* and *flirtatious* letter *F*, inasmuch as these two letters are so opposite in their essence. The *B* represents *bossy belligerence*, while the *F* is *fickle* and *fun-loving*. This uneasy alliance may account for the fact that fewer than 10,000 people in the United States have a *BF* name. These names come packaged with a split personality; as they oscillate from comedy to tragedy, you simply won't be able to predict what *BFs* are going to do next. But *BFs* won't mind if you stick around and watch the show; they thrive on attention and are clearly in love with the spotlight.

Besides slaying vampires, *BF* individuals are best suited for careers in which they can entertain and please others. While this might make them great comedians and actors, they also do well in the service industry, including hotel work, sales and customer service. They are not overly aggressive in the workplace, and although *BFs* will take the occasional risk, direct conflict makes them nervous and they will avoid the head-to-head competition that comes with direct sales.

In their intimate affairs, *BFs* will prove to be supportive and devoted mates who genuinely desire the best for their partners. Their innately childlike natures draw them to children, who appreciate their conspiratorial mind-sets, and there's nothing they enjoy more than lazy evenings playing games in the company of close friends. *BFs* are anything but selfish in their relationships and will place no undue pressure on their mates for attention. But if you've ever been romantically involved with a *BF*, you know that it can be difficult to know with which *BF* you're dealing . . . the brashly self-confident one, or the little boy (or girl) lost. Overall, you should consider yourself lucky that you have a "two-for-one" deal from your relationship.

Buffy
Buford

Buffy the Vampire Slayer The cult following of the Warner Brothers TV series *Buffy the Vampire Slayer* propelled the show into seven successful seasons. Was the show's success due to its quirky dark edges, or the incongruity of watching a girl named Buffy single-handedly render the undead dead? ■ The series, which spun off from a motion picture of the same name, starred Sarah Michelle Gellar as Sunnydale's kick-butt vampire slayer. The show remained on the cutting edge and retained its youthful audience by openly dealing with themes of homosexuality, devil worship and addiction. ■ When one of the show's popular lesbian characters was killed off, it triggered a howl of protests from gay advocates who noted that gay characters on prime-time television have a much higher mortality rate than the average character.

Charisma										
Career Success										
Love & Friendship										
Power										

Brave Firm Loyal
Impetuous Aggressive Unpredictable

If you're looking for a forceful name for your child, there is simply no stronger choice than a name with the *BK* root. For when the *belligerently booming* tones of the letter *B* interact with the *crisply cutting* edges of the letter *K*, it constitutes a sharp psychological impact that resonates with power and unyielding strength. These same sounds are often found in dynamic words, like *break*, *brock* (*badger*), *brick*, *backache*, *bicker*, *beak* and *buck*.

It's not easy to overcome a name that's so lopsided with abrasive tones, which is why the female *BK* names (*Becky* and *Becki*) are softened with the high frequency sound of the terminating letter Y. When a word ends with the playful letters IE or Y, its tone becomes indelibly associated with all that is diminutive and benign, as seen in the words *lovey-dovey*, *binkie*, *pinky*, *funny* and *whimsy*.

While the male versions of the *BK* root (*Brock* and *Buck*) are unquestionably power names whose personalities brook no disrespect, the feminine versions suggest women whose superficially brittle outward behavior belies a gentle core apparent only to those who know

Beck
Becky
Booker
Buck

them well. Significantly, most *Beckys* have chosen to shorten their names from the well-rounded Rebecca, which signals a rejection of the formal and conservative.

BKs are responsible people who flourish in positions of authority. Still, they have no problem when someone else takes the lead—being so secure with their own strength, they have little need to dominate others. Perhaps this is why so many *BK* individuals are so soft-spoken and exude the gentle self-confidence of an alpha male or female.

BKs' aggressive style can sometimes be off-putting to their friends, and they must compensate for this abrasiveness with constant reassurances. *BKs* understand the concept of teamwork and loyalty, and once they've bonded with a small and tight group, their relationships invariably prove to be stable.

When it comes to permanent relationships, most *BKs* will take their time before committing. Whether this stems from an abiding self-confidence or is just a reflection of being hard-to-please, there is no doubt that the *BKs'* emotional roots grow deepest when anchored in the bedrock of matrimony.

Beck Drawn from a complex array of influences from folk, hip-hop, country, and blues, Beck's musical style is quite impossible to pigeon-hole. Considered one of the most adventurous artists since John Lennon, his single *Loser*—with its funky beat, angst-ridden free-flowing lyrics—became the anthem for the slacker generation. Beck had more than just a passing connection to John Lennon; his grandfather was a key figure in the *Fluxus* art movement credited for launching Yoko Ono's career. ■ As a tenth grade dropout, Beck plied his wares as a folk and blues street busker. While playing music at an LA rock club he was invited by promoters to cut an album of folk songs with hip-hop beat. His recording of *Loser* was such a huge success that copies couldn't be pressed fast enough to meet the demand. His contract with Geffen allows him to release innovative and noncommercial work on smaller independent labels.

bl

Charisma	😊😊😊😊😊😊😊😊😊😊
Career Success	💰💰💰💰💰💰💰💰💰💰
Love & Friendship	🐦🐦🐦🐦🐦🐦🐦🐦🐦🐦
Power	💣💣💣💣💣💣💣💣💣💣

Relaxed Outgoing Positive
Thoughtless Elusive Know-it-all

There's a distinct air of self-assurance that surrounds the *BL* names. For even though the initial letter *B* is indelibly associated with *belligerence* and *boasting*, the *lyrical* and *loving* qualities of the letter *L* manage to soften its tone without sacrificing any of the *B*'s confidence. This explains why the *BL* phoneme dominates words like *blowhard*, *blurt*, *blunt*, *blame*, *blunder*, *bluff* and *bloated*. That's wju there's no real threat from a *BL* personality, just a lot of posturing to mask outward signs of weakness.

Those choosing to end their names with the diminutive IE or Y sound send the message that they take themselves less seriously. To illustrate, compare the flippant personalities of Billy Crystal, Billy Idol, Billy Barty and Billy Carter to the more staid Bill Clinton, Bill Moyers and Bill Gates. Billys are known for their good-natured optimism while Bills are more inclined to use intimidation as their primary tool for garnering resources.

The thing that's true for all *BL* personalities is that by being able to anticipate life's obstacles, *BLs* are capable of overcoming almost any challenge with an unparalleled sense of confidence. All in all, the *BL* names bestow upon their owners a sense of control in an unpredictable universe.

Their rough-and-ready constitutions make *BLs* naturally suited for physical labor, which is why so many are found in the construction industry. But *BLs* aren't going to be satisfied with doing menial jobs and many have a secret passion for recognition and titles. Whether it's foreman or president of purchasing, these designations serve to remind them that the world thinks as highly of them as they do of themselves. For similar reasons, *BLs* usually sport athletic physiques and much of their self-esteem is derived from their looks and physical prowess.

Despite their habitual bluntness, *BLs* can be surprisingly tender and sensitive. And even if intimate personal relationships don't come easily to them, given enough time, the *BLs'* suitors will often see right through their bluster and un-cover their softhearted core. Their ideal marriage partners are those with a big enough sense of humor to keep their voluble personalities at bay. And it's particularly important that *BLs* are one who can conform to them, because unless appropriately partnered, they're unlikely to live up to the responsibilities that come with long-term commitment.

Belen
Bailey
Bell
Bella
Beulah
Bilal
Bill
Billy
Blaine
Blair
Blaise
Blake
Blanche
Blanca
Blaze
Burl

Bill Clinton Love him or hate him, no one denies that Bill Clinton had a profound effect on the political and sexual psyche of late-twentieth-century American culture. ■ Judged by historians and political pundits to be one of the canniest politicians in U.S. history, Clinton soiled his legacy by giving fodder to a virulent pool of critics when he chose, while testifying in Paula Jones's sexual-harassment lawsuit against him, to lie about his affair with Monica Lewinsky. ■ Somehow Clinton maintained his dignity throughout the degrading process and left the White House with his head held high. ■ Says Bill: "I tried to walk a line between acting lawfully and testifying falsely, but I now realize that I did not fully accomplish that goal." ■ History, as always, will be the judge.

Charisma	👄	👄	👄	👄	👄	👄	👄	👄	👄
Career Success	💰	💰	💰	💰	💰	💰	💰	💰	💰
Love & Friendship									
Power									

**Creative Expressive Devoted
Negative Complacent Unrealistic**

An interesting thing happens when words beginning with the explosive letter *B* are infected by the negative implications of the letter *N*. The *brash, belligerent* and *bold* characteristics of the *B* are transformed into *benign* words like *benevolent, bouncy, beneficial, bountiful* and *bunny*. It's something akin to the personalities of the *BN* people, who initially come across as tough, energetic and resilient, but on further review, turn out to be surprisingly compassionate people who are full of exotic surprises.

Whether they're dreamy, poetic, or creative, these people display little of the overconfidence and pushiness associated with most *B* names. On the contrary, the *BNs*' survival strategies are rooted in their ability to harmonize their personal and business lives. But although they list among their many attributes a prodigious set of social skills, bold leadership is not one of them. So don't expect them to run for office or mount a campaign for "most popular." They have little interest in making waves and are decidedly better lovers than they are fighters.

You wouldn't call them easygoing, but *BNs* are social chameleons who relish the stimulation that comes from having a varied group of friends. They are outstanding communicators, and everything that gets

Ben
Benedict
Benita
Benito
Benjamin
Bennett
Benny
Benton
Beyonce
Bianca
Blane
Bonita
Bonnie
Bunny

churned around in their heads will sooner or later come out of their mouths. So don't be offended when your *BN* friends point out your faults with annoying bluntness; it's just their way of showing concern. Sure they're a little parental, but it's only because they expect the best from you.

Belief plays an important role in the *BN's* life. Religion, philosophy and moral principles motivate these people to their quick, and their values extend to the natural world for which they have an abiding respect. But because they have respect for other people's opinions, they are not the types to proselytize.

Both male and female *BNs* radiate a powerful appeal to the opposite sex, but these are people who adhere rigorously to their personal moral codes and are unlikely to take advantage of their popularity. It's in their intimate relationships that the *BN's* creative side is most visible; these are romantics in the truest sense of the word. On the downside, there is nothing *BNs* fear more than looking like "bad guys," particularly when it comes to breaking off failed relationships. These situations have a habit of dragging on while *BNs* drag their feet, and this tendency often results in missed opportunities.

Ben Affleck Ben Affleck's film debut, *School Ties*, a drama about anti-Semitism, was one of those rare films that launched a host of Hollywood notables, including Brendan Fraser, Chris O'Donnell and Affleck's best friend, Matt Damon. ■ Ben's big break came after co-writing the film *Good Will Hunting* with Matt Damon. Their high-spirited acceptance speeches for the Academy Award for Best Screenplay trumpeted their arrival on the Hollywood scene. ■ Although Ben has made his share of grab-the-money-while-you-can action pictures, he maintains his street credibility with small roles in independent productions like Kevin Smith's *Dogma*.

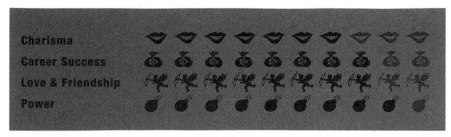

Charisma	
Career Success	
Love & Friendship	
Power	

Accepting Expressive Carefree
Unfocused Compulsive Passive

The *BR* phoneme is responsible for the uplifting qualities found in words like *breezy, bright, brash, brat, break* and *brilliant*, so it's not surprising that *BR* names are the evocation of youthful, enterprising individuals who are game for anything, at any time. If there's something exciting going on, *BR*s want to be right in the thick of things, even if they're not the actual provocateurs.

Quick-witted and outspoken, *BR*s place great stock in their communication skills and will always let you're know what's on their minds. They usually take active roles in organizing and counseling their friends, but with the exception of their social activities, *BR*s are not blessed with persistence. Life offers too many distractions for these talented people to spend much time on any one thing, and this often results in financial stress as they move from job to job. Ideal careers for a *BR* might include acting, teaching or politics—or just about anything that avoids the tedium of the nine to five.

In their personal lives, *BR*s are always ready to extend a helping hand or provide a sympathetic ear. If anything, they secretly wish that they could be the ones pouring out their hearts to someone as sensitive as they are. But *BR*s are simply too proud to reveal their insecurities, and despite their famous empathy, they have little patience for emotionally needy people who refuse to help themselves.

*BR*s are most definitely social animals, and when it comes to enjoying themselves, have few established limits. They relish the breaking of tradition and cheerfully push the boundaries of good taste when it means that a good time can be had by all. And although there's always a hint of a calculating air behind their social interactions, *BR*s have little time for logic and careful planning. Instead, these charismatic extroverts rely on their instincts to get them through life— even if that reliance repeatedly gets them into situations they're unable to handle.

*BR*s are known for acts of genuine generosity and—even if their first impulses are not always completely altruistic—you can utterly rely on them to come through when the chips are down. Being a partner to a bouncing *BR* and keeping up with his or her frenzied activities can prove to be tiresome for the average person, so if you're in love with a *BR* and are feeling a little overwhelmed, a little countermanipulation should redistribute the relationship's power balance. All's fair in love and war.

Barrie
Barry
Beryl
Braulio
Bree
Brielle
Bria

Barry Bonds When your godfather happens to be the great Willie Mays, you can't blame people for expecting great things from your baseball career. One of the few players in the history of the game who commanded enough respect to be given an intentional walk with the bases loaded, Barry Bonds is regarded as one of the sport's all-time best all-rounders. ■ When Mark McGuire set a league record in 1998, scoring seventy home runs in a season, a nonplussed Barry Bonds knocked in seventy-three just three years later. ■ With his distinctive compact batting style, he hit his five hundredth career home run and passed the 1,500-RBI mark in 2001. He is one of a handful of players to have stolen and homered five hundred in his career.

Charisma										
Career Success										
Love & Friendship										
Power										

Decisive Bold Self-reliant
Cranky Argumentative Obtuse

The *boldly belligerent* letter *B* imparts a sense of unqualified strength to names it initializes. And like all names that feature a double dose of the *brash B*, these women are imbued with a fiercely independent streak and an unparalleled sense of obduracy. When the *B* teams up with the *randy*, *ravishing* and *romantic* letter *R*, the resulting combination is accountable for the impetuosity found in the words *brat*, *brash*, *brilliant*, *brooding*, *braggart*, *break*, *brittle*, *bright* and Barbarian, the name given to the hordes that sacked Rome in 410 AD.

For all their brooding strength, *BRBR* women exhibit a complex set of emotional contradictions. On the one hand, these are bright and appealing people who are usually at the center of attention, but at some very deep level there lies a misunderstood compassionate softie. Paradoxically, it's this gentle core that fuels *BRBRs'* fierce outer behavior. Consider as an example how their strong sense of justice compels them to aggressively defend their positions, no matter how much discomfort they produce in their listeners. Caught up in the passions of their arguments, they are articulate, relentless and even a little intimidating. It's not that they would object to their ideas being challenged, but they don't suffer fools

Barbara
Barbra

gladly and certainly won't abide a line of reasoning that isn't carefully thought out. Friends and family soon come to understand these motivations, but to the casual eye these outbursts can be downright nerve-wracking. Nonetheless, these upstanding individuals refuse to kowtow to public opinion and will remain true to their core beliefs.

Even with their occasional failures of tact, the *BRBRs'* fundamentally altruistic natures make them ideal for any of the helping professions, particularly counseling, medicine or social work; and it's in these environments that their gentler side percolates to the surface. However, when trapped in jobs or lifestyles that chafe their independent spirits, they soon revert to their abrasive and sullen alter egos.

There is no more joyful creature than a *BRBR* in love (but you'd never know it from her behavior). Perhaps motivated by her internal fear of rejection, she has a tendency to restrain her affectionate instincts. This kind of behavior is apt to be misinterpreted as yet another sign of her controlling tendencies, but with the help of an insightful and persistent mate, it's inevitable that she'll reach her true potential as a lover.

Barbra Streisand The most expedient way to summarize this Brooklyn-born singer/ actress/ director's career is to encapsulate it as a series of firsts. ■ Her first Broadway role, in the musical *I Can Get It for You Wholesale*, won the New York Drama Critics Award. *The Prince of Tides* was the first female-directed movie to receive a Best Director nomination from the Directors Guild. Her first record, *The Barbra Streisand Album*, won two 1963 Grammy Awards, including Album of the Year. Her first film, *Funny Girl*, won an Oscar for best actress, and Barbra was the first woman to direct, produce, write and star in a major film. ■ She was also the first female composer to win an Academy Award, and has outsold all other female recording artists in history—second only to Elvis Presley.

Charisma										
Career Success										
Love & Friendship										
Power										

Intelligent Extroverted Inquisitive
Absentminded Temperamental Nosy

All names that begin with the *BR* phoneme evoke the *breezy* images found in the words *bright, brash, brittle, brilliant, brat, brave* and *break*. But the *BRD* names are spared some of this dizziness through the action of the *dominant, dignified, diplomatic* letter *D*, which anchors these names with its *brooding bravado*. Consequently, *BRD* names exude a sense of balanced, earnest personalities whose sovereign spirits are very much at peace with the universe. Those names ending in the playful high-pitched Y or IE (*Bradley, Brady* and *Brody*) typically exhibit a more casual and relaxed approach to life.

The outgoing *BRD*s are able to effortlessly attract friends but often have a hard time hanging on to them—thanks to their relatively short attention spans. They're much better off focusing on those one or two special friendships, which can last for decades, if not for life. Others don't always recognize the deep fondness that *BRD*s have for people, for these absentminded people have an annoying habit of forgetting birthdays, anniversaries and even appointment times. And no one would accuse *BRD*s of oversentimentality either; if it were up to them, Hallmark would go out of business. But if you don't mind forgoing the occasional birthday pres-

Brad
Birdie
Braden
Bradford
Bradley
Brady
Bradyn
Bridget
Brigitte
Broderick
Brody

ent, your *BRD* friend will make up for this inattentiveness with devoted loyalty and affection.

There's a certain naïveté to the *BRD* personalities—like children that never completely matured—and perhaps this is why *BRD*s feel most at home in the outdoors. As a rule, they aren't people who take themselves very seriously, but they're also not above serious reflection when it comes to their careers. They have the remarkable ability to focus (in short bursts) on the task at hand, and aren't liable to mix business with pleasure. *BRD*s also have a particular affinity for working with their hands and should consider careers that reward their creativity and artistic talents. Female *BRD*s have an outstanding fashion sense and are frequently called upon by friends for their clothing recommendations.

*BRD*s respond well to the call of domesticity, and although they tend to settle down later in life, have a natural affinity for commitment. Having children is another issue entirely, and *BRD*s are usually dismayed at the prospect of having their freedom encroached on by dependent beings. Still, should the opportunity present itself, they'll prove to be dutiful and devoted parents (but secretly can't wait for the newcomers to leave the nest).

Brigitte Bardot Most men who were adolescents in the sixties remember Parisian beauty Brigitte Bardot. ■ An appearance on the cover of *Elle* magazine led to her film debut in the 1952 movie, *Le Trou Normand* (*Crazy for Love*), but it was *Et Dieu . . . créa la femme* (*And God Created Woman*) a few years later that established her as an idealized French sex kitten. ■ After retiring from films in 1973, Brigitte became famous for her vocal advocacy of animals' rights. Her organization seeks to convince the public that it is wrong to consume such things as horsemeat, foie gras, frog legs and any foods involving unacceptable conditions of life and slaughter. ■ Brigitte has achieved a modicum of success in the U.S., where frog legs and horsemeat sales are at their lowest ebb.

Charisma										
Career Success										
Love & Friendship										
Power										

Energetic Whimsical Communicative
Fickle Self-absorbed Changeful

It's the *boisterous, bossy, bass* tones of the letter *B* that bestow these names with their characteristic stubbornness. The *B*'s belligerent effects are additionally enhanced by the resonating *BR* phoneme, which we unconsciously associate with the words *bright, brassy, brazen, brooding, braggart* and *break*. And when the sharp letter *K* kicks in with its incisively cutting influences (as in *kill, kidnap* and *king*), the overriding effect on the *BRK* names is the creation of an extroverted, forceful and dogged individual.

It's *BRK*s' unique combination of exuberance and patience that makes them eminently attractive, because for all their outward pushiness, they have an unmistakable magnetic charisma. This charm seems to extend to the animal kingdom as well, and *BRK*s are often found in the company of dogs, cats and horses—pretty much anything with fur or feathers. Physical activity is the *BRK*'s refuge, and their high metabolisms find release through competitive activities. They're certainly talented on the playing field as well, with many school trophies collecting dust in the attic.

Put *BRK*s in a box and they will quickly destroy it.

Brock
Brooke
Brooklyn
Brooks

These are people who hate being labeled and who need to constantly re-create themselves. They will change their career paths several times in their working lives, partly from boredom but mainly because they enjoy the challenges brought on by new people and environments. But *BRK*s run the danger of falling into a rut when the money is good (they have a particular fondness for material things) and will soullessly ply their trade in exchange for a high salary. They would do well to remind themselves that their inner happiness is ultimately more important than a BMW.

With a penchant for spice and variety, *BRK*s often have a tough time settling into meaningful relationships and tend to bounce around before finally putting down roots. And even when they do settle down, it's rarely in the traditional white-picket-fence sense; these are marriages in the fast lane, with exotic travel and frenzied socializing. Because they have an almost religious belief that "the truth will set you free," *BRK*s can always be counted on to give you the straight scoop. But in return, the *BRK*s will insist upon complete honesty from you, and would never dream of punishing someone who voluntarily fesses up to wrongdoing.

Brooke Shields Lauded as the most beautiful baby in America, one-year-old Brooke Shields pitched soap for Ivory in 1966. Her mother, Teri—perhaps in an attempt to fulfill her own frustrated acting ambitions—pushed the young Brooke into her first major film role, playing a twelve-year-old prostitute in *Pretty Baby*. ■ The controversial role seems incongruous in light of the squeaky-clean image of an actress who refuses to do nude scenes. Her "Nothing comes between me and my Calvins" campaign in the eighties did nothing to quell the controversy. ■ Critics panned her acting in *The Blue Lagoon* and *Endless Love*, but gave her kudos for the self-deprecating role on the sitcom *Suddenly Susan*. ■ The Princeton University graduate married Andre Agassi in a much-heralded 1997 wedding, but the couple divorced only two years later.

Charisma										
Career Success										
Love & Friendship										
Power										

Comfortable Affectionate Philosophical
Reticent Preachy Stubborn

The *brightly brash BR* phoneme is invariably associated with words like *break*, *brave*, *brilliant*, *brawny*, *brat* and *braggart*. But although the *BRN* names hold the promise of bright extroversion, they taper into a gentle and nonthreatening hum when coupled with the *negative* qualities of the letter *N*. In short, these *vibrant, brainy, brawny, firebrands* may talk big, but they are all heart when it comes to sharing their talents.

This popular name root is represented by over three million people in the United States and characterizes those impetuous, good-natured people whose buoyant outlook makes them popular figures. With their advanced set of communication skills, *BRN*s love nothing better than philosophizing and sharing their expert opinions on every subject under the sun. It's not that they're necessarily smarter than the next person, but their love for reading and watching documentaries helps them to hold their own on topics ranging from religion and politics to the supernatural. Still, their tendency to dominate discussions can be wearisome for others trying to interject their own views into the debate.

In terms of their career tracks, the *BRN*s' innate sense of logic makes them perfect candidates for law, politics or sales. But the biggest complaint leveled against these loquacious individuals is that they're constantly trying to win other people over to their ways of thinking. While this may be a useful sales technique, it fails to produce converts to their cause in their personal lives. All told, the *BRN*s would be well served to temper their passion for intellectual issues and focus instead on the emotional impact of their behavior.

There's something you should know about your *BRN* friends. Just because they're quiet doesn't mean they're not thinking. And just because they don't wear their emotions on their sleeves doesn't mean they don't have feelings. *BRN*s, more than most, have an enormous capacity for keeping things to themselves, and dating them will produce its share of surprises. Their true feelings will emerge when they're secure in the knowledge that their dark secrets are not going to be judged. Sometimes you'll find your *BRN* lover hiding some kind of quirky sexuality; just when you think you've landed yourself a run-of-the-mill lover, out come the rubber sheets. Either way, you can expect to be pampered, surprised and cajoled, but never bored.

Baron
Barney
Brannon
Branson
Bernice
Bernie
Brennan
Brianne
Brian
Bruna
Bruno
Brynn
Byron

Brian Dennehy When a movie script calls for an actor to play a wise older friend with a square jaw and world-weary eyes, Brian Dennehy is likely to get a call. ■ The burly Dennehy made his debut playing a football player in the Burt Reynolds vehicle *Semi-Tough* in 1977. He established himself as a reliable second man in films like Sylvester Stallone's *First Blood* and the genial alien in *Cocoon,* and his comedic talents were put to work playing Chris Farley's father in *Tommy Boy* in 1995. ■ Brian also enjoyed a successful stage career and won a Tony Award for his role as Willy Loman in *Death of a Salesman* in 1998. ■ His most challenging role to date was his portrayal of ornery Indiana basketball coach, Bobby Knight, in *Season on the Brink.*

Charisma	👄	👄	👄	👄	👄	👄	👄	👄	👄	👄
Career Success	💰	💰	💰	💰	💰	💰	💰	💰	💰	💰
Love & Friendship	🏹	🏹	🏹	🏹	🏹	🏹	🏹	🏹	🏹	🏹
Power	💣	💣	💣	💣	💣	💣	💣	💣	💣	💣

Steady Strong-minded Encouraging Myopic Willful Exclusive

As the definitive symbol of *boisterous belligerence*, when the letter *B* teams up with the *romantic, ruddy* and *randy* letter *R*, it takes on the *brash* qualities found in the words *brazen, brave, brilliant, brutal, brawn* and *braggart*. But under the influence of the *nurturing* qualities of the letter *N* and the *dignified* letter *D*, these names gain the air of soft familiarity that we find in the words *friend, fond, blend, garland* and *slender*. To further moderate the effects of the aggressive B, many women elect to end their names with the high-pitched tones of the Y or I (*Brandy* and *Brandi*), which injects a distinctly more approachable and feminine tone.

Complex names usually mean complex personalities, and *BRND*s are no exception. This high-energy group is poised, persistent and intelligent, and includes some of the steadiest and most loyal friends you'll ever encounter. These are people who will put aside their own needs in the service of others and who feel a duty to protect and nurture those around them. However, their steady natures do not preclude the occasional flare-up of passions; *BRND*s have a fiery underbelly that often manifests itself in times of stress.

Whatever a *BRND* decides to do, you can bet it'll be done with finesse and dedication; potential employers are often able to sense this from a single interview. But *BRND*s are freelancers at heart, and no nine-to-five job will ever completely satisfy these feisty souls. As long as they're feeling intellectually or creatively challenged, they prove to be perfect for careers in design, sales or writing. But *BRND*s are not political animals. They don't understand why anyone would play games to get ahead when all it should take is hard work and straightforward discussion.

*BRND*s are not people who know how to lose gracefully—in part because they simply don't have much experience in losing. One of the only things that *BRND*s are not good at is figuring out the motivations of the opposite sex. It's not that they don't have good communication skills; it's simply that they struggle to connect with feelings that they themselves have not actually experienced. But what *BRND*s lack in empathy is more than compensated for by a beguiling charm that can be turned on like a faucet. It's hard not to get swept off your feet when a *BRND* deems you worthy, but since these are not the world's most romantic people, don't expect fireworks in the bedroom. *BRND*s would rather put their energies into the practical issues of life: career, income and walking the dog.

Branda
Bernard
Bernardo
Bernadette
Bernadine
Brandi
Brandon
Brandt
Brandy
Brenda
Brenden

Brandi Chastain The United States women's soccer team got much needed publicity when they played in the hotly contested final game of the World Cup in 1999. Brandi Chastain provided them one of the greatest moments in the history of women's sports when, after beating the Norwegian goalkeeper with a game-winning penalty kick, the excited midfielder sank to her knees and ripped off her top. The incident triggered a wave of sports-bra sales across the country. ■ Her achievements had their price: Brandi had reconstructive surgery on both knees after damaging her anterior cruciate ligaments. ■ Brandi scored an unfortunate own-goal in the quarterfinals of the World Cup game against Germany in the fifth minute, but true to form, redeemed herself forty minutes later to tie the game.

brs

Charisma	👄	👄	👄	👄	👄	👄	👄	👄	👄	👄
Career Success	💰	💰	💰	💰	💰	💰	💰	💰	💰	💰
Love & Friendship	🦅	🦅	🦅	🦅	🦅	🦅	🦅	🦅	🦅	🦅
Power	💣	💣	💣	💣	💣	💣	💣	💣	💣	💣

Gregarious Dynamic Brave
Proud Unsettled Uncommunicative

The *brash BR* phoneme is responsible for the swaggering and self-confident air evident in those with *BRS* names. We instinctively associate this *breezy* letter combination with images like *brat, brilliant, brawny, braggart, break* and *brittle*. The softly sensual tones of the *S* sound (or soft *C*) manage to dilute these abrasive effects, but the overall upshot is still *brassy, brash, brisk, bristling, bruising* and *brusque*. In short, most *BRS*s are take-charge people with a sensitive side that is revealed only to people whom the *BRS*s completely trust.

There's something *bracing* about the *BRS* personality; if they were animals, they'd be stately bull moose or sable antelopes. Conscientious but casual about their physical appearance, *BRS*s usually present a nonintimidating and informal air. This laid-back approach may well limit their earning potentials, but *BRS*s will happily forgo fiduciary success in exchange for free time and autonomy.

BRS personalities are capable of creating wonderfully complex (but private) fantasies in which they are masters of the universe, using all their imagined power to create a world in which nobody has to work, bedrooms are automatically cleaned and everybody parties.

Brisa
Bruce
Bryce
Bryson

To them, life is a just a race in which to cram as much pleasure as the allotted time allows. Because they prefer to be recognized for their machismo and physicality rather than their intellectual prowess, *BRS* types generally steer clear of academic pursuits.

In their personal lives, *BRS*s prove to be extraordinarily loyal and protective of their family and friends. With a *BRS* at your side, you'll always have someone who will come to your aid without asking questions. So go ahead and pick a fight with the biggest bully you can find, and watch your *BRS* friend enthusiastically take care of business for you. While a *BRS* will never actually initiate these fights, their protective qualities make them great soldiers, policemen and bodyguards.

With so much buoyant energy, it's hard to bring a *BRS* down. But the biggest hindrance to these individuals is their exaggerated sense of pride that can impede communication with co-workers and loved ones. But even though his I'm-always-right attitude may trigger a great deal of resentment, when the *BRS* acknowledges his own shortcomings, his intimate relationships prove to be quite enduring and highly appreciated.

Bruce Willis A smirking and charismatic Bruce Willis (with hair) played the role of David Addison in *Moonlighting* in the 1980s series starring Cybill Shepherd. ■ Who knew that this cheerful former bartender would one day become one of the biggest stars in Hollywood? Bruce did. ■ He parlayed his notoriety into a one-man entertainment industry and set new standards for actors' salaries. He raked in five million dollars for his role in 1988's *Die Hard*, only to see his record fall to wife Demi Moore's twelve million dollars for *Striptease*. Demi and Bruce divorced in 2000. ■ Oddly enough, Bruce holds the world record for appearing in major motion pictures with numbers in their title: *The First Deadly Sin, Twelve Monkeys, Four Rooms, The Fifth Element, The Sixth Sense,* and *The Whole Nine Yards*.

THE ENERGETIC

brt

Charisma	
Career Success	
Love & Friendship	
Power	

Quick-thinking Innovative Witty
Short-tempered Insensitive Wild

When a name root begins with the *bossy* and *boisterous* letter *B*, we unconsciously expect its owner to posses a confident and assertive personality. The *BR* combination takes this one step further with its association to words like *brazen, brassy, breezy, break* and *brash*. And when we add the *triumphant* and *tooting* letter *T*, we end up with a hyperactive personality whose zest for life can be discerned in the words *bright, brilliant, brat, braggart* and *brittle*.

There simply is no other name root that comes closer to describing the frenetic energy of a mischievously restless individual whose main impetus is a taste for discovery. They'll try anything twice: rock climbing, scuba diving, spelunking . . . you name it. Their main objective seems to be to avoid routine and find ways to release some of that prepubescent energy. Even when they've slid into old age, the *BRT*s' youthful spirit will refuse to take a vacation. They'll insist on staying fit to better exploit new opportunities.

These passionately bright people hold strong convictions and lofty ideals that tend toward the conservative. Perhaps overly concerned about the judgments of others, *BRT*s keep their wild sides under quite vigilant guard, which often manifests in periodic outbursts of pent-up frustration. Those

Bart
Barton
Barrett
Berta
Bertram
Britney
Brittany
Brant
Brent
Bertie
Brenton
Britta
Bryant
Burton
Brett
Britt
Burt

*BRT*s who haven't established effective outlets for their accumulated dissatisfactions tend to express themselves with snippy comments and sharp-tongued diatribes. But for every sarcastic outburst uttered, there is a proportional amount of clever banter and cunning wit.

Like most people whose names begin with the letter *B*, *BRT*s are politically astute and will employ these skills to further their ambitions in the workplace. Did someone say ambitious? These people are so highly motivated that communicating with them is sometimes a one-way affair. They can dominate discussions with their high-energy styles, and their love for debate takes precedence over their desire to really hear what their partners have to say. But since *BRT*s appreciate a little challenge in their lives, potential partners are advised not to back down from the their sometimes-unreasonable demands.

Once *BRT*s choose their life partners (which they tend to do late in life), they'll obediently commit to the duties of marriage and family. Though *BRT*s are wary of being tied down, they fear being left to their own devices almost as much. It's a rock-and-hard-place quandary, with which the *BRT* never quite makes peace.

Britney Spears Britney Spears, the hyper-feminized teen pop star, is at the top of her game. With almost total saturation of the airwaves, she is a multi-million-dollar empire. ■ When, at the age of eleven, Britney landed a part on *Disney's Mickey Mouse Club*, she found herself in the company of two other future teen idols: Justin Timberlake and J. C. Chasez (both members of the band 'N Sync). Other notable alumni were Keri Russell (star of the TV show *Felicity*) and pop star Christina Aguilera. ■ When her debut album, *Baby One More Time* was released in 1999, the song soared straight to number one, with 'N Synch at number two. ■ There is no sign that the Britney train is slowing down. Her seven-figure deal as spokesinger for Pepsi even had Bob Dole's dog standing up to be counted as one of her fans.

48

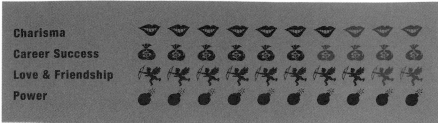

Charisma										
Career Success										
Love & Friendship										
Power										

Energetic Giving Courageous
Sarcastic Irritable Bossy

Names that begin with the *bouncing, brash* and *belligerent* letter *B* tend to herald an individual with a powerful self-image. Things get really interesting when the brazen *B* conjoins with the *slyly seductive* letter *S*, and the mere act of pronouncing the *BS* phoneme evokes visions of *busily buzzing bees bustling* through the *bush*. It's hardly surprising that the vigorous *BS* names spawn equally hyperactive personalities who almost always have a significant impact on the lives of people who know them.

It's not to say that *BS* people are over-achievers, but they are the kind of people who find it tedious to stop and smell the roses. There's simply too much dust to be vacuumed, too many books to be read, and not enough time in the day. They are goal-oriented, inveterate planners, capable of intense bouts of frenetic activity that leaves the rest of us feeling guilty.

Never underestimate the *BSs*' stubbornness; they can be real bulls when backed into a corner. And while there's rarely any indication of malice, their sharp tongues and active minds can be a deadly combination. But while you're recovering from your headache after the confrontation, their remorseful side is likely to put your friendship back on track in no time. This technique of pushing people down, then offering them a helping hand is a patented *BS* technique and reflects their need to feel like they're always in control of the relationship.

BSs' all-encompassing determination springs into action when they face difficult decisions or uncertain crises. Emergencies bring out the best in them, and the higher the pressure, the cooler they become. This ability to disconnect their emotional subroutines in times of stress permeates their social lives as well. If they ever perceive that they'd been challenged or insulted, the *BS* will react with annoying indifference and coolly withdraw.

But as mates, *BSs* are effusively attentive and extraordinarily generous with their time and energy. They're the type who will take charge of running the home with an efficiency that borders on downright fascism but show no signs of needing to control their mates' or children's personal lives. This kind of neutrality gives them the unique ability to act as both counselor and consoler to their loved ones.

Basil
Bess
Bessie
Boyce

Bess Truman It is said that there is no more challenging job than being the First Lady of the United States: you tend to take on all the responsibility without having any of the power of the office. The wife of Harry Truman, the thirty-third President of the United States, reluctantly found herself in the position of being counselor to the man who ordered the dropping of the world's first atom bomb. ■ Bess was born in the town of Independence, Missouri, in 1885, where she met her future husband after his family moved to a nearby house. ■ The couple was married in 1919 and moved to Washington when Harry was elected to represent Missouri in the U.S. Senate. When asked by a reporter about what she planned to do when her husband was no longer President, Bess replied, "Return to Independence."

Charisma										
Career Success										
Love & Friendship										
Power										

Daring Generous Confident
Scatterbrained Unruly Spoiled

As with all names that begin with the *brashly bullish* letter *B*, *BT* people flaunt a high degree of self-confidence and thrive on overcoming challenges. And when the *belligerent B* comes into close contact with the sharp tones of the *triumphant* letter *T*, it creates the *biting* texture found in words like *bitter, bitch, bait, batter, battle, betray* and *brittle*. Consequently, few names can compete with the *BT*s for sheer energy and grit.

It's impossible to keep *BT*s down for long. Their unquenchable optimism and seemingly endless supply of enthusiasm exude enough energy to power a small city. But beware the jagged claws of the *BT* personalities, for their sharp tempers are on a short fuse and can lay waste to even the hardiest souls.

But *BT*s prefer persuasion to intimidation and usually savor the chance to exercise their first-rate verbal skills. These individuals feel accountable for the advice they give, whether it's financial, moral or relationship-related, and because they have a vested interest in the outcome, have a tendency to take on the stress of the problem themselves.

*BT*s' homes reflect their eclectic taste in artwork

Betsy
Beatrice
Bette
Bettina
Betty
Braxton
Buster
Butch

and their genuine appreciation of function over form. Spartan and well organized, their living spaces are usually efficient and designed with entertaining in mind. *BT*s are certainly not shrinking violets, and these vivacious creatures will often pursue life in the public eye.

With such an affinity for the limelight, it's fair to say that even if they weren't the lead in their high-school play, you can bet they said their lines the loudest.

Maintaining social status is important to *BT* personalities, who are drawn to a tight group of alpha male and female friends with whom they'll spend hours scheming how to polish their reputations. These people exude sexuality of the highest order, and it's no coincidence that the word Betty is widely used as a colorful descriptive for woman. Ultimately, though, *BT*s' attractiveness to the opposite sex lies in their trademark irrepressible love for life.

As friends and lovers soon discover, bonding with a *BT* will have its ups and downs . . . but at least you'll always know where you stand. Things should hum along quite smoothly as long as you don't question their integrity or trifle with their daily routines.

Bette Davis Bette Davis was a screen presence unlike any that Hollywood had ever encountered. Referred to as The First Lady of the American Screen, Bette never backed down from difficult film roles, taking on projects that less powerful actresses could not have handled. In an industry dominated by men, Bette developed a reputation for standing up for her artistic standards. ■ The 1934 film *Of Human Bondage* was her first critically received project, and her performance in *Dangerous* a year later led to her first Oscar nomination for Best Actress. ■ Powerful stars in Hollywood often get the reputation of "being difficult to work with," and Bette did nothing to discourage the label. She was married four times, had one daughter and adopted two others.

Charisma										
Career Success										
Love & Friendship										
Power										

Exuberant Hospitable Dynamic
Controlling Overpowering Brooding

When the *brisk* and *belligerent* letter *B* combines with the spiritual aspects of the *TH* phoneme, it portends a boisterous individual with a gentle core toward whom people naturally gravitate. The soothing influence of the *TH*, which is found in words like *theology*, *motherly*, *thee*, *thou*, *pantheon* and *strength*, characterizes the *BTH* as someone who would never run away from trouble, meeting it instead with a booming laugh.

When a *BTH* walks into a room, everyone knows it. It's not that she's trying to garner attention, it's just that her natural buoyancy and warm energies inspire a great deal of interest. Legendary for her hospitality, the *BTH* will work hard at putting people at ease, and will be completely unselfish with her time and attention. When talking to a *BTH* you'll always get strong eye contact and an interested expression, leaving you with the feeling that you're the only person in her world.

Yet there is a dangerous quality to *BTH*s, and when you step into the path of one on a mission, the momentum can bowl you over. And once she's made a decision to judge you, it can be nigh on impossible to change her mind. There's no parole once you've been entered into a

Beth
Bertha
Bethany

BTH's book of bad graces, just permanent exile into her world of the cold shoulder.

The *BTH*'s relationship to her universe gives her the confidence to be true to her feelings. She feels as if she really belongs in the world, and it's from this stable platform that she shapes her life and relationships. One of the consequences of having such supreme self-assurance is that *BTH*s manifest an enviable combination of patience and empathy. These qualities are put to best use in careers as teachers, managers, medical practitioners, or simply as leaders in the workplace.

As a mate and mother, the *BTH* is more than capable of providing the best for her brood. Her tendency to rampage over minutia will require some flexibility on the part of her family, but the benefits of her loving, protective presence should far outweigh these negatives. Her children will enjoy a confiding relationship with this easygoing parent, who will shun traditional methods of discipline, preferring to deal with problems in rational and unemotional ways. With a *BTH* in the house, there will be plenty of warmth, visitors, team-spirit and no possibility of boredom.

Beth Henley Beth Henley's very first professionally produced play, *Crimes of the Heart*, was the co-winner of the 1979 Great American Play Contest. The dark comedy dealt with the fallout between three sisters after one of them shot her husband. It won a Pulitzer Prize and New York Drama Critic's Award for Best Play, and established Beth as a respected American playwright. ■ Beth went on to create a well-received play almost every year, including *The Miss Firecracker Contest*, *The Debutante Ball*, *The Abundance*, *Control Freaks* and *Impossible Marriage*. ■ Beth was also asked to write the screenplay adaptation of *Crimes of the Heart*, and the film version, featuring Diane Keaton, Jessica Lange and Sissy Spacek, was nominated for an Academy Award.

THE RED-BLOODED BV

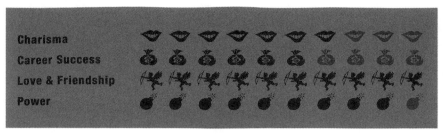

Charisma	😊😊😊😊😊😊😊😊😊😊
Career Success	💰💰💰💰💰💰💰💰💰💰
Love & Friendship	🦁🦁🦁🦁🦁🦁🦁🦁🦁🦁
Power	💣💣💣💣💣💣💣💣💣

Resilient Intuitive Sensual
Preoccupied Uncertain Distant

The *boldly brisk* letter *B* is dramatically transformed when brought under the spell of the *voluptuous, vibrant, vivacious* letter *V*. If the aggressive *B* is the *brashest* of all letters in the alphabet, the *V* is unsurpassed in its raw sexuality. Put them together and you have a name saturated with animal magnetism. The other sexually charged letter in the alphabet is the *romantic, randy, ravishing* letter *R*, and for those who choose to use the full version of the *BV* root (like *Beverly*), their names resonate with even more sensual intensity. We see the *VR*'s corporeal influence in words like *virgin, lover, fever, quiver, pervert* and *fervor*.

When you meet a *BV* for the first time, you might not notice her seductive elegance, for it's often disguised by a mantle of innocence and charm. In fact, while the *BV* can be quite approachable and friendly, you should know that she's sizing you up at the same time she's charming you with her witty repartee. Which is to say, you can only come as close to the *BV* as she will allow you to, while all the time you're thinking that she's the most open person you've ever met. Their attractive blend of wit and wisdom means that they're often regarded as modern-day sages, and anyone who puts a

Bev
Bienvenido
Beverly

BV on a pedestal will find that she's really quite comfortable up there.

*BV*s are renowned for their ability to blend into almost any social group, whether it's as an activist, a pacifist, a Hell's Angel or a member of the church choir. Her chameleonlike social behavior is born from her deeply rooted confidence that she can hold her own in any situation.

A friendship with a *BV* can prove to be quite an adventure, because no one, least of all the *BV* herself, is really sure what she's going to do next. Since they're often unclear about their destinies, *BV*s may change directions at any time without prior notice and can easily lose touch with loved ones.

Sensual beings that they are, *BV*s have a keen eye for beauty and style, and often find work as fashion consultants, hairdressers or photographers. They are comfortable doing anything that involves giving advice or critiquing others' artwork, clothing or career choices, and would never condescend by giving praise unless it was earned. Their ability to assess the motives of other people makes careers in counseling and teaching perfect for the *BV*'s amalgam of horse sense and honesty.

Beverly D'Angelo Most aspiring actors pay their dues by waiting tables or parking cars. Beverly D'Angelo did it in style as a cartoonist for Hanna Barbera. ■ Beverly received rave reviews for her performance as Patsy Cline in *Coal Miner's Daughter*, in which her own voice was used for Patsy's songs and fans of *The Simpsons* may remember her as the voice of Lurleen Lumpkin—Col. Homer's country-singing prodigy. ■ After her role as the matriarch of the Griswald family in three National Lampoon comedies starring Chevy Chase, Beverly was unable to shop in a supermarket without being recognized. ■ Beverly married Italian Duke Lorenzo Salviati in 1981, but they divorced in 1995. In 2001 she gave birth to twins, fathered by Al Pacino.

52

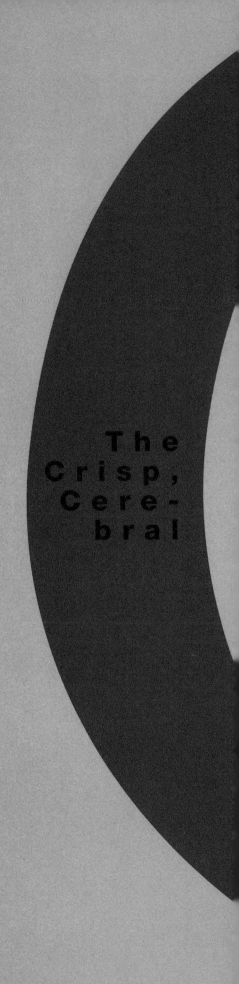

**Most Popular
Girl's Names**

Carol
Cynthia
Carolyn
Christine
Catherine
Cheryl
Christina
Crystal
Connie
Carmen

**Most Popular
Boy's Names**

Charles
Christopher
Carl
Carlos
Craig
Clarence
Chris
Curtis
Chad
Clifford

The
Crisp,
Cere-
bral

It's no coincidence that the value of a diamond is determined by the four Cs—color, carat, clarity and cut—for the letter C's crisp pronunciation is indelibly associated with all things sharp and unyielding. Having evolved from the Egyptian picture sign of a sharpened hunting stick, its very shape harks back to its boomerang origins. Its sharp edges are depicted in the words cactus, crack, cut, click, concise, carbon, clamor, clash, curse, claw and club. ■ These characteristics even manage to describe the sharp intelligence associated with the C in words like clever, civil, careful, capable, cranium, cerebral and the word capital, derived from the Latin caput, meaning head. ■ But when the C's keen intellect is moderated by the gentle letter H, it takes on a distinctly benign tone: champion, chancellor, chapel, church, cherub, chaperone, charisma, chastity, cherish, chivalry, charming and chief. And when the C is connected to the letter R, it assumes a distinctly creepy tone (crabby, crabby, crappy, cranky, cretin and crafty), but when linked to the laid-back L, it becomes clear, classical, clean, clever, classy and clinical. ■ We see the C's influence on the traditional meanings of the names Conan (knowledge bringer), Christopher (of Christ), Clementine (merciful), Cyril (of the Lord) and Clark (of the clergy).

Charisma	👄👄👄👄👄👄👄👄👄👄
Career Success	💰💰💰💰💰💰💰💰💰💰
Love & Friendship	👼👼👼👼👼👼👼👼👼👼
Power	💣💣💣💣💣💣💣💣💣💣

**Compassionate Friendly Gracious
Insecure Overinvolved Restless**

When the *classy* and *cerebral* letter *C* is pronounced like the sharp-edged *K* sound, it takes on the *capable* air found in the words *clever, canny, captivate, clear-cut* and *cocky*. And when coupled with the effects of the *brazen, brash, belligerent* letter *B*, these names are infused with an unmistakable sense of devil-may-care confidence. These distinctly masculine qualities account for the fact that there are no female names in this category at all.

CB individuals have a rock-solid feel to them. Once set in their opinions, they'll resist change in the way a mountain resists floating on air, so steering *CBs* from their charted course can prove to be an exercise in futility. They are driven by a profound belief that they are masters of their own ships and would rather sail against the wind than be swayed by popular opinion. Admired for their stick-to-it-iveness and steady temperaments, they almost always prove to be popular with the ladies, who particularly appreciate their willingness to commit. *CBs* have a strong sense of their places in the universe, and whether their destinies are to conquer the world or just to sweep its floors, they'll attack their tasks with abandon.

CBs also have an innate ability to motivate others. They tend to only see the good in people, and even

Caleb
Coby
Cobi
Colby

social misfits will discover themselves to be beneficiaries of the *CB*'s warm encouragement. They're the ones you'll want as your hiking guide, group activities coordinator or motivational speaker. Still, *CBs* don't like to be bothered with other people's problems because they're usually much too busy being successful.

It's not that *CBs* don't love their homes, but it would be extremely unusual to find them there. They're so often on the prowl looking for something exciting to do that they don't put many resources into their living spaces. So if you notice a worn couch in the living room, it's not that your *CB* friend doesn't have the money to replace it, it's just that he hasn't gotten around to it yet.

In terms of their romantic entanglements, *CBs* are serial monogamists who prefer quality to quantity. But when it comes to physical expressions of love, they often struggle to loosen up, and waiting for them to make the first move can prove to be quite exasperating. But once you've married a *CB,* you'll encounter a deeply involved lover who will depend heavily upon you for reassurance and companionship. It can be a heavy burden to bear if you're the independent type who needs a lot of space, but you're likely to get back just as much in terms of love, reassurance and support.

Cobi Jones Hockey had Gretsky, baseball Mark McGuire, football Joe Montana and basketball Michael Jordan. In the spirit of crowning its own star to generate public enthusiasm, the U.S. soccer team optimistically presented Cobi Jones. His photogenic good looks and distinctive Rastafarian locks made him a media darling. ■ In 2002, Cobi was a key player in the U.S. World Cup triumph, which put U.S. soccer on the map and gained the respect of countries that had—up to that point—routinely embarrassed them. The leading scorer in the 2000 season, Cobi became the first U.S. player in twenty-eight years to score goals in three consecutive international matches.

cd

Charisma										
Career Success										
Love & Friendship										
Power										

The *crisply concise* sounds of the letter *C* (when the *C* is pronounced like a *K*) infuse these names with energy, optimism and just a hint of the dark side, much as the *dominant* and *decisive* letter *D* anchors it firmly to reality. Both of these letters are inherently masculine, and when combined, give the overall impression of a person with an unyielding and dynamic personality. *CD* individuals are also noted for their combination of quick-wittedness and dependability, and with their uncanny ability to land on their feet, have the confidence to take the risks that most other people avoid.

The thing that primarily shapes *CDs*' approach to their lives is their search for the novel. Thriving on the excitement of new relationships and jobs, they'll attack their goals with signature joie de vivre and unequalled emotional strength. Even though they're not above bending the rules when it helps them get a leg up on the competition, *CDs* have strong moral compasses (and secretly want to be liked), and will draw the line when it comes to using unfair tactics. And when it comes to letting you know what they think of you, sarcasm is not a tool they feel comfortable using. They prefer the car-crash method: head-on, in-your-face and hope-nobody-gets-hurt.

Cade
Caden
Cadence
Caiden
Cody
Conrad
Cordelia
Cordell
Kadin
Kody

CDs will succeed where others fail, because of their ability to adjust to their environments. With their special blend of physical energy, emotional intelligence and natural charm, they can pull off the role as a judge or sports idol with equal ease. These people may be natural leaders, but because they have little desire to complicate things with the intricacies of office politics, *CDs* in the top echelons of management are rare. Exceptionally intelligent, *CDs* are often drawn to the intellectual stimulation that comes from careers in science, medicine or law, but will happily adapt to any position in which they feel suitably challenged.

CDs are quick learners when it comes to dealing with the opposite sex, and communicating with them on an intimate level is remarkably easy. Their emotions are neither subtle nor hidden, so you'll never have to wonder what they're thinking, and you can place as many physical or financial demands as you want on them, as long as you don't overload them with emotional neediness. But as warm and affectionate as they might be with casual lovers, *CDs* tend to avoid permanent commitment until the last possible moment. But once that commitment has been made, they will prove to be a source of strength, support and extraordinary loyalty.

Conrad Hilton Conrad Hilton's publicity machine billed him as the "Innkeeper to the World." The hard-driven entrepreneur single-handedly built his father's small business into a hotel empire that now owns 2,000 hotels in fifty countries. ■ His was the first hotel company to be listed on the New York Stock Exchange and the first to operate a hotel gift shop. His company was also the first to install air conditioning and direct-dial telephones, and the first upscale lodging company to franchise their hotels. ■ Hilton also became involved in sleep research and tried to find better ways to help his clients' sleep. Complimentary brandy was only briefly considered. ■ The durable Conrad also had an eye for the ladies. His marriages to Elizabeth Taylor and Zsa Zsa Gabor were both short-lived and expensive.

ch

Charisma										
Career Success										
Love & Friendship										
Power										

Shrewd Tidy Meticulous
Uptight Cloying Jealous

The *crisp* and *cutting* influence of the letter *C* takes on a more temperate tone—and a distinctly spiritual flavor—when coupled with the *hallowed*, *hushed* and *holy* tones of the letter *H*. We see this effect in action in the words *church, chapel, cherub, chaperone* and *chastity*. In the only female name in this group, *Chloe*, the *CH*'s clement timbre is infused with a *laconic* and *laid-back* air thanks to the *lilt* of the *loving* and *lively* letter *L*.

These are names with a strong inference of moral superiority and may even suggest the image of a self-important youth with a college sweater draped over his or her polo shirt. But this characterization might be a little unfair because there's also an emotionally generous aspect to these people that ultimately comes to define their essence.

Fastidious about their appearance, *CH*s like to keep physically fit and are perennially well-groomed (and insist on the same from their partners). The *CH*'s fondness for petty details can border on the obsessive, and while it may drive everyone nuts, it also makes them wonderful doctors, lawyers and accountants. Most people who have worked with *CH*s comment on their ability to complete projects with seemingly little effort. Opinions are divided as to whether this is a symptom of raw talent or a knack for finding shortcuts.

No one understands how *CH*s manage to ingratiate themselves with so many people, but perhaps it's because they studiously avoid conflict and can schmooze like a Hollywood agent. But a word of warning: *CH*s should not be provoked. They may be patient and hospitable, but they are certainly no pushovers. You are simply not going to impose your will on them, and the sooner you to accept this reality, the fewer headaches you're going to have. It's the same in their intimate relationships: if you aren't willing to pay attention to the niceties of a romance, don't get involved. So if it's a casual fling you're considering, consider flinging elsewhere.

Once settled into a mutually respectful relationship, odds are that the *CH* will mate for life.

With a proclivity for controlling their environments, *CH*s have a tendency to keep their spouses and children under their thumbs, but it's an iron fist in a velvet glove, and their shrewd minds and smooth tongues are the perfect tools for these kinds of subtle manipulations. Children are the best counterbalance to the *CH*'s traditionalist tendencies, for only the exuberance of youth has a chance of prodding them into a semblance of spontaneity.

Chad
Chaz
Chet
Chip
Chadrick
Chadwick
Chaim
Chaya
Chloe

Chet Baker Until his drug-related, violent death in 1988, jazzman Chet Baker lived the life of a modern myth. His melancholy trumpet and intriguing vocal style made him an icon to a generation of jazz fans, but his heroin addiction created a nightmare for his intimates. A year after Bruce Weber began filming his documentary on Chet's life, Chet plunged to his death from a hotel window after bingeing on cocaine. Weber's film, *Let's Get Lost*, earned an Academy Award nomination and 1997 saw the publication of Chet's unfinished autobiography *As Though I Had Wings: The Lost Memoir*.

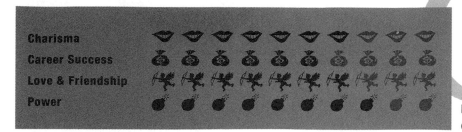

THE FORCEFUL Chk

Charisma										
Career Success										
Love & Friendship										
Power										

Dominant Fun-loving Encouraging
Complicated Boastful Secretive

The *CH* phoneme is responsible for the spiritual elements found in the words *church, chapel, cherub, chaperone* and *chastity*. And when coupled with the sharply cutting elements of the letter *K* (*kick, kill, kamikaze, kidnap* and *king*), the result is a name with a distinct sense of power and foreboding. People are instinctively on the alert when there's a *CHK* in the room—not because the *CHK* is dangerous, per se, but because it always seems as if something important is going to happen when they're around.

If there were one word that could accurately summarize these intensely masculine names, it would be *fearless*. These are people who are drawn to adventure and feel ill at ease unless something momentous is going on. So the best way to motivate a *CHK* is to tell him "no." Tell him he's not qualified for that executive-level job and he'll prove you wrong (whether he wants the job or not). *CHK*s eat boundaries for breakfast.

But these are also people with a strong sense of honor, and there are limits to the things they'll do to get ahead. For example, *CHK*s don't believe in taking shortcuts. A job worth doing is worth doing in the most chal-

Chakra
Chiquita
Chuck

lenging way possible. Strict self-disciplinarians, *CHK*s' schedules are carefully thought out and rigorously adhered to, and their social events are planned with the same intensity as their business lives.

Even with their best intentions, *CHK*s' impulses impel them to turn every situation to their advantage—a trait that often results in isolation in their personal lives. In their intimate dealings, *CHK*s sometimes have a hard time earning the trust of their partners, mainly because of their habit of overlaying their own agendas onto the relationship. Partners sense these ulterior motives in the *CHK*s' seemingly sociable advances and treat them with suspicion.

Consequently, the CHK's love affairs are often tempestuous—at least in the early stages. Compounding this problem is the *CHK*'s habit of choosing someone completely unattainable as the object of his affections, leaving him with an uphill struggle to convince his potential partner that he's worth taking a chance on. And even though *CHK*s can pull off this tactic better than most people, they are apt to lose interest when their partners succumb too easily to their forceful charms.

Chuck Norris Singled out as one of the most violent shows on network television, the success of Chuck Norris's *Walker Texas Ranger* is in no small part due to the perfectionist style of its leading man, who held the world's middleweight karate title for six years. ■ Chuck got his acting start by networking with celebrities traipsing through his L.A. karate school. In Bruce Lee's classic, *Return of the Dragon*, Chuck's character was kicked to death by Lee. ■ Chuck lent his voice to the animated TV series *Karate Kommandos*, in which his cartoon character killed five or six bad guys in every show. Although Chuck reminds his young audience that "violence is the last option," he kept on killing on his *Texas Rangers* series, which finally wrapped up in 2001.

59

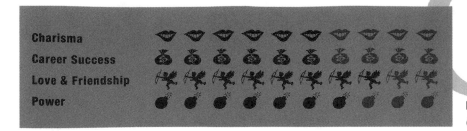

Charisma										
Career Success										
Love & Friendship										
Power										

Demonstrative Giving Hospitable
Overemotional Coy Distracted

The *CH* combination of letters produces the clear sense of *charming cheekiness* that we find in the words *cherub, champion, chafe, challenge* and *chipper*. But in the *CHN* names, the appearance of the *negative* letter *N* (*no, not, never, nyet, nada, nix, nein, nothing* and *naught*) colors these names with the self-doubt found in the words *chagrin, chink, chintzy, aching, chancy* and *chiding*. Although the name *Chandler* is in this group, these are largely feminine names that suggest the feminine virtues of nurturing and emotional awareness. In Elizabethan England, silence was considered to be the central feminine virtue. They had obviously never met a *CHN*.

*CHN*s are not shy about giving unsolicited advice or the occasional parental lecture, but their communication suffers when they demonstrate their tendency to get a little shrill in the face of conflict. On the bright side, the need to argue with these bright people is rare; their sense of fairness usually mitigates tensions before they have a chance to mature. Besides, few people can resist their big-eyed charming appeal for long.

There's a strange thing about *CHN*s of both sexes: No matter how much they achieve in their lives or how many compliments they get for their ability to handle themselves, they secretly believe that it's just a matter of time before they're "found out." If they had just a fraction of the confidence in themselves that others have in them, there is almost nothing that they couldn't achieve.

Even with their penchant to wallow in cynicism, these are people with distinctly clear agendas. So never mistake the *CHN*'s gentleness for fragility; these are no wilting lilies. Fragrant and charming they may be, but if you're looking for a *domesticated* partner, these are not for you. In fact, many *CHN*s have been known to place their relationships on hold to chase down a promising career, or just for the chance to wander freely.

Family life seems to require some effort on the part of the freedom-loving *CHN*s, for their fiercely defended independence dissolves into feelings of claustrophobia when there are too many demands on their time and emotional energies. But provided that their mates are prepared to tolerate their free spirits, they'll prove to be warmly affectionate and not the least bit needy. Oh, and with their love for physical challenges, be warned that *CHN*s are piquant lovers. Potential mates should be prepared for fireworks in the bedroom.

Chana
Chanda
Chandler
Chandra
Chanel
Chantal
Cheyanne
China

Chyna One look at Chyna and you understand why she's called the "Ninth Wonder of the World." With her six-foot frame decked with a layer of muscle a steer would envy, she steps into the ring mano-a-femme to tackle the biggest names in wrestling. ■ The WWF superstar began her wrestling career as a valet to wrestler Hunter Helmsley. Up until that point, women were simply a sideline curiosity in men's professional wrestling—limited to appearances in bikinis. ■ Her character was the brainchild of WWF owner Vince McMahon, and Chyna became the first woman to hold the WWF Intercontinental title. ■ Despite her suspiciously deep voice and impossibly broad shoulders, she fiercely defends her femininity and even had her jaw restructured to enhance her appearance.

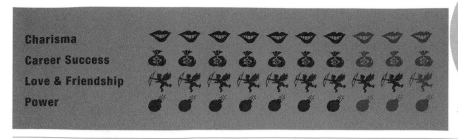

Charisma										
Career Success										
Love & Friendship										
Power										

Secure Fun-loving Encouraging
Complicated Two-faced Secretive

The gentle femininity of the *CH* phoneme—as pronounced in *church, cherub* and *churlish*—is very different from the crisper pronunciation (with its masculine overtones) found in names like *Christopher* and *Christina*. The softer articulation imbues these names with warmth and charm, and when teamed up with the passions of the *red-blooded, romantic* letter *R,* gives them an unmistakable quality of feminine sexuality. We find these characteristics in the words *cheery, chirpy, cherish, cherubic, charity* and *charming*.

The *CHR*'s feminine side rules her existence, and true to this romantic essence, she tends to operate on a subjective basis. Her gut instinct, rather than her powerful intellect, will rule the day. And to her credit, her assessments are usually accurate. The *CHR* only runs into difficulty when it comes to life's more mundane issues—such as holding down a job or getting up in the morning—for she's decidedly a creature of comfort. But because she's willing (and eminently able) to ply her feminine charms, there's usually someone willing to cater to her chocolate-and-champagne appetites. She'll even go so far as to hide her intelligence behind a flirtatious façade if it helps her avoid the stigma that brainy women sometimes have to overcome.

Cher
Charity
Charmaine
Cherie

The *CHR*'s sensitive and dramatic nature often steers her into some form of creative self-expression. Whether she's talented or not, she'll be drawn to acting, painting, photography or singing—or pretty much anything that can scratch her itch to create something. But before you write her off as an irreverent self-indulgent artist, consider that many *CHR*s feel a deep sense of responsibility toward humanity and will actually get off their butts to help out. Sometimes it just manifests itself in the way they play caretaker in the lives of those around them (they're also not above a motherly lecture at times), but often it takes the form of their charity work or social causes.

The *CHR* mate is affectionate and responsive as long as everything dovetails into her romantic notions of how her life should unfold. She won't rest until her house is immaculate, the garden blooming, and the kids obedient. But she's unlikely to be the one getting her hands dirty. That's what men are for. It's not laziness per se that makes her this way; it's simply how she's always believed that life should work. If you want to cohabit in her castle in the sky, just cater to her ladyship's requirements. She'll return the favor with the uncompromising love and loyalty of a storybook princess.

Cher Cher was born Cherilyn Sarkisian. Dropping out of high school to pursue a career in acting, she became smitten with a 28-year-old smooth-talking singer named Sonny Bono. ■ Sonny wasn't initially attracted to the gawky teenager, but after the two consummated their relationship, they crafted one of the most extraordinary singing duos in history. ■ Performing as "Caesar and Cleo," their first recordings were an unmitigated failure, but things started to look up when Sonny penned, "I Got You Babe." Cher's far-out hippie ensemble helped create their hugely popular seventies series, *The Sonny and Cher Comedy Hour*. ■ Cher split with Sonny to become an Oscar Award–winning actress (*Silkwood*), but maintained a soft spot for him until he died in a skiing accident in 1998.

Charisma										
Career Success										
Love & Friendship										
Power										

Spry Witty Involved
Snappish Petulant Flighty

The gentle sighing of the *CH* sound is responsible for the benignly gentle feel in the *CHRL* names and is distinctly different from the sharper pronunciation found in names like *Christopher, Christie* and *Christian*. When combined with the passionately *romantic* letter *R*, the *CH* phoneme conjures the placid images found in the words: *cheery, chirpy, cherish, cherubic, charity* and *charming*. These names are also significantly influenced by the letter *L*—the symbol of *life, love, liberty* and *laughter*—which suggests people with values rooted in the things that matter most.

CHRLs exude a sense of refined warmth and bubbly charm, which explains why they're so often found in the helping professions (medicine, therapy and hair care), where their soothing dispositions are put to good use. But don't be fooled by their pacific appearances; there's a crackling emotional fire raging just beneath that surface. With their strong desire (and talent) for flirting, these are people with a powerful need to be noticed and have proportionately powerful libidos.

Open conflict with *CHRLs* is something to avoid at all costs—they have long memories and equally long talons—so if you think you've offended one, you'll want to keep your distance for a while. When they have to,

Charla
Charlene
Charles
Charlie
Charlize
Charlotte
Cherilyn
Cheryl

CHRLs can be boldly outspoken, with a charismatic self-assurance that is sometimes confused with arrogance. They are often the ringleaders of their social group, and with their secret fantasies of being defenders of the weak, *CHRLs* will use inspiration (instead of intimidation) to rally their troops and to make sure that no one is left behind.

With their extraordinary sense of compassion, *CHRLs*' instincts are to put the needs of others before their own. They are wonderful hosts and are notorious for cooking army-sized meals and force-feeding their guests, and wouldn't think twice about taking anyone into their homes if they needed a place to stay. Many *CHRLs* have an assortment of stray animals and people sharing their living spaces. Since the *CHRL* is energized—rather than drained—by contact with people, you'll never find one turning down an invitation for a party or failing to show up for a celebration or a funeral.

When it comes to courtship, the *CHRL* can be quite a handful, and these playful sprites are practically bursting with a wanderlust that proves quite tiresome to the more sedate among us. Stable unions are more likely, therefore, with mates who will tolerate their penchant for socializing and can balance the *CHRLs*' extroversion with aloofness.

Charlie Chaplin Charlie Chaplin arrived at the perfect time to cheer up an America in the throes of the Great Depression, and the comedian was probably responsible for more laughs than anyone else in history. ■ As a child, Charlie's world fell apart after his father died and his mother suffered a nervous breakdown. His decision to join the circus as a mime proved to be a pivotal tangent for the young man destined to be the world's most famous silent-film star. In 1915 Charlie's tramp character debuted in the movie *The Tramp*. ■ Charlie's movie career was put in jeopardy when Senator Joseph McCarthy's act came to Washington and labeled Charlie a Communist. The pressure exerted by the government so affected his work that he never again achieved the degree of artistry that characterized his earlier career.

chrs

Charisma										
Career Success										
Love & Friendship										
Power										

Playful Altruistic Affectionate
Childish Petulant Unpredictable

The complex *CHRS* names define quite a broad range of personality types. With the spiritual and loving associations found in the *CHR* phoneme (*Christ, charisma, cherub, cheery* and *charming*), CHRS people are able to maintain a positive and energetic attitude in the face of life's challenges. But these names are also strongly influenced by the *sensuous* and *serpentine* sounds of the letter *S,* which is the classic icon of all things *sexy, sly, supple, slippery* and *soft,* so no matter what you say about *CHRS* people, it must include something about their ability to beguile the opposite sex.

*CHRS*s exhibit the quiet confidence that only a loving childhood can produce, and as children they probably enjoyed a supportive family environment in which education (or at least free thinking) was encouraged. With charm aplenty, *CHRS*s have no trouble in finding friends and don't have to expend huge amounts of energy keeping them. And don't even think about resisting these sweet-talkers, for once *CHRS*s have set you in their sights, you'll find yourself enchanted by their offbeat and oddly vulnerable appeal. It's a good idea, though, to be aware of the *CHRS*'s sensitive centers: any challenge to their integrity or insult to their self-esteem will almost certainly trigger an outburst. It's

Chris
Charise
Charissa
Cherish
Chrissy
Chrystal
Christa
Christen
Christian
Christiana
Christopher
Christiane
Christina
Christine
Cristobal
Christy

not that *CHRS*s would ever go out of their way to deliberately hurt anyone, but they will lash out with surprising ferocity to protect their feelings. The best way to avoid pulling their emotional hair triggers is to make sure that your communication lines are wide open.

Don't try to pigeonhole *CHRS*s either . . . particularly when it comes to their careers. These are people with such a wide range of talents that they can afford to ply pretty much whatever trade strikes their fancy. Still, because they thrive in social environments, they are better suited for careers requiring teamwork and problem solving. If there are any *CHRS*s in your office, they are probably the first ones that you'd turn to for information and advice.

Their powerful desire for companionship means that *CHRS* people are most satisfied in exclusive and nurturing relationships. They have no qualms about committing to family life, and if and when children show up, *CHRS* parents will be there to deliver unconditional affection, alternated with bouts of sharp discipline and preachy moralizing. At the end of the day, nothing is more important to *CHRS*s than being able to provide their children the kind of nurturing upbringing that they themselves experienced.

Christiane Amanpour, the face and voice of conflict for CNN, may be the best-known female journalist in the world. And it's not just the public that admires this brave and articulate reporter: her colleagues regularly praise her willingness to put herself in jeopardy to get the story. ■ Although many people believe Christiane to be of Lebanese descent, in fact she has a mixed pedigree. Born in Iran to British and Iranian parents, she is a British citizen. Critics point out that CNN declines to publicize her Moslem, Middle Eastern roots.

chs

Charisma											
Career Success											
Love & Friendship											
Power											

Loyal Sensual Subtle
Evasive Naïve Introverted

The words *church, cherish, chapel, cherub, chaperone,* and *chastity* all have a pacific and dreamy quality to them, and go a long way in describing individuals whose names begin with the *CH* sound. But there's much more to these complex people than mere gentility, for they are also endowed with an unparalleled sense of conviction that comes from words like *champion, chief, charming, chafe* and *chivalrous.* And because the letter *S* is the symbol for all that is *sensual* and *sassy,* it insinuates a subtle sexuality that reveals itself in slyly unexpected ways.

*CHS*s are much happier in the role of nurturer than that of leader, so you can count on them for loving support but not necessarily for perceptive advice. Being such free spirits themselves, they tend to go with the flow and don't see much point in telling others how to live their lives. Though certainly not timid, *CHS* people are not exactly extroverted either—tending to restrict their social activities to their small tight group of friends.

You'll never see a *CHS* out looking for trouble, but if you want to provoke one, just try hurting someone they love. Their strong protective streaks are underscored by an adamant sense of justice, so it will pay to

Chas
Chase
Chance
Chastity
Chauncey
Chelsea
Chester

have a *CHS* in your corner when you're down on your luck. They have an enormous amount of emotional strength and are quite willing to part with their time, money and energy to help you back onto your feet.

Unlike their love lives, the *CHS*'s professional path is well paved. They have an enviable ability to focus on their work, and whether it's in their careers or their schooling, this dedication helps to ensure their eventual success. Their combination of compassion and drive makes them ideal for careers in medicine, clergy and research, but as expected, *CHS*s will avoid sales and leadership roles whenever possible. They just aren't aggressive types.

As they grapple to maintain an even keel in their romantic lives, *CHR*s will find themselves drawn to others with similar struggles. Restless to begin with, they spend much of their lives running from one person to another in an attempt to find the perfect mate, but the most common reason that *CHS*s get into trouble is that they're reluctant to set boundaries for those they love. In their efforts to not rock the boat, *CHS*s run the risk of becoming human doormats when teamed with overly aggressive partners.

Chelsea Clinton The girl who was once a poster child for the orthodontics industry was named after the 1969 Joni Mitchell song, *Chelsea Morning*. In a classic retelling of *Swan Lake*, the young Chelsea Clinton, daughter of President Bill Clinton and New York Senator Hillary Rodham Clinton, was cruelly satirized for her gawky post-pubescent public appearances until ultimately blossoming into a confident, attractive young woman. Although much of the venom appeared to have been angular criticism of her father's presidency, it came at a time when Chelsea was most vulnerable. Taking her cue from her parents, she handled the criticism with stoic aplomb. ■ In 1997 Chelsea left the nest to attend Stanford University under a tacit agreement from the press corps to give her privacy. ■ In 2003, Chelsea accepted a six figure consulting job from the London-based McKinsey & Company.

THE EXPLOSIVE

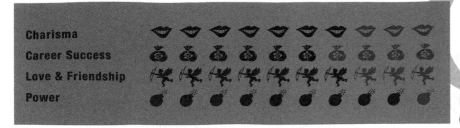

Charisma	
Career Success	
Love & Friendship	
Power	

Devoted Tenacious Hard-working
Overzealous Aggressive Cranky

There's a distinct sense of dynamite to the *CK* names as personified by the *crisply concise* letter *C* and the sharp-edged letter *K*. The letter *K*—one of the most aggressive letters in the alphabet—is responsible for the violence in words like *kick, kill, kidnap, keelhaul, knuckle* and *knife*. So while there's an implied threat looming over these names, there's also a refined aloofness . . . as if they were holding something in reserve. When the *C* is pronounced with the softer *S* sound, as in *Cedric*, we tend to find a more sensual personality without the rugged edges of a name like *Clark*.

For the most part, *CK*s are autonomous types who prefer to be left to their own devices. Though they are *able* to work well with others, they shun the anonymity of group efforts, preferring the glory that comes from self-achievement. It's not that they're particularly antisocial—on the contrary, *CK* individuals are quite drawn to large groups of people—but they aren't the types to actively pursue friendships.

When they *are* required to work with others, *CK*s will naturally take the lead with a leadership style that borders on domination rather than cooperation. Blessed with intelligence and vision, *CK*s tend to shun touchy-

Cedric
Cedrick
Clark

feely occupations like counseling or education, gravitating instead toward construction, design and engineering. They derive energy from problem solving, whether it's from their skill as hands-on repairmen or their extraordinarily well-developed sense of logic. In stereotypical masculine fashion, *CK*s will approach their friends' crises by trying to fix them rather than simply listening.

Reveling in their reputation for being strong, silent types, *CK*s enjoy the company of friends but won't ask for their affections. This often triggers a sense of unease in their companions, who find it hard to discern just what *CK*s are thinking or feeling. And rest assured, *CK*s are *always* thinking. As proof, they'll often they come out of left field with offhand observations that, upon examination, usually prove to be deeply profound.

In close familial settings, *CK*s will drop their natural reserve and allow their thoughtful and easygoing natures to bubble to the surface. They may not be known for their social graces, but they are certainly straightforward and considerate. And when they do finally decide to settle down, everyone seems to agree that *CK*s make for thoughtful and broad-shouldered mates.

Clark Gable In the light of modern standards, it seems quaint that Clark Gable created such an international firestorm when he uttered the word "damn" on the silver screen. Playing the scoundrel Rhett Butler in the movie *Gone With the Wind* wasn't a role he wanted. Worried that the public wouldn't accept his portrayal of the leading man from the widely read book, he almost quit the project after learning that he had to cry on-screen. It was only after co-star Olivia de Havilland assured him that his crying would denote strength that he agreed to stay. The sequence proved to be one of the most memorable scenes from the movie. ■ As was the trend for stars during the Second World War, Clark enlisted in the Air Force and achieved the rank of major before retiring.

65

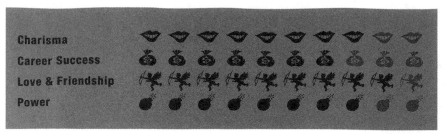

Charisma										
Career Success										
Love & Friendship										
Power										

Sexual Practical Productive
Boring Self-Involved Stubborn

A sense of *clarity* and *clearheadedness* emanates from the combination of the *crisp* letter *C* and the *lively, loving* letter *L*. With their personalities closely associated to words like *clever, classy, clarity, clean* and *clergy,* one can't help but be attracted to these energetic individuals who never seem to be without a clear sense of purpose.

CL names are steeped in an air of nobility that their owners carry quite well. It's as if they stepped straight out an English countryside smelling of Windsor roses and oiled leather. The charming *CL*s will be unfailingly courteous and polite even when things aren't going their way. In social gatherings, these people tend to gravitate toward society's elite, not out of any expression of snobbery, but simply because that's where they feel most comfortable. In fact, *CL*s are quite compassionate toward the less fortunate but are more likely to make their contributions from a distance, instead of actually mingling.

*CL*s are quite serious about how they conduct their business affairs and tend to choose careers that offer them the opportunities to fly solo—preferring the rewards that come with individual achievement. These are competitive people who enjoy activities that challenge their well-maintained bodies and sharp minds, but since they are not particularly patient or intuitive people, should avoid professions that involve intimate contact, like counseling or nursing.

In their personal lives, *CL*s are well organized and exhibit a need to be firmly in control of their relationships. Because *CL*s are big-picture people (they aren't the type to fret over things like putting the cap back on the toothpaste), potential partners are advised to pick their battles. Few things irritate *CL*s more than someone interrupting one of their many rants about politics, war or the family finances. One could accuse them of being in love with the sound of their own voices, but it's more likely a reflection of their love for any kind of debate.

*CL*s would never allow themselves to exhibit weakness by displaying their affections and putting themselves on the line. And because they can be so self-contained, their emotional motivations are sometimes hard to fathom. But this doesn't mean that they're not actively engaged in their choice of mates. Marriage to socially appropriate partners is very important to the choosy *CL,* who will often wait years for the right match to come along.

Clay
Cleo
Cleve
Caleigh
Cleveland
Columbus
Cali
Callie
Cayla
Cecil
Cecile
Cecilia
Celia
Cielo
Clarice
Cole

Cecil B. DeMille Cecil B. DeMille was one of the few Hollywood directors to survive the evolution from silent movies to "the talkies." ■ The sheer scale of his movies—in terms of extras and the massive size of his sets—will likely never be duplicated, especially considering modern technology and digital effects. ■ As a young man, having been turned down after trying to enlist in the army to fight in the Spanish-American War (he was too young), he enrolled in the Academy of the Dramatic Arts in New York. ■ After forming his own company and moving to Hollywood, Cecil rapidly established himself as one of the premier directors in the emerging industry. His interest in biblical and historical themes spawned the Academy Award–winning films *The Ten Commandments, Cleopatra* and *Samson and Delilah.* ■

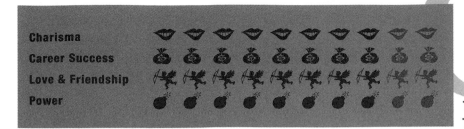

Charisma	😁😁😁😁😁😁😁😁
Career Success	💰💰💰💰💰💰💰💰
Love & Friendship	🏹🏹🏹🏹🏹🏹🏹🏹
Power	💣💣💣💣💣💣💣💣

Trustworthy Tender Creative
Temperamental Demanding Petulant

People whose names incorporate the *CLD* group of letters typically personify the good sense and steady temperament of the *clean-cut CL* phoneme, which is apparent in words like *clever, classy, clarity, clergy* and *clearheaded*. And while the *dignified* and *dapper* letter *D* adds an element of formality, those whose names end with the emotive *IA* or *IO* vowel combination (*Claudia* and *Claudio*), can be counted on to flaunt distinctly more playful and stylish attitudes.

Style or no style, these are dependable names and equally reliable people. You can always count on *CLD*s to come through in moments of crisis, for what they lack in intuition is more than made up for by their willingness to lend a sympathetic ear. Patient and kindhearted, they enjoy the simple things in life—children, animals and back rubs—and are never to be at a loss for a compassionate gesture.

The *CLD*'s steady nature can lose its equilibrium when subjected to prolonged stress. No one would think of them as being thin-skinned though, but it is true that they don't always cope well under pressure. And because these are individuals with stubborn minds and powerful

Claud
Claude
Claudia
Claudine
Claudio
Clyde

egos, anxious *CLD*s can prove to be difficult to counsel.

CLD lovers are adventurous and inquisitive but can be quite difficult to hang on to. But even though their flighty natures may prevent them from perching for too long on a particular branch, when confronted with life-changing decisions, *CLD*s aren't going to sit around and ponder their options. With uncommon faith in their instincts, they'll grab the moment, pop the question and begin building their nests.

As mates, *CLD*s provide strong shoulders to lean on and make fine matches for those with more timid personalities. Their parenting style tends toward liberality—leaving their mate to do the heavy lifting when it comes to the children—but when it comes to dealing with issues of finance and domestic blowouts, *CLD*s will roll up their sleeves and go to work.

The *CLD*s' laissez-faire parenting style makes them especially popular with their children, who adore their uncomplicated rules and earthy sense of fun. With their ability to retain an unruffled dignity against the onslaught of muddy faces and pleas for attention, many *CLD*s are the envy of harried parents everywhere.

Claudia Schiffer One night in a Dusseldorf nightclub, the director of the Metropolitan modelling agency approached an impossibly beautiful seventeen-year-old Claudia Schiffer, who refused to give him her phone number. Only after her mother met with the agency would she allow her daughter to go to Paris for photo tests. ■ The German teenager's career took off faster than you can say *Farfegnugen*, and after Karl Lagerfeld, Chanel's celebrated designer took her under his wing, Claudia was ready to conquer the United States. After Guess jeans linked fortunes with Claudia, they unleashed a stunning campaign featuring the emerging supermodel in tight pants. ■ Her engagement to magician David Copperfield created some controversy when the French magazine *Paris-Match* published a salacious story detailing a "love contract" between the two. The relationship ended six years later.

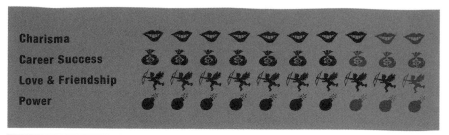

Charisma	
Career Success	
Love & Friendship	
Power	

Playful Shrewd Capable
Undependable Inconsistent Irreverent

Words that begin with *clarion call* of the *CL* letter combination tend to describe qualities that are lucid, logical and straightforward. We see these effects in the words *clean, clever, classy, clergy* and *clarity*. And when followed up with the *flirtatious, freedom-loving, frivolous* letter *F*, the *CLF* names take on a distinctly emancipated air—albeit with strongly masculine overtones.

These names represent people with clear plans for their lives, a strong set of principles and a sardonic sense of humor with an unpredictable streak. Maybe *CLFs'* need to overturn the status quo stems from a thirst for new challenges, or maybe it's just that *CLFs* are too bright for their own good. But more likely, their tendency to flirt with disaster is just an extension of their sexually teasing natures. With their innate abilities to put people at ease, *CLFs* are popular with both men and women, and no one seems to disagree that *CLFs'* libidos are as healthy as their sense of humor.

If you're moving to a new house and need someone to look after your kids, you can count on your *CLF* friends to offer their services. But don't ask them to get involved in any heavy lifting, for *CLFs* have no calluses on their hands and have no intention of getting any. Other than this, *CLFs* are not ones to put on airs and

Cliff
Clifford
Clifton

will readily interact with people on their own level.

With their hearty and oddball sense of humor, *CLFs* would do well to pursue careers in the creative fields of comedy, writing, journalism and acting. But their concise thinking patterns are also ideal for engineering, architecture and detective work. Like most people whose names begin with a *C*, *CLFs* must work a little harder than everyone else to make a buck, for the *CLF's* relationship with his job is tenuous at best and at worst is on the verge of a divorce.

If you're mated to a *CLF*, you're probably familiar with his cleft personality. One moment he'll play the insistent rationalist, and the next, a wildly spontaneous lover. And don't try to predict which side is going to emerge on any given day, for the *CLF* secretly delights in catching people unaware.

Ultimately, it's in their roles as parents and spouses that *CLFs* comes into their own. Their easygoing natures make them popular favorites with children, a situation that generally pleases them, even though they're likely to postpone having their own. And since *CLFs'* quirky sense of humor springs into action at the most unlikely times, their children will never want for laughter either. These are people unafraid of getting their hands dirty in the service of their families.

Clifford Irving In an example of art imitating life, author Clifford Irving was making the Orson Welles movie, *F for Fake*, featuring the story of an art forger, at the same time he was plotting his own insidious literary counterfeit. ■ Irving had penned a fake biography of Howard Hughes, relying on the fact that the reclusive billionaire had not been heard from in twelve years. ■ After the book was released, an incensed Hughes held a telephone conference in which he exposed Irving's lies. Although Irving stood by his story, he and his wife were convicted of fraud and served more than a year in the pen. ■ Confirming the entertainment dictum that even bad publicity is good publicity, Irving has written many successful novels since his release from prison.

Charisma										
Career Success										
Love & Friendship										
Power										

Elegant Genuine Soft-spoken
Coquettish Oversensitive Condescending

The *clean* and *clear* tones of the *CL* letter combination demonstrate their influence in the words *clever, clarion, classy, clarity, clergy* and *clarity*. But the addition of the *negative* letter *N* (*no, not, never, nyet, nada, nix, nein, nothing* and *naught*) somewhat dilutes these clearheaded qualities and creates a sense of detachment. We find these dispassionate effects in words like *clinical, clingy, decline, truculent, clunky* and *clannish*. This is why most *CLN*s exhibit a genteel and refined outer demeanor, while inwardly struggling to contain their inclination toward self-doubt and pessimism.

In between their forays into melancholy, these competent and talented individuals tackle life with enthusiasm. Their seemingly upbeat attitudes render them a big hit with friends and prospective lovers alike, so don't be surprised when your *CLN* date stops to chat with every member of the opposite sex they meet on the way to the theater. Everyone seems to know them . . . or at least know *of* them.

Their unique sense of style helps *CLN*s to stay plugged into the social scene. Female *CLN*s are perfect for careers in design or art, while male *CLN*s lean toward pursuits such as computers or architecture— anything where they can apply their sharp minds and talent for working with their hands. As co-workers,

Calvin
Celina
Celine
Coleman
Colin
Colleen
Cullen

*CLN*s prove to be competitive creatures with an annoying habit toward condescension, especially when they sense someone edging into their niche. They take pride in their work and will go out of their way to make sure that they get the credit for work they do. Employers appreciate their perfectionism, and *CLN*s are usually handsomely rewarded.

Some people are social chameleons; *CLN*s are social statues. This is a good thing, mind you, for at least you know where they stand and never have to guess which *CLN* is going to show up—even when they're in the grip of one of their downbeats. Consistency, thy name is *CLN*.

It's as mates that *CLN*s' sensitive aspects emerge, and few things hold more terror than the stigma of a failed relationship and the emotional consequences of rejection. Perhaps that's why *CLN*s place so much emphasis on having first-rate *friendships* with their mates before concentrating on issues of mere romance. However, if the partnership does happen to become untenable, *CLN*s will be the last to give up, obligingly traipsing to marital counseling or springing for trips abroad. This explains why *CLN*s are so careful about picking their partners: it's part of their perfectionist credo; something worth doing, is worth doing once.

Celine Dion James Cameron's Academy Award–winning film *Titanic* created superstars out of its lead actors, and although Celine Dion was already a bona fide pop star, she became the hottest singer in the world . . . overnight. ■ So it was a complete surprise and shock to her fans when, at the top of her game, Celine announced plans to take a six-year hiatus from the business, citing her wish to have a baby and spend time with her husband, Rene, who was battling cancer. ■ Celine had recorded her first demo at the age of twelve, and as fate would have it, the man who first heard the demo was none other than René Angelil, the man who managed her career and eventually became her husband.

Charisma										
Career Success										
Love & Friendship										
Power										

Like most names that begin with the letter *C, CLR* names resound with a *clean-cut, concise* ring that announces their presence with confidence and poise. When combined with the *loving, lively* letter *L*, the *C* takes on the *classy* appearance found in the words *clever, clean, clergy, clarion* and *cleave*. Rounded off with the *romantically robust* letter *R*, the *CLR* names paint a portrait of a clearheaded and passionate individual with distinctively feminine wiles.

Gifted with quick tongues and even quicker thought processes, the clever *CLRs* don't have to go far to find success in life. Their enviable combination of intellect and sensuality serves them well in their professional lives, though their inclination for dreaming sometimes prevents them from excelling in jobs that require strictly left-brained logic. *CLRs* aren't known for their killer instincts and prefer teamwork over rugged individualism, but since they are intuitive when it comes to discerning the motives of others, they are ideally suited for people-oriented careers like teaching, medicine or management.

As a friend, *CLRs* are *the* people you want to have around when you're in trouble or simply down in the dumps. Their instinctive understanding of the inner workings of the human mind gives them the kind of

Claire
Clara
Clarence
Clarissa

insights rivaled only by professional therapists. They are incomparable listeners (and articulate speakers) with the talent to point out people's shortcomings without crushing them. It's a rare gift, and one that might explain the incessant ringing of her phone and ceaseless stream of emails.

CLR mates are spontaneous, romantic and love surprises. But unless their emotional curiosity is occasionally tickled, they're likely to grow bored and will feel the urge to get out and roam. So if you're planning to marry a *CLR*, there's something you should keep in mind. While an occasional bouquet of flowers might go a long way, don't try to keep them happy simply by flattery. They're way too canny for that, and you run the risk of appearing condescending—the cardinal sin in the *CLRs'* book. They also hate it when people assume that their improvised lifestyles mean that they're not able to make their own decisions, and are best when paired with mates who appreciate their thirst for adventure.

CLRs are natural nurturers and were born to have children. Their kids will benefit from having a parent who still remembers how difficult it is to grow up, and will (eventually) come to appreciate their insightful and accurate advice.

Claire Danes Claire Danes's acting career began with a series of morbid roles: she played a molested child in the film *Dreams of Love* and a murderous teenager on television's *Law and Order*. ■ Claire became a symbol of disaffected teen angst when she portrayed Angela Chase in the TV series *My So-Called Life*. Among her many fans was actress Winona Ryder, who facilitated the casting of Claire in the film *Little Women*, and later in *How to Make an American Quilt*. ■ Claire starred opposite Leonardo DiCaprio in the modernistic film version of *Romeo and Juliet*, and was cast in the critically impaled movie based on the successful 1970s TV series *The Mod Squad*. Joining the current trend of actress/spokespeople, Claire recently became the face and voice of the trendy cosmetics company, *Za*.

clt

Charisma										
Career Success										
Love & Friendship										
Power										

Bold Charismatic Outspoken
Aggressive Manipulative Closed

Like all names that begin with the *crisply concise* letter *C*, the *CLT* root conjures up images of those confident individuals who know their own minds and always get what they want. In part, it's because the *CL* phoneme is associated with words like *clear, clever, clergy, clarion* and *classy*, while the terminating letter *T* lends a masculine air of *triumphant tenacity*. These forces conspire to give the *CLT* names an intensity and dogged intelligence that is impossible to ignore.

With such supreme self-confidence, *CLT* people can't help but give off an intimidating vibe—though their intent is usually just the opposite. They are natural extroverts who relish any opportunity to sharpen their minds and exercise their powerful wills. There's also a "hail-fellow-well-met" quality to *CLTs*, who thrive on meeting new people and experiencing fresh challenges. Trying to redirect *CLTs* from something they've set their mind to is like trying to stop the U.S. 3rd Infantry Division.

When set on the right track, the *CLT*'s considerable focus can be harnessed to accomplish nearly anything—although there's always the risk that innocent bystanders will get the wind knocked out of them in the process. Close friends soon learn to stand on the sidelines when the *CLT* steamroller gets moving. But *CLTs* have no interest in harming others as they barrel toward their goals, even if they are often accused of being insensitive to the feelings of those around them.

And if it seems that the *CLT* is incapable of lying—even to flatter someone by telling them what they want to hear—it's probably because they simply have no clue what someone else might want to hear.

Marriage and parenthood suit *CLTs* just fine as long as they can stay firmly planted on center stage, and the most compatible mates for the *CLTs* are those who don't have a particular agenda of their own. Riding in the freight train is easier than trying to steer it and promises an exhilarating adventure for someone who's happy just to check out the scenery. But the rewards for hitching yourself to the *CLT*'s star can be deeper too; they have rich inner lives, which they'll obligingly share with anyone who wins their heart.

Because *CLTs* are naturally curious themselves, they can relate to their children on a level that makes other parents envious. The children of the *CLT* will be treated to the same wild ride as everyone else, and will be expected to keep up with their parent's idealistic lifestyle.

Calista
Celeste
Celestine
Claudette
Clayton
Clement
Clementine
Cletus
Clint
Clinton
Colette
Colt
Colton

Clint Eastwood Clint Eastwood's name is an anagram of Old West Action. Outpolling even the venerable John Wayne, the leathery actor's movies have grossed over a billion dollars. ■ Clint "Make My Day" Eastwood has dominated over his competition in a variety of eclectic enterprises, including his stint as mayor of his hometown of Carmel, California. As a director, he won an Oscar for his 1992 Western, *The Unforgiven*, something he had been unable to achieve as an actor. ■ Clint's trademark laconic style and attention to detail lent authenticity to his characters. In all three of his *Man with No Name* movies he wore the same unwashed poncho. ■ Clint shows no sign of slowing down. He starred recently in the 2002 film *Bloodwork*, and appeared once again behind the camera in 2003's *Mystic River*.

Charisma	👄	👄	👄	👄	👄	👄	👄	👄	👄	👄
Career Success	💰	💰	💰	💰	💰	💰	💰	💰	💰	💰
Love & Friendship	👼	👼	👼	👼	👼	👼	👼	👼	👼	👼
Power	💣	💣	💣	💣	💣	💣	💣	💣	💣	💣

Artistic Serene Comforting
Stubborn Passive Repressive

When the *crisply concise* letter *C* initializes a name, it's usually associated with someone with a *clean-cut* and well-defined personality. But there's more to the *CML* names than mere simplicity. While it's true that *CML* personalities have the *cutting* edges and *canny* minds associated with the letter *C,* the *maternally merciful* letter *M* and *lyrically loving* letter *L* moderates these names with an exceptionally feminine and womanly charm—evoking the flowery image one associates with youthful innocence. Lurking under the veneer of a dry wit and a sharp intelligence is a doe-eyed creature incapable of hurting anyone's feelings even to protect her own.

Camelia
Camilla
Camille

The key to the *CML*'s personality is most evident when she's chiding someone for splurging on an expensive new car, or for playing golf instead of going to the office. To the casual observer, her rebuke may sound like nagging, but those in the know recognize her motivation to be of genuine maternal interest—the same quality that keeps her up late baking pies to deliver to a sick friend. That's why the best careers for *CML*s are those in the nurturing fields: nursing, catering, teaching or social work.

The *CML*'s down-to-earth qualities have the side effect of letting people know, in no uncertain terms, where they stand. If there's any argument or discussion to be had, she'll be the first to broach the subject, and even if her bluntness leaves a few bruised egos here and there, she's not going to stop talking until she's sure that you've understood her point. So it's best to keep your mouth shut in the face of a *CML*'s lecture and act like it's the most sensible thing you've ever heard.

Just remember that she really believes she knows what's best for you. She's no dummy, either; she's giving you advice because she's been there and done that and is sincerely trying to save you from the same hard lessons.

As mates, *CML*s are legendary for standing by their men. For her, settling down to marriage and raising children is a logical step in her life process. She has always been thrilled at the prospect of motherhood, and is the kind of woman who picked names for her kids when she was just a child herself. But the judicious *CML* isn't the type to rush into a commitment without first carefully vetting potential mates to make certain their words are in synch with their actions. Perhaps this is the reason that *CML* marriages tend to be so stable and why the *CML*s' children are universally well adjusted.

Camilla Parker-Bowles Camilla Parker-Bowles was cast as villain in one of the greatest passion plays in British history. Although her protracted love affair with Prince Charles had long been an open secret, Princess Diana's accidental death in 1997 caused a mourning public to blame her for the sequence of events leading up to the accident. ■ Camilla had long been disparaged by the British press for her boring style, and many felt that were it not for her, Prince Charles's marriage might have survived. ■ In recent years, Charles and Camilla have attempted to legitimize their relationship with both the royal family and the public, and after a relationship of over thirty years, the couple appeared together in public for the first time in 1999.

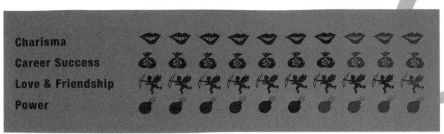

Charisma	👄	👄	👄	👄	👄	👄	👄	👄	👄	👄
Career Success	💰	💰	💰	💰	💰	💰	💰	💰	💰	💰
Love & Friendship	🏹	🏹	🏹	🏹	🏹	🏹	🏹	🏹	🏹	🏹
Power	💣	💣	💣	💣	💣	💣	💣	💣	💣	💣

Easygoing Nonjudgmental Dependable Distracted Careless Extravagant

The energetic qualities of the *CMRN* names emanate from the *crisp, clear, clean* sounds of the letter *C*, which taper off into the *maternal* embrace of the *motherly* letter *M*. But there are two distinct components to this complex name root: the *CM* phoneme—which brings to mind the benign images of words like *companion, campy, comical, cameo, comedian* and *comrade*—and the nurturing *RN* phoneme (reminding us of an *RN* nurse), which appears in the words *friend, concern, eternal, renew, reunion*, and *matron*.

All told, the defining aspects of the *CMRN* personalities pivot around their liberal attitudes and emotionally resilient temperaments. The *CMRN*s' strongest asset is their ability to live life with apparent ease, laughing along with the funny parts and drawing on their flexibility to get through the rough parts. Candid, casual and carefree, the *CMRN*s' energies are appealing to anyone who doesn't mind an unexpected visit from a rambunctious friend. And because these affable people don't react to stress the way the rest of us do, you can expect your *CMRN* friends to be the ones knocking back mai tais at the beach while the world is coming to an end.

With their liquid approach to life's complexities, *CMRN*s are the perfect buddies to help you through

Cameron

those tough emotional times. But you'll have to stand in line to get a date with these popular individuals, for *CMRN*s have a steady stream of suitors knocking at their doors. If you do manage to impress one enough to get him or her to spend some quality time with you, you'll benefit from having an introspective partner who understands that relationships are the most important things in life.

Despite their relaxed approach, *CMRN*s are not lazy people, and their ambitious energies drive them in both work and play. Being natural entertainers (with quirky senses of humor to boot), *CMRN*s feel responsible for maintaining the group's social calendar and for keeping everyone's spirits up. This alpha-male/female approach can grate on other type-A friends who resent the *CMRN*s' power.

When it comes to their children, *CMRN*s take the "best friend" route: choosing to be confidantes and co-conspirators rather than disciplinarians. It proves difficult for the *CMRN*'s spouse to compete with this special kind of relationship, and they're often relegated to the job of "bad cop." As the *CMRN* would say . . . it's a small price to pay for being married to such an exceptional person.

Cameron Diaz Shortly after high school, Cameron Diaz was working as a model when she decided to try her hand at acting. After twelve unsuccessful auditions, she landed a dream role in the movie *The Mask* with Jim Carrey, where her bubbly beauty smote the Hollywood critics. ■ Proving she would do anything for a laugh, Cameron took the leading role in the movie *There's Something about Mary* and made the list of all-time most memorable scenes when she daubed co-star Ben Stiller's "mousse" into her hair. ■ Cameron played the voice of the princess in the movie *Shrek*, and she stole the show as Tom Cruise's neurotic girlfriend in the film *Vanilla Sky*. Cashing in, Cameron appeared in both of the hugely successful *Charlie's Angels* movies.

Cn

Charisma	😗	😗	😗	😗	😗	😗	😗	😗	😗	😗	
Career Success	💰	💰	💰	💰	💰	💰			💰	💰	
Love & Friendship	🕊	🕊	🕊	🕊	🕊	🕊	🕊	🕊	🕊	🕊	
Power	💣	💣	💣	💣	💣	💣	💣	💣	💣	💣	

Gregarious Hospitable Communicative
Quick-tempered Judgmental Bossy

An examination of the *CN* names reveals the effect of the *crisply clean-cut* letter *C* and its association with the pessimistic letter *N* (*no, never, not, nyet, nein, nix, nary* and *negative*). When these two letters get together, they create the shadowy tenor found in the words *conquest, censor, cunning, conflict, control, conman* and *connive,* reminding us not to take the congenial disposition of the *CN* personality at face value. These are individuals who, although competent and outgoing, must secretly fight their desire to rule the world (or at least their personal environments).

*CN*s are not natural socializers, but what they lack in instinct is more than made up for by their enthusiasm for being part of a group. They are the types who can pull off elaborate parties with seemingly little effort, or who can sit down to lunch with complete strangers to discuss intimate issues without batting an eyelash. It's important for them to feel like they're part of the "in" crowd, and the *CN* is the one to call when you need the latest gossip. They may seem cliquish—like most attractive and popular people—but in the *CN*s' case, the elitism proves to be transitional. Deep down, *CN*s have the common touch.

*CN*s are very much career-minded and feel most in control when their careers are stable. And the need to be

Connie
Connor
Constance
Consuelo
Cornelia
Cornelius
Cornell

in control is usually at the heart of *CN*s' motives, especially their need for control over their financial affairs. Employers love their steely dedication and the single-minded sense of purpose with which they tackle their work, and although these multitalented individuals could have their choice of jobs, they prove to be remarkably unfussy about the work itself. Inasmuch as money plays such a big role in *CN*s' lives, they will almost always choose a lucrative job over one that offers personal satisfaction.

When it comes to their personal lives, *CN*s enjoy a great deal of attention from the opposite sex, who are attracted to their air of earnest responsibility. But *CN*s are picky about with whom they commit, so you shouldn't think that your casual relationship is going anywhere unless they've given you specific reasons to think otherwise. And because most *CN*s marry late in life, their unions are usually permanent.

The *CN*'s children will enjoy a somewhat spoiled existence when it comes to material wealth, but they'll have to hurry to catch this parent between appointments. When *CN*s are on a mission, their families will have to accept being just another component of the intricate machinery that is the *CN*s' life.

Connie Chung Connie Chung was the first Asian to co-anchor a major network's national news broadcast and the first woman to do so since Barbara Walters annoyed Harry Reasoner on ABC. ■ Originally signed by CBS to cover stories for the local evening news, her preference for soft stories quickly earned her the nickname Connie Fun. ■ Many people wrote her off when CBS unceremoniously dumped her from the anchor position in 1995, but Connie simply wouldn't go away, reappearing in 2002 as host of her own show, CNN's *Connie Chung Tonight*. ■ Her most controversial moment came when she interviewed the mother of former Speaker of the House of Representatives Newt Gingrich. Pulling the woman aside to "privately" ask her what her son thought of First Lady Hillary Clinton, Newt's mother whispered "a bitch," and Connie proceeded to announce the comment to the world.

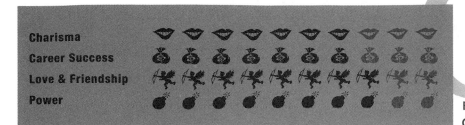

THE UNDECIDED
cnd

Charisma	👄	👄	👄	👄	👄	👄	👄	👄	👄	👄
Career Success	💰	💰	💰	💰	💰	💰	💰	💰	💰	💰
Love & Friendship	💘	💘	💘	💘	💘	💘	💘	💘	💘	💘
Power	💣	💣	💣	💣	💣	💣	💣	💣	💣	💣

Engaging Refreshing Lively
Conflicted Snobbish Cranky

The *crisply* sharp pronunciation of names beginning with the letter *C* suggests an individual with a *candid* and *clearheaded* approach to life. But there are forces at work in the *CND* name root that lend a gently egalitarian feel to this otherwise sharp letter. When the *nurturing* qualities of the (usually negative) letter *N* and *dignified* letter *D* combine, they form the basis for the gracious overtones in the words *fond, kind, mend, friend, bland, Godsend* and *garland.* Perhaps this is why virtually all names containing an *ND* combination belong to women.

Those who bear *CND* names inspire respect (never fear) with their straightforward attitudes, and adamantly refuse to back down from good arguments. But there's always a hint of chaos looming in the *CNDs'* lives: they're as unpredictable as the Dow Jones. They just can't be bothered with making the same old schedules every day or, for that matter, any schedule at all. Still, *CNDs* are detail-oriented women with a tendency to become irritated when people suggest shortcuts or try to give them how-to advice. Outside interference, no matter how well intentioned, is simply not appreciated.

Consistent with their laissez-faire philosophy, *CNDs* will steer clear of controlling the lives of her friends and family. And since *CNDs* love the element of surprise, hardly a celebration goes by in which they're not actively

Candi
Candice
Candida
Candy
Candyce

involved. *CNDs* also make perfect rally leaders, and their impulsive energies can be hard to resist once they've glommed onto a new idea. This cheerleading style makes them ideal people for drawing attention to a project. *CNDs* take great pride in their personal appearance, dress in contemporary styles and—as their families will attest—spend way too much time primping in the bathroom. So if you have a *CND* as your hairdresser, masseuse or palm reader, chances are you're going to be spoiled.

CNDs are not above an occasional drama-queen performance—especially when they fail to monitor their emotions, which have a tendency to overheat. If you want to short-circuit these moods, don't try ignoring them. Bite the bullet and give them the attention they're really asking for. Still, since 90% of *CNDs'* energies are spent on others, no one can begrudge them the occasional self-indulgent rants.

In their romantic lives, *CNDs* are drawn to men who make them feel feminine. Because they have enough power in their professional and social lives, they don't want to be the ones wearing the pants at home as well. *CND* marriages are typically stormy for the first few years, before settling into a gentle rhythm when both parties have worked out the relationship's hierarchy.

Candice Bergen The daughter of ventriloquist Edgar Bergen, Candice Bergen began her career as part of his show alongside his puppets, Charlie McCarthy and Mortimer Snerd. Her big-screen debut was in the film *Carnal Knowledge*, and she later received an Oscar nomination for her role in the movie *Starting Over*. ■ In 1988 Candice found her niche playing the sarcastic, independent and liberal anchorwoman, *Murphy Brown*. With Candice at the helm, the show won five Emmy Awards. ■ The show was given a huge boost when Vice President Dan Quayle attacked Candice's single-mother character for being a poor role model. Amid guffaws from the media reminding Quayle that it was only a TV show, Candice actually seemed supportive, commenting, "His speech was a perfectly intelligent speech about fathers not being dispensable. Nobody agreed with that more than I did."

cnth

Charisma	👄	👄	👄	👄	👄	👄	👄	👄	👄	👄
Career Success										
Love & Friendship										
Power										

The *CNTH* name root is comprised of two distinct phonemes with very dissimilar qualities. Although the letter *C* is associated with all things *cool*, when it's combined with the *negative* letter *N,* it takes on the *controlling* essence found in the words: *connive, censor, convict, cunning, conquest* and *conflict*. Thankfully, the pacific influences of the *TH* (*thoughtful, father, mother, theology, theatre* and *theoretical*) remind us that these strong and controlling personalities are ultimately benign.

The powerful *CNTH* personality is incapable of entering a room without creating some level of tension. It's not that they're trying to cause any discomfort; their presence just seems to lend an electrical charge. Likewise, if you've ever had a *CNTH* as a friend or mate, you understand the meaning of the phrase *high-maintenance*. Appreciative of the status that money and fame can buy, *CNTH*s have a tendency to choose their friends with material wealth as a guide. But before we relegate them to the shallow end of the friendship pool, remember that there's little malice residing in their hearts—at worst, just a little neediness.

The ideal careers for a *CNTH* are those that allow

Cynthia

her to take charge and make her own decisions. It's also not unusual to find these strong-willed individuals owning small businesses in which they express their creative and intellectual talents. It's a rare *CNTH* who doesn't achieve her goals, either as an athlete, musician, businesswoman, artist, class president or homemaker.

When it comes to their love lives, most *CNTH*s enjoy the benefit of having a powerful pull on the opposite sex. Even if they're not stereotypical beauties, there's something enormously attractive about their strong-willed personalities. Earthy? Definitely. *CNTH*s are usually the aggressors in dating and mating situations (even if most potential lovers never realize it). While this may not always prove to be a successful mating strategy, don't waste your time pointing out their faults. They're resourceful enough to solve their own problems.

*CNTH*s are comfortable in the role of parent, and even those who aren't in a hurry to have children prove to be capable and unconditionally loving mothers. *CNTH*s understand the value of a good education, and even when their children don't attend private schools, they are bound to learn all the *right* lessons from their patient and insightful mother.

Cynthia Rothrock Cynthia Rothrock is one of the most respected female martial arts/action film stars in the world. ■ Starting her martial arts training at the age of thirteen, she soon began competing and winning titles in male karate tournaments. With five black belts under her belt, she more than proved her mastery of the Eastern martial art disciplines, and for four years she was the undefeated World Karate Champion, a feat no one has been able to duplicate. Thrust into the spotlight by her success in competition, she soon became a superstar in martial-arts circles. ■ As her bio points out, "She has a ponytail better than Steven Seagal, a chest superior to Arnold, looks superior to Van Damme, and unlike Stallone and Willis, can obliterate bad guys while perched on three-inch heels."

Charisma	
Career Success	
Love & Friendship	
Power	

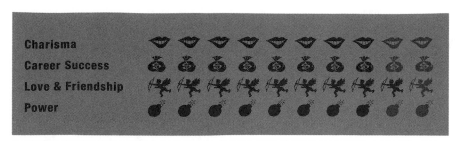

Daring Vivacious Devoted
Inconsistent Undependable Uptight

It's unusual to encounter an individual whose assertive nature is rooted in pure audacity, but it's arguable that that is precisely what defines the *CR* personality. When the *crisply concise* letter *C* combines with the *ribald* and *randy R*, it imparts the air of robust passion found in the words *courageous, coercion, cobra, conquer, cougar, crisp, curvy* and *carnality*. Names tailed by the playful letter *Y* or *IE*—as in *Carrie, Cory* and *Carey*—are imbued with a bit more of an approachable aspect, but *all CR* names incorporate the elements of romance, passion and resilience that enable these people to weather life's rough patches.

Never without a sense of humor or a perpetually impish grin, *CR*s present a cheerful, if unpredictable face to the world. And while you may think you know a *CR*, be prepared for surprises! With a tendency to switch directions in midstream, their whimsical and unpredictable dispositions can quickly throw relationships out of balance, which is why it's common for *CR*s to move in and out of relationships several times a year. But there's a price to pay for this high emotional metabolism, for without the constant stimulation of fresh people in their lives, *CR*s are prone to mood swings and bouts of ennui.

The *CR*s' volatility can land them in trouble in other ways, and at its worst it manifests itself in out-

Cara
Cari
Carissa
Carrie
Carson
Ciara
Cierra
Cira
Cora
Corey
Cyrus

bursts of aggressive sarcasm that can alienate even the most loyal friends. But at their best, *CR*s are exciting, well-meaning friends with a vast reservoir of emotional energy. The best way to deal with these occasional outbursts is to give them a respectful distance in which they can collect their composure.

*CR*s exhibit a deeply spiritual side that articulates itself in a variety of artistic forms (mainly music, writing or painting) and these talents are often parlayed into successful careers in entertainment. But their indifference to more concrete forms of labor often excludes them from high-paying careers. Fortunately, because most *CR*s are not driven by a need for money, their creative talents more than compensate for their occasional diva behavior.

With a strong sense of destiny and the belief that karma is looking out for them, *CR*s are by and large happy people who are at peace with themselves and the universe. *CR*s don't *have* to be married and function quite well as singles. But if the right person does happen to stumble into their busy lives, they'll probably at least *consider* it. There's a great deal of power that comes from not wanting something too badly, and *CR*s take full advantage of it. Still, they'll do their part, and family life will be firmly anchored by their intelligent guidance.

Carrie Fisher When Carrie Fisher was still a child, her father, Eddie Fisher, received a mating call from Elizabeth Taylor and left Carrie's mother, Debbie Reynolds, to raise Carrie and her brother, Todd, on her own. ■ Cavorting around in a spaceship wearing a revealing white dress was not exactly what Carrie's parents had had in mind for their daughter. But after *Star Wars*, in which she played the winsome Princess Leah, created a worldwide commotion in 1977, they became converts. ■ Through her friend comedian John Belushi, Carrie was introduced to the drugs that would impair her career for years to come, cutting short her marriage to songwriter Paul Simon and resulting in a near-fatal overdose. Her experiences led her to write a best-selling book and movie, *Postcards from the Edge*.

Craig

Charisma										
Career Success										
Love & Friendship										
Power										

**Strong Dependable Precise
Short-tempered Uncommunicative Aggressive**

The staccato rhythms of the crisply pronounced name *Craig* fall under the influence of the *CR* phoneme, which evokes images of *crafty, cranky, crabby, crawly, creepy* and *crud.* When terminated by the *guttural* sounds of the *gruff* letter *G,* these names describe a masculine individual with a powerfully driven sense of purpose and a lot more going on than he's prepared to fess up to.

In his everyday life, the *CRG* struggles somewhat with his communication style—or, more accurately, *everyone else* struggles with his style of communication. *CRG*s believe that the less said the better. These are the strong, silent types who would rather let their actions represent their feelings instead of their (occasionally tongue-tied) mouths. But *CRG*s sometime pay for their silence by being unable to achieve intimacy with their partners. And yet, *CRG*s are eager to please and work hard to make up for their stoicism with demonstratively thoughtful acts. If you happen to receive an unexpected bouquet of flowers from your *CRG* mate, chances are he hasn't done anything wrong—it's just his way of saying something without having to open his mouth.

Though they hide it well, these are men with extremely sensitive centers. Perceived criticisms will provoke a strong defensive reaction, which, if true to form, will be in the form of prolonged sulks or sullen silences. Trying to get *CRG*s to open up is probably a waste of time; it's best to allow their moods to run their course. Consequently, *CRG*s tend to bond closely with small groups of people while their wider circle of casual acquaintances are held at an emotional arm's length.

In the workplace, the *CRG*'s loyalty and strong focus are usually well rewarded by regular promotions and raises. These are providers par excellence, and their families and close friends will appreciate their customary acts of generosity. The word on the street is that if *CRG*s had their druthers, they would work from home, not because they don't want to commute but because they think it would be cool to work in their pajamas.

As a friend, the *CRG* can be tenaciously loyal, and it's virtually impossible to shake his camaraderie once it has been established. To those outside his inner circle, however, the *CRG* is a different story, a stony man who is quick to find fault with others. Despite this seeming inconsistency, those close to a *CRG* are fully aware that he is an earnest perfectionist with a strong moral backbone.

Craig T. Nelson Although best known for his portrayal as Hayden Fox on the award-winning series *Coach*, Craig Nelson made a name for himself long before that as a competent writer and actor in major motion pictures, co-starring with Keanu Reeves in *Devil's Advocate* and appearing in Rob Reiner's *Ghosts of Mississippi*. ■ The hugely popular *Poltergeist* movies, in which Craig played father to the unfortunate Freeling family, made Craig a star, but the role also came with its own eerie curse which the actor felt lucky to survive. Two of its young stars died shortly after the movie's release: Heather O'Rourke (who played Carol Anne) died from a congenital intestinal condition, and twenty-two-year-old Dominique Dunne (who played the older sister, Dana) was strangled to death by an ex-boyfriend.

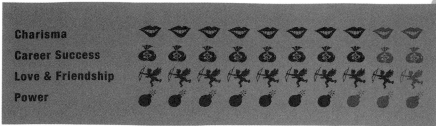

Charisma										
Career Success										
Love & Friendship										
Power										

The *crisply cerebral* sound of the letter *C* lends a sense of vigor and cordiality to the names it initializes and perhaps explains why *CRL* people exude such a strong sense of self-confidence. The *crystalline* features of the *CRL* names are brought under the influence of the rolling cadence of the *romantic* letter *R* and the *loving* qualities of the letter *L,* where their whimsical connotations make their influence felt in words like: *girl, twirl, whirl, droll, choral* and *curly.* Perhaps this is why many people tend to associate *CRLs* with flights of fancy and why *CRLs* consider themselves to be on a different (and somewhat higher) plane.

If you are drawn to idealistic, intellectual and arty types, chances are you know a *CRL.* These are dreamers, but not hopelessly so, for they clearly possess the intellectual tools to implement their ambitions with determination and grit. So don't be surprised if your *CRL* friend comes out with a hot scientific discovery or an innovative style of interior design.

You can sometimes spot *CRLs* at parties before you even know their names. They are socialites, flitting from group to group and leaching snippets of information from each conversation. On the surface they may seem flighty and even shallow, but you can be sure they

Carl
Carla
Carlo
Carlos
Carlotta
Carlton
Carly
Carol
Carolee
Carroll
Coral
Coralee
Corliss
Cyril

are busily processing everything they hear and stockpiling it away for future use.

CRLs are the soul of friendliness, and they would never consciously make enemies. They take great pleasure in surprises—preferring the role of surpriser to that of the surprisee—but beware the fickle downside. These are people with a strong need to be liked, and they will do or say anything to garner the approval of others. Only when they're wholly confident in the strength of the relationship will they drop their gushing façade.

In their intimate relationships, *CRLs* are unlikely to be accused of having firm grips on reality, for many of them cling to the belief that they're able to transform the world to fit their ideals. This has the effect of leaving some people to feel manipulated, which is made worse by the *CRLs'* habit of walking away from problems rather than confronting them early on.

Because their worst nightmare is to be left alone and friendless (as unlikely as this may be), *CRLs* rely on their relationships to be the source of their self-esteem. This might explain why they're so determined to use their chameleonlike social skills to gain the cherished social status of "most popular."

Carl Sagan There may be billions and billions of stars in the galaxy, but there was only one mega star in the astro-entertainment business. ■ Carl began teaching astronomy at Harvard University while moonlighting as an astrophysicist at the Smithsonian Observatory. As a respected astronomer in his own right, his belief that intelligent life existed elsewhere in the universe inspired him to bring his case to the public. He brought his galactic saga to many through the award-winning PBS series *Cosmos.* ■ His screenplay for the movie *Contact* resulted in a major motion picture starring Jodie Foster and Matthew McConaughey, but Carl never lived to see its success. He died in 1996 after a two-year struggle with bone marrow disease.

Charisma	👄	👄	👄	👄	👄	👄	👄	👄	👄	👄
Career Success	💰	💰	💰	💰	💰	💰	💰	💰	💰	💰
Love & Friendship	💘	💘	💘	💘	💘	💘	💘	💘	💘	💘
Power	💣	💣	💣	💣	💣	💣	💣	💣	💣	💣

Positive Outgoing Confident Willful Harsh Moody

The *CRLN* name root is a complex amalgam of conflicting messages. The *crisp* and *crystal clear* tones of the initial letter *C* suggest an idealistically motivated individual, but its conjunction with the carnal letter *R* (*racy, ribald, randy, ravishing, romantic*) implies someone whose powerful emotional impulses are kept barely under control. We see these effects in the words *cranky, crabby, crafty, creative, crackling, crude* and *cruel.* Then there's the influence of the *loving, lively* and *learned* letter *L,* and the *nurturing* aspects of the letter *N,* which contribute the feminine intelligence found in the words *élan, clean, feline, flaunt, fluent, talent* and *learn.*

So if people tend to be drawn to the *CRLN* personalities, it's because unraveling their complicated spirits often proves to be a delightful challenge. These are women who are generous of spirit and who have an altruistic desire to see others do well. But the sharper aspects of their personalities—expressed by their acerbic tongues and critical tone of voice—often prove to be impediments to their social lives. Still, once you've befriended the complex *CRLN,* you'll have someone you can trust with your life. Even if you happen to lose touch with her for years, there's that comforting feeling that you can pick up right where you left off.

Carlena
Carlene
Carline
Carlyn
Carolann
Carolina
Caroline
Carolyn

With an agreeable mix of intellectual and emotional intelligence, *CRLN*s gravitate toward jobs in education, customer service, physical therapy and the medical fields. When they put their minds to it, they really know how to put people at ease. Their intuition and sense of responsibility combine to make them effective managers of people, and as long as they don't overstep their abilities, they'll be able to maintain a heavy workload without sacrificing their attention to detail.

The *CRLN* mate will be companionable and charming, upholding her idealistic values both inside and outside the home. And yet, finding common ground with a potential mate sometimes proves difficult for the picky *CRLN.* Unless her mate is one who fully shares her convictions, the relationship can denigrate into a series of backbiting spats.

Perhaps this is why many *CRLN*s tend to delay getting married. Though they thrive in intimate situations, their persnickety tastes require somebody very special. Once happily ensconced in loving relationships, however, *CRLN*s will apply their high standards to the upbringing of their children, who will enjoy the benefits of an energetic mother concerned with their proper moral education.

Carolyn Kennedy The tragedy dogging the Kennedy clan embraced the recently married Carolyn Bessette Kennedy when she boarded a private plane bound for a family wedding in Martha's Vineyard. ■ Piloted by her charismatic husband, John Jr., the popular son of President John F. Kennedy, the couple was looking forward to the celebration. Carolyn had chosen a black silk Alber Elbaz gown for the event, and the salesperson who sold it to her later recalled that Carolyn was "not looking forward to flying." ■ Significantly, the flight was John's first solo flight since he had broken his foot in a paragliding accident. He inexplicably decided to forgo the services of his regular co-pilot that day. ■ The plane plunged into the ocean, and there were no survivors. The bodies, when recovered, were still strapped to their seats, but in such poor condition that full details were never released.

Charisma										
Career Success										
Love & Friendship										
Power										

Mysterious Wide-eyed Artistic
Picky Elusive Inconsistent

It's hard to ignore the sexy and mysterious overtones of the *CRM* names. The *crisply* pronounced letter *C* suggests an individual of decisive intelligence, while the *racy* qualities of the *randy* and *rambunctious* letter *R* combine with the warm embrace of the *motherly* letter *M* to hint at a passionate and charming individual.

But there's also a dark—and even creepy—aspect embodied in these names that stems from the *CRM*'s association with words like: *cremate, crime, scream, crummy, acrimony* and *cramp.* Perhaps this is why we instinctively (if not a little unfairly) associate the name *Carmine* with being the quintessential Mafia hit man, or why these names are often chosen to represent mysterious fictional characters like *Carmen San Diego* (the elusive heroine of the popular children's computer game) and George Bizet's ill-fated Spanish gypsy *Carmen* (the title character from the most famous of his operas). It's also significant that the *CRM* root shares the same core letters as the words *charming* and *chiromancy* (another name for palmistry).

The unique combination of inscrutability and strength in the *CRM* names evoke romantic and dreamy spirits whose mystique is their greatest asset. There's no question that *CRM*s make for nurturing and loyal friends, but it's wise to keep in mind the wild side of their personalities, in which their gypsylike natures make it hard for them to settle down in the traditional sense.

When it comes to their careers, the *CRM*'s enigmatic powers are suited less to concrete pursuits than they are to the creative fields. *CRM*s shine in professions like design, computer software, science and the arts, but you probably won't find a *CRM* in corporate leadership. This is not because they're ineffectual leaders but because they adamantly refuse to work under someone else's set of rules. *CRM*s need to be in firm control of their emotional wellbeing, and exhibit a strong sense of their own destiny. But don't make the mistake of assuming that simply because they're dreamers, they're incapable of making sharply rational decisions.

*CRM*s need their intimate relationships to be tinged with a sense of adventure, and when family life gets too predictable, they'll simply move on in search of more exciting settings. Since *CRM*s are comfortable with physical expressions of love, you can expect them to be experimental and inventive in the bedroom, and in the living room as well. But don't ever take them for granted. *CRM*s know how special they are and will expect some effort on your part. Romance—the old-fashioned kind with wine and roses—is the ideal tool for hanging on to your *CRM* lover.

Carmel
Carmelita
Carmella
Carmelo
Carmen
Carmina
Carmine

 **Carmine Galante** Carmine Galante was one of the most ruthless of all the New York Mafia bosses, with an uncountable number of murders to his credit. When he received a twenty-year jail term for narcotics trafficking in the 1960s, the underworld breathed a sigh of relief. ■ But even from his prison cell, the cigar-chomping Carmine continued to run his "family" business, and the prospect that he would be paroled in 1974 set everyone on edge. An all-out war was expected. ■ Within ninety days of his release, eight Genovese crime family members lay dead, and Carmine was once again in control of the lucrative New York drug operation. ■ "The Cigar" seemed unstoppable until three masked gunmen cut him down in a Brooklyn restaurant in 1979. Carmine died with his cigar still in his mouth.

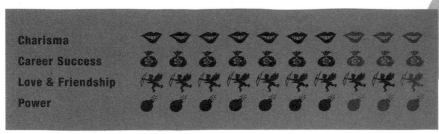

Charisma										
Career Success										
Love & Friendship										
Power										

crn

Thoughtful Capable Faithful
Reticent Reclusive Closed

When a name begins with the *crisply concise* tone of the letter *C* (pronounced as a *K*), we expect to find an individual with a strong intelligence and well-defined personality. However, the letter *C* takes a somewhat dubious turn when it comes into close contact with the letter *R*, forming words like *creepy, crawly, cranky, crazy, cryptic, crappy* and *crud*. And these harsh overtones are hardly helped by the appearance of the *negative* (*no, not, never, nix, naught, nothing*) letter *N*. All told, these names suggest a person with a precarious balance of brains and shrewdness kept under tight emotional control.

*CRN*s take a "yellow-light" approach to life, carefully testing the waters before jumping in with both feet. Though they're not shy, they certainly are cautious and would never make important decisions without first weighing the repercussions. Still, *CRN*s always seem to know exactly what they want from life; it's just a question of how to get there with the least expenditure of energy. Emotions are kept carefully under guard to ensure that sloppy sentimentality won't cloud their judgment or reduce the efficiency of their decisions.

The *CRN*s' knack for keeping their feelings in check (or is it numbness?) gives them emotional stamina that most people take years to develop. With this ability to separate their heads from their hearts, *CRN*s thrive in emotionally challenging professions, which may explain why so many of them are found in the medical, social and rehabilitation fields. *CRN* people are also generally methodical—one might even say that they find comfort in simplicity. While other people might be cracking under the pressures of stressful situations, *CRN*s are busily getting organized and preparing their counterattacks.

There's a sentimental current running just beneath the surface of the *CRN*'s everyday life, which displays itself in unexpected ways. You might be friends with a *CRN* for years, until the levelheaded person you think you know reveals what's really in his or her heart. Once the floodgates are opened, you might find a passionate and idealistic dreamer, or a person with some sort of mysterious past. The danger to *CRN*s is that in hiding themselves so well, they sometimes miss out on the best part of their relationships.

Perhaps this is why *CRN*s take a cautious approach to marriage. They like the idea of commitment; they're just not convinced that they're up to the challenge. So don't take it personally when your *CRN* lover gives you that "it's not you, it's me" speech. Odds are, they really mean it.

Carina
Corbin
Coreen
Corina
Corinne
Corrin
Corrina
Corrine

Corbin Bernsen Sturdy, durable and handsome, Corbin Bernsen's notoriety stems mainly from his portrayal of a manipulative and sleazy attorney on the television show *L.A. Law*. His career success was helped by the fact that both of Corbin's parents were in "the biz": his mother, Jeanne Cooper, is a long-time actress on *The Young and the Restless* and his father, a film producer, gave Corbin his first role in a movie. ■ Even with substantial feature films under his belt, including *Major League*, *Radioland Murders* and *Tales from the Hood*, Corbin's television work mostly pays the bills. He starred as the Southern Poverty Law Center founder Morris Dees in NBC's *Line of Fire* and also had a key role in the NBC miniseries *Grass Roots*. In 1996, he played the lead in the syndicated action series *The Cape*.

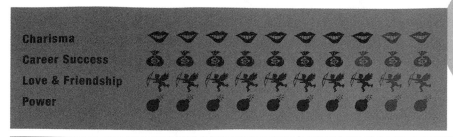

THE LEADER
crt

Charisma	
Career Success	
Love & Friendship	
Power	

**Straightforward Honest Driven
Gruff Temperamental Aloof**

People whose names begin with the *crisply cerebral* letter *C* (or *K* sound) are very straightforward in their interactions with the universe. And when their names feature the equally abrupt letter *T*, you can expect them to be forthright, brusque and even a little bit demanding. These people are *curt, certain, critical* and *crotchety*.

There's something inherently clean-cut and noble about the *CRT*s. With their precise balance of self-discipline and foresight, they would make ideal Boy or Girl Scout leaders even if they'll tend to keep an emotional distance from their charges. Athletic and strong, *CRT*s prefer team sports (which give them the opportunity to display their gift for motivating others) and can be quite competitive as long as no one is going to get hurt. Their easy laugh and dry sense of humor marks them as *the* person to be invited to any social gathering.

*CRT*s are also the ideal people to have around when you're running late on a deadline, mainly because they're so skillful at prioritizing their schedules and cutting out excess work. Concrete planning is the *CRT*'s modus operandi, and they're never without either an appointment book or a laptop to help them strategize their hectic lives. *CRT* people will always come through

Carter
Catrina
Cortez
Carleton
Courtney
Courteney
Crystal
Curtis
Kurt

with their promises, get quickly to the point and to hell with the funny stuff. It's not that they lack a sense of humor (for *CRT*s have an exceptionally wry wit), but when they do get down to business, their keen concentration manages to exclude all else.

Like most hyper-organized people, *CRT*s don't take kindly to change. The status quo is the *CRT*'s refuge, and anyone who threatens to rock the boat is treated with suspicion. So if you have any ideas about how things could be done differently, it would be better to keep them to yourself.

The easiest way to reach any *CRT*'s heart is to impress him or her with how responsible a citizen you can be. The *CRT* male is going to be most influenced by a female who doesn't expect him to spend a lot of money, while the *CRT* female is attracted to men able to whip up a decent meal on a budget. All told, *CRT* mates are generous, loving and team-oriented, and are usually willing to rework their priorities for the benefit of the relationship.

Marriage and family are intrinsic parts of *CRT*s' overall plan for their lives, and they take to domestic life like ducks to orange sauce. Children are welcomed into *CRT*s' busy lives but will be forbidden to usurp their parent's well-planned routines.

Courteney Cox In a memorable scene from the music video for the Bruce Springsteen song "Dancing in the Dark," the Boss performed an impromptu dance with a fan pulled from the audience. The pretty brunette was an unknown Courteney Cox, chosen for this role months before the shoot. Her exposure lead to what culminated in one of the highest-earning careers on television. ■ After appearing as Michael J. Fox's girlfriend on the television show *Family Ties*, Courteney's break came when she won a role in Jim Carrey's hugely successful *Ace Ventura: Pet Detective*. Based on the strength of that performance, Courteney was later cast as Monica on NBC's sitcom *Friends* after originally auditioning for the role of Rachel. ■ Courteney also has the distinction of being the first person to say the word "period" on national TV in a Tampax commercial.

83

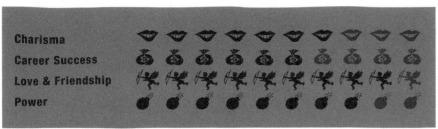

Charisma	
Career Success	
Love & Friendship	
Power	

Lively Thrifty Clever
Vain Immature Spoiled

The *CS* root evokes both the brusque *and* the sensual characteristics of the letters *C* and *S*. The strong *cadence* of the *crisp* letter *C* instills a sense of *conviction* and *clearheadedness*, while the *sensual* letter *S* lends an air of *slinky sexuality* that infuses these names with a coy *sensuality*. Those whose parents terminate their children's names with a diminutizing *Y* or *IE*—as in *Casey, Cassie* and *Cicely*—bestow an even more playful aspect to their children's lives.

*CS*s are those people who enjoy life and its simple pleasures. In fact, one could say that their most solemn characteristic is the effort they put into finding new adventures. *CS*s strive to be around like-minded people who also take pleasure from always being on the go, although it's less about companionship than about the camaraderie. The last thing you'd ever describe *CS*s as being is *dependent*, for they are fiercely autonomous people whom you wouldn't expect to find in dependent relationships: they function best in the company of others who have a life.

Anyone who dates the energetic *CS* shouldn't be afraid of having too much fun. Nor should they be worried about what friends would think about hanging around such an irrepressible party animal. And they shouldn't even think about spending a quiet night at

Caesar
Casey
Cason
Cassidy
Cassie
Cecily
Cicely

home, for *CS*s will expect their friends to be active co-conspirators in their quest for merriment. This positive outlook makes *CS*s a particular favorite with the younger set, and anyone in need of a mentor will find them to be supportive and unselfish with their time. If there's a downside to this enthusiastic altruism, though, it's that *CS*s have a difficult time stretching their attention spans for more than a few minutes at a time, giving the impression that they simply can't hold a deep conversation.

Careers for the *CS*s will have to include plenty of opportunities for socializing. Look for them to enter occupations that involve working with the public, like catering, performing, retail or teaching. But anything that allows them to be outdoors or gives them opportunities to travel will also be perfect for the convivial *CS*s.

A corresponding need for excitement and variety pervades the *CS*s' family lives, where they don't feel comfortable unless surrounded by noise, activity and laughter. *CS* lovers are passionate enough, but also hard to please; they want more out of life than just marriage and children, but are not really sure what that might be. Ideal mates are those who will accompany the *CS*s on their search for meaning.

Casey Stengel Charles "Casey" Stengel is remembered for his comic antics around the baseball field as well as for his successes as a major league baseball player and manager. Before his baseball career, though, Casey was a dentist in his hometown of Kansas City.■ Casey was a topnotch outfielder for the Dodgers, Pirates, Phillies, and Braves, and played in three World Series' with theGiants. He is probably best remembered, however, for his managerial accomplishments. After stints with Brooklyn, Boston, and Milwaukee, Casey landed a job with the New York Yankees and the team won ten pennants in twelve years, including five straight world championships. After three dismal seasons with the Mets' expansion team, though, Casey called it a career. He died in 1975 at the age of 86.

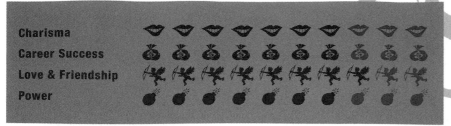

Charisma	👄👄👄👄👄👄👄👄👄👄
Career Success	💰💰💰💰💰💰💰💰💰💰
Love & Friendship	💘💘💘💘💘💘💘💘💘💘
Power	💣💣💣💣💣💣💣💣💣💣

Classy Intelligent Loving
Fussy Predictable Lazy

Like may people with complex names, *CSNDR* women sport extraordinarily complex personalities but it's important to note that those who have shortened their names to *Cassie* or *Kassie* are signaling their discomfort with the intricacies of the three-syllabled *Cassandra*. On the other hand, those who insist on being called by the full version display the complexity of character that corresponds to their larger-than-life names.

To understand the forces at work in these names, consider what happens when the *crisp* letter *C* couples with the *sublime* and *sensual* letter *S:* it takes on a distinctly *casual, cozy* and *classical* feel. The flexible *ND* phoneme produces the welcoming images found in the words *lend, blend, friend, fond, Godsend* and *garland,* and like most names that incorporate the *robust, randy* and *romantic R,* there's a suggestion of a self-assured individual who's always willing to clamp you in a warm and friendly embrace.

*CSNDR*s love to pamper themselves and will spare no expense on their clothing, entertainment and hobbies. You'll rarely find *CSNDR*s shopping by themselves, however, for these are eminently social animals who draw their energy from human interaction. But as extro-

Cassandra

verted and flirtatious as they are, they prefer limiting their social connections to just a few close friends.

*CSNDR*s are often so secure with themselves that it borders on complacency. They take life in bite-size pieces, as if to savor every nuance of flavor, and are not the types to allow themselves to be rushed into anything, particularly when it comes to their careers. But they are flexible workers, as happy behind an espresso machine in a local café as they are as chairwomen of the board.

Often, the *CSNDR*'s insatiable curiosity about the world translates into a fear of commitment, a trait that often costs her dearly in the workplace. But fortunately this circumspection doesn't extend to her personal relationships, where she proves to be most stable when connected to a partner who shares her angular view of the universe.

When it comes to romance, the *CSNDR*'s complex sensual appeal is responsible for a long line of would-be lovers knocking hopefully at her door. But in true *CSNDR* fashion, she's going to take her own sweet time before deciding to grant anyone access to the mysteries of her heart.

Cassandra Peterson Remember Elvira, Mistress of the Dark, the hostess of late-night movies destined never to see the light of day? Were fans tuning in to watch the movies—or were they instead checking out the purrings of the vampish thirtysomething Cassandra Peterson? ■ Originally a conservative-looking redhead, Cassandra penetrated the film industry by playing a naked woman in the 1973 movie *The Working Girls*. Her acting roles were thereafter confined to cameo appearances, like the Biker Mama in *Pee Wee's Big Adventure*. ■ Squeezing into a tight black evening gown as hostess of the TV series *Movie Macabre*, her incessant stream of double entendres captured the imagination of her largely male audience. Her success led to the unfortunate release of a 1988 film based on the same character: *Elvira, Mistress of the Dark*.

Charisma										
Career Success										
Love & Friendship										
Power										

**Determined Powerful Compassionate
Overbearing Miserly Impatient**

The feminine *CTH* root practically oozes likeability and character, and the bearers of these names exude an extraordinary charisma. The sharp edges of the *crisp* letter *C* take the credit for all her *cutting* edges, while the *TH* combination injects the kind of altruistic dignity associated with all things *thoughtful, thankful, fatherly, motherly, theological, theatrical* and *theoretical.*

Never ones to beat around the bush, you'll never have to guess where you stand with a *CTH.* This might prove a little intimidating to the more timid personalities, but as far as the *CTH* is concerned, if you can't take her heat, stay out of her kitchen. The phrase "the best man for the job is a woman" could well have been written with a *CTH* in mind, so don't make the unfortunate mistake of telling her that she can't be the best at something. If she wants to be a fighter pilot or a mob boss, no one's gonna stand in her way. This is why *CTHs* are most comfortable in management and supervisory positions where their natural authority can be applied with characteristic fairness.

CTHs have the capacity to feel genuine empathy for people, but their dictatorial styles often cloud the source of their intended compassion. *CTHs* believe that the more control people have over their lives, the better off they'll be. So their approach to counseling others includes a not-so-gentle shove here and there, and many employees and acquaintances end up having love-hate relationships with them. They soon learn, however, that *CTH* is not being unreasonable, she's just having a little trouble suppressing her desire to improve the lives of those around her.

CTH's spiritual side (which lends itself to astrology and poetry) reflects her refusal to accept reality at face value. Their sense of well-being comes from a place deep within and certainly not from the trappings of a prestigious job or a fancy car (which is fortunate, because *CTHs* are unlikely to make it onto the *Forbes 1000*).

CTHs respect autonomy in others and seek to be matched with life partners who are their equals in strength and conviction. As usually occurs when two strong people get together, there is likely to be some tension in the relationship. But *CTHs* are calm in battle, holding their emotions in reserve for a time when they can befriend the "enemy" once again. They exhibit this same coolness in their parenting styles: always fair and always in control.

Cath
Catherina
Catherine
Cathleen
Cathy

Catherine Zeta-Jones At the age of eleven, future Oscar Award–winner Catherine Zeta-Jones endured her obligatory rite of passage for budding actresses by appearing in a stage production of the musical *Annie*. By the time she was sixteen, the Welsh actress was mature enough to steal the show in David Merrick's *42nd Street*. ■ Catherine's performance in the four-hour English TV docudrama *Titanic* was spotted by director Steven Spielberg, who plugged her for a leading role in *The Mask of Zorro*, in which she co-starred with Anthony Hopkins and up-and-coming Antonio Banderas. ■ It is reported that the first time she met Michael Douglas, he told her that he was going to father her children. Although the couple shares a birthday, their actual birth dates are twenty-five years apart.

**Most Popular
Girl's Names**

Dorothy
Donna
Deborah
Debra
Diane
Doris
Denise
Diana
Dawn
Debbie

**Most Popular
Boy's Names**

David
Daniel
Donald
Dennis
Douglas
Danny
Dale
Don
Derek
Darrell

*Discerning
difficulties,
dangers and
distances is
the test of a
great general.*

—SUN TZU,
The Art of War

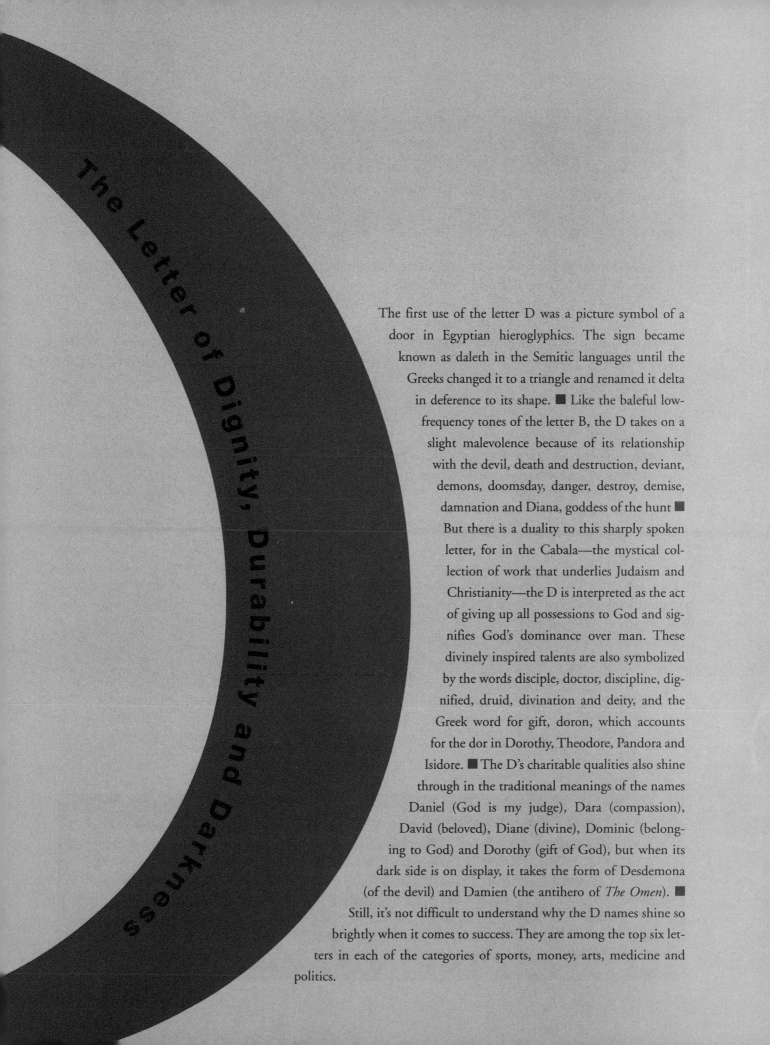

The Letter of Dignity, Durability and Darkness

The first use of the letter D was a picture symbol of a door in Egyptian hieroglyphics. The sign became known as daleth in the Semitic languages until the Greeks changed it to a triangle and renamed it delta in deference to its shape. ■ Like the baleful low-frequency tones of the letter B, the D takes on a slight malevolence because of its relationship with the devil, death and destruction, deviant, demons, doomsday, danger, destroy, demise, damnation and Diana, goddess of the hunt ■ But there is a duality to this sharply spoken letter, for in the Cabala—the mystical collection of work that underlies Judaism and Christianity—the D is interpreted as the act of giving up all possessions to God and signifies God's dominance over man. These divinely inspired talents are also symbolized by the words disciple, doctor, discipline, dignified, druid, divination and deity, and the Greek word for gift, doron, which accounts for the dor in Dorothy, Theodore, Pandora and Isidore. ■ The D's charitable qualities also shine through in the traditional meanings of the names Daniel (God is my judge), Dara (compassion), David (beloved), Diane (divine), Dominic (belonging to God) and Dorothy (gift of God), but when its dark side is on display, it takes the form of Desdemona (of the devil) and Damien (the antihero of *The Omen*). ■ Still, it's not difficult to understand why the D names shine so brightly when it comes to success. They are among the top six letters in each of the categories of sports, money, arts, medicine and politics.

Charisma										
Career Success										
Love & Friendship										
Power										

Lively Giving Exciting
Manipulative Repressive Biased

The letters *D* and *B* are both pronounced with an explosive action designed to attract attention. The letter *D*—created by the tongue making light contact with the palate—evokes an individual of quiet *dignity* and self-*discipline*, while the *belligerent* letter *B* suggests *bellicosity*. Some of the unyielding and forceful qualities of the *DB* phoneme can be seen in the words *admirable, disobey, disbar, debauch, debate, drub, durable, laudable, redoubt* and *hardbound.* This is why many women (for example, *Debbie*) choose to mitigate these severe effects by appending the infantalizing *IE* or *Y* sound at the end of their names in the way a mother of small children uses words like *booties, doggy, kitty* and *footsies.*

Strength of character is unquestionably *DBs'* hallmark trait, though in their worst moments, it can appear to be more like pure muleheaded stubbornness. So don't be dismayed when your *DB* friend criticizes you to your face: they truly have your interests at heart, and at least they aren't bad-mouthing you behind your back. This is at the root of the *DBs'* legendary loyalty; short of insulting their mothers, there's little you can do to shake their friendship. Still, *DBs* are quite competitive, and in some situations, will try to outshine those whom they perceive to be rivals.

Deb
Darby
Debbie
Deborah
Delbert
Dilbert

Female *DBs* in particular are famous for these "queen bee" complexes, while male *DBs* have the persistence of telemarketers.

It's easy to overlook the dark sides of these charismatic individuals, for their weakness are only revealed to those they trust. And it's not like they get jealous in the traditional sense—it's more of a competitive thing born of insecurity. *DBs* have such a strong need to wield power in their relationships that they even subconsciously sabotage their unions in an effort to leverage control.

For all their hardheaded obduracy, *DBs* are not without their sensitive sides. With powerful instincts for empathizing with people's feelings and motivations, *DBs* tend to unconsciously respond to the underlying meaning of a conversation rather than the actual *words*. And since they tend to trust their instincts so completely, trying to change their minds once they've passed judgment on someone is likely to be impossible.

DB mates are one third idealistic, one third practical and one third impossible. Often they will be more like one of the kids than like the heads of the household. The key with *DBs* is to hit on something they care about, then harness their emotional energies to get things done.

Debbie Harry Deborah Harry broke the old-boy's network of rock stars when her band, Blondie, brought a more digestible brand of punk rock to the musical mainstream. Debbie played the part of a sexy, glamorous and distant platinum blond, and took advantage of the attention she received wearing skimpy dresses and torn bathing suits. ■ Adopted when she was three months old, one of the most decisive moments of her life was meeting Chris Stein in 1973. It was love at first sight, and the beginning of a long personal and professional relationship. ■ When Blondie scored its first international hit album in 1979 with *Heart of Glass*, the album included the song "Rapture," which was credited as the first commercially successful rap song ever recorded.

Charisma	💋 💋 💋 💋 💋 💋 💋 💋 💋 💋
Career Success	💰 💰 💰 💰 💰 💰 💰 💰 💰
Love & Friendship	🦅 🦅 🦅 🦅 🦅 🦅 🦅 🦅 🦅
Power	💣 💣 💣 💣 💣 💣 💣 💣 💣 💣

**Kind Supportive Obliging
Disturbed Shy Escapist**

The *dignified* and *daring* letter D casts its *dominating* shadow over the names it initializes and instills a distinct sense of someone with *dynamic drive*. The *DD* names—influenced by a double dose of the vigorous D—suggest people in whose hidden depths any number of demons might lurk. Don't let their intensity put you off, though, for with great passions come great works. When *DD*s are allowed to express their prodigious energies, there are no limits to the feats they can accomplish.

No matter what their personal convictions or political leanings are, those with double D names are almost always direct and honest and somehow manage to see right through the games other people play. Not ones to beat around the bush, they are quick to condemn activities they find frivolous—and "frivolous" to the *DD* is anything that doesn't address the great mysteries of life. Their spare time will likely be spent pursuing their music, art, philosophy or religion (they are constantly revamping their theories of the world in their search for the authentic), and with all their soul searching, *DD*s have an extraordinary range of conversation topics and know *just* enough to debate any issue over a round of cocktails. Perhaps this is why the

Dee
Deandre
Dee Dee
Deirdre
Dudley

DD is on everyone's invitation list . . . and why *DD*s have such an eclectic band of friends.

Always reluctant to completely commit to a particular job, *DD*s may wander indefinitely before settling into steady careers. But when they do finally pledge their loyalty to a particular employer, they seem to care less about the amount of money they're going to earn than the validity of the work itself. It's not that they aren't practical about money issues, but since they recognize they have only one life to live, they believe it should be lived in a socially responsible way. Maybe this explains why so many *DD*s are drawn to social work, teaching and the medical fields.

When it comes to their intimate relationships, *DD*s know exactly what they want and aren't going to be put off by a few rejections here and there. But romance presents some danger for *DD*s when they become involved with partners who cannot (or will not) reciprocate the *DD*s' feelings. In these cases, *DD*s are prone to compulsive fantasizing, which results in obsessive, unbalanced unions. But when *DD*s carefully manage to negotiate the landscape of their relationship choices, their unions have the potential to become great works of art.

Dudley Moore Anyone who saw the movie *Arthur* remembers British actor Dudley Moore as a lovable, cuddly teddy bear. In reality, Dudley was the proverbial crying clown. Born with a deformed left foot, he was teased unmercifully as a child. ■ As a young man, Dudley enjoyed outrageous success as a composer and jazz artist, but these successes did nothing to ease his lack of confidence and admitted self-loathing. ■ His role in the movie *10* mirrored his own remarkable prowess in matters of romance; his numerous marriages—though mostly failures—were to women of unusual beauty. ■ His odd speech pattern, thought by many to be a result of too much drinking, was actually the result of supranuclear palsy, a degenerative condition related to Parkinson's disease, which eventually took his life.

dg

Charisma	😈	😈	😈	😈	😈	😈	😈	😈	😈
Career Success	💰	💰	💰	💰	💰	💰	💰	💰	💰
Love & Friendship	🏹	🏹	🏹	🏹	🏹	🏹	🏹	🏹	🏹
Power	💣	💣	💣	💣	💣	💣	💣	💣	💣

Observant Friendly Idealistic
Reckless Needy Awkward

When the *dominant*, *durable* and *dignified* letter *D* teams up with the *gregarious*, *gracious* and *genial* letter *G*, it creates a set of names that embodies the unyielding masculine qualities found in the words *badger*, *dagger*, *cudgel*, *budge*, *dignity*, *dogged*, *dogmatic*, *handgun* and *prodigious*. These are people who are easily recognized by their steadfastly moral behavior and who manage to retain their dignified tough-guy images under the most extreme of circumstances. Those whose names are terminated by the emotionally expressive letter *O* (like *Diego*) tend to be more personable and approachable.

If *DG*s were animals, they'd be wild dogs; friendly and sociable when relaxed, persistent and resolute when on the hunt. And like their canine counterparts, *DG*s do best in careers in which they can utilize their highly effective social skills, whether as a team leader or simply a member of the pack.

Although *DG* individuals have strong creative streaks, they are more apt to express themselves though some form of physical activity. Many *DG*s make a living with their hands, and whether they're mechanics, chefs, builders or sculptors, they will never fail to color their creations with their distinctive *DG* style. But when *DG*s aren't at work, chances are they're in a local dive bar

Diego
Doug
Douglas

watching the game over a pint with a core group of fellow hounds.

If you're in love with a *DG*—and he's in love with you—you can look forward to a solid partnership from an uncommonly attentive mate. You may have to put up with a few hare-brained ideas (like that rocket launcher he's building in the back yard), but life with the *DG* is almost always going to be emotionally stable.

They love the inquisitive minds of children, and in some respects, having a *DG* around is like having a very large child. Not that he's immature, of course; it's just a reflection of his prodigious imagination and boundless energy.

If you've ever mothered, partnered or married a *DG*, you'll know how sensitive he can be . . . even an accidental slight to his ego can put him in a funk for days. And once you've lit the eternal flame in a *DG*'s heart, you may as well burn all those old prom pictures and forget you ever had other relationships, for he's going to want you all to himself. But if he's a little possessive, it's just his way of letting you know how special you are to him. Don't be surprised when he comes up with something completely unexpected: even if he's a little clumsy on occasion, he'll never stop trying to impress you.

Douglas Fairbanks By the time the talkies arrived in Hollywood, Douglas Fairbanks had already established himself as a star of the silent screen. The stage-trained actor eagerly embraced the new medium, but his first attempt was an utter failure. ■ The expensive 1929 film *Taming of the Shrew*, in which he starred alongside Mary Pickford, seemed to alienate his silent-picture fans, who had grown accustomed to his over-the-top facial expressions and acting style. ■ Douglas later created the film studio United Artists with wife Mary Pickford, friend Charlie Chaplin and director D. W. Griffith. The studio, which is still around today, encouraged other actors to experiment with producing their own films. ■ Douglas died peacefully in his sleep, leaving behind a son, Douglas Jr., who also became a successful actor.

Charisma	💋💋💋💋💋💋💋💋💋
Career Success	💰💰💰💰💰💰💰💰💰
Love & Friendship	👼👼👼👼👼👼👼👼👼
Power	💣💣💣💣💣💣💣💣💣

Dynamic Capable Loyal
Power-absorbed Restless Self-serving

There's a decided difference in the makeup of people who choose to use the name *Dick* over the more sophisticated *Richard*. *DK*s clearly prefer the masculine edges in their names—the same qualities that spawn the manly words *dukes* (fists), *dirk* (dagger), *drake* (a male goose), *dyke* and *deck* (to fell). Of particular interest is the way some *DK* names are invigorated by the addition of the *racy, randy* and *ribald* letter R (*Derek, Drake* and *Dirk*). In the film *Boogie Nights*, the lead character, Eddie, felt that his name was holding back his career as male porn star. After changing it to Dirk Diggler, his career took a decided turn for the better.

Notwithstanding the intimidating presence of these names, *DK* people exhibit a steady fairness and protectiveness toward those they love. Their stoic temperaments allow them to handle stressful situations without any outer signs of emotional overload, and their unruffled air proves to be quite useful in their careers. Their strong sense of self-preservation, coupled with their steely nerves, makes them perfect spies or FBI agents; but mostly, *DK*s use their strong personalities to make friends and influence people. Whether it's in politics, sales or management, they typically earn more money than most people.

Dakota
Danica
Daquan
Declan
Dedric
Dequan
Derek
Derrick
Drake
Duncan
Dickie
Dick
Dirk
Duke

In their personal communications, *DK*s are men and women of few words and have a distinct tendency toward bluntness. And if you're tempted to think of them as dogs that are all bark and no bite, *DK*s are definitely not *those* dogs. When sufficiently roused, they'll exhibit a temper that can take chunks out of a lesser ego, and the only way to handle *DK*s in this inflamed state is from the working end of a ten-foot pole.

Having *DK*s as friends can be tiresome at times because of their kinetic mode of existence. They're always out too late, never in one place for long, and can not unwind without a little libation. But take heart. There will be times when you'll be able to settle into some gentle petting with a companion who's had a lot of practice in making up after a fight.

This is why the *DK*s' most successful relationships are with perceptive and no-nonsense types, who will give them room to rage and not dissolve under the weight of their bluster. They won't make the mistake of messing with the *DK*s' ideals either, knowing full well that *DK*s are fierce defenders of their beliefs. Such partners will reap the rewards that come with having such an extraordinarily vigorous and capable mate.

Dick Butkus It must have been a difficult experience to grow up with a name like Dick Butkus, and some say the experience was responsible for shaping one of the most feared football players in the history of the NFL. ■ His mobility and bone-crunching tackles were enough to make teams plan entire plays around avoiding him, and he was one of the few big men with the speed to attack receivers in passing situations. A serious knee injury closed out his career in 1997 but his induction into the Football Hall of Fame in Canton, Ohio, proved to be the high point of his career. As a radio and TV broadcaster, he writes a column called "Friends of the Dick," and he played the role of Coach Katowinski on NBC's *Hang Time*.

THE REALISTIC **dl**

Contemporary Spirited Impulsive
Frustrated Overconfident Impatient

Charisma										
Career Success										
Love & Friendship										
Power										

The *dignified*, *dapper* and sometimes *dark* letter D instills names with a conservative and traditional air. But names featuring the *DL* letter combination are saved from tedium by the diametrically opposed *L*—the letter of *love, laughter, life, liberty* and *learning*. This bright combination gives rise to words that exhibit the benign and devoted tones found in *delightful, delirious, delicate, docile, idol, fondle* and *kindly*. It should be noted that those whose names end with the *sexy, sensual* and *sultry* letter S (*Delores* and *Dallas*), exhibit an even more *delicious* personality than most. As is typical of names featuring letters with opposite inferences, there is a distinct *duality* to the *DL* personalities that manifests itself in a variety of ways.

There's the diligent and driven aspect of the *DLs*' character (which reveals itself in their careers and casual friendships), and there's the laid-back romantic side that percolates through their intimate relationships. But in both cases, the *DLs*' salient trait is a firm grounding in reality: no matter how fanciful their dreams, they usually adhere to their internal budgets and will rarely overspend—financially or emotionally.

To know a *DL* is to have a ready source of laughter.

Dale
Dalia
Dallas
Dalton
Del
Delia
Delilah
Della
Delois
Delores
Dillard
Dolly
Doyle
Dulce

Relaxed, flexible and fun-loving in their personal lives, *DLs* make a delightful addition to any circle of friends. Their strong physiques and ready sense of adventure often put *DLs* in pioneering, outdoorsy activities such as surfing, climbing, extreme skiing or sky-diving. They need an outlet for their overflowing energies and are adept at finding stimulating opportunities to play.

In their work lives, however, *DLs* are another story. Co-workers quickly learn to recognize the focused look that flashes in *DLs'* eyes when engrossed in a project—a warning to stay out of their way until the job is done. Rather than be sidetracked by the distractions that come with socializing, *DLs* would rather work on their own. They have a need to be in control of their work environments and will gladly accept responsibility for both their successes and failures.

Although settling down may not be high on their list of priorities, *DLs* tend to fall in love when they least expect it—and usually with partners who share their love for learning and philosophy. Anyone that ends up cohabitating with *DLs* will find that even though they are prone to periods of dark moods, the *DL*'s essence is one of unrestrained dependability.

Dale Earnhardt The son of race-car-driver Ralph Earnhardt, Dale fell in love with speed and power as a boy and, as a young man, made his presence felt on the NASCAR circuit. There was a reason that the race-car press referred to him as "The Dominator," "The Intimidator" and "The Man in Black." With characteristic aggression and energy, he took top titles in every major race including the Winston Cup and the Daytona 500. ■ In 1998, NASCAR honored both Dale and Ralph Earnhardt by naming them among the fifty greatest drivers in NASCAR history. Dale's tragic death on the last lap of the 2001 Daytona 500 shook the racing world to its core and prompted a public outcry to improve safety standards.

THE VERSATILE dln

Charisma	😙	😙	😙	😙	😙	😙	😙	😙	😙	😙	
Career Success	💰	💰	💰	💰	💰	💰	💰	💰	💰	💰	
Love & Friendship	🏹	🏹	🏹	🏹	🏹	🏹	🏹	🏹	🏹	🏹	
Power	💣	💣	💣	💣	💣	💣	💣	💣	💣	💣	

Multifaceted   Sensitive   Mentally Quick
Procrastinating   Restless   Indiscreet

When the *dominant, durable, dignified* letter *D* teams up with the letter of *love, life, liberty, libido, lyrical* and *learning,* the resulting combination generates the benign and devoted tones found in the words: *delightful, delirious, delicate, docile, idol, fondle* and *kindly.* But inasmuch as the letter *N* is associated with all things *negative (no, never, not, nix, nada* and *naught),* these names also imply an individual beset by bouts of pessimism and self-doubt. Consequently, while *DLN*s might make great engineers, teachers and doctors, they're really better suited as artists, writers and political and environmental activists.

*DLN*s feel a great sense of responsibility for their fellow human beings, and whether or not they choose religion as their spiritual compass, they live by a strict personal code that puts compassion and empathy over vengeance and retribution. This belief system comes from a thinking mind and not from any bleeding heart, and you can depend on a *DLN* to put friendships over money every time.

And yet there's a bit of a dark streak to these people, for *DLN*s have an unusual fascination for strangeness, mystery and even violent behavior. Not that they would participate in this world mind you; they're simply responding to some deep voyeuristic urge. So if you're dating a *DLN*, you might want to choose the movies

Dallin
Dalena
Dalton
Delaine
Delana
Delaney
Delena
Delfina
Delphine
Dylan

you rent lest you be subjected to every *Friday the 13th* movie ever made. On the bright side, many *DLN*s channel their dark sides into their creative endeavors as artists and writers.

*DLN*s' native caution is especially evident in their intimate relationships, where it's rare for them to enter into serious relationships until they've matured. But *DLN*s have plenty to occupy their time, for as students of life, they're always reading, traveling or watching the *History Channel*'s gladiator specials to broaden their horizons. Where family is concerned, *DLN*s are loyal to a fault. This doesn't mean you'll receive unbridled affection from these sometimes-taciturn people, who tend to be miserly in matters of love and dole out affection as if it were in limited supply, but you *will* be able to count on them to stand up for you, even if they know you're in the wrong.

In relationships, *DLN*s make for steady and charming mates, willing to endure routine (like putting the kids to bed) in order to get to the fun stuff (like putting their partners to bed). But as relaxed and carefree as *DLN* mates can be, they tend to flip into single-minded stress mode when things aren't going well financially. Children seem to mitigate these tensions in their lives, and *DLN*s are superbly equipped to raise them with understanding and intelligent discretion.

Dylan McDermott The star of ABC's *The Practice*, Dylan McDermott made his film debut in 1987 in *Hamburger Hill*. Considering the flops he experienced after *Hamburger*, he considers himself lucky to have stayed in the business. ■ Dylan came to acting largely his father's second marriage to playwright Eve Ensler. His new stepmother opened his eyes to the world of the stage and, after observing his natural talent for acting, drove him off to acting school and steered him onto Broadway. ■ During the making of *Steel Magnolias*, Dylan fell in love with co-star Julia Roberts, only to lose her to Kiefer Sutherland.

95

Charisma	👄	👄	👄	👄	👄	👄	👄	👄	👄	👄
Career Success	💰	💰	💰	💰	💰	💰	💰	💰	💰	💰
Love & Friendship										
Power										

**Gentle Dignified Deep
Emotional Complicated Clingy**

People who bear the *DM* phoneme tend to display a curious mixture of masculine and feminine traits. The *dynamic* and *dominant* letter *D* is brought under the influence of the *maternal, motherly* and *merciful* qualities of the letter *M,* to create a personality that's altogether strong, perceptive and nurturing. So while *DM* males tend to be those strong sensitive men that are in such high demand, *DM* females are warmly engaging women with assertive, albeit sometimes intimidating, personalities.

Both sexes display the deeply emotive core that draws them to artistic expression, which often comes in the form of their love for music. It wouldn't be surprising to find them involved in garage bands when they were young, and photography or computer art as adults. And even if they're not ones to actually play the guitar, you can bet they're the type of people who sing in the shower. *DM*s are also natural actors with a penchant for the dramatic, and their big hearts are worn right on their sleeves (or at least tattooed on their shoulders).

On the surface, it would seem that a relationship with one of these romantic sweet-talkers would be smooth sailing for all concerned, but you'd better be on guard for hidden rocks. For like most people who bear a

Delma
Damaris
Delmar
Demarco
Demarcus
Demario
Demetria
Demetris
Demetrius
Dimitri
Demi

D name, *DM*s have their dark sides, and it's not in your interest to put your emotional trust in them until you've discovered exactly what it is.

Perhaps it has something to do with the fact that the *DM*'s loving side comes with a persistently roving eye. It's not that they're deviant in any way, but one moment they'll be wooing you over dinner with promises of eternal passion, and the next, making eyes at the waiter or waitress. And it's not that they aren't capable of loving their partners either; it's just that they seem to love everyone else as well. But even if settling into a permanent relationship isn't the *DM*'s first choice, it often turns out to be just what they need. Married life with a *DM* will be nothing if not exciting, and if you're the type who enjoys roller-coaster rides, hang onto your hat.

*DM*s' track records in their careers are considerably more dependable than in their personal lives. These are people who take great pride in their work and their ability to compete with the best of them, and their ideal careers are those that allow them the freedom to express themselves creatively. And if they're lucky enough to find a job that will reward their unique brand of artistic expression, they'll perform above the call of duty.

Demi Moore The star of the blockbuster movies *Ghost* and *Indecent Proposal* was already a teenager when she learned that her stepfather—who died from inhaling car exhaust fumes—was not her real father. ■ Demi began a three-year affair with Emilio Estevez on the set of *St. Elmo's Fire*, where she was fired for reporting for work under the influence of drugs. Her widely publicized marriage to Bruce Willis ended in 1998. ■ Her later films—1996's *Striptease* and *G.I. Jane*—drew hoots from critics who considered it unlikely that Demi would ever again earn the millions of dollars she commanded during her heyday. They were wrong. ■ The forty-year-old actress recently made her comeback in *Charlie's Angels: Full Throttle*, and generated buzz by cavorting in public with the much younger Ashton Kutcher.

Charisma										
Career Success										
Love & Friendship										
Power										

Skillful Magical Visionary
Fatalistic Controlling Disturbed

There's something disquieting about the *DMN* combination of letters. It vaguely reminds one of the words *damn* and *damnation*. This condition arises from the close proximity of the *dominant* letter *D* to the *motherly* and *maternal M,* which creates the conflict seen in the words *doom, damn, dumb, dump, drama* and *dogmatic*. Things are made exponentially worse by the addition of the *negative* letter *N*. The letter *N* is the very personification of negativity as seen in the words *no, not, never, naught, nada, naughty* and *nasty*.

All told, these three letters create the ominous qualities we find in the words *demon, madman, damned, demented, domineering, dominant, demean, Doberman* and *demanding*. And if this name root makes us think of a wolf in sheep's clothing, it doesn't help that the name *Damien* is synonymous with the Antichrist in The Omen series of feature films.

Still, the intimidating power of the *DMN* names can be constructive if channeled in the right direction; for the *DMNs'* mysterious persona affords them a special charisma that is eminently attractive to members of the opposite sex. This kind of social power affords *DMNs* opportunities for leadership that most people rarely enjoy, and many *DMNs* take full advantage of their charismatic influence. And while their moods may be dark, they are also gifted with a kind of street-smartness that allows them to uncannily understand the motivations of their fellow man. Since kindness from unexpected quarters is more appreciated than kindness taken for granted, *DMNs* can get a great deal of mileage from the occasional compliment or flattering remark.

In the working world, *DMNs* are attracted to conventional niches like business management or corporate pursuits, although they will occasionally end up in the arts, particularly music and drama. But like all people whose names begin with the letter *D,* no matter what *DMNs* decide to pursue, they invariably end up in the top percentage of wage earners.

Since the *DMNs* attract the opposite sex like nobody's business (especially those who appreciate an element of emotional danger), they can afford to be choosy when it comes to selecting their mates. But even though landing a *DMN* might prove to be an emotional rush at first, it can lead to major heartbreak if the *DMN* fails to keep his or her runaway impulses under control.

Damien
Damon
Demond
Desmond
Diamond
Domenica
Dominga
Domingo
Dominica
Dominique
Dominic

Dominick Dunne Author/journalist Dominick Dunne's fascination with the dark side may have something to do with the 1982 murder of his only daughter. The young actress, who starred in *Poltergeist*, was stalked and strangled by her ex-boyfriend. The trial of the killer—who received a sentence that could have freed him in less than three years—sparked Dominick's contempt for the justice system and drove him to air his grievances by reporting the ins and outs of high-profile murder cases. ■ Dominick's most visible work came during his coverage of O. J. Simpson's trial for the murder of Nicole and Ronald Goldman. His incisive reporting for *Vanity Fair* made him the period's most sought-after talk-show guest and led to his 1997 book *Another City, Not My Own: A Novel in the Form of a Memoir.*

THE DARING
dn

Charisma										
Career Success										
Love & Friendship										
Power										

Idealistic Faithful Devoted
Demanding Self-Indulgent Isolated

The popularity of the *DN* names reached its peak in the 1970s, and although many baby boomers sport one of its many incarnations, these names are quite rare among today's newborns. Its declining status may have something to do with the inherent conflict created when the *determinedly decisive* letter *D* teams up with the *nasally* pronounced letter *N*. While the letter *D* denotes people of upstanding fortitude, the *N* is the archetypal expression of *negativity*: *no, never, nada, naught, nothing* and *nowhere*. Consequently, this letter combination is the source of the contentious tones found in the words *damn, darken, demand, deny, dingy, demon, dank, dragon, drunk, madman* and *debunk*. So while these people carry themselves with dignity and exhibit a capacity for genuine caring, there's also a wry streak of pessimism flowing through their veins.

DN people have a distinct aura of stubbornness that *they* consider quite attractive. Employers, parents and friends might disagree, but no one will argue that *DN*s take advantage of their fierce focus and put it to work in their business ventures. The fact that they have such a vast reservoir of enthusiasm means that they have no problem attracting people who are willing to take advantage of their emotional and material resources, and the nice thing is that *DN*s *don't* usu-

Dan
Dana
Dandre
Dane
Danette
Dania
Danita
Danny
Dante
Daphne
Dean
Deana
Deangelo
Deeann
Denny
Denveer
Deondra
Deonte
Diana
Dinah
Dino
Dione
Don
Donita
Donny
Donta
Duane

ally expect anything in return, except someone with whom to team up in their quest for diversion.

Of course, being an idealist has its downside; life cannot always be counted on to go the way you had expected. And failure and *DN*s don't get along very well, and *this* is where they tend to manifest their depression. *DN*s will feel sorry for themselves and try to co-opt their friends for commiseration. You get the sense that *DN*s could snap out of it anytime they wanted to, but there's nothing like a good wallow every now and then. Once they've had their fill of melancholy, they'll step back into the sunshine—reinvigorated and refreshed—to resume their productive ways.

When it comes to relationships, *DN*s absorb their energy from other people and are known for their devotion to friends and family. Intimate affairs with *DN*s can be a little touchy at times, not because of their occasional huffs but because of their high ideals and their habit of placing impossible expectations on their mates. *DN*s also need to be high on their partners' priority lists: being snubbed even in an insignificant way can trigger one of their sulks. To get the most out of these dynamic souls, those who mate with *DN*s are advised *not* to walk around on eggshells but roll with the punches.

Diana Ross Diana's first taste of solo stardom came after Motown Records decided that she should be the center of an all-female group, The Supremes. Diana began her solo career with the hit "Ain't No Mountain High Enough." ■ When a security guard frisked Diana Ross at Heathrow Airport in 1999, an indignant Diana was arrested after grabbing the woman's breasts in retaliation. ■ The incident set off a debate as to whether Diana had a right to protect the integrity of her body or whether she was simply demonstrating the petulance of a star.

Charisma										
Career Success										
Love & Friendship										
Power										

These unisex names have enjoyed undiminished popularity for the past fifty years, and their complex combination of letters makes for equally complex personalities. The letter *D*—the icon of *dignity* and *dominance*—is associated with the qualities of *demonstrativeness*, *discipline* and *divinity*. But the letter *N* is unquestionably the symbol of *negativity* (*no, not, naught, nil, nada, never, nowhere* and *nothing*) and conspires with the *D* to form *dank* words like *damn, demand, deny, demon, dragon* and *kidnap*. Happily, these negative influences are largely offset by the appearance of the letter *L*—the icon of *love, laughter, life, liberty* and *lip-licking*—so it's not surprising that *DNLs* are invariably described as having an expansive set of emotional and intellectual talents.

It's easy to understand why *DNL* people are popular with the opposite sex, for these are people who clearly enjoy life's little pleasures and are very willing to share their emotional wealth. With supreme confidence in their ability to handle themselves in any kind of situations, *DNLs* are not going to be thrown off-balance by anything short of a full emergency. It's not that *DNLs* are oblivious to what's going on around them—in fact they are extraordinarily aware of their surroundings—it's that *DNLs*

Danelle
Dangelo
Daniel
Daniela
Danielle
Danille
Danilo
Donald
Donella
Donnell

have that rare ability to use their intellects to overpower their emotional responses.

The *DNLs'* keen observation skills help them to understand the motivations of others and are put to good use in their business dealings. With an ability to communicate effectively, *DNLs* naturally gravitate to taking the lead in social and business situations and have the killer instinct necessary to lead large corporations. Still, *DNLs* have an instinctive understanding of the rules of hierarchy. So while they might be the top dog at any given moment, they'll happily concede their leadership role if a bigger dog comes along. (If *DNLs* do have a few control issues, they hide it well.) Like all names that begin with the letter *D*, *DNLs* are likely to make a lot of money. And this is not because they are particularly materialistic, but because they enjoy the challenges of business and have an outstanding work ethic to boot.

Despite their warm dispositions and gregarious natures, becoming intimate with *DNLs* can prove to be a challenge. In part, it's because it can be difficult to believe that someone can be so consistently optimistic. Once you accept that their glass *is* really ? full, you'll be surprised at how quickly you'll become a disciple of one of these effervescent souls.

Donald Trump The name Donald Trump has become synonymous with the word mogul. Famous for his lavish lifestyle, aggressive business tactics and choice of wives, Donald survived a near bankruptcy in 1990. After struggling back from being almost a billion dollars in debt, he emerged once again on top of the competitive New York real-estate industry. ■ No one knows exactly how wealthy Donald is. By his own estimate, he is worth over two billion dollars, but was rated at only $450 million by *Forbes* magazine. ■ There is no disputing the amount of power he wields, in a city in which power is akin to royalty. A darling of the New York press, his divorces from Ivana Trump and Marla Maples created controversies which Donald showed no interest in quelling.

Charisma										
Career Success										
Love & Friendship										
Power										

**Playful Inventive Intelligent
Unpredictable Restless Escapist**

Spell the name *Dennis* backwards and you'll get a fitting insight into the personality of those that bear a *DNS* name. Mischief is a strong force in these people's lives and perhaps explains why Hank Ketcham selected a *DNS* name for his impish character: *Dennis the Menace*. Although the letter *D* is usually associated with all things *dignified, disciplined* and *dominant*, the negative qualities of the letter *N* (*no, not, never, nix, nincompoop, naught* and *nada*) create the sense of *dank darkness* found in the words *demand, deny, dingy, dragon, drunk* and *madman*. And while the appearance of the *sexy, sultry, sensual* letter *S* plays its part in diminishing some of these menacing qualities, it is still responsible for the words *dinosaur, damndest, demonism, downcast, hedonist, defensive* and, perhaps the scariest of all, *dentist*.

It's not surprising, then, that most *DNS* people turn out to be risk-takers who find adventuring an irresistible temptation. With their puckish sense of humor and penchant for tomfoolery, people either love 'em or hate 'em, but will almost always admire 'em for their capacity to do precisely as they please and take their lumps without complaining.

The rebel streak in most *DNS*s means that no matter what job they choose, they're likely to perform it with maverick flair. And did we mention that *DNS*s love the limelight? Whether it's in sports, acting, music, or simply entertaining their friends, they are suckers for attention. But it's important to note that *DNS*s have the talent to match their showboating ways, and if they have something to say, you can bet that it will be intelligently considered. Unsurprisingly for such unconventional characters, *DNS*s work best on their own, and it's not uncommon to find them setting up shop as restaurant owners or graphic designers. Only when they're able to socialize freely are they able to express their artistic visions.

Denise
Dennis
Denzel

In their intimate relationships—as in their vanilla lives—*DNS*s can be quite demanding of attention, and it's hard to predict how they will react to a given romantic situation. But if you're willing to ride the roller coaster of the *DNS*'s heart, you can be guaranteed of two things: you'll never be bored and you'll always have a dependable friend. *DNS*s are generous with their time and resources, and loved ones can expect to be treated with respect and dignity. And since *DNS*s have never met a party they didn't like, birthdays will always be celebrated with elaborate festivities and imaginative carousing.

Dennis Rodman It's difficult to predict whether Dennis Rodman will go down in history as one of basketball's all-time greatest defensive players or whether he will simply be remembered as one of the most extraordinary showmen of the twentieth century. ■ As an athlete, Dennis won an extraordinary five NBA Championships (two with the Detroit Pistons and three with the Chicago Bulls), and was twice named the NBA Defensive Player of the Year. ■ As a showman, Dennis's intermittent cross-dressing made him a favorite target and guest of TV talk shows. His countless arrests for disturbing the peace and alleged assaults have kept his lawyers busy. ■ Dennis owns a restaurant in Newport Beach, California, where he lives. Annoyed by his frequent parties, local residents pressed the Newport Beach city council to amend its public disturbance laws to thwart his raucous lifestyle.

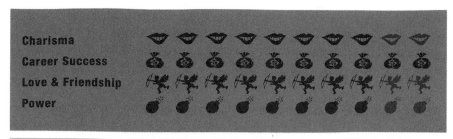

Charisma	👄👄👄👄👄👄👄👄👄👄
Career Success	💰💰💰💰💰💰💰💰💰💰
Love & Friendship	🏹🏹🏹🏹🏹🏹🏹🏹🏹🏹
Power	💣💣💣💣💣💣💣💣💣💣

THE DIRECT dr

Forceful Realistic Indomitable
Unyielding Rebellious Judgmental

The letter *D* may be associated with the upstanding aspects of *dignity* and *discipline*, but it also has its shadowy side. When coupled with the carnal ardor of the *randy, ribald, racy, roguish* letter *R*, for example, an astonishingly high percentage of *DR* adjectives embody some kind of dark aspect: *drained, dreadful, dreck, drunk, drivel, drool, drone, droop, drub, drug, drown* and *drastic.* Perhaps this gloomy resonance explains why there are no names (with the exception of *Drew*) that begin with a *DR*—without a vowel appearing between the two letters. These are people with a powerful sense of self, a dark side second to none, and a mysterious sexual quality that proves irresistible to a select group of people.

These are no-nonsense names that belong to no-nonsense people, and one of the *DR*s' greatest strengths is their ability to view the world without illusions. When things aren't going well, you're gonna hear about it with no punches pulled. And if you don't like what you hear, it's really not their problem; you'll be expected to grow out of it. From their perspectives, they're not being unkind, simply honest. And because they really appreciate frankness and candor in others, you should always tell *DR*s what's on your mind, even if you're not wild about their new haircut.

Dara
Daria
Dario
Dora
Doria
Drew

Did we mention a mysterious sexual quality? The *DR*s' direct method of confrontation isn't going to be everyone's cup of chamomile, but there's a definite core of people who are powerfully attracted to their style. And these people find befriending *DR*s to be easy, for *DR*s tend to be open and trusting (even somewhat gullible). Like most people who are honest to their core, *DR*s rarely bother to put up barriers.

With an unshakable belief in themselves and a corresponding love for adventure, most people aren't surprised when *DR*s take unexpected turns in their lives. If you haven't seen your *DR* friend in a few years, for example, chances are, he or she has changed jobs, gotten a new relationship or moved to another city. But while their career paths may be varied, once *DR*s are in their groove, they can make money as effortlessly as the U.S. Mint.

*DR*s believe humor to be just another form of honesty, and their abrupt style of candor makes for great story telling, albeit usually with a self-deprecating premise. When it comes to their intimate affairs, "opposites attract" may not be the best motto here, for *DR*s need spouses with enough energy to match their own. Fortunately, their whimsical outlooks often extend to the bedroom, where *DR*s prove to be spontaneous and adventurous lovers and full of naughty surprises.

 **Drew Carey** With his fifties crew cut and teddy-bear appeal, Drew Carey is one of the few TV comedians who has made a success out of just being himself. What most people wouldn't guess is that the seemingly relaxed and jolly comic suffered years of depression and attempted suicides. After a regimen of self-help books and a stint in the Marine Corps gave him the discipline he needed to write jokes for a friend's radio show, Drew was offered his own TV show portraying a corporately challenged real-life Dilbert in his self-titled sitcom *The Drew Carey Show.* ■ Although the first season was an unmitigated disaster, the show began picking up viewers. Today, his battles with Mimi and quirky friendship with Kate, Lewis and Oswald make *The Drew Carey Show* one of the highest-rated sitcoms on television.

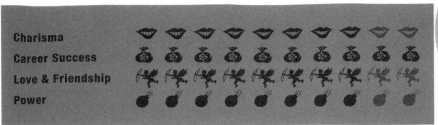

THE ADEPT
drl

Charisma										
Career Success										
Love & Friendship										
Power										

Versatile Motivated Attractive
Procrastinating Restless Unpredictable

When one examines words that begin with the *DR* phoneme, one finds that an astonishing number of these adjectives have some kind of reference to dark and ominous traits: *dreck, drudgery, droop, drivel, drab, drown, drubbing, drug, drag, dragon* and *drama*. These gloomy overtones account for the fact that there are no names in the U.S. (with the exception of *Drew*) that begin with a *DR* without a vowel appearing between the two letters. Fortunately, these ominous associations don't survive the addition of the *loving, laughing, liberating* letter *L*, which confers upon these names a relaxed gentility and thoughtful overtones. So, while we expect these individuals to be sober, dependable and clearheaded, there's a loving and inventive side that's almost always on display.

Darla
Darrel
Daryl
Derrell
Dorla

DRLs' ply their natural charms and parlay their sense of humor to keep them in the spotlight. And though it can be taxing to constantly be the center of attention, DRLs pull it off remarkably well. In fact, DRLs tend to thrive under pressure and use it to keep themselves motivated. This might explain the famous DRL procrastination: consciously leaving things to the last minute is their way of making sure things get done properly. DRLs also have a penchant to try new things,

and an unchallenged DRL will likely end up on the couch with a bag of potato chips, channel-surfing aimlessly. Buoyed by their multifaceted talents, DRLs will often change careers in midstream just to see if the grass really is greener on the other side.

Dating or marrying DRLs can be a treat if you don't mind sharing your partner with their wide circle of eclectic friends. DRLs are always in demand in the social arena and require a flexible, non-possessive mate who is prepared to actively participate in their rich personal and professional lives. Sharing the DRLs' interests and, more importantly, lavishing lots of praise on their accomplishments, is the key to romancing these energetic sprites.

Don't expect to settle down anytime soon, though, because even though DRLs respond well to intimacy, they are loath to relinquish their independence. Consequently, successful long-term relationships will have to have enough room for DRLs to breathe. Similarly, since children represent an even higher level of restriction to their freedoms, DRLs often take years becoming accustomed to the idea of parenthood. But once children arrive on the scene, DRLs will accept their parental roles with the same can-do style as they live the rest of their lives.

Daryl Hannah As a young girl, the step-niece of director Haskell Wexler (*American Graffiti* and *One Flew over the Cuckoo's Nest*) was diagnosed as being borderline autistic. ■ Daryl first came to prominence playing an android in the cult classic *Blade Runner*. Her performance as a sexy mermaid in Ron Howard's *Splash* cemented her as a box-office draw and enabled her to take on dramatic roles in *At Play in the Fields of the Lord* and *Steel Magnolias*. She was also well received for her performances in the comedies *Roxanne* and *High Spirits*. ■ Daryl's personal life made a splash as well. Her affair with singer Jackson Browne ended after it allegedly became abusive, and her romantic connection with John Kennedy, Jr. ended when his mother, Jacqueline Kennedy, put her foot down.

102

THE CONSTANT

drn

Charisma
Career Success
Love & Friendship
Power

Perceptive Expressive Devoted
Childish Restless Smothering

You'll notice that *all* the names in the *DRN* category have a vowel inserted between the *D* and the *R,* and there's a very good reason for this. Words beginning with a *DR* phoneme have an extraordinarily high chance of being associated with the more sinister aspects of life: *drained, dreadful, dreck, drunk, drivel, drool, drone, droop, drub, drug, drown* and *drastic.* But when the *DR* combination is separated by a vowel, the resulting names tend to take on the characteristics of their individual letters instead. Here the *dignified, disciplined* letter *D* bespeaks of an individual of upstanding fortitude, while the *randy, racy, robust* and *romantic* letter *R* lends an air of joie de vivre. The letter *N,* however, being the icon of all things negative (*no, not, never, nil, nix, naught, nothing* and *nowhere*), adds a lingering air of pessimism.

In summary, these are individuals whose personalities exude power and who approach life with aggressive zeal. Still, there's that tendency toward oversensitivity and moodiness when things don't go their own way. But these thin-skinned souls are anything but prissy—the *DRNs'* sensitivities emanate from their deeply held philosophical belief in fair play, and their reluctance to pass judgment on others. Female *DRNs,* for example, often display the sto-

Darian
Darion
Darlena
Darlene
Darnell
Darren
Darwin
Doreen
Dorian
Dorinda
Deron

icism and matter-of-factness typical of masculine personalities, while many male *DRNs* exhibit the feminine traits of intuition and empathy. Both sexes are comfortable with these cross-gendered traits and tend to disregard society's stereotypical boundaries in general.

It's true that *DRNs* often harbor a dark side that manifests itself in their professional lives. And because they feel most vulnerable when it comes to their careers, they often have a calculating approach and may even resort to some good old-fashioned manipulation if it gives them a leg up. While these actions may prove effective in certain politically oriented work environments, they are a guarantee of conflict when it comes to team pursuits like sales and creative situations. *DRNs* are more comfortable in leadership roles than most, in part because they feel less pressure to outmaneuver their co-workers. Like most people with a *D* name, *DRNs* are consistently high wage earners.

As mates, *DRNs* are unusually sensitive to their partners' needs, even if their emotional responses to problems tend to be bit melodramatic (especially if they sense that their partner is losing interest). But in general, these are loyal souls who are able and willing to provide unconditional love and support to their spouses.

Dorian Harewood Dorian Harewood is one of those actors whose face you know even if you don't remember his name. He holds the distinction of having played the most important role in the most widely seen network series in history. As Simon Haley, the father of the author Alex Haley, in *Roots* I and II, Dorian played a character who aged from seventeen to seventy. ■ Those who missed Dorian in *Roots* might have caught his award-winning portrayal of Olympic legend Jesse Owens in *The Jesse Owens Story.* ■ Dorian has appeared in numerous feature films including Kubrick's *Full Metal Jacket, Sudden Death* and *The Falcon and the Snowman.* He also starred alongside George C. Scott and Jack Lemmon in the remake of the MGM classic *Twelve Angry Men.*

Charisma										
Career Success										
Love & Friendship										
Power										

Fun-loving Humorous Genuine
Narrow-minded Controlling Dogmatic

As is typical of the *decisive* and *disciplined D* personalities, *DRS* people exhibit a quiet strength tempered by the occasional flare-up of control issues. Although a surprising number of adjectives beginning with *DR* phonemes have some kind of reference to dark pessimism (*dreck, drudgery, droop, drivel, drab, drown, drubbing, drug, drag, dragon, drama*), in the *DRS* names the *DR* combination is always separated by a vowel, putting the emphasis on the individual letters instead. The *dignified* letter *D* bespeaks of upstanding fortitude, while the *randy, racy, robust, romantic* letter *R* contributes a lusty sense of joie de vivre. The *slinky, sensual, sassy* letter *S* gives these names their distinctly sultry air.

In short, these are individuals who exude self-confidence and who approach life with aggressive enthusiasm. Because their conservative outer shell holds the promise of a mysterious sensuality, it's true to say that the more you get to know your *DRS* friend, the more you're going to be intrigued. So if, at first blush, your *DRS* companion seems to be one of those mellow types who get along with pretty much anyone, there's also an underlying bite to the *DRS* personalities (as those who accidentally prick their egos quickly discover). These counterattacks will be carried out with the *DRSs'* sharp tongues and sarcastic sense of humor, and perhaps

Darcy
Darius
Doris
Dorsey

because it seems so out of character, the strikes can wound quite deeply. Friends learn to steer clear of them when they're in one of their "funny" moods.

Like all people whose names begin with a *D*, finances play an important role in the *DRSs'* lives. These are people who know how to earn—and hang on to—their envious amounts of money. It's hard to stereotype *DRSs* in the workplace—they have so many options open to them, even *they* struggle to find their niche. So, if you're going to encounter them anywhere, it's probably going to be where their potential is unlimited. A *DRS* in a box is a *DRS* looking for a way out. But if you at least give them the *opportunity* to make a million, they'll be happy as dogs in a hubcap factory.

Marriage to *DRSs* is recommended to those with the gumption to take them on, and once someone enters their inner lives, *DRSs* bond deeply and permanently. As the relationship finds its rhythm, *DRS* mates will prove to be profoundly loyal partners who understand the value of communication. It's not that they don't have a stubborn streak, mind you, but because they always respect their partners' opinions, they'll usually find a compromise. Besides, conflict always leads to making up . . . and making up is the *DRS's* favorite pastime.

Doris Day One of pop music's premier postwar vocalists, Doris Day was born in Cincinnati in 1924 to German parents who stuck her with the name Doris Mary Ann Von Kappelhoff. A few years later, Doris's car was involved in a severe accident that almost ended her budding dancing career, not to mention her life. ■ But by the age of sixteen Doris had turned professional, married, had a son and divorced. Her crystal-clear singing voice made Doris a huge star, but her grueling schedule eventually led to a collapse from nervous exhaustion. When her third husband died in 1968, Doris found herself technically bankrupt after her fortune was misappropriated by her lawyer. A few years later, Doris was awarded $22 million by the court. Que sera sera!

THE MAGNETIC ds

Charisma										
Career Success										
Love & Friendship										
Power										

Alluring Exciting Visionary
Moody Obsessive Compulsive

People whose names fall into the *DS* category exhibit an agreeable blend of forthrightness and soft sensuality. In these names, the *dignified, dynamic* and *dominant* letter *D* is brought under the influence of the *sexy, sassy, sylphlike* letter *S* to create the suggestion of a uniquely feminine style of ethical traits.

Sensual and full of life, the *DS* exudes a magnetic vibe to which the opposite sex is powerfully attracted. Even when she plays at being naïve, she is keenly aware of the strong effect she has on others, and secretly relishes the attention. People respond to her, not only for her attractive feminine presence but also for her deeply spiritual and emotional side. For the *DS* is passionately enamored with life, and often expresses herself in her creative outlets: poetry, music and design.

At work, as well as in her personal life, the *DS* is a personable and free-spirited soul. She functions well in unstructured careers—that include writing, acting and graphic design—but her flair for the dramatic makes her perfect for those jobs in sales, advertising and even public speaking. Work is often an escape for these women, whose complex emotional makeups require a degree of distraction, and like most *D* names, *DS*s land on the upper end of the scale when it comes to income.

Dasia
Daisy
Dashawn
Deshawn
Desire
Desiree
Dessie

DS women have a powerful need to stay in touch with their friends and families and, if this need is not met, are prone to feeling as if their lives are incomplete. And a *DS* in a slump is a completely different creature from the otherwise smooth and confident woman that most people know. Although these moods will right themselves over time, friends might have to put up with a snappish and uncommunicative sulker until the *DS* works through her issues and finds her groove.

The *DS* loves the *idea* of love more than she does its messy consequences, and she proves to be a practical—instead of an overly passionate—lover. In marriage, she might even come to the altar with unrealistically high expectations on the part of her fiancé... who might be disappointed to discover that she wasn't the sex goddess she advertised. It's not that the *DS* isn't *capable* of creative lovemaking; it's just that the practical issues of life sometimes take precedence over what she considers to be frivolity. But let it be said, that the *DS* will expect to be romanced if she's going to get in the mood, and her partner will have his work cut out for him if he is to commune with her spiritual side. A persistent mate will be rewarded with the best friend and partner he could wish for.

Daisy Fuentes Daisy Fuentes was a news reporter and anchor for her local television station when she was targeted by MTV to host their show *MTV Internacional*. It was while she was at MTV that Daisy landed her recurring role on the ABC soap opera *Loving*. ■ Daisy became a household name when she began hosting *America's Funniest Home Videos* and was given a brief stint as host of her own talk show. ■ Under contract to represent Revlon's cosmetic lines, Daisy's career took a new tack when she become a professional hostess, hosting *The ALMA Awards*, *Dick Clark's New Year's Rockin' Eve* and the *World Music Awards*. More recently, she hosted the *Miss Teen USA*, *Miss USA* and the *Miss Universe* pageants. ■ Daisy's feature film roles included playing herself in Alicia Silverstone's *Clueless*.

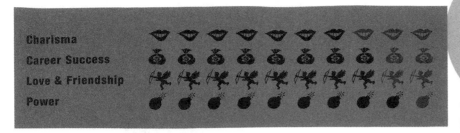

Charisma										
Career Success										
Love & Friendship										
Power										

Guided   Interesting   Admired
Restless   Secretive   Inflexible

When the *dominant, durable* and *dignified* letter *D* teams up with the *strong, straightforward, steady, staunch, steely* and *stoic ST* phoneme, it suggests a person with clear vision and solid ideals. We see these effects in the words *destiny, distinct, discreet, distill, headfirst, idealist, modest* and *steadfast.* People who bear the *DST* root are on a mission, and with a clear picture of where they're headed in life, they tend to arrive at their goals before most of us have even gotten out of bed. This isn't to say that there aren't going to be some twists and turns along the way, but these determined creatures will get there sooner or later—as long as their mission isn't "mission impossible."

And, of course, once a goal has been reached, then it's just a matter of resetting the goalposts to keep the challenge going. In the event that they happen to set the posts too high, they will fixate on the problem instead of moving on to try new challenges. It's just not in their nature to admit defeat.

It's hard to listen to *DST*s talk about their dreams without feeling inspired to do something great yourself. With their trademark belief that everything happens for a reason, they'll take their knocks with philosophical

Destin
Destiny
Dustin
Dusty

stoicism and trust in the universe to right its wrongs. This makes *DST*s ideal for any careers requiring long, hard hours with little short-term payoff, especially emotionally difficult jobs like social work or police work. If they actually had the time to create a motto, it would have to be "two steps forward, one step forward."

These just aren't the kind of people to have regrets.

DST people are lovers of harmony who strive to bring balance to their lives. It's not that they're above the occasional bouts of temper, depression or insomnia, but their habitual countenance is stoic and positive. Perhaps this is why so many people go out of their way to befriend *DST*s—to have one as a friend is to have a constant reminder that life is a journey and not a destination.

When it comes to love and marriage, *DST*s thrive on family life but usually center their activities outside the home. If it seems that *DST*s aren't interested in family life, it's not true. They are simply travelers at heart and the best advice for a nervous spouse is to let them slip away when the urge strikes, and trust that they will eventually return to where their hearts really are.

Dustin Hoffman Director Mike Nichols took a risk when he cast Dustin Hoffman in the role of the Benjamin Braddock in his 1967 film *The Graduate*. Back then, leading men were the all-American types, and Dustin certainly didn't fit the stereotypical look. ■ His Oscar-nominated role would be the first of many break-through performances, which included nominations for playing Lenny Bruce in *Lenny* and as a man struggling with divorce in *Kramer vs. Kramer*. ■ Considered to be an actor's actor, Dustin took home a second Oscar for his sensitive portrayal of an autistic savant opposite Tom Cruise in *Rain Man* in 1988.

106

Charisma										
Career Success										
Love & Friendship										
Power										

Constant Lively Loyal
Permissive Holier-than-thou Judgmental

The letter *D* is the essence of all that's *dominant, durable* and *dignified.* The *TH* phoneme, on the other hand, is the symbol of all things traditionally associated with the compassion and *thoughtfulness*: *theology, thankful, thorough, theory, thespian, theater, father, hearth, health, mother, author* and *sleuth.* Most who bear the uniquely feminine *DTH* names convey an air of inner strength without compromising their charming naïveté and innocence.

The *DTH* knows what she wants in life and has few qualms about going after it. Because she can be so focused, she's able to convince others that she means business, and even intimidate them without her knowledge. But there's a deeply compassionate side to her as well, and she has quite a reputation for her fairness and sense of justice. You may be able to count on your *DTH* friend for sound and ready advice, but you also need to be prepared for brutal honesty. She's not going to shrink from pointing out your faults, nor will she fail to compliment you when you deserve it. She knows where *she's* going and expects the same from you.

Careerwise, the *DTH's* introspective and spiritual nature makes her a natural for anything in the environmental, nurturing or medical fields. They are not partic-

Dorothea
Dorothy

ularly drawn to the limelight, preferring instead to control events from the wings, but like most *D* people, they are successful in almost everything they try. Even though money will not be a major motivator in their job searches, these people always seem to have more than enough cash on hand to maintain their comfortable existences.

*DTH*s approach their relationships in the same way they do their professional lives: with confidence, energy and helpful advice. *Plenty* of helpful advice. This can prove to be a little tedious for mates who are independent enough to fight their own battles, but for those who appreciate firm words of wisdom, she's a virtual fount. Marriage to a *DTH* will be nothing short of a complete intellectual and emotional package, and even though the *DTH* might grant her heart to just one man, friends and casual acquaintances will remain the mainstay of her social life.

Children are always a welcome addition to the *DTH* family, and the *DTH* parent is attentive to, and engaged with, her children—albeit more as playthings than as tiny humans. But she'll dole out enough affection and measured discipline that her offspring will come to respect her wisdom and worldly experience.

Dorothea Lange Without the images of migrant workers that Dorothea Lange captured with her camera lens, most people would never have known the profound social devastation wreaked by the Great Depression. ■ Dorothea opened a portrait studio in 1919 and, when the Depression hit in 1929, undertook to document the impoverished and displaced people she was beginning to see all around her. Plagued with a permanent limp caused by childhood polio, Dorothea had a special place in her heart for those who suffered. ■ Her well known photographs of migrant workers and sharecroppers in over twenty states were commissioned by the Farm Security Administration. Her portrait "Migrant Mother," showing a woman aged well beyond her years, looking into the horizon with steely determination, became the definitive image of the Great Depression.

THE WRY DV

Resourceful Intelligent Unassuming
Self-Centered Voyeuristic Misunderstood

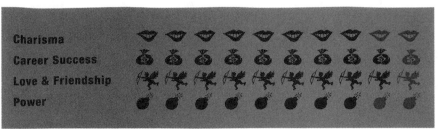

Charisma											
Career Success											
Love & Friendship											
Power											

When the *dashingly debonair* letter *D* is followed by the letter of *virility, voluptuousness, virtue* and *virulence,* it suggests the intriguing (and somewhat volatile) sexuality found in the words *divine, devilish, devoted, devour, deviant, ladylove, seductive, dervish* and *deprave.* These are the passionate qualities we come to expect from the *Davids, Devons* and *Donovans* of the world, who could be described as being iron fists in velvet gloves.

One of the surest traits of these idiosyncratic individuals is that they'll immediately destroy whatever pigeonhole they've been assigned to, and because they so strongly resent being stereotyped, they're not going to be particularly happy with this personality analysis. But if you *were* going to pick one thing that sets them apart, it would have to have something to do with their ability to take advantage of those fleeting opportunities that most of us miss: if it were raining gravy, they'd be out there with a frying pan. This is just one consequence of having a quick mind (even if it's not any bigger than the rest of ours).

*DV*s are drawn to outdoor activities and attack challenging physical tasks with gusto. Obstacles are met with stoic resolve and a healthy dose of humor, and since they tend to dismiss the expectations that society places upon them, their career

Dave
Davey
David
Davida
Davin
Davina
Davion
Davis
Davonte
Delvin
Devante
Devin
Devona
Devonta
Devonte
Devora
Divinia
Donovan
Dov
Draven

choices are usually off the beaten path. However, like most people whose names begin with the letter *D*, they are invariably successful in the workplace and are among the top wage earners in their social groups. Because they are somewhat unconventional in their approach to work, they have an inclination toward impatience when rules and procedures get in the way. Perhaps this sheds some light on why *DV*s are so often at odds with authority.

When it comes to relationships, *DV*s have a great capacity to bond. They're known for forming friendships that endure for lifetimes, but when it comes to those special intimate relationships, it will take a unique partner to keep up with their robust sexual appetites. And even though *DV*s tend to mellow with age, mates can still expect a lifetime of surprises. This often proves tiresome for the less adventurous, who find themselves bobbing in the wake of the *DV*s' enthusiastic wave making.

Children, although not always welcome additions to the *DV*s' busy lives, will be challenged to broaden their intellectual horizons. Chances are that their kids will quickly figure out a way around their parent's somewhat heavy-handed style of discipline, and if they can survive the *DV*s' frequent lectures, should profit from a rewarding friendship with them in later years.

David Geffen David Geffen's rise to top was a classic rags-to-riches saga shaped by a burning desire to succeed. ■ As the founder of Geffen Records, David made his billion-dollar fortune by spotting potential in young performers, like Tom Cruise, Bob Dylan, John Lennon and Elton John. David also has a reputation for being a cutthroat negotiator, but his contributions to AIDS research have made him a public hero. Even though he came close to marrying Cher, David publicly acknowledged his homosexuality in the nineties.

108

THE COMPLEX DW

THE COMPLEX DW

Charisma	😗 😗 😗 😗 😗 😗 😗 😗 😗 😗
Career Success	💰 💰 💰 💰 💰 💰 💰 💰 💰
Love & Friendship	🦁 🦁 🦁 🦁 🦁 🦁 🦁 🦁 🦁 🦁
Power	💣 💣 💣 💣 💣 💣 💣 💣 💣 💣

Productive Conceptual Talented
Stressed Ego-driven Picky

There is a bit of a contradiction intrinsic to the *DW* names. For while the letter *D* is associated with *dignity, discipline* and *dogma,* it's the *wild, wooly* and *wayward* letter *W* that is responsible for these peoples' mysterious life force. *DW* people are characterized by their blunt and honest dispositions and their gift for telling it like it is. People often seek out *DW*s for their honesty (which makes them outstanding judges and terrible lawyers), but there's an inherent awkwardness to the *DW* style that makes intimate relationships a little tricky to maintain.

When it comes to their careers, *DW*s in full stride are certainly a sight to behold. With their aptitude for mastering demanding situations, they usually end up in some type of leadership role, and like most people whose names begin with the letter *D, DW*s know how to make money—lots of it. One thing in their favor is that when the *DW*s settle on their career choices, they usually stick with them long enough for employers to reward them for their loyalty. But *DW*s are impatient with co-workers who aren't able to carry their own loads (which seems to be most of the time), for no one ever moves quite fast enough for the competitive *DW*s.

If working with these focused people proves to be nerve-wracking, try paying homage to their professional skills and you might just acquire an ally who'll help you get to the top. For despite the *DW*s' powerful drive to succeed, they are people-pleasers at heart who will go out of their way to help people willing to help themselves.

You'll probably never find a *DW* on the couch with a good book. In fact you probably won't find many books on their shelves at all. Life is too short for *DW*s to simply be reading about it; they're the types to be out there living it. These active people simply love to travel, and the more exotic the destination, the better. They enjoy traveling in style, mind you, so they'll likely disdain mixing with the natives and choose instead the pleasures of expensive hotels.

DW mates are responsible, hard-working and authoritative, and feel a strong sense of duty to their spouses and families. While this often translates into "all work and no play," you can bet that the household is going to be well organized with all the material needs taken care of. Unfortunately, romance and spontaneity aren't always their bag, and no matter how much *DW*s proclaim their desire for intimacy; a part of them will remain forever off limits.

Dawn
Dawson
Derwin
Dewey
Dewitt
Dwayne
Dwight

Dwight D. Eisenhower Dwight (Ike) D. Eisenhower's stature as the supreme commander of the European forces during World War II brought him the instant credibility that helped him become President of the United States. Dwight had been persuaded to run for President while in Paris in 1952, and his slogan, "I like Ike," proved to be irresistible to voters: He won by a huge margin. Dwight's administration embodied his notion that "America is today the strongest, most influential, and most productive nation in the world." ■ Before leaving the White House in 1961, Dwight issued his famous caution to the nation: "In the councils of government, we must guard against the acquisition of unwarranted influence, whether sought or unsought, by the military-industrial complex. The potential for the disastrous rise of misplaced power exists and will persist."

E

Most Popular Girl's Names

Elizabeth
Evelyn
Emily
Edna
Edith
Ethel
Ellen
Elaine
Esther
Emma

Most Popular Boy's Names

Edward
Eric
Eugene
Ernest
Earl
Edwin
Eddie
Edgar
Elmer
Erik

The Excitable, Emotional

The excitement of expectancy reigned upon each row of countenances.

HAROLD FREDERIC,
The Damnation of Theron Ware

The letter E is a singularly joyous letter that's impossible to pronounce without a brief grin flashing across your face. Originally the hieroglyphic and Semite symbol of a man with his arms raised in rejoicing, it stakes its claim as the initial letter of enthusiasm and Eros, the Greek god of love. It also stands for epicureanism, the philosophy that pleasure and happiness should be man's supreme goal and that emotional pleasures are far more powerful than physical ones. ■ Although it's the most commonly used letter in the English language, it's rarely used as an initial letter for people's names and thus occurs in fewer than two percent of the population. It is, however, more common among the British upper classes, perhaps because of its connection to the British royal family (Elizabeth, Earl and Edward). ■ It's possible that its infrequency is due to the fact that E names tend to be overly excitable as evidenced by the words earnest, ecstatic, eek, emotional, envious, exuberant, expressive, ego and empathetic. The most famous example of the E being used to express excitement and surprise emanated from the Greek inventor Archimedes, who exclaimed Eureka! upon his bathtime discovery that a weight of gold displaces less water than an equal weight of silver. ■ The traditional meanings of names beginning with E reflect these positive emotional qualities, as in: Ernest (sincere), Edward (happy guardian), Erasmus (to love), Edwin (prosperous friend) and Ezra (helper). Its enthusiastic, efficient, effective and excitable elements explain why E people are the second most likely to excel in professional sports. ■

Charisma										
Career Success										
Love & Friendship										
Power										

Charming Lighthearted Influential
Unstable Calculating Insulated

When a name begins with the *expressive* and *excitable* letter *E,* we expect to find a certain level of unpredictability and volatility emanating from its owner. In the case of the *ED* names, however, the modulating influence of the *dignified* and *dapper* letter *D* dampens some of the *E*'s *emotional* effects, and consequently, it would be unusual to find these people in the throes of emotional highs or lows. Still, most *ED*s exhibit the complex range of feelings typical of the vowel-initialized names, and for those who end their names with the youthfully good-natured letters *Y* or *IE* (*Eddie* and *Eddy*), there's an added element of zest and spunky playfulness.

If you're looking for a stimulating dose of banter sprinkled with dry wit, try getting acquainted with an *ED* during your next social outing. But don't be offended if you find your *ED* acquaintance keeping his or her distance, for these otherwise sociable individuals tend to avoid tangled emotional situations. So when the conversation switches to something personal or depressing—like your Aunt Gertha's bout with cancer—*ED*s will probably excuse themselves to check on the hors d'oeuvres.

Despite their carefree veneers, *ED*s are not known for being particularly compassionate. So if you're looking for sympathy over your latest heartbreak, you might want to give your Aunt Gertha a call (if she's feeling up to it). It's not that *ED*s aren't *capable* of empathy, it's just that they're a little uncomfortable in the face of raw emotion—either their own or that of others. Consequently, *ED*s function best when they're fully in control of the agenda.

What *ED*s lack in social grace is usually compensated by an exuberance that only a lighthearted spirit can impart. But although *ED*s love to spend time around close friends and family, they also carefully allocate themselves solo time to recharge their batteries, perhaps by hiking in the mountains or locking themselves in the bathroom for a stretch.

Dating an *ED* can turn out to be rather unfulfilling for someone who needs daily rations of romance and warm fuzzies. But if you appreciate being around a loyal and stimulating mate, you might want to consider giving an *ED* a test drive. Fortunately, the same childlike traits that retard *ED*s' intimate adult relationships make them popular favorites with younger kids and make them naturally suited for parenthood. You can expect your *ED* partner to want to have children early on in the relationship. Lots of them.

Ed
Eda
Edda
Eddy
Edgar
Edgardo
Edie
Edith
Eduardo
Eldridge
Enid

Ed Harris Ed Harris attended Columbia University on a football scholarship with aspirations of being a professional football player but dropped out to pursue a career in acting. After participating in one box-office flop after another, it seemed likely that his career was going to flounder, but everything changed upon the release of the 1983 movie *The Right Stuff*, which made Ed a star. ■ Even with his rugged Marlboro Man good looks it was six years before Ed managed another hit movie, this time with the innovative special-effects film *The Abyss*. He was given key roles in *Apollo 13* and *The Truman Show*, and he played a figment of someone's imagination in *A Beautiful Mind*. His portrayal of Jackson Pollock, however, in *Pollock* proved to be his most memorable role to date.

THE OLD-FASHIONED
edn

Charisma	👄👄👄👄👄👄👄👄👄👄
Career Success	💰💰💰💰💰💰💰💰💰💰
Love & Friendship	🐦🐦🐦🐦🐦🐦🐦🐦🐦🐦
Power	💣💣💣💣💣💣💣💣💣💣

Intense Methodical Influential
Intolerant Small-minded Impatient

Like most people whose names begin with the *excitable* and *effervescent* letter *E*, *EDN*s have deeply complex emotional lives and unpredictable tempers to match. But in the *EDN*s' case, the outward manifestation of their temperament is almost always under lock and key. Perhaps it's the *dignified, dominant* letter *D* that anchors them so firmly to reality, or the *negative* aspects of the letter *N* (*no, not, never, nothing, none* and *nary*) that's responsible for their introspective moods and self-absorption.

Self-controlled and perhaps even a little prissy at times, *EDN*s rule themselves with stern self-discipline and distrust open displays of emotion in others. Though they enjoy a good party as much as the next person, they never seem able to get carried away with the moment or relinquish the tight reign on their passions. Are *EDN*s uptight? It depends on who you ask. *They'll* tell you that it's just a symptom of healthy self-control.

Although there's a dark specter lurking just beneath the *EDN*s' surface, they do have a deeply developed sense of empathy. And even if their compassion isn't going to manifest itself in overtly demonstrative ways, they can always be counted on to come through in moments of need. If nothing else, *EDN*s are steadfast souls who

Eden
Edison
Edmond
Edmund
Edmundo
Edna

derive a great deal of their self-worth from being reliable.

When it comes to their careers, the no-nonsense *EDN*s prove to be well suited for managerial or administrative positions, inasmuch as they can be trusted to deal with crises with cool efficiency. But their strong notions about how things should be done, coupled with a reluctance to embrace change, means that *EDN*s often prove to be cantankerous co-workers. In other words, *EDN*s aren't people you'd want to use as guinea pigs for those new-fangled office procedures; they'll have to be dragged kicking and screaming up the ladder of success. If you want to try something innovative, you'll have to make them think it's their idea.

*EDN*s play free and loose with their advice on how others should run their lives, and even though they're well armed with a healthy sense of justice and fair play, their strong opinions border on meddling. But *EDN*s tend to take a more deferential approach when it comes to their life mates, where they'll only offer their counsel upon request. Unless you want to unleash the dark forces within, don't try any funny stuff on the home front—like picking out new wallpaper or changing the pizza toppings from pepperoni to pineapple—without consulting them first.

Dame Edna Although it may seem to many fans that Dame Edna is really Dr. Barry Humphries in gay apparel, the mauve-haired Edna considers herself to be a completely separate entity. ■ Her over-the-top performances, flamboyant frocks and gushing wit landed this Australian actor on Broadway, and Dame Edna's roles include the eccentric Claire Otoms in the final season of *Ally McBeal*. ■ But life wasn't always so kind to the adolescent Edna. "I always felt different from the other girls, somehow brighter, more on the ball. But the thing that set me apart most of all was my halo of bright wisteria curls." ■ According to her gynecologist, the feisty Edna shows no sign of slowing down. She is perfectly healthy and able to have grandchildren. Possums, who knew?

Charisma										
Career Success										
Love & Friendship										
Power										

Extroverted Bold Dignified
Oppressive Boring Conventional

People who bear *EDW* names display the same subtle internal conflicts that characterize most everyone whose names begin with an *ED*. In part this is due to the letter *E*'s association with *extroverted excitement* and its union with the *dignified* and *dapper* letter *D*. These two letters create the sense of enlightenment found in the words *educate, editorialize, edifying, edgy* and *edict*. The *wonderfully wild* and *weird* letter *W* lends a delicious hint of the dark side and may explain why so many *EDW* people consider themselves to be misunderstood. In addition, since all these people insist on being called by their formal given names (rather than the more casual *Eddy* or *Ed*), they tend to exude a more self-aggrandizing air.

There's an air of unshakable solidity to these individuals that many people misinterpret to be stuffiness. The fact is that *EDW*s are *not* antisocial. On the contrary, they make friends easily and their demonstrative advances are often quite irresistible to the opposite sex. Their quirkiness practically guarantees that that people will remember them, and their humor and fashion styles are deliberately chosen to avoid mainstream trends. More than any other, it's their idiosyncratic characteristics that define *EDW*s' "to-thine-own-self- be-true" philosophy, although its downside is their alienation from

Edward
Edwardo
Edwin
Edwina

conventional relationships. *EDW*s may not be particularly concerned about what other people think about them, but they are clearly emotionally driven and easily hurt by careless words. As much as *EDW*s can be loyal friends, they can also prove to be equally powerful enemies.

Even with their strong resolve and independent agendas, *EDW*s have a secret desire to please and have few problems with sustaining relationships—even with demanding partners. But any concessions *EDW*s make really only apply to the important issues in a relationship: where to live and how to raise the children. When it comes to the little things, you'll find they can be decidedly picky: how the living room is decorated, where the family spends its vacations and who gets the drumstick.

Despite these foibles, the *EDW* makes for a steady and dependable mate who, once settled, will be there for the long-haul. But always expect the unexpected. There will be occasions when the *EDW* gets a bee in his or her bonnet and charges off on a life-changing tangent without first checking to see if you're in tow. That's why the *EDW*s' children will be encouraged to find their own paths in life and will appreciate the nonpressure guidance from their wholly nonjudgmental parent.

Edwin Moses Even talking to a prostitute during the conservative Reagan era could irreparably damage one's reputation, and that's precisely what happened to one of America's most respected athletes in 1985 after his arrest by undercover officers for allegedly soliciting a prostitute. Even though he was acquitted in a jury trial, Edwin lost the bulk of his endorsement contracts because of his misadventure. ■ There are few, if any, athletes in the history of sports that dominated their fields as much as Edwin Moses. For ten years he owned the men's 400-meter hurdles. Edwin was literally unbeatable, stringing together 107 consecutive victories into his thirties—well past the age at which most athletes retire. He won gold medals at the 1976 and 1984 Olympic Games, but missed 1980 due to the fact that the United States (under President Jimmy Carter) boycotted the Games that year.

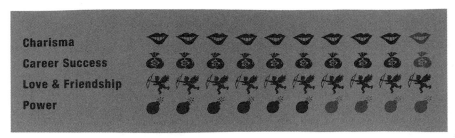

Charisma	
Career Success	
Love & Friendship	
Power	

Talented Sensitive Open-minded
Materialistic Controlling Indecisive

The emotional letter *E* is at its *elated* and *electrifying* best when its energy is combined with the *lively* and *life-loving* letter *L*. We see these emotionally flexible effects at work in words like *elastic, elusive, elevate, elfish, élan, elegant, elite, elixir,* and *eloquent.* These are personalities that exhibit none of the dark corners found in names that begin with consonants, even though *ELs* do experience occasional down cycles as a consequence of their whimsical natures. Emotional? Definitely. The *EL* will emote you right under the table.

The next time you interact with an *EL*, check and see if your emotions are subtly shifting to fit theirs. This uncanny ability to transmit their emotional states to those around them gives *ELs* an unparalleled ability to express themselves as artists, musicians and actors. But no matter what career path they choose, *ELs* take full advantage of the fact that people are so strongly drawn to them, and they almost always end up in positions where they can counsel and motivate others.

ELs are restless by nature and seek the stimulus of constant change. Consequently, to the chagrin of parents and mates, their career searches may turn out to be lifelong processes. Perhaps this is why so many *ELs* thrive in the entertainment world as singers, dancers and comedians—occupations that promise the uncertainty inherent in show business. Even on those rare occasions when *ELs* find themselves in the grip of laziness, their natural talents prevent them from ever reaching rock bottom.

ELs can be a bit overwhelming in their personal relationships, for one of the downsides to having such lively personalities is the temptation to manipulate other people whether deliberately or not. So if there's going to be trouble between you and your *EL* friends, it's going to arise from their insistence on getting their own way. And being defensive isn't going to help you either; it will only provoke resentment and make you look like the bad guy. The best way to handle these emotional maneuverings is to sit back and enjoy the ride.

When it comes to falling in love, *ELs* do it hard and fast. There are no half-measures in these expressive creatures' love lives, so you'd better be prepared to be swept off your feet. Once they've set you in their sights, it's just a matter of time before you'll be reaping all the benefits of being partnered with these teamwork-oriented sprites. If you manage to keep your cool in the face of *ELs'* sometimes-capricious moods and provide them safe harbor in their times of need, they'll return the favor with undying loyalty and extraordinary affection.

Eladio
Elba
Eli
Elia
Elijah
Ella
Elle
Ellie
Elma
Elmo
Elmer
Elmira
Elroy
Elwood
Eula

Ella Fitzgerald In 1934, during Amateur Night at the Apollo Theater in Harlem, New York, a trembling sixteen-year-old orphan made her way onstage. She launched into the song, "The Object of My Affection," won first prize, and gave birth to an American original. ■ Although she never received formal training, Ella's career spanned an amazing sixty years, with thousands of recordings to her credit. Her three-octave range and her spontaneous scat improvisations became her trademarks. ■ Songwriter Ira Gershwin paid Ella her most treasured compliment when he commented "I didn't realize our songs were so good until Ella sang them."

Charisma	👄	👄	👄	👄	👄	👄	👄	👄	👄	👄
Career Success	💰	💰	💰	💰	💰	💰	💰	💰	💰	💰
Love & Friendship	🐦	🐦	🐦	🐦	🐦	🐦	🐦	🐦	🐦	🐦
Power	💣	💣	💣	💣	💣	💣	💣	💣	💣	💣

Humorous Altruistic Loving
Flighty Distracted Scattered

When a name begins with the *excitable, emotional* letter *E*, its bearer usually projects a great deal of *enthusiasm* and *effervescence*. The appearance of the letter *L* (the flagship of *life, laughter, liberty, learning* and *love*) and the *nurturing* (if somewhat negative) letter *N* adds an air of thoughtful introspection. All told, the *ELN* letter combination conspires to produce names that bespeak of emotive, generous and decidedly animated individuals.

A number of *ELNs* report a strong attraction to bright colors, which is why their clothing and cars are unlikely to be in subtle shades—a preference that parallels their cheerful and colorful personalities. With their deeply rooted sense of self-assurance, *ELNs* won't stand for being ignored and will do almost anything to keep from being sidelined. At a party, don't be surprised to find an *ELN* hogging the limelight. Admittedly, they don't have to work very hard to attract attention; the spotlight often just seems to follow them around.

Lurking just beneath the *ELNs'* extroverted surface is an innate tenderness that draws them into the artistic and nurturing professions. These are right-brained individuals who are attracted toward musical and dramatic careers or jobs that involve creativity and dealings with the public. Nothing depresses an *ELN*

Eileen
Elaine
Elana
Eldon
Eleanor
Eleanora
Elena
Elian
Eliana
Elina
Ellen
Elnora

more than being confined to an office job in which their interactions with people are limited. *ELNs* are usually respectful toward authority, but their unwillingness to take their work too seriously often leads to clashes with corporate-minded bosses. So when *ELNs* insist on starting their own businesses, you should pay attention and buy shares if you can. When sufficiently motivated, *ELNs* are fierce competitors and their fortunes are almost always guaranteed.

Although this name root is shared by a significant percentage of men, the *ELN* letter combination has a distinctly feminine essence and *ELNs* tend to be responders rather than initiators when it comes to their relationships. This means that their social circle generally chooses them rather than the other way around, but it doesn't mean that *ELNs* are any less proud of their eclectic friends who they loyally nurture and emotionally sustain.

Still, *ELNs* are not always lucky in love and many endure the pain of a few false starts before they finally settle down with their permanent mates. They might claim that these failed relationships stem from their unwillingness to hurt others, but those who really know them suspect that it's simply another expression of their need for drama and attention.

Ellen DeGeneres Although Ellen DeGeneres was the first actress in history to announce her sexual orientation on a prime-time sitcom, her formal revelation actually came in a *Time* magazine interview a few years before. Her "outing" helped thousands of teens come to terms with their identities in a society struggling with traditional mores. ■ Her successful stint as a standup comedienne led to the film, *Mr. Wrong*, in which she describes her love scene as something akin to "Mary Poppins being naked." As evidenced by the film's meager box-office showing, fans were not very enthusiastic about such imagery. ■ Quips Ellen: "My grandmother started walking five miles a day when she was sixty. She's ninety-seven now, and we don't know where the hell she is."

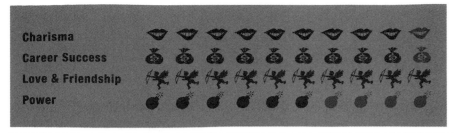

THE WINSOME
els

Charisma

Career Success

Love & Friendship

Power

Flirtatious Adventurous Practical
Scatterbrained Emotional Self-involved

The appealing *ELS* names herald personalities that strongly resonate with sensuality, emotionality and nurturing. The *energetic* letter *E* contributes its *emotive, exuberant* and *extroverted* aspects, while the *loving, life-affirming* letter *L* fortifies these names with its *learned* and *loyal* tones. Terminated by the *sexy* and *sensual* letter *S*, these names suggest creative and energetic people who are anything but inhibited. Eminently attractive to the opposite sex for their wit and enthusiasm, *ELS* people enjoy their lives and seem to want the same for everyone else.

The surest way to get acquainted with *ELS*s is to enter their living space. Their modest homes are likely to be inviting and comfortable, and if they're a little on the ethereal side, it's the perfect place for them to practice their unique concoction of ritual meditation. You'll feel welcomed by the scent of candles and patchouli, and also by the *ELS*'s bonhomie and hospitality, but there's also a sense that all is not as balanced in their lives as they'd like you to believe. As a consequence of the high expectations they've placed on themselves ever since childhood, many feel that they've never really "made it."

Because of their distaste for the world of hierarchy and competition, *ELS*s usually gravitate toward careers that give them a certain degree of self-expression, or at

Elias
Elisa
Elise
Eliseo
Elisha
Ellis
Eloisa
Eloise
Elsa
Elsie

least situations that promise them creative or athletic outlets. These aren't the one-person/one-career types, and true to their whimsical spirits, *ELS*s will readily flit between jobs. This kind of instability may well cost *ELS*s the kind of careers that could bring in the big money, but they're hardly the types to spend their lives chasing a dollar. Self-actualization seems far more valuable.

*ELS*s will be invaluable as confidants and helpmates in their close relationships, but it's not going to be easy to penetrate their inner circles. Whether their guardedness comes from their distrust of people's motives or simply the high standards they've set for themselves, prospective friends and suitors will be warily evaluated before being allowed into their lives. *ELS*s are keen observers of human nature, who unconsciously record all the little details of their conversations for later use, and woe-betide partners whose stories don't quite jibe with *their* recollections.

When it comes to intimate arrangements, integrity and honesty are high on their shopping lists, and *ELS*s aren't likely to grant a second chance to anyone who transgresses their rules. If there is going to be a breakup, chances are that *they* will be the ones to initiate it, and will handle it with sensitivity and good judgment.

Elisa Donovan Actress Elisa Donovan (*A Night at the Roxbury*, *Wolves of Wall Street*) did her obligatory stint as a waitress in New York City before garnering the attention of filmgoers when she co-starred opposite Alicia Silverstone in the film *Clueless*, playing Amber Princess Mariens, the snooty, misguided slave to fashion. ■ Elisa fell victim to two common problems faced by modern actresses: Nude pictures of her kept popping up on the Internet (even though almost all these images were elaborate fakes designed to take advantage of her celebrity), and after succumbing to "hard-core anorexia", her weight dropped to ninety pounds. ■ Capitalizing on the strong teen following she picked up from *Clueless*, Elisa landed a regular role as Morgan Cavanaugh on TV's *Sabrina the Teenage Witch*.

elt

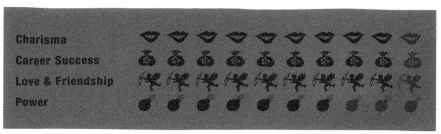

Charisma										
Career Success										
Love & Friendship										
Power										

Bright Optimistic Intellectual
Obsessive Reclusive Awkward

People who sport *ELT*s names exhibit all the *emotional* and *enthusiastic* qualities of the *excitable* letter *E* tempered with a distinct air of intellectualism. The letter *L*, symbolizing *love, learning* and *lightness,* moderates these names with its thoughtful spirituality. Bringing up the rear, the *triumphantly trumpeting* letter *T* infuses these names with a sense of contagious optimism and zeal for life.

Endearing and lively (although sometimes a little socially-awkward), *ELT*s are the type of person you'll find blazing trails in science or art. Their laid-back and unassuming natures mask sharp minds that are always on the prowl for stimulating conversations or challenging conundrums. Although their infectious energy is usually channeled into their intellectual lives, if you want to see their enthusiastic sides, just ask them about their latest project. You're likely to receive a garrulous lecture on cold fusion or sheep cloning. But the *ELT*'s delivery is rooted in a desire to educate and *never* from an egocentric need to seem intelligent.

However, there is more to the *ELT*'s life than hard work and research. For despite his occasional social clumsiness, this is a chummy fellow who requires ample amounts of human interaction to fulfill his emotional

Elbert
Elliott
Elton

needs. So even though he may struggle to make intimate connections (a trait that attracts all kinds of eccentrics), his extraordinarily well-developed sense of loyalty leads to rock-solid alliances.

Marriage, or an equivalent partnership, is essential to the *ELT*'s peace of mind, and he is most at peace when ensconced in an intimate affair. Because he finds dating to be somewhat intimidating, his mate will usually come from within his trusted group of friends. In this way, he is able to bypass messy romancing and go straight to the lasting and productive stage.

Those who enjoy hierarchy in their relationships will appreciate the *ELT*'s structured approach, for he is completely unfussy about whether his role is as leader or follower. He's not going to complain as long as things are running smoothly, nor will he have any expectations from his mate other than fidelity and loyalty.

The *ELT*'s parenting style, as one might guess, will be characteristically and refreshingly unconventional. Children will be welcomed into his life—provided that they know their place and don't put too many demands on his creative and intellectual time—and will be given the freedom that most kids only dream of.

Elton John Elton John was born Reginald Dwight to a middle-class family in England and went on to become one of the most commercially successful pop entertainers in history. ■ Like many talented musicians, Elton left school early to devote his time to his professional career and after a fateful newspaper advertisement introduced him to lyricist Bernie Taupin, his life was changed forever. ■ Reginald took the stage name Elton John from the names Elton Dean and Long John Baldry, both of whom he played with in the early sixties in a band called Bluesology. He began his solo career in 1967, singing songs created by him and Taupin. ■ Elton's live shows have always been marked by a flamboyant energy in which he flaunts six-inch platform shoes, feather boas and homemade sunglasses. His 1975 album *Captain Fantastic* was the first ever to debut at number one.

Charisma	💋	💋	💋	💋	💋	💋	💋	💋	💋
Career Success	💰	💰	💰	💰	💰	💰	💰	💰	💰
Love & Friendship	🦁	🦁	🦁	🦁	🦁	🦁	🦁	🦁	🦁
Power	💣	💣	💣	💣	💣	💣	💣	💣	💣

Refined Soft-spoken Positive
Petty Snobbish Manipulative

Is there something about the *ELZ* names that explains their extraordinary popularity over the centuries? It may have something to do with the *elegant* and *elusive* qualities of the *EL* letter combination, which can be seen in the words *elastic, elevate, elfish, élan, elite, elixir* and *eloquent*. Or maybe it's the *zany* and *zippy* qualities of the letter *Z*, which suffuses these names with an original and invigorating air. But for all their flair, there's a decided aloofness about people who insist on being called by their full four-syllabled name (*Elizabeth*), instead of the more obliging and manageable *Liz*.

Eliezer
Eliza
Elizabeth

The *ELZ* is not someone you'd call up out of the blue to join you for a night on the town. It takes a little more effort than that to socialize with these refined types who work hard at keeping up formal appearances. You might even affectionately describe them as being pretentious, but calling them arrogant would be too harsh. They certainly get a kick out of viewing the world from atop their well-groomed high horses, but they're also not afraid to get down in the mud as well. Sometimes, though, their self-imposed distances can isolate the *ELZ*s, who can't hide forever behind their decorous façades.

Affairs of the heart often prove to be tangled skeins from which they have difficulty extricating themselves. Their complex moods and emotions make it difficult for them to open up, and many are destined to search for a long time before finding appropriate matches. Unfortunately, there's no road map for those planning on having a love affair with an *ELZ*, and suitors will be expected to put up with a number of bewildering twists and turns if they expect to receive the *ELZ*'s prize of unconditional love and affection.

These are well-dressed women who excel in all manner of creative careers, and their personal styles are often reflected in their work output. They also like to tailor their careers to fit their own needs. Whether this stems from a sense of entitlement or simply from an inner confidence, *ELZ*s do have a knack for being able to find the most agreeable jobs. And once they've made themselves indispensable to their employers, they'll usually set about rewriting their job descriptions to make things even more comfortable. This isn't always a bad thing for the business, mind you, for when *ELZ*s are given the freedom to create, they are certainly productive.

An *ELZ*'s home is, more often than not, tastefully decorated with just the right balance of classic and contemporary styles. And as much as this doting mother will adore her children, they can expect to be well disciplined if they are to fit into her decorous world.

Elizabeth Taylor In much the same way the ancient empress Cleopatra represented beauty in the ancient world, Elizabeth Taylor has come to symbolize it in the twentieth century. The English-born violet-eyed actress was only twelve when she became a bona fide star, playing a young equestrienne in the 1944 film *National Velvet*. Elizabeth was nominated for three Academy Awards before finally winning one in 1960, for her role as a prostitute in the film *Butterfield 8*. ■ On the set of *Cleopatra* (for which she was paid the then-unheard-of salary of one million dollars), she fell in love with co-star Richard Burton and set the stage for a life-long tumultuous affair, which included two marriages. ■ All told, Elizabeth has been married seven times, including her short-lived partnership with construction worker Larry Fortensky, which left many fans scratching their heads.

THE DEMURE

em

Charisma										
Career Success										
Love & Friendship										
Power										

Affectionate Energetic Content
Nervous Petulant Childish

Whenever a name or a word begins with the *excitable* and *emotional* letter *E*, we anticipate its owner to project the *enthusiastic essence* found in the words *effusive, excited, excellence, exotic, expressive, erotic* and *earnest*. And since the letter *M* is the standard bearer of all things *maternal* and *motherly* (*mammary, Maid Marion, Mary Magdalene, madam, maiden* and *mild*), it's not surprising that *EM* names exude the demonstrative compassion found in the words: *embrace, emotive, embolden, eminent, empathy* and *empower*. To offset these feminine qualities, most male *EM* names (*Emmett* and *Emmitt*) are terminated by the masculine tones of the *triumphant, tough* and *taciturn* letter *T*.

The *EM* is someone you can count on for plenty of affection, but far less for levelheaded reasoning. For *EM*s live by their emotions and have a deep spirituality governing their actions. Though everyone seems to agree that *EM*s are quite bright, it's their *emotional* intelligence that enables them to function so well in their workplaces and social interactions. This is why you'll rarely find *EM*s resolving their differences through debate and argument; they're more liable to sidestep the surface issues and focus on the emotions that caused the disagreement in the first place.

Emma
Emerson
Emery
Emmett
Emory

With their easygoing and smooth approach to life, *EM*s find a multitude of career doors open to them but will most often choose jobs in which they can express themselves creatively. In corporate settings, for example, *EM*s might end up in the advertising or marketing department, while in the industrial world they might become technical writers. Since it goes against their grain to apply unwanted pressure on others, *EM*s function poorly in aggressive careers like law and sales.

If you're friends with an *EM*, you probably appreciate his or her ability to keep everyone in the group on an even keel, and *EM*s are happiest when their environments are harmonious. People instinctively trust their unbiased analyses, and *EM*s quite often find themselves to be adjudicators in squabbles among their friends and families. The downside of *EM*s' reflexive altruism is that in putting the needs of other people above their own, they often accumulate secret resentments that express themselves in mildly bitter ways.

Falling in love with an *EM* is easy. These loving people are full of surprises, and most prospective partners are happy to learn that the *EM*'s bracing bonhomie (and colorful language) transfers to the bedroom as well.

Emma Thompson Emma Thompson began her bright-light career as an earthy stand-up comic. It was while acting in her own TV series, *Thompson*, that Emma met a motivated young director with his own acting company. When Kenneth Branagh proposed to her on his knees in Central Park, the thirty-year-old actress headily accepted. They were divorced in 1994. ■ It wasn't until the Merchant-Ivory production *Howard's End* that Emma finally hit her mark. Not only did she walk away with an Oscar, but her performance earmarked her as one of the strong, independent woman en vogue in the nineties. ■ *Howard's End* also began a special chemistry between Emma and Anthony Hopkins, with whom she went on to make *Remains of the Day*. Though that role earned her her second Oscar nomination, she lost to Holly Hunter (for her role in *The Piano*).

THE ENGAGING
eml

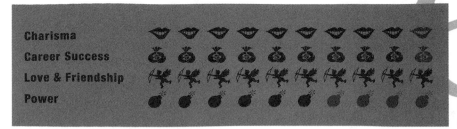

Charisma	😚😚😚😚😚😚😚😚😚😚
Career Success	💰💰💰💰💰💰💰💰💰
Love & Friendship	🕊🕊🕊🕊🕊🕊🕊🕊🕊🕊
Power	💣💣💣💣💣💣💣💣💣

Lighthearted Forgiving Gentle
Childish Flighty Interfering

When a word begins with the *effervescent* letter *E*, it tends to suggest the *enthusiastic essence* found in the words: *excited, erotic, excellent, eek, exotic, expressive,* and *earnest.* And because the letter *M* is the flagship of all things *maternal* and *motherly,* it's hardly surprising that the *EM* combination expresses the gentle compassion found in the words: *emotive, empathy, embrace, eminent,* and *empower.* When the letter *L* (the icon of *love, loyalty, life, lust* and *learning*) is added to the mix, it produces a uniquely engaging name whose *emotional* playfulness is firmly grounded in a spiritually empathetic core.

You often hear the word "genuine" when people are describing *EML* personalities, for these are people who are incapable of pretending to be anything other than what they are. Truth is their battle flag and shield, and you'll never have to worry that your *EMLs* friends are trying to flatter or protect you. When they do feel compelled to put their two cents in, they will be careful to do it in the most sensitive way possible. With these empathic instincts, *EMLs* will be the first to highlight your good points, offer you unconditional encouragement and watch your back at the ATM.

EMLs are happiest when they are climbing their own hand-built ladders to success while the rest of us

Emilio
Emilia
Emanuel
Emerald
Emil
Emiliano
Emmanuel
Emmeline
Emily
Esmeralda

are looking for the escalator. They are rarely swayed by the expectations of society, nor do they feel a responsibility to "make it" in a world they consider too focused on material possessions. It doesn't seem to matter to them what kind of work they're involved in; it's a matter of how they can achieve their goals without expense to others.

A powerful streak of perfectionism pervades everything they do, but this is also where they can get into trouble. They are often so afraid of failure that they have a tendency to freeze up at critical moments—particularly when situations call for important decisions or when success is close at hand. Fortunately, because *EMLs* are particularly self-aware, these setbacks are short-lived and ultimately trifling.

As much as they might shine in their careers, *EMLs'* inner lights are ignited by love and bonding. If you're married to one, you are probably already familiar with their steady affections punctuated with bouts of forthright advice and counsel, and you'll know that it takes a lot to get them riled up. Bumps in the road will be expertly smoothed over with the *EMLs'* dry sense of humor, and with them around, you'll never want for companionship, sexual gratification or chicken soup.

Emmeline Pankhurst Many historians believe that the achievements of activist suffragette, Emmeline Pankhurst, should be credited, ironically, to her husband, Richard. After all, Richard was the radical English lawyer who authored England's first woman's suffrage bill. ■ "Nonsense!" retort her supporters. For it was Emmeline who founded the Women's Franchise League in 1889, and the Women's Social and Political Union in 1903, with her rallying cry "Deeds, not words." A series of arson attacks orchestrated by her daughter Christable led to a series of arrests, but Emmeline's intelligent use of hunger strikes forced her and her daughter's release. ■ The unchallenged leader of the Women's Movement in England, Emmeline lived to see the passing of the Voting Rights Act for Men and Women only two weeks before her death in 1926.

121

en

Charisma										
Career Success										
Love & Friendship										
Power										

Protective Altruistic Talented
Controlling Stubborn Uncommunicative

When the emotional letter *E* brings its *excitable, energetic* and *enthusiastic* presence to names, it suggests people of noteworthy emotional intelligence. However, when it teams up with the *negative* elements of the letter *N* (as seen in the words *no, never, not, nowhere* and *nothing*), it creates a combination marked by the passionate negativism expressed in words like *enemy, enslave, enigma, enema, enrage* and *ensnarl.* These negative overtones might explain why—with the exception of the name *Ean* (which hit the top thousand list in 2002)—these names are at their lowest ebb of popularity in over one hundred years, and why there are fewer than 50,000 people in the United States who sport an *EN* name.

But all is not lost for these enigmatic names, for the letter *N* also has strong *nurturing* properties, which come through in the words: *endear, enable, encourage, enduring* and *enjoy.* Perhaps this is why *EN* people are so well known for having distinct dualities to their characters. In some ways, they are the strict unforgiving headmistresses or headmasters whose uncompromising styles of discipline are motivated by genuine desire to get the best out of their students.

*EN*s forge their way through life with determined energies and focused vision. Only the brave or foolhardy would step into their path while they're complet-

Ean
Enoch
Eunice

ing a task, and when they do, they'd better have a damn good explanation, or at least a note from their mother. It's not that they're unforgiving; it's that they value their time highly and expect others to acknowledge it accordingly. Challenge them if you must, but if you don't have your ducks in a row, you'll get one of their patented withering stares or a whipping from their acerbic tongues. But if you're the kind of person whom an *EN* deems worthy of their respect, you'll be a welcome ally in their private struggle to make the world a better place.

The *EN* is an early-to-bed early-to-rise type—all the better to get a head start on everyone else. The day is vigorously attacked, and their schedules, appointments and even relaxation times are carefully considered and flawlessly maintained. *EN*s are conservative dressers who usually adopt traditional styles of business wear, and even though they don't adapt very easily, they'll readily change their careers if their contributions are not being adequately appreciated.

Emotional security is an important component in the *EN*s' success, which explains why they always seem to be in stable relationships. When it comes to being parents, the only thing that takes priority over their children's education is going to be their children's discipline. Like *EN*s themselves, their offspring must always be presentable, polite and well mannered.

Eunice Kennedy Shriver Eunice Kennedy Shriver was born in Brookline, Massachusetts, the fifth child of Jospeh P. and Rose Fitzgerald Kennedy. She holds a degree in sociology from Stanford University and has, throughout her life, been a leader in the worldwide struggle to improve and enhance the lives of individuals with intellectual disabilities. She is the founder and honorary chairman of the Special Olympics, an organization dedicated to helping disabled people develop their skills through sparts training and competition. President Ronald Reagan summed it up nicely when he awarded her the Presidential Medal of Freedom in 1984, saying "her decency and goodness have touched the lives of many, and Eunice Kennedy Shriver deserves America's praise, gratitude and love."

erk

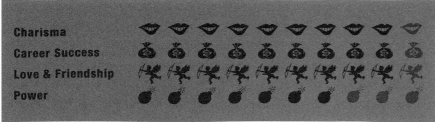

Charisma	👄 👄 👄 👄 👄 👄 👄 👄 👄 👄
Career Success	💰 💰 💰 💰 💰 💰 💰 💰 💰 💰
Love & Friendship	🦅 🦅 🦅 🦅 🦅 🦅 🦅 🦅 🦅 🦅
Power	💣 💣 💣 💣 💣 💣 💣 💣 💣 💣

Gregarious Dependable Mellow
Reticent Overstimulated Controlling

When the letter of *emotional energy* appears in close proximity to the symbol of *robust* passion—the *roaring, randy, romantic, raffish* and *roused* letter *R*—it suggests an individual on emotional overdrive with a libido to match. And since these names are terminated with the sharply pronounced *K* or *C* (as in *break, kick, brick, crack* and *jerk*), there's an unmistakable edge to these energetic people. The *ERK* names evoke the same urgently passionate traits found in the words *erotica, erection, acerbic, cherubic, eccentric, electric* and *erratic*.

Just because the *ERK*s' strong carnal drives aren't easily discernible by their implacable exteriors doesn't mean there isn't something smoking just under the surface. Many *ERK*s have mastered the art of relationship judo in which they've discovered that it's best to move *away* from the things you love in order to have them come to you. Manipulative? Maybe just a little. But if you really want to know what their motivations are, just ask them. These candid souls are happy to spill the beans as long as they are reasonably sure you're not going to use it against them.

*ERK*s are full of energy when it comes to their careers and their manic work schedule has the effect of galvanizing their co-workers, who often feel guilty for

Enrico
Enrique
Erica
Eric

not being able to keep up with their determined pace. This is why many *ERK*'s are destined to become leaders in their fields or owners of their own businesses. While success may *seem* to come easily to them, it's only as a consequence of their unrelenting physical efforts.

Looking for someone to organize your next party? Get an *ERK* involved and it'll be an experience to remember. *ERK*s take their entertaining as seriously as they do their wooing, and their creative minds are constantly rummaging around for novel ways to impress people. Just make sure that they're not responsible for the checkbook though: *ERK*s wrote the book on big spending

As might be expected from such emotionally charged personalities, stable relationships can present quite a challenge. Being naturally impulsive, *ERK*s will relentlessly hunt down the objects of their affection (which can prove to be quite an ego boost to their quarry), but the flipside to this is that once they've cornered their prey, they're likely to lose interest in the chase. Consequently, many hopeful lovers are abandoned without so much as a peck on the cheek. Fortunately, once *ERK*s commit themselves to lifelong unions, even these hungry hunters treat their vows with solemn respect.

Erica Jong Feminist author Erica Jong's best-known novel is *Fear of Flying* (1973), an intensely intimate take on the life and loves of the anti-heroine Isadora Wing. With over twelve million copies in print, Henry Miller applauded it as "a female Tropic of Cancer" and noted that the book encouraged women to "find their own voices and give us great sagas of sex, life, joy and adventure." ■ Erica's follow-up opus, *Fear of Fifty*, was published in 1994. The book was the biographical story of the author, who considers herself a member of the "Whiplash Generation," in which women were encouraged, as young girls, to be Doris Day, then went through adulthood aspiring to be Gloria Steinem, and finally had to raise their daughters amongst the likes of Madonna and Britney Spears.

erl

Charisma										
Career Success										
Love & Friendship										
Power										

Successful Inquisitive Poised
Ego-driven Repressive Self-centered

There's an extraordinary amount of *emotional energy* that emanates from the combination of the *emotional* letter *E*, the *randy* and *ribald* letter *R*, and the *life-loving, lusty* letter *L*. Words in which these three letters appear in order have the unmistakably effusive characteristics found in *enthrall, eagerly, fertile, earnestly, personable,* and *overflow.* These *effervescent* effects *percolate* into *ERLs'* psyches and give them the reputation for being completely unintimidated by the world at large.

With all their demonstrative shenanigans, it's easy to overlook *ERLs'* sensitive sides. Perhaps it's their belief that as long as they stay in motion there's little reason to reflect on issues that might knock them off balance. But one thing is sure: *ERLs* keep steely locks on their negative emotions and will only offer the key to a select few. Even if things are amiss with your *ERL* friends, it's unlikely that you'd even be aware of it. You'll be too mesmerized by their affable and impish hijinks.

ERLs love parties and come into their own in when they're in any kind of social situation. They certainly aren't shy about introducing themselves or putting their emotions on the line, and people seem to respect this unabashed honesty. They are well-liked by both sexes,

Earl
Earlene
Errol

although their popularity certainly doesn't stem from their underabundance of tact: it's their ebullient senses of humor and obvious delight at being alive. *ERLs* don't embarrass easily and privately delight in making comments that other people might find uncomfortable, but although they'd never admit it, their own feelings are easily bruised by sharp-tongued comments or snubs to their character.

ERLs often choose career paths that put them in the company of as many people as possible. They enjoy the unpredictably inherent in working with the public and would absolutely shrivel under the yoke of an unyielding system or a strict boss. This is why they steer clear of assuming authority positions themselves and avoid jobs that threaten to isolate their gregarious spirits.

The *ERLs'* mates should be willing to cater to their social addictions. *ERLs* don't respond well to overly dominant partners, but they're not looking for submissive domestics either. Their ideal choice for a spouse is someone who's willing to be their partner in crime, even if it's just an occasional no-holds-barred night out on the town. Their children will appreciate their ability to relate to them on their own level and will never be lacking in unconditional love and affection.

Errol Flynn The age of Australian heartthrob actors began with Errol Flynn—born in Tasmania, a windswept island off the coast of Australia. ■ In the now-fashionable style of Hollywood bad boys, the rabble-rousing Errol was expelled from some of the finest schools in England. ■ Errol became an overnight star with the film *Captain Blood* and went on to become the leading man in the talkies. His career highlights included *The Charge of the Light Brigade, Robin Hood* and the quasi-autobiographical *Adventures of Don Juan.* ■ His reputation for excessive drinking and predilection for young girls ultimately landed him a charge for statutory rape. The rakish star was married three times before his death by heart attack in 1950, and details of his iniquitous life were shamelessly confessed in his autobiography, *My Wicked, Wicked Ways.*

THE RESOLUTE
ern

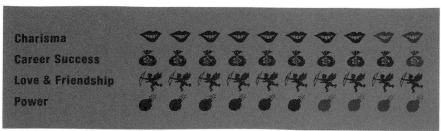

Charisma	
Career Success	
Love & Friendship	
Power	

Unassuming Sympathetic Demure
Passive Unmotivated Immature

The *excitable* and *emotional* letter *E* combines with the *ravishingly romantic* letter *R* to form an amalgam that positively oozes with ardor. We see the *ER*'s effects in the words *erotic, erectile, eruption, erratic, hero* and *erstwhile*. However, the *negative* letter *N* (*no, not, never, nowhere* and *none*) imparts a distinctly sobering element to these otherwise ebullient names (think of *stern, aversion, belligerent, concern, derision* and *errant*) and infers someone with contrary views on life. In short, *ERN* personalities are characterized by fervor and zeal, with just a pinch of pessimism and self-doubt.

Because *ERN*s mask their moods with superficial displays of perkiness, you can't tell from casual encounters if they are feeling low; in fact you're more likely to be won over by their finely honed social skills. You also aren't likely to encounter their darker moods in the workplace, unless their job involves some form of intimate contact with their co-workers. The darker aspects of the *ERN*s' personalities will only surface once they've decided that you're capable of keeping their secrets.

When *ERN*s are feeling frisky, there's little that can stop them from achieving their goals. At work, they prove to be highly motivated employees who are quite

Earnestine
Erin
Erna
Ernest
Ernestine
Ernesto
Ernie
Ervin
Erwin

willing to pick up the slack and do the dirty work that no one else wants to do, and they seem to be driven by a need to prove themselves to be a little better than the rest. This habit of trying their hardest in everything they do extends to their personal relationships, as well as casual pursuits like board games.

Many *ERN*s are drawn to intense occupations that trigger their adrenalin, and it's not unusual for them to flirt with danger as a way of making sure their emotional packages are in working order. This explains why such a high percentage of *ERN*s become policemen, soldiers, nurses and CIA agents, while the less adventurous among them will likely apply their emotional acuteness to counseling, childcare or teaching.

Like most people whose names begin with the letter E, *ERN*s are naturally empathetic, and in their social transactions demonstrate authentic concern for their friends. But while they form solid friendships easily, the same cannot be said for their intimate relationships. Here *ERN*s prove to be finicky creatures who often delay making "the big decision" until the last possible moment. *ERN*s are so emotionally independent, and their friendships so strong, that single life holds no terrors.

Ernest Hemingway It is rare for the details of a writer's life to actually overshadow the lives of the characters in his books, but Ernest Hemingway was a rare man. ■ Ernest learned to write while working as a cub reporter for the *Kansas City Star* when he was only seventeen. His status as an expert and practitioner of boxing, war, bullfighting, deep-sea diving and extravagant living provided the fodder for his critically acclaimed books *For Whom the Bell Tolls, The Old Man and the Sea, The Sun Also Rises* and *A Farewell to Arms*. ■ Ernest's manic temperament resulted in three failed marriages, an addiction to alcohol and long periods of literary inactivity. When asked what made a great novelist, he replied simply, "A writer's job is to tell the truth."

est

Charisma												
Career Success												
Love & Friendship												
Power												

Extroverted Fun-loving Sexy Clingy Domineering Selfish

When the *emotional* and *excitable* letter *E* teams up with the *sexy* and *serpentine* letter *S*, it forces a slight smile from the speaker that reinforces its *escapist essence*. The *ES*'s natural ebullience is undiminished when terminated by the *traditional* and *triumphant* qualities of the letter *T*, as attested to by the words *zest, best, esteem, established, quest* and *honest*.

EST people express their cheerful qualities through their sassy wits and energetic momentum. The whimsical *EST*s ride a roller coaster through life, and it's often difficult to know whether they're on their way up or on their way down. These fun-loving extroverts even take *themselves* with a grain of salt and never quite come to terms with their own unpredictable emotions. Their ethereal, idealistic natures can be roused with righteous zeal at one moment, or float off on some frivolous concern like what to have for lunch. For the record, the *EST*s' choice of restaurant will largely depend on whether the establishment is trendy or whether the lighting complements their skin tones. Heaven forbid if they get caught looking anything but *en vogue* while dining.

These gregarious characters love to socialize and consequently have an extraordinarily wide circle of friends. Outspoken and fearless in general, they would never let their natural sensitivities get in the way of saying something blunt (or even just plain rude) if they felt the situation called for it. Above all, *EST*s are honest to a fault and studiously avoid people who might interfere with their main goal: having fun.

Their zeal for life is evident in their career choices as well. Drama and music are right up their alley, but they also do well in more conventional roles like teaching and sales. Either way, money is rarely a factor in their career choices—which is surprising, since *EST*s certainly know how to spend it.

If you're mated to an *EST,* you should avoid the trap of believing that the relationship's rules will apply to them. *EST*s hate rules (unless they're the ones making and breaking them), and while your *EST* mate will have no qualms about expecting you to stay home on Friday nights, he or she won't understand how you could ask them to give up their weekend getaways. Still, for all their inequitable ways, *EST*s are loyal and affectionate, and their unions almost always prove to be passionate and long-lasting.

Esteban
Estefania
Estafany
Estella
Estevan
Estrella
Estelle
Esther

Esther Williams Esther Williams was already a beautiful teenage swimming champion when she was spotted by a talent agent at a Los Angeles department store. ■ Billed as "America's Mermaid," Esther had the ability to stay underwater forever (if we are to believe MGM's press releases). After the popularity of the aqua musicals thankfully waned, Esther attempted to make the transition to dramatic roles. Although she held her own with Cliff Robertson in *The Big Show*, it was clear that her skills were better suited for retirement. ■ Her autobiography, *The Million Dollar Mermaid* raised a few eyebrows when it was published in 1999. Esther revealed how she had experimented with LSD (on Cary Grant's advice), how she had been a victim of Gene Kelly's verbal cruelty and how Johnny "Tarzan" Weismuller had once pursued her naked.

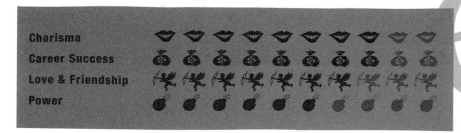

eth

Charisma										
Career Success										
Love & Friendship										
Power										

Conscientious Detailed Solicitous
Uncoordinated Predictable Clingy

The letter *E* is the symbol of *emotional expressiveness,* and the *TH* phoneme is the essence of all things *thoughtful, thankful, therapeutic, theological, theistic* and *thorough.* Unsurprisingly, when they come together to form the *ETH* root, they form the basis for words dealing with humankind's transcendental issues: *death, ethics, empathy, ethereality, free thought, health, weather* and *ether* (the mysterious substance once believed to fill the universe).

Perhaps this is why *ETH* names evoke such an impression of inscrutability. The truth is, although you never really know what to expect from these inscrutable souls, you can rest assured that they know *exactly* who they are and what they're trying to achieve in their lives. These are no-nonsense people, the type that you'd want to carefully pick your battles with . . . or put your weapons down altogether.

At work *ETHs* are the people who get handed those important but annoying projects, because everyone knows that they're going to get the job done with mechanical efficiency. *ETHs* approach their personal lives in the same perfunctory manner and tend to be very analytical when determining the motivations of

Eartha
Ethan
Ethel
Ethelyn

other people. The worst crimes in the *ETH*'s book are indecision and self-pity, and an *ETH* is unlikely to be sympathetic toward someone who's wallowing in self-imposed misery.

One can pretty safely rule out flexibility as one of *ETHs*' strong points, but this doesn't mean they're controlling or heavy-handed. They're quite willing to accept others as they are, as long as there's a genuine attempt at self-improvement. At most, *ETHs* will give you some well-meaning advice, which even if not taken, will result in no ill feelings.

Being married to an *ETH* can be frustrating for a partners who expect to maintain their independence, for *ETHs* are big on teamwork and always expect to have everyone included in their plans. And since they like to plan things in minute detail, you'll have every day and night of your vacation carefully coordinated. The biggest complaint about *ETHs*' is their tendency to micromanage their relationships, but once people realize that this is only the *ETHs*' way of showing affection and concern, most are quite willing to let the capable *ETH* maintain control.

Ethel Merman The engine of show business has always relied on unusual and extraordinary personalities, and few celebrities displayed more personality than Ethel Merman—born Ethel Agnes Zimmerman. ■ Success came easily to the brassy-toned dame, who wowed audiences with her brash New York style. Her crowning achievement came when she played Annie in *Annie Get Your Gun* on Broadway. According to the singing actress herself, her success had more to do with ebullience than style: "I just stand up and holler and hope my voice holds out." ■ There's a story about the night when she fired her prop rifle into the air, expecting a stuffed pheasant to drop onto the stage. The gun failed to fire, but the bird fell at her feet anyway. Picking it up, she exclaimed, "Well whaddya know? Apoplexy!"

THE UNSTOPPABLE

Warm Sensuous Creative
Maudlin Oversensitive Manipulative

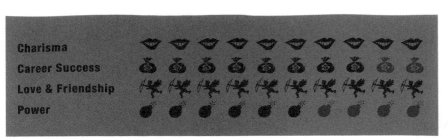

Charisma										
Career Success										
Love & Friendship										
Power										

In retrospect, it should be no surprise that the name *Eve* was given to the woman who (allegedly) caused the downfall of man's perfection. The letter *V* is the consummate symbol of feminine passion (*virginal, vampish, vexing, vague, vixen* and *Venus*), and when it's sandwiched between two *emotional* letter *E*s, there is an unmistakable sense of persuasive femininity. Even male bearers of an *EV* name can be expected to project a gentle brand of masculinity rather than a hardcore machismo image.

There is a subtle aloofness to the *EV* names, rooted in a quiet satisfaction that gives them an aura of intrigue when you meet them for the first time. Whether or not you actually befriend any *EV*s, you won't be able to deny the effects of their appealing charms. And it's not only friends and lovers who find themselves subject to their charisma: employers and co-workers alike are liable to be beguiled by an *EV*'s attractive essence.

To be fair, *EV*s rarely play the role of Medea or Casanova; they simply don't have to. Their brand of attractiveness is rooted in their genuine love for others and in their openly accepting ways. Anyone who suspects disingenuousness in the *EV*'s demonstrative behavior would be plain wrong. Sure their effusiveness

Elva
Elvia
Elvina
Elvira
Elvis
Eva
Eve
Evelia
Everett
Everette
Evia
Evie

may be over the top on occasions, but those with intimate knowledge of their true motives report them to be as authentic as bluegrass music.

When it comes to their career lives, *EV*s have any number of avenues open to their wide range of talents, but more often than not, will carve their own roads as small business owners or in independent ventures in the design or computer-related fields. *EV*s are particularly adept in sales-related fields, although if given the choice, they'd rather not be directly responsible for their employers' bottom line. *EV*s are particularly creative people who express themselves through their music and hobbies, and their homes are likely to be decorated with their own eclectic creations.

Dating and mating *EV* personalities can prove to be quite an adventure, for one can never be quite sure what these enigmatic souls are going to come up with next. The relationship is likely to flourish provided that their mates understand that *EV*s are never going to be happy as housebound domestics. But *EV*s have no problem with playing the traditional roles of supportive mate, and even though *EV*s aren't likely to forgo their extracurricular social activities, family life ultimately proves to be the most important component of their hectic existence.

Eva Gabor Of the three Gabor sisters, Eva was always considered to be the "good" one. But considering the cheeky antics of Zsa Zsa, that might not be much of a compliment. ■ Eva was the youngest of the three girls, and as a teenager, had the good fortune to marry Greta Garbo's personal physician. After signing a contract with Paramount Pictures and making two forgettable movies, her career perked up after she landed a part in a Rogers and Hammerstein Broadway show. But when Zsa Zsa arrived on the scene, having recently immigrated to the U.S., a lifelong competition for roles ensued. ■ Although her sister eventually gained more notoriety, Eva's softer personality landed her the choicest roles. The two finally teamed up for a theatrical production of *Arsenic and Old Lace*.

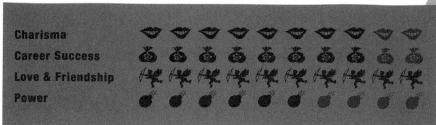

Charisma		
Career Success		
Love & Friendship		
Power		

Easygoing Attentive Sexual
Suspicious Emotional Cloying

Initialized by the *emotional* letter *E* and dominated by the *virile* and *voluptuous* letter *V*, the *EVN* names radiate a vigorous brand of sensuality. But because these names also fall under the influence of the *negative* letter *N* (*no, not, never, nix, null* and *nowhere*), there's also an element of cynicism and self-doubt that pervades their lives. Overall, most people agree that *EVNs* are all about avoiding conflict and finding ways to succeed without making waves.

These personalities are marked by genuine empathy enhanced by a lively intelligence. Friends and co-workers know them as playful, sensitive people with a deep capacity for caring. But don't be lulled into complacency by the *EVNs*' desire to promote harmony; flickering behind those smiles lies a sharp tongue backed by a rapier wit.

In the working world *EVNs* make for great physical and occupational therapists. Their ability to sense pain in others and go straight to its source also makes them great teachers, motivators and salespeople. Their hobbies often include artistic pursuits—particularly writing and music—which fulfill their need for intellectual and creative expression.

It's easy to form a friendship with the loquacious

Evan
Evangelina
Evangeline
Eveline
Evelyn
Evonne

EVN, but romance may not be so cut-and-dried. For one thing, they're reluctant to commit to just one person when there are so many fish in the sea—especially since they have so much bait to spare. But even if your most dashing attempts to lure them in fail, *EVNs* aren't cold fish by any means, and will usually reward their suitors with consolation prizes of affection even when no long-term relationship is in the offing.

When it suits their purposes, *EVNs* will camouflage their sharp minds by being a little coquettish. Sure it's manipulative, but these occasional demonstrations of control only highlight the fact that, once they've given in to love, they're quite happy to be the power behind the throne. In these intimate relationships, *EVNs* are insatiable in their appetite for togetherness, and potential mates will have to prove their stamina if they expect to keep up with them. As problems go, this is a good one to have.

The *EVN*'s consistency and staying power will prove useful when kids arrive. But as important a role their offspring play in their lives, children will never be allowed to intrude on the intimacy of the *EVNs*' primary relationships.

Evelyn Waugh Evelyn Waugh was born in London and educated at Hertford College in Oxford. By his own admission, his stint at Oxford was a complete waste of time, and even though he spent a brief period as a teacher, he was quickly dismissed for drunkenness. ■ Many scholars believe that Evelyn's conversion to Catholicism was responsible for his writing's mystical flavor. These themes were evident in the religious underpinnings of *Brideshead Revisited*, which was later turned into a successful BBC television series. ■ Evelyn is credited for a number of writing innovations, including the now-commonplace technique of assimilating several seemingly unconnected plots and bringing them together into an ordered whole. ■ Some believe his book *The Ordeal of Gilbert Pinfold*, detailing the tribulations of a novelist suffering from hallucinations, to be autobiographical.

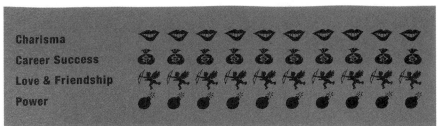

THE INTERESTING

eZ

Self-contained Intense Well-read
Overconfident Moody Diffident

When the *emotional exuberance* of the letter *E* combines with the *zealous* and *zany* letter *Z*, it forms the basis for the *EZ*'s inborn oddities. Few names can match the *EZ* root for sheer originality and funkiness, and these unusual names tend to herald individuals with remarkable personalities.

The *EZ* man is a traveler at heart, and you could find him living anywhere from the wilds of Africa to the lofts of New York City. But just because you know an *EZ* still living in his hometown doesn't mean that he doesn't have a well-developed sense of adventure. For if there's one thing you can always count on from an *EZ*, it's devotion to knowledge and exploration. Name any book to do with science, travel, religion, astrology or culture, and he's either read it, preparing to read it or secretly planning to write it.

As is typical of such erudite souls, *EZ*s love good debates as long as they're not about subjective issues, like who the world's best jazz singer is. But don't worry about offending them; it's virtually impossible to ruffle their feathers with an outrageous statement or controversial opinion. Don't let their absentminded-professor masks fool you into thinking they're one-dimensional—whether they show it or not, there's usually a roiling tumult just beneath the surface.

Ezekiel
Ezra

The *EZ* doesn't search for his career; it tracks him down and ambushes him when he least expects it. But even though things always seem to work out it the long run, *EZ*s sometimes seem to lose faith in the future. In keeping with their sensitivity, there's a paranoid aspect to their personalities that prevents them from fully trusting their own decisions. Part of them believes that everyone else is going to make it while they're going to be left in the dust. And even when they *do* achieve some professional notoriety, they often feel it's just a matter of time before people discover they're really not as capable as they seem.

While it takes the *EZ* a long time to settle into his life's work, it takes him even longer to settle into an intimate relationship. He's a little suspicious about love, and it's a rare *EZ* who has the instinctive faith that's needed to build trust. Given the chance, he'd choose the cool logic of his studies over the unpredictable fires of passion, but he can't hold out forever. When his emotional side finally takes control, he'll grudgingly succumb to the messy tangle of feelings that love entails. The good news is that many partners report being pleasantly surprised on finding that their studious *EZ* is far more carnal than he ever let on.

Ezra Pound Few American poets experience the kind of intense political fallout that was endured by Ezra Pound. On returning home after the Second World War, the giant of the American poetry scene was slapped with a charge of treason for making radio broadcasts on behalf of the fascist Italian government during the war. In a face-saving maneuver by a Justice Department unwilling to air its dirty laundry in public, Ezra was found not guilty by reason of insanity and committed to an asylum for twelve years. ■ His seminal work—which took fifty years to complete—was the encyclopedic poem: *The Cantos*. Begun in 1915, *The Cantos* was 800 pages of Ezra's personal reminiscences, detailing his political, religious and economic influences with metaphors from Greek and Chinese mythology.

F

The Flirtatious

Most Popular Girl's Names

Frances
Florence
Felicia
Faye
Fannie
Flora
Francis
Freda
Faith
Francine

Most Popular Boy's Names

Frank
Fred
Francis
Frederick
Francisco
Floyd
Franklin
Fernando
Felix
Freddie

There was a felicity in the flow of the first four words.

JANE AUSTEN,
Mansfield Park

The letter F is a relatively new addition to the alphabet and only entered the language when the Romans decided they needed a letter to differentiate the sound of a soft and hard V, around 200 BC. In Modern English the delicately pronounced F denotes all things festive, initializing words like fun, flirt, fresh, free will, fond, feast, folksy, friendly, flirtatious, flashy, fine and festoon. ■ Shakespeare was particularly fond of this letter's alliterative qualities and often used it to convey a sense of urgency as in "Fly, father, fly; for all your friends are fled" (*Henry VI*). And when he observed in The Merry Wives of Windsor that "fairies use flowers for their charactery," he paved the way for the letter F to become the banner for the gay lifestyle—flaming, flamboyant, fairy, fruity, fabulous, frolic, fellah, fag, fellatio, feminine, fashionable, fecund, fancy, fetish and fanny. ■ When the F teams up with the letter L, the resulting phoneme is associated with the flashy flapping of a bird's wings, as in flippant, flighty, flowing, flushed, flowery, flee, flap and fly, and when grouped with the letter R, words take on a decidedly frenzied quality, as in frantic, frazzled, freaky, free, frenetic, frivolous, frolic, fresh and frothy. ■ People whose first names begin with an F tend to be faithful and friendly, as borne out by the traditional meaning of the names Felicia and Felicity (happiness), Fidel (faithful), Forbes (prosperous), Frank (a free man), Fred, Fritz and Frieda (peaceful), Fremont (freedom mountain) and Fulbright (very light). ■ With the letter F's flippant overtones, it's not surprising that it doesn't appear on any of the success lists of politics, medicine, money or the arts. ■

Charisma	👄	👄	👄	👄	👄	👄	👄	👄	👄	👄
Career Success	💰	💰	💰	💰	💰	💰	💰	💰	💰	💰
Love & Friendship										
Power										

**Intelligent Sharp Adaptable
Shifty Deceptive Capricious**

When the *flighty, flirtatious* letter *F* (or *PH* phoneme) occurs in the same words as the *brash* and *bold* letter *B* (the symbol of *bellicose belligerence)*, the feminine *F* and the masculine *B* struggle to coexist. This explains why the *FB* combination produces the awkward qualities found in the words: *fumble, fib, feeble, fly-by-night, flub* and *goofball*. The only unambiguous aspect of the *FB* names is their sexual promise: The letter *F* evokes concepts of *fun, feelings* and *fooling around*, while the aggressive *B* backs this up with its sense of assertive action. There's very little suave subtlety to the *FB* personality, just an alluringly sexy character lurking behind a goofy, puppy-dog effervescence.

Fabian
Fabio
Fabiola
Phoebe

Like most people who flaunt an *F* name, *FB*s think of themselves rather highly and are hardly discreet about it. And if it's true that pride comes before a fall, then *FB*s are going to do most of their falling in public. But what might be an embarrassing situation for lesser personalities will sit quite easily with *FB*s, who easily bounce back with their charming and coy charisma. There's something inherently lovable about these flamboyant people, who always manage to convey a sincerity that appeals to the parental emotions of the opposite sex.

*FB*s have few vices, and although they'd never be accused of being profound or sensitive, displaying good-will toward others is an important part of their philosophy. It's not surprising that they integrate themselves into many different social circles, where they can reap the benefits of their extraordinary charms.

Like their loves, careers for *FB*s often take unpredictable turns. They may start out painting houses and end up doing dairy commercials on cable TV. But in retrospect, these twists are simply by-products of their unsettled natures and are no cause for alarm. At the end of the day, *FB*s get to enjoy a series of adventures that most of us only dream of.

In their intimate endeavors, *FB*s' tendency to exaggerate often creates problems. This natural optimism also works against them when they establish impossibly high standards for their relationships, so it's best to take the *FB*'s promises with a grain of salt—or an entire container of Morton's, to play it safe. It's not that they would ever overtly lie, it's just that no one—including *FB*s themselves—can really predict their fickle moods. When *FB*s find their soul mates in a fellow adventurer, the union has a good chance of lasting—at least until "change of heart do us part."

Fabio Lanzoni If someone handed you a business card in the 1990s that read "Professional Hunk," it probably belonged to the barrel-chested romance cover model, Fabio Lanzoni, better known simply as Fabio. ■ Fabio created a mini-empire by appearing on the cover of over five hundred (mostly paperback) formula romance novels. After landing an assortment of trifling television shows and movies (most often playing himself), Fabio tried his hand at writing a romance novel. His book, *Pirate*, which holds the record for the use of the word "turgid," was saturated with literary gems like "her sails unfurled around his mast." ■ In 1999, Fabio won the sympathy of his adoring fans after being hit in the face by a goose while riding a roller coaster. Both Fabio's career and the goose survived.

Charisma	👄	👄	👄	👄	👄	👄	👄	👄	👄	👄
Career Success	💰	💰	💰	💰	💰	💰	💰	💰	💰	
Love & Friendship										
Power										

fl

Giving Sexual Undaunted
Flamboyant Unrealistic Inconsistent

The showy *FL* letter combination is the undisputed icon for all things *flashy* and *flamboyant*, and we see its gaudy effects in words like *flighty, flirtatious, flippant, fluid, flubber, flounce* and *flaunt*. In a similar way, *FL* people aren't exactly known for having their feet planted on the ground; they're much more comfortable with their own rose-colored version of reality. So don't bother consulting an *FL* for insightful advice; it's better to sit back and let the positive energies of these engaging creatures flow over you. And don't try using logic to "set them straight" either, for *FLs* really have no intention of coming down to earth. Strong-willed and idealistic to their core, they approach life with childlike enthusiasm and innocent faith.

But for all their enthusiasm and apparent naïveté, *FL* people have two distinct sides: a sympathetic aspect, which makes them strong and loyal friends, and a happy-go-lucky side, which propels them into uncharted tangents. These competing forces sometimes give them a reputation for being fair-weather friends, and while it's true that their moods change like the tide and can leave a few friends stranded, there's simply no malice anywhere in the *FLs*' hearts. It's just a symptom of their inability

Fallon
Felice
Felicia
Felicita
Felicity
Felipa
Felipe
Felix
Felton
Fidel
Fletcher
Florentino
Flo, Flora
Florence
Florencia
Florencio
Florida
Florine
Flossie
Floyd

sail a straight course in a world that offers so many temptations.

The *FLs*' professional lives are likewise interesting and varied, and they can flit from job to job with relative ease without feeling the need to settle down. While this quirk may cost them financial security in the long term, *FLs* are so versatile that they can find a job at the drop of a hat. It's not unusual to find *FLs* making their living in exotic locations and enjoying their fortuitous encounters with chance and change.

Love comes to the *FL* often, but fleetingly. These fun-loving characters attract suitors like moths to a flambé, but they are up front about their reluctance to be tied down. Sociable as they are, they enjoy being in love (and are very physical in expressing it), but this doesn't mean they're in it for better or worse. If you want to keep your *FL* lover interested, the key is to maintain a high level of spontaneity in your relationship. Once you allow the gloss to wear off, your *FL* will flounce off in search of the next big quest.

It's a nonnegotiable requirement that the *FLs*' partners must be their best friends, and permanent bonding is only possible when mates share the *FL's* addiction for exploration.

Florence Nightingale The horrific sanitary conditions endured by wounded British soldiers during the years of the Crimean War prompted Florence Nightingale to conceive of an entirely new standard for nurses and hospitals. In those days, nurses were considered to be little more than maids, given such tasks as ferrying amputated body parts to the trash and emptying bedpans. ■ Changes began to appear in hospitals worldwide after Florence's innovative techniques noticeably lowered the mortality rates of injured soldiers. Recognition of her life-saving work was universal. Lauded by foreign governments and celebrated by her own, she became the first woman in the history of the British Empire to be awarded the Order of Merit.

THE FRIENDLY fn

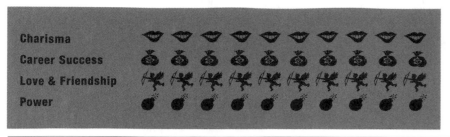

Charisma	👄👄👄👄👄👄👄👄👄👄
Career Success	💰💰💰💰💰💰💰💰💰💰
Love & Friendship	🏹🏹🏹🏹🏹🏹🏹🏹🏹🏹
Power	💣💣💣💣💣💣💣💣💣💣

**Sincere Youthful Soulful
Scattered Codependent Chaotic**

Although the nasally pronounced letter *N* is the symbol for all things *negative* (*no, not, never, nix, nada, nowhere* and *nothing*), when it occurs in words initialized by the *fresh* and *freedom-loving* letter *F*, the result is an impression of laid-back camaraderie. We see these effects in the words *friendly funny, fondly, fanny, fondle, fawning, fancy* and *Feniculi Fenicula*. There's nothing complicated in these *feminine* names and no complex sequence of letters fighting for control. They are simply self-satisfied creatures with an eye for *fun* and just a hint of pessimism.

Having an *FN* as a friend can be quite an ego-booster; they'll always have something positive to say about you. The problem is that sometimes people take advantage of this trait by using the *FN* as a confidante in times of need, then jumping ship when the *FN*s turn to *them* for help. And with the *FN*'s tendency to see the glass half empty, this fickleness in friendship is greeted not with surprise or hurt, but with stoic pessimism. It's difficult to disappoint an *FN*; they expect the worst while quietly hoping for the best.

These sage and philosophical creatures are so accustomed to doling out advice that they are naturally suited to enter the counseling or teaching professions.

Fanny
Fawn
Finn
Fiona

Clients, students and co-workers benefit from their encouraging energies, and even if they display a little gloom once in awhile, it only serves as a reminder that they are human. *FN*s are not particularly academically minded, and it's a rare *FN* who has the self-discipline to make it through medical or law school. But like most people whose name begins with the letter *F*, *FN*s aren't ones to worry much about money. They either have plenty of it, or they have very little need for it.

When it comes to casual relationships, *FN*s often surprise their suitors by emerging from their naïve façades and exhibiting a powerful libido that can knock the socks off an unsuspecting lover. When it comes to more permanent relationships, *FN*s are prone to falling in love and settling down quickly. But because they are not ones to put their eggs in a single basket, potential mates will have to accept sharing them with a wide circle of friends.

Those who marry one of these gregarious creatures should be aware that without sufficient variety in their lives, *FN*s are liable to fall into one of their funks. Mates must learn to balance these unpredictable moods with plenty of romance and the occasional box of chocolates.

Fiona Apple Fiona Apple began playing the piano and writing songs when she was only eight years old. But after suffering from a rape ordeal at the age of twelve, Fiona became emotionally withdrawn. ■ Music became her outlet, allowing her to vent her frustrations and give voice to a psyche that was mature beyond its years. In 1996, Fiona received a two-year contract to work on her debut album, *Tidal*. The album was an immediate success, entering the Billboard 100 while she was opening for Chris Isaak. Fiona explained that she called her album *Tidal* because the music poured out of her like a wave and symbolized the ebb and flow of life. In 1999, Fiona released her second album with a ninety-word title, *When the Pawn . . .* to rave critical

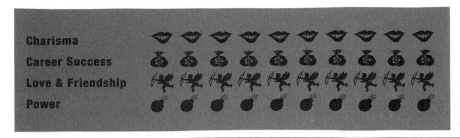

Charisma										
Career Success										
Love & Friendship										
Power										

**Physical Friendly Adaptive
Frazzled Frenzied Distracted**

The letter *F* is the icon of all things *free, flirtatious* and *fun,* and combination with the *romantic* qualities of the *randy, robust* and *racy* letter *R* imbues these names with an ebullient sense of *freshness, freedom, frivolity, fruitfulness, frankness, friskiness* and *friendliness. FR* people have a sense of forward momentum, and it often proves difficult to keep up with their crazy pace as they rush from one rendezvous to another. But somehow *FR*s always seem to have time for their friends, and their top priority is to maintain and nurture their wide circle of acquaintances.

*FR*s are decidedly romantic and spiritual people, who are sensitive to everything that goes on around them. There's very little of the dark side to these people, and the worst thing you could say about them is that they sometimes exhibit a charming case of foot-in-mouth disease. Their blunt mannerisms might cause some consternation among their close companions, but it's unlikely that *FR*s would actually try to hurt someone. In fact, *FR*s are usually puzzled when people react negatively to their frank approaches, for they are people pleasers at heart and can't bear the thought that others might hold them in low regard. This might be a reflection of the *FR*'s inherent vanity, for it could be argued that few people have

*Farrah
Farrell
Fermin
Forrest
Fritz*

such high regard for *FR*s as they have for themselves.

*FR*s sometimes demonstrate a little social awkwardness, particularly when they're out in public without their ubiquitous entourages in tow. But this unease in the presence of strangers certainly isn't an indication that *FR*s are shy in any way. It might have something to do with the fact that reading isn't high on their priority lists, so *FR*s aren't particularly confident about their grasp on current events. So when the conversation swings around to, say a Middle East theme, notice how quickly your *FR* friends will divert the dialogue back to their own zones of interest.

*FR*s can be quite competitive when it comes to their intimate affairs, especially when it comes to negotiating their position in the relationship's power structure. This should not be taken as a sign that *FR*s have to be the stars of their relationships (they will willingly take on a supporting role when they have to), but they simply won't tolerate being an extra. If their involvement isn't going to be appreciated, they'll simply find someone else who values their contributions. All it takes is a little bit of ego-massaging, and partners will be able to bask in the glow of the *FR*s' sunny dispositions for as long as the union lasts.

Farrah Fawcett At her high school in Corpus Christi, Texas, Farrah Fawcett was voted Most Beautiful four years running, and at the height of her fame in the 1970s, she became the most recognized blonde in the world. ■ In 1973 she married the *Six-Million Dollar Man* (Lee Majors) and was cast as Jill Munroe in *Charlie's Angels*—the role for which she is best remembered despite doing only one season. At one point, her signature feathered-layer hairdo became all the rage, and millions of adolescent boys hung her poster on their walls. ■ In 1984 Farrah was nominated for an Emmy for her role as a battered wife who kills her husband in *The Burning Bed,* but she remains best remembered for that shock of blond hair and impossible set of pearly whites.

frd

Intuitive Colorful Verbal
Superficial Volatile Caustic

Charisma										
Career Success										
Love & Friendship										
Power										

When the *flirtatious* letter *F* gets together with the *randy, racy* and *romantic* letter *R*, it creates the unmistakably refreshing and breezy combination found in the words *friendly, frolic, frenzy, fresh, frank, free, frothy, frilly, frisky* and *frivolous*. On the other hand, the letter *D* is the definitive letter of *dignified discipline,* and its upstanding forthrightness contributes an air of respectability to these otherwise flighty names. *FRD*s who choose the *IE* or *Y* ending (like *Freddy*) tend to project a more playful persona, while names that incorporate the dynamic letter *K* (*Fredrick, Fredricka*), exhibit a more forceful aspect.

But *all FRD*s know how to have a good time and love nothing better than entertaining and being entertained. These restless people have an unusual mélange of enthusiasm and cynicism, which acts as a magnet to their eclectic group of hangers-on. The *FRD*s' trademark dry sense of humor often leaves people to speculate a little uneasily about whether they really mean what they say, but *FRD*s aren't likely to give up on their edgy wit. Keeping people off balance gives them a sense of control (and is fun besides).

These are multitalented and keenly intelligent spirits, and *FRD*s can be found in a wide variety of careers. This is in spite of the fact that *FRD*s tend to perform poorly in formal education environments. Simply put, *FRD*s hate school. But this doesn't mean that *FRD*s aren't bright or ambitious, and when sufficiently motivated, will prove to be reliable and diligent employees. They'll mostly eschew manual labor in favor of white-collar jobs, but with their tendency to activate their tongues before engaging their sharp minds, they are sometimes written off as flippant or inconsequential. But as long as *FRD*s are made to feel that their contributions are appreciated, they'll knuckle down and do what's needed for the team. Since they enjoy intellectual challenges, they also make ideal lawyers and arbitrators.

When it comes to their romancing styles, *FRD*s often prove to be somewhat erratic. The problem stems from their habit for evaluating potential relationships based on physical attraction alone, ignoring issues of compatibility and shared values. And just because *FRD*s may be smothering and obsessive when they're in love, be aware that they can fall out of love without any prior symptoms. If you're dating an *FRD*, don't bother looking for signs that their attention may be wandering; just make sure that you're occupying their time with plenty of interesting events and copious physical attention.

Federico
Ferdinand
Fernanda
Fernando
Fred
Freda
Freddy
Frederick
Fredericka
Fredia
Fredrick
Frida

Federico Fellini When the film *Luci del varietà* first played in Rome in 1950, critics raved about the fresh new voice that had arrived on the filmmaking scene. ■ Federico's dark style reflected his brooding upbringing in fascist Italy, where, at the age of seven he had run away from boarding school to join the circus. Many of his subsequent movies mirrored his love for circus life. ■ His wry and affectionate commentary on human nature garnered his 1954 movie *La Strada* an Oscar Award and made a star out of his actress wife, Giulietta Masina. ■ Although *Le Notti di Cabiria* won him a second Oscar, his 1960 film *La Dolce Vita* was his first real commercial success, sparking a roar of protest from the Catholic church for its religious cynicism.

THE WELL-ROUNDED *frn*

Charisma	💋 💋 💋 💋 💋 💋 💋 💋 💋 💋
Career Success	💰 💰 💰 💰 💰 💰 💰 💰 💰
Love & Friendship	😇 😇 😇 😇 😇 😇 😇 😇 😇
Power	💣 💣 💣 💣 💣 💣 💣 💣 💣 💣

Intelligent Intuitive Popular
Anxious Meddling Hidden Motives

The *FR* letter combination is the source of the *frenetic* sense of *freshness* found in the words *frolic, frenzy, free, frank, frothy, frilly, frisky* and *frivolous*. On the other hand, the letter *N* is the definitive icon for all things *negative* (*no, not, never, nada, nix, naught* and *nowhere*), and it's not surprising that when these three letters get together, they color words with vigorous pessimism: *frenzy, frantic, foghorn, affront, confront, firebrand, inferno, flagrant* and *forbidden*. *FRN* people tend to display these same intense qualities and find themselves walking a line between their positive, fun-loving sides and the nagging sense that something is about punish them for having too much fun.

*FRN*s tend to set themselves apart from the rest of the world and are very choosy about with whom they socialize. This behavior is less a symptom of elitism than it is a sign that they're marching to a different drumbeat. Fortunately, this turns out to be a good thing most of the time, because many *FRN*s end up rising to the tops of their fields. People admire the seeming ease with which *FRN*s follow their hearts, but don't realize just how much they agonize over every major decision they make.

Ideal careers for *FRN* personalities include those that give them the freedom to make their own choices.

Faron
Fern
Fran
Frances
Francesca
Francine
Francis
Francoise
Freeman

While they do their best work in solitary pursuits, they're not averse to working on a team, provided that they still have an opportunity to claim individual glory. Because their industrious minds are so full of new ideas, any job that can tap their creative energies will be a welcome bonus. But once an idea has been born, *FRN*s often lose interest in their projects and seem quite happy to turn them over to others for implementation.

Mating with *FRN*s can be tough, for they tend to be loners (or need regular doses of solo time). And since partnerships are not on the top of their priority lists, they'll take their own sweet time before settling on mates. While some of them are better off remaining single, there's one thing you can be sure of: when an *FRN* does commit, he or she will never go back on his word. They may be loners, but they're loyal to a fault and appreciate a supportive partnership. So as long as their partners make the effort to balance their occasional anxiety attacks with positive reinforcement, harmony will reign.

If they choose parenthood, of course *FRN*s will be devoted to their children. But if kids aren't in their stars, it's not going to unsettle these independent spirits. Their nurturing instincts are just as easily sated by puppies, kittens or goldfish.

Frances McDormand When film directors want to cast an actress for an unglamorous and substantive character role, Frances McDormand is usually the first one they call. ■ The wife of Joel Coen of Coen Brothers fame (*Raising Arizona*; *Barton Fink*; *O Brother, Where Art Thou?*), Frances's film debut in *Blood Simple* initiated a long-term collaboration with the brothers. She married Joel the same year the movie came out. ■ Frances has appeared in many films, first coming to prominence in *Raising Arizona*, and won a Tony Award nomination for her performance in *A Streetcar Named Desire*. She also picked up an Oscar nomination in 1988 for her role in *Mississippi Burning*. ■ In 1996, she took home the Best Actress Oscar for her memorable performance as the very pregnant Sheriff Marge Gunderson in *Fargo*.

THE FORTHRIGHT
frnk

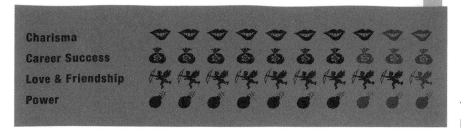

Charisma	💋	💋	💋	💋	💋	💋	💋	💋	💋	💋
Career Success	💰	💰	💰	💰	💰	💰	💰	💰	💰	💰
Love & Friendship										
Power										

Truthful Outspoken Charismatic Blunt Frazzled Dark

When the *flirtatious* letter *F* gets together with the *randy*, *racy* and *romantic* letter *R*, it creates a combination that is undeniably refreshing and breezy. We can see these effects in the words *frolic, frenzy, fresh, frank, free, frothy, frilly, frisky* and *frivolous*. However, the sobering effects of the letter *N* and the letter *K* (or hard *C*) stand in sharp relief to the *friendly FR* combination. For the *N* is the symbol of all things *negative* (*no, not, never, nada, nix, naught* and *nowhere*), and the *K* sound is the icon of aggressive action (*kick, cutting, crash, kill, kidnap, knife* and *knuckle*). This is why the *NK* sound terminates so many discordant words: *skunk, dank, tank, spank, prank, stunk, junk, clank, flunk* and *punk*. Some women (like *Frankie* and *Franky*) take the edge off the *NK* sound with the feminizing *IE* or *Y*, giving their names a distinctly more *spunky, kinky* and *slinky* flavor.

All told, *FRNK*s are the sort of confident, self-assured, and outgoing types who get a kick out of just being alive. But few people would deny that there's also a dark side to these complex souls, whether it takes the form of control issues, pessimism, mood swings or even a weakness for chemical dependency. Happily, no matter how this dark side manifests itself, people are so strongly drawn to *FRNK*s' ebullient spirit that they'll

Francesca
Francesco
Frank
Frankie
Franklin

often give them more leeway than they deserve. *FRNK* appreciate this kind of unconditional acceptance and return the favor by being correspondingly devoted to their friends.

Business and corporate pursuits integrate well into the *FRNK* personality, but *only* if they're given the freedom to ferment their creative juices. Perhaps this is why so many *FRNK*s are drawn to the arts, whether to acting, music, cooking or writing. Although *FRNK*s are sometimes accused of having their heads in the clouds, they more than make up for it with their frenetic energy and charming appeal. *FRNK*s work well under pressure, which is a good thing since they are often responsible for putting themselves into the stressful situations in the first place. Consequently, *FRNK*s suffer a little more anxiety than the rest of the population.

*FRNK*s aren't renowned for their cool logic, so it's best for them to live alongside someone who's relatively organized and calm. *FRNK*s' combative style of communication can be quite intimidating, and lovers may find themselves to be pushed around unless they take strong stands on important issues. Don't let the *FRNK*s' growling manner discourage you, though—they will bark just as loudly in your defense.

Frank Sinatra Known in entertainment circles as the Chairman of the Board and to everyone else as Ol' Blue Eyes, Frank Sinatra was a mega-international star who made men jealous and made ladies swoon. With his understated crooning style that everyone imitated but none could duplicate, Frank starred in countless films, romanced the beauty queens of his day and (allegedly) counted the members of the Mafia among his friends. ■ Frank's father was a Hoboken fireman who gave his son his street smarts, and his mother was an iron-willed Italian-born matriarch. (Word on the street was that she performed backroom abortions for girls in trouble.) ■ Having never finished high school, Frank become nothing less than a legend, putting his own inimitable touches on such songs as "My Way," "New York, New York," "Chicago," "The Lady is a Tramp" and "Strangers in the Night."

140

fth

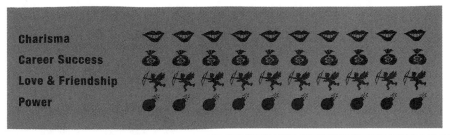

Charisma										
Career Success										
Love & Friendship										
Power										

The letter *F* is the icon of all things *friendly, flirtatious, fresh, folksy* and *fun-loving,* and when it encounters the high-minded *TH* phoneme, some interesting traits begin to emerge. The *TH* combination is responsible for the spiritually uplifting sounds found in the words *truth, theological, thankful, thoughtful, thorough, theory, hearth, health, thespian* and *theater.* So it's not surprising that the *FTH* names evoke the moral principles of the words *faith, father* and *Haftorah* (the holy book of the Jews). *FTH* people drift placidly through life with a reserved air and long-suffering expressions. While they undoubtedly have the strength of character to ensure success, they are not particularly competitive or highly motivated when it comes to financial issues.

These are people whose characters are built on rock, and with this kind of inherent stability, many *FTH*s find themselves acting as pillars of support for their wide circle of family and friends. Their career choices tend to reflect this quiet constancy, and it's common to find *FTH*s working as teachers, librarians, or in public-service positions. When *FTH*s allow their creative sides to come into play, it usually takes the form of writing, cooking, music or literature. But no matter

Faith
Firth

how they choose to express themselves, you can be sure their art will reflect their conservative and moralistic bent.

You can count on *FTH*s for honesty and straight shooting; these aren't the sort to beat around the bush when it comes to resolving conflict. Though it's true they are good listeners, they can also talk up a storm with the best of them, and their first instincts are to jump in with extensive advice (they *love* telling people what to do), although they might sometimes be better served by standing aside and letting people figure things out in their own time.

Provided their feelings are being reciprocated, *FTH*s will be exceptionally devoted friends and lovers. So if you're not the type who appreciates the value of commitment, it's best to step aside and let them find what they need. And if you *do* break up, chances are you'll be the one doing the dirty work. *FTH*s don't like getting their hands dirty and have a tendency to withdraw when it comes to awkward emotional issues. But when happily ensconced in a reciprocal relationship, she will be *very* family-oriented, and her home will be a comfortable haven for family and any strays that come along.

Faith Hill With a face that could have made her a model, Faith Hill instead became one of those rare singers who successfully crossed the music-genre divide from country-western into pop. ■ Growing up in Mississippi, Faith sang at every opportunity—rodeos, local fairs, birthday parties and (some say) bar mitzvahs. By the time Faith was nineteen, she had wound her way to Nashville, where she became a secretary in a music-publishing company. ■ While singing in a café, Faith was spotted by a Warner Brothers agent, and her 1994 debut album, *Take Me as I Am*, sold an astonishing two million copies. ■ Her second album was released in the midst of a grueling tour schedule and a marriage to touring partner Tim McGraw. Her third album, *Faith*, earned her five Country Music Awards.

THE WISTFUL

fy

Charisma	💋	💋	💋	💋	💋	💋	💋	💋	💋	💋
Career Success	💰	💰	💰	💰	💰	💰	💰	💰	💰	💰
Love & Friendship	🏹	🏹	🏹	🏹	🏹	🏹	🏹	🏹	🏹	🏹
Power	💣	💣	💣	💣	💣	💣	💣	💣	💣	💣

Ethereal Whimsical Intuitive
Disconnected Non-committal Preachy

The *feisty, fresh* and *freedom-loving* letter *F* gets a feminizing kick when its words end with the playful letter *Y*. This explains why the *FY* names embody the spirit of fanciful whimsy we find in the words *fairy, fancy, family, festivity, finery, flirty, fluffy* and *fussy*. These are women who are prone to flights of fancy and shooting off on unexpected tangents.

*FY*s enjoy being in the company of the opposite sex, and men seem to take pleasure in being around them as well. While she may not be the actual initiator in these personal encounters, the typical *FY* has an uncanny sense of other people's motives, and if you want to get to know her better, you'd better be prepared to be totally honest about your intentions.

*FY*s have a deep sense of empathy that they lug around like a heavy burden. Though not particularly melancholy, they *are* sensitive to life's injustices and feel deeply for anyone who's suffering. It's not surprising, then, that *FY*s gravitate toward jobs that allow them to express their compassionate sides, whether in the medical fields, teaching, coaching or simply being mothers. *FY*s derive a great deal of satisfaction from the camaraderie that the workplace brings, and these are team

Fay
Faye

players in the truest sense of the word. This team sprit extends to their relationships, in which they'll go out of their way to be their partner's best friend.

Like most people whose names begin with the letter *F*, *FY*s are going to be among the top wage earners in their social groups. And it's a good thing, too, because although most people don't know it, *FY*s have very expensive tastes. Nothing gaudy, mind you—they have a hankering for the sort of quality items that will last a lifetime. It might be an expensive couch, bed or chest, but is rarely a sports car or an extravagant fur coat.

If problems do crop up in an *FY*'s relatively idyllic life, it's likely going appear in her relationship, where she has a habit of lending a sympathetic ear to more than one suitor at a time. When forced to make a choice, she'll often vacillate wildly, to the chagrin of her potential partners. But the *FY* in love is a force to be reckoned with. Romance infuses her with a wild-eyed energy, and she's not going to listen to anyone but her heart. So if you're an *FY*'s best friend who doesn't approve of her intimate choices, stand by with Kleenex in hand and let nature run its course.

Faye Dunaway Back in the seventies, Faye Dunaway was the first choice for directors looking for a competent and beautiful leading lady. But time and tastes have not been kind to the star, who has been reduced to accepting roles she would not have even considered a few years ago. Faye was even dropped as the lead in the Broadway musical *Sunset Boulevard* after director Andrew Lloyd Webber snubbed her for Glenn Close. ■ First coming to international prominence for her performance in *Bonnie and Clyde* in 1967, Faye went on to win an Oscar for her role as a hard-bitten television executive in *Network*. ■ With over thirty motion picture credits—including *The Thomas Crown Affair* and *Chinatown*—under her belt, Faye's recent TV work has received a lukewarm response.

142

Most Popular Girl's Names

Gloria
Gladys
Grace
Gail
Geraldine
Gertrude
Gina
Georgia
Glenda
Gwendolyn

Most Popular Boy's Names

George
Gary
Gregory
Gerald
Glenn
Gordon
Greg
Glen
Gilbert
Gene

The Letter of Benign Leadership

I thank thee, Moon, for shining now so bright;
For by thy gracious, golden, glittering gleams…

—WILLIAM SHAKESPEARE,
Midsummer Night's Dream

The G is a direct descendant of the letter C, and although it retains some of the C's hotheadedness, its softer articulation imbues it with a more benevolent and thoughtful quality. To put it another way, G is a mature C, which may account for its association with God, glory, grace, good, governor and gubernatorial—derived from the Latin gubernator (helmsman). ■ G men and women embody the G's leadership characteristics tempered by a desire to serve others. In the Cabala and other mystical Hebrew writings, the name for the letter G is Gimmel, which symbolizes a rich man running after a poor man to give him charity. So it's not surprising that the traditional meaning of names beginning with the G reflect its gallant and gracious qualities: Sir Galahad, Gareth (gentle), Gaylord (brave), Gerald (warrior), Gilda (servant of god), Gallagher (eager helper), Godfrey (God's peace), Grace (of God) and Gloria (glory). ■ The G can be pronounced in two distinctly different ways: hard as in go-getter and grand, or soft and reflective as in genuflection, gentle, genial and genuine. ■ With their ability to lead and influence others, G people enjoy above-average success in business and politics, but are found at the bottom of the list when it comes to the arts and entertainment.

Charisma	💋💋💋💋💋💋💋💋💋💋
Career Success	💰💰💰💰💰💰💰💰💰💰
Love & Friendship	🏹🏹🏹🏹🏹🏹🏹🏹🏹🏹
Power	💣💣💣💣💣💣💣💣💣💣

Dependable Loyal Cheerful
Shallow Self-serving Cranky

Even though the G names are dominated by the *gruff* letter G (found in the words *grim, grievous, glory, governor, God* and *gumption*), whenever a name ends with a vowel sound, it has the effect of eliminating all traces of vanity and indulgence. This is why the names *Gay, Gia* and *Gaye* resonate with such an attractive combination of humor and strength, while the names *Gaige* and *Gage* (both recent additions to the list of top one thousand boys' names) are considerably more masculine in their appeal.

People are naturally drawn to the G's unassuming good-natured camaraderie. But because being friendly isn't necessarily the same as being faithful, those who bear G names must fight against preconceived notions that they are self-indulgent heartbreakers. It might be true that some deserve this reputation (for young Gs often *do* take advantage of their appeal to the opposite sex), but it would be unfair to characterize them as selfish. These are people-pleasers at heart, whose lives are dictated by what others might think of them. Under pressure to live up these expectations, Gs often have a tendency to bite off more than they can chew.

Careerwise, Gs don't have to struggle to find jobs. Most employers appreciate their good-natured knack for

Gage
Gaige
Gay
Gia
Guy
Gaye

being team players, and they are capable of making a living in anything from construction work to accounting. But many secretly yearn to own their own businesses, and they usually succeed because of their knack for inspiring others to do their best. Often, for the sake of doing the "right thing," Gs may stay in jobs that don't completely satisfy them. If nothing else, Gs have a well-developed sense of ethics and will err on the side of loyalty when it comes to staying on their boss's good side. Sooner or later, though, Gs will figure out that they're really not much use to anyone if they're not happy with themselves, and will then assert their desire to rebel. This is why such a high percentage of Gs end up working for themselves as small-business owners or consultants.

Casual dating with such a reliable person would seem like a cinch . . . except that it's not. The more intimate you get with a G, the more you'll sense their need to control the minutiae of the relationship. Still, determined Gs will eventually burrow their way into intimate relationships and thrive on the mutual give-and-take of exclusive partnerships. If there's any danger to this hunger for intimacy, it's their tendency to enter into premature commitments that both parties wind up regretting.

Guy Pearce As a fresh face in the growing field of Australian actors in Hollywood, Guy Pearce is a promising standout. His classically chiseled looks and acting versatility have catapulted him to the top of the list of the film industry's most sought-after. ■ Not that Guy's life was always easy. His father was killed in a plane crash when he was only eight years old, leaving his mother to care for him and his sister on her own. ■ After acknowledging that his slight build might stand in the way of his future career as an actor, Guy hit the gym and won the Mr. Junior Victoria bodybuilding award in high school. His first acting gig was on an Australian soap opera; from there it was a quick climb to success as a brooding memory-challenged man obsessed with avenging his wife's death in the thriller *Memento*.

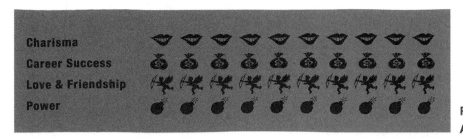

Charisma										
Career Success										
Love & Friendship										
Power										

Reasoned Capable Loyal
Abrasive Controlling Distracted

There's something rough and ready about the *GB* letter combination that stems from the union of the *gruff* letter *G* and the *belligerently bellicose* letter *B*. These two letters are responsible for the physicality in words like *rugby, arguably, vagabond* and *goblin.* This is why, with the exception of the masculine name *Gabe,* the aggressive connotations of these names are offset with the *rosy* tones of the *romantic* letter *R* and the *lyrically loving* letter *L.* The *RL* combination is responsible for the feminine spirit found in words like *pearl, whirl, girl, twirl* and *swirl.* The name *Gabby,* with its consciously diminutive high-frequency *Y,* escapes the full authority of the *GB* and suggests a blithely joyous spirit. All told, the incongruousness of the *GB* names suggest people with complex motivations and well-balanced emotions.

    *GB*s are great believers in destiny and will even sacrifice their personal relationships if it means they can follow their stars. But although their friends and family believe that *GB*s are destined for greatness, they will have a hard time convincing the *GB*s themselves. For *GB*s don't define success in the conventional way. To them, it's usually about fulfilling their lifelong hunger for adventure and exploration: "The

Gabby
Gabe
Gabriel
Gabriella
Gabrielle

one who dies with the most passport stamps, wins."

    These individuals don't have jobs; they have missions. *GB*s might find their calling as fishing guides on a remote Alaskan river or as Peace Corps volunteers in Africa, but their careers will usually revolve around some form of personal discovery: perhaps in the realm of medicine, teaching or counseling. Still, the actual work matters less than the opportunity to learn lessons. Any business would jump at the chance to have a *GB* in their customer service or human resources department, for with their innate understanding of human nature, they have that rare knack for making others feel important.

    While *GB*s may be emotionally rock-solid, they're the first to recognize that they're not impenetrable. Proving reluctant to sacrifice even the *prospect* of an opportunity for new discoveries, *GB*s conduct their love affairs with cautious foresight. Love partners will be measured against a list of qualities that the *GB* has squirreled away since second grade, and it's unlikely that they'll fall head over heels without having carefully considered the ramifications. But finding someone who can actually live up to the *GB*'s idealistic expectations is another story entirely. Ultimately they will have to settle for a mere human.

Gabriel Byrne Gabriel Byrne's acting career was almost as an afterthought. At the age of twelve, he had left home to make his way to an English seminary, where he was later expelled for smoking in a graveyard. ■ His next venture found him installing eyeballs at a teddy-bear factory. Not surprisingly, the job failed to ignite his passions, and he quit his job to go to college, where he studied archeology and phonetics. He also briefly taught Spanish at an all-girl's school, and slyly admits that it taught him a good deal more than college ever did. ■ Gabriel drew on his own experiences in *Stigmata* and *End of Days,* in which he played a priest and Satan, respectively. He does not reveal to which character he most closely relates.

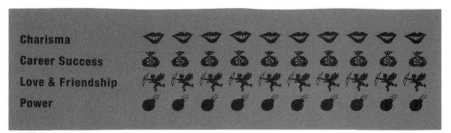

Charisma	😗 😗 😗 😗 😗 😗 😗 😗 😗 😗
Career Success	💰 💰 💰 💰 💰 💰 💰 💰 💰 💰
Love & Friendship	🦁 🦁 🦁 🦁 🦁 🦁 🦁 🦁 🦁 🦁
Power	💣 💣 💣 💣 💣 💣 💣 💣 💣

**Impetuous Sociable Animated
Preoccupied Thoughtless Ditzy**

Whenever the letters *G* and *L* occur together in names, they tend to remind us of the *glitzy* qualities found in the words *gleam, glossy, glamour, glimmer, glib* and *glow*. Perhaps this explains why those whose names who fall into this category are so often described as having such demonstrative and relaxed personalities. *GLs* are people who are drawn to the spotlight and relish the attention they get from anyone who'll listen. If a *GL* actually had the time to come up with a motto, it would have to be "all the world's a stage."

It's hard to pin down the source of the *GL's* outgoing effervescence, but many believe it stems from a hunger for attention. But whether or not it's a reflection of neediness, their frequent hogging of the limelight often proves draining to their close friends. Still, once *GLs* feel that people are responding to them, they'll calm down enough to reveal their intricate emotional workings.

GLs are people-pleasers par excellence. They rarely forget someone's face or name if they think they might meet them again, and never fail to send birthday or Christmas cards weeks before the event. And lest you think this is just another cry for attention, consider that *GLs* are simply uncommonly loyal and faithful. They're

Gail
Gala
Galilea
Gayla
Gil
Gilbert
Gilberte
Gilberto

also interesting to have around because they have so much to offer in terms of insights into how the universe really works: *GLs* consider themselves students of life and spend a great deal of their free time just pondering.

The *GLs'* career choices are ruled by their creative sides. While these job-selections may not always be financially prudent, *GLs* are quite happy to live on beans and noodles if it means having the freedom to do as they please. Whatever their chosen careers, *GLs* are likely to perform them with the verve that characterizes their existence—unless, that is, they get worn down by routine. *GLs* have a strong distaste for predictability, and when trapped in jobs without sufficient stimulation, are prone to becoming bored and ineffective.

When partnered with the right person, the *GL* will prove to be an attentive mate whose spontaneous affections add an element of freshness to any relationship. However, the *GL's* impatience will rear its moody little head when it can't have its own way, and any mate who gives a centimeter may lose a kilometer in the process. Marrying a *GL* doesn't set the future in stone, either, for these incorrigible extroverts are capable of easily forging new ties at any time. It's all about the *GL's* other motto: "till monotony us do part."

Gail Devers As the winner of two track and field gold medals at the Atlanta Olympic Games, Gail Devers was the odds-on favorite at the Olympics in Seoul, South Korea. But Gail was struggling in her training for Seoul with what she believed to be exhaustion from overtraining. As her symptoms mounted—migraines, insomnia, dizzy spells and vision loss—Gail learned that she had developed Graves' disease. ■ The debilitating chronic thyroid disorder left her in excruciating pain and forced her to discontinue her training. At one point, doctors even thought they might have to amputate both of her feet. ■ That's why everyone was astonished when, a year and a half later, Gail won her first gold medal in the 100-meter sprint at the Barcelona Olympics, landing the title of World's Fastest Woman.

Charisma										
Career Success										
Love & Friendship										
Power										

Passionate Impulsive Dedicated Impatient Picky Restless

Whenever two phonemes with radically different influences appear in a name, the resulting individual typically possesses a set of starkly contrasting personality traits. This is particularly true of the *GLD* names, where the *glamorous GL* phoneme hints at a bright and active person through words like *gleaming, glossy, glitter, glare, glitzy* and *glint*, while the *darkly dignified* letter *D* anchors them with a touch of sobriety. And those with the good fortune to have names that end on an *IE* or *Y* sound (like *Goldie*) take on an added feminine playfulness that often proves irresistible.

All *GLD*s exhibit a playful aura, and even in their darker moods, their trademark lightness-of-being percolates through. With their seemingly inexhaustible supply of enthusiasm, some of the *GLD*s' friends might even be tempted to ask them to "cheer-down" a little bit. Not that it would help, mind you; they'll never miss an opportunity to share their glass-half-full point of view, whether or not it's welcome. One criticism to which *GLD*s are often subject is that they're too full of surprises. Just as you think they're heading downhill, you'll find them marching to the top without you. And don't think that *GLD*s are unhappy with their ability to catch people with the occasional head fake; it's a source of great internal amusement for them.

Gilda
Gaylord
Glady
Gladys
Glayds
Golda
Goldie

*GLD*s often gravitate toward careers that reward their optimism: particularly sales, teaching and personnel management. But no matter what job they end up doing, they can be counted on to brighten their work environments with positive reinforcement, even if it means supervising a roomful of screaming children. Since *GLD*s secretly crave a place in the sun, perhaps the most fitting environments for them are those in which they have the spotlight all to themselves. So if your *GLD* friend expresses ambivalence for performing karaoke on stage, don't be surprised if you have to drag them off at the end of the night.

*GLD*s appreciate intellectual stimulation as well, so those who hope to capture their heart will have to appeal to both their playful *and* rational sides. Courtship will be a playful affair with few restrictions on inventive physical relations, but don't expect any breakthroughs too early on in the relationship. As impetuous as they might be in their daily lives, *GLD*s are quite cautious about surrendering their autonomy—accounting for why so many *GLD*s delay having children. Once they tie the knot, *GLD*s aren't going to make many demands, but they will expect absolute dedication from their mates. The favor will always be returned with corresponding loyalty and unconditional affection.

Goldie Hawn It could be that every blonde joke ever told has been inspired by one of Goldie Hawn's characters. As the accepted queen of ditz, her list of film credits, awards and achievements would make for a complete novella, while her cute face and perky screen presence belies a surprisingly canny professional producer and deal maker. ∎ Goldie, who describes herself as a "Jewish Buddhist," makes an annual pilgrimage to India and practices daily meditations in her "India Room" in the same home in which her Oscar statuette reposes—perhaps in a nod to the dual religions of simplicity and glamour. ∎ It took Goldie three attempts at marriage before settling into a twenty-year relationship with her common-law husband, Kurt Russell.

gln

Charisma										
Career Success										
Love & Friendship										
Power										

Loyal Attentive Long-suffering
Bullheaded Pushy Preachy

When the *growling* letter *G* combines with the *loving*, *laughing* letter *L*, it reflects the *glowing* aspects found in the words *gleam, glamour, glitz, glory* and *gladness*. When this *GL* phoneme occurs in the same name as the somewhat *negative* letter *N*, the upshot is an outgoing, exuberant individual with a distinctly shadowy edge to his or her personality.

Self-control is important to the *GLN*, whose emotional river runs deep. But since most people aren't going to be allowed to drink from that river, few realize how much is going on beneath the surface of the *GLN's* blasé currents. This suits them just fine. But once you prove to them that you're trustworthy, they'll let you in on their little secrets. Otherwise, all they will ask is that you give them the same level of respect that they give you.

Did someone mention conflict? When it comes to discord, *GLNs* are experts on the subtle sarcastic comment, and a not-so-subtle-in-your-face staredown. They can be intractably stubborn when they feel they are being taken advantage of—or, worse yet, being taken for granted. Their tenacity usually pays off, too, either by driving off unwanted suitors or by conditioning their casual friends to maintain a deferential distance.

Galina
Gaylene
Gaylon
Gillian
Glenda
Glenn
Glenna
Glinda
Glynn

Still, most of us who have a casual *GLN* friend in our lives find them to be easygoing and unassuming. And this suits *us* just fine. We get to have wonderfully stimulating conversations about everything from art to science to philosophy, while we don't have to be burdened with the heavier emotional aspects of a relationship. But those who dig into their underground wells will uncover a comrade-in-arms whose uncommon loyalty forms the basis of a lifelong friendship. You'll wonder what you ever did without them.

Like most *G*-named people, *GLNs* have the political instincts to succeed in high-pressure careers, but if it were up to them, they'd choose a job with some form of creative outlet. And although money is rarely their driving force in their job choices, they are pragmatic enough to make a stink when they're not being appropriately rewarded.

In their relationships, the *GLNs'* doggedness may result in bruised feelings here and there, but when the dust settles, they'll prove more than willing to take the first step in making up. Even though you might have to take your licks, you'll never be in doubt as to where their affections lie.

Glenn Close Up-and-coming actresses could take pointers from the success of Glenn Close, whose once-obscure career took off after her portrayal of a psychotic lover in *Fatal Attraction*. In a single motion picture, Glenn went from being a forgettable "nice girl" actress to the paragon of feminine obsession, becoming every man's nightmare and many women's secret alter ego. ■ Since then, the public has had an uneasy affection for Glenn; she's beautiful, talented and smart as hell, but any actress who could boil a bunny alive surely has a few issues. ■ Glenn ultimately proved how difficult it is to escape the typecasting that comes with being Hollywood's best-known psychotic bitch, and was the obvious choice for Disney's *101 Dalmatians*, in which she played arch-villain Cruella De Vil.

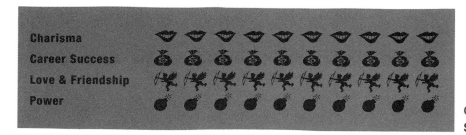

Charisma	👄👄👄👄👄👄👄👄👄👄
Career Success	💰💰💰💰💰💰💰💰💰💰
Love & Friendship	🦅🦅🦅🦅🦅🦅🦅🦅🦅
Power	💣💣💣💣💣💣💣💣💣

THE ROYAL glr

Graceful Dignified Generous
Self-centered Impatient Spoiled

The *glamorous* and *glorious GLR* names display all the *gleaming, glowing, glamorous, glittering, glitzy* qualities of the *GL* phoneme, colored by the *romantic* influence of the *royal* letter *R*, which lends a somewhat *rakish* essence. *GLR* people are certainly endowed with more than their fair share of fashion sense, and carry themselves with style and grace.

Moreover, *GLR*s manage to be dignified without being intimidating—charming others by making them feel important despite their own "obvious superiority." Many *GLR*s are accompanied by an entourage of doting admirers, and as long as you pay them the homage they believe they deserve, you too can count yourself as a member of the *GLR*s' court. *GLR*s aren't likely to become professional athletes. In fact, they aren't likely to become anything that involves any sweating at all. Their version of keeping in shape has less to do with pumping iron than it does with going power-shopping.

If you know any *GLR*s, you're probably familiar with their mysterious way of ending up at the top of their chosen professions. This could be anything from retail sales to rocket science, but like most people with a *G* name, they are natural politicians, who are well suited

Gloria
Glory
Guillermo

for any job that involves schmoozing. It's not that they're particularly driven, however—they just seem to know which buttons to push and with whom to associate in order to get where they want to go. Subtlety is part of their secret, and their easygoing nature hides an intent that only becomes apparent *after* they've achieved their goals.

*GLR*s don't like to be bothered much with other people's messy emotional issues; they're much too busy being the sovereign of their own affairs. So if it's just sympathy you're looking for, don't waste the *GLR*s' time unless you want further rejection. However, if it's guidance or advice you need, then *GLR*s (who love having their opinions polled) are the go-to people.

Marriage to a *GLR* can be an uplifting experience. But once someone has landed this noble creature (or typically the other way around), they'd be advised to cater to his or her romantic notions of marriage if they expect the *GLR* to hang around. Once *GLR*s' partners figure out that flowers, kind gestures and unreminded anniversaries are part of their courtly duties, they can expect a reciprocal royal treatment from these gracious souls.

Gloria Swanson Gloria Swanson was a woman for her times and filled the transition era between silent films and sound. She was also among the first to adapt to the changing roles of women on screen. ■ Gloria knew her place in the world and played her part with alacrity. Though she had a substantial stint in silent films, she is perhaps best known for her Oscar-nominated role as Norma Desmond in 1950's *Sunset Boulevard*, delivering the legendary line: "All right, Mr. DeMille, I'm ready for my close-up." ■ But acting wasn't Gloria's only creative outlet, and she enjoyed moderate success as a sculptress and painter. ■ Gloria also found time for six marriages and seemed to have a new man in tow for every phase of her long and successful life.

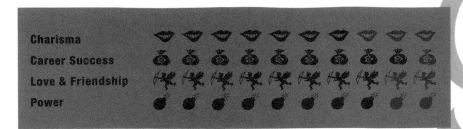

Charisma										
Career Success										
Love & Friendship										
Power										

gn

Giving Fun-loving Truthful
Unpredictable Blunt Gullible

When a name begins with the *soft* pronunciation of the letter *G* (as in *genuflect, genteel* and *genuine*), and is also colored by the *nurturing* qualities of the letter *N*, it suggests an authentically *generous* and *genial* individual. However, the letter *N* is also associated with *negativity*—as in *no, nonsense, not, never* and *naah*—so while *GN* people may exude an altruistic spirit, there's an element of dark mystery that underlies their motivations. If the *GN* were a drink, he or she would be a gin and tonic: effervescent and bubbly, but with an intoxicating kick.

*GN*s love to laugh and can't seem to enjoy themselves unless everyone around them is laughing as well. They'll call on their natural vitality to help them become the life of the party, and succeed so well that it's nigh unthinkable to have a social event without them. But although they are almost always surrounded with people who share their party-animal bent, they'll limit their lifelong intimacies to a select few.

The impish *GN*s cherish the element of surprise. Nothing is too unusual or far-out to try, especially when it comes to their travels, where they'll usually end up in funky, nontouristy locations to get to know the locals.

Gena
Gene
Gannon
Genesis
Genia
Genna
Giancarlo
Gianna
Gianni
Gieon
Gina
Gonzalo
Ginny
Gino

Their love of the novel rules their work lives as well and *GN*s will often switch careers several times before finding a combination that works.

The best careers for *GN*s should be those geared toward their ability to work well with people; perhaps in customer service, medicine, retail or education. And although most of the time co-workers will experience the personable side of the softly spoken *GN*s, woe betide those who assume a familiarity with them that oversteps their boundaries. *GN*s' sense of humor doesn't encompass laughter directed at themselves.

If there's anything that's going to slow the *GN*s down, it's that annoying tendency to lose focus when it comes to making big decisions. Perhaps out of fear of making the wrong choices, they have a habit of procrastinating until the last possible moment, and at no time will this be more evident than when it comes to choosing a mate. The interviewee will have to undergo a battery of tests and an unnerving period of indecision before the *GN* finally passes judgment. But the wait may prove to be worthwhile, for a relationship with these outgoing individuals is bound to be an intensely passionate adventure.

Geena Davis With brains, beauty and personality, Geena Davis seems to have it all. Not only is she a top-grossing Hollywood actress, but she is also a world-class archer, who was once invited to try out for the U.S. Olympic team. ■ Geena made her big-screen debut in what critics often refer to as the most disgusting movie of all time—*The Fly* with Jeff Goldblum, whom she eventually married. ■ Geena confirmed her talent when she starred opposite Michael Keaton and a young Winona Ryder in the 1988 cult comedy *Beetlejuice*, and later took home a Supporting Actress Oscar for her role in *The Accidental Tourist*. ■ Her most memorable role came in *Thelma and Louise*, when her character got to deflower the then-unknown Brad Pitt.

Charisma	💋	💋	💋	💋	💋	💋	💋	💋	💋	💋
Career Success	💰	💰	💰	💰	💰	💰	💰	💰	💰	💰
Love & Friendship										
Power	💣	💣	💣	💣	💣	💣	💣	💣	💣	💣

**Quick-thinking Adaptable Sociable
Caustic Temperamental Edgy**

In a good example of how the pronunciation of the letter *G* can affect the characterization of a name, consider the difference in tone between the names *Gunner* and *Ginger*. Although similar in structure, the hard *G* of *Gunner* gives the name the aggressive qualities found in the words *grim, grievous, Gatling gun* and *gumption,* while the soft and benign *G* in *Ginger* is more reminiscent of the words *genuflect, genial, genteel, genuine* and *generous.*

Both of these names are also significantly affected by the addition of the letters *N* and *R*. The somewhat *negative* qualities of the *N* (*no, never, not, none*) are offset to a significant degree by the *robustly romantic* letter *R*, which gives these personalities their sense of restrained passion. So while it's true that *GNRs* have an exuberant side, their conservative outlook keeps it very much under control.

GNRs make friends easily and tend to keep them for life; but this is due more to their level of honesty than their sweetness. People tend to instinctively *trust GNRs'* old-fashioned values, and even if they are not ones to pussyfoot around when it comes to letting others know how they feel, no one ever questions their integrity or genuine altruistic intentions. These frank

Genaro
Ginger
Gunnar
Gunner

characteristics spill over into the workplace, where *GNRs'* to-the-point management style and company loyalty are very much appreciated by their employers.

People who bear the *GNR* name root are not averse to intellectual pursuits, but their endeavors tend to be of a mostly spiritual nature, whether religion, music, philosophy, reading or other forms of self-expression. To them, the important thing in life is not what they accomplish, but what it is that they learn along the way. And *GNRs* are subscribers to the idea of noblesse oblige: being the sovereign of their own lives comes with the responsibility of improving one's knowledge of the universe and helping others do the same.

Just because they're a little brusque on occasion doesn't mean *GNRs* are not capable of love: in fact, *GNRs* are happiest and most productive when they're involved in a romance. But we're not talking about the mushy kind of love; *GNRs* are far more focused on the practical issues of relationships, like joint bank accounts and tax credits for children. To them, mates are for bouncing ideas off of, splitting the workload or as partners in mixed doubles. But life with a *GNR* will prove to be rewarding to those seeking a sensible and responsible partner who is easygoing and loyal to the end.

Ginger Rogers It's hardly possible to say the name Ginger Rogers without thinking of her leading man, Fred Astaire. ■ The magical duo wrote the book on dance musicals in the Hollywood world, and dominated the field for almost seven years. Astaire had all the grace and style of a classical dancer, while Ginger was the bold and down-to-earth part of the pair. As Katharine Hepburn once said of them, "She gave him sex, and he gave her class." ■ Despite such flattering accolades, Ginger wanted to run her own show and broke with Fred after seven magical years to pursue her own career as an actress. For a short while in 1945, Ginger was the most highly paid performer in Hollywood. Not a bad accomplishment for the "other half" of a dancing duo.

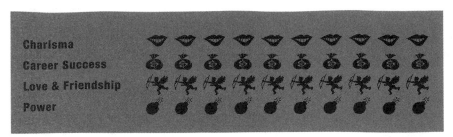

Charisma										
Career Success										
Love & Friendship										
Power										

**Strong Sophisticated Unyielding
Duplicitous Impatient Tricky**

When an aggressive dog admonishes its potential rivals, it retracts its upper lip and produces a low-frequency snarl that all animals instinctively recognize as a threat signal. This is why so many English words that contain both a *G* and an *R* have a distinct aura of menace: *grumble, grouchy, gruff, grim, grievous* and *grizzly*. In fact, when humans pronounce the *GR* sound, they tend to pull back their upper lip to reveal their teeth as well.

So don't be fooled when your *GR* friend appears to be terse and disinterested, for this cool outer shell belies an intensely involved individual whose ears are very open and whose antennae are constantly tuned to the social hum. *GR*s will often come out with some surprisingly astute observations after spending an evening in the company of friends, during which they seemed to everyone else to be fully involved in their own world. This trait, often mistaken for intuition, reflects the fundamental common sense that is at the core of the *GR*'s emotional makeup.

When choosing careers, *GR*s' main goals are to find positions that allow them to be in charge, or at least permit them to work on their own. But it's in running their own businesses that *GR*s really shine, for they possess

Garfield
Garland
Garrick
Gary
Geary
Geralyn
Germaine
German
Gerry
Gertha
Graham
Griffin

the kind of take-charge attitude that inspires respect and loyalty. And make no mistake, working for a *GR* can whip even the most reticent employee into shape. Anyone caught shirking their duties—if they're lucky enough to keep their job—will suffer the unwelcome storm of an angry *GR*.

Underlying the *GR*'s brusque relationship with the universe is an extraordinary self-confidence. When things go wrong, *GR*s are so certain of their ability to land on their feet that they're completely unafraid of putting themselves in risky situations. This self-assuredness is not born of arrogance; these people unquestionably have the walk that comes with their talk.

So although the *GR*'s gifts may not lie in the area of empathetic friendship, they have ways of showing that they care about others. If you have a *GR* at your side, you'll never lack for a staunch defender when there's a battle to be won. This kind of loyalty need never be second-guessed: The whole world could accuse you of a crime and the *GR* would be standing by you to vouch for your innocence. This innate love for a good fight and their reluctance to accept failure make them eminently desirable employees and love partners.

Gary Oldman Like most success stories, Gary Oldman's triumph was born in struggle and includes the usual suspects of alcoholism and divorce. If the ability to overcome obstacles is the mark of durability, then Gary has the personality of an M1 Abrams tank. ■ Gary set the tenor for his future roles after garnering critical acclaim playing punk-rocker Sid Vicious in *Sid and Nancy* in 1986. His reputation for playing complex villains crystallized with his dark characterization of Lee Harvey Oswald in Oliver Stone's 1998 feature film, *JFK*. ■ Often referred to as "the chameleon" for his unparalleled ability to absorb the essence of his characters, Gary wowed audiences with his portrayal of Ludwig van Beethoven in *Immortal Beloved* and terrified them in Bram Stoker's *Dracula*.

THE DEBONAIR
grd

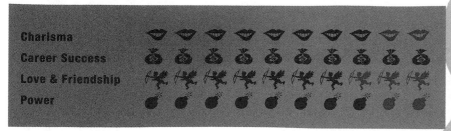

Charisma										
Career Success										
Love & Friendship										
Power										

Suave Artsy Sensitive
Smooth-talking Deceptive Non-committal

With the exception of the names *Gordon* and *Grady*, GRD names escape many of the aggressive connotations associated with the growling *GR* phoneme, which is at the heart of the threat words *grizzly, gruff, grab, gross, grimace, grimy* and *grouch*. This is because the softened form of the letter *G*—used in the names *Gerald, Geraldine* and *Geraldo*—tends to be associated with moderate words like *gentle, genuflect, genuine* and *genial*. The dignified letter *D* that terminates these names is associated with *distinguished, dark, daring* and *debonair*, instilling an air of noble gallantry.

In keeping with the complex nuances of their names, GRDs tend to have equally intricate emotional makeups. Typically, these are highly sexual people with open minds and a willingness to explore all kinds of interactions, and though they may not be the best-looking individuals in the world, their rough-and-tumble sex appeal often proves to be irresistible. Smooth? Absolutely.

In both their career choices and their relationship decisions, GRDs tend to delay making the transition into permanence until they've had the chance to sow their wild oats. But GRDs are responsible people who put their "growing up" time to good use, and whether it's a college degree, a trial relationship or a part-time

Gerald
Geraldine
Geraldo
Gerard
Gerardo
Gerda
Gordon
Gordy
Grady

job, GRDs consider *every* experience to be potentially valuable fodder for the future.

On occasion, GRDs can display an extraordinary level of sensitivity and intuition, revealing emotions that even their best friends never knew they had. But just because they have a wide emotional range, don't assume that your GRD friends are going to wear their hearts on their sleeves; they can be quite inscrutable about their motives and annoyingly reluctant to share them.

The GRDs' smoky sensuality often lands them in romantic entanglements from which they find it difficult to escape. They're famous for prolonging their brooding relationships well past the point of everyone's mental health, so when you sense your GRD partner losing his or her concentration in the relationship, it's best to cut your losses and run. In fairness, it's hard to be as irresistible as them.

If you're married to a GRD, don't take it for granted that the two of you are going to stay in lockstep forever. They may love you dearly, but they'll never lose the potential to love someone else as well. But if darkly obsessive romances are your thing, by all means let the GRD take the wheel. Enjoy the ride—just don't expect it to last forever unless you're willing to put some gas in the tank.

Gérard Depardieu No one would accuse Gérard of being just another pretty face, but he certainly does have a peculiar appeal. Maybe it's his brooding brow or soulful eyes, or maybe it's just that old saying about the size of a man's nose. ■ Gérard's entrée into the American film market was with his role in *Green Card*, in which he played opposite Andie MacDowell. The role earned him a Golden Globe award for Best Actor and the following year he was the logical choice to star as Christopher Columbus in Ridley Scott's epic, *1492: Conquest of Paradise*. ■ Gérard often works for little more than scale salary in order to play interesting characters, and while heart trouble caused him to take a short sabbatical, the quadruple bypass did little to diminish his workload.

Charisma	👄	👄	👄	👄	👄	👄	👄	👄	👄	👄
Career Success	💰	💰	💰	💰	💰	💰	💰	💰	💰	💰
Love & Friendship	🐾	🐾	🐾	🐾	🐾	🐾	🐾	🐾	🐾	🐾
Power	💣	💣	💣	💣	💣	💣	💣	💣	💣	💣

Generous Loyal Versatile
Mutable Indecisive Intimidating

The *GRG* names embody two distinctly different personality types depending upon how the first letter *G* is pronounced. In the case of the hard *G* (*Greg* and *Gregory*), there's a connotation of an aggressive and hard-edged personality. This is because the *guttural G* is the letter of *grumble, garish, Gatling gun, grim* and *grimy*. On the other hand, the softly pronounced *G* (as in *George* and *Georgina*) takes its milder cue from the words *gentle, genuflect, genial* and *genuine*. This is why *all* female *GRG* names utilize the softer pronunciation, and why "hard" male *GRG* names ooze such relaxed masculinity.

But no matter how the initial letter is pronounced, words that contain a double dose of the *G* are instilled with the air of forceful authority that contaminates the words *mugger, jagged, trigger, bugger, swagger, dagger* and *bigge*r. These aggressive qualities are hardly mitigated by the fact that names beginning with the *GR* phoneme tend to be associated with the warning sounds of: *growling, grimacing, grieving, grizzly* and *grave*.

With all these powerful influences, it should be clear that we're dealing with an emotionally strong individual with a self-confidence that borders on arrogance. *GRG*s are not the types to wait for life to come to them.

Greg
George
Georgetta
Georgette
Georgia
Georgiana
Georgie
Georgina
Georgine
Gregorio
Gregory
Jorge

They'll forcefully hunt it down and make it do their bidding.

Like most *G*-named people, *GRG*s usually succeed in everything they try. Of course, they're going to make their fair share of mistakes, but true to their dictum that "failure only occurs when you give up," nothing's going to keep these determined individuals down for long. Inasmuch as these are hard nuts to crack, *GRG*s are welcomed in careers that reward perseverance and fortitude. From policework to firefighting to the military professions, they are comfortable in positions of leadership and are particularly capable when it comes to hard-core business negotiations. They are concrete-minded people, who rely so much on their sense of logic that it's rare for them to get carried away by their emotions.

Once you've won a *GRG*'s respect, you'll have the eternal allegiance of a loyal and capable friend. And when it comes to the *GRG*s' intimate affairs, these occasionally gruff characters can be remarkably suave and sophisticated lovers when they're trying to make an impression. They are physical people, who love to touch and be touched, and in truth, their lovemaking has more to do with carnality than it has to do with romance. The casual lover will learn that their bite can sometimes be worse than their bark.

George Clooney The crinkly-eyed nephew of legendary crooner Rosemary Clooney has always seemed to have the world at his feet. Not only was he declared Sexiest Man Alive by People magazine, but he was also fortunate enough to inherit his TV commentator father's gift of the gab. ■ George's acting career has consistently improved since his appearance in *Return of the Killer Tomatoes* in 1988. His performance as Dr. Doug Ross on ABC's *ER* and his starring role in *O Brother Where Art Thou?* has kept his heartthrob status rising. ■ His role as the main character in the star-studded remake of *Ocean's Eleven* earned him top billing, over the likes of Brad Pitt and Julia Roberts.

Charisma	😗	😗	😗	😗	😗	😗	😗	😗	😗	😗
Career Success	💰	💰	💰	💰	💰	💰	💰	💰	💰	💰
Love & Friendship	🦅	🦅	🦅	🦅	🦅	🦅	🦅	🦅	🦅	🦅
Power	💣	💣	💣	💣	💣	💣	💣	💣	💣	💣

Astute Thoughtful Talented
Gruff Uncommunicative Threatening

GRS names are partially immune to the aggressive connotations associated with the *growling GR* phoneme (found at the heart of the threat words *grizzly, gruff, grab, gross, grimace, grimy* and *grouch*). The letter *S* (or its counterpart in the sibilant letter *C*) counteracts the effects of the forceful *G,* and infuses these names with a distinctively *sassy sensuality*. This dichotomy can produce in the *GRS*s an internal conflict that requires a special kind of intelligence to resolve, and although the pressures of this inner struggle might be manifested by symptoms of emotional instability, they are usually well hidden from the public.

*GRS*s' strongest point has to be their exceptional skill at steering their own ship and encouraging others to do the same. Many *GRS*s live their lives in unconventional ways—spending a year or two abroad, or earning an esoteric degree—but those that *do* enter the business world prove to be superbly well equipped to grease the wheels of commerce. Like most *G*-named people, *GRS*s are in the highest tax-brackets and derive a great deal of their self-worth from their careers and their accomplishments. With negotiating skills second to none and verbal dexterity that could shame Bill Clinton, you'd think that *GRS*s would make outstanding leaders, but you'd be wrong. They simply have no

Grace
Gracia
Gracie
Garrison
Graciela
Grayson

aspirations for controlling other people. They would much rather be part of a team in which every member contributes his or her own input, in which anyone unable to match the *GRS*'s gruelling pace will be gently eased out.

With their unique blend of poise and sensitivity, *GRS*s inspire respect in others and have an expectation of respect from their friends and lovers. *GRS*s are not above using their intellectual prowess or corporeal charms to manipulate others; but since they have no real malice in their hearts, the manipulatee is in very little danger of being taken advantage of.

A *GRS* is not the mate for you if you're into things like mysticism, UFOs and conspiracy theories. These are pragmatic people whose spiritual essence comes from a down-to-earth understanding of natural laws. But although they'd never admit it, the *GRS* personalities are true romantics at heart, and prospective suitors are advised to pay homage to the little things in their courtship regardless of the *GRS*'s protestations. Hallmark, roses and (expensive) champagne will win the *GRS* heart over an engaging intellectual debate any day. And once the *GRS*s are happily ensconced in a committed relationship, their barriers will come crashing down to expose a remarkably amenable mate.

Grace Kelly The story of Grace Kelly's life provides a prime example that royalty isn't always everything it's cut out to be. Still, there's nothing as flattering as having a king fall at your feet, and when the King of Monaco proposed to the American movie star in 1956, she accepted his offer and moved into his palace. ■ As Princess Grace, the former Hollywood star was pushed into the role of palacemaker for her princely husband—responsibilities she reportedly handled well. ■ Grace's death in 1982 was eerily similar to the 1997 death of Princess Diana: A car accident tragically ending a life full of romance and tragedy. Like Diana, Grace's gentle existence will remain forever etched in the mind of the American public.

THE POWERFUL
grt

Charisma										
Career Success										
Love & Friendship										
Power										

**Decisive In-charge Innovative
Controlling Obtuse Intimidating**

The *GR* phoneme is the de facto warning sound of the English language. Stemming from our instinctive reaction to a growling dog, it spawns the words *grimace, grumble, gruff, gripe, grimy* and *grizzly*, setting the tone for the *GRT*'s personality. And the explosive sounds of the *triumphantly trumpeting* letter *T* only aggravate these powerful effects. Together they are responsible for the forceful essence found in the words *grate, braggart, grit, ingrate, regret* and *bogart*. If there's something primal about these names that evokes an image of a dangerous animal, bear in mind that these are inherently self-assured people who have no need for overt blustering.

And yet these people, like their names, are straightforward and brook no nonsense. So if you're trying to befriend a *GRT*, you'll discover their ability to quickly cotton on to any game-playing. They'll also let you know, in no uncertain terms, that they disapprove of dishonesty in any form. Their brusque, even menacing style can prove to be somewhat intimidating (which is why many people find it so challenging to maintain close relationships with them), but if you're prepared to be honest, loyal and reliable, your *GRT* friends will return the favor with quiet and steady commitment.

Garnet
Garnett
Garrett
Garth
Gertie
Gertrude
Gretchen
Grant
Greta

GRT people are not the sort to be aggressors in their personal dealings, but they certainly aren't weaklings either. A powerful sense of self-esteem instills in them an almost unnatural confidence that they can handle any external crises. Their strong-willed dispositions express themselves not in aggressive physical flourishes, but rather in sharply honed intellects. And in keeping with someone with an active mind, many *GRT*s have a yen for brainteasers, crossword puzzles or simply higher education. This explains why so many of them are found in careers that reward deep concentration and attention to detail: engineering, medicine, research or the stock market.

In contrast to their sometimes-abrupt styles, *GRT*s are surprisingly gentle with loved ones. Compliant they may never be, but their honesty and willingness to communicate will prove to be great assets in their relationships. As you might have guessed, partnering a *GRT* is not for the weak-willed, for these headstrong personalities will run roughshod over a partner who fails to meet their high standards. And since there's nothing they hate more than whiners, the best way to gain their respect is to counteract their stubbornness with vigor and conviction.

Greta Garbo Greta Garbo, a Swedish-born American film icon, was one of the first actresses to make the transition from silent films to sound. Her screen presence and ability to act in both English and German set her apart from the hundreds of wannabes in the fledgling sound-film industry. ■ After leaving her fiancé John Gilbert at the altar, Greta made the decision never to marry. Her choice reflected the independent streak that was her hallmark—one that she fiercely defended throughout her life. ■ By the mid-1930s, Greta had achieved the distinction of becoming America's highest-paid female actress and was selected as *Variety* newspaper's Best Actress of the Half-Century in 1950. She remained fabulously reclusive until she died in 1990, at the age of eighty-four.

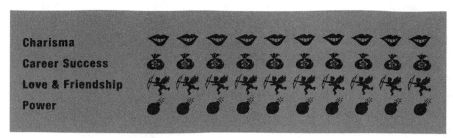

Charisma										
Career Success										
Love & Friendship										
Power										

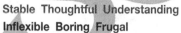

Stable Thoughtful Understanding
Inflexible Boring Frugal

Despite the *gruffness* of the letter *G* that dominates the *GS* names with its *grandly glorious gumption,* these names also enjoy the *softly sensual* influence of the letter *S.* There is strength here, but it's a quiet, internal strength. The *GS* is a behind-the-scenes person who prefers to facilitate events rather than direct them firsthand.

Since they have such a strong handle on their emotions, it's virtually impossible to stress *GSs* out. In fact, one of the defining characteristics of *GS* personalities is that they are remarkably competent at solving other people's problems. So much so that they have a tendency to seek out relationships with troubled individuals just so they can feel useful in putting them back together. Some would call this meddlesome or even codependent, but loved ones don't care what you call it, as long as they get to be the recipients of the *GS's* insistent benevolence. But *GSs* can also prove to be quite stubborn when making their point, and their conservative views can be somewhat wearing after a while.

Even if being an interesting person isn't the *GS's* strongest suit, you can always count on them to do their best. Even in failure, these people exhibit a remarkable tenaciousness that keeps them bopping up for more.

Gaston
Gisela
Giselle
Giuseppe
Griselda
Gus
Gussie
Gustavo

And if by chance you *do* catch a *GS* in the throes of a failed project, it's best to never rub it in. They don't always have the emotional tools to deal with self-caused disappointments.

With their outstanding work ethics, *GSs* are assets to any corporation or work environment, and take pride in their ability to be team players. Like most people whose names begin with the letter *G*, they are likely to earn more money than their peers, although in *GSs'* case, this has less to do with raw talent than it does with an uncommon attention to detail and a solid understanding of office politics. If you happen to have a *GS* for a mechanic or dentist, you can rest assured that you'll get terrific service at a reasonable price.

The best mate for *GSs* is someone who's not going to be too possessive of their time. Male *GSs* in particular are prone to making the rounds with their collection of friends and aren't likely to feel comfortable in the role of househusband. And even if both sexes of the *GS* group never lose their ability (or desire) to flirt like drunken teenagers, no one would ever expect these dependable creatures to even *think* of breaking their vows. They're far too aware of the rewards inherent in unions based on mutual trust.

Gus Grissom   But for a faulty piece of equipment, Gus Grissom would have become one of America's best-known astronauts. He was, after all, one of the first men to venture outside Earth's atmosphere, when, in 1961, he took a fifteen-minute trip through space. As fate would have it, Gus never got his chance at immortality. While returning from a mission in Liberty Bell 7, his safety hatch blew open and the little craft was sent to the bottom of the Atlantic. Gus survived, but his reputation didn't. As the sole passenger, rumors circulated that he had panicked and blown the hatch, making him responsible for the spacecraft's loss. ■ Later findings showed that technical flaws were the most likely culprits, and "Gus didn't do it" has become the new refrain.

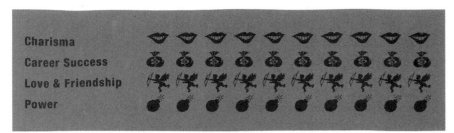

THE RED-HOT GV

Charisma										
Career Success										
Love & Friendship										
Power										

Smoldering Single-minded Romantic
Impatient Intimidating Hot-tempered

The fortunate combination of the *grand* letter *G* and the *vital, virile, vivacious* letter *V,* earns the *GV* names their spicy grandeur. It's not for nothing that these people are associated with a jaunty swagger and a devil-may-care attitude.

In their social lives, *GV*s enjoy being the center of attention and have a knack for seducing the spotlight. But in their work environments, *GV*s often prove to be somewhat restless. In part, this is triggered by their inherent discomfort with authority, but it's also because working indoors is anathema to these free-spirited souls. They'll usually let their views be loudly known (and some might even accuse them of being troublemakers), but they certainly have no intention of causing any harm. They live by the dictum "if you're not making waves, you're not paddling."

The best thing an employer can do is to allow their *GV* employees to work at their own pace in order to give free reign to their creative spirits, for it's only when the *GV*s are being creative that they don't feel like they're actually working. But like most people whose names begin with the *get-up-and-go* letter *G*, *GV*s prefer to work for themselves so they don't have to waste time trying to convince others of the importance of their ideas.

Gavin
Geneva
Genevieve
Genoveva
Giovanna
Giovanni
Granville
Grover

Even with their rebellious attitude toward work, *GV*s are quite canny when it comes to their money, even when they don't have much money to worry about. It's just that they place a great deal of emphasis on material comforts and have a healthy respect for the value of a dollar. *GV*s' homes are tastefully and expensively furnished, so when they go shopping they'll likely pass up on the bargain brands and select a few quality items that will last for years.

GV people often allow their emotions to run away with them when it comes to matters of the heart. So if you're married to a *GV* you can expect a few surprises, especially when it comes to creative boudoir romps, but mates should remember that *GV*s are strongly averse to being controlled and should not try and rule the roost.

*GV*s are big-picture people and would rather take care of the big things in the relationship in exchange for their mate taking care of the little details. It's not surprising that many people comment on how happy and well-adjusted *GV*s' children are. They will be raised under an old-fashioned philosophy that includes a focus on education, independence and sober-living.

Geneviève Bujold Geneviève Bujold could have written the book on the effects of a repressive atmosphere in an all-girl's Catholic school. Things got so bad for the young teenager that she engineered an "escape" by getting kicked out of the strict Montreal convent where, in her own words, she had spent twelve years in "a long, dark tunnel." ■ Her strict upbringing might explain why throughout her career, Geneviève portrayed complex women in difficult situations. She starred in Brian De Palma's *Obsession* and Michael Crichton's *Coma*—one of the biggest hits in her career. ■ Geneviève's rebellious nature asserted itself once again when she backed out of the film *Mary, Queen of Scots* because she felt that the studio was typecasting her. After Universal sued for $750,000, Geneviève retreated to Greece to make the film, *The Trojan Women*, alongside Katharine Hepburn.

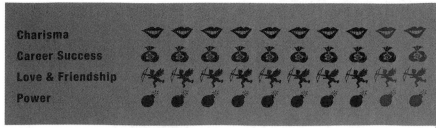

Charisma	😊 😊 😊 😊 😊 😊 😊 😊 😊 😊
Career Success	💰 💰 💰 💰 💰 💰 💰 💰 💰 💰
Love & Friendship	🏹 🏹 🏹 🏹 🏹 🏹 🏹 🏹 🏹 🏹
Power	💣 💣 💣 💣 💣 💣 💣 💣 💣 💣

**Original Daring Wise
Dark Moody Restless**

When the *gruff* and *growling* elements of the letter *G* team up with the *wild, weird, wise* and *whimsica*l qualities of the letter *W*, it reflects the darker elements of an unconventional spiritual soul. And while these mysterious qualities are exacerbated by the *negative* qualities of the pessimistic letter *N* (*no, not, never, nary* and *negative*), the *GWN* personality retains its enigmatic charm even in the face of occasional lapses into pessimism and cynicism.

*GWN*s are anything but pragmatists; they are dreamers of wild dreams and tempestuous lovers of the random universe. They are also restless characters whose quirky ways make them eminently attractive to fellow thrill-seekers. And this adventurous theme is visible not only in their social lives, it thoroughly infects their career choices and intimate relationships. *GWN*s feel a compulsion to shake things up every few years or so—maybe by moving to a new city, or by dropping a comfortable relationship, or simply by changing jobs.

It's not that *GWN*s are immune to anxiety, however, and there will be periods in their lives when they'll seem frozen by the number of decisions they have to make. But unlike most people, *GWN*s don't exhibit much apprehension when they take their leaps into the unknown; they have too much

**Gwen
Gwendolyn
Gwyn**

confidence in their ability to land on their feet.

Maybe it's symptomatic of the *GWN*'s right-brained tendencies that she's drawn to creative outlets like writing, sketching and music. When it comes to her career, the *GWN* should make sure that her work environment allows a healthy measure of self-expression and creative articulation. Her dramatic personality may lead her to the stage or send this plucky soul off on a wild adventure to join the Peace Corps, but no matter what she chooses, the *GWN* is happiest when she is in motion. The only thing she fears is having her future mapped out in concrete.

There's something charming about the *GWN*'s haphazard ways, and she's very aware of her appeal to the opposite sex. She's liable to be an incorrigible flirt who prefers the mystery of a dark nightclub to the glare of a walk on the beach. Late-night coffee shops are a particularly favorite haunt in which she can spend the night philosophizing about life, death and those unseen forces that shape our destinies.

If you're going to have an intimate relationship with a *GWN*, be warned that it can be a tricky proposition. It's a little like taking fruit from a cactus: there's always a tantalizing reward, but you're going to have to shed some blood.

Gwen Stefani Eric Stefani founded his band *No Doubt* in 1987 and asked his perky little sister Gwen to sign on as co-vocalist with their friend John Spence. The group played gigs at small venues in Orange County, and after Spence committed suicide, Gwen took over as solo vocalist. When Flea from the *Red Hot Chili Peppers* recorded the band's demo, the group landed a contract with Interscope Records. ■ Sales from their first release were so disappointing that the band's founder took a job as an animator for The Simpsons, but with the addition of a few new band members, *No Doubt* released *Tragic Kingdom*, a hugely successful album. In 2002, Gwen tied the knot with fellow rocker Gavin Rossdale, front man for the band *Bush*.

The Letter of Hope, Charity and Healing

Most Popular Girl's Names

Helen
Heather
Hazel
Holly
Heidi
Hilda
Hattie
Harriet
Hannah
Hope

Most Popular Boy's Names

Harold
Henry
Harry
Howard
Herbert
Herman
Hector
Harvey
Hugh
Homer

My heart, my house, my all; every hope in my breast is centered in her.

ANTHONY TROLLOPE,
The Warden

Words beginning with the letter H are practically whispered. Created by a gentle rush of breath directly from the lungs, its hushed tones are personified in the words holy, honor, heal, helpful, heavenly and hallowed. ■ Hegelianism is a philosophy that involves the elevation of spirituality and idealism above materialism and these spiritual aspects of the H are evident in the words healer, hope, harmony, hero, healthy, heart, harvest, Hasidic and Haftorah (the holy book of the Hebrews). ■ The H is also the flagship letter of home and hearth, and is commonly found in words describing family values; husband, house, heart, happiness and Hymen, the Greek God of marriage. ■ Even words that don't actually begin with an H benefit from its moderating influence. Note how it softens the meanings of words beginning with harsh letters like C and T: tank becomes thank, tinker becomes thinker, taut becomes thought and catty becomes chatty. Likewise, the name Telma is an anagram of metal, giving the impression of a strong and unyielding individual, but by softening the T with an H to create Thelma, the anagram is transformed into Hamlet, the tragic hero of Shakespeare's peerless play. ■ According to a survey conducted by Dr. Albert Mehrabian, people whose names begin with an H are five times more likely to be perceived as moral as opposed to masculine. These pious overtones are illustrated in the traditional meanings of Hayley (hero), Hannah (grace of god), Harmon (person of integrity and rank), Helga (holy), Homer (promise) and Humphrey (peace). ■

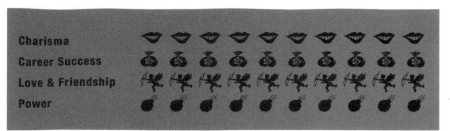

THE EVEN-HANDED

hb

Charisma										
Career Success										
Love & Friendship										
Power										

**Paternal Humorous Gentle
Stubborn Detached Mental**

In the *HB* names, the *hushed, harmonious* tones of the letter *H* come into direct conflict with the *belligerent, blustering, brash* and *brooding* tones of the letter *B*. This internal discord proves to be a source of tension in the *HB* names, and it takes a decidedly strong personality to navigate through this inherent friction. Perhaps this explains why the *HB* names are reserved solely for men.

If *HB*s were symbolized by a sign in the Zodiac, they'd be represented by *Libra*—a precarious balancing act of the Ying and Yang forces in his personality. He's aggressive in business but honest to a fault. He may also be helpful and full of advice, but he can also be bossy, obtuse and hard-headed enough to make Mike Tyson wince. Still, once he decides to take up your cause, he's yours, for better or worse. So while making a casual acquaintance with an *HB* may be easy, getting rid of him may present the *real* problem. This is one stubborn creature, and his successes in his career and relationships come in large part from his obstinate refusal to give up.

Unlike many people whose names begin with the letter *H,* failure doesn't seem to faze the *HB* much. Although he may shed a tear over a failed romance here

Herb
Herbert
Herbie
Herby
Heriberto
Hobert
Hubert

and there, in the scheme of things he recognizes failure to be simply another path to self-improvement.

What *HB*s have in common with most *H*-named people is that they rarely resort to dishonesty or deceit to get what they want out of life. They also strongly disapprove when others do that sort of thing and expect nothing less than brutal honesty from their business and social associates. But in terms of their careers, *HB*s shouldn't expect to achieve positions of top leadership. These are men whose talents are better utilized behind the scenes, where their work ethic is appreciated by others who are better suited for leadership.

*HB*s can be surprisingly intuitive in matters of the heart. These are men who are skilled in playing by the rules of romance, even if they're not immune to the occasional clumsily conducted courtship. But since *HB*s are not those for playing games when it comes to the important issue of love, they have limited patience for women who play hard to get. But if she accepts his initial advances, his wooing will be gentle but persistent. And after the nuptials are said and done, she'll be expected to cheerfully tend the hearth in exchange for the staunch devotion of her *HB* mate.

Hubert Humphrey As a champion of the liberal cause and civil rights, Hubert Humphrey commanded a level of affection and respect beyond that accorded to almost any vice president in history. ■ As a senator, Hubert's voting record attested to his commitment to the liberal agenda and he was pivotal in helping to win support for the Nuclear Test Ban Treaty. He also helped push the Civil Rights Act through the Senate. After an unsuccessful bid for the Presidency, Hubert became President Johnson's running mate in 1956. ■ Hubert's insistence on alienating liberals by staunchly defending Johnson's policy in Vietnam probably cost him his second bid at the presidency against Nixon. When he died of cancer, in 1976, his body was laid out in the Capital Rotunda, an honor befitting a head of state.

Charisma	👄	👄	👄	👄	👄	👄	👄	👄	👄	👄
Career Success	💰	💰	💰	💰	💰	💰	💰	💰	💰	💰
Love & Friendship										
Power	💣	💣	💣	💣	💣	💣	💣	💣	💣	💣

**Energetic Positive Intelligent
Unfocused Dissatisfied Restless**

Names that begin with the *hushed, harmonious* tones of the letter *H* usually suggest people with genteel and laid-back personalities, who would never think of using intimidation to accumulate their resources. And since these names incorporate the *dignified, dapper, disciplined* qualities of the letter *D*, one also expects to find a strong sense of *destiny* characterizing all of their life decisions.

While *HD*s are not the most spontaneous of individuals, they do exhibit a contagious verve that makes them perfect recreational partners and party planners. Their natural cheerleading attributes also make them ideal for mobilizing people toward a common goal. But few *HD*s are comfortable in front of large crowds and, for the most part, prefer to remain behind the scenes and control events from the wings. *HD* people tend to be very involved in the lives of people around them and are not shy about voicing their opinions, solicited or not. But it's hard to get too peeved at someone with such an impish sense of humor.

Co-workers might initially feel something vaguely deceptive about these individuals, not because they're dishonest or manipulative, but because they so often appear to be lost in thought. This taciturn exterior masks a great intelligence and a remarkable ability to perform under pressure, so it would be a mistake to underestimate the *HD*s' competitive drive. They can easily outclass their more aggressive and pushy colleagues and are usually the "go-to-guys" on those difficult projects that no one else wants to tackle.

As lovers, *HD*s are typically drawn toward casual companionship rather than torrid romances. To them, intimacy is just friendship carried one step further, and, while this apparent lack of passion might put off potential mates, *HD*s are far from cold: they're just very choosy. Once their relationships have had time to mature, their exterior coolness melts away to reveal someone whose sexuality is deeply connected to a desire to please. Submissive? Perhaps. But more likely *HD*s are driven simply by their altruistic impulses and their belief in Karma.

*HD*s are usually not overly anxious to become parents and will often wait until later in life to take this step. It's not that they don't *like* children, mind you; it's just that because they have such grand plans for their own lives, they're willing to delay their family obligations until their nests have been fully feathered.

Haden
Hadley
Harold
Haydee
Hayden
Haywood
Hedwig
Hedy
Heidi
Hudson
Heidy
Hiedi
Hilda

Heidi Fleiss If you were a single male actor in Hollywood during the 1990s, chances were that you would have at least heard of Heidi Fleiss. And if you were Charlie Sheen—who had just tied the knot with model Donna Peele—you received a subpoena to testify at her trial. Sheen confessed to having been one of Heidi's best customers, spending over $50,000 on call girls. (Charlie and Donna divorced soon afterwards.) ■ Heidi was anointed "the Hollywood Madam" and subjected to a set of charges that led to a three-year prison sentence. It was estimated that her empire grossed over five million dollars a year. ■ Heidi recently separated from her boyfriend Tom Sizemore (*Black Hawk Down*) who had allegedly cheated on her with prostitutes.

Charisma	👄	👄	👄	👄	👄	👄	👄	👄	👄	👄
Career Success	💰	💰	💰	💰	💰	💰	💰	💰	💰	💰
Love & Friendship	🦅	🦅	🦅	🦅	🦅	🦅	🦅	🦅	🦅	🦅
Power	💣	💣	💣	💣	💣	💣	💣	💣	💣	💣

**Quick-thinking Reliable Warm
Hyper Reactionary Calculating**

The complex *HG* personalities are defined by the combination of the *hallowed* letter *H* and the *gregarious* letter *G*—the symbol of *grace*, *goodness* and *governance*. These people are natural leaders, whose motivational style is derived from a quiet inner strength, a strong moral compass and an underlying core of altruism.

Working alongside an *HG* is not going to be all fun and games; you're going to have your work cut out for you if you expect to maintain their demanding pace. These are people who just adore routine and for whom working nine to five (or seven to six) doesn't faze them in the least. It's not that *HGs* are introverts or workaholics . . . it's just that business always comes before pleasure.

To the casual observer, the *HG* might appear to be shy and reserved; but this is just a smokescreen. In reality, these are quite intense and idealistic people who see themselves as champions of the common man. They'll insist on taking ownership of their projects and are usually drawn to careers in which they have a great deal of autonomy and creative control. Those fortunate enough to work for an *HG* will be surprised to find that someone so considerate can also be so driven and meticulous.

Helga
Hildegard
Hugh
Hugo

But that's the *HG* for you: full of contrasts and contradictions. And if you don't like their style of management, they'll be delighted to give you strong references for your job search.

Though the *HG's* gifts may not lie in the area of passionate romance, they have their own particular ways of showing they care. For example, if the whole world were to accuse you of a crime, the *HG* would be the first to volunteer as a character witness. Partly because of their uncommon loyalty, but mainly because they have the habit of seeing only the best in people, you'd definitely want an *HG* as your advocate. Their innate stubbornness gives them a stick-to-it-iveness that can overcome seemingly impossible odds.

Love will look less like romance and more like business when an *HG* is involved, but this doesn't mean you'll lack for affection and warmth. It's just that the *HG's* priorities are always pracitical first, and pleasure if there's any time left over. Still, when they do get around to indulging in a little intimate romping, it'll usually prove to be worth the wait. *HGs* always take their partners' needs into consideration, and their ideal lovers are those who can navigate the bedroom and the raising of children with equal ease.

Hugo Black Supreme Court Justice Hugo Black never really cared for the press, but he believed that the First Amendment was an inviolable idea which had to be protected. ■ Hugo was a controversial figure particularly because he had been a member of the Ku Klux Klan for two years as a political neophyte in Alabama. In the South in those days, politicians had to court the Klan as a necessary evil, but this fact did little to assuage his critics even though Hugo had supported school desegregation. ■ Hugo also took heat for his defense of the internment of Japanese-Americans during WWII but despite these criticisms, proved to be a staunch advocate of human rights and defender of the First Amendment during the communist witch-hunts of the McCarthy era.

hl

Charisma	😗😗😗😗😗😗😗😗😗😗
Career Success	💰💰💰💰💰💰💰💰💰
Love & Friendship	🐉🐉🐉🐉🐉🐉🐉🐉🐉
Power	💣💣💣💣💣💣💣💣💣

**Faithful Loving Companionable
Temperamental Unpredictable Oversensitive**

When a name begins with the *hushed* tones of the *helpful* letter *H*, and has the good fortune to incorporate the letter of *life, liberty, love, learning,* and *loyalty,* it's a sure indication that the resulting personality will reflect the gracious characteristics of the words: *help, hello, holy, halo, hallowed, shalom, homily, healthy,* and *humble.* While these aren't exactly cheerleader-types, you could say that *HL*s are more optimistic than a Britney Spears' ballad.

*HL*s usually keep themselves trim and fit, and have well developed tastes for the finer things in life. In the workplace, they are predictably upbeat and positive and can always be counted on to inspire their co-workers. They tackle challenges with verve, and overcome them with finesse; traits that serve them well in all their business endeavors. Being such social creatures, *HL*s seem equally happy when they're in charge of the factory or just being cogs in its machine . . . just as long as they don't have to work alone.

As courteous as *HL*s may be, they find there's nothing as satisfying as a good old-fashioned argument. Not one of those hotheaded and provocative kinds, mind you, but a lazy ill-defined debate over some mundane issue. And if they don't seem to care who wins these arguments, don't think it's because they give up easily. They will fight the good fight long after everyone else has thrown their towels into the ring, and failure simply doesn't faze them in the least. This is why *HL*s do so well as lawyers and CPAs: they're sticklers for accuracy and take pleasure in niggling over the details.

Although *HL*s project a consistently reassuring calm, they have their dark sides too—in the form of a slow-burning fuse on their tempers, which can blind-side even those who know them best. But no one can really begrudge them this occasional release of pressure, and once the storm has blown itself out, they prove to be experts in making up. But be cautious about crossing your *HL* friends. Their sense of justice runs deep, and they're not above giving Karma a helping hand in hauling a betrayer over the coals. You'll not only get not only the guilt trip, but the entire vacation package before being allowed back into their good graces.

When *HL*s decide to settle down, they'll do it with style and permanence. There may be a few false starts here and there, but once they accept that there is no such thing as a perfect mate, they'll direct all their energies into constructing a mutually rewarding union.

Hal
Hailee
Hailey
Hailie
Haleigh
Haley
Halie, Halle
Halley, Hallie
Harlan, Hilary
Hillary, Holley
Holli, Harley
Haylee
Harland
Hayleigh
Hayley
Haylie
Hollie
Hollis
Holly

Halle Berry Halle Berry's abusive father left her mother, a psychiatric nurse, when Halle was four. Even though the bi-racial Halle is largely deaf in the right ear as a result of an abusive boyfriend, she was a runner-up in the Miss USA pageant and won a role on the television sitcom, *Living Dolls*. She eventually won a Golden Globe for her title role in *Introducing Dorothy Dandridge*. ■ Spike Lee was responsible for Halle's big break when he cast her as the crack-addicted sister of his main character in *Jungle Fever*. Her greatest triumph came in 2002 when she won a Best Actress Oscar for *Monster's Ball*, in which she played an executed convict's wife involved with the prison guard who pulled the switch.

hln

Charisma	👄	👄	👄	👄	👄	👄	👄	👄	👄	👄
Career Success	💰	💰	💰	💰	💰	💰	💰	💰	💰	💰
Love & Friendship	💘	💘	💘	💘	💘	💘	💘	💘	💘	💘
Power	💣	💣	💣	💣	💣	💣	💣	💣	💣	💣

**Demure Attractive Humorous
Shy Reticent Enigmatic**

When a name begins with the *hushed* tones of the *helpful* letter *H*, and features the letter of *life, liberty, love, learning,* and *loyalty,* it is typically associated with personalities that reflect the gracious characteristics of the words: *helpful, hello, holy, halo, hallowed, shalom, homily, healthy,* and *humble.* The letter *N,* however, is usually connected to the *negative* aspects of life (*no, not, never, nada, nein, nyet,* and *naught*), and infects names with a distinct air of pessimism. These are men and women who carry themselves with gentle grace, but who occasionally indulge themselves in bouts of melancholy and ill-temper.

Since the dominant theme in the *HLN*'s life is serenity, it's a rare *HLN* that stands out in a crowd. But this certainly does not mean that they're not going to leave their mark on those who cross their paths, for these are people with a profound sense of destiny, who believe their lives are meant for some specific purpose. To befriend an *HLN* is to be introduced to a unique world colored by strong spiritual and mystical beliefs.

The *HLN*s' charms may be legendary, but you won't find them working as runway models or chairmen of the board; their attractiveness is more ethereal than that. The same could be said of their competitive drive, which is

Halina
Helaine
Helen
Helena
Helene
Hellen
Holden

better suited to helping people overcome their difficulties that it is about making money. But just because *HLN*s may be kind at heart, one shouldn't assume that they are also predictable. They are so bent on following their own stars that if others get in the way, *HLN*s will squarely set their jaws and defiantly push them out of their path. This is where the *HLN*'s normally altruistic spirit gives way to driven and sharp-minded individualism, which if you're not fully expecting it, can seem more like bullheaded selfishness than careful planning.

The *HLN*s' dating and mating lives are a bit ambiguous, and they tend to drift in and out of relationships without ever dropping anchor. But if their ship happens to appear on the horizon, you'll be surprised at how well they do the breaststroke.

The *HLN*s' nurturing aspects reveal themselves by the way they often end up with people for whom they feel a certain amount of responsibility. But there's a fine line between being needed and being smothered, and many *HLN*s struggle to find this equilibrium. Children, too, are apt to upset their delicate balance, but since their parenting skills increase exponentially with age, their family structures are likely to become more stable over time.

Helen Hunt Winning a Best Actress Academy Award takes skill and serendipity. It helps have a great director (James Brooks), a role in which you get to cry a little, and—if you're lucky—a leading man like Jack Nicholson. Helen Hunt's Academy Award in the film *As Good as it Gets*, was for her role as an overburdened "Carol the Waitress", playing opposite Nicholson and Greg Kinnear as "Simon the Fag." ■ In 1996, Helen starred in the summer action film *Twister*—helping it become one of the top-grossing films of the year, but it was her role as an urban career woman on the sit-com, *Mad About You* with Paul Reiser, that made Helen a household name. The show ran for seven seasons and earned her four consecutive Emmy Awards.

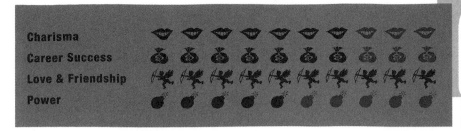

Charisma	😗 😗 😗 😗 😗 😗 😗 😗 😗
Career Success	💰 💰 💰 💰 💰 💰 💰 💰 💰
Love & Friendship	🦅 🦅 🦅 🦅 🦅 🦅 🦅 🦅 🦅
Power	💣 💣 💣 💣 💣 💣 💣 💣 💣

**Moderate Persevering Steady
Undefined Changeable Impatient**

The letter *M* is the icon of all things *maternal*, which is why it occurs in the words for *mother* in virtually every language on earth. It's also the key to the words *maiden*, *mammary*, *mother's milk*, and *marriage*, and when combined with the *hushed* and *hallowed* letter *H*, it creates a unique resonance of nurturing gentility. This is why so many words that incorporate the *HM* phoneme display such pacific qualities: *hum, hymn, humane, home, humble, homily,* and *shalom* (the Hebrew word for peace).

These are the nurturers among us, those sensitive types whose antennae are always vibrating to someone else's needs. But you won't find them dissolving into tears at the terrible state of the world; they're simply too confident in their own virtue to let life's tumult ruffle their feathers.

The *HM* man is the one who can go through an earthquake without spilling his glass of merlot, but won't hesitate to put it aside to comfort the family dog. And if you've ever seen a Renaissance painting of a woman ensconced on a velvet pillow accepting peeled grapes from an adoring lover, then you have a pretty accurate picture of the *HM* woman.

*HM*s have an intrinsic dignity that belies their sensitive natures. They live their lives with such confidence

Hamza
Harmon
Harmony
Herman
Hermina
Hermine
Herminia
Herminio
Hermoine
Humberto
Hiram
Homer
Hyman

in their superiority that they feel little need to assert their authority. Some might say this is complacency, but everyone seems to agree that theirs is a benevolent rule in which they are more than willing to take the needs of others into account.

When it comes to their leisure pursuits, *HM*s are always looking for outlets for their expressive natures, whether it's writing, painting, photography or playing music. But they will rarely make full-time careers out of such trifling activities, for they are far too practical to actually live lives of struggling artists. Instead, they are more likely to have lucrative day jobs that provide them the freedom with which to pursue their hobbies.

Family life in the *HM* household is almost always defined by stability, warmth and togetherness. It would be a faux pas to eat and run at the *HM*'s table—meals are meant to be indulged and washed down with interesting discussions. This kind of dignified pace will drive an impatient type crazy, which is one reason why *HM*s tend to end up with sedate partners who are comfortable with the finer pleasures in life. Children will be raised with extraordinary respect and instilled with the same level of self-esteem enjoyed by their *HM* parent.

Herman Melville Herman Melville stands alone among 19th century American writers in terms of literary stature. His most well known work, *Moby Dick*, was written in 1851 and went on to became a world classic; recognized not only as a great adventure novel, but as a metaphor for man's futile search for understanding. ■ At the age of twelve, Herman was forced to quit school after his father died and set sail for the South Seas on a whaling ship. His adventures became the fodder for his books. ■ *Moby Dick* was not initially well received, but the novel was rediscovered in the 1920's and took its place as a set-work for millions of high-schoolers across the country.

Charisma										
Career Success										
Love & Friendship										
Power										

Trustworthy Reliable Forward-thinking
Dull Hardheaded Closed minded

Although the letter *N* is strongly connected with all things *negative* (*no, not, never, nyet, nix, naught, nein, nada*), when it occurs in words initialized by the *happy* and *hushed* tones of the letter *H*, its pessimistic tones are converted to the warmly nurturing aspects found in the words *honey, harmony, honor, honesty, Hanukkah, handy* and *hunky-dory.* These are names that exude a sense of forthright dependability while still managing to retain their element of mystery.

Still, if you've ever known an *HN*, you know the meaning of the word *stubborn.* These are people who simply cannot to take *no* for an answer, whether in their jobs, their relationships or a losing hand of poker. Yet their hard-headedness is somehow endearing, and, even if your *HN* friends may resort to blustering to get their way, they usually have your best interests in mind. The *HNs'* hearts are as pliant as their exteriors are tough, and people who manage to get close to them are rarely disappointed by their uncommon generosity of spirit.

Their uncompromising dispositions can mean that *HNs* are tough to work with, but the payoffs are usually well worth the effort. As business leaders and entrepreneurs, *HNs* have few equals, and even though they may taste failure on occasion, they have the gump-

Hana
Hanh
Hank
Hanna
Hannah
Hans
Hassan
Haven
Heaven
Henning
Henrietta
Henry
Hernan
Honey

tion to rally themselves until they get it right. The *HN's* co-workers and employees respect this kind of stick-to-it-iveness and are usually willing to overlook the *HN's* pedantic approach to life.

HNs are private about their relationships and resent outside intrusion into their affairs. So to successfully partner an *HN*, you'll need a blend of patience, imagination and independence. Although they crave the closeness that comes from being attached at the hip, they will require plenty of room in which to experiment and explore. But at the end of the day, these are stay-at-home types who enjoy those lazy routines of backrubs and breakfast in bed. You can always count on your *HN* partners to be consistently conventional in their approach to both courtship and marriage.

HNs will also be focused on the practical issues of their relationships: 401ks, property values and mortgage rates. But if there are going to problems in your dealings with your *HN* mate, its source will probably be that annoying stubborn streak that crops up at the most inopportune times. And since there's no getting around it, you'll find giving in to their demands to be the most effective solution. *HNs* are willing to compromise as long as they get what they've always wanted: undying respect and admiration from the ones they love.

Henry Fonda If there were an Academy Award for Grand-Old-Man of American Cinema, Henry Fonda would be one of the nominees. ■ With a Hollywood career that spanned almost half a century, Henry's list of credits is longer than a 1977 Cadillac limousine, and his long-time association with director John Ford spawned some of Hollywood's classic movies: *The Grapes of Wrath, The Great Mr. Lincoln* and *My Darling Clementine.* ■ Henry's genes are also responsible for the acting talent of son Peter (*Easyrider*), daughter Jane (*Barbarella*), and granddaughter Bridget (*Jackie Brown*). ■ Many believe that Henry's greatest triumph was his final film, the Academy Award-winning *On Golden Pond* starring daughter Jane and Katherine Hepburn. Henry died the following year.

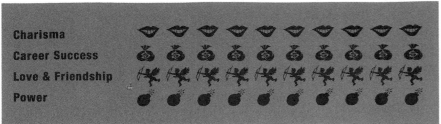

Charisma										
Career Success										
Love & Friendship										
Power										

The letter *P* is the symbol for all things *positive, parental, paternal* and *peppy*, so when it occurs in words initialized by the *hearty* and *healthy* tones of the letter *H*, it evokes the sense of carefree cheerfulness found in the words: *happy, hopeful, hoopla, hype, hippy, chirpy, whoop* and *chippy*. Under the influence of these two positive letters, the name *Hope* has come to symbolize an individual with an unquenchably optimistic outlook on life. But this is someone who doesn't have a lot of time to spend in introspection; she's far too busy making sure that her life runs flawlessly.

Because her name tends to have such a positive effect on others, the *Hope* learns early in life that people accept her with little effort on her part. So she comes across as a relaxed woman who knows what she wants and is confident of receiving it. With this uncommon brand of self-assurance, she is emotionally free to take on all sorts of difficult projects with inspirational and youthful enthusiasm. Still, people may be disappointed to find that a deeper friendship with the *HP* proves to be elusive; as friendly and outgoing as she is, she has little interest in the messier aspects of intimate relationships.

*HP*s are artists at heart and are incessantly seeking new modes of expression. But these are certainly not

Hope

starving artists, for they also have the drive and daring to power themselves through challenging and rewarding careers (usually those geared toward dealing with the public). Working in teams comes naturally for these closet cheerleaders, and *HP*s thrive on making significant contributions to their workplace's esprit de corps. But although these enthusiastic people may be fine motivators, they tend to shun leadership roles that require any kind of intellectual heavy lifting.

It takes a special someone to capture this wayward spirit, for the *HP* is notoriously choosy when it comes to giving her heart. Some people might even accuse her of being remote in matters of love, but the only thing cold about her, is her feet. And it's certainly not that she's commitment-shy. On the contrary, she respects commitment so much, that she's loath to consummate her relationship until absolutely sure that her partner is on the same page.

The *HP*s' tactile senses and fertile imaginations make for some interesting evenings, and a union with one of these blithe souls is recommended for men who appreciate sensitivity and demonstrativeness. The more concrete-minded types will be hoping for her to cheer-down just a little.

Hope Davis Hope Davis' first notable role was at the age of nine when she and her neighbor Mira Sorvino co-wrote and starred in a neighborhood play. By many accounts she has grown into a thinking woman's actress. With a penchant for portraying women wronged by disloyal men (like her breakthrough films *The Daytrippers* and *Next Stop Wonderland*), Hope has won an avid following among the exacting indie film crowd. ■ In hindsight, her rejection for a role on *Baywatch* was a windfall. Instead of watching her cavort in a high-cut bathing suit, fans got to enjoy her thoughtful beauty playing opposite Jeff Bridges in *Arlington Road,* and in the quirky comedy about a small-town psychiatrist in *Mumford*. Hope's commercial breakthrough was as Jack Nicholson's estranged daughter in *About Schmidt* in 2002, which helped earn Jack yet another Best Actor Oscar nomination.

hr

Charisma										
Career Success										
Love & Friendship										
Power										

Playful Exuberant Encouraging
Unbalanced Insecure Snappish

The letter *R* resonates with cheeky sexuality, which explains why it's the initial letter of *romance, rakish, rebel, risqué, ruddy, randy, racy,* and *robust*. But in combination with the *hushed* and *humble* tones of the letter *H*, the *R* also generates words that describe the more admirable aspects of human endeavors *heroic, honor, harmonious, heart, hardy,* and *humor*. These emotive qualities reflect the way *HR* people typically wear their hearts on their sleeves. To *really* know an *HR* is to find it difficult to resist his hearty and down-to-earth personality. *HR*s have that rare ability to put other people at ease without appearing smug or condescending.

*HR*s may be solicitous and gentle with their loved ones, but they're not overburdened with patience. Still, even if they vent with the occasional burst of bad humor, everyone knows that it's more bark than bite. It's a good idea not to push them too far or too often, though, for over time, even these otherwise-harmonious individuals will become cranky and unreasonable.

*HR*s amble through life with an abiding hatred of routine, which is why you won't find them slugging away at the nine-to-five grind unless forced into it by

Harris
Harrison
Harry
Harvey
Herschel
Hershel
Horace
Horacio

the prospect of poverty. These are capable people who have a lot to offer and aren't the kind to take a backseat to anyone. Typically, they're attracted to jobs that promise creative freedom (or at least a high degree of autonomy), and the most common complaint about the *HR*s is that they'll sometimes take their independent philosophies to the extreme and make far too many reckless decisions.

*HR*s are introspective people who are dedicated to their ideals and convictions. And as friends, *HR*s are almost without peer. Trustworthy, reliable and dependable, they understand that the responsibilities of friendship extend beyond casual familiarity and the occasional drink. To them, a friend in need is a call to arms, and they'll reflexively volunteer their services without having to be asked.

*HR*s tend to choose mates who can balance their adventurous aspects with responsible and grounded outlooks. But in their zeal to find mates who can offer them the stability they need, they run the risk of settling for women who don't appreciate their unconventional perspectives. Still, because *HR*s are quick learners and masters in the art of compromise, their marriages are more stable and permanent than most.

Harry Belafonte Harlem born Jamaican crooner and activist, Harry Belafonte, has one of the smoothest voices (and skin) of any Calypso singer in history. His song "Day-O" ("The Banana Boat Song") is still a staple of beach parties throughout the world. ■ A long-time friend of Martin Luther King, Harry's criticism of the South African apartheid government brought him close ties with Nelson Mandela. In 2002, Harry made headlines after using the words "Colin Powell" and "house-slave" in the same sentence. Made in connection with the looming 2003 Iraqi war, it was an extraordinary statement given that both Harry and Powell shared a Caribbean heritage. ■ Although roundly criticized for his statement, Harry refused to recant, noting that although he greatly respected Powell, men of greatness must do what they believe is right.

THE SURPRISING *ht*

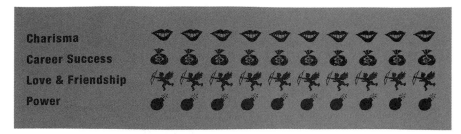

Charisma										
Career Success										
Love & Friendship										
Power										

Soft-spoken Spiritual Humble
Self-righteous Passive Distant

Most names beginning with the *hushed* and *harmless* intimations of the letter *H* make us think of a well-rounded personality with very few hard edges. But the *triumphant* tones of the letter *T* are rife with implications of self-assurance and outspoken confidence, which is why the words *hot, heart* and *heat* are so reliant on the *T* to convey their passionate significance. These are people who speak softly and carry a big stick of self-confidence.

*HT*s seem to cruise through life with enviable ease, and meeting someone as confident as them, can leave some people feeling a little insecure. In fact, if you've ever tried to befriend one of these cool-headed individuals, you'll know that it takes quite a bit of effort to get past their reserved exteriors. It's not that they're overly introverted; it's just that they prefer to maintain a low emotional profile until the other person has been proven worthy of their friendship. So while though they're unfailingly polite and considerate, their socially cautious attitudes give them reputations for standoffishness and keep many at bay.

*HT*s are inveterate measurers (in their relationships as well as in their careers), and carefully calculate the pros and cons of every decision. When they meet poten-

Harriet
Harriett
Harriette
Hattie
Heath
Heather
Hector
Herta
Hester
Hettie
Hilton
Hortense
Houston
Hoyt
Hunter

tial mates, it's difficult for them to simply go with the situation's emotional flow, and they can't help second-guessing whether their partners are tall enough, rich enough or beautiful enough. Perhaps this is why so many people think that *HT*s are judgmental, but it really comes down to the fact that they are far more critical of *themselves* than of anyone else.

When it comes to their careers, *HT*s integrate easily into the workplace and will obligingly accept the authority of their leaders. But these are proud people, who, unless they believe their contributions are being appreciated, will quickly fall into rebellion and seek more creative pastures. This combination of a quiet exterior and an unyielding core might seem a little passive-aggressive, but it seems to work perfectly well for the *HT*s.

*HT*s have plenty of spunk when it comes to their intimate relationships, and even though they will dutifully play the role of supportively loving mates, they're not going to be satisfied with just going through the motions. They're always the first to initiate new ways of romancing, and make sure that vacations are regular and exciting. Encouraging and positive, they are never happy until their loved ones are equally content.

Heather Locklear The perennially pretty Heather Locklear has been one of television's most sought-after actresses for over a decade. ■ After appearing on *Melrose Place*, *Texas Justice*, *The Return of Swamp Thing* and *T.J. Hooker*, Heather played herself in *Wayne's World II*—a nod to just how much of an icon she had become. ■ Heather's private life was as varied as her career, and she was romantically linked to Scott Baio, Tom Cruise and Mark Harmon. Her rocker period featured an unfortunate seven-year marriage to Tommy Lee of *Motley Crue* and a union to Richie Sambora of *Bon Jovi*. In 1997 the couple gave birth to a girl. ■ Interestingly, the blonde, blue-eyed actress claims to be part African. Her last name, she claims, is common amongst members of the Lumbee tribe.

173

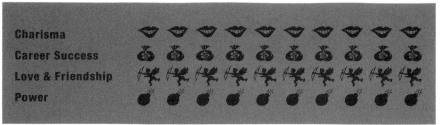

Charisma										
Career Success										
Love & Friendship										
Power										

Innovative Quick-thinking Shrewd
Selfish Hardheaded Arrogant

The letter *W* is the icon for all things mysterious and untamed. And as the initial letter of *wild*, *weird*, *wispy*, *werewolf* and *whimsy*, when it comes into contact with the *hushed* tones of the *humble* letter *H*, it takes on a distinct sense of the sardonic *shrewd*, *showy*, *thwart*, *hawkish*, *shallow*, and *hogwash*. In the case of the names *Howard* and *Hayward*, it's worth noting that the *RD* phoneme is usually associated with the impish qualities found in the words: *rude*, *ribald*, *sordid*, *crude*, *bastard*, *fraud*, *lurid*, *pride*, *torrid*, *turgid*, and *weird*. So, not surprisingly, *Howards* are people whose enigmatic personalities walk the fine line between good humor and bad taste, while *Howies* tend to take themselves decidedly less seriously.

Hayward
Howard
Howie

Like all people whose names begin with the letter *H*, *HW* personalities have a gentle side that is readily apparent to those who know them intimately. These are people who prize loyalty and friendship above all else, and even though they might drive you crazy, they'll always be there for you when it counts. Either way, you're unlikely to become jaded with an *HW* in your life. Annoyed and provoked, perhaps, but never bored. Their sense of adventure is legendary, and there's nothing an *HW* won't try, even if it means taking great risks.

So if you're in the mood to get crazy and stupid for a night, give your *HW* friend a call.

*HW*s function best in careers that allow them full rein to express themselves, and will easily grow frustrated when they feel their creativity is being repressed in any way. Co-workers love them, bosses are in awe of them, and customers are likely to buy from them. Even though their eccentricities provide plenty of distraction from their work routines, *HW*s have a work ethic that is second to none.

*HW*s pride themselves on being mysterious—even when they're being as transparent as picture windows. So don't let your *HW* friends discover that you've figured them out! It will simply challenge them to become more enigmatic and unpredictable than ever.

As mates, *HW*s are tricky propositions. They prefer their partners to be stable (all the better to counteract their erratic lives), but if the union is to succeed, their partners must be up to the challenges brought about by the *HW*s' non-linear thinking and whimsical ways. Having children seems to be the only thing that brings continuity to *HW*s' otherwise roller-coaster lifestyles, and because they secretly crave the anchoring effect of kids, they are probably going to be the first to propose having them.

Howard Stern Howard Stern once claimed that the sexually voracious character of his radio show was simply a character he played, and that his real personality was that of loving husband to his wife of twenty years. Only after his separation from wife Alison did he admit that his role as husband had been the act, and that he really was his obnoxious show-business persona. ■ Claiming the mantle of King of All Media, Howard leveraged his morning talk show into a media conglomerate that included best selling books *Private Parts* and *Miss America*. Whether it was showing up on *The Tonight Show* with scantily clad lesbians or flying butt-naked into the MTV music awards, Howard continues to stoke his reputation as the man to watch—and listen to.

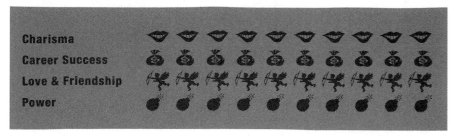

Charisma											
Career Success											
Love & Friendship											
Power											

**Creative Sociable Humble
Submissive Passive Fearful**

The letter *Z* is indelibly associated with all things *zesty* and *zany*. So when it occurs in words alongside the *humble, homey* letter *H*, it creates the sense of cheeky warmth that percolates through the words *chutzpah, schmaltz, schmooze, huzzah,* and *humanize.* These are softly gentle personalities, full of loopy surprises and the kind you want to have around when you need a little life in your cocktail party.

Like most people whose names begin with the letter *H*, *Hazels* are not particularly proactive about making waves, but have the uncanny ability to bring harmony and balance to any situation. Not that they're pushovers by any means; it's just that their philosophical aesthetic calls for things to be on an even keel.

If there's strife among the *HZ*'s family or friends, you can count on her inserting herself right in the middle as an arbitrator. But don't mistake her need for tranquility as an invitation to whine, for *Hazel* isn't always the best person to go to when you're looking purely for sympathy. Your *Hazel* friend may be incensed that your fiancée left you at the altar, but she's not going allow herself to be used as a human Kleenex. She's much more likely to dispense the type of sensible advice that makes

Hazel

a practical difference.

Hazels are industrious women but suffer from a lack of focus when they have too much on their plates. Rather than tackling the big issues in their lives (like paying the rent and feeding the dog), they're likely to be writing a poem to send in to the greeting- card company or debating where to move the couch. Occasionally, these distractions can adversely affect their intimate relationships, which over time can suffer from lack of nourishment.

But it should be remembered that although *Hazels* sometimes give the impression that they need more time to themselves, they genuinely enjoy company and value their friendships

If you're in love with an *HZ*, there's something you should know: If she seems to be putting her energies into other issues, it doesn't mean that she doesn't care about you. On the contrary, it's only *because* she knows that the relationship is stable that she is comfortable enough to futz around. The time to worry is when she starts making you her priority. So if you're the sort who needs constant attention, you should consider getting a puppy. As long as she's happily distracted with her many projects, you can rest easy that your *Hazel* mate will always be there for you.

Hazel Wightman In the age of powerhouse tennis stars who consider themselves lucky if they can dominate the court for a few years, Hazel Wightman stands alone in her fifty year domination of American tennis. ■ Hazel was arguably the greatest tennis player who ever lived. Winning an astonishing forty-five U.S. tennis titles over the course of her career, she won her first U.S. singles championship in 1909 and won the doubles and mixed doubles in the same tournament. ■ Hazel is credited for being the first woman to use the volley as a winning strategy, made more complicated by the fact that she played with her skirt down to her ankles. Before finally retiring, Hazel won the 1954 U.S. Senior Championships at the age of sixty-seven, beating players almost thirty years her junior.

**Most Popular
Girl's Names**

Irene

Ida

Irma

Isabel

Iris

Inez

Ina

Ingrid

Iva

Isabelle

**Most Popular
Boy's Names**

Ian

Ivan

Isaac

Ira

Israel

Irving

Ismael

Ignacio

Irvin

Isaiah

The Letter of Self Indulgence

The word I is the single most repeated word in the English language, and as the initial character of introspection, idealistic, indulgent, illuminating, id, illustrious, individualistic and identity, it's not surprising that I people exhibit a high level of self-esteem. This kind of confidence is commonly seen in the traditional meanings of names like Imogene (image), Irving (handsome and fair), Inez (pure), Ismael (God listens) and Ilyssa (rational). ■ Typically, I people are more intuitive than practical, and more ego-driven than most, and with the exception of the letter R, I people are more likely to become doctors or famous entertainers than any other initial letter. They suffer nonetheless from the same problem as the other ego-related vowel, the A: their self-assurance is often mistaken for conceit and egotism. This explains why surveys show that people almost never associate I names with either feminine warmth or robust masculinity. ■ But when it functions as a terminating letter, the I has an entirely different effect. There is no comparison, for example, from the arrogant pronunciation of the I in Ivan, to the feminine pronunciation of the I in Tammi, for whenever words end with a high pitched letter (I or Y), they invariably i,part a reassuring and spiritual texture found in the words yogi, rabbi, beauty, merry and chivalry. ■

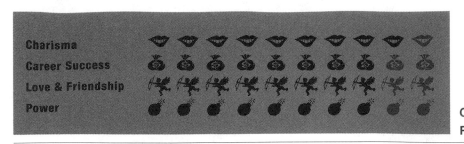

Charisma	👄 👄 👄 👄 👄 👄 👄 👄 👄 👄
Career Success	💰 💰 💰 💰 💰 💰 💰 💰 💰 💰
Love & Friendship	🦅 🦅 🦅 🦅 🦅 🦅 🦅 🦅 🦅 🦅
Power	💣 💣 💣 💣 💣 💣 💣 💣 💣 💣

Composed Secure Decisive
Repressed Dissatisfied Morose

Names that begin with the *idealistically intellectual* letter *I* almost always denote an individual with a strong sense of self-worth and high intelligence, and its union with the letter *L*—the symbol for *life, love, liberty, lust* and *learning*—suggests a feminine creature with an uncommon facility for philosophical introspection. It should be noted however, that people with names like *Ilene, Ilona* and *Ilana*—which incorporate the *negative* letter *N* (*no, not, never, nix, nada, nyet, nein, nothing*)—often have to cope with occasional mood swings and a propensity for pessimism.

Like all people with high intellectual and emotional intelligences, *ILs* possess a quiet strength that grows more apparent as you get to know them better. And while they are hardly ever outspoken about their opinions, you always get the feeling that they have a lot to say. Even in an all-out debate, *ILs* are more likely to stand on the sidelines with an enigmatic smile than they are to show-off their considerable verbal skills.

ILs are also more likely to stand up for others than for themselves, and if you want to test this theory, just try meddling with one of their loved ones. This is about the only time you'll experience the *IL's* darker aspects and, even though they don't have a temper worse than anyone else's, once they've built up a head of steam it can be virtually impossible to derail them. It's not easy to find people with this capable combination of protectiveness and obduracy, so it's not surprising that *ILs* have few problems with finding friends.

ILs, like most people whose names begin with an *I*, are drawn to the medical profession. But those that choose *not* to pursue the sciences manage to blossom in jobs that allow them to operate at their own pace. This is why they so often gravitate toward small business enterprises in which they'll sacrifice income for creative freedom. Teamwork presents no problems for the empathic *ILs*, but overall, they prefer solo ventures in which they can take credit for their own efforts.

When it comes to family life, *ILs* prove enthusiastic and dedicated mates who place great importance on establishing a friendship with their spouse. They are fastidious about keeping the channels of communication well maintained, and *IL* marriages are characterized by the teamwork with which they build their nests. Children are welcome additions to the *IL's* rich emotional network and can expect intelligent discipline and unconditional love.

Ileana
Ilene
Ilana
Iliana
Ilona
Ilse
Iola

Ilene Graff The thing about supporting actors and actresses is that they tend to be more well-rounded than the average one-dimensional Hollywood megastar. They have to be. To make a living in the competitive world of TV and film, you have to be ready to sing, dance and get into character at a moment's notice. At least that's how Ilene Graff makes her living. ■ Best known for her role as Bob Ueker's wife on ABC's popular comedy *Mr. Belvedere*, Ilene has also popped up in *Three's Company, Laverne and Shirley, Touched by an Angel, St. Elsewhere, Remington Steele* and *Mork and Mindy*. ■ At last report, Ilene lives in California, raising money for charity and singing for her supper on cruise ships.

THE DEDICATED im

Charisma	👄 👄 👄 👄 👄 👄 👄 👄 👄 👄
Career Success	💰 💰 💰 💰 💰 💰 💰 💰 💰 💰
Love & Friendship	💘 💘 💘 💘 💘 💘 💘 💘 💘 💘
Power	💣 💣 💣 💣 💣 💣 💣 💣 💣 💣

**Pragmatic Supportive Attentive
Fussy Self-sacrificing Driven**

Inasmuch as the letter *M* is the definitive icon of all things *motherly* (*maternal, mammary, matronly, mamma, milk, maiden*) and the letter *I,* the symbol of *idealistic introspection*, the *IM* combination implies a uniquely pensive name with an exceptionally high emotional intelligence. These are people who are unafraid to take a stand. Pick an issue, any issue, and they'll be right there to weigh in with their opinions.

IMs will stop at nothing to see justice done, even if their definition of justice is likely to differ from those around them. But while they may well be fierce defenders of their families and close friends, they're unquestionably dedicated to the preservation of their own reputations and status. What depresses *IMs* more than anything, is having no current passion in their lives: These are people who need a reason to get out of bed in the morning.

Few *IMs* travel without their cell-phones or stray too far from their email. *IMs* are experts at expressing themselves, and whether it takes the form of their exceptional verbal skills or letter writing prowess, they're the kind of people who hate being out of touch—even for a minute. These are people who have no problems with shyness and who will freely share

Ima
Imani
Imanol
Imelda
Ibrahim
Immanuel
Imogene

their effusive spirits with those in their lives. But supporting such a high-profile presence requires a constant output of emotional energy, which can sometimes leave *IMs* feeling drained. When life gets too overwhelming, they'll need to find a tranquil place to meditate and recharge their batteries.

IMs' protective instincts extend their home-lives, and they're quite proactive about nourishing the relationships that bond them to a rather wide circle of friends. The spiritual nature of *IMs* come to light when they become parents, where they're careful to instill their offspring with a sense of self-awareness that will provide them structure and direction long after they've left the nest.

Love and courtship are likewise very serious matters to the *IMs*—so much so that they'll think nothing of setting aside all their other activities to pursue a potential mate. And *pursuit* is one thing that *IMs* are particularly good at, for with their knack for subtle courting and sly flirtations, their quarry often has no idea that they are being pursued. By then it's too late, and the *IM's* new mate will find him or herself signed onto a lifetime of partnering someone whose interests lie exclusively in their family's well-being.

Imelda Marcos At the Miss Manila finals in the early 1950's, a shy teenager took the stage in a swimsuit to await the judges' results. Imelda Romualdez won the contest and went on to become one of the Philippine's most reviled personalities. ■ Her marriage to Ferdinand Marcos in 1954 spurred her husband's political ambitions, and in 1964 he achieved the Presidency. The Marcoses used their power to amass huge amounts of wealth but were eventually forced to flee the country amid allegations of corruption. Imelda's huge shoe closet became the locus for popular outrage represented her ambivalence to the suffering of the Filipino people. ■ Although she was later convicted of corruption, a revived Imelda went on to win election to the House of Representatives in her home province of Leyte in 1995.

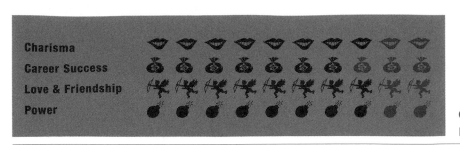

Charisma										
Career Success										
Love & Friendship										
Power										

Calm Self-aware Reassuring
Repressed Uncommunicative Egotistical

Because the letter *N* is the definitive symbol of *negative* influence (*no, not, never, nix, nada, naught, nein, nyet,* and *nowhere*), it tends to convey an air of pessimism and self-doubt in many of the words in which it appears. And even though names that begin with the *idealistic* and *intellectual* letter *I* almost always depict an individual with a high level of self-worth and intelligence, its conjunction with the *N* still tends to describe the downbeat motifs found in the words *inane, inept, inferno, infidel, inmate, insipid,* and *infirm.*

Despite the cynical implications of the *IN* names, these are very bright people whose inner reserves help them achieve balance in their active lifestyles. And while inwardly they might be warmly passionate, you won't encounter *this* side until you've gotten to know them fairly well: These are natural introverts who require some one-on-one work before they're going to lower their walls. And even though *IN* people prefer being the *approached*—rather than the *approacher*, it's unlikely that they will ever refuse a person in need. They recognize, at least intellectually, that everyone needs a hand now and then.

Like most people whose names begin with the letter *I*, the *INs* tend to view the universe through a prism of intellectualism rather than relating to it emotionally,

Ian
Ignacio
Ina, India
Ines, Inez
Infant
Inga, Inge
Ingrid
Iona
Ione
Iyana
Iyanna

which is why such a high percentage of them wind up in the medical fields as scientists or researchers. Even when they make their mark as artists (*I* names are on the top of the list when it comes to this), they tend to approach their work somewhat clinically, rather than being driven by their feelings. And because the *IN's* introspective nature often turns inward for answers to life's many questions, they are without equal as psychologists and counselors.

Making friends with an *IN* may take some effort, but it will usually prove to be worth the exertion. They are great listeners, if not the most forthcoming talkers, and will quietly listen to you for hours while you reveal your deepest secrets. And don't ever worry that your privacy isn't going to be safe: *INs* have deep contempt for gossip and meddling.

Partnering an *IN* will be an equally rewarding experience, unless you especially need excitement in your life. The price of being with these steady, internally controlled creatures, is having to cater to their need for predictability and routine. If you can deal with the occasional explosion of petulance, you're going to be blessed with one of the most steadfastly supportive mates on the planet.

Ingrid Bergman Arguably the steamiest love affair ever portrayed on the big screen was between Ingrid Bergman and Humphrey Bogart in the 1942 film classic, *Casablanca.* Those were the days of a heavily stylized form of acting popularized by Marlene Dietrich and Greta Garbo, and Ingrid's natural style proved to be hugely popular with international audiences. ■ Ingrid's intriguing accent and porcelain beauty gave her enormous power in an industry dominated by men and she used her influence to help destroy the studio contract system despised by almost all actors at the time. ■ She learned a bitter lesson about American culture after she left her husband for film director Roberto Rossellini. Ingrid was denounced by the U.S. Senate outraged at the "moral degradation" of Hollywood.

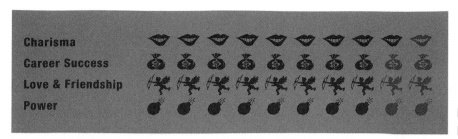

Charisma										
Career Success										
Love & Friendship										
Power										

Idealistic Creative Motivated
Distracted Disconnected Unrealistic

The letter *R* is one of the symbols for overt, cheeky sexuality. We see it's *racy* influence in words like *randy, ribald, raunchy, rapture, relish, ripe, ruddy* and *Romeo*. And when it appears in names initialized by the idealistic letter *I*, it suggests an individual with intensely creative qualities and a passion for living. These are people with the potential for greatness—whether it's in their art, work, or relationships—and are the kinds who throw themselves with unrestrained gusto into everything they do. Even when they don't always emerge at the top of their chosen fields, *IRs* consider it a success just to have been in the game.

IRs are strongly connected to the life forces in the universe, and anything to do with animals, people and nature seems to hold a special fascination. And this connection isn't simply an intellectual affair, for *IRs* have a wellspring of emotional reserve that serves to bind them to their loved ones. If it sometimes seems that *IRs* are looking at life through rose-colored glasses, it should be noted that their optimistic outlooks are very deliberately constructed. They see no reason to dwell on past mistakes, and have a capacity for forgiveness that almost seems reckless on occasion.

IR people are doers and it's unlikely that you'll ever see them at a loss for something to keep them occupied.

Ira
Ireland
Irena
Irene
Irina
Iris
Irma

They'll be the first to suggest a new movie or a trip to Las Vegas, and tend form close alliances with like-minded people. But this doesn't mean that life with your *IR* friend will always goes down smoothly: The flipside to the *IR's* active mind is an unyielding quality that often manifests itself in a little bit of bossiness.

When it comes to their intimate relationships, *IRs* enjoy nothing better than exercising their mental reflexes in debates and intellectual small talk. But a consequence of having a formidable mind is that many people overlook their gentle sides. You could know them for years and never fully experience the sensitive core underlying their keen intellect. In fact, many people comment on how surprised they were to discover that their *IR* friend felt a certain way about something.

As an expression of their self-doubt, *IRs* have a tendency to vacillate on even the smallest decisions when it comes to their relationships. Consequently, dating *IRs* can be like riding a roller coaster—one of those big wooden ones you think is about to fall apart. But if you enjoy wild romps with a partner who shares your passion for adventure, you'll find them to be perfect gems.

Ira Gershwin A decision by the Gershwin family to buy a piano for their music-mad fourteen-year-old changed their lives forever. Ira and his younger brother, George, went on to become one of the most heralded song writing teams in Broadway history. ■ In deference to his Jewish heritage, Ira was originally named Israel Gershvin and was the lyricist to George's music. But the brothers' greatest triumph was originally a box office failure. Written two years before George's death, *Porgy and Bess*—a depiction of an impoverished black man and his wife—eventually proved to be the high-water mark of their career. The show is now known as *The American Opera* and features the songs "Bess, You is My Woman Now," "I Got Plenty uh Nuttin'" and "Summertime."

IS

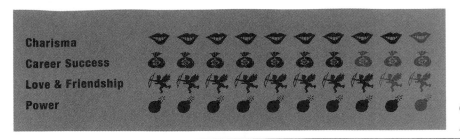

Charisma										
Career Success										
Love & Friendship										
Power										

Courageous Passionate Complex
Argumentative Conservative Compulsive

The letter *S* is the symbol for all things *sexy, sublime, sensual, sassy, slinky* and *sylph-like,* and when it occurs as the dominant letter in a name, we find these individuals to be passionate, hot-blooded and very much in love with life. And since these names begin with the letter *I*—the icon of *idealistic introspection*— these people exhibit a wonderful balance of enthusiasm tempered with practical know-how. If all of life's a stage, the *IS* doesn't mind not having a leading role as long as they have a speaking part.

Although these are people you definitely want to get to know, befriending an *IS* can be an exasperating experience. You might, for example, be caught up in a deep conversation with them, only to discover that their minds are running a mile a minute contemplating their daily to-do list. It's not that they don't *want* to listen to your ideas, but their lives are generally so full of activity that standing still isn't something they do very well. Still, if an *IS* ever senses that you really need his or her help, you'll be promoted to the top of their priority list, where you'll find few friends to be more attentive, accommodating and just plain helpful. This is just one symptom of the *IS's* intense nature: When something is important enough, they'll tap their deep reserves and

Iesha
Isai
Isaiah
Isaias
Isamar
Isiah
Isidro
Isis
Ismael
Israel
Isreal
Izaiah

come through with a surprising amount of emotional and physical strength.

But this expenditure of energy comes at a price, and there will be times that your *IS* friend is going to feel emotionally depleted. So if you're in an *ISs'* inner circle, you'd better be ready to reciprocate their support. *ISs* have long memories and will not forgive a slight without some kind of subtle retaliation.

When it comes to their intimate relationships, *ISs* often find themselves in the predicament common to many high-energy people. Unless their mates are able to match their high metabolisms and put up with the occasional emotional outburst, the imbalance of power can ultimately lead to disaster. This might be frustrating to those *IS* partners who require a great deal of attention, but the sooner they accept that *ISs* are independent people whose interests will not be confined just to them, the better. When partnered with the *right* person, the *IS* will prove as committed and loyal a mate as anyone could wish for.

If they choose to experience parenthood, *ISs* are not ones to smother their children with advice. They'd rather they follow their own stars and not to let society's conventions dictate their dreams.

Iris Murdoch Iris Murdoch was a prolific British writer who managed to complete a novel in the final stages of Alzheimer's disease. She was the subject of the 2003 feature film, *Iris*, starring Kate Murdoch. ■ Iris was a writer's writer, forbidding editors to make any changes to her text and completing twenty-six novels in forty years of writing. Her novels wove philosophical tensions intended to spark ideas in her readers. ■ Her first novel, *Under the Net*, was published in 1954 but it was her seminal work, *The Sea, The Sea* that won her the Booker Prize. ■ In 1956 Iris married a man six years her junior who was a self-described virgin. Eventually succumbing to the ravages of Alzheimer's in 1999, she became—as her husband put it—"like a very nice three-year-old."

isbl

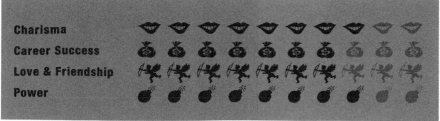

Charisma										
Career Success										
Love & Friendship										
Power										

**Expressive Provocative Original
Melodramatic Unrealistic Proud**

If complex names are a sign of complicated personalities, the *ISBL* names are amongst the most intricate in the world. The dominant letter in these names—the *introspective* and *intellectual* letter *I*—suggests a person of logical restraint, while the *sexy, sultry, slinky, sensuous* letter *S* suggests someone with a *sassy sexuality*. Still, we can't underestimate the *belligerent* power of the *BL* phoneme, for words shaped by the *BL* almost always denote some form of aggressive action: *blackmail, blowhard, blame, blast, blaze, blockade, bloodbath* and *bludgeon*. All told, these are women whose names proclaim a personality of exceptional depth, intelligence and enigmatic power.

The *ISBL* is always acutely aware of her surroundings: sensing the vibes from other people and acting accordingly. Although there's no question that she's strong and self-confident, she's a bit of a closet introvert in that she rarely makes the first move. Unfortunately, her intimidating essence can make the *ISBL* such a daunting proposition for prospective suitors that many *ISBLs* spend more than a few Saturday nights washing their hair.

If you could personify the essence of perpetual motion, the *ISBL* would come close—there's a bit of the Energizer Bunny inside every one of them. This kind of kinetic energy enables the *ISBL* to be an excellent motivator in both her work and personal settings in which she loves playing ringleader to her tightly knit circle of girlfriends. At work, she's usually the one to plan all the staff parties and birthday surprises; to the *ISBL*, life without frequent merrymaking is simply not worth living.

For all her effervescent deportment, it's easy to forget that the *ISBL's* volcanic impetuosity can detonate without warning. The trouble is that many *ISBLs* have a habit of denying the stresses that build up in their lives, and they're often as surprised as anyone when they reach critical mass. But like most eruptions, these outbursts are short-lived and functionally harmless.

If you fallen in love with an *ISBL* and suspect that her feelings are not reciprocal, chances are, there are no reasons to worry. At some point—perhaps triggered by her fear of losing you—the *ISBL's* romantic cavalry will arrive to protect her emotional investment. And even though a long-term partnership might wear off her rough edges, she'll never lose her charmingly convoluted essence.

Isabel
Isabela
Isabell
Isabella
Isabelle
Isobel
Izabella

Isabella Rossellini If it's true that it helps to have a pedigree in Hollywood, then the daughter of Ingrid Bergman and Italian director Roberto Rossellini has nothing to complain about. ■ Isabella's first introduction to American audiences was in the 1985 Mikhail Baryshnikov vehicle, *White Nights*, during the filming of which she was involved in a love affair with the Russian dancer. ■ While she was earning millions of dollars as the principal model for the cosmetic giant Lancôme, Isabella took a risk by appearing in the disturbing David Lynch film *Blue Velvet*. The movie's harsh depiction of Isabella's character prompted Roger Ebert to say that he had never seen an actress so humiliated outside of a pornographic movie. ■ In 1979, Isabella married director Martin Scorsese, but divorced him less than four years later.

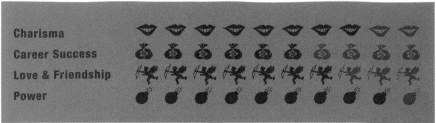

Charisma	
Career Success	
Love & Friendship	
Power	

Talented Attentive Loving
Temperamental Unpredictable Oversensitive

Words and names that end in the letter *K* (or hard *C*) tend to project the sense of forceful action and masculine power that we see in the words *kick, knock, smack, flak, crack, thwack* and *smack.* And because these names are initialized by the *intellectual* and *introspective* letter *I,* and followed up by the *sexy, slinky, sassy, sensual* letter *S,* they suggest a man whose intellect and passions are anchored by a resolute self-confidence.

The *ISK* is a man who knows what he wants and is willing to put his foot down if anyone tries to stand in his way. He is such an interesting blend of brains and masculinity that members of the opposite sex report an unmistakable sexual attraction to him (even though you wouldn't think so to look at him). *ISKs* may take themselves seriously but aren't above lightening up every now and then to pull the occasional practical joke—even if their sense of humor is sometimes so obtuse that only family members will get the joke.

Isaac
Isaak
Issac

ISKs often choose careers in which they don't have to associate too intimately with other people. They prefer the anonymity of larger groups to the forced familiarity of working one-on-one. They're certainly not incapable of forming close ties, but they're reluctant to invest the kind of emotional energy it takes to become close to "just" a co-worker. And although *ISKs* function well in unstructured environments, they're unlikely to take risks when it comes to their livelihoods. If there's going to be a layoff, they'll be one step ahead of the game with their exit strategies laid out well in advance.

And try not to mention that your car is having engine trouble around an *ISK:* You're liable to get a detailed explanation of the internal combustion engine. Not that he's going to get his hands dirty, mind you, but he'll certainly be willing to give you directions on how to replace your carburetor.

When it comes to marriage, *ISKs* may well prove to be devoted mates, but they're also going to be a little distracted. Not by other women, mind you, but by their work, hobbies, and the Internet. So don't allow your *ISK* husband to set up a home-office unless you're willing to see him only for a few hours a day.

Still, with a little judicious nagging you'll have a mate who's quite content to stay home and play Scrabble or chess with you every night. There may even be times when your *ISK* gets a rush of blood and presents you with a night to remember.

Isaac Newton Sir Isaac Newton—one of the greatest scientists in history—was also a leading practitioner of alchemy. Although largely discredited by modern science, alchemy included the notion that one element could be transformed into another. ■ The popular story that Isaac "invented" gravity after having an apple fall on his head was a simplification of what was really a laborious piece of detective work. While trying to explain the mathematical principles of gravity, he invented an entirely new branch of mathematics, the bane of every undergraduate engineering student: calculus. ■ After his "retirement," Isaac was appointed to the head of the British Mint where he figured out a way to stop people from shaving silver off the coin. The slightly raised edges on all U.S. coins are a remnant of this idea.

IV

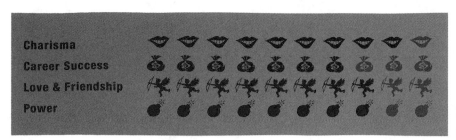

Charisma	
Career Success	
Love & Friendship	
Power	

Confident Charismatic Outgoing
Self-serving Egotistical Belligerent

The *V* is the unmistakable icon of both masculine and feminine sexuality, and its *virile* power can be seen in the words *vestal virgins, virtuous, vanquish, virgin, virtue, vixen, vamp, Venus* and *Viagra.* And when the *valiant V* occurs in names initialized by the *introspective* and *intelligent* letter *I*, it evokes a person of extraordinary ardor *and* the street smarts to pull it off. Assertive, but never heavy-handed, *IVs* know exactly what they want out of life and have few scruples about getting it. But these aren't the type of people who have to resort to underhanded tactics or throwing their weight around; their personalities are so compelling that most people seem happy to help them out.

IVs are going to be the dominant force in both their professional lives and in their relationships. Even these people's employers will learn to stay their good side, for they recognize the motivating effects that an *IV* can have on the rest of the workers. And when *IVs* are not happy with conditions at work, they will have no compunction about resigning and going into business for themselves.

The *IV* is capable of making and maintaining close relationships, provided their partners meet their high standards. And don't think the *IV* is going to cut you any slack when it comes to your contribution to the relation-

Irvin
Irving
Iva
Ivan
Ivana
Ivelisse
Ivette
Ivonne
Ivory
Ivy

ship: you'll have to earn their respect and you will be periodically evaluated. Because status is so important to the *IVs,* they like to surround themselves primarily with worldly and successful individuals. But beware. Even if you've been accepted into *IVs* inner circle, there will usually be an undercurrent of competitiveness in your relationship with them.

As with most alpha males and females, *IVs* have expressive faces that unconsciously convey whatever emotions they happen to be feeling. So while you'll always know what's going on inside their hearts, the downside is that *IVs* will make no attempt to convey what they're thinking. So intimacy with *IVs* can be a little tricky—and even a little harrowing—for those with less assertive personalities, but when *IVs* find mates with whom they are intellectually compatible, they will demonstrate more patience than you thought possible.

A marriage with such a commanding temperament can be a tempestuous affair, but because the *IV* hates to admit defeat, even an unhealthy union has a good chance at longevity. If you're going to choose an *IV* as a mate, it's best to find one who has been tempered with a healthy dose of humility from previously failed relationships.

Ivana Trump Many people expected the wife of real estate mogul Donald Trump to be eclipsed by her flashy husband, but anyone who knew Ivana before their 1977 marriage knew better. Ivana became VP of Interior Design for his organization and the President of the Plaza Hotel in New York City. ■ Ivana grew up in Czechoslovakia, but immigrated to Canada in the early 1970s. In 1976, in a bar in New York she was treated to drinks by a pushy stranger named "The Donald." The two were married a year later and Ivana gave birth to Donald Jr. shortly thereafter. ■ After a stormy marriage played out in news magazines everywhere, the couple divorced in 1990. As a single mother, Ivana became a successful entrepreneur in her own right, establishing her own lucrative jewelry and cosmetic companies.

**Most Popular
Girl's Names**

Jennifer

Jessica

Janet

Joyce

Julie

Jean

Joan

Judith

Janice

Judy

**Most Popular
Boy's Names**

James

John

Joseph

Jason

Josè

Jeffrey

Joshua

Jerry

Joe

Juan

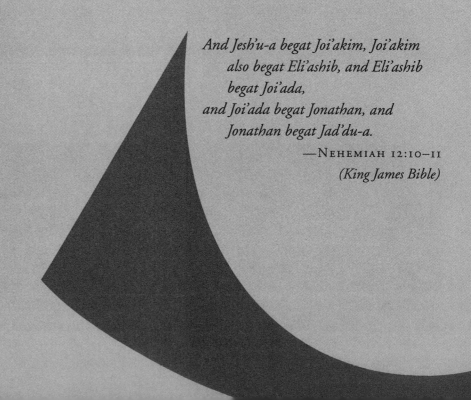

*And Jesh'u-a begat Joi'akim, Joi'akim
also begat Eli'ashib, and Eli'ashib
begat Joi'ada,
and Joi'ada begat Jonathan, and
Jonathan begat Jad'du-a.*
—Nehemiah 12:10–11
(King James Bible)

The Letter of Refined Judgement

Although the letter J initializes fewer than 1% of all English words, it is easily the most popular first letter for names in the Western world. In addition to accounting for over 11% of all names, it initializes four of the top twenty most popular male names— James, John, Jacob and Joseph—as well as two of the top five surnames—Johnson and Jones. What makes this all the more unusual is that the I and J only became wholly separate letters in the seventeenth century. ■ The pervasiveness of the letter J stems from its repeated use in the Bible, from John to Jacob, Jeremiah, Jezebel, and James to Jared. But since most biblical references to the letter J are masculine, female J's occur with only about half the frequency of their male counterparts. ■ With its special status as the initial letter of Jehovah, Jesus, judgment, Judicia, jury and Jupiter (the king of the Roman Gods), the letter J has become inextricably linked to the qualities of wisdom and justice. This can be seen in the traditional meaning of names such as Jarvis (conqueror), James (supplanter), Justin (truth), Jessica (God's Grace) and Jethro (outstanding). ■ As one might expect from a letter that begins the name of God, J people are hugely successful in everything they attempt and are found in the top four in each of the categories: professional sports, business, arts, medicine and politics. ■

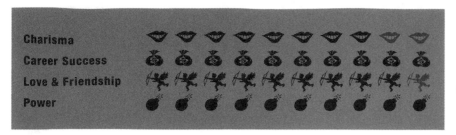

Charisma										
Career Success										
Love & Friendship										
Power										

Warm Intelligent Engaging
Distracted Overly emotional
Uncommunicative

The letter *J* is the icon of all things to do with *justice*: *judgment, judicious, jury, Jehovah, jail* and *Jupiter*, the head of the Roman Gods. It is also usually associated with all things conservative, deep-thinking, and sober-minded. But when names such as these are terminated with a vowel or the playfully *youthful* letter *Y*, it usually indicates people whose traditionalist leanings have many of the lighter aspects found in the words *joy, jelly, jaunty, juicy, jolly* and *jazzy*. These are well-balanced individuals who, for all their serious underpinnings live their lives with style and buoyancy.

J men and women are outgoing individuals who aren't going to allow themselves to be sidetracked by such trifling things as reality. It's not that they're flighty, mind you, for they have a very keen sense of how the universe works and of their places within it. It's that they adamantly refuse to kowtow to the expectations placed upon them by society. Their engaging sovereign spirits prove to be quite infectious, and many people quietly admire the *Js*' resilience and independence.

If you have any *J* friends, you can be confident that they'll always have something good to say about you, even when no one else is willing to sing your praises.

Jae
Jay
Jaye
Ji
Jo
Joe
Joey
Joi
Joy
Joya
Joye

But they aren't above poking fun at your foibles either. Still, most people don't seem to mind, because their sense of humor is the self-deprecating kind where they'll laugh at themselves too.

Like most people whose names begin with the letter *J*, *Js* are people with strong spiritual centers. And even when their philosophy doesn't translate into conventional religious beliefs, they will have strong connections to the earth and all living things (except certain people). The trouble is that because *Js* go out of their way to avoid conflict, it's not easy to pin them down. So, if you want to change a *J's* mind, arguing is *not* the way to do it. The best thing to do is to show them that you have their best interests at heart and they'll pretty much fall in line.

When it comes to their intimate relationships, *Js*' primary goals are to have fun and explore their partners' emotional construction. *Js* tend to mellow with age, so any initial problems are likely to dissipate over time, and in the final analysis, their marriages last longer than most. Many people report that *J* mates are spontaneous and passionate, but not particularly over-sexed. Perhaps this is a symptom of *Js*' tendency for being overly cautious when the stakes are too high.

Jay Leno When Johnny Carson vacated his desk on the *Tonight Show* in 1992, the word on the street was that David Letterman would take over the long-running ratings engine for NBC. The industry was understandably stunned when NBC gave the relatively untested, lantern-jawed Jay Leno the job instead. ■ The decision so incensed Letterman that he took his act to CBS in the time-slot opposite the *Tonight Show*. Everyone wondered who was going to win the ratings war. ■ Letterman held his own for the first few years, but Jay slowly crept up in the ratings and went on to win the war. ■ "On average, children laugh 400 times per day. Adults only laugh 15 times per day. The reason why adults laugh so much less—because adults have children!" — Jay Leno.

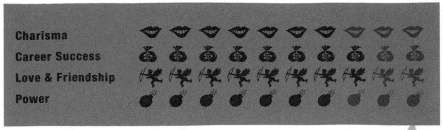

Charisma		
Career Success		
Love & Friendship		
Power		

Shrewd Straight-shooting Clever
Aggressive Moralizing Obtuse

If it's true that complex names herald complex personalities, *JCLN* names prove the rule. These are women who've elected *not* to contract their names to the friendlier *Jackie*, and the competing forces within these names suggest personalities whose outward fortitude comes at the price of a somewhat fragile emotional core. The *JCLN's* external strength comes from the combination of the *judicious* letter *J* and the *cool, cutting* tones of the *crisply* pronounced letter *C*. We see these decidedly combative tones in the words *jackboot, Jekyll, jerk, jackal,* and *hijack*. The letter *L*, on the other hand, is the indicator of all things that money can't buy (*love, life, laughter, learning* and *liberty*) and in combination with the *negative* letter *N* (*no, not, never, nada, nyet, nix* and *nothing*) evokes the pessimism and emotional brittleness found in the words *loony, loner, bland, lunkhead, lament, lesion* and *larceny*. Complex indeed!

If you knew a *JCLN* in high school, she was probably the kind of person that everyone respected. Not that she was universally liked, mind you, for there was something about her that made her inaccessible to all but her closest friends. Even when she laughed—which she often did—there was probably a distinct glint of sharp tooth in her smile.

Jaclyn
Jacalyn
Jacelyn
Jackeline
Jacqualine
Jacquelin
Jacqueline
Jacquelyn
Jacquelyne
Jacquelynn
Jaqueline
Jaquelin

It's important for the *JCLN* to present the outward appearance of being the epitome of a cool collected woman, mainly because she needs to protect her feelings. If the *JCLN* was a food-group, she'd be a dark semi-sweet chocolate with a sweet gooey filling. Somewhat of an acquired taste, but as rich as Donald Trump on the inside.

*JCLN*s who decide to take advantage of their impressive charismas usually do well in the professional world. But it's rare to find *JCLN*s who enjoy work for its own sake: These are women with a not-so-secret penchant for taking things easy. So once a *JCLN* feels she has enough money to take care of life's necessities (manicures, massages and shopping sprees) she'll probably settle into a more introspective and meaningful existence.

Even if they're not immune to the occasional clumsy relationship (especially with *bad-boy* types), *JCLN*s are skilled in the art of romance and can be surprisingly gentle lovers.

But *JCLN*s are not ones for playing games when it comes to the important issue of love and have limited patience for men who refuse to do their parts in the courting rituals. After the nuptials are said and done, they'll happily trade some of their cherished independence in exchange for their mates' unconditional devotion.

Jacqueline Bisset In the 1970s film *The Deep*, a special diving mask had to be constructed for Jacqueline Bisset so that her beautiful eyes could be seen in her underwater scenes. But it turned out that no one was interested in her eyes for Jacqueline was soon featured on dozens of magazine covers promoting her wet tee-shirt look. ■ Even though *The Deep* propelled Jacqueline to stardom, her first international exposure came when she played Mrs. Goodthighs in James Bond's *Casino Royale*. The film *Sweet Ride*—in which she lost her bikini top while surfing—ironically earned her a Golden Globe nomination. ■ Jacqueline has appeared in over sixty films and was nominated for a best supporting actress César Award for the French drama *La Cérémonie*.

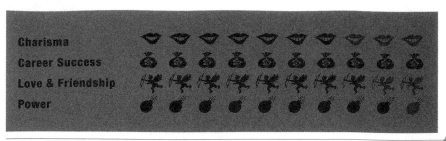

Charisma		
Career Success		
Love & Friendship		
Power		

**Pragmatic Honest Consistent
Stern Bossy Know-it-all**

The *judicious* quality of the letter *J* takes on a distinctly more sober aspect when coupled with the *darker* aspects of the *disciplined* letter *D*. The *JD* phoneme presides over words like *prejudice, jeopardy, jaded, jihad, jailbird, jaundice* and *judder*—all images we associate with disapproving *judgment*. Perhaps this is why *JD* people have reputations for being unyielding in their high expectations of themselves and their friends. It should be noted that because names that end with the letters *I* or *Y* tend to signify the more playful aspects of life (*silly, goofy, jolly, funny, happy, sunny* and *zany*), the *Judys*, and *Jodys* of the world will be appreciably more flexible the *Judiths, Jadas* and *Jeds*.

In general, however, because *JDs* see things in such starkly black-and-white terms, they have a nose for rooting out—and pointing out—any shortcomings their friends might have. It's not that they necessarily want everyone to conform to their own worldviews, it's that they believe all problems can be solved when taken in bite-sized logical chunks. So if you want technical advice on personal or business issues, by all means consult your *JD* friend. But if you're just looking for a soft place to lay your head, you're going to need a pillow.

That said, *JDs* manage to pull off their brand of

Jada
Jade
Jaden
Jed
Jedediah
Jodi, Jodie
Jody, Judah
Judd, Jude
Judith
Judson
Judy

judgmental behavior with a scrupulously maintained sense of fairness and honesty. If nothing else, you'll never have to worry about your *JD* friend hiding anything from you. If you want a second opinion on your new hairstyle, you'd better be prepared to hear the truth.

As is common with most *J*-named people, *JDs* rarely resort to dishonesty or deceit to get what they want out. The reason they strongly disapprove of this sort of thing is because they've learned that candor—brutal as it may be—is the most effective tool for achieving their goals. Paradoxically, in terms of their careers, *JDs* avoid positions of authority because they also believe that life is best lived by unburdening oneself of responsibility whenever possible. But *JDs* are attracted to money and will do what must be done when funds are running low.

The *JDs'* relationships are chosen for their practical value rather than any madcap romantic notions, and partners will be carefully vetted for potential character flaws before any commitment is forthcoming. Expect their relationships to be stable and enduring affairs without a lot of frills and wild romance. If there's an exception, it's going to involve the *Jodys* and *Judys* of this world, whose relationships almost always exhibit a level of volatility and experimentation.

Jodi Foster Jodi Foster is one of those few people who become famous for three entirely different reasons. ■ Her first claim to fame is that virtually every person in U.S. thinks they have seen her bare bottom. Rumor has it that Jodi was the model for the Coppertone billboards depicting a young girl with her shorts pulled down by a spaniel, but the actual model was the illustrator's daughter. ■ Jodi is also famous for being an Oscar winning actress and director. Her first nomination came for her role in the controversial film, *Taxi Driver*, when she was only fourteen, and she won awards for her performances in *The Accused* and *The Silence of the Lambs*. Jodi staked her third claim to fame when a deranged fan tried to assassinate President Reagan on her behalf.

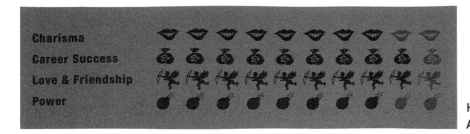

Charisma										
Career Success										
Love & Friendship										
Power										

Humorous Outgoing Daring
Argumentative Thoughtless Aggressive

The letter *F* is the icon for all things *fun, flamboyant, flirtatious, flighty, funky, flippant, fresh* and *friendly*. So though it's true that names beginning with the conservative letter *J* tend to describe personalities that are cautiously deliberate, *JF* people are almost always described as being unpredictable and friendly.

But no matter what else people say about the *JF* personalities, they will always some-thing about their undaunted optimism, and—even if this enthusiasm isn't readily apparent to the casual observer—the *JFs'* irrepressibility is never far from the surface.

JF people seem to cause a stir wherever they go, and even *they* would have to admit that it's because they enjoy showing off their ability to make clever jokes on the spur of the moment. But *JFs* also aren't known for their patience and won't waste their efforts on people who fail to deliver instant gratification. So if you want to keep your *JF* friend, make sure that he thinks that *you* think he's funny. Your *JF* friend will be particularly generous and considerate and won't ask for much in return other than a corresponding loyalty. The nice thing is that if your *JF* friend has a problem with you, he'll leave you no doubt as to where you stand.

When sufficiently motivated, the *JFs'* powerful emotional energies make them dynamic workers and formidable competitors, and since independence and

**Geoff
Geoffrey
Jeff
Jefferey
Jefferson
Jeffery
Jeffrey
Jeffry**

stubbornness are two of the *JFs'* salient qualities, they are usually best suited to working on their own. Whether they are owners of their own businesses or helping to run someone else's, they're natural sales-people and great negotiators. Teamwork doesn't come naturally to these independent creatures, and they're happy to assume the blame when things go wrong in exchange for taking all the credit when they don't. When they do take a leadership role, people seem to appreciate their unaggressive styles. The only downside of being among the highest wage earners in their peer groups is that *JFs* are typically the first people that others hit up for loans.

When it comes to matters of the heart, *JFs* usually take their own sweet time in deciding when to settle down, a situation that can be frus-trating for the women that see them as desirable mates. But these fun-loving flirts are nobody's fool and usually see no reason to rush their decisions. When the right one happens to come along, they'll waste little time in claiming their prize.

Married life will mirror the *JF's* professional life, in that he's going to insist on maintaining his independ-ence. As long as he hasn't married a jealous type, his union should prove fruitful, long-lasting and undeni-ably interesting.

Jeff Goldblum Jeff Goldblum's breakthrough performance was as a reporter in *The Big Chill*, and his first hit as a leading man was in the gruesome 1986 feature, *The Fly*. Cashing in on his fame, Jeff signed up to play a chaos specialist in Spielberg's *Jurassic Park* and an annoying computer hacker in *Independence Day*. ■ Tall, gangly and incongru-ously handsome, actor Jeff Goldblum is an unlikely sex symbol, but has a habit of romanti-cally hooking up with his co-stars. First there was actress Patricia Gaul (*The Big Chill*) whom he married and divorced. Next was Geena Davis (*The Fly*) whom he divorced before his proposal to Laura Dern who he met while filming *Jurassic Park*. True to form, the relationship ended a few years later.

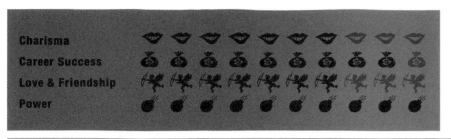

THE WILD CARD

jk

Irrepressible Daring Original
Unpredictable Rebellious Stubborn

Charisma	💋	💋	💋	💋	💋	💋	💋	💋	💋	💋
Career Success	💰	💰	💰	💰	💰	💰	💰	💰	💰	
Love & Friendship										
Power										

Names dominated by the letter *K*—the letter of forceful action—tend to denote the vigorous masculine power found in the words: *kick, knock, knuckle, knife, kill, keen* and *king*. And because the letter *J* is usually associated with people of considerable self-control, these names suggest those who walk softly and carry substantially large sticks. *JK* people can be a bit like those sour candies with sugary centers: you have to put up with a bit of mouth-puckering before getting to the sweet reward. Perhaps because of the inherent power in this root, many *JKs* find refuge in youthful names like *Jackie, Jacoby* and *Jacqui,* which imply the childlike energy found in the words *happy, funny, goofy, jolly* and *zany.*

At first blush these people may appear to be a breed of the strong silent type, for they're not your typical small-talkers and tend to keep their deeper emotional issues under wraps. This is why many people are surprised to uncover the *JKs'* sensitive underbelly that colors their existence and enriches their relationships. Although they can hold their own in just about any social setting, *JKs* are drawn to the inherent simplicity of small and tightly knit social groups.

Unpredictable but never reckless, *JKs* have a trademark charm that makes for trouble-free friendships. But the downside to flitting in and out of casual

Jack
Jacki
Jackie
Jacklyn
Jackson
Jacky
Jacob
Jacoby
Jacque
Jacques
Jacqui
Jakayla
Jakob
Jakobe
Jaquan
Jaquez
Jaxon
Jaxson
Joaquin
Jake

relationships—as *JKs* are apt to do—is that it tends to provoke jealousy and create as many enemies as it does allies. And if it's true that people either love them or hate them, it eminently suits the *JK's* own black-and-white view of the world.

When it comes to their careers, *JKs* are tactile people who are often found in jobs that require hand-to-eye coordination. But many *JKs* opt for a more aggressive approach in their professional lives, where they prove to be fierce competitors with an extraordinary will to win. With their strong belief in justice, these people live their lives in accordance with their own moral codes and aren't afraid of old-fashioned hard work. But because they're ultimately mavericks at heart—and because they honestly believe they know what's best—*JKs* often end up clashing with authority and must be mindful not to tread on anyone on the way up, lest they meet them again on the way down.

The *JKs'* approach to their relationships can be similarly intense, and when they've set their sights on prospective partners, there's little doubt in *their* minds that they're going to prevail. It could even be said that love and marriage are simply extensions of their *gotta-come-out-on-top* strategy, and their hunting instincts are so strong that their finest relationships only come about when their prey puts up a decent fight.

 Jack Nicholson When you have an unusual name like Madonna or Cher, it's easy to be remembered by only your first name, but Jack Nicholson has achieved the distinction of owning the name Jack. ■ His first hit film, *Easy Rider,* made him an emblem of the counterculture and Jack soon began piling up Oscar nominations. His performance in *One Flew over the Cuckoo's Nest* earned him his first Academy Award and he went on to accumulate a record eleven Oscar nominations. ■ Although it's difficult to pinpoint the moment Jack became a legend, a good argument could be made for his creepy "Heeere's Johnny!" from *The Shining.*

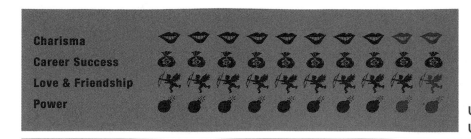

Charisma										
Career Success										
Love & Friendship										
Power										

Upbeat Involved Outgoing
Unrealistic Indecisive Inconsistent

The *lyrical* letter *L* is the symbol of all the things that money can't buy (*life, liberty, love, learning* and *laughter*) and has the power to soothe with its *lyrically languid lilts.* So when it occurs in names initialized by the *judicious* and *judgmental* letter *J*, it's indicative of people who have an attractive balance of wisdom, wit and poise.

These are socially intuitive men and women who know how to work a crowd. No matter what kind of hair-day they're having, it's important for them to be "up" when out in public. This kind of positive outlook pays dividends in the *JLs'* popularity, which might explain the wide circle of acquaintances who feel fortunate to be in their company. But the downside to being in such high demand is that *JLs* often subjugate their personal aspirations to the interests of cultivating these relationships. There will be times when emotional-drain proves too exhausting and triggers a retreat into the security of their private spaces.

Like most people whose names begin with a *J*, *JLs* are canny about the way they earn and spend their money. A high percentage of *JLs* own their own businesses or end up as leaders in their chosen professions. But whatever field they enter, *JLs* are likely to be successful and like most *J*-named people, are among the

Jill
Jaleel
Jalisa
Jaliyah
Jayla
Jenelle
Jewel, Jewell
Joel, Joella
Joelle, Jolie
Jule, Julee
Jules, Juli
Julia, Julie
Julio
Julissa
Julius

first that everyone goes to for a loan. While you would not characterize them as being profligate, they are usually quite generous when friends and family are involved.

The *JLs'* sense of fairness means that everyone gets the benefit of the doubt—at least until they do something to suggest they're not be trusted. They place such a great deal of importance on the qualities of emotional honesty that they wouldn't even consider dating someone unless they came with the recommendation of a trusted associate.

If you're married to a *JL* you can always rely on their emotional and physical generosity, whether it's uncomplainingly bringing home the bacon or dutifully tending the house and kids. With their fundamental philosophy of *loyalty-first*, it's unlikely that *JLs* will emotionally abandon the ship unless their partner rocks the boat too violently. But *JLs* will insist on emotional honestly from their partners, and if it's true that they can talk a dog off a meatwagon, it's only because they understand the value of open communication.

In typical *J*-name fashion, their children will be treated like young adults with the expectation that they achieve the high level of moral and ethical behavior that characterizes the *JLs* themselves.

Julia Roberts No one expected Julia Roberts to emerge as a star from her role as a prostitute in the Richard Gere vehicle *Pretty Woman*. A year before, Julia had received some attention for her performance in *Steel Magnolias*, but her portrayal of an ersatz hooker earned her the title of "America's Sweetheart." ■ Julia kept the tabloids busy by announcing her wedding to Kiefer Sutherland and then cancelling it three days before the nuptials, and the press had a field day when she married craggy-faced musician Lyle Lovett only to divorce him two years later. ■ Julia's biggest critical success came from playing the title role in *Erin Brockovitch*, for which she won an Oscar. Today, she is widely regarded as one of the most powerful actress in Hollywood and is probably the most highly paid.

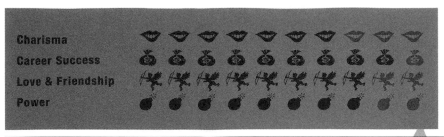

THE SUAVE

jln

Charisma	
Career Success	
Love & Friendship	
Power	

Genteel Well-spoken Smooth
Irritable Unrealistic Erratic

The *justice*-loving letter *J* imbues names with a sense of forthrightness and ethical values. And because the letter *L* is the flagship of the best things that money *can't* buy (*love, life, liberty, learning* and *laughter*), these are people who live their lives with a strong respect for tradition and always have time to smell the roses. It must be said, however, that the *negative* letter *N* (*no, not, never, null, nothing, nada,* and *naught*) is an important component of these names and will probably express itself in the *JLN's* occasional bouts of pessimism and irritability.

JLNs are undeniably intelligent, and they put a lot of effort into looking the part. Appearance is very important to them, and it would be unusual to find one schlumping around in anything but neatly pressed clothes. Even when they're in mufti on their days off, their outfits are likely to be *fashionably* grungy.

JLNs also have a strong sense of self-worth and expect to be listened to even when they have nothing to say. Fortunately, these are interesting people with well-honed conversational skills and usually have novel perspectives on everything from politics to religion to science. Debates are verbal sparring matches in which it's in everyone's best interests for the *JLN* to emerge victorious.

Jalen
Jalon
Jalyn
Jalynn
Jaelyn
Jailyn, Jaylan
Jaylen, Jaylene
Jaylin, Jaylon
Jaylyn, Jillian
Jocelyn, Joellen
Joleen, Jolene
Juliann, Julianna
Joline, Jolyn
Jolynn, Joycelyn
Julene, Julian
Juliana, Juliane
Julianne
Julieann
Julienne
Julien

When it comes to their careers *JLNs* will put aside their secret dreams to be artists or musicians and buckle down to make some serious money. Not that anyone would accuse them of being greedy, but they certainly understand the value of a dollar and its importance to their families. Many *JLNs* enter into some kind of entrepreneurial venture in which—even after a few missteps—they're likely to succeed. But it's almost certain that no matter what job *JLNs* end up accepting, they are going to rise to the top. Even when *JLNs* choose not to work, odds are, they're going to be the best homemakers since RuPaul.

It's in matters of the family where the *JLN* really shines, for like most *J*-named people, *JLNs* resonate strongly with the notion that blood is thicker than water. But this doesn't mean that the *JLN* is a soft touch when it comes to family handouts; they know that a tough-love approach is sometimes best.

If *JLN* marriages seem to work so well, it's not because they're the easiest people to live with. Rather it's because they're willing to put in the level of work that durable marriages require. These are proud people who feel that the best way to measure a person's character is by the quality of his or her relationships. And they cannot abide having their own character questioned.

jlt

Charisma										
Career Success										
Love & Friendship										
Power										

Quick-thinking Tactful Open-minded
Moody Unpredictable Closed

The letter *L* is the symbol of all the things that money can't buy (*life, liberty, love, learning* and *laughter*) and has the power to soothe with its *lyrically languid lilts*. On the other hand, the *triumphant* and *trustworthy* tones of the letter *T* are rife with self-assurance and outspoken confidence. So when these two letters occur in names initialized by the *judicious* and *judgmental* letter *J*, it's not surprising that they herald feminine personalities of uncommon wisdom, aplomb and prudence.

With their relaxed and tactful approach to life, *JLTs* rarely encounter difficulties in either their social or professional lives. In fact, if you ever need a reminder not to take life too seriously, take your *JLT* friend out for a drink and let her tell you how life should *really* be lived. *JLTs* also have a particular aptitude for dealing with difficult people and many look to her for counsel when going through a rough patch.

There will be times when you're going to encounter your *JLT* friend in an apparent funk. But these moods are rare and are usually a symptom that she's simply contemplating her next move. As much as *JLTs* seem self-assured and expansive, these are introspective people who believe that life should be lived with respect for Karma and a degree of thoughtfulness. Most of the time

Juliet
Julieta
Julietta
Juliette

you'll find her to be emotionally generous, unquenchably optimistic and fiercely independent. Her professional life will probably reflect this to some degree, and her combination of snappy energy and periodic moods of quiet observation make her ideal for jobs that require public trust. She'd make an ideal news anchor—not for the fluffy local news but for the more serious PBS kind—and an even better teacher. *JLTs* are terminally curious about life, which is why so many of them are drawn to intellectual careers like medicine, academia and law. But ultimately, their greatest interests lie in the realm of friends and family.

In their personal lives, *JLTs* are unlikely to settle on a mate before they've gotten all their ducks in a row. These are women who need the companionship that only intimate relationships provide but who also value their independence. Almost always though, *JLTs* will be able to retain their freethinking habits as long as their mates are chosen wisely. With a perceptive understanding of children, *JLTs* are naturally suited for parenthood, and their children will be raised in well-regulated households. Even if their offspring aren't the most coddled kids on the block, they'll be uncommonly educated in the ways of the world and will benefit from their parent's hard-won understanding of life.

Juliette Lewis Juliette Lewis dodged a bullet when her parents decided not to name her Snow Lake as they had originally intended. The intense teenager was legally emancipated at the age of fourteen and, as a young girl, Juliette was busted for being underage in a club. She so charmed the cop, though, that he released her without charges and even let her keep her mug shot. ■ Juliette first came to prominence when cast by Martin Scorsese in his remake of *Cape Fear*. Her performance as an innocent girl who sucked a psychotic Robert De Niro's thumb, earned her an Oscar nomination. ■ Juliette has played everything from the naive, dysfunctional girlfriend of a psycho-killer in *Kalifornia*, to the Marilyn-obsessed waitress in *Romeo is Bleeding*, to the dangerously sexy moll in Oliver Stone's *Natural Born Killers*.

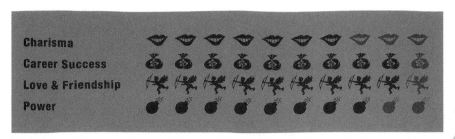

THE STERLING

jm

Charisma										
Career Success										
Love & Friendship										
Power										

Stable Bright Talented
Boring Unfocused Condescending

With almost four million individuals bearing some form of a *JM* name, this group is by far the most popular in North America. Perhaps it has something to do with the *judicious*, *judgmental* and *justice-loving* letter *J* and the letter *M's* close association with all that is *maternal*, *motherly* and *merciful*. These names herald personalities of uncommon strength and compassion, and *JMs* are statistically better prepared for life success than almost any other name. It should be noted that words ending with the high-pitched letters (*Y* and *IE*) are associated with all things *funny, sunny, silly, goofy, spry, happy* and *zany*, and the *Jimmys* and *Jamies* of the world are consequently a lot more approachable and a little less predictable.

There's a sense of self-satisfaction (and even a hint of smugness) associated with *JM* names. For even though they're not the types to throw their weight around, they are usually granted authority over their social groups. People naturally defer to their laid-back style of leadership, and *JMs* often emerge as pillars of their communities. They may not be particularly big on finesse, but they are certainly open-minded and generous to a fault.

If you know any *JMs*, you're probably familiar with their mysterious way of ending up at the top of the food chain. Not in the dominating sense—for these are remarkably easygoing people—but in the way they seem to know which buttons to push to get what they want.

These were the kids whose science projects actually worked and whose show-and-tell made everyone sit up and take notice.

It's often said that *JMs* refuse to grow up, and in truth, many of them seem to have a childlike curiosity and a knack for learning new skills. They are secretly very competitive people who see life in terms of winning and losing, so don't expect them to be graceful losers. They simply don't get much practice.

JMs have excellent language skills and it's difficult to compete with them when they're in one of their persuasive moods. They aren't shy about plying their influence to get what they want, but it would be unfair to label them as manipulative. Then again, *JMs* don't give a hoot about labels and aren't going to object in any case.

JMs can also be downright shmoozy when it comes to interacting with the opposite sex and often play the field while pondering about getting hitched. And although settling down may be a long time coming, once they've made their decision, *JMs* will waste little time getting to the child-rearing stage. Like most people whose names incorporate the maternal letter *M,* nothing pleases *JMs* more than being able to nurture, teach and influence their offspring.

Gemma
Jaheem
Jaheim
Jaime
Jamaal
Jamal, Jamar
Jamarcus
Jamari
Jamee, Jamel
Jameson
Jamie, Jamil
James, Jamila
Jamir, Jamison
Jammie
Jamya
Jem
Jim, Jimena
Jimmie
Jimmy
Jomar

James Dean James Dean's legend is as enduring as his career was short. The actor—whose life was immortalized by the Eagles' lyric "Too Fast to Live, Too Young to Die"—had all the qualities of a modern tragic hero: youth, beauty, success and a violent death. ■ James only had three major movie roles, of which two received Oscar nominations. The first was in *East of Eden* and his performance made him a symbol for disaffected post-war youth. The next was as Jim Stark in *Rebel Without a Cause*. James died while shooting his last movie, *Giant*.

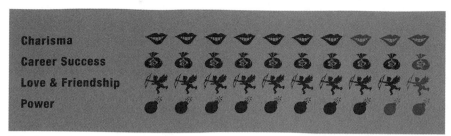

Charisma	🙂 🙂 🙂 🙂 🙂 🙂 🙂 🙂 🙂
Career Success	💰 💰 💰 💰 💰 💰 💰 💰 💰
Love & Friendship	🏹 🏹 🏹 🏹 🏹 🏹 🏹 🏹 🏹
Power	💣 💣 💣 💣 💣 💣 💣 💣 💣

Charismatic Convincing Shrewd
Two-faced Stubborn Overbearing

With the exception of the *JM* names, there are more people in the United States with a *JN* name than any other. This extraordinary popularity may be a tribute to the letter *J*'s ability to impart a sense of integrity, but the fact that these names also fall under the influence of the *negative* letter *N* is an indication of some dark secret, or a reflection of the *JNs*' occasional forays into self-doubt. Still, because these are people who have likely been treated since childhood as part of the in-crowd, they have extraordinary levels of self-confidence and equally resolute backbones. Since words ending with the high-pitched *Y* or *IE* tend to denote the emotional expressiveness found in *silly*, *goofy*, *funny*, *happy*, *sunny* and *zany*, the *Jeanies*, *Johnnys* and *Janeys* of the world are somewhat more approachable than the *Johns*, *Joans* and *Junes*.

Like most people whose names begin with the letter *J*, *JNs* have a strong sense of justice and will think nothing of putting themselves at personal disadvantage when they think they're doing the right thing. If your *JN* friend is a politician (as many *J*-named people are), he or she would be neither a hawk nor a dove: your *JN* friend is likely to be an owl. They are driven by the belief that the universe will take care of itself (as long as we take care of each other), and you can count on them for clearheaded counsel. But

Jan
Jana
Janae
Janelle
Jane
Janie, Jayne
Jean, Jeanie
Jen, Janiya
Jaren, Jaron
Jena, Jina
Joan, John
Johna, Jon
Joni, Juan
Joanie, Johan
Juana, June
Johanna
Johnie
Johnna
Johnpaul
Jonah
Junior
Juwan

remember, as much as the *JN* will be your staunch defender in times of trouble, he or she will be a dangerous enemy if you contradict their definition of fair play.

When it comes to their work lives, *JNs* aren't going to be satisfied unless they feel they're making a difference. But whether they own their own businesses or work as artists, they're happiest when they're making the rules. These capable people have a propensity to take the lead in both their social and professional lives, and though hardly tyrannical, it's not unlike them to put their foot down when they sense their integrity has been challenged. If *JNs* have an Achilles heel, it has to be their stubborn streak (a consequence of believing that they really know how the world works). But *JNs* mellow well with age, the *JNs*' assertive nature rarely condenses into outright aggression.

JNs crave companionship and shine in relationships when their mates meet their internal criteria. They function best with steady spouses who aren't addicted to constant change, but will probably be disappointments to lovers looking for fluffy expressions of romance. These are dignified, introspective individuals, who simply don't have much time for games. *JNs* are into the nitty-gritty: nest building, upward-mobility, child rearing and retirement plans.

John Kennedy Jr. When John F. Kennedy Jr.'s airplane crashed into the Atlantic near Martha's Vineyard in 1999, it seemed as if the Kennedy's were indeed a family cursed. ■ John's love life had always been public information. Rumor had it that as long as his mother Jacqueline was alive, John could never allow his relationship with Daryl Hannah to become serious. His mother was also against his dream of becoming an actor, so he went to law school. After graduation, John launched George; a political satire magazine. ■ Eventually, the man People Magazine called the Sexiest Man Alive married a more suitable woman—Carolyn Bessette.

Charisma										
Career Success										
Love & Friendship										
Power										

Comfortable Self-assured Resourceful
Judgmental Distant Insensitive

Complex names are usually a harbinger of complex people. This is particularly true when the name bearer chooses the longer version of their name when a contraction is readily available: in this case, *Jenny* or *Jen*. The name *Jennifer* (and its spelling variants) are the fifth most popular names for girls in North America and are only slightly behind the stalwarts: *Mary, Patricia, Elizabeth* and *Barbara*. The fact that *J* names are the most popular overall has to do with the fact that the *J* is associated with *justice* and spiritual strength, while the *FR* combination—comprising of the *fun-loving F* and the *red-blooded R*—is a particularly strong indicator of all things *frisky, frantic, frazzled, freaky, frenzied, frenetic, frivolous, frothy* and *frolicking*. These names bespeak women full of bubbly effervescence with backbones made of solid titanium.

Confident, complex and intelligent, the *JNFR* is someone you'd expect to do well in life and counts among her many talents an extraordinary set of social skills. There's a friendly yet no-nonsense aura about her, and she'll make it her business to know the name of every person in a room. And even though her outgoing nature suggests that she's quite comfortable in social sit-

Jenifer
Jeniffer
Jennefer
Jennifer
Jenniffer

uations, there is also a shyness that manifests itself when she feels out of her depth. On these occasions, the *JNFR* is likely to resort to her people-watching mode and quietly absorb the social milieu until she feels more at ease.

JNFRs like to think ahead, and are the kind of people who are constantly scanning the horizon for anything that might upset their future plans. Being that they are long-range thinkers, they're apt to miss out on life's daily pleasures while obsessing about tomorrow. But it's poetry in motion when a *JNFR's* plan comes together: these are women who know what they want and aren't afraid of a little sacrifice in order to get it.

JNFRs make energetic and playful mates. But when they sense their mates aren't as committed as they are, they can be as cool as the other side of the pillow. This kind of chilly reception is their trademark way of expressing displeasure, and mates had better be able to interpret its origins without having to ask.

So if you're going to tie the knot with a *JNFR*, you'd better be the sensitive type or, better yet, a mind reader. In the main, most men agree that life with one of these impish sprites is worth just about any sacrifice . . . including the occasional night on the couch.

Jennifer Anniston To fans of Brad Pitt, Jennifer Anniston is the luckiest girl in Hollywood. From a producer's point-of-view, Jennifer is a canny businesswoman tiptoeing her way around the pinnacles of stardom with a savvy eye for self-promotion. ■ The daughter of a Greek immigrant turned soap-opera actor, Jennifer auditioned for—and won—a role in a pilot for *Friends Like These* (later renamed *Friends*). Declining the role of Monica, Jennifer stole the show as the quirky Rachel with just enough hipness to curry favor with the largely teen audience. She even launched a hair-cult—a neo-seventies 'do that fell nicely around her oval face. ■ Her marriage to Brad Pitt came with some less likable side-effects when her mother's unwelcome gossip got her name crossed off the wedding guest list.

Jnn

Charisma										
Career Success										
Love & Friendship										
Power										

Creative Intellectual Unselfish
Indecisive Worried Fitful

Names that begin with the letter *J* usually denote individuals with a solid set of core values and an outlook on life that's positive and self-assured. However, the *JNN* names are also dominated by the letter *N*, which is usually associated with *negativity* (*not, never, nada, null, nothing, nada, nyet* and *naught*), and as such, tend to suggest pessimism and sarcasm. But an interesting thing happens when *two N's* appear in a name: an example of two negatives making a positive, these words tend to convey the joyful aspects found in the words *nun, granny, manna, sunny, innocent, funny, canny, feminine, bonny* and *hosanna* (a shout of praise to God). For the *Jennys* and *Johnnys* of the world there is the added effect of the playful letter *Y* that creates words like *silly, goofy, gay, happy, zany,* and *joy*.

In short, these are men and women with the ability to charm anyone they meet with their unique blend of carefree humor and uncommon affability. It's not to say that *JNNs* don't have their share of problems, but these issues don't seem to disrupt their ability to maintain social harmony. *JNNs* like to think of themselves as champions of the weak (at the very least they want to be viewed as being accommodating) and no one will ever be excluded from *JNNs'* lives on the basis of status or wealth.

Everyone agrees that *JNNs'* lives are more hectic

Jann
Janeen
Janene
Janina
Janine
Janna
Jeanene
Jeanine
Jeanna
Jeanne
Jeannie
Jeannine
Jenine
Jenna, Jenni
Jennie, Jenny
Joann
Joanna
Joanne
Joeann
Johnnie
Johnny
Jonna
Jonnie

than most. It's hard to know what they're going to come up with next, but as they say, if you're never going to change your mind, why even have one? It could be argued that the *JNNs* use their chaotic lives as a way to escape their problems, but it's probably because many *JNNs* confuse the dictum; *anything's possible* with *everything's possible*.

These are capable and multi-talented people, and *JNNs* are able to choose from a broad range of careers. Whether they decide to employ their creative talents or their extraordinary people skills, the one thing *JNNs* have in common is the pursuit of intellectual stimulation. *JNNs* are happiest when learning or teaching but don't fit well into traditional institutions. Whatever they happen to choose will be tackled from their own unique angles.

JNNs' mates will find themselves to be alternately enchanted and frustrated by their partners' whimsical natures. Mates who expect structure and hierarchy in their relationships are going to be disappointed, but if they're into art, socializing or schmoozing, then they've made the right choice. As one might guess, *JNNs'* parenting style is going to be refreshingly unconventional and children will be expected to behave like little adults—not with any intent to stifle their childhoods, but to encourage their growth as ethical human beings.

Johnny Depp Johnny Depp had the words Winona Forever tattooed onto his upper right arm. "I love Winona and I'm going to love her forever" (like that's not going to jinx things). The tattoo was later changed to Wino Forever. ■ Johnny's nomadic charm might have something to do with his Cherokee blood. His gift for trespassing on the edges of reality shone through in *Don Juan DeMarco* and *Edward Scissorhands*. His other credits include *Ed Wood, Benny and Joon, Chocolat, Blow, Donnie Brasco* and Disney's *Pirates of the Caribbean*.

jns

Charisma										
Career Success										
Love & Friendship										
Power										

Intuitive Appealing Witty
Indecisive Oversensitive Impulsive

Like most people whose names begin with the *judicious* and *justice-loving* letter *J*, JNS people are described as having the kind of personalities you'd want in your doctor, lawyer or investment advisor: innately trustworthy and awash in common sense. The fact that these names end with the *sexy, sassy, sultry* sounds of the *S* (or soft *C*), intimates that these are also people with fresh and vigorous perspectives on life, but it must also be said that when the *nasal* letter *N* shows up in names, it's an indication that something is amiss. (The *N* is the definitive symbol of negativity: *no, not, never, nada, null, nothing, nada, nyet* and *naught*.) So for all their outward I-have-it-under-control dispositions, *JNS* people are often prone to mood-swings and even occasional bouts of depression.

These men and women must work hard to overcome their tendency to freeze when the going gets rough, and most *JNSs* learn early in life that inertia is the hardest thing to overcome. To put it bluntly, they're procrastinators. But *JNSs* take this all in stride and will adamantly refuse help when it comes to (eventually) getting the job done. Although this might be mistaken as a form of egocentricity, it's just a symptom of an intelligent person struggling to fulfill his or her enormous potential.

Only when *JNSs* channel their emotional energies into their professional lives are they likely to make their marks in their chosen fields. And although *JNSs* can hold their own in science, business and law, these intuitive people are best suited for jobs in which they can guide other people to overcome their problems: counseling, teaching, or social work. One thing is sure, *JNSs* will always choose stability over excitement and you'll rarely find them skipping from job to job just to make an extra buck.

When it comes to choosing intimate partners, a *JNS* can be as picky as a five-year old at a salad bar. So if you're considering taking a *JNS* as a life partner and they're taking an awfully long time to commit, it's just a symptom of their look-before-you-leap philosophy and is certainly no reflection on you. They simply aren't going to be rushed when it comes to such important issues. By the same token, once they've decided against getting married, not even the most artful suitor will be able to sway their hearts.

JNSs are high-maintenance lovers—but this is a good thing. They appreciate quality in all its forms and will yield a high return on your emotional and physical investments.

Janis
Janessa
Janice
Janiece
Janyce
Jeanice
Jenice
Johnson
Jonas

Janis Joplin When Janis Joplin belted out a raspy rendition of "Ball and Chain" at the 1967 Monterey Pop Festival, it was a revelation to those who had never heard her sing. The electrifying performance was responsible for her going gold with her first album, *Cheap Thrills*, and the success of her hit single, "Piece of My Heart."■ With the flowering of the 60's peace culture, Janis became the voice for a generation dissatisfied with a bourgeois way of life. Living an openly free sexual life and pursuing a dangerous love affair with heroin, she was a free spirit who lived with the same uncompromising honesty as her contemporaries Jimi Hendrix and Jim Morrison. ■ Life was equally uncompromising with Janis, who died of a heroin overdose at the age of twenty-seven.

	Rating
Charisma	🔴🔴🔴🔴🔴🔴🔴⚪⚪⚪
Career Success	🔴🔴🔴🔴🔴🔴🔴⚪⚪
Love & Friendship	🔴🔴🔴🔴🔴🔴🔴🔴⚪
Power	🔴🔴🔴🔴🔴🔴🔴🔴🔴

Droll Quick-witted Focused Cunning Dictatorial Unpredictable

Names beginning with the letter *J* usually signify self-assured personalities with none of the cockiness often associated with successful people. But when the *negative* letter *N* comes into close contact with the *triumphant* letter *T*, it creates an element of intransigence that leaves no room for debate about the *JNT's* authoritative presence. We see this unyielding presence in the words *defiant, urgent, regent, serpent, taunt, torment, cement* and *taint*. All in all, *JNTs* are intricate and effective people with strong wills and equally sharp minds.

There are many reasons why *JNTs* have reputations for being old-fashioned, but the most commonly cited reason is their insistence on staying true to their down-home values in the face of societal pressure. There's a natural reserve to these people, and as gracious as they can be with strangers, they're not particularly forthcoming with their feelings. By no means does this mean that *JNTs* are stuffy or uninspired; these are people with powerful creative urges that manifest in an appreciation for music, art and literature. But you'll have to win their trust before you'll win their affection, and only after you've made it past their initial coolness will you encounter all the warmth these gracious creatures have to offer.

When it comes to career opportunities, the versatile *JNTs* have plenty of options from which to choose.

Janet
Janett
Janetta
Janette
Janita
Jannet
Jannette
Jaunita
Jeanett
Jeanetta
Jeanette
Jeannetta
Jeannette
Jenette
Jennette
Jonty
Juanita
Junita

They pride themselves on their willingness to bite off more than they can chew—seeing it as an expression of fearlessness rather than short-sightedness—and can be quite competitive in the workplace. The only real impediment to their professional success is their susceptibility to romantic entanglements that disrupt their career trajectories. Still, even if they're going to be financially penalized for these idealistic choices, they aren't going to have many regrets—hearts trump diamonds every time. Because *JNTs* are vulnerable to these kinds of distractions, they rarely find themselves in upper-level positions or in jobs requiring six-day work weeks.

JNTs can be quite brusque when it comes to getting what they want, but despite their dictatorial essence, they are quite popular with the opposite sex. So if you're wondering why your *JNT* friends are still unmarried, it's not because they've scared anyone off; it's just that they haven't found the right person to share life's simple pleasures—a warm bed, a kind word and nightly foot rubs. But once they've found what they're looking for, their single-mindedness is ideal for the hurly-burly of marriage. *JNTs* have a strong need for structure in their households, which requires a healthy system of communication, and their ideal partners will be easy-going enough to act as foils to their somewhat gritty styles.

Janet Jackson Janet Jackson was born into music. As the ninth child in a family of musicians, she was already performing by the age of seven. ■ Janet had a long haul if she was going to emerge from under the shadow of her brother, Michael, who was already the greatest pop star of all time. Sales of her first two albums were modest, but *Control* was a huge success with five singles topping the charts. Her status as a pop icon was cemented by her follow-up album, *Rhythm Nation*. ■ The fiasco surrounding Janet's "wardrobe malfunction" at the 2004 Superbowl has, if anything, increased her notoriety.

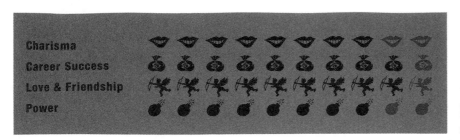

Charisma										
Career Success										
Love & Friendship										
Power										

Intelligent Outgoing Creative
Sarcastic Prickly Unpredictable

The *romantic* letter *R* reverberates with the cheeky sexuality evident in words like: *ribald, rakish, rebel, risqué, ruddy, randy, racy* and *robust*. So when it occurs in names beginning with the *judicious* letter *J*, it tends to indicate people who are capable of sober introspection and have impudent senses of humor to boot. And since words and names that end with the letters *I* or *Y* tend to signify the more playful aspects of life (*silly, goofy, funny, happy, sunny, jolly* and *zany*); it's not surprising that the *Jerrys* of the world tend to have even more of a mischievous twist to their personalities.

Witty, bright and even a little sarcastic at times, these are people who are comfortable with their relationships and with life in general. There are few unlit rooms inside *JRs'* psyches (other than their annoying habit of not taking "no" for an answer), but this doesn't mean they are predictable in any way. Expect to be constantly surprised by their uncommon intelligence and angular outlooks on life.

Like most people who live their lives with a high level of emotional control, *JRs* are the right people to approach when you're having personal problems. Not only will they be happy to lend an ear, but when *JRs* give you advice you can take it to the bank. And speaking of banks, *JRs* almost always have quite a tidy sum stashed away for those rainy days. These are people who respect

Jabari
Jairo
Jarrell
Jerel
Jeri
Jerilyn
Jerrell
Jerri
Jerrica
Jerrie
Jerry
Journey

money and know how to make it—even if it means sacrificing some aspect of their relationship to their professional lives.

If you know any *JRs*, you've no doubt noticed their ability to laugh at other people's foibles. But *JRs* don't take criticism from other people quite as easily (why are you pointing out their mistakes when their intentions are so good?). And while it's true that *JRs* don't have a mean bone in their bodies, they are often accused of being insensitive, even negligent, when it comes to other people's feelings. A word to the wise: since *JRs* are particularly astute when it comes to solving relationship issues, if there's something that your *JR* friends are doing that you don't like, simply explain that their behavior is hurtful and let *them* figure out how best to solve the problem.

JRs are charming and inventive mates, and their playfulness is likely to carry over into the bedroom. Nothing gets their goat more than a mate who refuses to share their feelings, and they're not the kind of people to allow potential problems to go un-addressed. They might even go a little overboard at times—perceiving problems that don't really exist—but all-in-all, they are romantics at heart, who will ask for nothing more than a little harmony and a pinch of spice.

Jerry Seinfeld After being fired from the sitcom *Benson*, Jerry Seinfeld swore he would never work for anyone again. When offered his own show, Jerry and friends George, Kramer, and Elaine went on to make TV history. ■ Most actors have a hard time surviving the end of their sitcoms, but when *Seinfeld* voluntarily went off the air, it was the viewers who were left hanging, while Jerry happily went back to his former life as a stand-up comedian. ■ Jerry's personal life was often difficult to distinguish from the role he played on TV. In real life he snatched away a newlywed right after her honeymoon. In a revenge attempt worthy of a Seinfeld episode, the abandoned husband reportedly considered suing him for alienation of affection.

jrd

Charisma										
Career Success										
Love & Friendship										
Power										

Admired Reliable Outgoing
Self-gratifying Repressive Inflexible

Like most people whose names begin with the *judicious* and *justice*-loving letter J, *JRD* people are awash in common sense and exhibit an old-fashioned sense of honor and homespun values. The *dignified*, *dapper* and *disciplined* letter D has an equally traditionalist influence on these names, but the appearance of the *red-blooded* letter R—the symbol of all things *raunchy*, *racy*, *randy*, *rapturous*, *ravishing* and *robust*—means that *JRDs* aren't as conservative as they might lead you to believe.

While you wouldn't exactly call these people charismatic, *JRDs* engender near-universal respect from those that intersect their lives. They are uncommonly well-meaning individuals with a sense of justice that draws people into their realms, but you shouldn't mistake their kindness for sympathy: these are goal-oriented people who believe that others should take care of themselves.

JRDs shine in jobs that reward concentration and attention to detail. They're quite content to work as accountants, bankers or lawyers, and even if they harbor secret desires to take off and join a circus, they're far too responsible to do anything of the sort. As long as they feel they're making a contribution to society, they're not particularly fussy about their working conditions, either. Sure, they'd love an office with a window, but they'd happily trade it for a little appreciation or a nice fat raise.

Things aren't as straightforward when it comes to the *JRDs'* relatively cool romantic styles. Their social inhibitions prevent them from making the first advances to a prospective partner and they'd rather spend the night alone than risk rejection from someone they're interested in. So don't be disappointed if your *JRD* lover isn't the type to light your fireworks every night; they're just a little on the old-school side and wouldn't want you to think they're being aggressive. That's why *JRDs* are notoriously choosy about to whom they give their hearts, and why it wouldn't be fair to characterize them as cold. The only thing cold about them (in matters of romance) is their feet.

Children will truly be welcome additions to the *JRDs'* lives, as it gives them an opportunity to show off just how dependable they are. But because *JRDs* aren't micro-managers when it comes to other peoples' lives, they tend to be hands-off parents who will allow children to explore for themselves. Even when their children make mistakes, they're going to have to draw their own lessons. *JRDs* are providers, not babysitters.

Jared
Jarod
Jarred
Jarrett
Jarrod
Jerad
Jerald
Jeraldine
Jered
Jerod
Jerold
Jerrod
Jerrold
Jordan
Jorden
Jordon
Jordy
Jordyn

Jared Leto When actor Jared Leto's four year relationship with actress Cameron Diaz fell apart, rumors swirled that Jared had become jealous of Cameron's career successes. Some even suggested that the split had something to do with Jared swearing off sex for two months while preparing for his role as a heroin addict for the film, *Requiem for a Dream*. ■ Twice named by *People* magazine as one of the Fifty Most Beautiful People, Jared's career took off in 1994 when he played Claire Danes' love interest in the TV series *My So-Called Life*. Their on-screen chemistry led to their feature film the following year, *How to Make an American Quilt*, and his role in the box office hit, The Thin Red Line. ■ Jared also appeared in David Fincher's *Fight Club*, alongside Brad Pitt and Ed Norton, and in *Panic Room* with Jodi Foster.

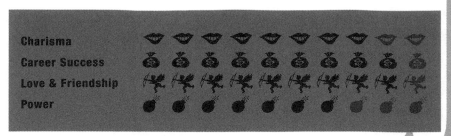

Charisma	👄👄👄👄👄👄👄👄👄🤍
Career Success	💰💰💰💰💰💰💰💰💰💰
Love & Friendship	🐦🐦🐦🐦🐦🐦🐦🐦🐦🐦
Power	💣💣💣💣💣💣💣💣💣💣

Connected Creative Thoughtful Obsessive Repressed Moody

Since *JRM* names are initialized by the *judicious, judgmental,* and *justice-loving J,* they suggest rather conservative individuals concerned with tradition and old-fashioned values. But very often, people who have names containing the letter *R*—the icon of all things *romantic, rakish, rebellious, risqué, ruddy, randy, racy* and *robust*—also exhibit a rather cheeky sexuality. The letter *M,* on the other hand, is the symbol for all that is *maternal, motherly* and *merciful,* and suggests a man in touch with his feminine side. All told, we expect the *JRM* to be a man of uncommon bonhomie, grounded by a nucleus of rationality. It's worth noting that since words ending with the high-pitched letters *Y, IE or I* are associated with all things *funny, sunny, silly, goofy, happy* and *zany,* the *Jeremys* of this world tend to be more flamboyant than their *JRM* counterparts.

Unless you know them well, you might think that *JRMs* are just regular nice guys with a bit of a conformist streak. It's only when you've been exposed to them in an intimate way that you'll discover that they more than meet RDA requirements for emotional receptivity. But don't expect to be welcome into their personal realm without an invitation; *JRMs* are quite protective about their inner lives and it will take some patience on your part before you'll discover if you've been deemed worthy. But even if you only know them superficially, you'll have to concede that they are wonderful listeners (if not the most forthcoming talkers) and are always willing to help you through your issues. And don't ever worry that your privacy isn't going to be safe; like most *J*-named people, *JRMs* are as dependable as passports.

Money is important to *JRMs,* but you'll rarely see them flashing it around. These are people who save their money for rainy days and who need the security that only a fat savings-account can provide. Still, *JRMs* would never trade job satisfaction for money, and when it comes to their careers, they are independently minded enough to end up owning their own businesses. While they don't have an inordinate need to be in the spotlight, they do have a strong need to be noticed for their efforts, and it isn't uncommon for *JRMs* to have their diplomas, awards and trophies prominently displayed in their homes.

Most *JRMs* will put off choosing their mates until they meet someone who shares their traditional values. The intermittently narrow-minded *JRMs* may prove to be a little bull-headed at times, but the best way to get their attention is through patience and persistence. The *JRM* responds better to a whisper than a shout.

Jeramie
Jeramy
Jeremey
Jeremiah
Jeremie
Jeremy
Jermaine
Jermey
Jerome
Jeromy

Jeremy Irons With eyes as cold as steel and a bearing verging on creepiness, British actor Jeremy Irons gave a chilling performance in David Cronenberg's *Dead Ringers*, playing two insane gynecologists whose motives had nothing to do with the well-being of their patients. He struck another sinister chord as Claus Von Bülow in *Reversal of Fortune*, winning a Best Actor Oscar for his efforts. ■ Jeremy seems drawn to literary classics, having played leading roles in Karel Reisz's *The French Lieutenant's Woman*, Steven Soderbergh's *Kafka*, and sympathetically portraying the aging protagonist in the 1997 version of Nabokov's *Lolita*. ■ One of his lesser-known contributions—but biggest box-office hit—was Disney's animated movie *The Lion King*, where he lent his menacing voice to the villain, Scar.

JS

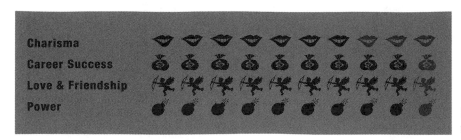

Charisma										
Career Success										
Love & Friendship										
Power										

Original Straight-shooting Charismatic Volatile Rebellious Bullheaded

The letter *S* is the symbol for all things *sexy, sassy, sensual, serpentine* and *sly*, and the letter *J* is the harbinger for a personality full of self-righteous *judgment*. So if you've ever met a person who's simultaneously charmed you and challenged your core beliefs, there's a good chance it was a *JS*. These people have the admirable—albeit somewhat annoying—ability to beguile just about anyone and turn them into co-conspirators.

JS people are attractive and intimidating. They have the ability to lighten tense situations with their sly sense of humor and youthful vigor, but they also give the feeling that at any minute they're going to switch into authoritative mode and start calling the shots. Perhaps it's because they have such strong confidence in their understanding of the universe that they're willing to put themselves on the line in this way.

You'll never find a *JS* following the crowd—they're the ones dressed in consciously unconventional clothes while somehow managing to make themselves seem stylish. They enjoy marching to a different beat and sometimes even garnish their reputations by being deliberately contrary, but *JSs* would never dream of making apologies for who they are; they have an unshakable

Jace
Jacey
Jacinta
Jacinto
Jasper
Jayce
Jaycee
Jess
Jesse
Jessi
Jessia
Jessie
Jessy
Jesus
Jesusa
Jose
Josie
Josue
Joyce

belief in their own values and moral direction. *JSs* are enterprising individuals who can smell opportunities from miles away and have a compelling need to be at the head of the action. They're typically the first to take advantage of new business trends and it would be unthinkable for them to be twiddling their thumbs while everybody else is making money. And when it comes to their verbal and motivational skills, *JSs* really shine. Quick thinkers with extraordinary street smarts, they make ideal salespeople and even better sales managers. But while they may be expert tacticians, *JSs* are not the world's best strategists. Long-range thinking just isn't their thing, which may explain why they tend to live so much in the moment.

Most *JSs* approach their intimate affairs with the same zeal as they do their careers. They are intensely passionate people, and although they are sometimes accused of pushing too hard, most lovers appreciate their unrestrained demonstrativeness. Long years of marriage aren't likely to diminish the *JS's* ardor one iota, although partners will have to cede some level of control if they don't want the union to disintegrate into a struggle for power.

Jesse Jackson A formidable orator and arguably the most prominent civil rights leader of his day, Jesse Jackson has tried his best to be the moral and spiritual head of the African American community—taking over from his mentor Dr. Martin Luther King, Jr. As King's assistant, Jesse became the center of attention when he claimed to have cradled King when he died. ■ Combating racism through community-based organizations like PUSH, Jesse became the first African American to run for the Democratic presidential nomination. ■ Jesse's tenure has been marred by controversy. He made waves by openly supporting Arafat and generated a tsunami when he referred to New York as Hymietown. His moral authority took another beating after he admitted to having a love-child as a resulf of an extramarital affair.

jsf

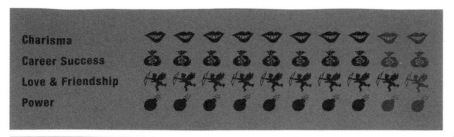

Charisma										
Career Success										
Love & Friendship										
Power										

Successful Persuasive Sensual
Underhanded Manipulative Moody

The letter *S* is the symbol for all things *sexy, sassy, sensual, slippery, serpentine* and *sly.* And since the letter *F* (and the *PH* sound) is the icon for all things *fun, physical, festive, phat, flamboyant, flirtatious, flighty, flippant, fresh* and *friendly* these two whimsical letters suggest a personality of extraordinary vivaciousness and brash sociability. And because the *judicious* (if somewhat *judgmental*) letter *J* initializes these names, these are also people with a tinge of egocentric self-righteousness.

Although most people find it difficult to resist *JSF's* unique appeal, there's also the school of thought that they sometimes go overboard in their sanguinity and many people secretly wish that they would cheer-down just a little bit. But no matter who you are, or what your opinion of the *JSFs* is, they can probably talk you into buying whatever it is they're selling. For when it comes to selling, *JSFs* are as subtle as flying bricks and their enthusiastic optimism almost always proves to be contagious. Although these are potent personalities whose powers of persuasion *could* be used for all sorts of wicked deeds, the *JSFs'* sense of justice is well-developed enough to guarantee that they'll rarely abuse their influence.

JSFs approach their relationships in a similarly frenetic fashion, and once they deem you worthy of being

Joesph
Josef
Josefa
Josefina
Josefine
Joseph
Josephina
Josephine
Josphine

their friend, there's little you're going to be able to do about it. Fortunately, these fiercely loyal people hold the belief that friendship is something that should last forever. *JSFs* also rarely forget a good deed, and even if they're not in a position to return a favor immediately, it's just a matter of time before you'll be rewarded with a reciprocal gesture. Life is one big adventure to the *JSFs* who see the people in their lives as accomplices for their merrymaking. They never want to miss an opportunity for fun and, thanks to their intuitive powers, seldom do.

Career choices for a *JSF* aren't limited to sales positions; their extroversion lends itself to all kinds of creative expression. Many make their mark as artists, musicians and writers, while law and politics provide fertile soil for their willingness to bend—and occasionally break—the rules.

JSFs are going to take control of the emotional aspects of their relationships, expecting their partners to sit back and enjoy the ride. So if you're in love with a *JSF,* you won't have much to worry about as long as your feelings are being reciprocated. But *JSFs* must respect their mates before they're able to love them, and you'll have to accept the *JSFs'* philosophy of loyalty *über alles* if you expect to preserve balance in your married life.

Josephine Baker Josephine Baker came to embody the liberal views of 1920 Europe. Famous for her titillating costumes and no-holds-barred dance routines, the "Creole Goddess" took the Paris nightclub scene by storm. ■ Initially shut out because she was "too dark," she received an invitation to perform at La Revue Nègre in Paris, where she made her entrance wearing nothing but a feather skirt and a big smile. Her next gig was at the Follies-Bergère where her costumes included a skirt made from sixteen bananas. ■ During World War II, Josephine smuggled secret messages for the French Resistance and was awarded the Medal of the Resistance. ■ In 1975, changing attitudes in America encouraged Josephine to perform at New York's Carnegie Hall, where she wept upon receiving a standing ovation even before her show began.

THE INTERNAL JSH

Charisma										
Career Success										
Love & Friendship										
Power										

Insightful Thoughtful Determined Shy Sensitive Needy

The names *Josh* and *Joshua* enjoyed a popular resurgence in the 1990s and are now on the top-ten list of names of boys under the age of twelve. This popularity may have something to do with the *JSH* phoneme's rare combination of insight, sensitivity and wisdom. For when words contain the *SH* phoneme, they usually convey a sense of sensitivity and calm like a mother protectively soothing a crying child (*hush, shh, shy, shalom* (peace), *shade, shield* and *shroud*). And like most people whose names begin with the *judicious* and *just* letter *J, JSHs* are introspective and intuitive when it comes to interacting with the world at large.

But because of the high expectations imposed on him by parents or teachers, it's not unusual for a *JSH* to get off track. They are certainly more sensitive than most, and are particularly vulnerable to getting stepped on by more aggressive personalities. *JSHs* also have a tendency to let their hearts rule their lives, and often make major life decisions based on their emotional states instead of relying on their intellectual judgments. If some people underestimate their uncommon intelligence, it's because *JSHs* are much more likely to listen than talk.

When it comes to their careers, the *JSH* seems to

Josh
Joshua
Joshuah
Josiah

have a mixed-brain-dominance; his ambidextrous mind operates equally well in right-brained and left-brained pursuits. But having so much potential has its drawbacks, too, and he often battles to find a career path that will keep them stimulated. Still, once he's found a job that provides the kind of emotional and financial rewards he feels he deserves, he'll probably prove to be an extraordinarily loyal worker. If given the choice, the *JSH* will choose a job that allows him to flex his mental muscles: teaching science or philosophy would be right up his alley.

If you're looking for a steady source of support and dependability in your love life, a *JSH* is the mate for you. Once he makes the leap (for he'd never actually fall) into love, he's in it for better or worse. You can gain thirty pounds, shave your head or become a nun, and he'll still remain by your side. He is every girl's *mother's* dream, but he's not the type to write impassioned poetry or strum a guitar outside anyone's window. At best he'll slap a ring on your finger and expect you figure out what to do with it.

But don't let his apparent aloofness put you off. If you want to know the secret motivation in the *JSH's* romantic life, it's that all he wants to be is the shining star in your universe.

Josh Hartnett Josh Hartnett's engaging innocence and promising manhood epitomizes the image of the Midwestern boy that Hollywood loves in its younger stars. ■ After a stint on ABC's remake of the drama *Cracker*, Josh auditioned for *Dawson's Creek* but failed to get the part. If he had, he would probably never have broken out of the TV trap. ■ With his accessible and vulnerable looks, Josh is able to take on a wide variety of film roles, and his appearances in *Here on Earth*, *Pearl Harbor* and *Black Hawk Down* fixed his place in the panoply of young, fresh-faced Hollywood stars. His latest role, opposite one of Hollywood's all-time leading men, Harrison Ford, in *Hollywood Homicide*, was designed to package Josh as an action hero.

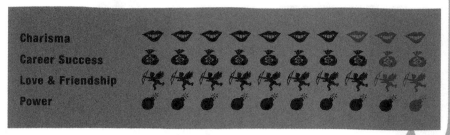

THE SHARP

JSK

Self-assured Efficient Controlled
Abrasive Illogical Possessive

Charisma	
Career Success	
Love & Friendship	
Power	

When the *sassy* letter *S* comes into close contact with the sharply pronounced letter *C*, the resulting combination tends to evoke the intensely brisk images found in the words, *screech, schism, scold, skittish, skillful, skid, scrape, scream* and *scare*. Fortunately, the *judicious* and prudent aspects of the letter *J* tend to ground these names and suggest a person who is sharp-witted, capable and thoughtful.

When you first meet a *JSK*, it's hard to know what to expect. On the surface they might seem friendly enough, but you always get the sense that you're being analyzed and evaluated. But this is par for the course when dealing with someone who is very selective, so don't count on having the *JSK* warm to you before you've proved yourself worthy of her attentions.

If *JSKs* are usually considered to be somewhat glamorous figures, it might have something to do with the fact that they're a little inaccessible, but it might be because they comport themselves with such dignity and fortitude. *JSKs* can be quite unyielding when it comes to controlling things that affect them directly and often give the impression that their own happiness is their top priority. If they don't actually believe that they're the center of the universe, it's not going to keep them from

Jesica
Jessica
Jessika

insisting on having their own way, and even *they* will have to admit that they sometimes get carried away with dispensing unwanted advice. And just because *JSKs* happen to be uncommonly smart doesn't mean they have a lot of common sense, and their desire to be helpful is often misinterpreted to be meddling. Still, from their perspective they have nothing but the best intentions and are quite happy being themselves.

Like most people whose names begin with the letter *J*, *JSKs* never have to worry much about money—probably because they're so willing to make the effort to go out and earn it. As much as they might secretly desire to spend their lives in the pursuit of art, relationships and music, they're still practical enough to put moneymaking near the top of their priority lists.

JSKs never do anything unless it's carefully planned in advance, so if you're married to a *JSK*, chances are that she was the one who initiated the process, whether you realized it or not. Just be flattered that you've been handpicked. The *JSK's* good taste is legendary, and her judgment seldom faulty. You can rest assured that she thinks you're the cream of the crop; and you could do a lot worse than living up to her expectations.

Jessica Lange After the dismal reviews she received playing the part of King Kong's defiant little victim, Jessica Lange must have thought her movie career was finished. But her second chance came when Jack Nicholson recommended her for Bob Rafaelson's remake of *The Postman Always Rings Twice*. Her role as a sultry adulteress landed her firmly on the Hollywood A-list and reignited a film career that would include an Oscar for Best Supporting Actress (*Tootsie*) and best actress nominations for *Frances, Country, Sweet Dreams* and *Music Box*. ■ Jessica met actor/playwright Sam Sheppard on the set of *Frances*, and although they were both attached to other people at the time, it didn't stop them from beginning a relationship that would endure for more than two decades.

Charisma										
Career Success										
Love & Friendship										
Power										

Enthusiastic Adaptable Independent
Closed Judgmental Cryptic

Names beginning with the letter *J* are usually associated with people who are sensible and judicious. But it's also true that names that feature the letter *S* (or *Z*) in close proximity to the letter *N* trigger a cautionary reaction. For when the *S* combines with the nasal *N*, it creates the off-putting tones found in the words *snarl, snide, sneer, snake, snivel, snoop* and *sniper*. These are the kinds of people who, while coming across as poised and rational, are usually dealing with powerful undercurrents of emotional tumult.

JSNs are known for their sensitivity to what they consider to be life's little injustices. And since *JSNs* aren't the kind of people to contain themselves in the face of perceived unfairness, they will rally to the aid of complete strangers if they believe they can make a difference. The problem is that they often find themselves reacting purely emotionally—rather than giving matters due thought—and this gives them a reputation for hot-headedness. But if you happen to be a friend of a *JSN*, you'll appreciate this super-hero rescue syndrome.

In their social lives, *JSNs* are the quintessential coffee-shop types who thrive on the company of close friends and stimulating conversation. They are terminally inquisitive people—particularly when it comes to the dynamics of their social groups—and are always ahead of the gossip curve. This natural curiosity proves useful in their careers, and many *JSNs* are drawn to jobs that enable them to acquire even more knowledge. It wouldn't be surprising to find them becoming marine biologists, scientists or professors, but they're just as happy as entrepreneurs, salespeople and computer boffins. Many *JSNs* have a talent for art and music, but because they consider making a good living more important than job satisfaction, these skills usually aren't given an opportunity to flower. Nothing unnerves them more than an underwhelming bank balance.

In their intimate relationships, *JSNs* follow a strict personal code of honor and are the kinds of people who'll treat you with absolute respect rather than unrestrained passion. So if you're considering a *JSN* for a possible love match, don't expect to be swept off your feet; their style of wooing is quite subtle, and they'll slowly grow on you instead. This is not uncommon for people whose names begin with a *J*—they simply aren't the most animalistic species in the zoo.

But if you're the kind of person with a little patience—and a willingness to overlook some imperfections—you'll find your *JSN* to be a real *mensch*. Just remember that while you're making up your mind, your *JSN* may well be reconsidering *you*.

Jasen
Jasmin
Jasmine
Jasmyn
Jason
Jayson
Jazlyn
Jazmin
Jazmine
Jazmyn
Jazmyne
Jesenia
Jessenia
Joselyn
Joslyn

Jason Priestley With his way-too-cool demeanor, boyish features and perfectly coifed hair, Jason Priestley once hoped to evoke the legend of James Dean but is now struggling to be taken seriously as a dramatic actor. ■ Jason didn't have any problems opening doors when he first moved to Los Angeles and landed guest appearances on *21 Jump Street* and *MacGyver*. The problem was that his role on *Beverly Hills, 90210* typecast him as a cute and not-to-be-taken-seriously TV personality. ■ Fans didn't want him to act . . . they just wanted him to be pretty, but his effort to reinvent himself in the movies *Tombstone* and *Coldblooded* did less to shatter his heartthrob image than his 1999 drunk-driving conviction.

Charisma										
Career Success										
Love & Friendship										
Power										

The letter *S* is the symbol for all things *sexy, sassy, sensual, slippery, serpentine* and *sly,* and the *triumphant* tones of the letter *T* are rife with allusions to self-assurance and outspoken confidence. So when these letters occur in names initialized by the *judicious* and *judgmental J,* they suggest savvy people with sly senses of humor and bucketsful of common sense. However, some of these *JST* names (*Justin* and *Justine*) are also influenced by the *nasal* letter *N,* which is the symbol for all things *negative: no, not, never, nada, null, nothing, nada, nyet* and *naught.* So for all their surface optimism, the *Justines* and *Justins* of the world are also prone to bouts of cynicism and occasional emotional outbursts.

Like most people whose names begin with the letter *J, JSTs* aren't the sort to make waves on their way to achieving their goals; it's far more important to find the right balance between making money and maintaining their relationships. Because their philosophical aesthetic calls for things to be on an even keel, it's rare to find *JSTs* rising to any great height in the business world. These are responsible people who often end up as small business owners, mid-level managers, accountants and lawyers.

JSTs love to dispense advice whether it's wanted or

Jestine
Josette
Justen
Justice
Justin
Justina
Justine
Juston
Justus
Justyn

not. From their perspective, it couldn't hurt to have an extra mind working on the problem, and they're also not too proud to accept help from others when struggling with their issues. *JST* people can also be counted on to offer a compassionate ear, but don't expect these commonsensical creatures to play the role of human Kleenexes: they are practical-minded folks who are only interested in dishing out pragmatic and effective advice.

The downside to the *JST's* principled outlook is that it borders on being controlling. This doesn't stem from any particular desire to meddle in the lives of others, but they do have a tendency to micro-manage situations that directly affect those they love. This sometimes-annoying trait is a little more tolerable if you consider that the *JSTs* are exceptionally good tacticians who can see things that most of us can't anticipate.

When it comes to their love lives, *JSTs* are conscientious about expressing their emotional needs and quickly learn that communication is at the heart of a successful relationship. Still, the *JSTs'* mates are going to need a thicker skin than most, inasmuch as *JSTs* are quite liberal when it comes to pointing out their mates' shortcomings.

Justin Timberlake When curly-haired pop star Justin Timberlake appeared on stage with Mick Jagger and the Rolling Stones in Toronto in 2003, he found himself dodging water bottles flung by the audience. The audience's displeasure was understandable; they were rockers and Justin was the meister of all that is bubblegum. ■ Justin was the frontman of the mega-popular boy-band 'N SYNC whose singles—"Tearing Up My Heart, "God Must Have Spent a Little More Time on You" and "I Want You Back"—created flutters in the hearts of teenage girls worldwide. His youthful love affair with fellow popster Britney Spears ended uncomfortably when he publicly tattled that Britney was no longer a virgin. "Every relationship I've been in, I've overwhelmed the girl. They just can't handle all the love," says Justin.

Charisma											
Career Success											
Love & Friendship											
Power											

Gentle Mannerly Softhearted
Controlling Stuffy Emotional

The name *Jonathan* has a distinctly more complex essence than the name *John* and many *JTHs* switch names depending on the situation. The soft sounds of the *TH* phoneme are responsible for the reassuring qualities found in the words *mother, father, thanks, therapy, thoughtful, theism* and *thrive*. So when it occurs in names initialized by the conservative and *judicious* letter *J*, it strongly implies a personality that is both prudent and encouraging.

Like most men whose names begin with the letter *J*, these determined people have a strong relationship to money—either making it or looking after it. There's something about *JTHs* that engender confidence in others, and their careers are quite often built around this trust. If they're not working in banks, accounting firms or in the legal profession, chances are they're in some form of leadership positions. *JTHs* have a reputation for stamina in both their professional and personal lives and have aptitudes for solving problems that require long periods of concentration.

These aren't the kind of people to take center stage in their jobs, and *JTHs* are rarely the initiators or innovators in the workplace. They prefer to slipstream and control things from the behind the scenes, and they're always there to pick up the slack and make sure things

Jethro
Johnathan
Johnathon
Jonatan
Jonathan
Jonathon

get done right. They're serious about their work and resent outside interference to their methodical approach. Still, this trait doesn't keep them from successfully working under powerful authority figures, and they will follow direction as long they're given *some* autonomy to make their own decisions.

It's not easy for *JTHs* to reveal themselves emotionally, and if something's bothering them, they'll likely suppress it until the dam bursts. These kinds of internal restraints can place a great deal of pressure on their relationships, and those trying to commune with them must be willing to coax their inner demons to the surface. Surprisingly for such reserved fellows, *JTHs* often express themselves through their art, whether it's painting, computer graphics, writing or music. And like most things in their lives, *JTHs*' ability to finish everything they start means that they're likely to show some promise in their artistic endeavors.

Family plays an extremely important role in *JTHs*' lives, and no matter how busy or preoccupied they are at work, their families will always be at the top of their priority lists. Easy and eager to please, these unassuming people don't expect their mates to provide them with happiness. All they need is honesty, loyalty and for someone to watch their backs.

Jonathan Winters Younger audiences probably remember Jonathan Winters for playing the son of Mork (Robin Williams) on *Mork and Mindy* in 1982. The age-reversed role was an ironic casting device given that Williams was the obvious heir to Jonathan's agile improvisational humor. ■ The only son of a "monstrously" alcoholic father, Jonathan enlisted in the Marines and spent two years in the South Pacific before winning the talent competition that kicked off his television career. In 1954, the moonfaced comedian was cast as a regular on the NBC comedy-variety series, *And Here's the Show*. ■ Jonathan's career was haunted by the specter of bipolar disorder that led to two nervous breakdowns and an eventual institutionalization. Since taking regular doses of lithium and swearing off alcohol and caffeine, Jonathan has been symptom free.

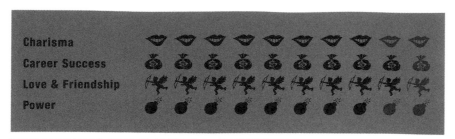

Charisma										
Career Success										
Love & Friendship										
Power										

In-charge Reflective Original
Self-centered Pushy Stubborn

Since the letter *V* is the undisputed flagship of all that is *virile, vibrant, voluptuous, virtuous, vampish* and *valiant*, it tends to imbue words with a sense of *vim, vigor* and overt sexuality. Even when it occurs in words initialized by the conservative letter *J*—the symbol of all things *judicious* and *judgmental*—the *V* manages to suggest an intrepid, flamboyant personality who is *jovial* and *juvenile*. Like most people whose names begin with the *J, JV* people are not ones to publicly draw attention to themselves but will usually turn out to be the ringleaders of their large social groups.

When growing up, the *JV* was probably a bouncy, even hyperactive, child who found release in competitive sports. One thing is certain: the *JV's* talents include a highly competitive instinct *and* the talent to pull it off. Although *JVs* have little time for those who can't pull their own weight, they are not the types to gloat over their successes. They would much rather see *everyone* doing well—even if it means that they aren't going to stand out in the crowd.

Even with (or maybe *because* of) their childlike perspectives, you can always expect courtesy and politeness from a *JV*. These are people with old-fashioned values

Jarvis
Javen
Javier
Javion
Javon
Javonte
Jevon
Jovan
Jovani
Jovanny
Jovany

and an affinity for keeping things simple. They also have an uncommon set of communication skills, which is put to work in their professional lives, and they often choose careers that involve writing, politics or management. This is why such a high percentage of *JVs* end up as company spokespeople, lawyers and arbitrators.

By carefully picking their battles and keeping a lid on negative emotions when tensions are running high, *JVs* prove to be formidable and successful negotiators. But *JVs* are sorely lacking when it comes to patience and don't suffer fools gladly. This is why they are rarely found in the helping professions such as counseling, medicine or education.

It takes a special partner to keep up with the *JVs'* robust sexual appetites and even though they will mellow with age, mates can still expect a lifetime of surprises. This may prove tiresome to less adventurous personalities who find themselves bobbing in the wake of the *JVs'* enthusiastic wave-making, but for those able to keep up with these energetic creatures, *JVs* will prove to be loyal, flexible and unconditional life long friends.

Javier Pérez de Cuéllar While it's certainly not the most powerful appointment in the world, the position of UN Secretary General affects the lives of more people on the planet than any other. With far reaching mandates—including the protection of non self-governing people—the Secretary General must walk a fine line between defending the world's poor and offending the world's rich. ■ Peruvian born Javier Pérez de Cuéllar served two terms as leader but did not seek a third term. He was replaced by Boutros Boutros-Gahli. ■ His tenure oversaw the end of the cold war and a restoration of UN prestige. He personally negotiated the cease-fire that ended the Iran-Iraq War and the Soviet withdrawal from Afghanistan. ■ After stepping down he entered local politics and was appointed Peruvian Prime Minister in 2000.

K

The Letter of Forceful Action

*And when I have stol'n upon these
son-in-laws, Then kill, kill, kill, kill, kill, kill!*
—WILLIAM SHAKESPEARE,
King Lear

Formed by the explosive sound of the tongue's contact against the back of the palate, the letter K casts a decidedly aggressive shadow and is inextricably linked to words of power and violence as in kick, knight, king, kidnap, keen, knave, Kaiser, knock, knife, knuckle sandwich and kill. ■ As one of the rarest initial letters in the English language, the K accounts for less than 1% of all words and isn't even pronounced in 25% of these cases (e.g. knitting and knowledge). ■ This powerful letter, however, carries far more influence than its meager use suggests. In most cases, the K sounds like the hard letter C, and its strong and unyielding qualities are exemplified in the traditional meanings of Karl (manly), Kim and Kimberly (diamond rock), Klaus (leader in victory), and Kevin and Kenneth (handsome). ■ Wherever it appears, its masculinizing power influences the tone of names in letter order, accounting for the K's extraordinary frequency on Dr. Albert Mehrabian's survey of names connoting masculinity. No fewer than 25% of the top fifty names on this list contain a K, for example Buck, Duke, Hank, Kurt, Jake, Mark, Chuck, Jock, Keith, Rick, Mike, Derek, Kevin, Drake and Kirk. Conversely, only two names appear on the list of names indicating femininity, both of which have a diminutive form: Katie and Kitty. ■ With all their assertive self-confidence, it's not surprising that K people are among the most likely to have professional sports careers. But as an indication of their sometimes over-the-top forcefulness, they are the least likely to have successful political careers. ■

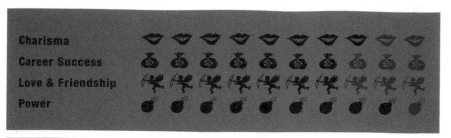

Charisma										
Career Success										
Love & Friendship										
Power										

Talented Outspoken Communicative
Rash Choosy Unstable

Dominated by the commanding letter *K*, an aura of strength, charisma and bluntness surrounds these names and suggests a motivated individual with a keen intellect. In the female names of this group we find the *K's* masculine overtones modulated by the feminizing action of the high-pitched *I* or *Y* sounds (as in *Kay*, *Kai* and *Kya*) or the softening action of the *S* sound (*Kacy*). Most male names—as in *Kirk*—utilize a double dose of the *K* and suggest a man especially comfortable with his masculinity.

While these aren't the most romantic people you'll ever meet they are amongst the most dependable and forthright souls in the universe. You're also unlikely to sink into pessimism with a *K* around—not because they're overly buoyant—but because they're guided by reliable moral compasses and are solidly grounded by compassion and altruism. Sure it's an intellectual approach but this doesn't mean that *Ks* are incapable of connecting emotionally. It's just that in the war between their hearts and heads, their heads remain undefeated.

Surprising for such sensible people, *Ks* exhibit quite an artistic bent. This may take the form of a musical talent or perhaps a flair for decorating their homes with decidedly eclectic tastes. When it comes to their careers, the *Ks'* sharp minds make them attractive prospects for employers looking for responsible and motivated

Kacy
Kai
Kaia
Kaiya
Kay
Kaya
Kaycee
Kaye
Keiko
Kirk
Kiya
Kya

employees. But although people with *K* names have a higher than average probability of success in the arts and in professional sports, they don't stand out when it comes to making big chunks of money. This could be due to the *Ks'* priorities being more attuned to what (they consider) to be the most important elements of life: having fun and exploring their universe.

When it comes to their intimate relationships, *Ks* are in high demand as marriage partners. Potential mates are drawn to their strength of character and unique blend of resourcefulness and creativity. But it should be noted that because *Ks* are creatures of independence who require an unusual amount of personal space, prospective partners are advised to give them time to recharge their emotional batteries.

Even though they'll indulge in periodic bouts of solitude, *Ks* have a powerful need for emotional reassurance. This is why they are drawn to partners who are more sensitive than they are, and why most *K* marriages are a little lopsided in the power department. Still, they are remarkably good listeners and quite willing to share their most private thoughts. Parenthood comes naturally for these family-minded individuals and their offspring will find them to unconditionally loving—if a little heavy handed when it comes to discipline.

Kirk Douglas Kirk Douglas, the dimpled-chinned square jawed father of Michael Douglas was a powerhouse box-office draw whose career spanned almost six decades. ■ His breakthrough performance came from his title role in *Spartacus* in 1960. The film was considered to be an intellectual epic and broke from traditional Hollywood ending by allowing its hero to be crucified. ■ Kirk's accolades included three nominations by the Academy for Best Actor, an Honorary Oscar in 1995 and a Golden Globe for *Lust for Life*. In 1995 he suffered a stroke that left him with limited speaking abilities but continued his public appearances anyway.

Charisma	😚😚😚😚😚😚😚😚😚😚
Career Success	💰💰💰💰💰💰💰💰💰💰
Love & Friendship	🐉🐉🐉🐉🐉🐉🐉🐉🐉🐉
Power	💣💣💣💣💣💣💣💣💣💣

**Adventurous Talented Independent
Untrusting Impetuous Distracted**

There are two letters in the alphabet that compete for the title of most assertive: the letter *B*—the symbol of all things *belligerent, brave, bulwark, badgering, biting, bossy, brawny* and *bouncy*—and the letter *K,* the symbol of forceful action found in the words. *kick, kill, knuckle, king, knock, knigh* and *knife.* When these two resolute letters occur together in words or names; they reflect the determined qualities seen in the words *backbite, jackboot, brickbat, bulwark, bark, brisk, rebuke* and *bulkhead.* It's not to say that *KB* people are exceptionally aggressive, it's just that they have a strong sense of who they are and where they're going; even if they don't know exactly how they're going to get there.

These are people who were accorded the kind of respect from their peers that most of us never experienced. But because doors were so often opened for them when they were young, *KBs* often struggle to find their direction. In later life, in trying to live up to the expectations of such a powerful label, many *KBs* take a while to find their way. But rest assured; once *KBs* discover their wings there's almost nothing that can hold them back from taking flight and exploring the mountaintops. Sometimes their discovery takes the form of an almost compulsive literary craving, but more often than not, it expresses itself in the *KBs'*

Kaleb
KB
Kelby
Kirby
Kobe
Koby
Kolby
Korbin

appetite to travel to the furthest reaches of the planet. These are people with such deep self-confidence that they can leave their comfort zone at the drop of a hat when opportunities beckon.

The *KBs'* extraordinary communication skills when combined with their steely self-confidence inevitably commands attention, and as is typical of people whose names begin with the letter *K,* the *KBs'* inner strength gives them an almost bottomless volume of emotional energy, which they're quite happy to share with others. But if they're the types of people who seem to cruise through difficult emotional situations, don't think for a minute that *KBs* aren't fully cognizant of what's going on around them. With their keen emotional intelligence they intuitively understand their limitations and take appropriate action to ensure that they never lose control.

Nothing beats having a *KB* watching your back when it comes to intimate relationships. When the world's against you, you can count on having at least one person who believes in you. Even if you happen to displease your *KB* mate, don't expect an overtly aggressive response. Like most powerful personalities, *KBs* prefer communicating their feelings by what they *don't* say rather than resorting to fancy verbal outbursts.

Kobe Bryant Depending on whom you ask, Kobe Bryant was either named after a Kobe steak listed on the menu of a Japanese restaurant or, after the restaurant itself. Kobe spent eight of his childhood years in Italy where his father, Joe Jellybean Bryant, spent the waning years of his basketball career. Kobe is fluent in Italian and owns an Italian basketball team. ■ One of the youngest players ever to play in the NBA, Kobe downplayed the reports of tensions between him and the Shaquille O'Neal. Kobe and Shaq took the Lakers to their first championship in 2000 and followed it up with another title in 2001 before three-peating in 2002. ■ Kobe married his long time sweetheart Vanessa in 2001 who stood by his side during his sexual assault trial in 2004.

Kl

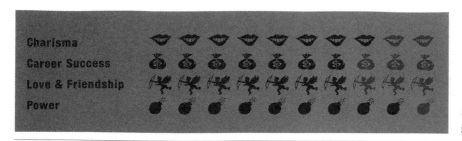

Charisma										
Career Success										
Love & Friendship										
Power										

Smart Strong Adaptable
Stubborn Abrasive Demanding

Although the commanding tones of the letter *K* project a rather masculine essence, the letter *L* is a gentle letter that represents all the things that money can't buy: *love, life, laughter, lust, learning* and *liberty*. When these two letters appear in combination, they *twinkle* with a *silky* resonance. To further emphasize these names' feminine tones, many women (*Kelly, Kaylie, Kylie* and *Kelley*) terminate their names with the diminutizing tones of the high-pitched *I* or *Y*.

KL names are undergoing a surge in popularity and their acceptance is perhaps a tribute to their attractive combination of strength and vulnerability. And while *KLs* might sometimes be mistaken for being too deferential, it's just because their iron core tends to be masked by a disarmingly quiet exterior. Stubborn? You bet. If you want to change their minds, it's much smarter to seduce them with the promise of something better. As for all headstrong people, the carrot is more conducive than the stick.

Don't be fooled if your *KL* friends seem to be in high spirits all the time—even if something *were* bothering them you'd likely never know. Denial is not their only flaw, but they'd never admit to that either. *KLs* often come across as people who're having a love affair with life itself and man-

Kaela
Kaelyn
Kaila, Kailey
Kailyn, Kalen
Kaley, Kaliyah
Kallie, Kalyn
Kayla, Kaylyn
Kaylynn, Keeley
Keely, Keila
Kelcie, Keli, Kelle
Kellee, Kellen
Kayleigh, Kelley
Kelli, Kellie Kelly
Kellye, Kelsea
Kelsey, Kelsi
Kelsie, Keyla
Khalil, Kiel
Kiley, Kole
Kolton, Kyla
Kylan, Kylee
Kyleigh, Kyler
Kylie

age to make everyone around them feel like the most important, charming, intelligent people in the world. Perhaps this is why so many people are drawn into the *KLs* realm and why they're talked about in such glowing terms. *KLs* are keen observers of their environments and rarely miss the fine details that are often overlooked by the rest of us. An extraordinary "street-smartness," or at least an instinct for what makes people tick, amplifies this trait, and if you ever want the latest scoop on what's going on in the social milieu, you'd want to consult a *KL*. You'll find that even though gossip isn't their bag, they're very interested in the human drama underlying it all. These characteristics make them ideal candidates for trouble-shooting careers: psychology, law, medicine, accounting and even teaching.

You're unlikely to find yourself in a casual fling with a *KL*. They are drawn to relationships in which they can deeply delve into the psyches of their partners. They enjoy interacting at the deepest levels but aren't always as quick to share their own dark secrets with their mates. Mates are advised to tread softly around their *KL* spouses when it comes to deciding household issues. *KLs* hold their own opinions in such high regard that conceding you're wrong will get you everywhere.

Kelsey Grammer Kelsey Grammer's Emmy winning portrayal of the voluble and vulnerable psychologist on *Cheers* and *Frasier*, earned him a spot on America's funny bone. Anyone familiar with *The Simpsons* knows him as the malevolent Sideshow Bob. ■ Kelsey's early life was a tragedy of Shakespearean proportions. He lost his father in a shooting death and his grandfather, who helped to raise him, died before he entered high school. His sister was murdered and a diving accident killed two of his half-brothers. ■ Few were surprised then, when Kelsey was arrested for drunken driving and cocaine possession in 1988, leading to a month in jail. Kelsey checked into the Betty Ford Center after a 1996 car accident widely rumored to be the result of alcohol.

THE ENIGMATIC km

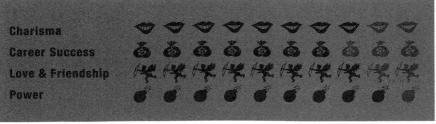

Charisma	
Career Success	
Love & Friendship	
Power	

Determined Energetic Spunky
Indecisive Conflicted Uncomfortable

The letter *M* is the symbol for all things *motherly* and *maternal*. Its *mellow* and *mellifluous* tones create the feminine resonance of the words *maiden, matron, merciful, mild, mama* and *mammary*. So when the *M* is teamed up with the forcefully masculine letter *K*, the resulting combination could be said to create an enigma of biblical proportions. This is why one can never be sure which facet of the *KM* is going to be the dominant theme on any given day: their protective and emotional aspects or their ambitious and goal-oriented sides.

If *KMs* were automobiles, they'd be one of those little foreign jobs. Not because they're overly flashy or powerful, but because they're performance-oriented people who appreciate quality and style. And *KMs* don't seem to mind if some critics describe them as stuck-up; they're the first to agree that their world-view is a little unusual and have long since come to terms with the consequences of being "different." Even when young, *KMs* learned to take care of themselves and are quite capable of living life without having someone make a fuss over them.

KMs are driven and successful individuals with a lot to prove... both to the world and to themselves. When there's nothing to temper their adventurous spirit, exploration and self-discovery will rule the *KM's* life. That's why there's no point in trying to pigeonhole

Kami
Kareem
Kim
Kimber
Kimmi
Kwame
Kym

them into a particular career path; they are creatures of excitement who get antsy at the thought of being professionally tied down. But if and when *KMs* do settle down into a job, they will avoid work that brings them directly into contact with the public. They're more likely to tackle some kind of technical or artistic challenge even if it means biting off more than they can chew.

People are both drawn to, and envious of, *KMs* without really knowing exactly why. Some believe this to be a symptom of the *KM's* snobbishness (they often give the impression that they consider themselves to be a cut above the rest) but it usually has less to do with vanity than it does their complex emotional makeup.

Friendship with *KMs* is an illusion of sorts and they can be tough nuts to crack when it comes to intimacy, for even in their most extroverted moments *KMs* will hardly ever reveal their true intentions. It's not that they don't know what they are, but they'd rather let their achievements speak for them instead. In matters of the heart, a good sign that you're winning a *KM's* trust is when they lose some of their restlessness and become a little more reflective. If you're lucky, you'll uncover their clandestine sensitivities and even enjoy one of their patented meaningful conversations.

Kim Basinger Most people don't know that Oscar winning actress Kim Basinger suffers from shyness verging on agoraphobia. ■ Kim's career breakthrough came when she played the lead opposite Mickey Rourke in the *Nine and 1/2 Weeks*, an exploration into the realm of erotic games. The next few years saw a series of debatable choices where Kim disastrously purchased the town of Braselton in Georgia and faced near-bankruptcy when sued by the producers of *Boxing Helena* for breach of contract. ■ Kim orchestrated her comeback by playing Vicky Vale in *Batman*, winning an Oscar for her performance as a hooker in *LA Confidential*, and igniting her love-affair with Alec Baldwin. ■ Kim's portrayal of Eminem's mother in *8 Mile* was criticized only by Eminems' real mother—who reportedly said that she never drinks beer nor combs her hair.

kmbl

Charisma	👄	👄	👄	👄	👄	👄	👄	👄	👄	👄
Career Success	💰	💰	💰	💰	💰	💰	💰	💰	💰	💰
Love & Friendship	🦄	🦄	🦄	🦄	🦄	🦄	🦄	🦄	🦄	🦄
Power	💣	💣	💣	💣	💣	💣	💣	💣	💣	💣

Thoughtful Strong-minded Talented Closed Pushy Two-faced

Complex names are a sign of complicated personalities and few names are more intricate than *KMBL* group. This is particularly true when you consider that *Kimberlys* have the option of the more accessible *Kim* or *Kimber* at their disposal; suggesting they consider themselves worthy of a more complex name. The letter *K* initializes these names with a forcefully masculine presence but is in direct opposition to the *maternal* letter *M*—the symbol of all things *merciful, mild,* and *matronly.* A second set of competing influences comes into play with the *belligerent, brave,* and the *bullying* letter *B*'s connection with the *languid, lazy, life-loving* letter *L*. These two sets of contrasting forces hint at the dichotomy that is the *KMBL,* and explains why she's able to exhibit a wide range of emotional states; ranging from a light-on-her-feet ingénue to a woman of pig-iron grit.

But one thing is consistent about the *KMBL* personalities. While others are rushing into promising opportunities, *KMBLs* tend to be prudent about their decisions—particularly when it comes to their relationships. Perhaps this is a necessary consequence of the precarious balancing act in maintaining their internal equilibriums, and *KMBLs* are very aware that ill-chosen relationships can dramatically upset their delicate poise.

These women exhibit a calm and stable temperament under fire. Even though one might be tempted to describe them as refined or aloof, a sampling of the *KMBL's* fiery temper quickly dispels *this* myth. Like most explosions though, the *KMBLs'* burn out quickly and they are not prone to long-term mood swings or protracted episodes of aggression.

The *KMBL's* career path is carefully chosen. Always up for a good challenge, she favors jobs where she can shine on her own, and would rather compete against herself than against anyone else. This might give the impression that she's actually somewhat shy, but anyone who knows her well, knows that she's anything but milquetoast. Getting to know her is like unwrapping a present: you can't tell what's in there by the color of the paper.

Where it comes to finding romance, *KMBLs* don't seem to make much of an effort; they're usually content to let it hit them over the head. Under the influence of persuasive suitors, some *KMBLs* are beguiled into signing onto marriage before they're ready and these affairs tend to be destabilized as both parties vie for power. Unless an early truce is called, it's likely that these unions will dissolve prematurely. *KMBLs* who stave off marriage—and allow the right partner to choose them—will enjoy above-average relationships and blossom as the union matures.

Kemberly
Kimberely
Kimberlee
Kimberley
Kimberli
Kimberlie
Kimberly
Kymberly

Kimberley Locke Many consider Kimberley Locke to be an American Idol without the title. As the only female finalist in the second season of Fox's mega-hit talent search, Kimberley narrowly lost out to Ruben Studdard and Clay Aiken, who were both in her original group. Kimberley had beaten out 35,000 other female contestants from across the United States with her signature rendition of "Somewhere Over the Rainbow." Even the show's caustic judge, Simon Cowell, grudginly conceded that any of the top three finalists deserved to win. This after Kimberley had lashed out at him rather brusquely in the very first episode. "Sometimes I wanted to smack him . . . people can be very cruel. ■ Like most of the to finishers in Idol, Kimberley landed a major recording contract.

THE DIVIDED

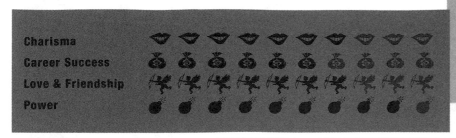

Charisma										
Career Success										
Love & Friendship										
Power										

Intelligent Detail-oriented Creative Eccentric Awkward Withdrawn

The letter *N* is the defining symbol for all things *negative*, which is why it is the initial letter for *no, not, never, none, nyet, nada, nix, naught* and *nothing*. When this pessimistic force combines with the dynamic influence of the letter *K*, it tends to create words that denote toughness and dogged action: *knife, knight, knuckle, kingly, kinky, keen* and *kinetic*. This is why many *KNs* (*Kenny, Kinsey, Kenya, Kalyn,* etc.) utilize the playful letter *Y*—the symbol of youthful innocence—to reduce their name's inherent aggression.

There's no way to tell which aspect of the *KN's* personality is going to be dominant on any given day; it's entirely up to the gods of randomness. For like most people whose names begin with a *K*, *KNs* march to the beat of their own drummers and have little time for people who don't accept them for who they are. And if the *KNs* aren't everyone's cup of chamomile, that's perfectly fine with them. The truth is, *KNs* seem to live in a parallel universe and don't fully connect with the humdrum issues that occupy the rest of us.

If you're an acquaintance of any *KNs*, you'll have a sense of the bull-headed loyalty that marks their social style and explains their faithful following of core supporters. You can count on them to deliver on every promise they make, and because they have an old-fashioned sense

Kane
Keagan
Keanu
Keegan
Keena
Keenan
Kegan
Ken, Kena
Kent, Kenton
Kenia, Kenna
Kenny, Kenya
Kenzie, Keon
Keyshawn
Kian, Kiana
Kenyatta
Kenyon
Keshaun
Keshawn
Keyon
Kianna
Kina
King
Kinsey

of duty, they will always do what they think is right regardless of the personal cost. This can be both a pro and a con for the headstrong *KNs,* who will often ignore sound advice when barreling in the wrong direction.

Even if their social skills aren't on a par with their intellectual capacities, *KNs* are undeniably smarter than most and can be formidable business opponents. Their ability to focus on problems makes them ideal computer programmers and technical advisors and their affinity for logic makes them perfect for law, medicine and the teaching professions. And even if they're not the most colorful crayons in the box, people are often surprised to learn that *KNs* have the ability to read other people's emotions quite accurately, a quality that serves them well in people-oriented careers like sales.

KNs often have a tough time when it comes to their intimate endeavors… it can be difficult to find someone who can tolerate their obstinate ways. But because relationships with these individuals hold the promise of a solid commitment and stable home, *KNs* have more than enough people from whom to choose. *KNs* aren't hell-raisers, nor are they likely to play the field. They're much more interested in finding someone who understands them so they can focus on more important things—like raising a house and children.

Ken Starr History will judge whether Ken Starr was villain or hero but there is no doubt that he was a major player in the Clinton presidency. As the special prosecutor appointed to investigate the President's business dealings, his pursuit earned him a reputation as a political hitman. ■ After Linda Tripp revealed that Monica Lewinsky had an affair with Bill Clinton. Ken made it the focus of his investigation. He managed to convict a number of Clinton associates but was ultimately unable to prove criminal behavior in the White House.

Charisma	👄	👄	👄	👄	👄	👄	👄	👄	👄	👄
Career Success										
Love & Friendship										
Power										

As with most people whose names begin with the forcefully masculine letter *K, KNDs* are active people with strong minds and equally strong shoulders. There is, however, an unmistakable sense of pessimism—or is it cynicism?—that permeates their lives, and is perhaps due to the influence of the letter *N*—the definitive symbol for all things *negative*; *no, not, never, none, nyet, nada, nix, naught* and *nothing*. On the other hand, the letter *D*—the icon of *dignity, discipline, divine* and *drive*—colors these names with a distinct air of eminence and gives these people a reputation for being unyielding in their principles and beliefs.

In short, *KNDs* are quandaries—as much to their friends as they are to themselves. Many people report that upon first meeting a *KND,* they sensed a measure of conflict underlying their personalities, but at the same time were fascinated by their obvious intelligence and indefinable mystique.

KNDs are roamers at heart and have hearts that roam. They are driven by a sense of adventure and dissatisfaction for the status quo and—like heat-seeking missiles—will hone in on potential "growth experiences" whenever the opportunities present themselves. They certainly know how to have a good time, but they're definitely not frivolous. In fact, they're so dedicated to wringing the most out of their lives that their quests lead them on adventures most of us will never

Kandace
Kandi
Kandice
Kandra
Kendall
Kendra
Kendrick
Kennedi
Kennedy
Kindra

consider. So don't count on finding your *KND* friend in the same place (or relationship) from one year to the next. These restless individuals will stay just long enough to get antsy before moving on to the next challenge. But like most people who struggle to connect with themselves, the *KNDs'* journey into self-exploration eventually pays off with a solid understanding of themselves and their place in the universe.

Autonomy is important to *KNDs* and because nothing bothers them more than being dependent on others . . . they have to feel financially independent. Their career choices almost always reflect their passion for creativity and personal freedom—writing, designing and the culinary arts are high on their list of things to try—but they're usually careful to have something solid to fall back on.

Falling in love with a *KND* can be problematic if you're looking for predictability in your life. And even though many people are drawn to their free-spirited and non-conformist ways, *KNDs* are apt to leave a trail of puzzled hearts in their wake. It may be hard to pin these gypsies down but togetherness (even if it's not in the traditional sense) will prove to be quite rewarding. *KNDs* will also benefit from the steadying influence of family and their children will inherit their sense of fun and adventure, and enjoy a supportive, if avant-garde home environment.

 Kennedy Montgomery Maybe it's the "Kennedy" curse, but when you're a hip young VJ hosting MTV's grunge show *Alternative Nation*, people reflexively assume you're part of the liberal left. Instead, Kennedy Montgomery's in-your-face conservatism made her a hero to her generation's right wing. ■ She has a pink Republican elephant tattooed in her pelvic region and once confessed to having a crush on Dan Quayle. ■ As conservative as she is, Kennedy believes that marijuana laws should be loosened and gays should be allowed to marry. On the flip side, she believes that gun laws are too strict. Her view on the death penalty? "Fry 'em."

THE YOUTHFUL
Kr

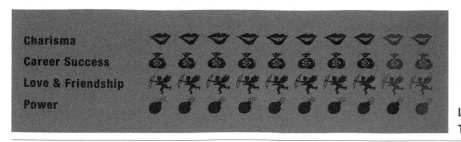

Charisma											
Career Success											
Love & Friendship											
Power											

Lively Playful Wholesome
Temperamental Annoying Imperceptive

The letter *R* is the classic icon of all things *romantic, racy, randy, ravishing* and *robust,* while the letter *K* the predicator of sharply decisive physical action. When these two positive letters dominate a name, they evoke the unambiguous image of someone with a defiant disposition and uncommon self-confidence.

The firm and fun-loving *KRs* know how to balance work and play. In their professional lives, they are renowned for their fierce focus and willingness to compete, while their private lives are characterized by their hard-driving sense of adventure. The one thing that stands out about the *KR* personalities is their particularly close and long-lasting friendships. Mind you, these friendships aren't stable because they're effusive or demonstrative; *KRs* prefer to express their affections obliquely—through quiet devotion and off-handed gestures—rather than through overtly emotional displays.

KRs are not averse to taking chances in their careers but avoid undue risks by always having a plan B at the ready. Since they aren't particularly well organized, their skills are best utilized in careers involving people or animals. Their somewhat ethereal approach to life tends to limit their advancement in the professional world, and for the same reason, *KRs* don't mesh well with left-brained practical types.

Kara
Karey
Kari
Karie
Karri
Karrie
Karry, Kary
Keara, Keira
Keri, Kerri
Kerrie, Kerry
Kiara, Kiera
Kierra. Kira
Korey, Kori
Kory
Kyra
Kyree

But whatever they decide to do for a living, you can count on them bringing a positive energy and a resolute commitment to getting the job done right.

KRs prove to be elusive intimate partners, for they are not only hard to come by but also hard to keep. You can track them down by following a trail of broken hearts and—while you'd never accuse a *KR* of being cruel—there's a little ice water running through those veins. *KRs* know exactly what they want from their relationships and have no qualms about brushing up the blue suede and walking out when things aren't going their way. And don't count on appealing to these wayward spirits with the offer of a traditional family setting; the *KRs'* opinion of a white-picket-fence is akin to most people's opinion of a funeral.

Married life with a *KR* will be a loosely organized but affectionate institution. Not being overly methodical, things function better when they're not the ones in charge of the social calendar, although there is something to be said for the *KR's* spontaneity when it comes to throwing parties.

Children will appreciate their parent's emphasis on fun. They will be gently disciplined and instilled with the same individualistic principles that rule the *KRs'* lives.

Kiri Te Kanawa Not since Maria Callas has opera had such a celebrated diva in Dame Kiri Te Kanawa. Kiri, who once described herself as a fat anorexic was born in New Zealand of mixed Maori-European descent. ■ Undeterred by professional advice that she wait a few years before beginning serious voice training, Kiri enrolled at an early age at St. Mary's Catholic School for Girls in Auckland and studied with the best voice teacher in New Zealand; Sister Mary Leo. ■ Invited to sing at the marriage of Charles and Lady Diana, Kiri was made a Dame of the British Empire as a token of appreciation. ■ She recently stepped out of the limelight to spend more time with her children.

223

THE DETERMINED

Krl

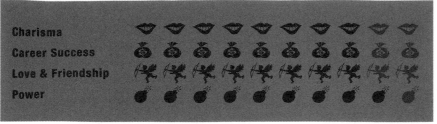

Charisma										
Career Success										
Love & Friendship										
Power										

Honest Forward-thinking Dutiful
Harsh Judgmental Hasty

Since the letter *K* is the symbol of all things masculine, forceful and brave, and the passionate letter *R* is the embodiment of all things *romantic, racy, randy, ravishing* and *robust,* these are clearly names with a great deal of focus on physical energy. And because the lyrical *L* is the harbinger of the important things that money can't buy (*love, life, laughter, liberty* and *learning*), these names also suggest someone full of passionate bravado ready to fight for his or her beliefs. A *KRL* is someone in whom you could entrust your life, your spouse and your wallet.

If the *KRL* were an animal, he or she would be a lion. Not a full-maned African lion mind you, but a lithe and flexible cougar always ready to battle the forces of nature: their instincts are always on the alert and they exhibit a remarkable reservoir of emotional strength. Sometimes this emotional reserve flows from a spiritual well, but it mostly stems from a methodical and practical approach to problems. *KRLs* are people who believe that any lock can be opened if you're persistent enough to find the key. But while this approach may serve them well in their business affairs, they find that in matters of the heart, not everything can be pried open with logic.

Forthright and outspoken, *KRLs* are appreciated for their sound advice even if those with delicate constitu-

Karl
Karla
Karlee
Karley
Karli
Karlie
Karly
Karol
Karole
Karyl

tions flinch when they encounter their blunt styles. But *KRLs* never say something without thinking and everyone seems to agree that they do have helpful insights into how life works. It's precisely this deliberate nature that gives them such an advantage in competitive work environments where *KRLs* are in demand as arbitrators and consultants. Because people tend to instinctively trust *KRLs*, they're also suited for leadership and motivational jobs where *KRLs* are always happy to oblige with elaborate advice.

Given their sense of responsibility to the people in their lives, *KRLs* thrive in relationships. Married life, in particular, is a natural environment for their protective natures and *KRLs* bond confidently and enthusiastically. Still, the *KRLs*' sometimes-inflexible approach may be somewhat exhausting to mates unable to cater to their determined mindsets. Mates unwilling to subjugate their personal power for the good of the relationship might want to trade in their *KRL* partner for someone who's not quite as sure of themselves.

If you're going to pick the one arena in which *KRLs* excel, it's in fulfilling their parental duties. Even if *KRLs* sometimes confuse material resources for affection, children will be raised in synch with their own moral codes and retain a life-long respect for their dutiful parent.

Karl Marx Karl Marx's influence in western philosophy cannot be overstated, but it's usually those who have never read a word that he wrote who vilify most. Karl would be horrified to learn that his name is now associated with the authoritarian communist regimes of the twentieth century; he was a child of the Enlightenment, who believed mankind was destined to be free. ■ Born in 1818, Karl studied law but soon became enchanted with philosophy. Ironically, the young Karl had problems with money and struggled to make a living as a lecturer after his radical ideas proved to be quite unpopular. Fortunately, Karl met Friedrich Engels, who became his patron and helped him publish *Das Kapital*. The work remains to this day, the most comprehensive critical analysis of the capitalist system.

224

THE MODEST

Krn

Charisma	🫦🫦🫦🫦🫦🫦🫦🫦🫦🫦
Career Success	💰💰💰💰💰💰💰💰
Love & Friendship	🦅🦅🦅🦅🦅🦅🦅🦅🦅🦅
Power	💣💣💣💣💣💣💣💣💣

Confident Focused Persevering
Inflexible Reticent Self-deprecating

The letter *R* is the classic icon of all things *romantic, racy, randy, ravishing* and *robust* while the letter *K* is the predicator of physical action. Even though both these letters are symbols of positive energy, it must also be mentioned that the letter *N* is the herald of all things *negative* (as in the words *no, not, never, nyet, nada, nothing* and *naught*). Chances are, when you really get to know one of these vital and unpretentious spirits you can also expect to encounter someone beset by bouts of pessimism and self-doubt. Interestingly, the name *Karena* has recently become the very definition of a desirable woman—as witnessed by a number of "nu-skool" lexicons listing the following entry: *karena: n. a pretty girl. ("She is such a karena").*

*KRN*s don't derive their undeniable popularity from being soft and cuddly; these are women who make their mark by being upfront and forthright. And while those who bear *KRN* names hardly ever display open aggression, there's a powerful bite to their disposition that manifests in an extraordinarily acerbic tongue. Still, the *true* essence of the *KRN* is that of a kind and nurturing spirit that reveals itself in the way they wrap themselves in their closely-knit circle of friends.

Though you'll never find them advertising it publicly, *KRN*s have a powerful inner drive that is quietly put to use in their careers. Like most people whose names begin with the letter *K*, the *KRN* isn't going to be the wealthiest woman on the block, but she really won't give a hoot as long as her work is intellectually and emotionally satisfying. *KRN*s are drawn to jobs that offer a level of creativity, and though she has no problem interacting with others, she'll usually choose to work alone or in small groups.

Friends of the *KRN*, once allowed to get past her initial barriers, will get a kick out of her unadulterated honesty. These are not women who hide behind superficial small talk or mince words when the time comes for honest intervention. This is tough love at its most intelligent and you'll never have to worry that she's hiding her true feelings on a touchy subject.

*KRN*s are fiercely loyal when they're in intimate relationships; but it's usually an all or nothing situation. Unless they are completely certain about their partner's intentions they find it difficult to loosen up. For this reason, many promising relationships simply fail to take root. Perhaps it's their tendency to intellectualize their feelings—rather than allowing nature to take its course—but sometimes it's just a symptom of their underlying self-doubt. So if you're just looking for a good time, pass her by. But if it's lifelong companionship you have in mind, throw away your little black book and hang on for all you're worth.

Karan
Kareen
Karen
Karena
Karin
Karina
Karine
Karon
Karren
Karyn
Keren
Kieran

Karen Carpenter It was Karen Carpenter's older brother, Richard, who initially recognized her gift for music. Karen was given a drum set with which to accompany Richard's guitar, and the brother-sister duo, The Carpenters, was born. ■ Thanks to Karen's extraordinarily pure singing voice, The Carpenters became one of the most successful bands in the history of pop. With hits like "Close to You," "Rainy days and Mondays" and "Yesterday Once More," they generated eight gold albums, five platinum albums and ten gold singles. ■ The story ended in 1983 when Karen died at the age of thirty-two after a long battle with anorexia. Thousands attended the singer's funeral.

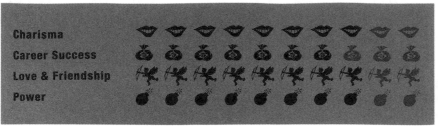

Charisma										
Career Success										
Love & Friendship										
Power										

Intellectual Pioneering Bold
Nonconformist Defiant Misunderstood

The letter *R* is the harbinger of naughty romance—*randy, ribald, ruddy, racy, ravishing,* and *robust*—and the *sultry S* is associated with all things *sensual, sexy, sassy, silky* and *slinky.* Whenever a name features these two letters, you can bet that it's going to belong to someone with a passionate lust for life and an extraordinary sensual promise. But it's the forceful letter *K* that gives these names their real kick, and like most *K* people, *KRSs* are confident and self-assured people who view life as one big adventure.

If you work with a *KRS*, your daily routine is sure to be peppered with jokes, laughter and friendly insults. And if you find this routine tiresome, take your *KRS* friend out for a drink and you'll get a meaningful conversation about life and the universe. But don't expect your *KRS* friend to dwell too deeply on these issues; a key component of their philosophy is that nothing in life is too serious that it can't be laughed at. An unfair consequence of the *KRS'* outgoing behavior is that some people mistake their natural ebullience as an attempt to gain attention and status. While there might be a germ of truth to this, having a good time needs no justification in the *KRS'* mind.

In the workplace, *KRSs* are typically drawn to occupations that allow them to express their unique brand of irrepressibility, or they might go a completely different

Karisa
Karissa
Karson
Kris

direction and end up in the scientific or medical fields. In fact there's a bit of the mad scientist in every *KRS*, which can be quite aggravating for anyone who's ever shared a room with them.

KRSs have a quiet strength that grows more evident as you get to know them. They aren't shy about expressing their opinions and are always ready to defend their ideas if necessary, and if you want to feel the force of a *KRS's* temper, just try questioning their loyalty for their friends and loved ones.

KRSs have a great capacity for spiritual communion—even if it's a concoction of their unique brand of introspection and out-of-the-mainstream philosophy—and personal space and private time is critical for the *KRS'* spiritual and emotional rejuvenation.

Love and marriage with a *KRS* can be alternately charming and frustrating. While your *KRS* partner will undoubtedly prove to be an energetic lover, he or she will be equally enthusiastic about pursuing interests outside the relationship. This doesn't mean they'll actually break their wedding vows, but it often involves maintaining past friendships that interfere with their primary relationships. Life is one big experiment to the terminally inquisitive *KRSs,* who are unlikely to feel fulfilled unless they have the freedom to sate their extraordinary curiosity for the universe.

Kris Kristofferson After landing a helicopter in Johnny Cash's backyard to pitch a new song, Kris Kristofferson teamed up with Cash to record "Sunday Morning Coming Down" and created one of the '70's biggest country hits. ■ His union with singer Rita Coolidge resulted in a number of albums and three babies, and the troubadour's performance in *A Star is Born* earned him a Golden Globe for Best Actor. ■ But Kris made some bad choices . . . particularly his decision to appear in Michael Cimino's *Heaven's Gate.* The film was such a disaster that it bankrupted the studio. Some blamed his poor judgment on his affair with Jack Daniels ,and Kris was sent to acting purgatory for a few years. He resurfaced as a chimpanzee in Tim Burton's remake of *Planet of the Apes.*

krst

Charisma	👄	👄	👄	👄	👄	👄	👄	👄	👄	👄
Career Success	💰	💰	💰	💰	💰	💰	💰	💰	💰	💰
Love & Friendship	🦅	🦅	🦅	🦅	🦅	🦅	🦅	🦅	🦅	🦅
Power	💣	💣	💣	💣	💣	💣	💣	💣	💣	💣

Self-assured Motivated Playful
Pushy Gullible High-maintenance

The names *Kristen* and *Kirsten* are anagrams of the word *stinker*, which aptly describes the essence of these cheekily feminine sprites. It's hardly surprising when one considers that the letters *R* and *S* are both symbols for sexual cockiness; the *R* is the initial letter of *racy, randy, romance, ruddy, relish, ripe, rapture* and *ravage*, while the *S* is the symbol of all things *sexy, sensual, sassy, sinful, sultry, sublime,* and *slinky*. The letter *T* adds its audacious resonance with a suggestion of *twinkling, tremendous, terrific,* and *trumpeting*. All in all, like most people whose names begin with the unyielding power of the letter *K*, these are women with considerable determination and a strong desire to be noticed.

Even though the *KRSTs* will always speak their minds, they are far from being abrasive and there's a submissive twinkle in their eyes even when they're asserting themselves. In time you'll come to know your *KRST* friend as a well-rounded soul whose passion occasionally gets in the way of their intuition. The heart of a *KRST* is almost always pure, but these occasional lapses in judgment often prove to be their undoing—particularly when it comes to life-changing decisions about her relationships and career. These people pay so much attention to the moment that they often forget that the future may have different plans for them, so even though your *KRST* friends appear to be happy-go-lucky, chances are they're battling some weighty internal issues all by themselves.

Kerstin
Kiersten
Kirsten
Kirstie
Kirstin
Krista, Kristal
Kristel, Kristen
Kristi, Kristian
Kristan, Kristeen
Kristianna
Kristie, Kristin
Kristina, Kristine
Kristle, Kristofer
Kristy, Kristyn
Krysta, Krystal
Krysten, Krystin
Kristoffer
Kristopher
Krystina
Krystyna
Krystle

KRSTs live their social lives to the fullest and usually apply the same level of intensity to their work. Not that they'd ever allow their jobs to intrude on their voracious appetites for socializing, but if they were working at a coffee shop for example, they'd know everything about each type of bean: its origins, essence, grain and nuance of flavor.

KRSTs also enjoy the creative side of life, which is often expressed through their music, painting or prose. But since many have learned the hard way that you can't pay rent with dreams, most decline to make careers of such self-indulgent pursuits.

Forging intimate relationships with *KRSTs* will undoubtedly be a rewarding experience but expect there to be a few strings attached. They are not the type to thrive in traditional white-picket-fence marriages, and value their autonomy so highly that they're not going to relinquish it without a struggle. Their ideal mates will have no problem with their eclectic social groups, and will be willing to keep them stimulated with more than just good conversation and the occasional night on the town.

Kristen Scott Thomas Critics who reviewed Kristin Scott Thomas' performance in the 1998 film, *A Handful of Dust*, likened the effect of watching her on-screen to being drunk on love potion. ■ With just the right balance of elegance, aloofness and subtlety, her performance in *The English Patient*, playing Katherine Clifton, earned her an Oscar nomination. ■ Kristen reinforces her iconic reputation by playing up her Parisian background even though she had crossed the Channel into France when she was already an adult.

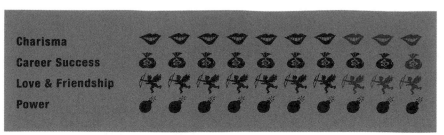

Charisma	😗😗😗😗😗😗😗😗😗😗
Career Success	💰💰💰💰💰💰💰💰💰💰
Love & Friendship	🦅🦅🦅🦅🦅🦅🦅🦅🦅🦅
Power	💣💣💣💣💣💣💣💣💣💣

Affectionate Straightforward Extroverted
Snappish Quick-tempered Changeable

The letters *K* and *T* are both pronounced with brittle and explosive tones. The letter *K* is the symbol of forceful action (*kick, kill, kidnap, knock, knuckle,* and *knife*) while the *triumphant* tones of the letter *T* convey a sense of *truth, tradition, thankfulness, triumph,* and *toughness.* This is why words incorporating both the *K* and *T* impart the no-nonsense grit seen in the words: *knight, kinetic, knotty, kaput, kraut, kryptonite, backbite,* and *cockfight.* These are hard-driven people who know how to get the things they want—even if they don't always know exactly *what* they want.

KTs have a reputation for sharp-tongued intelligence and an unhesitating dedication to 'telling it like it is'. Their occasional caustic outbursts may intimidate casual observers, but those close to them know it to be a carefully cultivated ploy designed to keep people at arm's length, *KTs* will reveal their extraordinarily sensitive hearts once you've proved yourself worthy of their emotional investment. This is why *KTs* spend most of their spare time with small groups of confidantes rather than hanging out with superficial air-kissing companions.

In their professional lives, perfectionist *KTs* are driven by a powerful urge to shine. Whether this ambition is fueled by confidence or lack thereof, this kind of fierce resolve serves them well whether they choose sci-

Kait
Kat
Kate
Katerina
Katarina
Kati, Katia
Katie, Katina
Katrina
Katy
Keaton
Kelton
Kermit
Kirt, Kit
Kittie
Kitty

ence, arts or athletics. If they weren't the ones in high school voted most likely to succeed, they almost certainly had an outstanding academic record or a role in varsity sports. But many *KTs* hold themselves to standards that are simply impossible to attain and these self-imposed stresses often result in a (difficult to diagnose) low self-esteem. But regardless of how they feel on the inside, *KTs* are experts at convincing people that they're the outgoing and powerful personalities they really want to be.

Love, marriage and parenthood suit the *KTs'* industrious personalities quite well—*if* they can lower their emotional walls enough to achieve true intimacy. Like many people in charge of their own lives, letting go on a deep emotional level represents a surrender of power with which *KTs* simply aren't comfortable. They prefer to operate from positions of emotional strength and their mates will have to able to roll with their sharp-tongued punches. Still, because there's enough of a softie in every *KT* to want to be romanced, prospective suitors are advised not to take the *KT's* nonchalance too literally. When it comes to having children; *KTs* usually do it for the right reasons. Instead of being motivated by a selfish desire to reproduce, they seem more interested in having genuine relationships with their children. Either way, the gene pool is definitely going to be improved.

Kate Hepburn When Kate Hepburn was described as "a cross between Donald Duck and a Stradivarius," it was probably a commentary on her uncommon beauty and her distinctive New England accent. ■ Kate was the only woman to win four Academy Awards and is best remembered for her performance in *The African Queen*. She won her second Oscar for *Guess Who's Coming to Dinner*, her third for *The Lion in Winter*, and her fourth for *On Golden Pond*, in 1981. ■ Kate earned a record twelve Oscar nominations and enjoyed a long love affair with fellow icon Spencer Tracy until his death in 1967.

Kth

Charisma	💋	💋	💋	💋	💋	💋	💋	💋	💋	💋
Career Success	💰	💰	💰	💰	💰	💰	💰	💰	💰	
Love & Friendship	😈	😈	😈	😈	😈	😈	😈	😈	😈	😈
Power	💣	💣	💣	💣	💣	💣	💣	💣	💣	💣

Composed Creative Original
Frigid Uptight Perfectionist

The softly comforting sounds of the *TH* phoneme are responsible for the reassuring essence found in the words *mother, father, thanks, therapy, thoughtful, theism* and *thrive*. So, when the *TH* occurs in names initialized by the forcefully aggressive letter *K*, it implies someone with iron self-control and an obliging disposition. Since the letter *N* is the symbol for all things *negative*—*no, not, never, nyet, nada, nix, nothing* and *naught*—we expect to find a certain level of pessimism from the *Kathleens, Kenneths* and *Katherines* of the world. On the other hand, those who choose to end their names with the playful letter *Y* or *IE* sound (*Kathy* and *Kathie*) are signaling that they don't take themselves quite as seriously.

As gracious as *KTHs* appear to be, there's an unmistakable energy humming just beneath the surface. *KTHs* would never deign to reveal the source of these powerful currents, for they are a dignified bunch for whom social modesty is very important. These powerful personalities are quietly confident in their own strengths and rarely exhibit outright aggression. And while you would agree that *KTHs* are habitually composed, they can be as cold as a Leona Helmsley scowl if you happen to betray their confidence.

KTHs are focused in the workplace, but it must be said that getting ahead isn't the only entry on their to-do list. They are less concerned with financial success than they are about the quality of their relationships and will even bench their careers when push comes to shove. Mostly, they prefer to intertwine the two: filling their workspaces with keepsakes from home and bringing work back from the office.

Although *KTHs* may change careers once or twice in a lifetime, they're pretty consistent about what they want. If some people believe there's only one *best* way up the mountain, *KTHs* believe that every path has its own unique view and there are no wrong ways to get there. Even if they can't remember where they put the road map, *KTHs* are quite happy to get lost on their journey.

If your ideal mate is someone who will do everything you ask, then marriage to a *KTH* isn't for you. Instead, you'll get a competitive partner who will push you to do *your* best. And if you want to know if your *KTH* likes you, it's not going to be easy to tell. Perhaps out of insecurity (or perhaps for control reasons) they aren't going to reveal their intimate emotions until they're good and ready, and suitors are often left blundering around in the dark while the *KTH* blithely acts as if everything were normal. With this kind of coquettishness it's a wonder that any of them actually survive their intimate relationships, but it's a reflection of just how much their company is valued by the opposite sex that they do.

Kathe
Kathey
Kathaleen
Katharina
Katharine
Katharyn
Katherina
Katherine
Kathi, Kathie
Kathleen
Kathlene
Kathline
Kathlyn
Kathrin
Kathryn
Kathryne
Kathy
Keith
Keitha
Keneth
Kenneth
Kieth

Kathleen Turner Few modern actresses can lay claim to a filmography as wide-ranging as Kathleen Turner's. Her debut as a femme fatale in *Body Heat* was followed up with another seductress role in the comedy, *The Man with Two Brains*. In *Romancing the Stone*, she played a good-hearted heroine trying to rescue her sibling, and in *Crimes of Passion* opted for the dark side by playing a hooker. ■ Kathleen appeared on *Friends* as Chandler's transvestite father, and also electrified Broadway when she played Mrs. Robinson in the stage production of *The Graduate*.

Charisma										
Career Success										
Love & Friendship										
Power										

Witty Determined Quick-thinking
Hypersensitive Unstable Suspicious

The *KTLN* names are dominated by the forceful letter *K*—evoking images of *kick, kill, king,* and *knife*—and the *triumphant* letter *T*, which conveys a sense of *truthfulness, tradition, thankfulness, triumph,* and *toughness.* The Gaelic derived *KTLN* names and all their derivative spellings have recently become *the* most popular girls' names in the United States. It's also undergoing an evolution in spelling as parents attempt to and differentiate their own daughter from the millions of others who bear a *KTLN* name. There are currently over one hundred and forty spelling variations on this name, but the prize for creative spelling must go to the parents of *Q'heightlynne.*

All told, these names herald a personality of uncommon internal resolve and mental toughness to boot. The *KTLNs'* strength lies in their ability to work *around* tense situations without fully absorbing them into their emotional core. This is why *KTLNs* rarely lose their cool and why people are drawn to them in moments of stress.

When it comes to the little things in life, *KTLNs* can change their minds as often as a butterfly with a lobotomy. But if they can't be depended on for showing up for movies or making appointments on time, when it comes to the big issues—loyalty, fidelity and love—they're as reliable as dial tones. Many *KTLNs* seem to take secret satisfaction in their ability to keep

Caitlin
Caitlyn
Caitlynn
Kaitlin
Kaitlyn
Kaitlynn
Katelin
Katelyn
Katelynn
Katlin
Katlyn
Katlynn

people a little off balance but will stop well short of taking advantage of anyone.

KTLNs may be exceptionally bright but this isn't always reflected in their academic record. They're simply not turned on by formal education; preferring to discover the workings of the universe in their own unique ways. The source of their intelligence is a healthy mixture of emotional and street-smartness that gives them a huge advantage in the workplace, but doesn't mean that they will achieve the kind the success of which they're capable. In fact, like most confident personalities, they have a propensity to procrastinate and take things too lightly. Oftentimes, they find themselves struggling to catch up to their peer groups.

KTLNs approach their relationships in a similar devil-may-care fashion. With unmatched emotional self-confidence, they often give the impression that they really aren't looking for anyone special. Nothing could be further from the truth. *KTLNs* are attention-hungry creatures who thrive on being in the spotlight. Because they are choosy about their relationships, every gesture and nuance from prospective suitors will have some significance. A careless word or thoughtless act can leave them feeling resentful for weeks and suitors must have an extraordinary set of communication skills if they hope to construct a peaceful alliance with these dynamic women.

Caitlin Thomas In 1936, a young **Caitlin Macnamara** met an intense twenty-two year old named **Dylan Thomas** in a London pub, thus initiating a tempestuous affair with a man destined to become one of the twentieth century's most respected poets. Caitlin and Dylan were married the following year and moved to Wales where she gave birth to their first child. ■ Their marriage was marked with hard drinking and infidelity and after yet another of Dylan's affairs, Caitlin was briefly institutionalized. After Dylan's death, Caitlin began expressing herself through writing and published the pathos-ridden, *Leftover Life to Kill.*

THE IMAGINATIVE

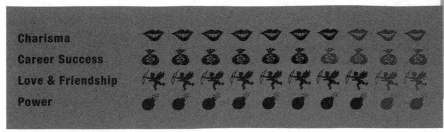

Charisma										
Career Success										
Love & Friendship										
Power										

Friendly Energetic Intelligent
Inattentive Changeable Nervous

The *vibrant* letter *V* is the classic symbol for masculine and feminine *vigor*. It is also the letter of *virility, virtue, voluptuousness, Viagra, va-va-voom, vixen* and *vamp*, and when it appears in words initialized by the forcefully masculine letter *K*, it defines an individual whose passion for life is directed by powerfully hedonistic urges. It should be pointed out, however, that the letter *N* is the symbol of *negativity* (*no, not, never, nyet, nada, nix, nothing, naught*) and introduces an element of pessimism that can manifest itself in the *KVNs*' bouts of self-doubt.

And yet the quirky *KVNs* have a unique ability to be everyone's best friend without ever being completely understood. Simply put… they are extraordinarily likeable. These are also people with a great sense of humor—often lost on others who don't grasp their sly witticisms—and animated modes of self-expression. The live-and-let live *KVNs* aren't ones to be slowed down by misunderstandings of their intentions, however, for they're sincere in their belief that people would get through life easier if they could only laugh in the face of adversity—like they do. There's nothing *KVNs* hates more than conflict. Throw them into a debate and they'll likely just walk away.

Many people whose names begin with the letter *K* are politically minded, and *KVNs* are political animals

Kalvin
Kelvin
Keven
Kevin
Kevon

in the extreme. They have no illusions about how life works and if you're trying to out-maneuver them in the workplace, you'd better have your ducks in a row. *KVNs* don't really care if you consider them to be perfect and—in the spirit of all's fair in love and war—they're not above using every trick in the book including making you look bad. They have enough confidence in their fundamental magnanimity to afford the occasional foray into self-interest.

If there's any real criticism about the way *KVNs* live their lives, it usually comes from the women in their lives, for *KVNs* like to think of themselves as creatures of the wild and aren't about to cage themselves without a fight. This reticence to make decisive choices in his relationships makes him a risky wager for women who lack their own sense of purpose. Still, while his romantic oscillations may prove maddening to potential lovers, no one will argue that the *KVN*—with his strong sense of justice—isn't a desirable prize; the problem is that the kind of women that the *KVN* needs is the same kind that won't put up with undulating behavior. Women that do, live in hope that he'll one day have a rush of blood and throw himself into the affair without first dissecting every eventuality. In the *KVN's* life, there's not much difference between fearing failure and fearing success.

Kevin Bacon Kevin Bacon counts himself lucky to have a self-perpetuating publicity machine. Anyone who has participated in a round of *Six Degrees of Kevin Bacon* (played by connecting him to other celebrities via his resumé) is reminded of Kevin's diverse body of work. ■ Kevin made his feature debut in the classic fraternity movie, *Animal House*, before starring in Barry Levinson's critically acclaimed, *Diner*. The fact that he had a fever when he auditioned for *Diner* worked in his favor; his character spent most of the movie slightly drunk. ■ Everyone agrees that Kevin bought home the bacon with his role as a big-city boy crusading against anti-dancing forces in *Footloose*. The film established him as one of the few white guys who can actually dance and made him a bona fide star.

The Letter of Love and Learning

Most Popular Girl's Names

Linda
Lisa
Laura
Lori
Louise
Lois
Lillian
Leslie
Lucille
Lauren

Most Popular Boy's Names

Larry
Lawrence
Louis
Luis
Leonard
Lee
Leroy
Lloyd
Leon
Leo

And lay my arms before the legs
of this sweet lass of France.

WILLIAM SHAKESPEARE,
Love's Labour's Lost

When pronouncing the letter L, the lips part and the tongue becomes highly visible as it embraces the roof of the mouth to produce the distinctively musical sound that is responsible for lullaby, lilt, la-la-la, lyrical and languid. Perhaps this is why the letter L has become the flagship letter of some of the most important elements of human existence: life, liberty, love, learning, luck and lust. As the initial letter of lip-licking, leering, lascivious, loyal, like and Luna (the Roman goddess of the moon), this lyrically pronounced letter is a lifelong member of the romance and passion letter group, along with M, V, R and S. ■ The L was originally a hieroglyphic symbol of an oxgoad, a tool used to control cattle, and its sense of authority is felt in the many words describing the judicial system: legal, legislation, legitimacy and law, all of which are derived from the Latin word lex. Its learned qualities are further reinforced by the words linguistic, literacy, lecture, language, logic, legible, laud, lexicon, license and library. ■ When DC Comics introduced Superman to the world in 1938, they symbolized his commitment to truth, justice, and the American way by surrounding him with the letter L: his birth name was Kal-El, his girlfriends were Lois Lane and Lana Lang, and his arch-nemesis was Lex Luthor. ■ Lacking that aggressive edge, it's hardly surprising that L people are at the very bottom of the list when it comes to professional sports and the medical profession, but as a measure of their laid-back popularity, are more likely than most to have successful political careers. ■

Charisma										
Career Success										
Love & Friendship										
Power										

Strong-minded Capable Hardworking
Impatient Obtuse Intimidating

Because the letter *L* is the herald of *love, laughter, life* and *learning*, we anticipate these names to project the *lilting, lyrical* and *lively* qualities to which people almost universally respond. Although these names are uncomplicated in structure, *L* personalities project a lordly air that inspires confidence and demands respect. If you need someone to get things done in a hurry and are thinking about putting an *L* in charge, chances are you won't even need to call on them. *L*s are the first to step up to the plate whenever there's an organizational need.

You might find that your initial encounter with *L*s to be a little intimidating. It's usually because they are focused on something other than the meeting at hand and don't feel it's their responsibility to make everyone feel comfortable. The problem is that the *L* mind is never at rest; it's always concocting some creative scheme (or wondering if it left the iron on) and the important thing to remember is that they don't mind playing the role of the absentminded professor when it suits their purposes. Still, these are forthrightly genuine people who are gentle to their core and who, once done wrestling their problems into submission, will be happy to offer

Lai
Le
Lea
Lee
Leia
Leo
Li
Lia
Lou
Louie
Lu
Lue

solace to anyone who's been bruised in the scuffle.

Friendship with an *L* personality can be a rocky road if you lose sight of that gentle heart, for their stubborn and willful ways will fray the nerves of even the most patient allies. To be truly compatible with the *L* personality, you'll need a great sense of humor and an equally masterful spirit. They are the kinds of people with whom you can get into a knock-down drag-out fight in the morning and then go out beering it up in the evening.

*L*s appreciate candor on the part of their lovers and will unflinchingly accept criticism as long as it's given in the spirit of beneficial counsel. They are equally frank when it comes to expressing their own beefs, which might be interpreted to be an aggressive and insensitive streak, but it's not. It's simply another symptom of their lively style of social interaction.

With their penchant for spice and variety in their personal lives, *L*s sometimes have a difficult time settling into meaningful relationships and—even when they do settle down—it's rarely in the traditional white-picket-fence sense. These are marriages in the fast lane, with exotic travel and frenzied socializing the order of the day.

Louis Armstong Louis Armstrong's nickname "Sachmo" was derived from "Satchel Mouth," because it was said he had the biggest grin on the jazz circuit. But Louis's real claim to fame that he was the greatest jazz musician of his age. ■ Louis's music career can be traced back to the time when he was arrested for firing a pistol into the air and sent to the New Orleans Colored Waifs' Home for Boys, where he was taught to play the trumpet. ■ Upon his release, Louis immersed himself in the sounds of the burgeoning jazz movement and became a regular feature on the New Orleans jazz scene. While working with jazz great Oscar Peterson, Louis recorded his first big hit, which became one of his trademark songs: "Mack the Knife."

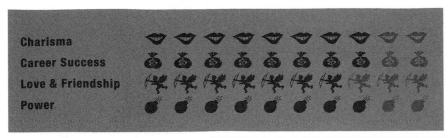

Charisma										
Career Success										
Love & Friendship										
Power										

Ebullient Sensitive Communicative
Self-conscious Dogmatic Petulant

The combination of the letters *L* and *B* produces an interesting meld of conflicting forces. The letter *L* is the herald of *love, learning, liberty, laughter* and *life*, and when combined with the flagship letter of *brashness, belligerence* and *boldness,* it makes for names that are alternatively laid back and conservatively dominant. We find these oscillating good/bad effects in the word groups *lamb/lambast, celebrate/celibate, clubby/club, pliable/playboy* and *lifeblood/bloodbath.* So although these are people whose outer deportment is gentle and spiritually uplifting, we cannot ignore the fact that they're also unyielding and uncompromising.

The *LB* personality is one to take charge in all aspects of her productive life. It's worth noting that her style of leadership isn't derived from aggression or coercion, it's that other people quickly cotton onto the fact that she is an Alpha female and trust that she will use her authority in good faith. Whether her leadership skills are expressed in the workplace or in her relationships, the *LB* is quite comfortable with her dominant role and will rarely abuse her influence. When the *LB* finds her leadership position challenged, she isn't going to tackle the interloper in a face-to-face confrontation. Secure in the knowledge that time will prove her to be a superior leader; she will coolly keep her distance and allow nature to take its course.

Because of her open acceptance of people from all walks of life, it's hard to land on an *LB's* list of undesirables. Whether she's hosting a casual picnic or attending a high-visibility fundraising event, her primary focus will be the feelings of the people around her. This is the kind of girl you can dress up or down without affecting her fundamentally unpretentious attitude.

LBs in their personal lives are typically stoic and conservative—particularly when it comes to their families. There's very little that can distract them from wholehearted intimate commitments and they fully accept that married life is going to have its ups and downs. They have so much confidence in the choices they make that they don't feel obliged to micromanage every little crisis that all families experience. But don't misinterpret the *LB's* non-involvement as a sign of disinterest; behind her implacable visage lies a fiercely concerned matriarch who puts family unity above all else.

Libby
Liberty

Libby Larsen It isn't easy to make a living as a composer of classical concert music in the age of hip-hop, rap and Broadway musicals, which is why Libby Larsen is one of America's few successful, living composers. She is also one of the most prolific. With a catalogue of hundreds of works, her music has been commissioned by major artists and orchestras around the world. ■ In 1994, Libby was awarded a Grammy for producing *The Art of Arleen Augér,* and her opera *Frankenstein: The Modern Prometheus* was judged as one of the best classical music events of 1990 by *USA Today.* ■ The first woman to serve as a resident composer with a major U.S. orchestra, Libby co-founded the American Composer's Forum, which acts as a resource for living composers.

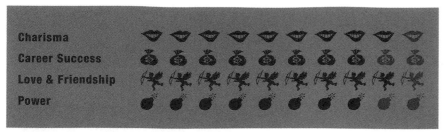

THE TWO-SIDED Ld

Charisma	👄👄👄👄👄👄👄👄👄👄
Career Success	💰💰💰💰💰💰💰💰 💰💰
Love & Friendship	👼👼👼👼👼👼👼👼👼👼
Power	💣💣💣💣💣💣 💣💣💣

Dogged Focused Good listener
Moody Self-indulgent Tempestuous

LD names convey an impression of a well-rounded intelligence modulated by a loving core and carried off with exceptional style. The letter *L*—the symbol of *love, liberty, laughter, learning* and *law*—contributes a sense of spiritual awareness, while the *D*—the flagship letter of *dignity, dapper* and *drama*—tells us that these names belong to men and women who glide through life with enviable ease. But there's also a shadowy side to those who bear *LD* names, for the *L* is also known for its association with the darker aspects of *love—lust, leering, lasciviousness* and *lip-licking*—and the *D* is responsible for *Devil, demon, destruction, doomsday, danger* and *damnation.*

So don't be surprised to find your usually easygoing and genial *LD* friend retreating into a surly mood for no apparent reason—as if *Dr. Jekyll* was struggling for equal time with *Mr. Hyde*. In the scheme of things, it's not much of a problem (at least from the *LD's* perspective) as both these aspects are essential to smooth operation of the *LD's* complex personality. Friends are well served by bearing in mind that with darkness comes light and with intensity comes passion.

LDs are political animals with an aptitude for creating alliances and a nose for ferreting out enemies. This serves them well in the workplace, where like most people whose names begin with the letter *L*, they find themselves in the highest tax brackets. Careers for these extraordinarily capable people will usually encompass a creative component—all the better to express their dramatic sides—and *LDs* genuinely seem to enjoy hard work. *LDs* are at their most productive when working alone and employers are often frustrated by their reluctance to join the team. It's not that *LDs* aren't willing to listen to advice: they seem genuinely interested in hearing other points of view before doing it their own way regardless. Still, at the end of the day no one questions the *LD's* ability to get the job done right.

LDs' brand of unrepentant individualism may well trigger friction in their intimate relationships, but as long as they keep a tight rein on their impulsive instincts they almost always prove to be fiercely committed mates. Still, the success of their relationships will have a lot to do with the patience of their partners and mates expecting predictability in their marriages will have their work cut out for them. But those partners who allow the *LDs'* moods to wash over them—instead of building dams to contain them—will enjoy truly fruitful relationships.

Ladarius
Ladonna
Leda
Leida
Lida, Lidia
Lloyd
Loida
Lourdes
Loyd
Lyda
Lydia

Lloyd Bridges Lloyd Bridges stole the show in the 1970s cult classic *Airplane!* when he parodied himself as a hard-bitten, hard-drinking, chain-smoking airport manager. With a career that spanned six decades, the squinty-eyed actor was one of Hollywood's most dependable action heroes. ■ Some may remember him for his supporting role in the film *High Noon*, but Lloyd really owes his fame to the 1950's TV series, *Sea Hunt*, in which he played a navy frogman on the *Argonaut*, presaging *Star Trek*'s *Enterprise*. Interestingly, Lloyd was turned down for the role of Captain Kirk on the Star Trek series. ■ Both Lloyd's sons, Jeff and Beau, are well-known actors who also appeared in *Sea Hunt*. The tireless serial hero worked until his death in 1998.

lh

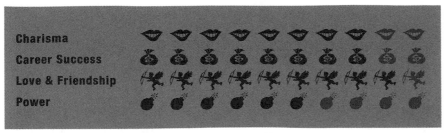

Charisma										
Career Success										
Love & Friendship										
Power										

Nurturing Caring Understanding
Homebound Apprehensive Puritanical

There is no stronger symbol of a *loving heart* than those with an *LH* name; the letter *L* is the definitive representation of *love, life, liberty, lust,* and *loyalty,* and the letter *H* is the essence of the *heart, home, hospitable, happiness, hearth, health, hope* and *harmony.* It's not surprising that the *LH* names project such a feminine air, and those whose names also feature the gentle *-GH* suffix (*Leigh, Leigh-Ann* and *Leigha*), are even more connected to the lighter side of the human experience as demonstrated by the words *laugh, high* and *sigh.*

There are considerable expectations placed on children with *LH* names. Society subconsciously expects them to be unconditionally understanding—even to the point of neglecting their own emotional needs. It's true that most *LHs* live up to these expectations, but don't think for one minute that they are all altruism and no self-interest, for they are very conscious of the personal benefits that come from helping others. They also understand that there are givers and takers in life, and having so much to give, genuinely don't mind helping out those who don't. Problems arise when their energies are sapped by constant appeals for their attentions, and loved ones must learn to recognize when their wells run dry.

LH people are not overburdened by self-confidence and are consequently uneasy in the presence of

Leah
Leigh
Leigha
Leighann
Leigh Anne
Leigh-Ann
Leigh-Anne

strangers—which is odd considering that the *LHs'* strong sensual appeal attracts others with such little effort. This lack of assuredness often leads them to befriend stronger personalities who complement their tentative approaches to exploring new physical and intellectual territories. Unless they're safely ensconced in one of these unions, it's safe to say that you'll find them washing their hair or painting their room on a Friday night. But this is fine with them because *LHs* are natural homebodies who don't feel a need to be particularly outgoing. At some point though—after they've had enough of the ennui that comes from isolation—they'll dry their hair and paint the town instead.

LH people place a high value on home and hearth and tend to settle down relatively early in life—as do many people whose names begin with an *L*. With their highly developed tactile senses, there's nothing better than spending a lazy afternoon cuddling in the arms of their partners.

LHs are devoted mothers whose children are nourished by their intelligent mothering. It would be rare for them to raise their voices or lay down the law: their style is far more co-conspiratorial than that, and their children will happily toe the line if it means maintaining their mother's approval.

Leah Remini When Leah Remini dropped out of school at the age of fourteen, she had the full support of her mother, who just knew she was going to achieve something great. Her mother must have been somewhat disappointed, then, when Leah took a job as one of those annoying telemarketers. But after a few lucky breaks, Leah's acting career coalesced. ■ The uninhibited New Yorker parlayed her Brooklyn accent into an appearance on *Head of the Class,* and for two years she made occasional appearances on *Cheers,* playing Carla's rebellious daughter, Sarafina. Leah is now a nationally recognized TV actor and co-stars in the sitcom *The King of Queens.* ■ When not on the set Leah finds time to manage three commercial web-sites with her friend and business partner, Jackie Guerra.

lk

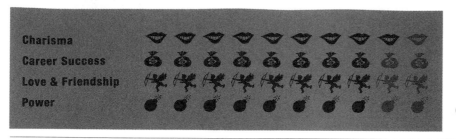

Charisma										
Career Success										
Love & Friendship										
Power										

Compassionate Kind Sharp
Dark Antagonistic Single-Minded

The letter *K* is a powerful symbol of forceful action and always manages to inject a sense of masculinity into words and names in which it appears. Consider the words *kick, knock, knuckle, crack, thwack* and *smack.* On the other hand, the letter *L* with its softly pronounced lyrical tones is the flagship of the highest expressions of human culture: *love, life, laughter, liberty* and *learning.* When the *L* and *K* get together in the same words, they create the sense of benign power found in: *hulk, luck, flake, balk, bleak, sulk* and *lock.* This is why *LK* names are such an enigmatic mesh of conflicting personality traits: sensitive yet abrupt, altruistic but short-tempered, approachable and judgmental.

For these reasons it can be tough to discern an *LK's* personality from a single encounter and he or she will continue to surprise you even after you've established a close relationship. Perhaps this is what makes *LKs* so intriguing and earns them the near universal admiration they enjoy. Conversely, it can be a little frustrating for those who have intimate relationships with *LKs*, because their ambiguous natures can leave you in totally in the dark as to their intentions. Even *LKs* themselves can't be quite sure what they're about and spend a great deal of their lives in search of the "right" job or the "perfect" partner.

Luca
Lucas
Lakeisha
Lakesha
Lakeshia
Lakia
Lakisha
Laquita
Lenka
Lincoln
Lucretia
Lukas
Luke

The *LK* can be described as someone who presides over the rest of humanity with cool indifference. Though not particularly aggressive, they consider it their place to sit in judgment on others and will secretly weigh the actions of their associates against their own standards. You might be surprised to know some of the things your *LK* friend has observed about you, but you need not worry that it will affect your friendship: Loyalty is an *LK* hallmark characteristic.

LKs succeed in careers that require physical as well as intellectual stamina. Their active minds require constant stimulation if they're to keep from getting bored and explains why they avoid routine as much as possible. *LKs* really come into their own when it comes to decision-making or problem-solving, and once they've been tasked with a job are unlikely to quit until it's perfectly accomplished. Ask them a riddle and they'll drive everyone nuts until they've cracked it.

LKs are not the types to fret about "finding someone," figuring that if the fates want them to hook up then there's not much they can do about it. So when it comes to having families, the paradoxical *LKs* might put it off for what seems like an eternity, until one day—*boom.* Marriage and children will follow in quick succession and the *LK* will live happily ever after (mostly).

Luke Perry Along with co-stars Shannen Doherty, Jason Priestly, Tori Spelling and Jennie Garth, Luke Perry became an icon of pop-culture in the 1990's thanks to his role on *Beverly Hills 90210.* ■ Despite his screaming success as the troubled Dylan McKay, Luke never managed to really make it on the big screen, even though his cheeky good looks and James Dean smolder were sufficient to land him roles in popular films such as *Buffy the Vampire Slayer* and *The Fifth Element.* ■ Because Luke's primary goal was to become a film star, he left 90210 to make his way in the movie business. He returned to the show with his film career still solidly parked in the driveway. Still, Luke managed to score some success with his multi-episode commitment to the gritty HBO prison drama, *Oz.*

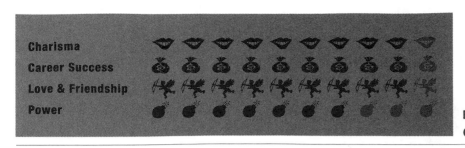

Charisma										
Career Success										
Love & Friendship										
Power										

Relaxed Strong Self-assured
Condescending Overly dramatic Smug

The letter *L* accounts for the *lusty* qualities found in the words *lively, lip-smacking, liberty, laughter* and *love,* and implies a person who is keenly aware that the important things in life have nothing to do with worldly goods. And since these names feature a *double* dose of the likeable *L,* they are exceptionally connected to the gentle comeliness found in the words *lilt, ladylike, belle, laurel, loyal, moll* and *lovelorn.*

LLs are men and women who seem to enjoy friction-free lives and make few enemies as they glide along. Although they hide it well, *LLs* are extremely protective of their emotional cores and any perceived criticisms will provoke strong defensive reactions—usually in the form of prolonged sulks or sullen silences. Trying to get *LLs* to open up during these down spells is a waste of time and you're better off allowing their moods to run their course. Consequently, *LLs* tend to bond closely with small groups on whom they can emotionally depend, while their wider circle of casual acquaintances is kept at an emotional distance.

LLs approach life with an abiding hatred of routine and their affairs are arranged accordingly; you won't find them slugging away at the nine-to-five grind or volunteering to work overtime. Yet for as little effort as they put out, they somehow always seem to have enough

Lael
Layla,
Leila
Leilani
Laila, Lala
Lela, Lelia
Lila, Lili, Lilia
Lillian, Lilla,
Lilli, Lillie, Lilly
Lily, Lilyan
Lemuel, Leola
Lola, Lilliana
Lolita, Lorelei
Lula, Lulu
Louella
Luella
Lyla
Lyle

money left over to buy gifts for their close friends. It also wouldn't surprise anyone to find *LLs* spending their spare time volunteering for worthy causes. But just because you don't bump into them at the local soup kitchen doesn't mean they aren't quietly supporting local charities or helping their friends through bad times.

So why are *LLs* so often the recipient of backbiting and gossip? It seems that some people have a problem with *LLs'* holier-than-thou syndrome and goody-two-shoes attitudes. And even if it's true that the comfortable *LLs* are a little smug on occasion, if this is the worst thing they're going to be accused of then everything is going according to plan.

Those who are out to find true love should definitely knock on the *LL's* door for even if you're not invited all the way in, you're likely to get a gracious smile and a peck on the cheek. But if you're lucky enough to have the door thrown open you'll find that *LLs* are experts at life's little luxuries. Once they've tied the knot, they're likely to become the self-appointed gardener of the family tree, impulsively tracking birthdays, anniversaries and nurturing all things familial. It's not difficult to successfully partner an *LL.* All you'll need is a little imagination, a modicum of patience and a lot of love.

Lyle Lovett Country singer Lyle Lovett's marriage to Julia Roberts drew more attention to his music than all the publicists in Nashville combined. After their short-lived marriage reverted to "bestfriend" status, Lyle began to make serious inroads into the music scene with his fusion of country, soul, folk, jazz, blues, and gospel. ■ Lyle's dry sense of humor verges on the absurd, as the lyrics to his first song demonstrated: "If I Had a Boat (and if I had a pony, I'd ride him on my boat)." ■ To date he has recorded eight albums, two of which earned him Grammy Awards. Befitting a modern Texas knight, instead of horses Lyle rides a *Ducati* motorcycle.

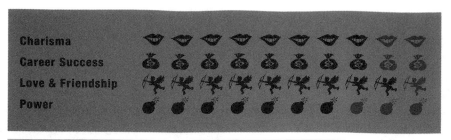

Charisma										
Career Success										
Love & Friendship										
Power										

Simple Confident Encouraging
Wishy-washy Defensive Bland

The letter *N* is the definitive letter of all things *negative* (*no, not, never, nada, nyet, nix* and *nothing*), and even though these names begin with the *life-loving* and *liberating* letter *L*, the *LN* combination still manages to evoke the pessimistic (if benign) images found in the words *loony, loner, bland, lunkhead, lesion, lament* and *larceny*. These are people who have a wonderful sense of direction in their lives but who also keep their emotions under wraps until they're absolutely sure it's safe to let them show.

Even though *LNs* have an instinctive understanding of how *other* people work, there's usually some personal aspect with which they haven't really come to terms. This can manifest itself in a variety of ways—maybe mood swings or a phobia or two—but these characteristics in no way detract from the caring essence of the *LN* personalities who are deeply appreciated by everyone in their lives.

LNs' natural compassion enables them to maintain a wide range of friends with whom they form close ties. If you've ever spent much time around *LNs* you'll know the benefits of having competent and self-motivated people on the scene. Their open acceptance of others is well known within their circles and *LNs* can blend into pretty much any social group with unobtrusive ease.

Lan
Lana
Lance
Lane
Laney
Lanny, Launa
Leann, Leanna
Leanne
Leeann
Leeanna, Lannie
Len, Lena
Lenna, Lennie
Lenny, Leon
Leona, Leone
Leonia, Leonie
Liana, Liane
Lianne, Lin, Lina
Ling, Linnie
Linsey, Logan
Lon, Lonna
Lonnie, Lonny
Louann
Louanne
Luana, Luann
Luanne, Luna
Lyn, Lynn
Lynne
Lynsey
Lynwood

Simplicity is the name of the game as far as they're concerned; they cannot abide having their lives bogged down in detail. Because things have to be neat and predictable, they will avoid relationships that are ill-defined and don't seem to be leading anywhere.

LNs are talented enough to tackle any kind of work, but perform at their best when their jobs are centered on people. Social interactions are their specialty, and being more politically astute than most, *LNs* know how to maneuver their way around both bosses and coworkers, but despite their social intelligence, *LNs* are unlikely to percolate to the top of the corporate pile. Their placid dispositions simply aren't cut out for competitive environments and they are far happier pursuing their relationships than fighting for material gain. Teaching would be a great choice for these socially comfortable creatures, but even if they happen to work in technical fields, you can be sure that they'll migrate toward leading the team— or at least being its cheerleader.

LNs are well equipped for married life. Their matrimonial success comes not from any particular set of secrets but from the work they're willing to do in understanding the emotional needs of their partners.

LeAnn Rimes LeAnn Rimes was a child prodigy. Her singing career began at the age of two, and her first platinum album, *Blue*, was recorded by the time she was fourteen. ■ LeAnn has won more awards than she knows what to do with and even tried her hand at acting, making her debut in the 1997 ABC movie *Holiday in Your Heart*—based on a book she had co-written with Tom Carter. ■ But there's a downside to being a child-star and Leann is reportedly suing her estranged father for allegedly pocketing seven million dollars of her earnings.

Lnd

Charisma											
Career Success											
Love & Friendship											
Power											

Creative Composed Giving
Restless Moody Controlled

No letter in the English alphabet expresses the higher levels of humanity better than the letter *L*—the flagship letter of *life, liberty, laughter, language, learning* and *love*. And when the *L* initializes words terminated by the *ND* letter combination, it creates the sense of benign feminine stability that we find in the words *blend, slender, garland, friend* and *fond*. These reassuring associations give the *LND* names the gentle appeal that offers comfort and engenders trust. Those fortunate enough to have names that end with an *-SY* (*Lindsey*) tend to for example, evoke the breezy images found in the words *daisy, sassy, classy, glossy, ecstasy, whimsy* and *artsy.*

LND individuals are often pillars of their communities to whom others turn for guidance. And when it comes to relationships, *LNDs* are about as solid as it gets and are always willing to offer their dependable shoulders to anyone in need of a little understanding. They instinctively know how to distinguish 'real' people from those with hidden agendas and their circle of friends includes everyone from the local butcher to the village idiot. But don't make the mistake of marking them as happy homemaker types; they also have exotic sides that express themselves in subtle but effective flirting techniques.

Landen
Landon
Leander
Leandra
Leandro
Leland
Leonida
Leyland
Linda
Lindsay
Lindsey
Lindy
Londa
London
Lynda
Lyndia
Lyndon

LNDs are lovers at heart and are always interested in new modes of expression, or acting as idea generators for their eclectic groups of acquaintances. *LNDs* are also tactile people who relate to their environments in terms of touch, smell and taste. So when *LNDs* choose their hobbies and careers, they'll usually have some emphasis on the senses either in the design arena, cooking, or graphic arts. No starving artists here though—*LNDs* have the drive and daring needed to power them through practically any career path.

Teamwork is what this cheerleader personality is about and *LNDs* are generous when it comes to sharing ideas. They are fine motivators but tend to avoid taking those formal leadership roles that might alienate them from their group. They'd rather use their social skills to lead from within and avoid being seen as the bad guy.

It takes a special someone to capture these elusive hearts, for *LNDs* are extraordinarily picky about with whom they're going to spend the rest of their days. Those *LNDs* that make the youthful mistake of taking the plunge before learning to swim usually end up regretting it, but those who follow their instincts and bide their time will find marriage to be as gratifying as they had hoped.

Linda Hamilton James Cameron's blockbuster, *The Terminator*, single-handedly made a star out of Linda Hamilton. ■ Linda's buffed-up action look may have helped her to escape robotic perils, but she couldn't escape being typecast as an archetypal action lady-who-endures-all-kinds-of-hardships-but-never-gives-up. This may help explain her appearance in such films as *Children of the Corn*, *Black Moon Rising* and *King Kong Lives*. ■ Linda's marriage to *Terminator*'s director James Cameron ended after less than a year, when Cameron was reportedly caught fooling around with Suzy Amis, the actress who played the granddaughter of *Titanic* survivor Gloria Stuart in Cameron's 1997 film. ■ Explains Linda: "I keep saying I'm Lucy Ricardo trapped in somebody else's body."

Charisma										
Career Success										
Love & Friendship										
Power										

Caring Committed Faithful
Heavy Cloying Hypersensitive

When a name begins and ends with the same letter, the properties of that letter tend to be amplified. And since the *life-loving* letter *L* accounts for the lusty qualities found in the words *leer, lascivious, lust, loyalty, like* and *love*, it tends to define people in love with life and with strong connections to the notion of loyalty and devotion. But then, there's the matter of the letter *N*. Even though it's bracketed by two *Ls,* the *N* is the classic letter of negativity (*no, not, never, nincompoop, nix, nyet* and *nada)* and these cynical qualities are evident in the words *lonely, longingly, malignly, leeringly, clinical* and *sullenly.* In summary, these are people whose lust for life is tempered by bouts of self-doubt and unpredictable shifts of mood.

Perhaps because they lack the imagination to be duplicitous, these are people you instinctively trust. But it's also because they are earnestly optimistic about life and don't seem to have a mean bone in their bodies. Even though *LNLs* live close to the ground and rarely indulge in flights of fancy, they will occasionally allow their emotions to carry them away. This tendency is most evident when they're going through an insecure phase, in which they might even become clingy. Because *LNLs* sometimes feed on their own negativity and find it difficult to pull

Lanell
Lanelle
Leonel
Leonila
Lionel
Lynell
Lynelle

themselves out of their own funks, they are well-served by having a few understanding friends to call on. Fortunately these downtimes are rare and *LNLs* usually enjoy solid relationships in their career and families.

In their work lives *LNLs* are best suited for jobs requiring long-term commitments and steady routines—they don't like surprises when it comes to their livelihoods. These are individuals who are precise, punctual and loyal, and even if they're not the most creative souls, this doesn't mean they don't appreciate creativity in others. Many *LNLs* are connoisseurs of music, literature and art.

One of the special treats in dealing with an *LNL* is that you don't have to say much to be understood. If you think that no one could possibly grasp your complex problems, your *LNL* friend will elegantly summarize your predicament and offer you an entirely new insight. On the other hand, it's not quite as easy to understand *their* motivations. It's not that they aren't willing to articulate their feelings, it's just that they have an unusual and convoluted set of emotional needs. But if the *LNL's* complexity could be distilled into a single phrase, it would definitely have the words *devoted, loyal* and *unconditional* in it. No matter what discord may evolve between you and your *LNL* companion, they'll be there for you in the long run.

Lionel Richie One of the biggest musical hits of the 1980s was the all-star performance of "We Are the World," a song created to aid victims of world hunger. Eclipsed by the performances of Paul Simon, Michael Jackson, Billy Joel, Cyndi Lauper, Kenny Loggins, Willie Nelson, Diana Ross and Bruce Springsteen, was the fact that Lionel Richie co-wrote the song. ■ Lionel's velvety voice and meaningful lyrics were responsible for many of his hits, which include "All Night Long," "Dancing on the Ceiling," "Easy," "Three Times a Lady," "Endless Love," "Sail On" and "Lady," which he wrote for Kenny Rogers. ■ "Lionel Richie now stands at the pinnacle of pop music, recognized around the world as the most successful singer/songwriter working today." —Charles Whitaker *Ebony* magazine

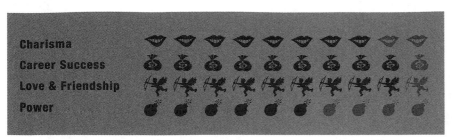

Charisma										
Career Success										
Love & Friendship										
Power										

Demonstrative Unconventional Dynamic
Unpredictable Moody Self-critical

People whose names feature the complex *LNR* letter combination typically embody the *loving, laughing,* and *liberating* qualities we associate with the letter *L.* However, since the letter *N* is the symbol of all things *negative (no, not, nada, nix, naught, nyet* and *nincompoop),* its union with the letter *R* creates the awkward nasal downturn we find in the words *sneer, snarl, whiner, nervous, narcissistic* and *neurotic.* These opposing forces serve to split the *LNR's* personality into two distinct groups: one light and loving—the other pessimistic and insecure. But no matter which *LNR* you encounter on a given day, you'll probably agree that they are well-meaning and highly-strung.

The *LNR's* social instincts abhor a vacuum and their preferred method of offsetting boredom is in entertaining their unconventional groups of friends. In this way, they get to indulge in both sides of their elaborate personalities: the personable entertainer and the self-critical host. They're the kinds of people who can be having a charming conversation with their guests—then suddenly erupt over the overcooked linguini.

The *LNR's* nervous disposition has its benefits.

Lanora
Leanora
Lenard
Lenora
Lenore
Leonard
Leonarda
Leonardo
Leonor
Leonora
Leonore

They're always on guard for potential problems and conduct their lives with extraordinary foresight and attention to detail. So if you're an employer looking to hire someone with precision, thoughtfulness and follow-through, interviewing an *LNR* is a good place to start.

Like most people whose names begin with the letter *L, LNRs* are unlikely to have money problems. And if it's true that the richest people are those who need the least, then *LNRs* are millionaires. They have little false modesty in tightening their belts in lean times—even if it means giving up the BMW—and always seem to have a tidy sum stashed away for those rainy days. They are cautious investors who will typically favor mutual funds over high-risk stocks.

There's something appealingly vulnerable about *LNRs* that complements their excitable natures and makes them all the more desirable to the opposite sex. Still, marriage with an *LNR* will be bipolar experience with some of the highest highs and lowest lows. Partners will be well advised to take advantage of their good moments and smooth over the rocky ones with well-placed praise, patience and plenty of encouragement.

Leonardo DiCaprio Leonardo DiCaprio's name came from his mother's infatuation with fifteenth century Italian artist/scientist Leonardo da Vinci, or so the story goes. ■ Before Leonardo became an international megastar in the wake of his role in James Cameron's *Titanic*, he found his niche in roles occupying the uncertain zone between adolescence and adulthood, including the mentally challenged youth in *What's Eating Gilbert Grape*, and the troubled teenager in *Basketball Diaries*. ■ Then came *Titanic*, the most expensive, highest-grossing film of the century. Although the film catapulted Leo into millions of young hearts, he carefully avoided being typecast as a teenage homme fatale by opting for darker roles in the films *The Man in the Iron Mask*, *The Beach* and Martin Scorsese's *Gangs of New York*.

THE TRUTHFUL
Lnt

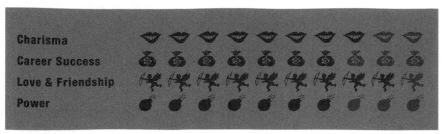

Charisma										
Career Success										
Love & Friendship										
Power										

Hopeful Soft-spoken Trusting
Gullible Withdrawn Unrealistic

The *lyrical* letter *L* is the icon of the best things that money can't buy: *love, life, laughter* and *loyalty*. And even though the letter *N* tends to be associated with *negativity*, it is offset by the *terrific* letter *T* (the symbol for all things *triumphant, truthful, tangy, tingly* and *teenaged*). When all three of these letters occur in words they create the sense of feminine flexibility found in: *lenient, talent, plenty, fluent, reliant, jubilant* and *pliant*. Fewer than thirty thousand individuals in the United States bear *LNT* names, but with their fiercely independent and outgoing personalities, these people stand out in a crowd.

Despite their natural vigor you won't find *LNTs* taking center stage at the local karaoke joint. It's not that they're shy by any means, it's just that at some level they believe it's a bit unseemly to draw attention to themselves. If they're going to reveal something intimate, it'll be quietly done in the presence of one or two close confidantes. If their reluctance to go out on a limb means they might miss out on some career or social opportunity, it's just fine with them. They have too hard a time forgiving themselves for their mistakes.

Like most people whose names begin with the letter *L, LNTs* are socially adept and easy going. But they're also extraordinarily accommodating people

Lamont
Lanette
Lanita
Lenita
Linette
Lynetta
Lynette
Lynnette

who know how to keep everyone around them happy. While some might see this as an unhealthy need to please, *LNTs* prefer to think of it as being loyal and devoted. Whatever the reason, *LNTs* must be on their guard lest people take advantage of their compliant natures.

When comfortably surrounded by people who have their best interests at heart, there's something quite charming about the way *LNTs* give of themselves and plenty of potential suitors are attracted to their wide-eyed innocence. But only when they're in a secure relationship are they likely to flower and reveal the more assertive aspects of their otherwise retreating demeanor.

LNTs' desire for intimacy makes communication a pleasure—even if most conversations revolve around emotional issues. *LNTs* can't help but say what's on their minds although they will need some time to pluck up the courage to express their deepest secrets. And because *LNTs* are so easily wounded, constructive criticism will only be acceptable when it comes from a loving partner.

Don't try and change their behavior with harsh words. *LNTs* respond far more readily to a whisper than they do a shout.

Lynette Jennings Few people influence the color schemes of people's houses more than Lynette Jennings, the creator, executive producer and host of *Lynette Jennings Design* on the Discovery Channel. Without the baggage of rival Martha Stewart, Lynette is arguably the most trusted name in American home design. ■ Like Martha, Lynette maintains a tight rein on all aspects of her show and works without a script because she believes it gives the show a spontaneous feel. ■ Lynette believes that everyone has an innate fashion sense and it's just a matter of paying attention to one's environment. She's also discovered that "most people are afraid of making an expensive mistake and that fear overpowers their confidence." She advises people to start with their bathrooms.

THE COLORFUL *lr*

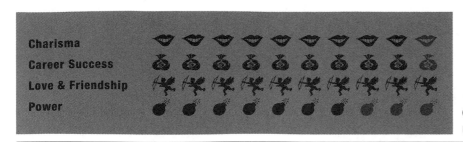

Charisma	
Career Success	
Love & Friendship	
Power	

Giving Creative Kindhearted
Unmotivated Restless Irresponsible

The letter *L* is indelibly connected to the ideas of *love, learning* and *laughter* and the *romantic* letter *R* is associated with the cheeky sexuality of the words *racy, rapture, ribald* and *ravish*. It's no surprise then, that the combination of these two passionate letters projects such a defiantly lusty ambience. Their upbeat tones explain why the *LR* dominates such words as *color, flora, clear, pallor, lurid* and *claret*, and why we associate these names with people whose outlook on life is positive, creative, and free thinking.

LRs present an inquisitive and inviting façade to the world and seem to derive much of their energy from their interactions with other people. With their natural ability for being all things to all people, you could even say that *LRs* are social chameleons. But in their quest to synchronize themselves with the needs of others, *LRs* often lose touch with their *own* desires and have trouble staying motivated. This is why many *LRs* approach new experiences with initial excitement before losing interest and turning away.

Like many people whose names begin with the letter *L*, *LRs* have the political skills to succeed in their professional lives. Their talent for creating alliances while avoiding making enemies enables them to achieve great heights in business—usually in the realm of people

Lamar
Lara
Larae
Laree
Larry, Lars
Larue, Laura
Laure, Laurel
Laurie, Leora
Lera, Leroy
Lore, Loria
Lorie, Lorri
Loura, Lourie
Lura
Lyric

management, motivation and sales. But there's a flightiness to them that prevents them from settling into their ideal careers until relatively late in life. Perhaps this is indicative of being so full of talent that life simply holds too many options to settle on just one. And don't bother trying to pin *LRs* to commitments; they'll make their minds up when they're good and ready, thank you very much.

The reluctance to accept responsibility is evident in the *LRs'* personal lives as well. And if this proves to be too frustrating for their potential mates, don't expect any sympathy from the *LRs* . . . just look elsewhere. By the same token, *LRs* will not tolerate partners who take them for granted, and when teamed with mates who appreciate their need to keep their options open, these romances will be experiences to remember. These warm-hearted individuals know how to make their mates feel like they're the only people in their world.

With their highly developed tactile senses, the *LRs* favored refuge is spending canoodling time in the arms of their partners. With such vigorous schedules they usually aren't looking to do anything particularly exciting, but when their blood is up, their active imaginations can make for some pretty intersting evenings.

Lara Flynn Boyle In *Men in Black II*, Lara Flynn Boyle played an alien disguised as a Victoria's Secret model who eats a man whole. In real life, she's something of an alien to the Hollywood crowd as well. Vociferously proclaiming to be a bad girl, she displays a brutal honesty uncommon among her Tinseltown peers. ■ When Jack Nicholson had his assistant call her to ask her on a date, the plucky beauty instructed him to make all future calls personally. Her on-and-off relationship with Jack was a favorite subject of entertainment talk shows. ■ Lara continues to star in the TV hit *The Practice*, and leads a double life between the big and small screens. Like all true bad girls she has tattoos: a Celtic cross on her ankle and a shamrock near her pelvis.

lrn

Childlike Attentive Loving
Obsessive Immature Passive

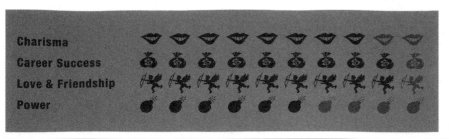

Charisma										
Career Success										
Love & Friendship										
Power										

Both the *LRN* names and the personalities they represent are complex in their construction. The letter *R* represents the youthfully *romantic* qualities found in the words *ripe, reproductive, racy, rapture* and *randy,* but the letter *N* is the authoritative letter of *negativity* (*no, not, never, naught,* and *nada*) and suggests a measure of cynicism and conservatism. The letter *L*, on the other hand, is the definitive symbol of *love, laughter, life* and *learning* and bespeaks an individual with an uncommon emotional intelligence. All told, the *LRN* combination suggests the feeling of a romance not quite realized in the words *lovelorn, alluring, forlorn, flowering* and *leering.* Although only about a quarter of a million people in the U.S. bear a *LRN* name (of which *Lorraine* and *Lauren* comprise the vast majority), this mainly feminine root is currently enjoying an extraordinary surge of popularity.

These amenable people may *appear* to be demure and submissive, but they're held up by a backbone of pure titanium. And if *LRNs* are capable of summoning up an impressive tantrum from time to time, it's usually just to make a point. The downside to having people think that you're an innocent is that it's somewhat inconvenient to grow up. So many people are willing to shield them from harm that their maturation is often

Laraine
Laron
Larraine
Lauran
Laureen
Lauren
Laurena
Laurence
Laurene
Loraine, Lorean
Loreen, Loren
Lorena, Lorene
Lorina, Lorine
Lorna, Lorne
Lorenza
Lorenzo
Loriann
Lorraine
Lorriane
Lorrine

compromised. Perhaps this is why so many *LRNs* retain their childish outlooks well into adulthood.

Having few insecurities, *LRNs* have little need to dominate others. Soft-spoken and exuding the gentle self-confidence of alpha males or females, they are responsible workers who flourish in positions of authority and have no problem with ceding control to someone else. Exceptionally intelligent, they are drawn to careers in science, medicine or law, but will readily adapt to any job that provides sufficient intellectual stimulation. If you're ever going to encounter the *LRN's* inclination for pickiness, it's going to be in the workplace. A healthy work environment is critical to their mental well-being and productivity: desks must be shiny, computers fast, and pencils and coworkers sharp.

LRNs' cool reserve can be off-putting and—because many people believe them to be *too* self-sufficient—*LRNs* must exert themselves to make friends. But once they've sown their seeds in their primary relationships, their roots grow strong and deep. *LRNs* make for low-maintenance marriage partners who aren't into flashy demonstrations of love. All they need is a little nourishment and the occasional dash of spice.

Lauren Bacall When director Howard Hawks spotted Lauren Bacall's face on the cover of *Harper's Bazaar*, he cast her opposite Humphrey Bogart in 1944's *To Have and Have Not.* Lauren was so nervous that to keep from shaking she kept her chin pressed against her collarbone and glanced upward every time she spoke. The posture earned her the nickname "The Look." ■ Lauren later married Bogart, and the couple became the ultimate movie-star pair. But her marriage to Bogart triggered the criticism that she wasn't able to be a star in her own right, even though she received raves for *Young Man with a Horn* and *How to Marry a Millionaire.*

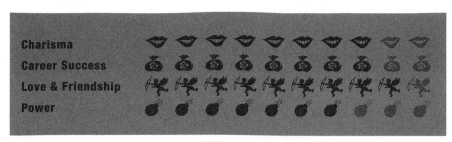

Charisma										
Career Success										
Love & Friendship										
Power										

Sexual Irrepressible Outgoing Permissive Self-indulgent Immature

The spontaneity and impulsiveness embedded in the words *blurt, flirt, stalwart* and *alert* stem from the *life-loving* and *lip-smacking* letter *L's* association with the *RT* suffix, which is indelibly connected to defiant sexuality (*consort, pert, tart, court, pervert, spurt* and *squirt*). *LRTs* are positive people who have full confidence in their ability to charm their way through life; anyone who shows the slightest immunity to their appeal becomes irresistible prey.

Most people agree that *LRTs* are aware of their sensuality and won't hesitate to use it. But they are also very approachable people who are easy to fall in like with. You'll want to stay on your guard, though; the charismatic *LRTs* are hardly impervious to the baser elements of human nature: jealousy, manipulation and anger. *LRTs* are not afraid of expressing their feelings openly and while *they* would argue that their transparent emotions are all about honesty, some critics believe it to be a sign of simple indulgence. But who cares about critics anyway? For people as confident about their motives as *LRTs* are, there's little fear of being judged and they'll simply take their knocks and walk away.

Drawing outside the lines comes naturally to *LRTs* and their quirky sense of mischief is more than enough to get them into recurring trouble. Fortunately, their gift for finding something positive in every situation helps to soothe any hurt feelings. People are advised to *never* underestimate their *LRT* friends; a keen sense of humor is often a symptom of a keen intelligence.

Young people are especially charmed by their zesty ways, which is why *LRTs* are naturals in front of first-grade classrooms or even university lecture halls. Since they have no false modesty about the status of their jobs, they aren't fussy about what they do for a living as long as the work is creative and gives them a chance to interact with the public.

You'll always know how your *LRT* friends are feeling even if you don't know what they're thinking. This is quite useful when it comes to intimate relationships, in which *LRTs* prove to be as intuitive as they are expressive—they'll take time to smell the roses and emotionally pamper their spouses. However, it's also in the realm of intimacy that *LRTs'* inherent insecurity shows up. When they're not being treated to the level of their expectations, they become as cold as airline food and communication begins to break down. This is the true test for the *LRT's* mate. Only if he steps up to the plate and becomes the man she really needs will the relationship have any chance of survival at all.

Larita
Lauretta
Laurette
Loreta
Loretta
Lorette
Lorita
Lorretta

Loretta Lynn Loretta Lynn's life was an all-American Cinderella story told through the Academy Award-winning movie, *Coal Miner's Daughter*, starring Sissy Spacek. ■ Loretta was born in the coal country of Kentucky, and even compared with the norm of that region whe married young, being only thirteen when she became Mrs. Doolittle "Doo" Lynn. Loretta was the mother of four by the time she turned eighteen when she and Doo moved to Washington to kickoff her professional singing career. ■ Loretta's career achieved liftoff after she wrote and sang the song "Honky Tonk Girl." With Doo at her side, Loretta drove all over the country to promote the song to radio stations. Loretta Lynn went on to become one of country music's best-loved singers and today owns her own music-publishing company.

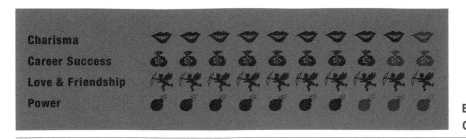

Charisma										
Career Success										
Love & Friendship										
Power										

**Bright Irreverent Witty
Childish Impatient Tempestuous**

The letter *S* and the soft pronunciation of the *C* evoke the air of sexual promise found in the words *sexy, sultry, soft, sassy, sensual, sin* and *slinky*. And because the *lusty* letter *L* is the symbol of all things *lively, laughing* and *life-loving*, its combination with the letter *S* stirs up an unmistakable sense of unbridled carnality: *flesh, classy, lush, loose, lust,* and *flush*. These names suggest people who are in love with life and who infect those around them with bubbly idealism.

Spontaneity is the key to the *LS*'s allure and they conduct their lives with unique flair and in their own particular time. If you're the structured, morally rigid type and happen to work in a cubicle next to an *LS*, they'll probably prove to be the bane of your life. For *LS*s respect no boundaries and follow no rules when it comes to finding conspirators for their energetic lifestyles. They'll alternately charm you and drive you insane with their coy ways but you could never deny that they know how to have a good time.

*LS*s are drawn to careers in which they can show off their talents for design and creative thinking. But since it takes them a little longer than most to find their paths in life, it's not unusual to find them working in McJobs until they get their act together. Climbing the corporate ladder isn't the *LS*'s cup of tea, and if their work doesn't fit into a conventional niche, it really isn't a big concern. They'd sooner be starving writers than stuffed into a pigeonhole in some anonymous office. The *LS*'s impulsive natures may cost them dearly when it comes to their long-term careers but they're surprisingly savvy when it comes to financial matters. When they're lucky enough to find a job that highlights their fiduciary acumen and people skills, they're capable of doing anything from running restaurants to controlling corporations.

*LS*s are quick learners when it comes to dealing with the opposite sex and because their emotional states are neither subtle nor hidden, prospective mates never have to wonder what they're thinking. But when it comes to courtship, *LS*s can be quite a handful; these playful sprites are infected with a wanderlust that the more sedate among us might find rather difficult to stomach. Stable unions are more likely found, therefore, with mates who can tolerate their penchant for socializing and balance the *LS*'s' extroverted nature with grounded reserve.

Lacey
Laci
Larissa
Lashawn
Lashonda
Leesa, Leisa
Les, Leslee
Lesley, Leslie
Lesly Lessie, Lisa
Lisandro, Lise
Lissa, Lois, Louis
Louisa, Louise
Lucero, Luci, Lucia
Luciano, Lucien
Lucienne, Lucille
Lucinda, Lucius
Lucy, Luis
Luisa
Luise

Lucille Ball Lucille Ball shortened her name to the diminutive Lucy to highlight her playful side for her eternally popular *I Love Lucy* television series. ■ Lucy began her career as a model and because at the time models were expected to be somewhat zaftig, Lucy was often presented in fur coats to hide the fact that she was so skinny. It was during a stint in the Broadway musical, *Too Many Girls* in 1940 that Lucy fell madly in love with a Cuban conga player named Desi Arnaz. ■ After Lucy was chosen to play the lead in the TV adaptation of radio's *My Favourite Husband*, she insisted that her real-life husband play her on-screen husband. The *I Love Lucy* show became a sensation and has been rated as television's all-time most popular show.

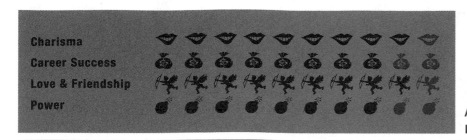

Charisma	👄 👄 👄 👄 👄 👄 👄 👄 👄 👄
Career Success	💰 💰 💰 💰 💰 💰 💰 💰 💰 💰
Love & Friendship	🐉 🐉 🐉 🐉 🐉 🐉 🐉 🐉 🐉 🐉
Power	💣 💣 💣 💣 💣 💣 💣 💣 💣 💣

Adaptable Expressive Outgoing
Escapist Inconsistent Opportunistic

The youthful qualities of the letter *T* are clearly discernible in the words *triumphant, truthful, terrific, tangy, tingly* and *teenager.* And since the letter *L* is the icon of the best things money can't buy (*love, laughter, life, learning* and *liberty*), it's hardly surprising that when these two letters get together, they evoke the effervescent images of *lightness, laughter, lust* and *loftiness.* These are people who live their lives with uncommon style and quite a bit of fanfare.

LTs are adventurers. No one seems to know where they're going to end up—least of all themselves. They are constantly on the move—as if they were afraid of their wake catching up to them—and while it may not be actual chaos they leave behind, there are plenty of people left *tsk-tsking* as they blaze by. Despite their tendency for running people over, there is little malevolence in their approach and they take great pains to protect people's feelings. Their strong belief in Karma explains why they're usually the first to offer a conciliatory token after a spat—even when they don't believe they were wrong.

These are multi-talented people whose skills run the gamut from the concrete (accounting, medicine and law) to professions involving people (management and sales), but you probably won't find them in corporate leadership. Not because

Latanya
Latasha
Latisha
Latonia
Latonya
Latosha
Latoya
Latrell
Latrice
Latricia
Layton
Lester
Leta
Leticia
Letitia
Lettie
Lisette
Lissette
Lita
Lottie

they're ineffectual leaders, but because they refuse to submit to the constraints of employee handbooks.

LTs are very much in control of their emotional well-being and have a strong sense of their own destinies, so don't assume their irrepressibility means they're incapable of making sharply rational decisions.

Loving and affectionate, the *LT's* parenting style tends toward liberality—leaving their mates to do the heavy lifting when it comes to the children. But when it comes to dealing with tantrums and domestic blowouts *LTs* like to be in the thick of things. They understand emotional outbursts better than most and are quite capable of being on the receiving end without taking anything personally. Their laissez-faire style of discipline makes them especially popular with children, and their ability to retain their poise against the onslaught of muddy faces makes them the envy of harried parents everywhere.

The *LTs'* marriages parallel the way they live their lives—wildly adventurous. The minute life gets too predictable they'll feel the call of the wild and their feet start itching. So, forget about romancing them the old-fashioned way. Take them on a balloon ride over Kilimanjaro and you'll have a mate for life.

Latoya Jackson Growing up in the shadow of her talented brothers and sisters was an ego-deflating experience for Latoya Jackson. Although she struggled gamely to keep up, her star was not destined to shine as brightly as Michael's or Janet's and she watched helplessly as her musical attempts faded into oblivion. ■ Still, Latoya managed to perform backup for several *Jackson Five* songs and gained some recognition for her participation in the *We Are the World* collaboration. The nineties also brought her moderate successes with the release of a bestselling autobiography.

THE HONORABLE lth

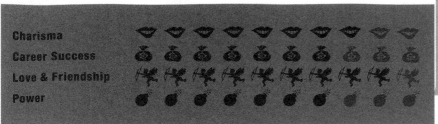

| Charisma |
| Career Success |
| Love & Friendship |
| Power |

**Clear-headed Steadfast Dependable
Demanding Self-absorbed Holier-than-thou**

The *TH* phoneme is usually associated with the spiritual aspects of the words *theology, thoughtfulness, therapy, thinking, thespian, theism,* and *thankfulness.* And since the letter *L* is so connected to the noblest things in life (*love, laughter, learning, law,* and *loyalty*), these names evoke people whose deep moral idealism acts as a magnet to those seeking guidance. The *LTHs'* lives are directed by a sensitive moral compass and they are unconditionally accepting of themselves and others.

LTH people love it when others ask them questions, for there's nothing quite as satisfying as being able to dispense wisdom. Their pride in their intellect is not rooted in arrogance, mind you, for their essence is one of genuine concern for others, and never self-aggrandizement or condescension. In light of this, one can forgive their occasional tendency to moralize from their pulpits, even if it wears a little thin at times.

Goal-oriented *LTHs* never take the easy way out, particularly when it comes to their careers. There's nothing like hard work to cleanse the soul, and if you can make a buck in the process, so much the better. And like most people whose names begin with the letter *L,* they're probably going to earn oodles of money from their ventures. Even if they aren't the highest paid peo-

Leatha
Letha
Luther

ple in their chosen fields, they'll certainly invest their assets carefully and successfully.

LTHs tend to get uncomfortable when people probe their innermost feelings, preferring to hang back until the relationship has had time to mature. Once someone does make it into the *LTHs'* inner lives, they tend to bond deeply and permanently. Getting married to an *LTH* may not be most exciting thing you'll ever do but if you're the type who's drawn to a steady and dependable mate, then they're the people for you.

Relationships in *LTHs'* world are strictly regulated according to their traditionalist ideals. But there's a downside to being so optimistic about love. *LTHs* have such a clear understanding of how they expect their marriages to play out that they project idealistic images onto their partners. The result is disenchantment when their mates can't meet these standards. But even if things aren't running smoothly in their primary relationships, nothing softens *LTHs* up like having their own offspring around. The role of doting parent was something they had been looking forward to from the time they were children themselves and they'll attack the challenges of parenthood with the same gusto as exhibited in their professional lives.

Luther Vandross It will be impossible to write the history of R&B music without mentioning Luther Vandross. His Grammy Awards and industry tributes would fill a spare bedroom and his thirteen albums have all enjoyed platinum recognition. ■ Luther first hit it big with his song "Here and Now" (still a staple at many weddings) and if there's a common theme to his music, it's his fascination with issues of love. Almost all his songs deal with the subject: "Stop to Love," "There's Nothing Better than Love," "The Power Of Love/Love Power," "Any Love" and "Your Secret Love." ■ Although Luther suffered a stroke in 2003, his ability to adapt to the latest musical trends without sacrificing his soulful R&B style is not expected to be adversely affected.

250

Charisma										
Career Success										
Love & Friendship										
Power										

**Outspoken Outgoing Irrepressible
Annoying Blunt Uneven**

Because the letter *L* is so strongly connected with all things connected to the most important things in life (*love, learning, laughter, language* and *law*), its association with the letter *V* is of particular significance. The *V* is the embodiment of human sexuality as seen in the words *vestal virgin, virtue, vixen, vamp,* and *vagina,* and when teamed up with the letter *L,* denotes *love, liveliness, vulva,* and *alive.* Thanks to the effects of the *romantic, racy, ripe* and *randy* letter *R,* this carnal association is even more palpable for the *Lavernes* and *Levars* of the world. Few names can compete with the *LV* for passion and ardent vigor.

These are people who view life like one big apple, taking huge bites and passing around the leftovers. And if *LVs* tend to bogart the apple at times, no one much seems to mind. What *LVs* take, they give back in spades.

LVs aren't overly concerned with "making it" in the career world; they're too engrossed with exploring the universe and utilizing their extraordinary social skills to collect as many friends as they can. Work to an *LV* is not about a paycheck. It's an opportunity to show off and maybe get a few phone numbers at the same time. They certainly do have an appreciation for money (supporting such an outgoing personality costs a pretty penny) and are the type of people who have a ready sup-

ply of cash—even if no one is quite sure from whence it came. *LVs* are subscribers to the dictum that it's not *what* you know but *who* you know, and few people milk their associations more than they do. But as we said, *LVs* are always willing to reciprocate and no one should dismiss them as *takers.*

In their personal lives, the *LVs'* tendency to exaggerate sometimes gets the best of them. Maybe it's just their way of reassuring themselves that everything is going according to plan, but their natural optimism often sets such high standards that failure and disappointment is common. In fact, *LVs* can be annoyingly optimistic, and anyone trying to cheer them down, or prod them back to reality, runs the risk of being cut off from their social sphere. They certainly care about what people have to say, but they're just too involved in their own lives to waste time dissecting it.

These people are specialists—and really come into their own—when it comes to making romance. They'll use every trick in the book to make their lovers feel like they're most important people in the world and will back it up with ample physical and emotional affection. Marriages (when they last) will be intense affairs with the *LV* firmly planted in the emotional driver's seat.

Lavada
Lavern
Laverna
Laverne
Lavina
Lavinia
Lavon
Lavonda
Lavonne
Levan
Levar
Levi
Liv
Livia
Lovie

Liv Tyler Liv Tyler grew up believing that her father was musician Todd Rundgren, but became suspicious after meeting Steven Tyler's daughter Mia. The girls looked so alike that her mother was forced to confess that Liv was actually the love-child of Aerosmith's legendary lead singer, Steven Tyler. ■ Liv was an awkward teen but after making the transition from ugly duckling to swan, her nubile performance alongside Alicia Silverstone in the video for her dad's song "Crazy" thrust her on to the big screen. Her most well known role to date is Arwen, the elf princess in the wildly successful *Lord of the Rings* trilogy. ■ In March of 2003, Liv married Royston Langdon, of the music group Spacehog.

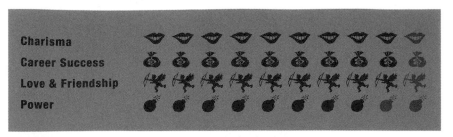

Inventive Witty Pragmatic
Distracted Stuffy Nerdy

The letter *W* is the symbol for the mysterious and dark aspects of human nature and it effects are clearly visible in the words: *weird, wild, warlock, wicked, warning, weapon* and *Wodin* (the Norse god of *war*). The letter *L,* however, is the polar opposite . . . the icon of everything noble about the human condition (*love, life, learning, laughter* and *liberty*). Consequently, the *LW* names represent people with appealing complexity and powerful insights into the workings of the universe and themselves.

If the *LW* was a stereotype, he would be a dignified college professor. With intelligence, humor and absent-mindedness all rolled up in one, he can expound for hours on quantum physics or the history of language, but for heaven's sake don't ask him where he's left his wallet. These endearing—if somewhat exasperating—traits may well charm your socks off, and when you're in his presence you'd better be ready for something unexpected to happen.

LWs would rather rely on their wits instead of taking advice from others. If it's true that their instincts serve them well, it's because they're constantly conducting experiments on life and carefully evaluating their outcomes. They are astute note-takers (even if they're only mental notes) and have a great eye for tiny details,

Lew
Lewis
Lawrence
Lawson
Linwood
Lowell

as long as they don't involve the location of their car keys.

The articulate *LWs* often employ their intellectual talents in education or in the creative fields, but if they have a weakness, it's that they are not particularly patient and must avoid professions requiring repetitive tasks like bookkeeping, manufacturing, or quality control. These are inventive and curious people, always willing to discuss the mystical aspects of the cosmos (more than a few *LWs* believe that aliens assassinated Kennedy), and are better off teaching, marketing or lawyering.

For all his romantic notions about how the universe works, the *LW* is not your dreamy knight in armor by any means. His idea of a hot date is taking a girl to a bookstore to illuminate her with his latest idea for a perpetual motion machine. But as life-partners, *LWs* are willing to provide strong shoulders for their mates and prove to be providers par excellence. If their marriages are going to have frustrations it's because their struggle with intimacy limits the depth of their relationships. Once they've broken through and achieved their unspoken understandings, however, they'll prove to be powerful allies with whom long-term partnerships are the norm.

Lewis Carroll Few writers have the authority to create new words that find their way into the dictionary. Shakespeare certainly was one, and so was Lewis Carroll. Arbitrarily inventing words as he saw fit, he created the word "chortle"—a morph of "snort" and "chuckle"—for his poem "Jabberwocky." ■ Lewis was born Charles Lutwidge Dodson in Chesire, and in typical Carrollian fashion created his pen name by taking the Latin version of his first names, switching them around and anglicizing them. ■ Known primarily for his fictional works *Alice in Wonderland* and *Alice through the Looking Glass*, Lewis was a prolific writer who penned dozens of short stories. His symbolic writing style has been so thoroughly analyzed that it's easy to forget that his timeless stories were written for children.

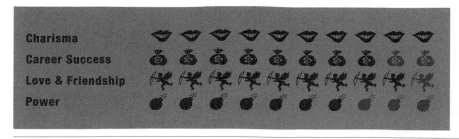

Charisma	
Career Success	
Love & Friendship	
Power	

Exciting Romantic Original
Harsh Unfocused Unrealistic

Names that incorporate the rare and unexpected letter *X* usually signify a personality with a hidden agenda, or at least the carefully cultivated illusion of one. And even though these names begin with the *learned* letter *L*, it is the dominant letter *X* which defines our impression of them. When he *X* comes into close contact with the *L*, its mysterious qualities can be discerned in the words: *elixir, lynx, complex, flummox, dyslexia, galaxy* and *Luxor* (the home of the Egyptian god *Serapis*). *LXs* will surprise you at every turn. These taciturn people posses a quiet strength that grows more noticeable as you get drawn into their realm.

The *LX's* abrupt social style has the advantage of letting people know where they stand in no uncertain terms. They'll be the first to broach the subject when there's an argument to be had, and even if their bluntness may cause a few bruised egos, they simply won't back down until matters are resolved. So if you've done something to warrant an *LX* lecture, it's best to act like it's the most sensible thing you've ever heard. They really believe that they know what's best for you and unfortunately, they're mostly right. Remember that you're not dealing with a neophyte; you're getting advice from someone who's been there, done that, and is

Lex
Lexi
Lexie
Lexus
Lexy

only looking to save you from the same hard lessons.

Although *LX* personalities aren't the kind to luxuriate in the spotlight, they're never silent about their opinions and are ever-willing to fight for them. Their philosophy of life is invariably left of center and they'll happily stick up for the little guy by acting as his self-appointed spokesman. But as liberal as they may be, these are no bleeding hearts. They're subscribers to the dictum that people should be held responsible for their own actions, and that education, rather than handouts is the best solution to all social problems.

LXs function best in careers that encourage them to grow at their own pace and often gravitate to small business enterprises that allow them to work on their own terms. The potentially messy complications of teamwork are a bit threatening to the organized *LXs* and unless they're able to take leadership roles, prefer to work on their own.

LXs make for enthusiastic and dedicated mates as long as they can rely on their spouses to watch their backs in an otherwise inhospitable world. Children will be welcome additions to their close-knit families and will be raised with the same protective slant that marks all of the *LXs* relationships.

Lex Barker Lex Barker was a member of a prominent New York society family. He attended Princeton, but dropped out to become an actor, about which his family was not especially happy. Lex's first starring role was as Tarzan in *Tarzan's Magic Fountain* (1949) and he went on to star in five more Tarzan movies before graduating to American Westerns. Lex then moved to Europe—he spoke Italian, Spanish, French and German—and made more than fifty films all over the world. He was especially popular in Germany, where he was awarded the Bambi Award for Best Foreign Actor of 1966. ■ Lex was married five times, including once to Lana Turner. He died in 1973.

Charisma										
Career Success										
Love & Friendship										
Power										

Wholesome Unconventional Original
Pushy Sarcastic Stubborn

When paired with the *zany, zippy, zingy Z*, the *laidback* letter *L* loses its *laconic* qualities and takes on the razor's edge that characterizes most people whose names contain the letter *Z*. *LZs*' modus operandi when it comes to dealing with difficult people is short, blunt and to-the-point, but if you're fortunate enough to be in their good graces, you'll be treated like royalty.

You'll be able to pick *LZs* out of the crowd by their quirky dress, irrepressible curiosity and the random firing of their brains (as evidenced by their inclination to jump from one subject to the next with dubious segues). But beware the patented *LZ* slicing which will be unleashed on everyone careless enough to step on their toes. Even *they* will admit that their sarcasm is a sign that they're just too lazy to talk things through, but no one should think of them as mean-spirited. Besides, they can take it as well as they can dish it out, and close friends understand that *LZs* banter because they love.

Routine is the *LZs'* worst enemy and they'll fight tooth and nail to keep their daily routines from becoming predictable. Still, boredom dogs their lives and often overtakes them in middle age when the kids leave home and the career loses some of its luster. Even if *LZs* aren't

Lazaro
Lazarus
Lisbeth
Liz
Liza
Lizabeth
Lizbeth
Lizeth
Lizette
Lizzie
Luz

the most assertive people in the world, they always seem to get their way by massaging relationships with those higher up the food chain. This technique serves them well in their careers where *LZs* prove to be formidable ladder climbers, if not the hardest workers in the cubicle.

Despite their bent for excitement, *LZs* can't escape the call of the hearth and will choose settling-down over the freedom and opportunities of single-hood. But this certainly doesn't mean that they're going to lose their zeal for life. Once they get through their middle-age crises, their unconventional natures will invariably reassert themselves.

Dating an *LZ* is a high-temperature experience characterized by a whirlwind courtship and passionate lovemaking. But *LZs* become wholly new animals under the influence of family and kids, and their children will be raised with the same open mind and liberal discipline that rules their own lives. In keeping with their belief that everyone should be encouraged to find his or her own way, *LZs*' will encourage their children to pursue untraditional careers—if that's what's going to make them happy. In the *LZs'* scheme of things, the universe is simply too unpredictable to waste time planning for the future.

Liza Minnelli Few people have lived in the public eye as utterly as Liza May Minnelli. Born to actress Judy Garland and director Vincente Minnelli, she became the youngest actress to ever win a Tony Award, for *Flora, the Red Menace*. ■ Liza's Oscar-winning performance in *Cabaret* extricated her from her mother's shadow and her follow-up films included *New York, New York* and *Arthur*. Her stage delivery evokes her mother's emotional intensity, and she is the only singer to ever sell out Carnegie Hall for three straight weeks. ■ Married four times, Liza's widely publicized nuptials with David Gest ended in an ugly lawsuit. Cynics wonder if Gest's decision to marry Liza had anything to do with the fact that he was an avid collector of Judy Garland memorabilia.

The Letter of the Maternal Embrace

Most Popular Girl's Names

Mary
Maria
Margaret
Michelle
Melissa
Martha
Marie
Mildred
Marilyn
Marjorie

Most Popular Boy's Names

Michael
Mark
Matthew
Martin
Mike
Manuel
Marvin
Melvin
Mario
Marcus

*In a nook
That opened south,
You and I
Lay mouth to mouth*
JOHN MILLINGTON SYNGE,
In May

It's difficult to resist the mellow tones of the onomatopoeic M. This initial letter of music, melodies and musings was originally used to denote water in hieroglyphic writings, and recalls these origins by mimicking the murmuring sound made by gently flowing water. ■ Created by pursing the lips and projecting a gentle hum, the M resonates maternal comfort in words like mother, madam, maiden, matronly, maternal, mercy, mild, moan, mama and mmm. In fact, the mmm sound is one of the first to be uttered by infants when demanding mother's milk, and the word for mother contains an m in just about every language on earth: mater (Latin), mama (Italian), mutter (German), mer (Vietnam), imma (Sanskrit), and mama (Zulu). ■ Form follows function when it comes to the physical shape of the letter m, for the two prominently rounded forms are reminiscent of female mammary glands. Perhaps this is why the letter M has come to symbolize those most enduring of human institutions: marriage and mistresses. With this strong reference to the mother image, it's not surprising that twice as many girls' names as boys' names begin with an M (Mary is the single most popular girl's name in the U.S.). Even when M names are anagrammized, the letter's gentle overtones bring warmth to the new words: Marcel (calmer), Mallory (morally), Maribel (balmier), Marlon (normal) and Miles (smile). ■ The sexual allure of the M is unlike that of the sensual S or the carnal R. It's more manipulative, with none of the in-your-face implication of imminent action. It plays on deep desires springing from one's association with one's mother, evoking warmth and nourishment while holding out the promise of a more meaningful relationship. But because of the M's deep sentimental qualities, it makes words like menace, malice, murder, maniac, mayhem, misery, maim and madman seem all the more malevolent. ■

Charisma	👄 👄 👄 👄 👄 👄 👄 👄 👄 👄
Career Success	💰 💰 💰 💰 💰 💰 💰 💰 💰 💰
Love & Friendship	🐉 🐉 🐉 🐉 🐉 🐉 🐉 🐉 🐉 🐉
Power	💣 💣 💣 💣 💣 💣 💣 💣 💣 💣

**Romantic Protective Seductive
Clingy Oversensitive Image-conscious**

When the *mellow* and *maternal* letter *M* initializes a name, it evokes an air of reassuring calm, much as a mother hums soothingly to her child. As the initial letter of *mother, maiden, matron, merciful, mama,* it's understandable that female *M* names occur with twice the frequency of male *M* names and that they manage to project such a powerful feminine presence. It is also significant that all the names in this category terminate in vowels which tend to convey cheerful characteristics found in words like *happy, gay, pixie, yippee, joy, cutie, funny* and *whoopee.*

These are women, who—true to their maternal self-image—tend to see themselves as the primary nurturers in everyone's life and try to keep loved ones close to their bosoms. Even when the situation calls for them to project authority (which they readily do) *M*s never lose their sensible center. Paradoxically, because *M*s operate from such a loving base, their outward behavior is often construed to be controlling: like strict schoolmarms who care deeply about the well-being of their charges. Those in the know realize that their somewhat inflexible methods are simply ways of expressing concern.

These passionate women are often drawn to professions in which they're able to express their artistic viewpoints. If *M*s have the opportunity to find work in the design, writing, or music fields they're going to be fulfilled and challenged, but if they find themselves in the nine to five grind with no way of unleashing their creativity, they simply aren't going to be satisfied. *M*s aren't only sweetness and light in the business world and they can be quite successful in cutthroat situations as well. The fact that many people underestimate their toughness plays right into their hands and they're not above a little feminine manipulation when it suits their objectives. Even though many *M*s enjoy success as small business owners and corporate managers, like most people whose names begin with the letter *M*, money is rarely their primary focus.

Just because children instinctively trust these protective people doesn't mean that *M*s are going to be delighted to have them around: nurturing and the responsibilities of child-raising sometimes take more energy than the *M* can afford. But *partnership* is a natural state for the *M*s, who love being part of a couple even at the expense of their autonomy. Most of the time, it's the *M*s' mates who are more likely to give up *their* freedom when the *M* co-opts them into all kinds of bonding adventures. As long as her partner seems to be making an effort to keep her happy, the *M* will reciprocate and be as loyal a mate as anyone could wish.

Mae
Maia
Mamie
May
Maya
Mayme
Mi
Mia
Mimi
Mya
Myah

Mae West Back in the 1930s, no one needed Dr. Ruth, *Cosmopolitan* magazine or Hugh Hefner to tell them that women could be sexually free. All they needed was Mae West. ■ The Brooklyn-born Mae was attacked by the conservative forces of her day for her flamboyant sexual style but refused to tone down her racy dialogue or mute the double entendres running throughout her films: "Between two evils, I always pick the one I never tried before," "The curve is mightier than the sword," "Don't make the same mistake twice unless it pays" and "Too much of a good thing can be wonderful." ■ Mae retreated from the screen after nine films and although she made a few appearances later in life, she lived out her years as a Hollywood recluse.

mb

Charisma										
Career Success										
Love & Friendship										
Power										

**Determined Feisty Affectionate
Unforgiving Dogmatic Belligerent**

The *bass* tones of the letter *B* are typically associated with the *belligerence* and *bellicosity* found in the words *beat, break, bash, battle, bully* and *bluster*. And even though the letter *M* is the symbol of all things *motherly, maternal,* and *matronly,* the *MB* combination still exudes a particularly powerful essence: *ambush, numb, rumble, somber, tomb, tumble* and *zombie*. Even names that end with the *lyrical* and *lively* letter *L* (*Mabel* and *Maribel*) are only marginally lighter in spirit (*fumble, rumble, ramble, bumble* and *tumble*). Due to these forceful elements, the *MB* names have largely fallen out of favor and today are represented by fewer than 80,000 individuals in the U.S., most of whom are over the age of forty.

MBs have the gift of single-mindedness and once they've made their decisions, they aren't going to be distracted from doing exactly what they've planned. Their innate compassion keeps them from running roughshod over other people on the way, but their decisive resolve ensures that they'll get the job done. These are no starry-eyed dreamers . . . *MBs* are firmly grounded in reality and expect their friends to be equally ambitious.

Those who've been startled by their *MB* friends' frank manners should just chalk it up to a little social clumsiness on their part, or to a replication error in their tact genes. But if *MBs* have a tough time making friends, they compensate with a refreshing determination to make sure that their friendships are successful.

Many *MBs* dare to do things their contemporaries would never dream, and their pioneering spirits put them in the forefront of whatever profession they choose. They'll even pick jobs and that are challenging just to prove to themselves that they still have *it,* even if it means sacrificing income for job satisfaction.

When it comes to the *MB's* intimate relationships, potential suitors often encounter an emotional wall of sorts, erected to protect the *MB's* fragile center. But once they get past the *MB's* tough-girl façade they soon discover a softly beating heart and a rich wonderland of gentle femininity. If she's a little reticent to show this gentle side at first, she'll warm up once she's reasonably sure of not being rejected.

It's hard to feel lonely when you have an *MB* watching your back and her solicitous attentions will make you feel cherished and special. As mothers, *MBs* embrace their children with their maternally nurturing spirit and won't withhold the no-nonsense discipline they'll need in later life.

Mabel
Mabelle
Mable
Maribel
Maribeth
Marybeth
Maybell
Maybelle
Melba

Mabel Normand Actress Mabel Normand's life was a study in tragedy and comedy. As a star of the silent screen in the early days of film, her brilliance rivaled that of her frequent co-star, Charlie Chaplin. ■ Mabel made a niche for herself as a hare-brained ingénue who performed all sorts of crazy onscreen stunts. In those days, stunt doubles were rare, so it was she who jumped off cliffs, engaged in swordplay and jumped into icy water. Even though Mabel suffered several injuries, nothing seemed to slow her down. Someone once described her as "a frisky colt that would take no bridle." ■ When Paramount director, William Taylor was murdered, Mabel's close ties with him permanently damaged her reputation and may well have contributed to her own premature death at the age of thirty-five.

Charisma	👄	👄	👄	👄	👄	👄	👄	👄	👄	👄
Career Success	💰	💰	💰	💰	💰	💰	💰	💰	💰	💰
Love & Friendship	🏹	🏹	🏹	🏹	🏹	🏹	🏹	🏹	🏹	🏹
Power	💣	💣	💣	💣	💣	💣	💣	💣	💣	💣

**Feminine Honest Original
Complicated Inscrutable Impassive**

The letter *D dominates* the *MD* names and imbues them with a *decisive* sense of *decency, dignity* and *discipline*. And since names that begin with the *maternal* letter *M* are associated with so many things that are *motherly* and *merciful*, the *MD* combination understandably creates the strongly humane effect found in the words *medicine, mediation, Madonna, modest, modulate* and *mindful*. There's something comforting about *MD* personalities even if their independent spirits make them impossible people to rely on.

MDs are explorers at heart who insist on learning about life through first-hand experience, even if it means enduring some hard knocks on the way. People seem to appreciate their frank approach to relationships and hardly anything comes out of the *MDs'* mouths that isn't carefully calculated. And even when *MDs* do happen to do something boorish, they are largely self-correcting: their feminine instincts quickly kick in to patch up any damage.

MDs are perfectionists with a self-critical streak to rival a Quaker. But despite their cool exteriors, they are emotionally quite sensitive and you shouldn't be fooled into thinking they weren't hurt by that unkind remark you just made. The thing that galls them more than anything is when someone talks about them

Maddie
Maddy
Maud
Maude
Meadow
Modesto

behind their backs. This is one behavior *they'd* never stoop to and they can't abide any form of disloyalty or betrayal.

Many *MDs* were tomboys growing up, but as adults, *MDs* are paragons of femininity. Still, there are remnants of childishness that manifest in impetuous display of autonomy, and sometimes leads to strange life choices. For example, a *MD* may be a homemaker one day, then with bee firmly in bonnet, careen off and take up karate. Even if they're not as extreme in their career choices as some, the *MDs'* dual nature certainly gives them an advantage in the workplace where they're happy doing anything that doesn't involve a commute or a nine-to-five routine.

Courtship and marriage with this energetic creature requires a suitor who can deal with her ups and downs. Her ready smile and warm spirit may *seem* like an invitation to potential mates, but she's going to be choosy. For like most people whose names begin with the letter *M*, *MDs* are protective of their feelings and have no compunction about turning down partners who they suspect don't have their best interests at heart. Partners that *are* willing to put her feelings first will find the relationship to be remarkably free of complications but are advised never to take her for granted.

Maude Adams It's arguable that the childhood hero Peter Pan owes his spunky personality to actress Maude Adams. It was Maude—who starred as Peter Pan in over two hundred shows of the famous play—who inspired James Barrie to create the magical little boy who refused to grow up. ■ Maude got her start in show business before she was even a year old. When she filled in as the star of a play called *The Lost Child*, the audience was so taken by Maude's little smile that her family was persuaded to keep her on the stage. ■ Since most of her fans were young, Maude carefully preserved their image of Pan as a male and never left the theater until all the children were gone.

Charisma	👄👄👄👄👄👄👄👄👄👄	
Career Success	💰💰💰💰💰💰💰💰💰💰	
Love & Friendship	💘💘💘💘💘💘💘💘💘💘	
Power	💣💣💣💣💣💣💣💣💣💣	

Comforting Intuitive Generous
Blunt Complex Uptight

As with all names that begin with the *maternal* letter *M,* MDN names exude the feminine and motherly qualities of the words *mother, mercy, mama, maiden* and *mellow.* The *dominant* letter *D,* on the other hand, is the icon of *decency, dignity* and *discipline* and its combination with the *M* reminds us of the benign strength found in the words *medicine, mediation, Madonna, modest, moderate* and *mindful.* It is also noteworthy that the nasal letter *N*—usually associated with *negativity, no, not, never, nyet, nix, nothing, naught, nincompoop, ninny*—infects these names with an air of pessimistic conservatism. If you were to describe *MDNs* in terms of food, perhaps they'd be a bar of dark chocolate: sweet, easy to digest, but with a bitter aftertaste.

People marvel at the *MDNs'* calm dispositions when crises arise, for they are focused people whose old-fashioned work ethic dominates their careers and relationships. Consistent with their emphatic essence, *MDNs* have a tendency to run roughshod over people in their quest for personal control and are often accused of trying to run the show. It's not that they *mean* to leave social chaos in their wake, but they can be so focused on driving the boat that they wouldn't even know if the skier had fallen off.

Madalyn
Madelaine
Madeleine
Madeline
Madison
Madlyn
Madonna

Their unwavering drive enables *MDNs* to get through all kinds of adverse situations and makes them inordinately well suited for medical and relief work (and second-grade teachers). Money is rarely their prime concern, and whether their chosen field is as CEOs, wives, chefs, or healer of scraped knees, *MDNs* take a good deal of pride in jobs well done. But on days when their pessimistic voices are in control, *MNDs* can feel so overwhelmed by life that the only cure is going to be a long vacation or a bottle of wine.

MDNs can be quite unpredictable in matters of the heart, so don't be surprised if your romancing fails to sweep them off their feet. *MDNs* do not give their hearts lightly, and though many will try, only a small number of suitors will actually make headway in their wooing. It's not that they're closed to love, it's that they place so much value in it, that they're unwilling to grant it to just anybody.

When they do lose their hearts, don't expect them to lose their heads as well, for these prudent souls are not about to place all their eggs in one basket. Only when they're securely encapsulated in wedding bands will they choose to fork over their hearts.

Madeline Albright Women all over the world rejoiced when President Clinton chose Madeline Albright to be the United States' sixty-fourth Secretary of State. During the Clinton administration, Madeline represented the United States with keen intellect, dignity, and a forceful vision of the world order. ■ Madeline was the daughter of a political refugee who had twice fled from his native Czechoslovakia. Raised as a Catholic, she had no idea of her Jewish heritage until her nomination for Secretary of State sent people scrambling to unearth her past: her grandparents had died at Auschwitz. ■ Madeline had a penchant for shooting from the hip and for pooh-poohing criticism of U.S. policy—"What's the point of having this superb military if we can't use it?"

Charisma	👄	👄	👄	👄	👄	👄	👄	👄	👄	👄
Career Success	💰	💰	💰	💰	💰	💰	💰	💰	💰	💰
Love & Friendship	🦅	🦅	🦅	🦅	🦅	🦅	🦅	🦅	🦅	🦅
Power	💣	💣	💣	💣	💣	💣	💣	💣	💣	💣

Direct Unpretentious Well-meaning
Overbearing Critical Condescending

When the *gruff* letter *G* dominates a name it imbues it with a sense of benign determination. This is why words that begin with the *G* often denote the qualities found in *goodness, grace, glory, God, governance* and *gentility*. The letter *M*, on the other hand, as the initial letter (or key component) of the word *mother* in practically every language on earth, resonates with maternal compassion. It's not surprising then that the *MG* combination occurs in female names significantly more often than in male names, or that they describe the inviting qualities found in the words *magical, magnetic, marriage, mitigate* and *massage*.

In short, these are men and women who—although they may advertise themselves as tender and caring—have a high sense of self-esteem that they will protect at all costs. Although they aren't ones to stand out in a crowd, there's a lot of depth to these uncommonly intelligent creatures, which will become apparent when you engage them in debates or ask them for advice. *MG's* like to surprise people who underestimate them. So if they're not making waves, don't think be fooled into thinking that they're not paddling.

Although *MG* people don't have any great desire to lord it over others, they do have a need to be in control of their own lives and will even engage in

Meg
Madge
Maegan
Magda
Magdalena
Magdalene
Maggie
Maggy
Magnolia
Margene
Margo
Margot
Meaghan
Megan
Meghan
Meghann
Migdalia
Mignon
Miguel
Morgan

one-upmanship if they sense that someone is getting the better of them. But it's less of a competitive drive than it is a self-defense instinct and even though *MGs* will enjoy the occasional game of Scrabble or tennis, it's never about winning. The game's the thing.

If you're floundering on a project that's way past deadline, cross your fingers and hope your *MG* friend is around. These hardworking powerhouses love it when their advice is needed but you may well have to pay a price for their assistance. A token gesture will do, or better yet, a dollop of the heartfelt admiration that *MGs* secretly crave.

Love and romance with an *MG* can be a one-sided affair, with the *MG* being a somewhat indifferent recipient of passion. Their personal spaces are so important to them that many partners will be unable to give them enough room to grow. Until the *MGs'* hearts are touched by partners who demonstrate an understanding of their needs, these romances have little chance of becoming permanent. As a result, many *MGs* will have to wait until later in life before they settle down—if it happens at all. If marriage isn't in the cards, *MGs* are likely to feel no great loss; their careers and creative endeavors are enough to keep them happily distracted.

Meg Ryan The blue-eyed blonde actress made her memorable star debut in 1989, when she faked an orgasm for co-star Billy Crystal in the movie *When Harry Met Sally*. Today Meg Ryan is recognized as one of Hollywood's greatest comic/romantic actresses. ■ Though she eventually married Dennis Quaid, it was with Tom Hanks that she found true on-screen chemistry. The two starred together in *Joe Versus the Volcano*, *Sleepless in Seattle*, and *You've Got Mail*. ■ In recent years Meg has forayed into drama and suspense, rounding out her screen presence to include the darker aspects of human nature.

THE GRITTY

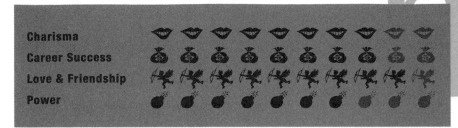

Charisma										
Career Success										
Love & Friendship										
Power										

Hard-working Moral Generous
Bitter Rigid Negative

Like most names that begin with the *maternal* and *mellow* letter *M*, *MGRs* hold the promise of nurturing, motherly concern. The *GR* phoneme, though, is linked to the threat sound that many animals make when they're showing *aggression,* and is why it initializes so many words that instinctively put us on alert: *growl, gruff, grimace, gross, grim, grizzly, grouchy* and *grave.* So while your *MGR* friend might behave with warm effusiveness on your first meeting, there'll also be a disquieting suggestion of an unyielding core. But no one would accuse *MGRs* of being wolves in sheep's clothing; their gracious and bighearted behavior is authentic and heartfelt.

It won't take long to discover the *MGR's* true essence if you spend some solo time with her. Her pithy style of communication has the advantage of letting people know where they stand in no uncertain terms, and she's not going to pull any punches when doling out advice or criticism. If you *really* want to know if you're gaining weight or if your new haircut makes you look like a chipmunk, you can count on your *MGR* friend to be as honest as a four year-old (and only a wee bit more tactful).

MGRs dream few impossible dreams. They approach their lives in practical and pragmatic fashion,

Margaret
Margareta
Margarete
Margarita
Margarite
Margarito
Margart
Margeret
Margie
Marguerita
Marguerite

and since the element of surprise is severely overrated as far as they are concerned, draw strength from their carefully planned routines. If they're sometimes accused of being rude or thoughtless it's a price they're prepared to pay for taking leadership roles. And if they make enemies along the way, you shouldn't expect them make apologies: they may be able to look ten moves ahead but they're not very good at looking back.

The *MGRs'* pragmatic approach to their lives might lead them to careers in law, sales, or politics, but they'll usually steer clear of pursuits requiring creativity. They are too down-to-earth for that, and although these assertive qualities may ensure success in the career world, it often hinders them in their personal transactions.

Intimate relationships highlight the *MGRs'* inner strength instead of bringing out their tender sides. When confronted with emotional hardships like death or divorce, they'll simply buckle down and pull harder to compensate for the loss—their resilience keeping them on their feet long after everyone else has dropped from emotional exhaustion. This is why the *MGR's* home and family life are characterized by the fierce allegiance only an *MGR* can give.

Margaret Thatcher With its history of strong female sovereigns, it's surprising that it took so long for Britain to elect Margaret "Iron Lady" Thatcher as their first female prime minister in 1979. ■ Standing side by side with Ronald Reagan, Margaret became the poster-girl for the brash brand of social and economic conservatism of the 1980s. She privatized many of Britain's state-owned industries and manhandled Britain's irritable trade unions. ■ Despite her plans to revitalize the country, the economy—and her popularity—continued to slide. So when Argentine President Leopoldo Galtieri played into her hands by invading the Falkland Islands in 1982, she attacked the islands and won a decisive victory. Her conquest helped her to become the first prime minister in British history to serve three consecutive terms.

THE CONSECRATED mhmd

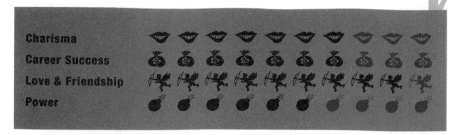

Charisma	😊😊😊😊😊😊😊😊😊😊
Career Success	💰💰💰💰💰💰💰💰💰💰
Love & Friendship	🦅🦅🦅🦅🦅🦅🦅🦅🦅🦅
Power	💣💣💣💣💣💣💣💣💣💣

**Zealous Involved Truth-seeking
Jealous Temperamental Addictive**

The name *Mohammed* is the most popular first-name on earth and owes its status to the prophet *Mohammed,* the founder of Islam. Its association with tensions in the Middle East has given these names a negative bias (to Western sensibilities) and one cannot talk about them without acknowledging the prejudices that envelop them. But the reality is that all names that feature a double dose of the *maternal* letter *M* stand above the crowd in terms of compassion and sensitive hearts. Augmented by the *holy, hallowed, helpful, happy* letter *H* and the *dignified, dapper, disciplined* letter *D,* these names resonate with a unique spiritual aura and denote people who take their responsibilities to their fellow man quite seriously.

Men who bear these names share a common sense of destiny, and whether their duties lie with family, society or the world at large, *MHMDs* have a powerful drive to live up to their expectations. The *MHMD* personalities always seem to be on a quest, whether it's for money, love, power, or simply higher spiritual awareness. No matter how much they've achieved in their lives, or how well things are going in their professional lives, *MHMDs* are unlikely to quit pushing. They project an air of intense restlessness and always seem to have a few tricks up their sleeves in those situa-

Mohamed
Mohammad
Mohammed
Muhammad

tions where most other people would simply give up.

The problem with having such a proactive mindset is that *MHMDs* can sometimes be deaf to reason when it comes to restraining themselves from things that might not be in their best interests. For example, they are particularly susceptible to focusing on their work to the exclusion of all else, and many pay a lonely price in their lost relationships

In the workplace *MHMDs* often crop up in sales, manufacturing, and the travel industry, all of which suit their restless energies. Success seems to follow them and, even if they're not rolling in riches, they'll be financially comfortable, finely dressed, and generous to a fault.

When it comes to love and marriage, *MHMDs* prove to be protective husbands and fathers who are prone to spoiling their loved ones with extravagant displays of affection and material offerings. Although they are fiercely loyal when it comes to their families, intimate relationships tend to bring out their jealous streaks and they'll need a strong partner to keep things on an even keel. The general rule is that when *he's* happy, everyone around him will be too. When he's not, peace will be a rare commodity in the *MHMD* household until he finds his sweet spot once again.

Muhammad Ali Of all the phrases you could use to describe three-time world heavyweight boxing champion Muhammad Ali, "shrinking violet" would not one of them. When Mohammad boasted that "I am the greatest," no one could disagree. ■ As Cassius Clay, Muhammad won his first Olympic gold medal at eighteen and, with his "float like a butterfly, sting like a bee battle cry, took boxing to a new level of grace and media hype. He changed his name after converting to the Muslim religion and stood as a symbol of black pride and dignity during the racial tumult of the 1960s. ■ In recent years Muhammad has struggled with Parkinson's disease—an ailment that many believe to have been caused by the repeated head trauma he received during his boxing years.

264

Charisma										
Career Success										
Love & Friendship										
Power										

All-rounder Understanding Motivated
Myopic Proud Preachy

The letter *K*—the symbol of forceful action—creates the vigorous masculine power found in the words *kick, knock, knuckle, knife, kill, keen* and *king.* On the other hand, the letter *M* is strongly connected to all things *maternal, mild, motherly, maidenly* and *matronly,* and suggests people who are very comfortable with *both* their masculine and feminine sides. Even though the overwhelming majority of people with *M* names are female, those who bear an *MK* root are mostly male. The exceptions are those names feminized by a terminating vowel (or the letter *Y*), as in *Mickey, Mackenzie, Minky* and *Monique.*

If there were one word to describe *MK* personalities, it would be *game.* For the *MKs* are the kinds of people to try anything once—or even twice if things don't work out the first time. Totally unafraid of hard work, *MKs* are irresistibly drawn to challenges, and their youthful curiosities give them considerable advantages when it comes to mastering new technologies.

If there's a drawback to having such a determined spirit, it's that *MKs* are apt to get a little impatient when other people are unable to keep up with them. It's not that they mind shouldering the load, but they're not the kind of people who'll stop what they're doing just to bring other people up to speed.

Mac
Mack
Malik
Mika
Mike, Miki
Mackenzie
Makena
Makenna
Makenzie
Malachi
Malakai
Malcolm
Mckenna
Mckenzie
Mekhi, Micah
Michaele
Mickey
Micki, Mickie
Mikki, Minky
Miyoko
Monika
Monique
Mick

MKs are incurably inventive. If someone is doing something a certain way, chances are they'll come up with a better way of doing it. It can be a little annoying at times because you often get the sense that they're only trying to show how good they are. And unfortunately, they're mostly always right. But like most capable personalities, there's nothing more dangerous than an *MK* who's made a miscalculation and is heading for disaster. Nothing's going to stop this train as long as it believes that it's on the right track, so you're better off getting out of the way and watching the wreck from a safe distance.

As mates, *MKs* tend to be the dominant partners . . . eager in bed and a bit pushy to boot. They may descend into petty lecturing when peeved but will ascend to heroic heights in their efforts to show how much they're in love. Their demonstrativeness might be based on a need to assuage their guilt for being so dogmatic, but their families will always be well cared for, and adored by, these larger-than-life dynamos.

If adults find their energetic spirits attractive, children find them positively irresistible. *MKs* respond well to the vigor of youth and usually can't wait to have their own children who will be co-opted into all sorts of misadventures.

Mickey Rourke If Mickey Rourke and Jerry Lewis have anything in common, it's that they both have the distinction of being big in France. It's not that Mickey lacks a U.S. fanbase—his early work was much lauded in the films *Body Heat, Diner* and *Rumble Fish*—but when his focus shifted to more violent and misogynistic roles (*9 1/2 Weeks, Year of the Dragon* and *Wild Orchid*), he began to lose his flavor to American tastes. ■ Even though his tough-guy reputation has hurt his career, no one questions Mickey's on-screen versatility.

mkl

Charisma	😊	😊	😊	😊	😊	😊	😊	😊	😊	😊
Career Success	💰	💰	💰	💰	💰	💰	💰	💰	💰	💰
Love & Friendship	🕊	🕊	🕊	🕊	🕊	🕊	🕊	🕊	🕊	🕊
Power	💣	💣	💣	💣	💣	💣	💣	💣	💣	💣

Responsible Stoic Appreciative Workaholic Preoccupied Diffident

Over three million men and women in the U.S. go by some form of *MKL* name and its enduring popularity is a testament to these names' inherent flexibility and the fact that its primary forces run the gamut from gentle to decisive to spiritual. The letter *M* is the flagship of *maternal* and *motherly* compassion while the vigor of the *K* can be discerned in the words *keen, kick, knock, knuckle, knife* and *king*. Since the letter *L* is the symbol for all the higher aspects of humanity (*life, love, liberty, learning* and *laughter*), your *MKL* friend is probably a compassionate and resolute individual with a strong moral kernel.

It is significant that *MKL* people choose to use the long form of their names (eg. *Michael*) instead of the available contractions (*Mike*). In opting to use the more complex version—requiring extra effort on the part of others to pronounce—it's fair to say that these people have stronger egos than most.

MKLs are restless creatures who need to feel that they're making a difference. They may not be the most colorful crayons in the box, but they do seem burdened by a sense of destiny to play an important role in whatever they do. Whether they make their marks as parents, businesspeople or artists, these are talented people with ever-bubbling creative juices, who even when they seem to be marking time, are simply pondering their next move.

When it comes to business issues, *MKLs* are like many people whose names begin with the letter *M* in that they are not driven by money alone. In fact, *MKLs* without family obligations tend to be dreamy and impractical. Fortunately, married *MKLs* take their responsibilities seriously enough to put their personal desires aside and get down to work.

The *MKLs*' insistence on doing things their own way asserts itself in the romance department where, instead of roses for your birthday you might get dahlias or hollyhocks—or a few dandelions stolen from the neighbor's yard. The good news is that, despite their oddities, they're as happy as turkeys on Boxing Day when it comes to committing to long-term relationships.

When it comes to these intimate unions, *MKL* mates will require heaps of attention from their partners if their relationships are to be kept running in tip-top condition. It's a little like owning a racehorse . . . the more hay you put in, the more you'll get out. So if you're a little peeved at having to clean the stalls, just remember why you married them in the first place.

Makaila
Makayla
Mckinley
Michael
Michaela
Michal
Michale
Micheal
Mikaela
Mikaila
Mikala
Mikayla
Mikel
Miracle

Michael Jordan Michael Jordan (aka Number 23) is widely regarded as the best basketball player in history and is arguably the most widely recognized sports figure in the world. ■ Under his reign, the Chicago Bulls won an astonishing six championship titles, with Michael winning the MVP in every final. He also led the U.S. men's basketball team to Olympic gold in 1984, but suffered a personal tragedy when his father was callously murdered by two young men who drove his father's Lexus for four days after the murder. ■ When he played his last professional game for the Washington Wizards against the Lakers before an appreciative crowd of 21,000, a fan waved a sign that read "Good-bye, Michael, Hello Kobe" (The king is dead. Long live the king.)

ml

Charisma	👄 👄 👄 👄 👄 👄 👄 👄 👄 👄
Career Success	💰 💰 💰 💰 💰 💰 💰 💰 💰
Love & Friendship	🕊 🕊 🕊 🕊 🕊 🕊 🕊 🕊 🕊
Power	💣 💣 💣 💣 💣 💣 💣 💣 💣

Astute Warm Forgiving
Easily hurt Clinging Effusive

The *lyrical* letter *L*—the symbol of *life, liberty, love* and *laughter*—has the power to soothe with its *lyrically languid lilts*. And when it occurs in words initialized by the *motherly, maternal* letter *M*, the resulting combination creates the calming resonance we find in: *family, calmly, comely, female, mellifluous, milk, smile* and *warmly*. It's not surprising that these names evoke a spirit that is *mild, mellow* and with a laid-back sense of humor.

MLs are those people who always manage to find something redeeming in other people. It's not that they're wearing rose-colored glasses mind you, it's just that their natural sensitivities and canny intuitions give them powerful insights into people's motivations. *MLs feel* their way through life rather than *thinking* their way through it.

The flip side to these gentle personalities is that the *MLs* are easily hurt when they perceive ill-will—even where there is no malicious intent. Some might even say that *MLs* are highly-strung or hypersensitive, but even if they are, their high level of emotional intelligence balances this out. And if they tend to take parental roles in their relationships, they're just trying to reassure their friends that they really want what's best for them.

Maleah
Malia
Maliyah
Mallie
Mallory
Mel
Mellie
Mila
Millie
Milly
Milo
Mollie
Molly

When it comes to their professional lives *MLs* aren't your typical corporate animals. Because it's important to them to pack as much variety into their lives as possible, *MLs* aren't known for their workplace stability, and like most people whose names begin with the letter *M*, have no real drive to make money for money's sake. Since they're happy to forgo earning potential in lieu of creative freedom, they're typically found in jobs with unusual flavors. If they had their druthers, they would prefer working with the public or with children.

MLs' need for diversity dominates their relationships and—as potential suitors often discover—the *M* in *ML* doesn't stand for *monogamy*. This doesn't mean that *MLs* are going around cheating on their partners; it's just that these roving Romeos and Juliets will play the field for as long as they're allowed to get away with it.

Ultimately, *MLs* know that there is nothing more important in life than their relationships. The self-appointed gardeners of the family tree, *MLs* are the ones that everyone goes to for news on the rest of the family. They'll keep their small circle of friends close and their families even closer.

Mel Gibson Mel Gibson has a little secret that it would be in his best interest to keep. The actor was actually born in New York, not in Australia as many people believe. Mel's father moved the family to Australia in 1968 with money he had won on *Jeopardy*, partly to prevent his sons from being drafted into the Vietnam War. ■ After debuting in *Mad Max*, Mel carved a reputation as an energetic hothead and box-office draw. He showcased his talents in everything from comedy (*Maverick*) to tragedy (*Hamlet*), romance (*Forever Young*) to epic heroism (*Lethal Weapon* and *Braveheart*). Any film with his name attached to it became a harbinger of a successful box-office gross. ■ Mel is a bit of an anomaly in Hollywood . . . he has seven children and has never been divorced.

Charisma		
Career Success		
Love & Friendship		
Power		

The letter *M* is the definitive symbol of the relationship between mother and child and is unambiguously associated with all that is *maternal, motherly* and *merciful.* The *lyrical* letter *L*—with its benignly lilting tones—has the power to soothe with its *languid lullabies,* which is why the combination of these two inviting letters creates the powerful feminine resonance found in the words *family, calmly, comely, female, milk, mellow, smile* and *warmly.* The *dignified, dapper, disciplined* letter *D* adds element of *distinction* and it's surprising that these names are not more popular than they are. Only about 100,000 individuals in the U.S. bear an *MLD* name . . . most of whom are over fifty years old.

If *MLDs* were animals, they would probably be giraffes. Noble in gait and countenance, these people lope through life with few natural enemies and no reason to make them. They are emotionally available, strong shouldered, and always ready to lend an ear to a friend.

MLDs' social circles are expansive and refined, and the guest lists at their weddings would read like a *Who's Who.* It's the little extravagances —*Dom Perignon* and lace doilies—that give *MLDs* their reputation for being consummate hosts, but it must be said that they can be awfully picky about with whom they mix, particularly

Malinda
Melinda
Melodi
Melodie
Melody
Melynda
Mildred
Milford
Millard

when it comes to their intimate relationships. Because *MLDs* would never dream of stooping below their station in life, they don't have all that many choices when it comes to marriage partners and must rely on introductions from mutual friends.

MLDs are also apt to show signs of being professional worrywarts, fretting about anything from bad weather to paying the bills. There is nothing so bad in their lives that *MLDs* couldn't imagine being worse, although the upside to being such worriers is that their lives are meticulously organized and carefully planned.

MLDs aren't the adventurous type and would prefer it if their friends weren't either. They are conservative souls with an aversion to change and will usually stay in the same place and hold the same job for many years. Once again, there are benefits to these characteristics; the dependable *MLDs* become the center of gravity for their friends and loved ones.

MLDs' marriage vows are taken seriously and they expect to be in it for the long haul (unless their partner doesn't reciprocate their fidelity). Children in the *MLD's* life almost always benefit from their parent's firmly rooted existence and will be raised in traditional, if somewhat predictable, style.

Millard Fillmore It's understandable that most people don't remember that Millard Fillmore was the thirteenth President of the United States; he simply never had the impact we associate with men like Jefferson, Lincoln or even Grover Cleveland. ■ Born into the harshness of frontier life in upstate New York, Millard was educated in a one-room schoolhouse (he ended up marrying the teacher), and worked as a young boy on his family's farm. Working his way up the social ladder to become a lawyer (some say down the ladder), Millard became President in 1850 when President Zachary Taylor died in office. Millard was denied a second term, partly because he signed into law the Fugitive Slave Act, which required runaway slaves to be returned to their owners no matter whether slavery was legal in the state in which state they were captured.

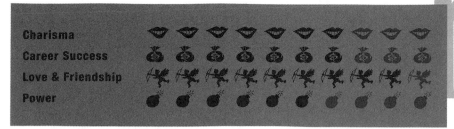

Charisma	
Career Success	
Love & Friendship	
Power	

**Impulsive Refreshing Spontaneous
Fickle Irresponsible Spacey**

When names begin with the letter *M* they are unambiguously associated with all that is *maternal, motherly,* and *merciful.* The letter *L,* on the other hand, is the symbol of *life, laughter, love* and *learning,* and when combined with the letter *M* takes on the warmly reassuring air of the words *female, melody, smile, mollify, mellow* and *dreamily.* But when the negative qualities of the letter *N* (*no, not, never, nothing, naught, nowhere*) are injected into these words, we get: *complain, humiliation, molten, imbalance, malevolence, malign, maudlin* and *Mussolini.* Perhaps this is why the most popular *MLN* name (*Melanie*) ends with the playful *IE* sound, which lends the disarming influence found in the words *bonny, funny, fanny, harmony, sunny* and *zany.*

In summary, *MLN* personalities are richly complex with a balanced combination of maternal compassion, irrepressible optimism and sober-minded conservatism. And while some might even call them living contradictions, *MLNs* have no time for labels or pigeonholing; they're too busy living life to its fullest.

Daydreaming is one of the hallmarks of an *MLN* personality. And because of a remarkable ability to retreat into rich fantasy worlds, these people aren't prone to being bored or boring. With their uncommonly fertile imaginations, *MLNs* are probably capable of solving every problem society has ever faced—if they could only remember their ideas long enough to write them down. It's not that the *MLNs* feel that they have any great mission to save the universe, mind you. From their spiritual perspectives if everyone were to take care of themselves and those around them, the world would be a much better place. It's not their job to teach people lessons; Karma will take care of that.

If there's a downfall to the *MLN* personalities, it's that they often forget that they have brains when it comes to matters of the heart. Fortunately, *MLNs* find compensation in their extraordinarily high emotional intelligences and take comfort in knowing that their gut instincts are rarely wrong.

Even though love and marriage with *MLNs* will inevitably be full of surprises, it will also feature more ups than downs. Their main focus will be on companionship and teamwork, and mates who expect a lot of fluff and romance will be in for a letdown. Even though *MLNs* demonstrate their feelings in the ways that count—like uncompromising loyalty and unconditional love—there will be moments when they have a rush of blood and present their mates with nights to remember.

Melani
Melanie
Melany
Melina
Melton
Milan
Milton

Melanie Griffith The daughter of Tippi Hedron—star of Alfred Hitchcock's *The Birds*—Melanie Griffith's life has been marked by triumph and turmoil. Her big-screen break came with her role in Brian De Palma's *Body Double* in 1984 and her trademark kittenish voice and classic looks made her a Hollywood darling throughout the 1980s. She received an Oscar nomination for her role in *Working Girl.* ■ Melanie moved in with actor Don Johnson at the age of fourteen, and the two were twice married and divorced. Between these affairs Melanie had a son with actor Steven Bauer and a daughter with Johnson. ■ After recovering from a publicly painful addiction to painkillers, things came together when she married actor Antonio Banderas, with whom she had her third child.

mls

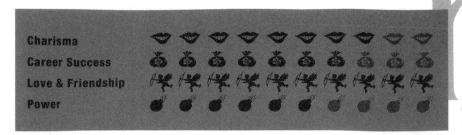

Charisma										
Career Success										
Love & Friendship										
Power										

Gracious Wide-eyed Maternal
Diffuse Dawdling Indecisive

The *lyrical* letter *L* is the symbol of things that money can't buy: *life*, *liberty*, *love* and *laughter*. And when it occurs in words initialized by the *maternal* letter *M*, it generates the powerful feminine resonance found in the words *family*, *calmly*, *comely*, *female*, *mellifluous*, *milk*, *mellow*, *smile* and *warmly*. So when the *ML* combination occurs in words followed by the *sassy*, *sexy*, *sensual*, *slippery* letter *S*, you can expect to find blithe spirits who act like butter wouldn't melt in their mouths. But although there are few hard edges to these people, never underestimate their power. Whether *you* know it or not, they know they can wrap you around their little fingers.

MLSs are steady and easy-going people who'll go out of their way to avoid conflict. In fact, since *MLSs* are reluctant to openly display their emotions, conflict tends to trigger a passive-aggressive response, which can lead to withdrawal and alienation. If there's any *real* criticism directed toward *MLSs*, it's that it's nigh on impossible to tell how they feel. You'll certainly know what they *think*, mind you, for these are exceptionally bright people with a great deal of creative and intellectual energy.

When it comes to their careers, *MLS* people aren't particularly driven by financial incentives. Their main

Malisa
Malissa
Melissa
Melissia
Milagros
Miles
Millicent
Myles

motivation comes from a need to please and a sincere desire to do the best job they possibly can. In general, *MLSs* are meticulous workers who thrive on praise and have few demands of their own. "Reliable under pressure" is the key phrase here, for these people have long fuses and tempers that only ignite under extreme heat.

Thanks to this combination of cool heads and warm hearts, *MLSs* make for great teachers, government workers, emergency technicians and personnel managers.

Because the *MLS'* downfall is their tendency to drift out of touch with their emotions, they've learned that they should never make decisions when their blood is up, especially when it comes to love relationships. Nothing is too innocuous for *MLSs* to take personally when it comes to romance and even the slightest criticism, no matter how well intended, is liable to drive them into a funk.

Once ensconced in healthy relationships, *MLSs* exhibit the same high level of commitment they display in their work. Potential partners soon discover that their *MLS* partners are apt to put their family's feelings before that of their own, and that only those who don't abuse their altruistic essence will be rewarded with loyal and enduring marriages.

Melissa Etheridge Fame came to raspy-voiced singer Melissa Etheridge in two different forms. She is both a Grammy Award–winning rock star and the first openly gay female rock singer in history. ■ Melissa never shied away from her identity and she developed a loyal following playing in lesbian bars in Long Beach, California. Her self-titled 1989 album took only four days to record and brought her positive critical attention. Her follow-up albums, *Never Enough* and *Yes I Am*, guaranteed her a position in the rock firmament. ■ Melissa's sexuality made headlines in 1993 when she came out at President Clinton's inauguration celebration in D.C. In the years since, her sexual orientation and forthright lyrics helped pave the way toward society's acceptance and understanding of homosexuality.

THE ENDEARING

mn

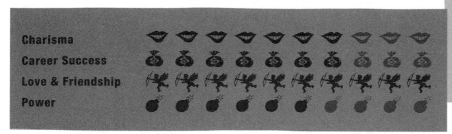

Charisma										
Career Success										
Love & Friendship										
Power										

Playful Entertaining Encouraging Flighty Forgetful Whiny

The nasally pronounced letter *N* is the symbol for all things *negative, naysaying* and *nullifying,* and injects an undeniable air of pessimism into the words it initializes (*no, not, never, nyet, nada, nix, nothing, naught, ninny* and *nowhere*). On the other hand, the letter *M* is the symbol for *maternal, motherly* love and, together with the *N,* produces a warm resonance. This is why so many words that feature the *M* and *N* exude the reassuring hum of *clemency, humanity, communal, harmony, money* and *hymnal.* In names like *Monnie* and *Minnie,* this soothing effect is augmented by the diminutizing *Y* sound found in such words as *doggy, kitty, silly, goofy* and *blankie.*

With the exception of the name *Monica* (which has the *cutting* edges of the letter *C*) there are no rough edges in the *MN* names and it's not surprising that Walt Disney chose an *MN* name for his second-favorite mouse. If we instinctively sense that these are benign and trustworthy people, you can be sure that *MNs* use this to their full advantage. But as unassuming and gentle as they can be, everything is not sugar and spice when it comes to these highly intelligent individuals; these are people with clear insights into what they want, and they are not shy about cranking up the charm to get it.

While many adults appreciate *MNs'* candidness and emotional openness, children universally seem drawn to

Manuel
Manuela
Manny
Mina
Minnie
Mona
Monica
Monnie

their simplicity and sense of fun. About the only time you'll see *MNs* display open irritation is when they've been denied something they believe was their right . . . like everyone's full attention. And because these people have impeccable tastes you'll have to think Dom Perignon, crystal flutes and orchids if you're going to keep them happy. If this is too much to ask, just remember that there's someone else who'll be more than willing to do it. Most *MNs* have been treated with kid gloves ever since they were young, and every lover they've ever had has probably reinforced this belief.

You're in for a treat if you're lucky enough to marry an *MN.* Their ability to see silver linings in every cloud makes them low-maintenance partners and high-spirited companions. At worst they'll be a little whiny when they don't get their way, but on the bright side, they're apt to give their partners the same kind of unconditional attention that they themselves crave.

The *MNs* star shines brightest when they become parents, and their children will never have to guess where they stand on the issues. They may take some criticism for their liberal style of discipline (especially from the traditional schools of thought), but the proof of the pudding will be in their brood's high self-esteem.

Minnie Driver With her multi-cultural upbringing and mastery of various accents, actress Minnie Driver is truly a girl of the world. She was born in London, raised in the Barbados and schooled in Paris, Grenoble and England. Born Amelia Driver, she was given the nickname Minnie by her younger sister who was unable to pronounce her name. ■ After a brief stint in television, Minnie gained twenty pounds for her role in *Circle of Friends*—winning kudos from the critics. Her versatility landed her roles as everything from a Bond girl (*GoldenEye*), to a dark comedienne (*Grosse Pointe Blank*) to a star-crossed lover (*An Ideal Husband*). But it wasn't until her performance opposite Matt Damon in *Good Will Hunting* that Minnie hit the big time with an Oscar nomination for Best Supporting Actress.

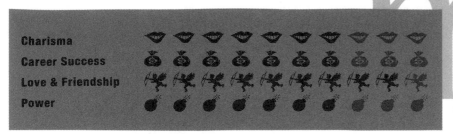

Charisma	💋💋💋💋💋💋💋💋💋💋
Career Success	💰💰💰💰💰💰💰💰💰
Love & Friendship	💘💘💘💘💘💘💘💘💘💘
Power	💣💣💣💣💣💣💣💣💣💣

mnd

Sober Genuine Affectionate
Impatient Immature Petty

When the *mellow* and *maternal* letter *M* initializes names it evokes an air of reassuring calm . . . much in the way a mother hums to soothe her child. The *nasal* letter *N,* on the other hand, is the symbol of all things *negative* (*no, not, never, nyet, nada, nix, nothing, naught* and *nowhere*) and when it comes into close contact with the *dignified, diligent* letter *D,* loses little of its pessimism. This is why the *M, N* and *D* letters are so commonly found in words conveying a melancholy air: *mundane, moribund, damnedest, reprimand, impound, demand* and *monody* (a mournful poem). In an attempt to lessen these negative effects many female *MND* names (*Mindy, Mandy* and *Mendy*) end with the playful letter *Y.* Words ending in the high-pitched *Y* are usually associated with diminution and youth: *silly, baby, kitty, joy, happy, doggy* and *puberty.*

To keep themselves from being bogged down in their own issues, *MNDs* will even take on projects that seem to have no financial gain; they are they volunteers, counselors, and soccer coaches that every community appreciates. But don't think for a minute that *MNDs* are entirely unselfish; at the end of the day they will always put their own families first. These are men and women who—like most people with names beginning with the letter *M*—are not motivated primarily by money. Job

Mandi
Mandie
Mandy
Maynard
Mendy
Mindi
Mindy

satisfaction, relationships, and family will always be more important.

As is also true with many people whose names begin with the letter *M, MNDs* are worriers. And even though most of the time they're not sure why they're putting so much pressure on themselves, it manifests in an almost frantic need to predict the future. Their weeks are planned with precision, their desks immaculately organized, and they'll check in religiously with their mates. And though this kind of stress exacts a heavy toll on the *MNDs'* energy reserves, they always have enough left over to indulge in their other passions: entertaining and home-building. *MNDs* are unquestionably nesting animals who need to be surrounded by friends to feel complete.

Although *MNDs* are most at ease when ensconced in intimate relationships they can sometimes lose their way on the twisted road to marital bliss. When problems occur in their relationships, they'll probably arise from their quest for perfection. This isn't always a bad thing mind you but it can place undue strain on *MNDs'* mates if they are laid-back types. But let it never be said that *MNDs* don't know how to roll with the punches; they know their limitations and have a great deal of experience in correcting their mistakes as well.

Mindy Sterling In Hollywood, it's either feast or famine. You can slave away for decades as an unrecognized journeyman, then boom, one hit movie and you can't go grocery shopping without sunglasses. That's what happened to Mindy Sterling after she landed her role as Dr. Evil's right-hand Nazi-esque henchwoman, Frau Farbissina in Mike Myers's *Austin Powers.* ■ The unexpected success of the movie spawned two sequels: *The Spy Who Shagged Me* and *Goldmember*, both of which brought Mindy worldwide attention. ■ In real life, the soft-spoken Mindy is nothing like the domineering and sinister Frau and actually gave acting lessons to Lisa Kudrow and Keanu Reeves at the Groundling Theatre. It's also where she first met Mike Myers who invited her to audition for the part in *Austin Powers.* Mindy ordered her sunglasses.

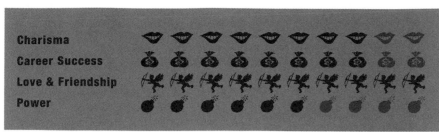

Charisma										
Career Success										
Love & Friendship										
Power										

Solicitous Hospitable Giving
Clinging Insecure Repressive

MR names have traditionally been some of the most popular names in the U.S. and have recently seen a surge in usage. Their prevalence may have something to do with the fact that the letter *R* is the symbol for all things cheekily *romantic*—as the initial letter of *racy, randy, raunchy, rapture, ravish, reproductive* and *ravage*, its rolling tones infuse a sense of impudent passion into names in which it appears—while the letter *M* is the harbinger of all things *merciful* and *maternal*. The *M* is also the key component in the word *mother* in practically every language on earth, and it's hardly surprising that the combination of the *M* and *R* evokes the warmly sensual resonance of the words *summer, glamour, demure, murmur, merry* and *shimmer*.

Careers for these gregarious people nearly always include a lot of people-contact in jobs like customer service, teaching, or retail. If there's any *MRs* in your office, chances are that they're the ones everybody looks to for the latest news on who's doing what and who's doing who. They have their fingers on the social pulse as well and are always up on the best dance clubs, restaurants and parties. Even if they're not the center of attention, they thrive on the feedback that comes with being part of a group.

Maira
Maire
Maria
Mariah
Mara. Mari
Marie, Mario
Mary, Marya
Maura, Mauro
Mayra, Meri
Merri, Merrie
Merry, Meyer
Mira, Mireya
Moira
Monroe
Mora
Moriah
Murphy
Murray
Myr

For all their childlike exuberance and altruistic leanings, it's sometimes difficult for *MRs* to accept reality as it is. They really want to believe the vision they see from behind their rose-colored glasses, and while this may keep them on an even emotional keel, it doesn't always serve them well in their professional lives. But one advantage to having this kind of optimistic perspective is that if they can at least envision the world the way they *want* it to be, then at least they have a shot at making it a reality. *MRs* are extraordinarily capable people when they set their minds to something, and even if they occasionally lack focus, can be counted on to make positive impacts in their workplaces and social lives.

Unfortunately *MRs'* idealism sometimes takes a beating in the realm of romance, for it's a rare lover who can live up to their glossy notions of love. Luckily, time has a way of weathering the sheen from their romantic sanguinity and those *MRs* who get married later in life have an excellent chance of success. It should be said that *MRs* are at their best when they're in committed relationships. Once there's someone is watching their backs, they can relax enough to do the things that matter most: nurturing and providing for their families.

Mariah Carey The drama surrounding Mariah Carey began early in the pop star's life. Prejudice against her parents' interracial marriage (her father was half-Venezuelan and her mother, Irish) was the suspected reason why their dog was poisoned and their family car blown up. ■ Kicking off her career as a backup singer for popster Brenda K. Starr, Mariah moved into the circle of music mogul Tommy Mottola, who engineered her 1990 debut album, which sold over six million copies. Mariah was named Artist of the Decade and received the Best selling Female Artist of the Millennium award from the World Music Awards. ■ Mariah and Tommy's subsequent half-million-dollar wedding rivaled the nuptials of Charles and Diana. The divorce that followed five years later left Mariah with a sullied reputation from which she is only now beginning to recover.

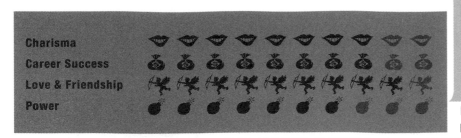

Charisma										
Career Success										
Love & Friendship										
Power										

Fair Sensible Earthy
Pessimistic Judgmental Egotistical

The letter *M* is the flagship letter for all things warmly *maternal, motherly* and *merciful*. The letter *R*, on the other hand, is the icon for all things *raffish* and *racy* and initializes words like *ribald, randy, raunchy, rapture* and *ravish*. It's not surprising, therefore, that when the *M* and *R* come into close contact they evoke the romantic resonance found in the words *summer, glamour, demure, murmur, merry* and *shimmer*. The letter *G* (or *J*) can be pronounced in two ways, each of which has diametrically opposed implications. The hard *G* is the symbol of *gruff, grizzly* and *grumbling*, while the soft *G* (as it appears in these names) is the icon of all things *genial, gentle, genuflection* and *genuine*. That's why people who bear the feminine *MRJ* name root glide gently through life with a strong sense of justice coloring their actions.

If these women have an uncommon sense of duty, it probably stems from their spiritual relationship to the universe. Most *MRJs*—even if not overtly religious—have rugged moral compasses and philosophies rooted in Karma. They believe that they can (and should) make a difference in the world, and often act as if they're on some kind of preordained mission (even if it's just keeping others on the straight and narrow). This is why

Majorie
Marge
Margery
Marjorie
Marjory
Maryjane
Maryjo

MRJs don't need to have hidden agendas. They're so confident they know what's best for others that they're often astonished—and even a little hurt—when people spurn their advice.

MRJs aren't out to make money for money's sake in their professional lives. Money would certainly be welcome—after all, they could always use another pair of sensible shoes—but like most people whose names begin with an *M*, they have no plans to be topping any *Forbes* lists. Fortunately there are good jobs out there for people who aren't afraid of being a little bossy and *MRJs* function particularly well in workplaces in which their co-workers appreciate a mother-knows-best attitude. The fact that they're nearly always right is a reflection of their down-home wisdom and common sense, but *MRJs* are not ones to lord it over others. They're just not the "I told you so" types.

Marriage and motherhood intersect perfectly with the *MRJs'* practical and protective personalities. When it comes to home matters, their mates will appreciate the fact that they've got their feet planted so securely on the ground and will find there is no job so menial that their *MRJ* won't give 100%. They might even be pleasantly surprised by their *MRJs'* intermittent spicy advances.

Marjorie Tallchief Born on January 24, 1925 and October 19, 1927, respectively, in Fairfax, Oklahoma, a town on an Osage Indian reservation, Maria and Marjorie Tallchief are of Osage and Scots-Irish descent. Both sisters began dancing at an early age and went on to have extremely successful careers as ballerinas. Maria, who was married to George Balanchine, is considered to be one of the greatest American ballerinas but Marjorie also left her mark on the ballet world, joining the American Ballet Theater in 1944 and then dancing with the Ballet Russe de Monte Carlo and the Ballet de Marquis de Cuevas. In 1957, Marjorie joined the Paris Opera Ballet, becoming the first American to serves as the company's premiere danseuse etoile. ■ Marjorie and Maria founded the Chicago City Ballet in 1980.

mrk

Charisma	👄	👄	👄	👄	👄	👄	👄	👄	👄
Career Success	💰	💰	💰	💰	💰	💰	💰	💰	💰
Love & Friendship	🏹	🏹	🏹	🏹	🏹	🏹	🏹	🏹	🏹
Power	💣	💣	💣	💣	💣	💣	💣	💣	💣

Generous Motivated Stable
Impatient Hardheaded Possessive

The letter *K* is the definitive icon of authoritative and commanding action. This is why it so commonly initializes forceful words like *kill, kick, kidnap, knife* and *knock*, and why we instinctively associate it with a not-too-subtle warning of impending danger. On the other hand, the letter *M* is the flagship of *motherly* love and the letter *R* is the symbol for audacious *romance*: *racy, ribald, randy, ravish, romp, ruddy* and *red*. So when these three letters coincide in words they convey the sense of sly nonconformity found in the words *maverick, smirk, malarkey, limerick, shamrock, murky* and *muckrake*. The *MRK* personalities are the very embodiment of these cheeky attributes and these men and women would surely describe themselves as lusty individualists.

MRKs are strong, stoic people who can endure enormous amounts of mental and physical pressure without showing signs of cracking. They will be quite upfront about what they want and seem know exactly how to go about getting it. And while you could say that *MRKs* are stubborn, it would probably be an understatement. They're more like granite; a monument to persistence that first surfaces in childhood where they never accept *no* for an answer.

Marc
Marco
Marcos
Marcus
Mariko
Mark
Markel
Markie
Markus
Marquerite
Marques
Marquez
Marquis
Marquise
Marquita

The *why* of things is especially important to *MRKs*—an interest that grows stronger as they grow older. This kind of curiosity drives them to all sorts of experimentation, and it's rare for them to turn down opportunities for new experiences even when they know they're in for a rough time.

In their professional lives, the *MRKs'* skills tend toward practical applications. Solving problems are among their greatest passions and they're quite adept at working with their hands. They might even create problems for themselves in their spare time just so they can fix them later and were the kind of children who took watches apart with no idea how to put them back together.

As stable as they are in matters of business, *MRKs* often lose their footing when it comes to matters of the heart. Problems occur when they realize that their emotions aren't quite as predictable as they believed them to be. When the *MRKs'* dreamy side comes to life, it usually does so unexpectedly and catches them off guard. They're certainly not the first to be fools for love, but they're arguably the most amusing. And if love and marriage come late for them, it often turns out to be a blessing: *MRKs* need a little more time than most to quench their natural curiosities.

Mark Hamill The role of Luke Skywalker in George Lucas's Star Wars trilogy transformed Mark Hamill from a small-time actor into a megastar. ■ Mark signed on to do all three movies in the trilogy, but before he completed *The Empire Strikes Back*, his facial features were altered in a car accident. George Lucas worked the mishap into the movie and wrote the "Wampa" scene to explain his new face. ■ Mark's repertoire includes work in the theatre as well. His most challenging role to date—playing Tony Hart in *Harrigan 'n Hart*—included both singing and dancing and won him a Drama Desk nomination for Best Actor in a Musical. In recent years, Mark lent his voice to the television cartoon characters *Batman* and *The Hulk*.

Charisma

Career Success

Love & Friendship

Power

As the initial letter of *racy, randy, raunchy, rapture, ravish, reproductive* and *ravage*, the letter *R* is the symbol for all things cheekily *romantic*. The letter *M*, on the other hand, is the key component of the word for *mother* in practically every language on earth, and so it's not surprising that the combination of these two emotionally-rooted letters evokes the warmly sensual resonance found in the words *summer, glamour, demure, murmur, merry* and *shimmer*. Since the letter *L* is the flagship of the best things that money can't buy (*love, life, liberty, laughter* and *learning*) those who bear *MRL* names are typically characterized by a nurturing warmth, an impish sense of humor, and an extraordinary passion for living.

There are no sharp edges in either the *MRL* names or in their embracing personalities. But while these certainly are altruistic people who have a knack for putting other people at ease, it doesn't mean that *MRLs* don't have their own agendas or the gumption to make things happen. Like most people whose names begin with the letter *M*, *MRLs* have high levels of emotional intelligence that are often parleyed into careers that include a significant degree of human contact. These are people-oriented souls who make wonderful teachers, medical personnel and public relations executives. Because of the *MRLs'* aversion to conflict, however, very few of them are destined to achieve heights in corporate leadership or politics.

Thanks to the natural equilibrium built into the *MRLs'* psyche, stormy weather is of little consequence unless it happens to be focused directly at them. It's then that these dreamy pacifists retreat into their shelter of avoidance (and even denial) in an effort to keep themselves dry. Emotional self-preservation is of highest importance to *MRLs* and they'll go to great lengths to ensure that their self-esteem remains healthy and intact. Perhaps this is why *MRLs* are so sensitive to the emotional needs of others and why they're initially so suspicious of the motives of potential partners.

Still, intimacy comes naturally to *MRLs* who are at their best when paired with partners appreciative of their gentle spirits. An *MRL* trait—that's annoying to some and endearing to others—is that they have a strong need to be coddled and can be quite demanding about receiving expressions of desire from their mates. But the flipside is that the *MRL* also loves to pamper and you can expect scads of hot chamomile and foot rubs in return.

Mariel
Mariela
Mariella
Marilee
Marilou
Marilu
Marla
Marlee
Marley
Marlo
Marylee
Marylou
Merle
Merrilee
Merrill
Meryl
Mireille
Mirella
Muriel
Myrl
Myrle

Meryl Streep Blond and beautiful (although not in the classic Hollywood way), Meryl Streep exudes a feminine intelligence that has made her the discriminating moviegoers' leading woman. ■ She received the first of an astonishing twelve Oscar nominations for her portrayal as Christopher Walken's fragile girlfriend in *The Deer Hunter*, and won her first Oscar as a troubled wife in *Kramer vs. Kramer*. The full force of her artistic brilliance hit home in *Sophie's Choice*, where she transformed herself into an Eastern-European refugee haunted by her past and she even took on the challenges of comedy in such films as *Defending Your Life* and *Death Becomes Her*. ■ Meryl remains intensely private about her personal life and lives a quiet anti-Hollywood existence in Connecticut with her sculptor-husband and their four children.

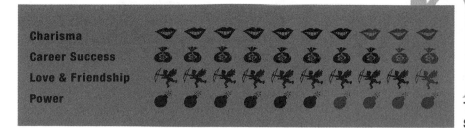

THE SENSUAL mrln

Charisma	👄	👄	👄	👄	👄	👄	👄	👄	👄	👄
Career Success	💰	💰	💰	💰	💰	💰	💰	💰	💰	💰
Love & Friendship	🦅	🦅	🦅	🦅	🦅	🦅	🦅	🦅	🦅	🦅
Power	💣	💣	💣	💣	💣	💣	💣	💣	💣	💣

Tranquil Seductive Versatile
Superstitious Controlling Morbid

The letter *R* is the definitive symbol for all things sexually *robust*. Its *rolling* tones conveying the *romantic resonance* found in the words *racy, randy, ravishing, ruddy* and *red* (the traditional color of passion). So when it occurs in words in close proximity to the *maternal* letter *M*, it radiates the warmly sensual glow of words like: *summery, merry, gossamer, glamour, demure, murmur* and *shimmer*. The *LN* letter combination, on the other hand—evokes an association with isolation and independent living: *alone, alienation, longing, lean, lynx* and *feline*, and explains why most *MRLNs* have reputations for withdrawing their warmth without warning. If *MRLNs* were drinks, they would be twenty-year-old brandies . . . warmly inviting and full of nuance, but not easy to swallow until you've acquired a taste.

It's unlikely that you'd find *MRLNs* in careers that require high levels of aggression. Even though these individuals are not above competing for their resources, their emotional metabolism runs so high that it saps much of their energy. They'd rather leave the bickering to someone else; like a stronger friend who's been designated to watch their backs.

MRLNs feel the need to control the events and people in their lives and avoid entanglements that might

Marilyn
Marilynn
Marlena
Marlene
Marlon
Marlyn
Maryellen
Marylin
Marylyn
Merlin

upset their carefully laid plans. It's not that they have any particular control issues, it's just plain insecurity. For *MRLNs* believe that once they lose the upper hand in their relationships they're liable to being taken advantage of. And since negative relationships can leave them in emotional paralyses for years, these sensitive individual are picky about with whom they place their trust. *MRLNs* have long memories and hold equally long grudges.

MRLNs conduct themselves in such an open way that people can't help but be drawn to them. If you're thinking about dating a *MRLN*, go for it, but remember that these are not easy people to befriend unless you're willing to accept a relationship dictated on their terms.

Love is a testing-ground for *MRLNs*, who are unwilling to relinquish their individuality no matter how enthusiastically their partner embraces the relationship. But they are sentimental souls who are quite willing to make sacrifices to keep the union together . . . even the ones that border on being destructive. Children—because they're able to take the edge off the *MRLN's* hectic existence—usually prove to be a welcome relief and will be parented in the way that only *M*-named people know how.

Marilyn Monroe With so many contradictory views on the life of Marilyn Monroe, it can be argued that she was *the* enigmatic figure of the twentith century. ■ As Marilyn's persona imprinted itself into the American psyche, she fell prey to drugs and depression. Her romantic life reflected her private turmoil when she married and divorced Joe DiMaggio in the space of a few years, later marrying and divorcing playwright Arthur Miller. Her rumored affair with John F. Kennedy didn't help her reputation for instability. ■ Marilyn died at the height of her star power and will be remembered as a vivacious young beauty sucked dry by the Hollywood machine. ■ Laments Marilyn: "Hollywood is a place where they'll pay you a thousand dollars for a kiss and fifty cents for your soul."

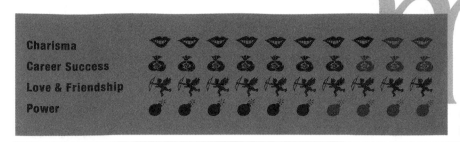

THE SUBTLE
mrm

Charisma										
Career Success										
Love & Friendship										
Power										

Serene Steadfast Faithful
Sentimental Condescending Diffuse

Names that begin with the *maternal* and *motherly* letter *M* hold the promise of a personality full of warmth and motherly affection. And since these *MRM* names feature a double dose of the gentle *M*, they suggest women very much in touch with their femininity. But it's not only sweetness and light in the *MRM's* world, for the rolling tones of the *R*—the initial letter of *racy, randy, raunchy, rapture, ravish, reproductive* and *ravage*—infuses these names with a sense of impudent passion. When the *R* gets together with two *Ms*, it predictably creates the sweet *murmuring* of the words *summer, mesmerize, mammary* and *shimmer.*

The calm and unflappable *MRMs* fairly brim with self-satisfaction and—thanks to their pacifying influence—you won't find many type-A attitudes in their social groups. *MRMs* express themselves through their musical tastes and their choice of art, but also through the way they live their lives. And because *MRMs* feel a strongly connection to style and creativity they always reserve a significant portion of their emotional reserves for artistic endeavors.

MRMs have that wonderful gift of being able to point out other people's shortcomings without hurting anyone's feelings. They would never say anything in an overtly derogatory way, but they'll certainly make it

Mariam
Maryam
Miriam
Myriam

known what they think about other people and how they should live their lives. Friends and lovers will find it to their advantage to avoid their moralizing lectures, even if they know that *MRMs* are almost always right.

MRMs aren't exactly self-starters and often need external motivation to get out of bed in the morning. Their idea of torment is spending an afternoon with nothing to do, or no one with whom to talk. *MRMs* might take the day off with the best of intentions—clean the house, do the shopping, and catch up on bill paying—only to see five o'clock roll around with nothing accomplished. Then, when their roommates come home, they'll start complaining about what a hectic day they've had. If you want to see their to-do lists, it's the same list of things they had to do yesterday.

MRMs gravitate toward careers that involve human interaction (rather than "concrete" jobs like science and business), and like most women whose names begin with an *M*, are more interested in job satisfaction than financial rewards. It's not that they wouldn't appreciate a little extra money—they are creatures of comfort and have expensive tastes—but all they're planning to do with their lottery winnings is to lavish it on family and friends.

Miriam Makeba "Mama Africa," as Miriam Makeba is known by thousands of her fans, spent most of her life beating the odds. Born into the apartheid of South Africa, she spent the first six months of her life in jail with her mother. ■ Miriam's musical breakthrough came in 1959, when she played the lead in a black jazz opera, *King Kong*. Taken under the wing of Harry Belafonte, her outspoken activism resulted in her being unable to return home for almost thirty years. ■ After the collapse of apartheid rule, Miriam returned home to take her place among the heroes of the anti-apartheid struggle. ■ "Given a choice," she says, "I would have certainly selected to be what I am: one of the oppressed instead of one of the oppressors."

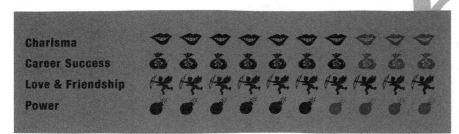

Charisma	
Career Success	
Love & Friendship	
Power	

Demonstrative Prudent Emotive
Dependent Subjective Inconsistent

The letter *M* is the flagship of all things *maternal, motherly* and *merciful* and tends to infuse names with an aspect of nurturing femininity. The letter *R*, on the other hand, is the definitive symbol of extroverted sexuality, with its rolling tones conveying the *romantic resonance* found in the words *racy, randy, ravishing, ruddy* and *red*. When these two passionate letters occur in the same name, they create the warmly sensual glow found in the words *summery, merry, gossamer, glamour, demure, murmur* and *shimmer*. But there's a shadow hanging over these names in the form of the *negative* letter *N*, which is responsible for the downbeats in the words *no, not, nonsense, never, nyet, nada, nix, nothing* and *nowhere*. This explains where *MRNs* get their reputations for being easygoing, but also why they are known for having distinct bites to their personalities.

When people describe *MRNs* as being successful, they aren't necessarily measuring them by conventional yardsticks. *MRNs* aren't the smartest, best looking or the most athletic people in the world, but they are clearly at peace with the universe and the role that it has allocated them.

MRNs aren't afraid of rolling up their sleeves and getting into the messier aspects of humanity. Being more intelligent and compassionate than most,

Maren
Marian
Mariana
Marianna
Marianne
Mariano
Marin, Marina
Marine, Marion
Marna, Marnie
Maryann
Maryanna
Maryanne
Maureen
Maurine
Meranda
Merna
Miranda
Mirian
Mirna
Myranda
Myrna
Myron

they are drawn to the medical fields where they often end up as doctors, nurses and counselors. But just because they are unselfish, it doesn't follow that they're going to be unconditionally sympathetic. When their compassion runs into their common sense, you'll find they have little patience for people who can't solve their own problems. They aren't going to stand on the shore while you're wallowing in misery, they're liable to wade in and give you a swift kick in the swimsuit.

These are men and women who aren't afraid to speak their minds and will let you know what they think of you in no uncertain terms. But there's nothing openly malicious about the way they deal with the rest of the world, and because they release their frustrations in small doses, it would be unusual to find them actually erupting into full-blown tantrums.

MRNs take to intimacy like fish take to water, and it follows that married life is going to suit these affectionate people quite well. If and when problems arise they'll probably have something to do with the way they try to mold their partners into their own images of perfection (a problem common to many successful people). Still, *MRNs* are quick learners and will prove to be extraordinarily adept at keeping their relationships on track.

Marion Ross At the age of thirteen, Marian Ross changed the spelling of her first name to "Marion," figuring that it would look better on a marquee. She went on to have one of the longest-running and most successful TV careers in history. ■ Although well received in her debut movie, *Forever Female*, and recognized for her performances in *The Glenn Miller Story* and *Sabrina*, Marion seemed to have been destined for the small screen. Her best-known role was as Mrs. Cunningham on *Happy Days*. ■ In total, Marion has made over four hundred appearances on various programs, including *The Love Boat*, *Night Court* and *Life With Father*.

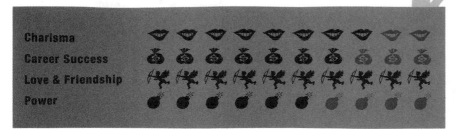

Charisma	😗	😗	😗	😗	😗	😗	😗	😗	😗	😗
Career Success	💰	💰	💰	💰	💰	💰	💰	💰	💰	💰
Love & Friendship	🦅	🦅	🦅	🦅	🦅	🦅	🦅	🦅	🦅	🦅
Power	💣	💣	💣	💣	💣	💣	💣	💣	💣	💣

Lively Sensual Artistic
Insecure Abrasive Antagonistic

It's not difficult to discern the feminine influences in the *MRS* names. The letter *M*—the unmistakable icon for all things *motherly, maternal, merciful* and *mellow*—contributes a sense of compassion and tenderness while the letter *R* is the symbol for all things cheekily *romantic*. As the initial letter of *racy, randy, raunchy, rapture, ravish, reproductive* and *ravage*, the *R's* rolling tones infuse words with a sense of impudent passion, and its combination with the *M* evokes the sensual resonance found in *summer, glamour, demure, murmur, merry* and *shimmer*. Since the *S* sound (and the soft pronunciation of the letter *C*) is the symbol of *sultry, slinky, sensuality*, these three emotional letters (and the absence of any aggressively pronounced letters) represent a placid spirit with an extraordinarily high level of emotional intelligence.

Whether they know it or not, *MRSs* are natural actors; not because—like some people—they have a need to be in the spotlight, but because they are so in touch with their own emotional mechanisms. This characteristic allows them to be social chameleons who can effortlessly adapt to any situations, although an unfortunate side effect of this talent is that it's sometimes difficult to discern whether *MRSs* are actually angry or just putting on a show to make a point.

Marcel
Marcela
Marcelino
Marcell
Marcella
Marcelle
Marcellus
Marcelo, Marci
Marcia, Marcie
Marciela
Marcy, Marica
Maricela, Maris
Marisa, Marisela
Marisol, Marissa
Maritza, Marlys
Marshall
Maryrose
Maurice
Mauricio
Mercedes
Mercy
Merissa
Morris

One thing to keep in mind about people who bear *MRS* names is that they are almost always liberal in their outlook. This doesn't mean they have any particular political agendas, mind you, but their natural empathy always has them coming down on the side of the little guy. Perhaps this is why they typically attract such an eclectic group of friends that inevitably profits from the *MRS's* generous spirit.

MRS people gravitate toward the unconventional when it comes to their careers. But like most people whose names begin with the letter *M*, the *MRS's* vocational choices are not driven primarily by money, which is why they're more likely to be happy than rich. Even if their primary interests don't earn them enough bread to grow fat, they'll happily eat crumbs in order to pursue their real passions: stewing in their creative juices and cultivating their relationships.

Marriage to *MRSs* will prove to be happy adventures, for these sensual, creative, and fun-loving people also have a natural affinity for monogamy. Their mates will enjoy the benefit of a soft shoulder from an attentive spouse, while their children will benefit from the most important thing that parents can provide: unconditional love and life-long support.

Marisa Tomei When Brooklyn-born Marisa Tomei was a child, her English-teacher mother tried to convince her to drop her accent. Headstrong Marisa resisted and went on to win an Oscar for playing a spunky and foul-mouthed girl opposite Joe Pesci in *My Cousin Vinny*. ■ But Marisa seemed to catch the best-supporting actress curse—a breakthrough followed by a series of flops from bad scripts. Still, she received critical kudos—and a Screen Actors Guild Award nomination—for her portrayal of a single mom in *Unhook the Stars*.■ Her second Oscar nomination, for her role in *In the Bedroom*, proved that she was no one-hit-wonder.

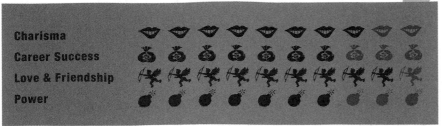

Charisma										
Career Success										
Love & Friendship										
Power										

**Tenacious Thrifty Disciplined
Miserly Critical Preachy**

Because the letter *T* is the symbol for all that is *triumphant, tremendous, truthful, terrific* and *talented,* whenever it occurs in words and names it manages to infuse them with a lively twinkle and a brisk effervescence. On the other hand, the *MR* combination—composed of the *maternal* letter *M* and the *racy, randy, ravishing, ruddy* letter *R*—radiates the warm sensual glow of the words *summery, merry, gossamer, glamour, demure, murmur* and *shimmer.* These are people who, despite their laid-back warmth and easy bearing, have the drive and intelligence to succeed in anything they set their minds to.

MRTs are capable of great playfulness and will take delight in driving you nuts if you let them get under your skin. But they are also compassionate, caring and parental, and truly seem to want the best for whom they love. If there's a particular drawback to these people, it's that they have pretty itchy trigger fingers when it comes to pointing out other people's shortcomings. So *MRTs* probably aren't the first people you'd go to for help if you're in need of a loan. They'll certainly be delighted to lend you a hand, but you just *know* you're going to have to endure an unnecessary lecture. By the time your money-conscious *MRT* friend has finished rebuking you, you'll probably decide that you're better off getting a job.

Marietta
Mariette
Marita
Marta
Marti
Martin
Martina
Martine
Marty
Maryetta
Maurita
Mertie
Mirta
Morton
Myrta
Myrtie
Myrtle

Even though *MRTs* are no more power-hungry than anyone else, it's not unusual for them to end up in powerful positions in the workplace. Employers value their natural leadership abilities and showcase them as company examples. Manual labor really isn't their thing; they are detailed oriented with excellent motor skills and are perfect for accounting and computer-related fields. Their ability to maintain their composure under stress also makes them great candidates for emergency services and teaching.

MRTs often seek out relationships with troubled individuals so they can feel useful in putting them back together. Some would call the *MRTs* meddlesome, but loved ones appreciate being the recipients of their persistent attentions. Almost always, *MRTs* will be leaders in their relationships and marriage to one of them can be quite an emotional whirlwind. These dynamic people are nothing if not passionate, and once secure in their roles as lovers, will prove to be wonderfully affectionate and hardworking partners.

Like most people whose names are initialized by the letter *M*, *MRTs* are at their best when surrounded by children. If there were pageants for best parent, *MRTs* would make it into the final four. As far as they're concerned, children should be seen *and* listened to.

Martina Navratilova When Martina Navratilova was twelve years old she lamented to her father that she looked like a boy. In an attempt to console his daughter, her father and tennis coach told her that if she looked liked a boy then she needed to play tennis like one. ■ Born in what is now the Czech Republic, Martina came to the U.S. in 1975 to pursue her tennis ambitions. By the time she retired, more than twenty years later, she was the undisputed queen of tennis, and could boast world records in singles titles (167), doubles titles (165), and mixed doubles (7). ■ Her rivalry with American darling Chris Everett was the stuff of legend, but their competitiveness never intruded on their off-court friendship.

Charisma	👄	👄	👄	👄	👄	👄	👄	👄	👄	👄
Career Success	💰	💰	💰	💰	💰	💰	💰	💰	💰	💰
Love & Friendship	🐦	🐦	🐦	🐦	🐦	🐦	🐦	🐦	🐦	🐦
Power	💣	💣	💣	💣	💣	💣	💣	💣	💣	💣

**Unruffled Comforting Steadfast
Stubborn Uninvolved Passive**

As the symbol of *slinky sexuality*, the *S* sound (and the softly pronounced letter *C*) is responsible for all things, *sexual, celebratory, sassy, sultry, sensual* and *slippery*. So when it occurs in words initialized by the maternal letter *M,* it's responsible for the soft seduction in the words *massage, moist, misty-eyed, mushy* and *modesty*. That's why, even though most *MS* people are known to be warm and emotionally available, there's a little of the cheeky flirt in every one.

If, on your first meeting with an *MS* he or she appears shy and reserved, you should be aware that this is just a smokescreen. The reality is, these are driven people who know precisely what they want from life and have few qualms about how they go about getting it. Mind you, *MSs* are not particularly selfish in fulfilling their ambitions; they're just committed to living life to its fullest and see no reason to beat about the bush. Things usually fall into place for these people even if they don't seem to be working any harder than anyone else, so if it seems strange that your *MS* friends are never in a hurry, don't make the mistake of thinking they have nothing going on. With such a clear sense of direction there's no need to get their bonnets in a knot.

Despite their unruffled exteriors, *MS* people tend to feel a touch of claustrophobia when their lives get too busy or cluttered. They don't require a great deal of space in which to be productive, but there's an inner restlessness that drives them to keep reinventing themselves. This is why, when it comes to their careers, they're almost always better off taking jobs in sales, customer service or even the travel industry . . . anything that allows for easy transfers and a high degree of freedom. The *MSs'* blend of natural caution and worldly intelligence also makes them ideal small business owners and managers. In most cases they are frugal and shrewd about how they spend their time and money, and although you wouldn't characterize them as miserly, it's unlikely that they'd be the ones to buy the first round.

When it comes to friendship and relationships in general, *MSs* are invariably demonstrative and can be counted on to come through in a pinch. Romance, while welcome in the *MS'* world, is not always at the top of their priority lists, although flirting certainly is. It's not that *MSs* aren't able to function in monogamous relationships, it's just that they don't have the same enthusiasm for them as do traditional romantics. The longer they take to settle down, the better their chances for enjoying enduring unions.

Macey
Maci
Macie
Macy
Mason
Misael
Missy
Moises
Moses

Macy Gray Critics stumble over adjectives in their quest to define Macy Gray's singing style . . . "passionate," "smoky," "soulful," "opaque," etc. But the one that Macy prefers is "real." Her trademark raspy sound has helped define the distiction between hip-hop and the genres of rock and rap. ■ As a child, Macy had an admittedly "strange speaking voice." Not only did she not sing as a youngster but she refused to speak for a long time as well. It was only after some musician friends asked her to help out that her career took off. ■ Macy's "I Try" video landed her the award for the MTV Video Music Award's Best New Artist, and even though she is unlikely to ever enjoy mainstream status, her distinctive music has found a group of hardcore fans.

THE FLIRTATIOUS *msh*

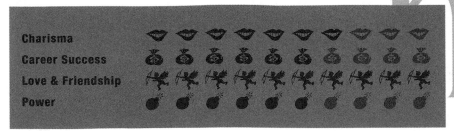

Charisma
Career Success
Love & Friendship
Power

Youthful Lively Graceful
Immature Sarcastic Complacent

Machelle
Marisha
Marsha
Marshalll
Mechelle
Michel
Michele
Michell
Michelle
Misha
Moshe

The soft hush of the *SH* phoneme signifies a sense of warmth and safety. It is the sound that mothers make to soothe their babies and its gentle tones account for the words *hush, mushy, bashful, shalom, shy* and *elfish*. And since the letter *M* evokes a *motherly* and *maternal* resonance, these are clearly names that proclaim people with delightfully placid spirits. But make no mistake, *MSHs* are not milquetoasts who need to be told how to live their lives. These are people who know their way around the universe and have the drive and ambition to go anywhere they damn well please.

The first thing you'll notice about *MSH* personalities is their penchant for broad displays of affection (at least toward their close friends). They are so filled with goodwill that there's more than enough to go around. They'll be the first to offer you a happy-injection when you're feeling down then buy you a drink if it doesn't take.

Stress doesn't affect these people as much as the rest of us, but for all their devil-may-care attitudes they are extraordinarily focused and deliberate. They are goal-oriented people who plan for the worst and hope for the best.

MSH people are talented at so many things that it's hard for them to stay humble . . . at least that's how *they* view themselves. Such is their self-confidence that it doesn't matter to them if others agree. While they may struggle with their egos here and there, there's no denying that the world benefits from their talents and positive outlooks. If *MSHs* always seem to be taking a stand about something, it's usually altruistic in nature and always with good intentions. It's this combination of selflessness and self-assurance that enables them to fulfill their larger purpose . . . making the world a better place.

It's true that *MSHs* are willing to laugh at themselves, but everyone knows that their emotional poise is easily disrupted by personal conflict. Their response to friction in their intimate relationships is to ignore the problem for as long as possible in the hope it will go away by itself. So if your *MSH* friend has done something to embarrass him or herself, you should pretend that you didn't notice.

MSHs make for dependable and affectionate mates even if they often fall into the high-maintenance category. It may be too much to call them *demanding,* but partners who expect their relationships to maintain their equilibrium had better have strong backbones and correspondingly healthy egos.

Marshall McLuhan In a memorable scene from Woody Allen's Academy Award-winning film *Annie Hall,* Woody humiliates a self-important Marshall McLuhan "expert" who's waiting in line for a movie by pulling Marshall out of a poster to tell the man, "You know nothing of my work." ■ As an author and communications technologist, Marshall made his mark as a culture and media critic. He is best-known for his works *Understanding Media* and *The Medium is the Message,* in which he postulates that the form of media is more significant than its actual content. ■ Marshall eventually became a consultant to General Electric, IBM and Bell. "Ads are news," he said. "The problem is that they are always good news." ■ "Marshall was a serious-faced Lewis Carroll. Nobody knew what the hell he was saying."—Tom Wolfe

Charisma	👄	👄	👄	👄	👄	👄	👄	👄	👄	👄
Career Success	💰	💰	💰	💰	💰	💰	💰	💰	💰	💰
Love & Friendship										
Power	💣	💣	💣	💣	💣	💣	💣	💣	💣	💣

**Decisive Confident Outgoing
Condescending Insensitive Pushy**

Although the letter *M* is the symbol of all things *motherly, maternal, matronly* and *maidenly*, it loses some of its knee-jerk sentimentality when combined with the *tightly-wound, triumphant* and *trumpeting* letter *T*. This is why *MT* combination so often appears in words that exhibit a distinct bite: *mint, mettle, molten, mutiny, martyr, meaty* and *metal*. If *MT* people exude confident and self-assured airs that sometimes border on smirks, there's usually a good reason for this: they are people who manage to get their own way without being overbearing or offensive (most of the time).

MTs are adept at hiding their inner motives and many people think that they're a little too smooth for their own good. But *MTs* aren't intentionally malicious and really don't understand why anyone would ever question their motives. To their way of thinking there can't be anything wrong with going after what you want. Besides, isn't it all just part of the game of life in which nothing is so serious that it can't be laughed over a round of drinks?

Still, *MTs* aren't above putting their own needs ahead of others when the stakes are high enough, and even close friends will sustain a few bruises if they inadvertently get in the way of the *MTs'* carefully laid plans.

Mateo
Matilda
Matilde
Mat
Matteo
Mattie
Meta
Misti
Mistie
Misty
Mitch
Mitchel
Mitchell
Mitzi
Montana
Monte
Monty

If you rarely see *MTs* procrastinating, it's because they are experts at making themselves at least *look* productive. But they aren't the sort to dawdle when they get up in the morning and usually have their entire days planned in advance. This kind of single-mindedness proves to be beneficial in the workplace where employers often hold them up as examples. Their ability to sniff the wind for new business possibilities makes them ideal in sales, R&D, design, and computer programming, but *MTs* work best alone and don't like to be bothered with what they consider trivialities: office gossip and social affairs. But just because *MTs* don't like to mix business and pleasure doesn't mean that they're loners. On the contrary; they thrive on emotional exchanges and are quite unsettled when deprived of intimate human contact for any length of time.

MTs' confidence really comes to the fore when it involves matters of the heart. If someone happens to catch their eye, they won't believe for a second that they're not going to be able to make headway. Even an outright rejection will be taken as a direct challenge and many *MTs* admit that their current spouse had to be won over with some perseverance. Judging by the high success rate of *MT* marriages, it pays to have the persistence of a telemarketer.

Matt Damon Many people's first exposure to Matt Damon was when he and long-time friend Ben Affleck accepted their Best Screenplay Oscar for *Good Will Hunting* in 1998. ■ Matt's acting career had never strayed far from that of his buddy Ben. At the age of sixteen, the pair decided to try to hit it big in New York (against the wishes of their parents) and Matt quickly landed parts in *Mystic Pizza* and *The Good Mother*. After a brief stint at Harvard, he returned to L.A. where his filmography includes some of the biggest money-makers of the decade: *Dogma, The Talented Mr. Ripley, All the Pretty Horses, The Legend of Bagger Vance, Finding Forrester, Ocean's Eleven, The Majestic* and *The Bourne Identity*.

mth

Charisma	👄👄👄👄👄👄👄👄👄👄
Career Success	💰💰💰💰💰💰💰💰💰💰
Love & Friendship	👼👼👼👼👼👼👼👼👼👼
Power	💣💣💣💣💣💣💣💣💣💣

Insightful Forward-thinking Amiable
Holier-than-thou Unrealistic Defiant

The softly comforting sounds of the *TH* phoneme are responsible for the reassuring essence found in the words *mother, father, thanks, therapy, thoughtful, theism* and *thrive*. So when it occurs in names initialized by the *maternal, motherly* and *merciful M*, these names take on a distinctly parental flavor that suggests people who are very comfortable with themselves but perhaps a little too concerned with the issues of others.

It should be said that *MTHs* aren't the kind of people to make rash decisions. While most of us don't even know what we're going to do tomorrow, your *MTH* friend probably has the next ten years all planned out. These are take-charge people who won't sit around waiting for something to happen; they know where they're going and spend a lot of time reckoning how to get there.

MTHs have a sense of obligation to all living things and are typically enmeshed in rich and profoundly spiritual philosophies. They're believers in the dictum that everything happens for a reason and their unquenchable faith in the ways of the universe is the foundation on which they build their successful lives. Their outstanding communication skills make them fine motivators and leaders, although with their aversion to confrontation they are not the proselytizing types.

Marth
Martha
Mathew
Matthew
Meredith
Merideth
Meridith
Mirtha

The *MTHs'* natural leadership skills come in handy in the workplace and, even though people with *M* names are on the bottom of the list when it comes to making money, *MTHs* are notable exceptions. This is particularly true when *MTHs* feel a sense of ownership in their work, and employers would be well advised to allow their *MTH* employees to write their own job-descriptions.

Falling in love with an *MTH* is easy. But before they're going to fall in love with *you*, you're going to have to prove your mettle. As approachable as they are, these aren't the types to leap into romantic trysts unless secure in the knowledge that you are capable of loving them unconditionally. This is why *MTHs'* lovers are usually introduced to them from within their tight circle of friends, and why they always seem to share common interests and values. Having an *MTH* to cherish is definitely worth the trouble: few people pour as much energy and affection into their families as they do.

It seems fated that the nurturing *MTHs* will have children, and when they do, these offspring will be nourished with intelligent discipline and total commitment. In return for their parent's infinite patience, children will do everything they can to make their parent proud.

Matthew Broderick Matthew Broderick's personality and charm have taken him a long way in the competitive world of Hollywood and his boyish face is forever etched in his fans' minds as the title character in *Ferris Bueller's Day Off* (1986). ■ Matthew's life took a tragic turn in 1998 when, while vacationing in Ireland, he lost control of his vehicle and struck an oncoming car killing a mother and her daughter. With hospitalization and legal problems behind him, Matthew returned to the stage in Mel Brooks's adaptation of *The Producers*. His triumphant performance opposite Nathan Lane set box-office records for over a year. ■ Recently, Matthew's marriage to *Sex and the City* star Sarah Jessica Parker fruited with the birth of a son. Ferris Bueller has finally grown up.

Charisma	💋	💋	💋	💋	💋	💋	💋	💋	💋	💋
Career Success	💰	💰	💰	💰	💰	💰	💰	💰	💰	💰
Love & Friendship	🕊	🕊	🕊	🕊	🕊	🕊	🕊	🕊	🕊	🕊
Power	💣	💣	💣	💣	💣	💣	💣	💣	💣	💣

Generous Expansive Artistic
Awkward Exaggerating Clingy

The letter *V* is the unquestioned flagship of all that is *virile, vibrant, voluptuous, virtuous, vampish* and *valiant,* and whenever it occurs in a word, injects it with a sense of *vim* and a *vigorous* sexuality. The *V's* combination with the letter *M* (the symbol for all things *motherly, maternal,* and *merciful*) produces the aspect of spontaneous passion found in *motivate, movingly, impulsive, marvel, emotive, mover* and *primeval.* If your *MV* friend was an animal, he or she would be an Energizer Bunny . . . full of restless energy and (some say) a fluffy white bottom that people find irresistible.

MVs usually have plenty of irons in the fire and function best in jobs in which they can indulge their wide range of interests. *MV's* are drawn to the spotlight like commuters to Starbucks, and whether they're on stage or standing in front of a classroom, they know how to hold an audience. The *MVs'* restless energies are attractive to young children who appreciate their enthusiasm and encouragement, and those who enter the field of education are invariably successful. In addition to these talents, the *MVs'* right-brained creativity lends itself to working in the design and computer fields.

Maeve
Malvina
Marv
Marva
Marvin
Maverick
Mavis
Melva
Melvin
Melvina
Mervin
Minerva

Like most people whose names begin with the letter *M,* you wouldn't expect to find *MVs* in politics or in corporate boardrooms. *MVs* are definitely lovers, not fighters, and conflict of any kind just isn't their thing. It should also be said that even though the *MVs* are usually physically active, they're more likely to be involved in sports in which they only compete with themselves. Besides, there's that reputation for being a little klutzy.

Generous and sympathetic, *MVs* sometimes get to into trouble when they bite off more than they can chew. This particularly applies to the *MVs'* intimate relationships where they often over-invest their emotional capital, but most of the time *MV* mates prove to be devoted consorts who approach each relationship as if it was their first.

The *MVs'* most reliable unions are those that stem from comfortable best-friend relationships, but then again, if they were looking for reliability they'd buy toasters. That's why most *MVs'* get involved with partners who promise some element of excitement or even danger. For these relationships to work, their partners will have to keep up with their high-energy lifestyles: high-maintenance mates need not apply.

Marvin Gaye Marvin Gaye, the king of Motown, was born in 1939 into a strictly regimented religious world. His father's small fundamentalist Christian church permitted no drinking, no dancing and certainly no back talk. ■ Marvin got his start in music after his honorable discharged from the Air Force. Soon after marrying Anna Gordy—the sister of the founder of Motown Records—Marvin's innovative music took him to the top of the charts. His exploration of social issues ("What's Going On") and celebration of eroticism ("Let's Get It On") made a deep impression on the industry. ■ When visiting his parents' home in 1984, his father began verbally abusing his mother. While Marvin intervened, his father pulled out a gun and shot him dead. One of the music world's greatest voices had been stilled.

mx

Charisma	👄👄👄👄👄👄👄👄👄👄
Career Success	💰💰💰💰💰💰💰💰💰
Love & Friendship	🏹🏹🏹🏹🏹🏹🏹🏹🏹
Power	💣💣💣💣💣💣💣💣💣

Idealistic Quick-witted Clever
Reckless Temperamental Hard-headed

Names that incorporate the unexpected letter *X* are usually an indication of people with strong agendas (or at least the carefully cultivated illusion thereof). And even though these names are initialized by the *maternal* and *motherly* letter *M*, it's the letter *X* that gives them their individualistic flair and indelibly colors our opinions. *MXs* are full of surprises and the characteristics that separate them from the crowd can be discerned in the words *complex, flummox, mixup, minx, moxie* and *lummox*. It should be noted that the letter *N* (as in the name *Maxine*) is the symbol for *negativity* (*no, not, never, nyet, nada, nix, nothing, naught*) and suggests a hint of cynicism underlying her intricate façade. But it's true to say that *all MXs* are people with unusual destinies; the roads down which they travel are circuitous and unpaved.

As children, *MX* people were probably quite stubborn but also uncommonly intelligent. As adults, they have the potential to achieve blinding success or spectacular failure—it's a toss up whether you'll find them on the dean's list or on the list of the FBI's Most Wanted—and their sometimes-bullheaded behavior often lands them in trouble with authority. If not judiciously handled, these dynamic packages can be quite a handful. What most people don't realize is that *MXs*

Max
Maxie
Maxim
Maximilian
Maximillia
Maximus
Maxine
Maxwell

have a genuine (if secret) desire to please. This doesn't mean they're compliant in any way, but if they do have to take care of business, they'll go to great lengths to ensure that they don't come off looking like bad guys.

When *MXs* aren't out exploring, they're throwing themselves into their work. These high-energy individuals must keep moving if they hope to stave off boredom and the resulting irritability, which is why they gravitate toward careers in the travel industry or intellectually based professions like law, counseling, or accounting. As capable as they are, *MXs* typically steer clear of competitive arenas. If the *MXs are* going to compete, it'll be against themselves, so if they are going to be involved in sports or sales, it'll probably be as mentors or coaches.

Like most people whose names begin with the maternal *M*, it's almost impossible for *MXs* to turn their backs on their friends. But they don't always express their feelings in overly sentimental ways. They believe the whole mushy romantic thing to be quite overrated and are the types who give their lovers practical gifts for Christmas. If you have any gripes with their rather perfunctory styles, you shouldn't try and manipulate them with expressions of hurt; the best way to handle them is to appeal to their logic and sense of justice.

Max von Sydow Very few actors could have portrayed such a wide range of characters as successfully as Max von Sydow did. He played the gamut from the avenging father in Ingmar Bergman's *Virgin Spring* to the tormented knight in *The Seventh Seal*, to the compassionate father in *Pelle the Conqueror*. ■ Film buffs know him as Bergman's leading man, for together they created some of the greatest movies in the history of film, including *The Seventh Seal*, *Wild Strawberries*, *Brink of Life*, *Virgin Spring* and *Winter Light*. ■ Commenting on his role as Jesus in *The Greatest Story Ever Told*, Max revealed that many people on the set believed the film was a holy mission and expected him to behave in character even when not working. A number of fans thought his role was typecast.

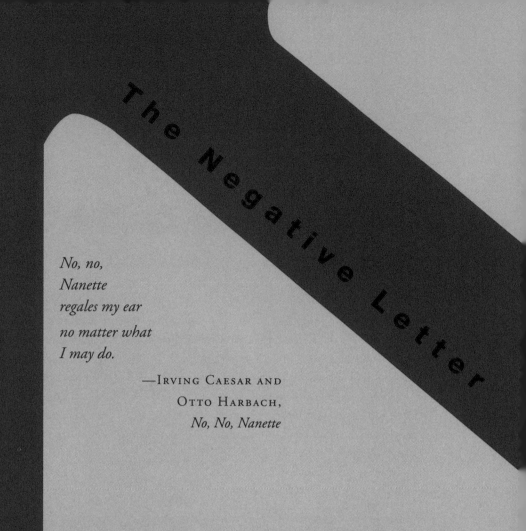

Most Popular Girl's Names

Nancy
Nicole
Norma
Natalie
Nellie
Nora
Nina
Naomi
Natasha
Nichole

Most Popular Boy's Names

Nicholas
Nathan
Norman
Nathaniel
Neil
Nelson
Nick
Neal
Noel
Nicolas

No, no,
Nanette
regales my ear
no matter what
I may do.

—IRVING CAESAR AND
OTTO HARBACH,
No, No, Nanette

The Negative Letter

The nasal sound of the letter N is similar in pronunciation to the letter M except that it's the tongue—rather than the closed lips—that modulate its humming sound. Even though the N is a close cousin to the letter M, its impact is decidedly different. There's a distinct downbeat to the letter, which initializes more negative words than any other letter in the English language and many other languages as well. ■ Consider the words no, never, none, nein, nyet, nope, not, nil, nothing, nowhere, naught, nada, nai (Japanese) and nix—all expressions of nonentities; and adjectives like nasty, naïve, nitwit, nutty, nag, Nazi, nerdy, niggle, nausea, nebbish, nefarious and nuisance. These are only a small fraction of pessimistic words that begin with the letter N. And then there's the issue of the N word, which has recently become so socially explosive as to be nigh on unutterable. Most negative prefixes also contain an N, like *non*event, *anti*social, *un*happy and *in*sane. ■ But all is not lost for the letter N, which manages to retain a number of the nurturing aspects of its cousin the M. The n even looks like half of an m, and comes somewhat close to representing motherhood in words like nana, naïveté, nanny, natal, nursing, natural, nun and Nymph—the spirit that oversees water, trees and mountains. Thses nurturing qualities may explain why N people are high on the list of people in the medical profession.■ As an initial letter for a name, the letter N occurs with only $^1/_6$ the frequency of the more maternal letter M, but as is the case with the letter M, twice as many girls' names as boys' begin with the letter N. Its nurturing influence is highlighted in the traditional meaning of Nani (charming), Nannette (gracious), Nigel (gift of God), Nalo (lovable), Naomi (pleasant) and Nathan (giver) ■

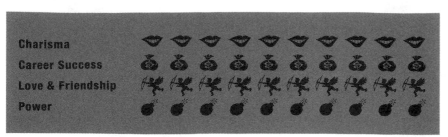

Charisma	
Career Success	
Love & Friendship	
Power	

Intelligent Warm-hearted Socially Adept
Pessimistic Impersonal Distant

The letter *N* is the icon for all that is *negative* (*no, not, never, nowhere, nyet* and *nada*), and when the *N* is the dominant consonant in a name—as in *Noah, Nia* and *Nya*—these names tend to be more conservative than most. *Ns* are determined but prudent individuals who avoid drawing attention to themselves so that they can quietly go about their business.

Nothing seems to disturb the tranquility of these steadfast creatures. One can yell, threaten or bully and *Ns* will calmly ignore the ruckus and pretend that all is well. But threaten the security or well-being of their families, and distinctly darker creatures emerge. Anyone unlucky enough to have stirred the *Ns'* passions should be prepared to backpedal immediately.

Just because *Ns* tend to avoid conflict doesn't mean that they aren't going to put in their two cents when they happen to disagree with you. The one thing that most *Ns* have in common is a love of reading, which when combined with their own quiet observations of the world, makes for quite an intimidating intellect. There's a touch of cool in the stoic *Ns*, which stems from the knowledge that they're able to handle themselves in any intellectual confrontation.

Their ability to disconnect their emotional subrou-

Nia
Noah
Noe
Nya
Nyah

tines in times of stress is a salient feature of their personal lives, for when *Ns* feel attacked or criticized, they'll react with annoying indifference and simply withdraw. The higher the heat, the cooler they become. And although it's quite astonishing how effectively *Ns* use silence as a weapon, they'll spring into action with surprising physicality when the honor of one of their loved ones is at stake.

Ns function best in careers which require attention to detail. But if you've got a big project that's been delayed and needs immediate attention, you're better off *not* giving them a call. It's not that they're lazy or slow-minded; it's just that they're so detail-oriented and pedantic that the job is going to take a while. They're likely to work themselves into a tizzy over the small things—instead of stepping back and seeing the big picture—so while they're not cut out for sales jobs or positions calling for dynamic leadership, they're perfect for design, bookkeeping, government work, or manufacturing.

When it comes to relationships and commitment, *Ns* tend to marry young. And although their marriages may lack fiery passion, unions with these faithful creatures will prove to be constant, predictable and enduring.

Nia Vardalos In the summer of 2002, a little independent movie arrived in theaters to compete with the likes of *Spider-Man* and *Star Wars: Attack of the Clones*. ■ *My Big Fat Greek Wedding*, written by, and starring Nia Vardalos, was given little chance to recoup its production costs. The film went on to become the highest grossing romantic comedy of all time. ■ Nia had been performing her one-woman show when she was approached by a number of studios interested in turning her show into a film. But none would take the risk of producing a movie with an unknown star and Nia turned down their offers. ■ Rita Wilson, wife of Tom Hanks and a second-generation Greek herself, offered to make the movie with Nia as the star, and history was made.

Charisma										
Career Success										
Love & Friendship										
Power										

**Warm Talented Gracious
Perfectionist Narrow-minded Preachy**

Although the letter *N* tends to be associated with *negativity* and pessimism, it enjoys a special relationship with the *dignified, dapper,* and *daring* letter *D*. When these two letters get together they express the kind of benign thoughtfulness found in the words: *candid, tender, kind, bland, languid, bend,* and, *mindful.* These aren't names that belong to people who make headlines; they the kind of names that go about their business in a deliberate way and make the best out of what they have.

NDs have the ability to adapt to just about any situation, which is why you'll find them in almost every career field except those that require public speaking. They are intelligent and reliable but are definitely not ladder-climbers. Seldom aggressive or pushy, *NDs* are behind-the-scenes people who prefer to facilitate rather than direct and function best as members of a team where they can rely on the group's approval before having to make major decisions.

As much as they enjoy working with others, *NDs* often choose to follow their own stars when it comes to their personal lives. Their hobbies lean towards solo pursuits, and whether it's hiking, stamp collecting, painting or just listening to music, *NDs* are secretly proud of the fact that they march to the beat of their own drums. Whatever they choose to do will bear their own unique stamp.

Nada
Nadia
Nadine
Naida
Ned
Neda
Nedra
Neida
Nelda
Nereida
Nida
Nidia
Nilda
Nydia

One nice thing about the *ND* personalities is that they're always willing to lend a sympathetic ear without expecting much in return. The only thing they'll ask is for people to take their counsel seriously (few people are as enthusiastic when it comes to doling out advice), and while their guidance is rarely intrusive or overtly controlling, they do have an unfortunate tendency to sermonize until they're satisfied that everyone has learned his or her lesson.

Even though *ND* personalities can't help but say what's on *their* minds, their own fragile emotional makeups are easily wounded by criticism. So don't try to modify their behavior unless you have a degree in diplomacy or psychology.

Since *NDs* almost never assume leadership roles in either their personal or professional lives, they need to be paired with mates who aren't going to take advantage of their pliant ways. *NDs* view marriage as a partnership of equals and will readily accommodate their mates' needs without being submissive, but when it comes to their children, these easy-going personalities reveal surprisingly resolute cores. They have that unique ability of relating to their offspring as equals without compromising their discipline or losing their respect.

Nadia Comaneci Anyone born before 1970 remembers a teeny Romanian gymnast at the Montreal Olympic Games in 1976. Up to that point, no gymnast had ever been awarded a perfect ten for any exercise in international competition. When the petite twelve-year-old finished her uneven bar, the judges were forced to award her a 1 because their scoreboards were not designed for tens. ■ After retiring from the sport, rumor had it that she was involved with the son of discredited Romanian dictator, Nicolae Ceausescu. After defecting to the U.S. in 1989, *Rolling Stone* magazine suggested that Nadia suffered from bulimia as a result of her harsh training regimen. ■ Nadia married Bart Conner, the gymnastic champion and owns a gymnastic training club in Oklahoma.

Charisma									
Career Success									
Love & Friendship									
Power									

Strong-minded Steadfast Loyal
Irritable Judgmental Defensive

When the *negative* connotations of the letter *N* combine with the forcefully pronounced letter *K*, they impart the *cantankerous* (but ultimately harmless) assertiveness found in the words: *funky, kinky, cranky, punk, drunk, junk, prank, skanky* and *flunky*. Many women (*Nikki* and *Nikky*) soften these harsh aspects through the *youthful Y* sound, which has the effect of infantilizing their names (*funny, coy, silly, goofy, happy* and *zany*). Others (*Nicole* and *Nicolette*) employ the *lively, loving, learned,* and *likeable* letter *L* to remind us of their gentle and altruistic sides. All these subliminal messages coalesce to imply willful and headstrong people bent on serving their own purposes, but with a gentility and chutzpah that suggests both sides of the equatorial spring.

Perhaps their imperviousness to criticism encourages them to behave without regard to social norms or the expectations of others. Or maybe it's simply that their unique personal styles are unencumbered by self-doubt. Whatever the reason, if you've ever befriended *NKs*, you'll be familiar with their dark moody sides *and* their beguiling charms. The problem is that you can never be quite sure, from one moment to the next, if your *NK* is going to shut you out or invite you in for homemade cookies. This pervasive sense of uncertainty creates the mystique

Nakia
Nectar
Nichol
Nicholas
Nicholaus
Nichole
Nicholle
Nick, Nicki
Nickie
Nicklaus
Nickolas
Nicky, Nico
Nicol, Nicola
Nicolas
Nicole
Nicolette
Nikhil
Niki
Nikia
Nikita
Nikki
Niko
Nikolas
Nikole

which separates the *NK* from the crowd.

If *NKs* were animals, chances are they would be foxes. Like their canine counterparts, they cannot succeed using brute force alone but must rely on their charms and sharp minds to garner resources. Consequently, *NKs* spend a lot of time in their heads, giving the impression that they're trying to outsmart their friends. But no one who really knows them would accuse them of manipulation; they are generous to a fault and their intensity is tempered with a sardonic sense of humor.

NKs expect others to be as honest about their strengths and shortcomings as they are of their own. They are anything but snobbish and are unimpressed by the usual symbols of success and status. All they need is a simple demonstration of loyalty and they'll return the favor by being faithful and dependable friends.

When cupid's arrow nails these otherwise autonomous spirits, they sometimes lose their composure and end up as helpless as shrimps on the barbie. But when they pull themselves together, you won't find any lover more devoted than they are. If you happen to be the love object of an *NK*, you may never have a sonnet written on your behalf, but you *will* be able to count on constant attention and unswerving loyalty.

Nick Nolte When a ruggedly good-looking Nick Nolte first appeared in TV's highly-rated, *Rich Man Poor Man* in 1976, his performance set the stage for a Hollywood career that would span the progression from brooding young man to kindly old father. ■ *New York* magazine called him a dysfunctional version of a Hollywood leading man and given his public struggle with drugs and three turbulent divorces. ■ Nick received an Oscar nomination for his role opposite Barbara Streisand in *The Prince of Tides* and a second Oscar nomination for the 1999 film *Affliction*. His drunk driving arrest for in 2002 did nothing to diminish his appeal.

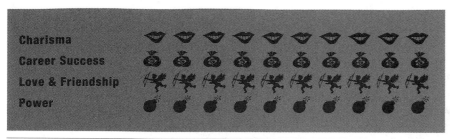

Charisma	
Career Success	
Love & Friendship	
Power	

Creative Involved Giving
Unrealistic Coquettish Over-sensitive

There are few sharp edges in the *NL* names and without any of the harsh consonantal stops of the letters *B, K, T,* and *D,* they roll off the tongue in a smooth blend of non-confrontational sounds. The *N* may be strongly associated with the *negative* aspects of the English language (*no, not, never, nowhere, nix, naught* and *nada*) but its combination with the letter *L*—the icon of the most important things in life (*love, loyalty, learning,* and *laughter*)—reflects the more altruistic aspects of human nature. This is why the *NL* phoneme plays such an important role in the words *genial, hymnal, noel, nicely, gentle* and *paternal.*

NLs are the people to call when life becomes too demanding and you need a break from reality: *NLs* don't just think outside the box, they *live* outside it. With their love for breaking convention, friends must be willing to go along with these lusty explorers lest they be left behind. They're not flighty by any means, but they always reflect a refreshingly unique point of view which can sometimes be a little annoying for the more logic-based personalities. Annoying or not, *NLs* also have a healthy dose of horse-sense, and when situations call for cool-headed logic, they'll snap out of their dreamy states long enough to get the job done.

Nallely
Nayeli
Nayely
Neal, Neely
Neil, Nelia
Nelida, Nell
Nella, Nelle
Nellie, Nelly
Napoleon
Nelson
Nigel
Nila, Nilsa
Noel, Noelia
Noella
Noelle
Nola
Nolan
Nyla

The thing to remember about *NLs* is that they're easily offended when they think they've been snubbed. Living life in such an exposed way has its risks, and *NLs* expect their friends to cut them some slack for their occasional lapses in judgment. And since it's a short distance from the *NLs'* warmly forgiving sides to their sensitive and touchy sides, friends must learn to carefully tread on the middle ground. *NLs* aren't particularly vindictive but they can make life very unpleasant for someone whom they feel has treated them with disrespect. Unfortunately, it's difficult to know when you've crossed the line because the line moves in rhythm with the *NLs'* moods.

Even though *NLs* might be formidable debaters, they are not necessarily good communicators. The problem is that they can get so caught up in what *they're* trying to say, they never get around to listening to what *you've* got to say.

With the right partner the *NLs'* potential is practically unlimited and their biggest challenge is in finding mates that can complement their tendency for emotional over-sensitivity. The danger that many *NLs* face is their tendency to make relationship choices based on their immediate emotional needs, rather than taking stock of the more practical and long-term issues of their relationships.

Neil Armstrong The most famous quote of the 20th century was a misstatement, In 1969, after years of careful planning, Neil Armstrong carefully lowered his right foot onto the surface of the moon and put his foot in his mouth with the words; "This is one small step for man, but one giant leap for mankind". What he meant to say was "... one small step for *a* man..." which has a very different meaning. ■ In the excitement of the moment no one really cared. After all, the event was of profound significance for the human race; marking the first time anyone from planet Earth had ever set foot on another world. ■ Today, the press-shy astronaut is chairman of the board an electronic systems company.

nm

Charisma	👄	👄	👄	👄	👄	👄	👄	👄	👄	👄
Career Success	💰	💰	💰	💰	💰	💰	💰	💰	💰	💰
Love & Friendship										
Power										

Elegant Warm Focused
Self-serving Smothering Irritable

Although the *nasally* pronounced letter *N* often conveys an element of *negativity* to words it initializes, it also has a *nurturing* side that can be seen in the words *nanny, natal, nourish,* and *nice.* And when the *N* teams up with the letter *M*—the powerhouse of *maternal, motherly* goodness—it generates the unmistakable sense of sensual vigor found in the words *nymph, dynamo, nimble, enigmatic* and *animalistic.* At heart, *NM* people are emotional caretakers who work hard at nourishing the people around them. Whether they do this through domestic avenues like cooking and mothering, or professional avenues like nursing, counseling or relief work, these people derive a great deal of their self worth from their altruistic exploits.

Naomi
Nehemiah
Neomi
Noemi

The *NM's* nurturing bent can prove a bit cloying to those who don't appreciate having a caretaker in their lives, and every now and then she may find herself being avoided or rebuffed. But because nothing makes the *NM* happier than when someone pays attention to their advice, they don't allow these occasional setbacks to sway them from what they believe to be their duty. Still, there are limits: An *NM's* friends will be showered with gifts and parties but far less so with hugs and kisses. Indeed, the *NM's* affections often manifest themselves with lectures and sermons on how their loved ones should conduct their lives.

NMs are humble people who derive no particular satisfaction from materialistic symbols like owning the biggest house on the block; the perfect setting for them is one in which they are surrounded by family or close friends. Their peace of mind comes from the knowledge that their relationships are growing and that their roots are strong.

Even though *NMs* would never be accused of hogging the spotlight, they're not above indulging in a little smugness from time to time . . . especially when family members achieve something special. But this kind of attention-getting is really a small part of the *NMs'* persona, and they're much happier when orchestrating events from the wings. This is why *NM* women love their homes which usually reflect their unassuming dispositions: immaculately clean kitchens and understated furniture.

But as much as *NMs* crave the security of rooted home lives, they'll be ready to move at the drop of a hat if it it's going to help their spouse with a new job or their child with a new school. This knee-jerk philanthropic attitude really defines the *NM* personality, and those who are lucky enough to have one in their lives, should *never* take them for granted.

Naomi Campbell Naomi Campbell was the first black model ever to appear on the covers of *Time* magazine and *Vogue*. As one of the original supermodels, Naomi's unique style and sophisticated approach to her profession helped break down race barriers within the fashion industry. ■ Not content with simply plying the catwalk, Naomi flirted with a career as a recording artist, and in 1995 released her debut album *Babywoman*. One of her songs, "La, La, La Love Song," even reached number one on the Japanese charts. ■ Her personal life took her to the brink of marriage with U2 guitarist, The Edge. But the pressure of being in the public eye was taking its toll. In a widely publicized spat with her flamenco dancing boyfriend, Naomi reportedly suffered a self-induced drug overdose.

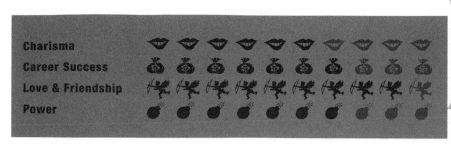

Charisma		
Career Success		
Love & Friendship		
Power		

Loving Inspiring Steady
Absent-minded Unfocused Myopic

If you need an explicit example of two negatives making a positive, consider the action of the double *N* in the *NN* names. While the letter *N* may be the symbol of *negativity* (as in the words; *no, not, nothing, never, nowhere* and *nix*), the double *N* is a manifestation of the more benign and maternal aspects of human nature: *nun, granny, manna, sunny, innocent, funny, canny, feminine, bonny* and *hosanna* (a shout of praise to God). *N* names which also incorporate the letter *C* pronounced like the *sexy S* (*Nancy* and *Nance*), are buoyed by the feminine brand of winsome charm found in the words: *fancy, flounce, dance, elegance* and *nicety*.

NNs don't have large personalities. They succeed in life by studiously avoiding the spotlight and acting as counselors to their small sets of tight friends. Like many non-aggressive people, *NNs* have highly developed instincts and powers of observation, and with penchants for ferreting out all kinds of trivia, they would make terrific news reporters or private detectives. But few *NNs* achieve great heights in their professional lives; they simply lack killer instincts and feel no great need to prove anything (at least when it comes to work). If *NNs are* going to succeed, it's because they intuitively understand that there is no future in being right when their bosses are wrong. This is why many *NNs* are drawn to the fields of education and medicine and why they excel

Nan
Nana
Nance
Nancela
Nancey
Nanci
Nancie
Nancy
Nanette
Nannette
Nannie
Nena
Nina
Nona

in endeavors that require a certain amount of patience and sensitivity.

If *NN's* cultivate an aura of nourishing energy, it's because they always seem willing to lend a helping hand. Many *NNs* have secretly concluded that there is no greater thrill than feeling needed, and they relish the fact that people turn so readily to them for advice. Their main danger in life is getting trampled on by those with bigger personalities—especially since they're so willing to give in to the needs of others—and this plants the seeds of resentment in the *NN's* caring bosom. Many grow wary as they mature, estranging old friends and keeping new ones at bay.

Honest? Absolutely. But these are people who believe the arrow of truth should be dipped in honey. At worst you'll get a gently sarcastic comment here and there, but they aren't the kind to actually put anyone down (at least to their face).

If you're looking for love, you're in luck, but if you're expecting a lot of physical demonstration you'll probably be disappointed. The *NNs* will certainly bring you chicken soup when you're feeling under the weather and their bedside manners have all the touchy-feeliness that nine out of ten patients prefer, but their brand of sensuality has everything to do with emotional connectedness and much less to do with overt physicality.

Nina Simone Jazz legend Nina Simone was born Eunice Kathleen Waymon in 1933, and like almost all disadvantaged child prodigies of that era, got her musical start at the local church singing in the choir. ■ By the age of ten, Nina had her first encounter with racism during a public performance at the town library. Her parents were evicted from their front-row seats in order to make room for some late arriving white patrons. ■ Taking a job in a piano bar in Atlantic City, she adopted the stage name, Nina Simone. (Nina means girl in Spanish and Simone was a nod to actress Simone Signoret.)

Charisma										
Career Success										
Love & Friendship										
Power										

Passionate Romantic Persistent
Repressive Gloomy Nagging

When the *negative* letter *N* initializes a name that features the *racy, randy, romantic, randy* and *ravishing* letter *R*, it invokes an image of a passionate person tempered by a conservative core. This is why the *NR* phoneme is responsible for so many zealous words with a veneer of controlling authority: *anger, blunder, snarl, enrage, control, hunter, nervy* and *snort*. *NRs* are authoritative people with a strong paternal (or maternal) bent. It's not that they don't have a sense of humor mind you; it's just that they're so focused on getting the job done that they don't have much time for life's more genteel pleasures.

It's hard to offend *NRs*—but don't think it's because they aren't smart enough to know when they've been insulted—their skins are just too thick to take someone's uninformed opinion to heart. They go about their lives with steady and purposeful airs, their feet planted firmly on the ground and their minds looking ten moves ahead. And if you want to see an *NR* in super-hero mode, wait until a loved one needs their assistance. Their extraordinary protectiveness has them recognized as the parental figures within their peer groups, so if you're tired of single-handedly slaying life's dragons, you'll be relieved have an *NR* in your corner. Exciting? Maybe not. Dependable? To the core.

Nasir
Nora
Norbert
Norberto
Noreen
Norene
Norine
Norma
Norman
Normand
Norris

You'll never have to worry about motivating these energetic souls. They're the ones who have the day's to-do list completed before the rest of us even get out of bed. The problem is that all this 'doing' can take precedence over 'being', which often proves a source of frustration for their mates. Still, there'll be plenty of time for intimate conversation as long as you're willing to join your *NR* friends on their hiking jaunts up Mt. Neverbeenclimbed.

As parents, it's hard for *NRs* to abandon the notion that old-fashioned discipline is the best way to establish control. It's not that they believe that dictatorial control is a means to an end, but if it worked for them when *they* were kids then dammit, it's good enough for their children. These conservative characteristics are typical of personalities who find life relatively easy and don't understand why other people seem to struggle so much. Still, they'll be willing to concede that old ideas aren't necessarily best, as long as *you're* willing to concede that new ideas aren't automatically better either. All things considered, *NMs* are the most protective parents anywhere. "All" they'll ever ask from their children is to make them proud by living up to their expectations.

Norman Schwarzkopf The first General Norman Schwarzkopf served in World War I and was the man in charge of the investigation of the Lindbergh baby kidnapping. The second General Norman Schwarzkopf was destined to outrank his father and lead his country to a resounding military victory in the First Gulf War. ■ Norman Schwarzkopf says that the Army was his life. His official title became Commander in Chief, United States Central Command, and Commander of Operations of Desert Shield and Desert Storm, but to his troops he was just The Bear. ■ The burly commander always had the unquestioned respect of his men and women. "It doesn't take a hero to order men into battle. It takes a hero to be one of those men who goes into battle."—Norman Schwarzkopf

THE SOFTIE

nsh

Charisma	👄	👄	👄	👄	👄	👄	👄	👄	👄	👄
Career Success	💰	💰	💰	💰	💰	💰	💰	💰	💰	💰
Love & Friendship	🕊	🕊	🕊	🕊	🕊	🕊	🕊	🕊	🕊	🕊
Power	💣	💣	💣	💣	💣	💣	💣	💣	💣	💣

**Intelligent Independent Enigmatic
Aloof Uncommunicative Inattentive**

Because the letter *N* is the definitive symbol of all things *negative,* names that begin with this *nasal* letter are usually accompanied by a sense of pessimism and self-doubt. In the case of the *NSH* names, however, the *N*'s effects are modulated by the gentlest sound in the English language: the *SH* phoneme. When a mother wants to soothe or *hush* a crying baby she instinctively makes use of its non-threatening high-pitched tones to communicate *shelter* and *friendship,* which is why the *SH* sound dominates protective words like: *shroud, shade, shepherd, shield, sheepish, shrink* and *cherish.*

NSHs glide through life with natural grace, as if some higher cause were sanctifying their path. But these are also are people who, upon first meeting them, can come across as closed and standoffish. You can't quite put your finger on it. Is it arrogance, shyness, or just plain bad-manners? After taking just a *little* effort to get to know them, you'll find out that it's their reluctance to intrude on your personal space. When dealing with these gentle sprites you'll also discover that more can be communicated with a few well-chosen moments of silence than could ever be said with words. But these elusive personalities aren't just wandering flower children; there's a bit of the wise guy in the way they partic-

Nash
Nastassja
Natascha
Natasha
Natashia
Natisha
Natosha

ipate in life with raised eyebrows and an appreciation of irony. Some may say this is sarcasm, but to the *NSH,* it's simply realism tinged with a dry sense of humor.

NSHs believe that self-improvement can only come through hard work and they almost always rise to the top of whatever field they enter. They are drawn to careers that offer challenges beyond the normal, but would rather not work too closely with the general public. They prefer jobs that offer more intimate one-to-one personal contact.

Never ones to parade their stellar qualities, *NSHs* prefer keeping their profiles low. This doesn't mean they're not above showing off every now and then (like when potential mates come along), but it can prove difficult to *really* get to know them in matters of the heart. Although they'll make little attempt to disguise their emotions and will readily display their moods, their communication style is somewhat abstract. And if your relationship with the *NSH* is plagued by chronic mood swings, remember that these are restless souls whose inner voices are constantly nagging them to find that one true love. This isn't to say that they don't have a huge capacity for intimacy; they just can't bring themselves to settle for anything less than perfection.

Nastassja Kinski German born Nastassja Nakszynski once served five days in prison after failing to pay for public transportation and refusing to take care of the fines. ■ One of her biggest fans was director Roman Polanski (now on the lam from U.S. charges of statutory rape) who gave her the title role in *Tess.* Even though the film was a critical success, Natasha was unable to maintain the kind of substantial roles actresses need to fuel their careers. ■ Her role in *Cat People* in 1982 did make people sit up and take notice, but probably had more to do with her epidermis than her acting talents. ■ Natasha, who has a child with music producer Quincy Jones, was also famous for her best-selling poster which depicted her naked embrace with a python.

297

Charisma	😗 😗 😗 😗 😗 😗 😗 😗 😗 😗
Career Success	💰 💰 💰 💰 💰 💰 💰 💰 💰
Love & Friendship	🕊 🕊 🕊 🕊 🕊 🕊 🕊 🕊 🕊 🕊
Power	💣 💣 💣 💣 💣 💣 💣 💣 💣 💣

**Reverent Faithful Capable
Stuffy Distant Evasive**

Many *N* names are known for their conformist bent but the *NT* names fairly vibrate with sober traditionalism. The letter *N* is the symbol of all things *negative* and the letter *T* is the icon of all things *traditional* (*truth, theology, Ten Commandments, testament, tabernacle* and *Torah*). So when these letters occur in the same word , they predictably describe people with hardcore *earnest* and *pedantic* views: *senator, knight, gentleman, saint* and *tyrant.* These are people who often take positions of quiet leadership within their communities and to whom friends are comfortable turning for advice and guidance. But if few people seek them out for their sympathetic ear, it's because with all their high-minded ideals, they tend to be somewhat dismissive of those who can't (or won't) fix their own problems.

If you're looking for someone with a wacky sense of humor, you might want to look elsewhere. For *NTs* are mostly serious people who don't see the point in wasting time with games when they could be doing something useful. These sober-minded individuals are more likely to spend their downtimes refining their tax returns than kicking back in a hammock.

The *NTs'* serious approach pays off in the workplace where they're in high demand for jobs with high levels of trust and responsibility. And whether it's as

Nestor
Nettie
Newt
Natividad
Newton
Nita

accountants, lawyers, community leaders, or managers, the *NTs'* brusque style gets results. A significantly high percentage of *N*-names are found in the medical fields and, if *NT* were doctors, they'll probably end up administering the hospital.

You can often recognize *NTs* by their stature and carriage. Whether tall or short, overweight or skinny, the dignified *NTs* carry their heads high with a focused expression that serves to reminds you that their minds are in constant operation. On first meeting them, you'll notice that they like to take control of the conversation—peppering you with questions about where you went to college and what your goals are. And this is no small talk either. They are genuinely interested in what you have to say and it all will be stored for later retrieval for when next you meet. But just because *NTs* are patient listeners doesn't mean that they're going to follow your advice. While they might confide in you about some personal issue, they are more apt to internalize their feelings and dissect their problems in their own way.

Partnering such a high-minded person can be exasperating if you're the type that prefers shopping malls to serious debates on the issues of the day. But if you share the *NT's* optimistic ideals and old-fashioned views, you just might have a match made in heaven.

Newt Gingrich There was a time in American politics when it seemed that Newt Gingrich was firmly on track towards the ultimate political job of President of The United States. ■ In 1995, the then Speaker of the House had ushered in a new era in politics with his powerfully popular conservative agenda and as the architect of the Republican's Contract with America, Newt rode roughshod over congressional Democrats. ■ Although history has yet to fully pass judgment, it might conclude that Newt's obsession with impeaching President Clinton led to a lack of focus in the Republican agenda and the loss of five Republican seats in the House in the 1998 elections. ■ Newt shouldered much of the blame for his party's poor showing and stepped down from his powerful position as Speaker of the House.

Charisma									
Career Success									
Love & Friendship									
Power									

Idealistic Prudent Meticulous
Proud Meddlesome Proud

Although the letter *N* tends to be associated with negativity and conservatism, it enjoys a special relationship with the thoughtful *TH* phoneme, which is associated with the introspective words: *thoughtful, theological, thankful, thorough, theory* and *thespian*. When words contain both the letter *N* and the *TH* combination, they tend to express an energetic brand of meditative *strength* found in the words *zenith, anthem, enthuse, enthrall, top-notch* and *neolith*. *NTHs* are highly principled personalities who would never use their strength to intimidate others, but for some reason, it can take some time for people to warm up to them. People often report feeling simultaneously vulnerable and protected in their presence.

NTHs embody a masculine gentility that recalls the romance of a bygone era. With an abiding respect for loyalty and honesty, they make for valuable business partners and priceless friends, but if you think that *NTHs* are the very definition of Renaissance men, that would be going too far. Let's just say that *NTHs* seem to have their whole lives planned out and their decisions are always carefully and logically constructed.

If people (eventually) end up putting their faith in their *NTH* friends, it's not only because of their quiet

Nathan
Nathanael
Nathanial
Nathaniel

certainty but also for their eerie insights into human nature. They are quite adept at making snap judgments about people and even if they happen to be wrong, they'll simply chalk it up as a learning experience. But it's a wholly different story when someone else points out *their* shortcomings: the guarded *NTHs* don't believe that anyone knows them well enough to make these kinds of judgments.

The *NTHs'* abundant emotional capital makes them perfect for jobs requiring high levels of trust and strength of character . . . perhaps as judges, airplane pilots or even politicians. Though people draw strength from their presence, they don't always feel a need to return the sentiment—preferring to work on their own or with carefully selected groups of close associations.

Because the opposite sex is so readily attracted to their respectable appeal, *NTHs* usually have a plentiful supply of lovers and feel no urgency to settle down. When *NTHs do* decide to tie the knot, it's usually with someone who offsets their conservative styles and imparts some much needed levity. Partnering these headstrong men will be no picnic but will be an educational experience for anyone with the patience to break through their self-satisfied dispositions.

Nathan Lane Nathan Lane seemed to come out of nowhere when he bowled over critics and audiences with his flamboyant rendition of Robin Williams' partner in *The Birdcage*, Mike Nichols remake of *La Cage aux Folles*. ■ The truth is that Nathan had been making movies since 1997. His films included *Ironweed*, *Joe Versus the Volcano*, *Frankie and Johnny* and *Addams Family Values*. Nathan also lent his voice to the meerkat, Timon, in Disney's big-budget animated *The Lion King*. ■ It's rare when a motion picture star makes bigger waves on the stage than he does on the screen, but Nathan arguably did exactly this as Max Bialystock in the hugely successful Mel Brooks Broadway production of *The Producers* in 2001. Co-starring Matthew Broderick, the show was responsible for a Broadway revival.

THE BALANCED
ntl

Charisma										
Career Success										
Love & Friendship										
Power										

Self-assured Loving Elegant
Repressive Self-centered Scattered

Although the letter *N* is usually associated with expressions of pessimism, its *negative* qualities are somewhat moderated by the *N's* close contact with the *triumphantly trumpeting T* and the letter *L* (the symbol of *life, laughter, love, liberty* and *learning*). It's significant that most of the *NTL* names are terminated with the youthful letter *Y* (or *IE*): its high-pitched sound adds a distinctly playful aspect to these otherwise steady names. These women have a spiritual poise that's difficult to define and quite irresistible to those whose paths they cross.

Aesop once said that no act of kindness, no matter how small, is ever wasted, and it seems as if *NTLs* have taken him at his word: *NTLs* make it their business to know everyone in town (and be on good terms with them), so if you ever need an introduction to someone, you should start by giving them a call. Appearances are important to *NTLs* who enjoy the finer things in life, but it would be a mistake to dismiss them as prissy; they have no problem with getting their hands dirty in the service of their friends.

NTLs are known for their sense of style and tend to be the fashion leaders within their social groups. All the world's their stage and they're star players. Their genteel style works for them in other ways as well... they're frightfully well spoken with a flair for

Natalia
Natalie
Nataly
Natalya
Nathalia
Nathalie
Nathaly

saying the right things at the most awkward times.

When it comes to their careers, *NTLs* usually parley their abundant social skills into personal—if not financial—advantage. Like most people whose names begin with an *N*, they are well suited for the arts (music, acting, writing and design), which dovetails nicely with their strong affinity for the spotlight. As long as their work holds the promise of a creative outlet, they'll be satisfied and stable.

There's something about the graceful way the *NTL* carries herself that makes her eminently attractive to the opposite sex. For all her natural poise, the *NTL* is never condescending and has a strong sense of justice and fair play that is particularly evident in her intimate affairs. Perhaps it stems from her (sometimes frantic) need for balance, but she has the gift of seeing both sides of an issue... even when emotionally embroiled in one of her infrequent arguments.

The *NTL* will simply not tolerate playing second fiddle in her relationships. She's not seeking to dominate her partner or anything; it's just that she expects the respect that comes from being an equal partner. The *NTL* was born to be a parent and will fret endlessly over the well-being of her brood. She may be overprotective, but her children will always feel safe and wanted.

Natalie Portman Natalie Portman startled film critics by demonstrating a range far beyond her twelve years when she played the sidekick of a professional hit man in *The Professional*. ■ The extraordinarily demanding emotional role was an auspicious debut, but it's ironic that she's best known for playing a role that demands almost nothing of her generous acting talents—that of Princess Amidala in the prequels to the *Star War Trilogy*. ■ Natalie's beauty was evident even as a child and she was encouraged to pursue a career in modeling. After catching the acting bug and landing her role in *The Professional*, Natalie followed up by appearing in *Heat, Beautiful Girls* and *Mars Attacks*. She also played key roles in the comedy dramas, *Anywhere but Here* and *Where the Heart Is*.

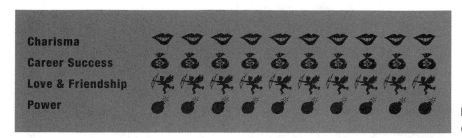

Charisma	
Career Success	
Love & Friendship	
Power	

Devoted Truthful Subtle
Cranky Maudlin Critical

The letter *N* is usually associated with the *negative* aspects of the human condition, and when it occurs in words that contain the *virile, valiant,* and *vigorous letter V*, tends to express concepts with edgy emotional dispositions: *nervy, envy, naïve, pensive, snivel, invalid, connive, anvil* and *vindictive.* So while these names may proclaim vitality and verve, there's also a distinct element of disquieting pessimism that pervades the *NVs'* lives.

Many *NVs* seem to have a nagging case of foot-in-mouth disease. These people may mean well, but their irrepressible enthusiasm often clouds their better judgments and makes them appear a little socially clumsy. But somehow, *NV's* trundle though life collecting more friends than they know what to do with (although they certainly don't do it the classical *Dale Carnegie* way). What they lack in tact, they more than make up for with their disarming honesty and engaging smiles.

NVs enjoy a little mystery in their lives and are not above cultivating reputations for being unpredictable. For all their social nonconformity, *NVs* are surprisingly articulate with a flair for saying the most interesting things at the most interesting times. And if it's true what they say in the insurance business—that there are no

Nev
Neva
Neve
Nevaeh
Neville

accidents, only mistakes—*NVs* certainly make more than their fair share of mistakes. Perhaps it's all their nervous energy that makes them so accident-prone but, whatever the cause, *NVs* are quick to apologize and move on with their lives. They also have extraordinarily expressive faces; so don't be surprised if they're walking around with self-satisfied grins. Just chalk it up to another example of the *NVs'* peculiar combination of gracelessness and charm.

Like most people whose name begins with the letter *N, NVs* are musically and artistically inclined, with many nursing secret dreams of playing the big-time. These aren't your typically overly-communicative types, mind you, for when problems crop up, they'd rather dip into their own emotional wells rather than taking their issues public.

Change is hardly threatening to *NVs*. In fact they welcome it and, on occasion, will even hunt it down. If there is something that can destabilize their otherwise productive lives, it's that creeping sense of ennui when things get too predictable. Whether it's a work project, a new relationship, or just a good book, *NVs* have to have *something* passionate in their lives if they're going to get out on the right side of the bed in the morning.

Neve Campbell Neve (pronounced Nev) Campbell took her stage name from her mother's maiden name, which means snow in Italian. At age nine, she was accepted into the prestigious National Ballet of Canada, but the pressure of five years of training proved overwhelming and Neve had to quit: "I basically had a nervous breakdown." ■ Taking a cue from her drama teacher father, Neve took up acting and made a name for herself on Fox's hit television show, *Party of Five*. ■ Her first film, *The Craft*, enjoyed moderate success but her next movie, Wes Craven's *Scream*, cemented her to young audiences. In her role as an angst-ridden teen, Neve's character dealt with a killer inspired by Hollywood's horror movies. ■ Neve divorced her husband of two years, actor Jeff Colt, in 1998.

**Most Popular
Girl's Names**

Olga
Opal
Olivia
Olive
Ora
Ollie
Ola
Ofelia
Odessa
Ophelia

**Most Popular
Boy's Names**

Oscar
Otis
Oliver
Orlando
Omar
Owen
Orville
Otto
Ollie
Odell

*And there, in fright, with one foot out,
Made one dead step and turned about.
Heeh, hee, oh! oh! ooh! oo! Look there!
And oh! so playsome, oh! so fair.*

—William Barnes,
The Surprise

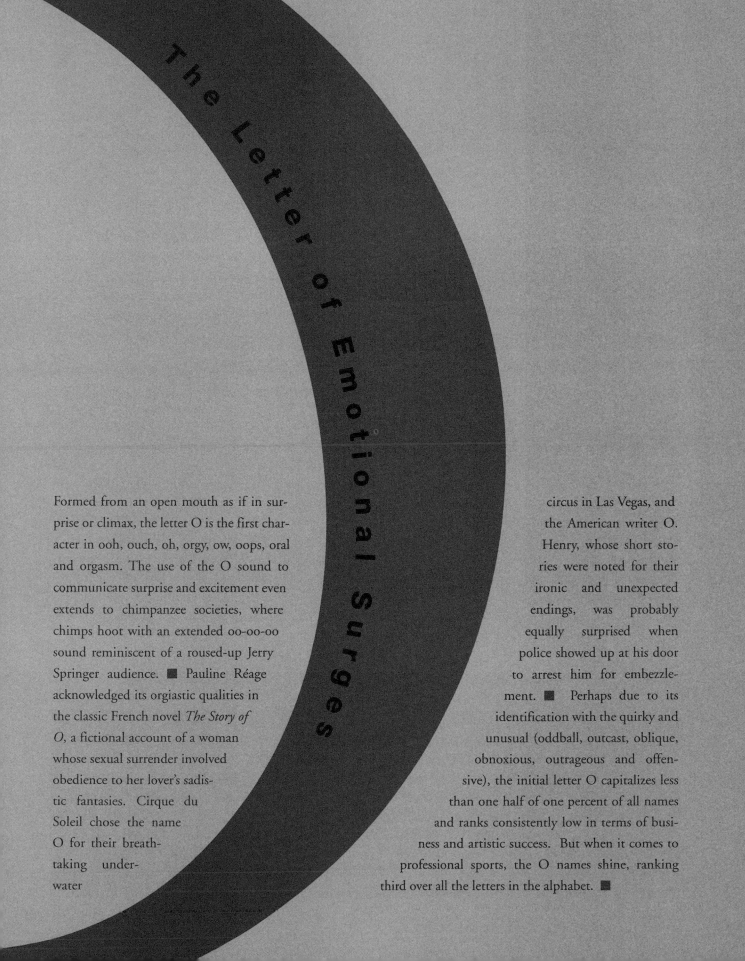

The Letter of Emotional Surges

Formed from an open mouth as if in surprise or climax, the letter O is the first character in ooh, ouch, oh, orgy, ow, oops, oral and orgasm. The use of the O sound to communicate surprise and excitement even extends to chimpanzee societies, where chimps hoot with an extended oo-oo-oo sound reminiscent of a roused-up Jerry Springer audience. ■ Pauline Réage acknowledged its orgiastic qualities in the classic French novel *The Story of O,* a fictional account of a woman whose sexual surrender involved obedience to her lover's sadistic fantasies. Cirque du Soleil chose the name O for their breathtaking underwater circus in Las Vegas, and the American writer O. Henry, whose short stories were noted for their ironic and unexpected endings, was probably equally surprised when police showed up at his door to arrest him for embezzlement. ■ Perhaps due to its identification with the quirky and unusual (oddball, outcast, oblique, obnoxious, outrageous and offensive), the initial letter O capitalizes less than one half of one percent of all names and ranks consistently low in terms of business and artistic success. But when it comes to professional sports, the O names shine, ranking third over all the letters in the alphabet. ■

THE UNLIKELY
od

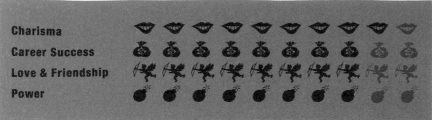

Charisma										
Career Success										
Love & Friendship										
Power										

**Emotive Generous Excitable
Spoiled Bossy Conceited**

The emotionally impulsive letter *O's* promise of excited surprise gives these names a flighty and restless quality. But it's the *darkly disciplined* letter *D*, that grounds the *OD* names and suggests a woman with a firm grip on reality. This girl has a big heart; one she wears boldly on her sleeve while always maintaining her quiet sense of dignity.

Though her extroverted persona might prove somewhat intimidating to some, an *OD* would never think of acting with malicious intent. She is simply an independent spirit who believes in spreading her goodwill to everyone. This is because the *OD* loves nothing so much as being loved, and can't (happily) exist without feeling admired by others. So when she *does* feel disrespected, expect her dramatic side to kick in and produce a great deal of bluster. Still, it must be remembered that it's a warm heart that beats at the core of her tempest, and the *OD* is more than willing to salve any wounds she may have opened.

OD personalities also display an independent streak that borders on bossiness. While not impossibly overbearing, those who share a workplace with *ODs* soon come to understand that they're compelled to do things in their own way and time. And they're not shy about cajoling others to follow their leads either, for it can be said that in climbing the ladder of success, the *OD* will use whatever foothold she can find . . . including other people's heads. Still, for the most part, they're driven by a desire to see their employers' businesses succeed.

Those who have fallen in love with an *OD* should know that the surest way to her heart is through a little flattery. It's not that she's more vain than the rest of us, but is a little more needy than most when it comes to feeling appreciated. If you're worshipping her, you're probably overdoing it, but by all means pull out all the stops when it comes to courting her—flowers, puppies and champagne will do nicely. And no matter how diffident she seems, as long she believes that you're making a genuine effort she'll topple like a tree in the wind. Just be ready to sow what you've reaped, for the emotional *OD* never outgrows her thirst for attention.

Children of an *OD* can expect a well-defined routine of discipline from their somewhat over-protective mother. But when it comes to birthdays and holidays, with her childlike approach to having fun, she knows how to show her kids and mate a good time.

Odalys
Odell
Odessa
Odette
Odile
Odis

Odette Hallowes Odette Hallowes was a French wartime resistance heroine. Married to an Englishman and living in London in the 1930's, she responded to a BBC appeal for information about the coast of Northern Europe. ■ Trained as a spy and sent to France in 1942, Odette was arrested by the Gestapo and sent to Paris for interrogation where she suffered horrifying tortures—including having her toenails pulled out. After refusing to make any admissions of importance, she was condemned to death and sent to Ravensbrück where the sentence was never carried out. ■ After her liberation, Odette returned home unable to walk properly until an operation restored her mobility. Her exploits were transformed into the successful 1950's film, *Odette*, which brought international fame to her and her husband, Peter Churchill.

THE GENTLE Ol

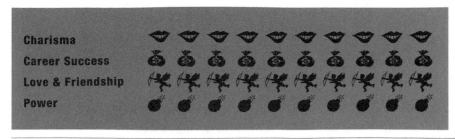

Charisma	👄	👄	👄	👄	👄	👄	👄	👄	👄	👄
Career Success	💰	💰	💰	💰	💰	💰	💰	💰	💰	
Love & Friendship	🏹	🏹	🏹	🏹	🏹	🏹	🏹	🏹	🏹	
Power	💣	💣	💣	💣	💣	💣	💣	💣		

Gracious Simple Hospitable
Absent-minded Predictable Distracted

The letter *O* is responsible for the sense of emotional surprise in words like: *ooh, ouch, oh!, orgy, ow* and *oops*. And when teamed up with *learned, loving, lively* and *liberating* letter *L*, it creates an ideal balance of emotional benevolence that bespeaks gentility and goodwill. Few names can beat the *OL* for sheer openhearted affection, and even though it is a unisex name root, the feminizing effects of the *O* and *L* account for the fact that 92% of these names belong to women.

You'll rarely find an *OL* rubbing people the wrong way . . . it's simply not in their nature to create friction. On the contrary, they're always actively looking for new ways to bring harmony and balance to their relationships, and if there's to be any criticism of the way *OLs* live their lives, it's that they sometimes try too hard. Their overarching need to maintain harmony in their social interactions means that these are *not* the people to go to for an honest appraisal of your new outfit or hairstyle. Your *OL* friend will reflexively love your new look even if you're naked and bald.

The *OLs* occasional indiscretions are exacerbated by an annoying forgetfulness that can make them seem diffident and cold, for it's a strange truth that most of

Ofelia
Ola
Olen
Oleta
Olga
Olin
Ollie
Olo

them have no memory for names and faces and will often forget an acquaintance as soon as they've met one. *OLs* compensate for their absentmindedness by carefully organizing their lives. They're the kind of people who will agonize over which outfits to pack when getting ready for trips. Perhaps it's their secret vanity that compels them to spend hours fretting over their clothing and hair, but no one will argue that it doesn't pay off in an immaculately groomed façade. All this worrying over their appearance (and what other people think) takes an emotional toll on the sensitive *OLs*. Whether it's a tendency to drink a little more than they should or falling into occasional funks, *OLs* must be careful to monitor their emotional levels lest they spiral completely out of kilter.

These are people who believe in the old fashioned values of chivalry and expect the same kind respectful behavior from others. Everyone can always expect unfailing courtesy from an *OL*, and as for their mates, the benefit of living with one of these charming souls far outweighs the downside of dealing with their precarious emotional states. Mates can expect an unconditionally loving partner, who's gifted in the ways of giving and is never at a loss for a caring gesture.

Olga Korbutt When the world fell in love with a pixie-faced Russian gymnast at the 1972 Munich Olympics, it wasn't simply her meticulously crafted routines; people fell in love with Olga Korbutt's bubbly personality and impish style. Even though she lost the overall individual medal to a teammate, she won three gold medals and one silver. ■ Although she never achieved the perfect 10s of the then up-and-coming Romanian, Nadia Comaneci, Olga was feted by the news media for many years following the 1972 Olympics. After retiring from active competition, Olga gave back to her sport by becoming a gymnastics instructor. ■ Olga's hometown of Minsk was precariously close to the Chernobyl nuclear accident of 1986 and she used her celebrity to campaign for relief aid.

305

Charisma										
Career Success										
Love & Friendship										
Power										

Inventive Forward-thinking Charming Hyperactive Over emotional Contrary

The letter *O* is responsible for the essence of emotional surprise that we find in words like *ooh, ouch, oh!, orgy, ow* and *oops*. And when conjoined with the letter *M* (the flagship of *maternal* love and *motherly* sustenance) creates words with a defiant sense of fun that resonate with feminine sensuality. Consider the *OM's* influence in the words: *bosom, womb, blossom, buxom, comical, comfort, home, homily, woman, aplomb* and *romance*.

So how do these explicitly feminine names (which represent only 1/100 of one percent of the entire population) manage to produce so many notably strong male personalities like General *Omar* Bradley, *Omar* Sharif, and *Omar* Khayyam (the heralded Muslim poet)? Perhaps it's a symptom of the *boy-named-Sue* syndrome, in which male *OMs* are forced to come to terms with their masculinity at a very early age.

But whatever the reason, these are men and women whose offbeat charisma effortlessly pulls people into their orbit. And while they certainly have a serious side, they also have a knack for raising the spirits of others with their crackling senses of humor. You can trust an *OM* with your life, though not necessarily with your

Oma
Omar
Omari
Omarion
Omayra
Omer

heart, for their strong libidos propel them to hunt down more than their fair share of the opposite sex. These people are also driven by their passions for work, and *OMs* are unlikely to settle for menial jobs especially when doors are so thrown so wide for them.

Fortunately, the earning potential of the *OMs* is willingly shared with those in their sphere of influence and the *OMs'* generosity is legendary in their social circles.

OMs have grand taste in design and clothing, and make a pretty good show of living the high life. And if *OMs* have trouble making enough money to support their profligate spending habits, they're certainly not above marrying into it.

Those that are planning to live with an *OM* will be happy to know that they're not prone to dark moods, though they are liable to let loose with the occasional bouts of theatrical storming in which their thunder can be quite intense. But the *OM's* benevolent essence is not interested in holding grudges and these tempests will quickly blow themselves out. The *OMs'* partners will discover that the benefits of being spoiled by such charmers more than make up for the temporary storms that come from living with these restless souls.

Omar Sharif It was an extraordinary feat for an Egyptian actor to make such an impact in the competitive international film business. Omar Sharif did exactly that, starring opposite some of the biggest names in the acting world. ■ Omar's break came when he played Sherif Ali Ibn El Karish in David Lean's blockbuster film *Lawrence of Arabia*. His role featured one of the most impressive delayed entrances for a leading man. ■ It was another Lean movie that propelled him to stardom—the Oscar nominated *Dr. Zhivago*, in which he played the title role. His 1968 movie *Funny Girl*, in which he starred opposite Barbra Streisand, was banned in his native Egypt because his character made love to a Jewish girl onscreen. ■ Although some have called him the Arab Sean Connery, supporters point out that Connery is simply a Scottish Sharif.

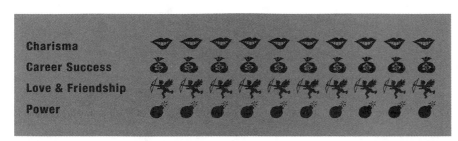

Charisma										
Career Success										
Love & Friendship										
Power										

or

Enthusiastic Innovative Authentic
Sarcastic Temperamental High-strung

When the emotionally excitable letter *O* teams up with the *romantic*, *red-blooded* and *randy* letter *R*, the resulting combination infects words with a profusion of passionate, fiery characteristics as found in the words: *orgasm, oral, consort, corporeal, horny, orbs, orifice* and *euphoric*.

There are only two colors in the *OR's* emotional makeup: red and black. Either they're totally in love with you or they have absolutely no time for you. Not that they'd be boorish or impolite mind you, it's just that their ardor takes up so much of their energy that they have very little oomph left over for casual relationships. This also explains why people either love or hate them. So if you're going to embark on an amorous adventure with an *OR* it's advisable to show no sign of fear, for anything less than total passion and commitment from a partner is the *OR's* bête-noir.

ORs' unconventional habits often land them in trouble in the workplace, which bothers them not in the least, for they are free thinkers and proud of their "I did it my way" style of problem solving. But there's a touch of hypocrisy in their refusal to accept advice from others, for they're the first ones to weigh in with their opinions even when it's decidedly unwelcome. But while some may resent their pushy style, most are eventually charmed by their fiery passion for getting the job done.

In intimate relationships, *ORs'* quicksilver minds and fickle emotional structures can present quite a challenge to anything less than a type-A partner. It's easy to misinterpret their quirky routines as being inconsistent, but the key to winning their hearts lies in unconditionally accepting the entire package. And if you think that their willingness to admit to their own shortcomings is a sign of an under-inflated ego—you'd be dead wrong. In fact, they're so confident of their value as human beings, they figure that even *with* all their faults, they're still blue-ribbon prizes.

It takes a special individual to keep up with the *ORs'* robust sexual appetites and the only medication they're going to need in the bedroom will be aspirin for their partners. And even though *ORs* tend to mellow with age, their mates can still expect a lifetime of surprises. This can grow tiresome for the less adventurous who find themselves bobbing in the wake of the *OR's* enthusiastic wavemaking, but the *OR's true* love will enjoy every minute of it.

Ora
Oralia
Oren
Orion
Orlando
Orpha
Orville

Orville Wright As a young adult, Orville Wright teamed up with his younger brother Wilbur to open a printing shop and eventually a bicycle repair facility. ■ The early years of the twentieth century was a time of intense interest in heavier-than-air flight, and the brothers attacked the problem from a novel angle by attempting to control the forces acting on a flying craft. ■ The brothers carted their prototype airplane to Kitty Hawk—where there was plenty of wind to assist take-offs and enough sand to soften any hard landings—and succeeded in getting the plane into the air. The first flight lasted only twelve seconds but went down in history as the first time a machine carrying a man had achieved free flight under its own power.

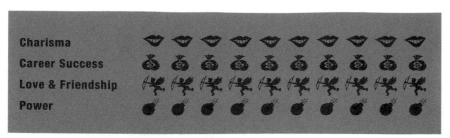

Charisma										
Career Success										
Love & Friendship										
Power										

Thoughtful Intuitive Dignified
Stubborn Demanding Fussy

The promise of excited surprise created by the emotionally impulsive letter *O,* imbues the *OS* names with a distinctively restless quality. And its union with the *sensually sultry S* (or *Z*) sound, generates words laden with the naughty sensual overtones of *rosy, posy, bosom, cosmic, floozy, cozy, flossy, goose* and *loose.*

So it's not surprising that people whose names fall under the *OS* category are often described as having an endearing air of irascibility and a feisty (but unintimidating) presence. It may be hard to know what's going on in their heads at times, but this suits the *OSs* perfectly; they relish the *man-of-mystery* reputation that comes with being oh-so enigmatic.

Perhaps because of their emotionally sensitive natures, *OS* people like to ponder and pontificate. With minds that effortlessly digest and index information, *OSs* have quite a scientific approach to problem-solving… it's almost as if they never outgrew their childhood curiosities for how and why things work. They'll spend much of their time in their heads mulling over everything from philosophy, to money and relationships. They also possess the gift of self-expression and often turn to the written word,

Oscar
Osbaldo
Osvaldo
Oswald
Oswaldo
Oz
Ozzie

which makes them ideal journalists, researchers, and speechwriters. When *OSs* have the benefit of solid educational backgrounds, their passion for knowledge can make them authorities on practically any subject, including the vagaries of the opposite sex.

Marriage to an *OS* will be nothing short of a complete intellectual and emotional package. Dinner parties, replete with witty table repartee and home-cooked meals, will be the norm. And even though an *OS* might have given his heart to one woman, friends and casual acquaintances will remain the mainstay of his social life. She who would marry an *OS* should possess a natural evenness to balance his outgoing personality, and might have to accept the stigma of being the wet blanket covering his restless lifestyle.

Children—although not always a welcome addition to the *OS's* family—will be doted upon and constantly challenged to broaden their intellectual frontiers. Still, chances are that they'll quickly figure out their way around their parent's somewhat laissez-faire style of discipline, and if they survive the *OS'* frequent lectures, will profit from a rewarding friendship with him in later years.

Oscar Wilde While he was studying at Oxford, Oscar Wilde made waves with his irreverent attitude towards religion and his deliberately provocative style of dress which included velvet knee breeches. Moving to London after receiving his degree, from Oxford, he began writing and producing plays. ■ Oscar achieved notoriety through the enormous success of his plays—including *A Woman of No Importance, An Ideal Husband* and *The Importance of Being Earnest*—but after falling in love with Lord Alfred Douglas, his life took an ugly turn. He was tried for homosexuality and sentenced to two years of hard labor. ■ His lover stood by his side while he served his sentence in Naples. ■ "The only way to get rid of a temptation," said Oscar, "is to yield to it."

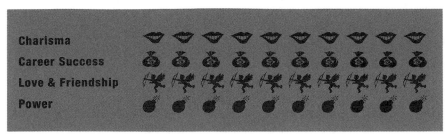

Charisma		
Career Success		
Love & Friendship		
Power		

Honest Sensitive Trusting
Immature Volatile Gullible

The emotional letter *O* is full of surprises, and when teamed up with the *vibrantly voluptuous, vivacious* and *virile* letter *V*, exudes an unmistakable air of excitement and anticipation. We find these boldly provocative attributes in the words *jovial, groovy, lovable, novelty* and *provocateur*. So if you detect a veneer of velvety good manners from the *OV*, be aware that it's probably a ploy to distract you from their charismatic and cheeky true selves. These are bright individuals who have fetishes for challenging the status quo.

Utterly charming and endlessly witty, these personalities comprise an unexpected combination of subtlety and flamboyance that is hard to beat for sheer animal magnetism. And while they don't necessarily seek the limelight, they're certainly willing to make the most out of any publicity that may come their way. It's quite common for the *OVs'* devil-may-care attitude to annoy family and friends who consider them to be somewhat reckless in their life decisions. But even though *OVs* may sense the discomfort caused by their careening lifestyles, it certainly isn't going to deter them from the exhilaration of making waves.

Octavia
Oliva
Olive
Oliver
Olivia

In terms of their careers, *OVs* are quite at home being the center of attention and manage well with the pressures that come from being in the limelight. This explains why *OVs* make such great company spokespeople and arbitrators in petty disputes. By carefully picking their battles and keeping a lid on their negative emotions when tensions are running high, *OVs* prove themselves to be formidable negotiators.

But it's in their home lives that the *OV* personalities come into their own, and prospective partners can expect an exhilarating ride. Sexually, *OVs* are quite adventurous—willing to try anything at least twice—and their lovers will find themselves the happy recipients of all manner of experimentation lifted from the pages of *Cosmopolitan* or *Playboy*.

As parents, *OVs* remember their own childhood struggles to express themselves freely, so their children are given plenty of leeway and will appreciate their parents' calm patience. These are parents who will even tolerate overt disobedience if it means giving their children free rein to their imaginations—as long as the kids don't pinch the *OVs'* personal freedom too tightly.

Oliver Stone With the possible exception of Woody Allen, Oliver Stone is the most controversial screenwriter-director on the American film scene. Known for his conspiratorial views, his films challenge audiences to reconsider their understanding of government's role in society. ■ At a time when most young men were signing up for college to avoid the Vietnam War, Oliver dropped out of Yale to join the army. Oliver was credited for single-handedly wiping out a machinegun nest and won bronze star. ■ Oliver seems addicted to controversy. The conspiracy film, *JFK*, made him a media target with its seemingly un-American portrayal of the sinister machinations of government, and his ultra-violent take on American youth in *Natural Born Killers* resulted in numerous lawsuits after several murders were allegedly inspired by the film.

OW

Charisma	👄	👄	👄	👄	👄	👄	👄	👄	👄	👄
Career Success	💰	💰	💰	💰	💰	💰	💰	💰	💰	💰
Love & Friendship										
Power										

**Innovative Playful Ingenious
Unpredictable Absent-minded Wild**

When the emotionally expressive letter *O* conjoins with the *wild, wooly, whimsical* letter *W*, it creates a howling sound that conjures images of the untamed spirit found in the words *rowdy, billowy, cowboy, flowing, power, showy* and *growl*. The saying *you can't keep a good man down* might well have been coined for an *OW* personality, for his devil-may-care mode of existence comes with its fair share of mishaps. But what defines this person's resilient and restless spirit, is his ability to casually shrug off defeat

If you want to impress an *OW*, buy him a set of luggage for his birthday, because this guy is going places. He may not know where (nor have the money to get there), but sooner or later you're going to get a postcard from a country you've never heard of. The *OW* is simply not designed to sit still and will resent and avoid anyone who tries to clip his wings. And while he may slow down with age, you *still* won't find him holding down the couch unless there's a good travel show on the tube. His love for discovery sometimes expresses itself in unexpected ways; perhaps he'll sign up for pottery lessons, or maybe he'll take up the bagpipes. Neighbors usually pray for the former.

Owen

OWs require a little more money than most people. And it's not because they're profligate, it's just that running an *OW* life can be expensive what with all that generous giving and expensive exploration marking his social style. If people leave him to his own devices and trust his intentions, the *OW* will come through every time. He has enough indefatigable energy to go around and he'll happily spend his spare time selling others his philosophy of living one's dreams. So don't idly wish for something in his presence ("*I've always wanted to go to Nepal*") or he'll hound you until you have the plane tickets in your hands. Because he's not the type to break a pledge, he's careful about what he promises and is unlikely to over-commit his limited free time.

Though settling down is not high on his list of things to do, the *OW* will fall in love from time to time, and will be happiest when bound to a partner who shares his wanderlust. His need for companionship may even trump his need for adventure for a short while, but it's just a matter of time before he resumes his wandering and eremitic ways.

Owen Hart When World Wrestling Federation star Own Hart fell fifty feet into the ring while being lowered from the ceiling in 1999, virtually everyone in the crowd thought it was just another in a long line of impressive stunts. But by the time the spectators realized that they had just witnessed a horrific accident, Owen Hart was dying from his fifty-foot fall. ■ The event was played out on live pay-per-view television but the actual fall was not shown. Owen was given CPR in the ring and taken to hospital where he was pronounced dead. After a fifteen-minute break, the show went on. ■ Owen had always wanted to spend his life in the public eye, and with Hollywood studios vying for his story, he has done so even in death.

Most Popular Girl's Names

Patricia
Pamela
Phyllis
Paula
Peggy
Pauline
Pearl
Patsy
Penny
Priscilla

Most Popular Boy's Names

Paul
Patrick
Peter
Phillip
Philip
Pedro
Perry
Pablo
Preston
Pete

"The populace is restless in the provinces; it is not in Paris. These are very pretty men, Sire. There is nothing to be feared on the part of the populace of Paris the capital. It is remarkable that the stature of this population should have diminished in the last fifty years; and the populace of the suburbs is still more puny than at the time of the Revolution."

—Victor Hugo,
Les Miserables

The Paternal and

Benign

Victor Hugo artfully conveyed the passive qualities of the Parisian populace by salting the above passage with P words and highlighting the P's association with pax, Latin for peace. ■ The pacific qualities of the P also connect it to all things paternal, and its benign and fatherly properties can be seen in the initial letters of Peter, Paul, Pontiff, Pope, pompous, patronizing, powerful, providence, papa and Psyche—the Roman goddess of the soul. ■ Its strong connection with the paternal explains why P words of insult tend to have such a masculine form—prick, pimp, pedophile, parasite and paparazzi—but when combined with the languid letter L, words take on a decidedly placid tone, as in pliant, plaintive, placate, pleasant and playful. (The word platonic, stemming from the Greek philosopher Plato, derives from the theory that the perfect relationship can only reach its spiritual zenith in the absence of sex.) ■ Particularly interesting is the way the PR phoneme embodies the authority of the paternal figure: prince, priest, president, prefect, professor, prelate, prosecutor, principal, primacy, pride, prostate and provider. Watched over by Priapus, the god of male inherited power, the Prestons, Prescotts and Princes of this world probably have no problem with prodigious procreation. ■ When used to initialize female names, the P tends to reflect its peaceful qualities, as in the traditional meaning of Paloma (dove), Philippa (loving) and Pia (pious), while male names tend to embody more dignified qualities, as in Paddy (nobleman), Pedro (a rock) and Prescott (priestly). Ps of both sexes tend to be proud, presentable and popular, which explains their high rankings in the lists of politicians and entertainers. ■

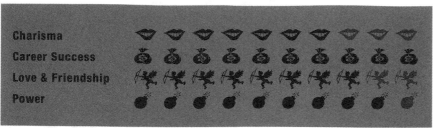

Charisma										
Career Success										
Love & Friendship										
Power										

Cautious Helpful Motherly
Conservative Stubborn Manipulative

Although female *PD* names have fallen out of fashion in recent times, there *has* been a slight rise in the use of the male version. Perhaps this is due to the decidedly conservative—and even puritanical—combination of the letters *P* and *D*. The *P* is the flagship of *paternal* authority, and when it conjoins with the *dominant, disciplined D*, gives rise to words like *prudish, padre, pedagogue, pedantic, perdition* and *pedigree.*

There's a recognizable aspect of the traditionalist in the *PD* names, and these are people whose values are firmly tuned to the importance of family, reputation and old-fashioned hard work. The *PDs*' orderly personalities abhor uncertainty, and they can be counted on to organize and arrange the work setting. And it's in the work environ that the prim and proper *PDs* prove to be the self-appointed guardians of the rulebook; , taking it upon themselves to monitor the workflow and motivate the rank and file. And while the *PDs* can be a little overbearing to those not accustomed to being micromanaged, those with a vested interest in the project's outcome will appreciate their calm presence.

The *PDs*' rare combination of patience and empathy gives them the ability to hold other people accountable without offending them. A rebuke from a *PD* boss

Pedro
Prudence

will be so gently applied that most people won't even realize they've been reprimanded until someone else points it out. *PDs* are intuitive as well, and will readily drop their bossy dispositions when they sense that someone is being intimidated.

In the workplace *PDs* are those go-to- guys who will shoulder any burden without complaint. This doesn't mean that *PDs* are without their own selfish needs, for they'll always manage to find a way to meet their goals even it means putting on a mask for the occasion. Shrewd thinkers with foresight and logic, there's always an air of purpose to their actions, and even though they'll make time to have some fun along the way, these are no wild party animals. When a *PD* entertains, don't expect any unpredictable shenanigans. It's going to be a sedate affair with just the right amounts of alcohol and witty repartee.

The *PDs*' intrinsic calm is especially welcome in touchy situations where their social graces go a long way in smoothing out conflict. But don't think for a second that the sensitive *PDs* are pushovers. For although their emotions may sometimes need stroking, their uncommon intellects will subtly put control of the relationship in their capable hands.

Pedro Almodóvar If any twenty-first-century man can lay claim to the mantle of "Renaissance Man," Spanish film director, composer, producer and actor Pedro Almodóvar would certainly be that man. ■ Pedro's first "acting" role was in the Madonna documentary *Truth or Dare*, but it was as a director that he made his mark. Consistently strong reviews of his provocative treatment of sexual themes, like the Oscar-nominated *Mujeres al borde de un Ataque de nervios* (*Women on the Verge of a Nervous Breakdown*), cemented his status as one of the few foreign directors able to penetrate the American market. ■ Pedro's films deal with the darker side of human behavior, as shown in his comedy-drama *All About My Mother*, which won both a Golden Globe and an Academy Award for Best Foreign Film.

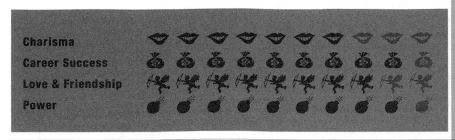

Charisma	
Career Success	
Love & Friendship	
Power	

Energetic Knowledgeable Positive
Predictable Moody Excitable

The *potent* and *paternal* letter *P* brings an air of *pomp* to the *PG* names, and when teamed up with the *gallant* (if sometimes *growling* letter *G*), produces a combination that is at once proud and earthy. Typically, people who bear *PG* names project an aura of goodwill and common sense, while those who choose to end their names with the youthful *Y* or *IE* sound, (for example, *Peggy* and Peggie), are likely to be even more approachable and friendly.

Paige
Peg
Peggy

You can count on *PG*s to spice up a party with lively discussions covering their extensive knowledge of the issues, for *PG*s are serious students of the world and are always up with current events. And yet, even though they know how to have a good time, they are not above the occasional descent into bouts of biting sarcasm. Usually these moods are triggered when *PG*s over-extend themselves by trying to be all things to all people, or when they believe that their unflagging generosity has been taken advantage of. But you can hardly blame other people for wanting to bask in the glow of the *PG*s' auras; their upbeat energies offer an uplifting promise to even the most demoralized soul.

Money is important to the *PG*, but not for flashing-around purposes. These are people who like to stash their money for rainy days and enjoy the security that only comes from having a chunky savings book. But *PG*s would never trade job satisfaction for money and, with their love for intellectual challenges, are drawn to pursuits that allow them to flex their mental muscles. Teaching science or philosophy would be right up their alley, but they also love to read and write.

*PG*s seem to have a mixed-brain dominance in which their ambidextrous minds operate equally well in right-brained or left-brained modes. This gift has its drawbacks though, for *PG*s often vacillate on which career path is going to keep them most stimulated. You might find *PG*s in physically demanding activities like dancing, sports or entertainment, but don't expect to find them on the stand-up comic circuit. If they have any drawback, it's their rather predictable sense of humor.

*PG*s tend to choose their relationships for their practical values rather than any madcap romantic notions, and partners will be carefully vetted for potential character flaws before *PG*s commit their hearts. Once ensconced in a marriage, it will usually be the the *PG*s' strong influence that gives the relationship its color and direction.

Peggy Fleming With the bitter fallout from the Tonya Harding incident in the 1994 Olympic women's figure skating event, it's easy to forget that women's skating was once a sport of grace and sportsmanship. Peggy Fleming was the epitome of that old-fashioned elegance, winning three world titles and ushering in the modern era of women's skating in the late sixties. ■ Her effortless style and girl-next-door charm ignited an ongoing American love affair with the sport, which intensified when Dorothy Hamill won the gold medal in the 1976 Olympics in Innsbruck. ■ In 1998, a lump in Peggy's breast turned out to be cancer. After her treatment and recovery, Peggy became an outspoken advocate for breast cancer awareness. ■ In 2000, *Sports Illustrated* named Peggy one of the most influential athletes of the twentieth century.

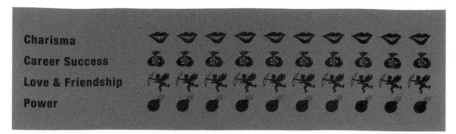

Charisma										
Career Success										
Love & Friendship										
Power										

Tasteful Shrewd Consistent
Snooty Inflexible Scattered

When the *paternal* letter *P* combines with the *hopeful* and *hushed* tones of the letter *H*, it takes on the inscrutable aspects of the words *phantom, physics, sphinx, prophecy, sophism* and *zephyr*. And even though the letter *L* (the symbol of *loving, laughing, living* and *learning*) plays a role in providing these names a sense of higher purpose, the *PHL* phoneme remains strongly connected to the commanding masculine images found in the words *physical, phallic, Philistine, phlegmatic, phalanx* and *philanderer.* This is why many female *PHLs* (*Phillis* and *Phyllis*, for example) employ the *sensual* letter *S* to *soften, sensitize* and *sweeten* their names.

With these aloof and pensive characteristics, *PHL* people can often prove difficult to warm up to when you first meet them. Perhaps it's because they don't encourage familiarity with outsiders and prefer to keep them at arm's length, but *PHLs* are unfailingly polite and respectful and will always reciprocate gestures of goodwill from strangers.

Remaining admirably unruffled in the face of pressure, *PHLs* don't adapt to situations so much as situations adapt to them, and they are therefore, the ideal people to have around in emergencies. Their innate calm makes them perfect candidates for being doctors,

Phil
Philip
Phillip
Phillipa
Phyllis

EMTs, or simply the go-to- people when cool heads are needed. *PHLs* are standouts in the fields of law and business, in which they handle themselves with shrewd intelligence.

These aren't overtly aggressive individuals, and you'll hardly ever see *PHLs* losing control of their tempers. They exude a quiet strength to which others usually defer, and negative emotions are cleverly channeled into their work efforts to better increase their earning power.

These intelligent people also have sardonic senses of humor, and these qualities go a long way to making them popular choices with the opposite sex. But since not everyone gets their wry wit, *PHLs* use this as a test to winnow their field of potential suitors. Even so, mating with *PHLs* can be challenging undertakings. Because intimate communication is a priority for these introspective souls, the burden will be on their partner to keep up with some pretty deep conversations.

If you want to witness the transformation of a sober purist into a puddle of goo, visit a *PHL* when he or she is taking care of their infant. Nothing brings out the *PHLs'* nurturing side more than marriage and parenthood and their families will thrive under their prudent sense of direction.

Prince Philip It's not easy to spend one's life in the shadow of tartan skirts and yapping corgis, but with his characteristically stiff upper lip and dapper demeanor, Prince Philip has uncomplainingly served as the consort of Queen Elizabeth for over fifty years. ■ In the aftermath of the Greek revolution in 1920, the Prince's family was rescued by the British Navy from execution. With the official title of His Royal Highness The Prince Philip, Duke of Edinburgh, his many social gaffes have made him something of a Dan Quayle to the British press. The Prince raised eyebrows when he reportedly asked a blind woman in the crowd "Do you know they have eating dogs for anorexics now?" ■ Only time will tell if his oldest son Charles will inherit his wife's throne.

THE SHARP

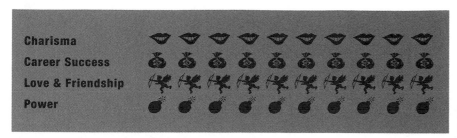

Charisma										
Career Success										
Love & Friendship										
Power										

Intelligent Perceptive Entertaining Mischievous Moody Restless

The abrupt pronunciation of the two key letters in these names suggests a personality of decisive and perceptive action. Inasmuch as the letter *P* is the flagship letter of *paternal* authority (*papa, padre, power, priest, patron,* and *pedantic*), and the *K* is the symbol of forceful power (*kick, knight, king, kidnap, keen, knuckle, knife* and *kill*), these individuals almost always exhibit a no-nonsense, can-do impression of confidence. We find these edgy *PK* effects in the words *spike, dropkick, peak, poker, pike* and *outspoken.*

If you're in need of a little self-discipline in your life and aren't sure where to start, give your *PK* friend a call. Not only have they gained mastery over their own willpowers, but also they're also more than willing to share their techniques with anyone who asks. Admittedly the *PK* can be a little stiff and reserved at times, but when in the company of close friends, they often take it on themselves to be the group's entertainment director, which they accomplish with relaxed aplomb. Once they put their minds to a task, they'll maintain focus until the job is efficiently and expertly complete.

Dignified, formal and rather on the overbearing side, *PKs* have a healthy self-image and don't like to reveal their personal weakness—like the holes in their

Paco
Parker
Pasquale
Pinkie

socks or their offbeat tastes in movies. They're also more likely to hole up in their private spaces, rather than destress with friends at a local bar. Their strict self-disciplinarian attitude is also directed at those in their group who aren't pulling their own weight: they're not ones to burden themselves with the loads of others.

You might be tempted to put them down as being wet blankets in the social arena, but this would not be entirely accurate. *PKs* aren't out to spoil anyone's fun; they're just trying broaden their horizons. Whether it's their (strong) religious beliefs or their (centrist) views of world politics, *PKs* are convinced they have the right answers and will willingly share them with anyone who'll listen. This sense of righteousness—combined with the *PKs*' sharp intelligence—makes them formidable debaters and mindchangers par excellence.

No one would argue that the *PKs*' hearts aren't in the right place. With a genuine desire to see people perform at their best, they are natural leaders with clear vision. Married to a *PK* ? Count your blessings. For all their unyielding qualities, *PKs* are decidedly passionate about their partners, and, although they would never reveal it in public, there are traditional and romantic hearts beating within their powerful bosoms.

Parker Posey Named after the 1950s supermodel Suzy Parker, Parker Posey emerged from the suburbs of Baltimore to make her acting debut as the nasty Tess Shelby in *As the World Turns*. ■ Her popularity on the show led to her getting the part of Stephanie in the *Saturday Night Live* spinoff movie *Coneheads*. It wasn't a big role, but the winsome actress was nevertheless cast next in another cult comedy, *Dazed and Confused*. Her co-stars were the likes of the then-unknown Matthew McConaughey, Renée Zellweger and Ben Affleck. ■ The woman that *Time* magazine once described as "Queen of the Indies" went on to make over twenty-five movies in five years, all but three being independent features. ■ For trivia buffs: While attending the State University of New York, Parker was roommate to *ER's* Sherry Stringfield.

pl

Charisma										
Career Success										
Love & Friendship										
Power										

**Charismatic Intellectual Talented
Flighty Unrealistic Over-analytical**

The combination of the *patiently paternal* letter *P* and the *loving, learned* letter *L* gives these names their *pleasant* and *playful* imprimatur. We see these effects in the many words that incorporate the *PL* phoneme: *pliant, plaintive, platonic, placid, pliable* and *placate.* These are people pleasers at heart who, even in the grip of their most philosophical moments, will always take the thoughts and opinions of others into consideration. These trendy philosophers flex both their mental and emotional muscles in cultivating their relationships.

PL people are always up for a good gab session about the meaning of life and the universe. Their endless fascination for how things work—especially the dynamics of their own relationships—is central to their personalities, and very little escapes them. But unlike other amateur philosophers, *PLs* are not the straight-laced intellectual types. Their theories are more likely to be bantered over a glass of ale and a slice of pizza.

A wide and varied circle of friends is drawn to the *PLs'* charming combination of wit and wisdom. One reason they're so popular, is that *PLs* are social chameleons who have a different hat for every occasion. And *PLs* seem to relish their status as someone you can't quite define, and are also happy to play the part of either the insightful intellectual, the social facilitator, or the spiritual guru.

The self-assured *PL's* ego really doesn't need stroking, and their career choices are made without regard to the social status they may bring. Anything from janitor to CEO, to professor or perpetual student will do, as long as the *PL* is stimulated by the work they're doing.

In their relationships, their willingness to socialize with just about anyone gives them an abundance of choices for their life mates. In fact, they often have trouble settling with just one person and may change partners in mid-stream more than once in their lives. Not that this deters potential suitors, though, for the *PLs'* easy laughter and invigorating brand of sexuality makes them treasured prizes.

Prospective mates can take heart in the knowledge that, once given, the *PLs'* love is designed to last, but they should tread lightly on sensitive emotional issues lest they discover the *PL's* surprisingly volatile temper. Children of the *PL* will enjoy an affectionate parent who provides gentle discipline and a laissez-faire attitude. This liberal approach springs from the *PL's* trust in the natural order of things; children will find their own way, just as they themselves have done.

Pablo
Paloma
Paola
Paul
Paula
Pauletta
Paulette
Paulina
Pauline
Paulita
Polly

Paul Newman Paul Newman's marriage to actress Joanne Woodward has proven to be one of the most enduring love affairs in Hollywood history. His portfolio of films is among the most respected in Hollywood, and his salad-dressing empire has raised millions of dollars for charity. ■ The man with the pale blue eyes first gained critical attention for his role as boxer Rocky Graziano in the 1956 classic *Somebody Up There Likes Me*, and his credits include an enviable lineup of classics: *Cool Hand Luke, Butch Cassidy and the Sundance Kid* and *The Sting*, just to name a few. ■ As Paul matured, he took on a number of senior roles in a series of successful feature films including *Absence of Malice, The Verdict* and the Coen Brothers' *The Hudsucker Proxy*, and he won a Best Actor Oscar for *The Color of Money*.

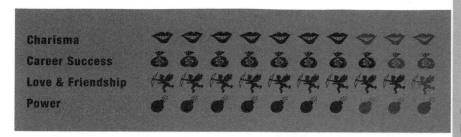

Charisma											
Career Success											
Love & Friendship											
Power											

pm

Quick-thinking Motivated Caring
Repressive Inconsistent Aloof

There's a decided conflict that underscores the essence of the *PM* names. The letter *P* is the fundamental symbol of male authority that we find in words like *paternal, power, priest, patron, papa* and *pedantic,* while the *M* is the icon of feminine *maternal* love demonstrated by the words: *matriarch, maiden, madam, mama, mother* and *Mary Magdalene.* So there's an internal battle waging war for control of the *PM* heart, a classic struggle between male and female, which expresses itself in a variety of ways. Perhaps it will be in bouts of depression or the occasional emotional outburst; but one thing is sure: With two parental icons at the core of these names, these women are amongst the most sensitive and attentive mothers in the world.

Those *PM*s who choose to use the shortened version of their given name (e.g. *Pam* from *Pamela*) are saying much about how they perceive themselves. When people contract their names from two to one syllable, they subconsciously portray themselves as no-frills, unpretentious individuals whose unselfishness is evident through their insistence on informality.

Beware a *PM* on the rampage out to prove a point, for the flipside of her sensitive personality is a stubborn

Pam
Pamela

streak that rivals a rhinoceros in heat. Once she's managed to build up a head of steam, changing her direction is nigh on impossible, even when she senses that she's on the wrong track. The key to handling a *PM* under these conditions is to short-circuit her high-energy fireballs by keeping a cool head and playing "catch-me-if-you-can."

PM people are those no-nonsense types whose inherent curiosity makes them great sources for the latest news and updates on the social scene. These natural-born newshounds are never out of the loop, chasing down everything from the great issues of the day to the gossip on the Estrogen Network. Their perceptive side may be a great tool for discerning other people's moods, but is of little help in understanding their own intricate emotions.

*PM*s tend to rely on their partners to be their sounding boards, but sharing physical activities falls pretty low on their priority list. Most partners understand that the *PM* has far more important things to do in life—after all, she has a family to run and social appointments to keep. With just a little warm understanding from her mate, the *PM* will prove to be the most aggressively loyal partner a man could ever want.

Pam Dawber As the girl who played Mindy on the wildly popular seventies TV show *Mork & Mindy*, Pam Dawber's winsome characterization left an indelible mark in the minds of many male baby-boomers. ■ But it was her starring role in TV's *My Sister Sam* that had the most dramatic effect on Pam's personal life. Co-starring with husband Mark Harmon (another seventies heartthrob), the show featured Rebecca Schaeffer, a promising young actress with whom she shared her Los Angeles home. Shortly after moving into her own apartment, Rebecca was hunted and killed by a deranged fan. ■ Pam is picky about the roles she accepts, claiming to have practically put herself out of the business by turning down work. "If I wouldn't want to watch it," she asks, "why would I be in it?"

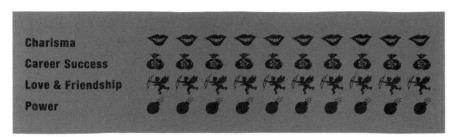

Charisma	
Career Success	
Love & Friendship	
Power	

Solid Inventive Encouraging
Severe Impatient Repressed

The *paternal power* of the letter *P* bestows these names an authoritarian tone. And because the letter *N* is the flagship of all that is *negative* (*no, not, never, nary, none* etc.), the combination of these letters confers the sense of autocratic discipline that reverberates through words like: *punishment, punitive, pain, punch, punk, pensive,* and *penal.* Most *PN* women (*Penny* and *Penni*) avoid these antagonistic effects by terminating their names with the high-pitched *Y* sound, for names that end with the *youthful* letter *Y* have the playful ambience of the words *joy, goofy, sassy, play, happy* and *zany.*

Penelope
Penny

*PN*s are survivors in the true sense of the word, never giving up no matter what the odds and making every effort to ensure that those around them are surviving too. They are consummate team players as well. Not through any sense of altruism, mind you, but from the realization that if everyone fulfills his or her responsibilities to each other, then everyone is bound to benefit. You need only look a *PN* in the eyes to sense her moxie and intelligence, and those who look deeper will find a trusted companion and utterly loyal friend. People are irresistibly drawn to her no-nonsense style, and her strong moral structure coupled with her bright (if not always open) mind, earns her a fair share of admirers.

*PN*s like to stretch their limits, which is why they often end up in challenging professions like medicine and science. But if anything is going to slow them down, it will be their lack of desire to compete on a head-to-head basis. *PN*s are only interested in competing against themselves and don't have the fighting instinct needed for careers in law, politics or big business. In fact, given the choice, most *PN*s will prefer to stay at home with their families, and center activities on their partners and children. But in any case, you can count on the *PN* to be well-read, well-spoken and well-disciplined.

Even with all their positive energy, however, *PN*'s are not immune to burnout. And although these bouts of depression can be quite acute, the *PN*'s willingness to lean on others means that they are also short-lived.

The *PN* lover is a focused and reciprocal partner. In keeping with her teamwork philosophy, she views married life as a working partnership in which both parties should take care of each other, and won't allow outside pressures to come between her and her mate. Firm discipline will guide her children as they grow up, but the *PN* must keep an eye out for potential mutinies once they reach their teens.

Penny Marshall Most people associate the name Penny Marshall with her ditzy character Laverne DeFazio from the hit seventies sitcom *Laverne & Shirley*. ■ Penny got her start after older brother Garry Marshall (director/producer of *Pretty Woman*) helped her land jobs on *The Odd Couple* and *The Mary Tyler Moore Show*. ■ During her stint on *Laverne & Shirley*, Penny met and married Rob Reiner from *All in the Family*. In the ten years they were together, they raised Penny's daughter from a previous marriage. ■ But Penny's real legacy is as an Academy Award–winning filmmaker, with over half a dozen major films to her credit. Her feature film directorial debut was the 1986 Whoopi Goldberg showcase, *Jumpin' Jack Flash*, while her Tom Hanks vehicle, *Big*, managed to garner two Academy Awards.

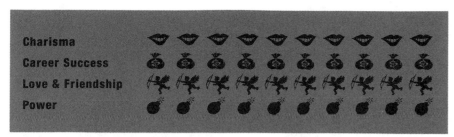

Charisma										
Career Success										
Love & Friendship										
Power										

pr

Dynamic Carnal Punctual
Prissy Demanding Temperamental

The letter *P* bestows the *PR* names their sense of paternal power, while the *randy, racy, romantic, ruddy, raring-to-go* letter *R* evokes a distinct air of *ribald* ardor. Together, these two letters create the strong implications of the masculine drive found in the words *primal, pride, preachy, prick, predictable, priest, prostate, protector, profound, prizefighter, provocateur, profane* and *priapism* (a condition of constant male arousal). So it's no surprise that the names *Pierre* and *Paris* evoke images of a lean, romantic Frenchman with a fervor for all things carnal. Perrys on the other hand—as if a little uncomfortable with this powerful libidinous association—terminate their names with the playful and high frequency letter *Y*.

Paris
Perry
Pierre
Piper

PRs' passion for socializing permeates all aspects of their vigorously active lives. In fact the boundaries between *PRs*' work lives and social lives are so blurred that it's difficult for anyone to tell the difference. Even when the *PRs* are relaxing they're never really at rest. Everyone they meet is a potential business associate, which is why *PRs* rarely forget names and faces. Conversely, *PRs* often look like they're goofing off when they're actually working.

With their intrinsic abilities to put people at ease, *PRs*' social skills are largely responsible for their successes. They will gladly take leadership roles in the workplace, but *PRs* tend to gravitate toward jobs in which their individual efforts can be more clearly recognized. They are ideal for careers in sales, design, entrepreneurship, teaching and, predictably, public relations (PR).

PRs' tendency to be slaves to fashion is perhaps a comment on their need to feel accepted. They are at the height of their game when they are surrounded by admirers and feel disheartened when they sense the spotlight slipping away. But routine and predictability are *PRs*' natural enemies, and it's important for them to maintain autonomy in their work. Many *PRs* change jobs every three or four years just to hold ennui at bay.

Partnering a *PR* is not for the indecisive; it's an all or nothing proposition. So if you're the kind of person who expects to maintain your independence, you might want to keep on looking. Once hitched, *PRs*' lovers will find themselves at the center of an affectionate maelstrom, for like everything else in life, they pursue their relationships with a never-say-die approach. And while it's a pleasure to be on the receiving end of such efforts, prospective partners must be on the alert for an element of possessiveness in the *PRs*' courtship.

Pierre Curie At the turn of the twentieth century, it was unheard of for a man of Pierre Curie's stature as a world-class researcher to be eclipsed by his wife in the same field, but Pierre was the ultimate team player, who put his love for discovery above the petty concerns of ego. Together with his brother Jacque, Pierre had demonstrated that the magnetic properties of substances change at a specific temperature. ■ With wife Marie at his side, Pierre began an extensive study of radioactivity and announced the discovery of radium and polonium in 1898. ■ Pierre and Marie won half of the Nobel Prize for Physics in 1903, and the Curie family was oddly connected with the prize thereafter. Marie won the Chemistry prize in 1911, their daughter, Irène, won the Chemistry prize in 1935, and his son-in-law received the Peace Prize on behalf of UNICEF in 1965.

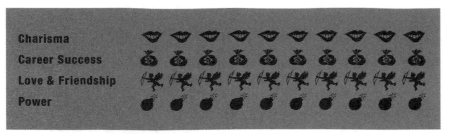

THE GRACIOUS
prl

Charisma	😗 😗 😗 😗 😗 😗 😗 😗 😗 😗
Career Success	💰 💰 💰 💰 💰 💰 💰 💰 💰
Love & Friendship	😇 😇 😇 😇 😇 😇 😇 😇 😇
Power	💣 💣 💣 💣 💣 💣 💣 💣 💣 💣

Resourceful Gifted Generous
Isolated Terse Mundane

It's always interesting to observe how the addition of a single letter in a name can have such a dramatic effect. Ordinarily, *PR* names evoke the strict masculine images we find in the words *provocateur, pride, profane preachy, prick, priest, prostate* and *protector*. But when modulated by the letter *L*—the flagship of *life, liberty, learning, lust* and *love*—these potentially prickly *PR* names are steered into symbols of gracious gentility: *primly, prolific, pearl, prettily, parental* and *parasol*.

But the genteel *PRLs* are not exactly known for their calm disposition and serene outlook on life. These are determined individuals who know what they want, and will do whatever it takes—short of hurting other people—to achieve their goals. It's not easy to get a *PRL* upset, for she seems to handle everything with a wise restraint and a philosophical air. But her ire will be up and her passion on full power when it comes to fighting injustice, particularly on behalf of the disadvantaged.

PRLs carry with them a sense of an old soul, as if they've seen more than their years would suggest. As children they often set themselves apart from their peers and act as arbitrators rather than co-conspirators. This

Pearl
Pearlie
Perla

may account for the *PRL's* independent streak, in which she never feels as if she quite belongs. And while it would be an exaggeration to say that the *PRL* is a solitary sort, she is certainly autonomous and has no qualms about doing things on her own. It wouldn't be unusual for a *PRL* to take off on a mini-vacation by herself (during which she'll prove to be very capable company).

The "lonely" professions (writing, design and research) suit *PRLs'* self-sufficient personalities perfectly. Spending time alone gives them a chance to recharge their batteries and smell the roses. Still, PRLs genuinely enjoy the stimulation that comes from small groups of close friends but, not being the flashy types, would rather hang around the local watering hole than the hottest new nightclubs in town.

When *PRLs* mate, they do it for life, even if it results in a long-suffering union. They simply don't have time to waste in flitting from one partner to the next, and that's why they are so careful in choosing their spouses. The only problem with *PRLs'* approach to parenthood—if they choose to be parents—is in encouraging their children to hang around long after they should have flown the nest.

Pearl Bailey Pearl Bailey's husky drawl and spirited singing style made her a darling of stage and screen. ■ Pearl started performing when she was just a teenager, and her break came when she was cast in the Broadway musical, *St. Louis Woman* and was named "Most Promising Newcomer of 1946." ■ Her 1947 film *Variety Girl* was a huge success, but performing on stage was always her first love. In the sixties she earned a Tony Award for her title role in the all–African American cast of *Hello Dolly* on Broadway. ■ Her reputation for impromptu asides on stage caught the eye of network executives who gave Pearl her own TV variety show in 1971. After retiring in 1975, the U.S. government honored her by naming her to the United States' UN delegation.

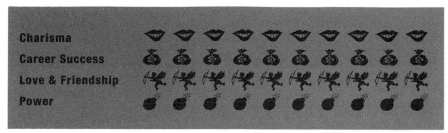

Charisma											
Career Success											
Love & Friendship											
Power											

Gracious Objective Sexy
Vain Miserly Manipulative

The *PRS* name root is a convoluted blend of intricate influences that make for equally complex personalities. There's the *pompous* and *patronly P,* which, when combined with the *randy* and *ribald* letter *R,* evokes the sternly masculine images found in the words: *protector, provocateur, primal, pride, prick, predictable, priest, prostate, prizefighter* and *profane.* Fortunately, a great deal of these names' severity is tempered by the addition of the *sensual* letter *S* (or the soft pronunciation of the *C*), which transforms them into symbols of benign power: *precious, princess, prosperous, personable, presentable, purist* and *praise.*

These self-assured people inspire respect with their coolly elegant carriage. Their outlook on life is one of calm ownership—as if the world was is their oyster and they're playing the part of the pearl. With an uncommon ability for convincing others to do things for them that they wouldn't do for anyone else, it's not surprising that *PRS*s are famous for their perpetually pleased smiles. These aren't devious manipulators by any means—it's just that people readily respond to their commanding charm. The *PRS*s' gracious thank-yous are sufficient reward for those who have fallen captive to their charisma.

These are realistic and levelheaded individuals who

Percy
Pierce
Porsha
Precious
Presley
Preston
Prince
Princess
Priscilla

will rarely permit themselves a leap into the deep end without careful consideration. But on those occasions when the *PRS* has a rush of blood and does something they're going to regret in the morning, it'll be done with the consummate flair that only a *PRS* can muster.

Going to a *PRS*'s party? Make sure you take caviar and champagne, because hotdogs and beer aren't going to cut it. *PRS*s appreciate quality and beauty in all forms, and are drawn to professions in which they can be surrounded by them. Whether their careers are in interior design, modeling or the health industry, these discerning souls are also delighted to help others unlock their own inner beauty. The *PRS*s' elegant aura can be intimidating to the less confident among us (it's not easy to shine around someone who's always so trim and fresh), but few people resent these gracious individuals who work hard at putting others at ease.

If *PRS*s have an air of royalty to them, it comes with the expectation that their partners will be of noble birth as well. Their ideal lovers are those who treat them with dignity, loyalty and commitment, and they will be rewarded in turn with lavish praise, affection and sensuality.

Priscilla Presley Priscilla Ann Beaulieu's precocious personality would probably have led to fame in her own right even had she not married The King in 1967. The couple divorced in 1972, just five years before Elvis's ignominious death in a Las Vegas hotel room. ■ Priscilla went on to become the director of the board of Metro Goldwyn Mayer, and as executor of Elvis Presley's estate, took it from a market value of three million dollars to an enterprise with annual revenues of over $75 million. ■ Following in the footsteps of many female celebrities, Priscilla began development of an international fragrance line in 1988. Her keystone fragrance, *Moments*, currently grosses over ninety million dollars a year.

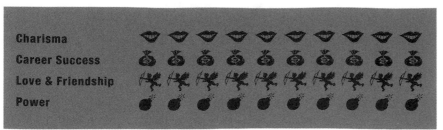

Charisma	😙😙😙😙😙😙😙😙😙😙
Career Success	💰💰💰💰💰💰💰💰💰
Love & Friendship	🐉🐉🐉🐉🐉🐉🐉🐉🐉🐉
Power	💣💣💣💣💣💣💣💣💣💣

Inspiring Energetic Hardworking
Controlling Worrisome Snappish

The concise elements in the *PT* names reflect the power and strength of character of these energetic people. The *powerfully potent,* and sometimes *pompous* letter *P,* initializes these names with a benevolently *paternal* feel, while the *triumphant* letter *T* introduces a sense of urgency. When these two letters team up in a name, they reflect the forceful themes found in the words *capture, contempt, adept, kryptonite, uptight, potent, sculpt* and *Baptist.* Some people (the *Peteys, Pattis* and *Patsys*) find this brusque intensity too much to live up to and choose to terminate their names with the playful and diminutizing *Y* or *I,* which diminishes some of its overwhelming authority.

*PT*s have the remarkable ability of making hard work appear effortless, but if things seem to magically turn out right for them, it may be because they have an extraordinary fear of failure. So maybe you'd be right in thinking that your *PT* friends are stress cases, but at least they have the ability to recognize impending anxiety it, deal with it, and move on. And when *PT*s hit the rocks after sailing along quite smoothly, a small voice in the middle of the vortex reminds them that they're the captains of their own ships and guides them safely back to port.

Pat
Patience
Patsy
Patty
Paxton
Pete
Petey
Peyton
Portia

Because their deliberate demeanor has a way of calming others in times of crises, *PT*s are highly sought after in stressful careers. They are the people we turn to when a hurricane is on the way, or when the cat gets stuck in the toilet. But the *PT*'s style of management isn't exactly what you'd call subtle, and even though their commanding presence may be appreciated by the rank- and- file, their brusque approach can grate on other Alphaalpha- personalities in the workplace. *PT*s hate to waste time and are famous for their multitasking abilities. They can simultaneously type a memo, answer the phone, send out an email, and still find time to retrieve the cat from the toilet.

The *PT*s' personalities are so strong that they rarely need to lose their tempers to back up their point. Other people sense that *PT*s are not ones to trifle with and avoid butting heads with them. This is why most of them never discover the full potential of their own anger.

*PT*s treat their lovers with the same boisterousness that characterizes their professional lives. Although this can prove arduous for the more aloof among us, when teamed up with a similarly energetic partner who is able to meet their touchy-feely requirements, the resulting relationship will be vital, interesting and long- lasting.

Pat Boone No one was more surprised than his loyal fans when the all-American Christian gospel singer shocked everyone by appearing on stage in black leather chaps and tattoos to promote his album *No More Mr. Nice Guy.* His transformation to heavy-metal rocker was considered by some to be the worst news since Donny Osmond chose rock over country. ■ Stunned by the vehemence of his public's reaction, a subdued Pat quickly moved to repair the damage by explaining that his actions were an attempt to communicate with the grunge generation. ■ Still, Pat was not really acting completely out of character. After all, he had made a name for himself by singing cover songs of black artists at a time when listening to such music was considered to be quite radical.

THE PROVIDER

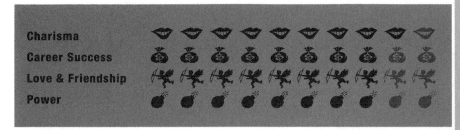

Charisma									
Career Success									
Love & Friendship									
Power									

**Steadfast Honest Willing
Bigmouthed Complicated Vain**

When the *prudent* letter *P* combines with the *triumphant* letter *T,* it creates vigorous words that orbit around the forceful themes of the words: *kryptonite, capture, contempt, adept, potent, uptight, sculpt* and *Baptist.* Fortunately, these tightly wound effects are saved from testosterone overkill by the *relaxed* letter *R,* whose rolling contours infuse these names with a sense of *paternal* and *protective* wisdom.

The conflicting elements in the *PTR* names suggest personalities that encompass a spectrum of possibilities from the stern, to the playful, to the capricious. Though they might appear to be relatively uncomplicated on the surface, this all-American façade masks complex and multi-faceted personas. When you interact with *PTR*s you'll find that they are analysts at heart, looking at you from various angles and running subtle internal tests (which is why conversations with them can leave you feeling like a bit like a lab rat). But armed with the knowledge that *PTR*s are simply trying to deepen their understanding of their relationships, most friends will be tolerant of the *PTR*'s persistent probing.

A ravenous curiosity forms the basis for the *PTR*'s' rich store of information, which they're quite happy to share with others. For *PTR*s are natural teachers and,

Patrice
Patricia
Patrick
Peter
Petra
Porter

with strong feelings of responsibility towards their fellow man, prove to be wonderful counselors. This might take the form of frequent debates or gentle arguments, but it also subtly expresses itself in their dabblings in art and music.

*PTR*s would never tell you what you want to hear simply in the interests of making you an ally; these are honest, forthright people with strong moral compasses guiding them in all aspects of their mostly- triumphant lives. If things *are* going to go a little wonky in the *PTR*s' day-to-day transactions, it'll probably be a result of their inability to handle life's finer details. These are big-picture people, and keeping track of their keys, wallets and paperwork simply isn't on their priority lists. It might also explain why their closets and underwear drawers are so meticulously organized.

As mates, *PTR*s will weather all sorts of adverse conditions if it helps to keep their marriages alive. But there's a fine line between stubbornness and blindness, one that the *PTR* straddles even in the face of obviously impending failure, and many *PTR*s simply don't know when to quit. But whether this stick-to-itiveness is an expression of constancy or simply hardheadness, no matter what the odds, *PTR*s are the kind of people to have in your corner when the chips are down.

Peter Jennings As one of the most influential and powerful voices on network television, Peter Jennings has held his anchor on ABC's *World News Tonight* since 1983. ■ Television executives took a major risk when they first hired the youngest (twenty-six) network anchor ever, especially since the venerable Walter Cronkite was purveying the news on CBS at the time. ■ In the twenty years Peter has held his position, he's seen other networks change anchors while his own stature has only grown. His reassuring voice reveals only a trace of a Canadian accent, and his position at the helm of ABC news has helped the network achieve consistently high ratings (at least in the news division). ■ "I don't mind offending people," says Peter. "Journalists should not mind offending people if they're in search of the truth."

**Most Popular
Girl's Names**

Queen
Queenie
Quiana
Qiana
Quyen

**Most Popular
Boy's Names**

Quentin
Quinton
Quincy
Quinn
Quintin

"It is qui, quae, quod; if you forget your quis, your quaes, and your quods, you must be preeches."

—WILLIAM SHAKESPEARE,
The Merry Wives of Windsor

In the Semitic languages, the letter Q is called qoph (monkey). This mischievous animal seems to aptly personify this unusual letter, for while words that begin with a Q are rare enough, names beginning with a Q are even more unusual and occur in less than 1 in 2,000 people. ■ But it's not just the scarcity of these names that makes Q people so unusual; it's their indelible association with all things quixotic, queer, questionable, quaint, quirky and quizzical. The Q is also the initial letter of the mysterious quantum theory, which forms the basis for all known matter where particles of matter appear and disappear at random. ■ After the American Cereal Company introduced its extraordinarily successful Quaker Oats breakfast food and the world's first cereal mascot, the Quaker Man, it returned in 1965 to the idea of featuring the Q sound in its breakfast food line with Quisp and Quake cereals. The early Quisp boxes featured a space alien holding a ray gun, which was eventually removed under pressure from the peace movement in the 1960s. ■ Individuals whose names begin with this underutilized letter are typically unconventional in their approach to life, work and relationships. Practically immune to criticism, they'll follow the beat of their own drum no matter where it takes them. ■ While Q people aren't featured on the top of any lists for success in sports, politics, arts or medicine, they aren't on the bottom of any of them either. ■

The Eccentric Letter

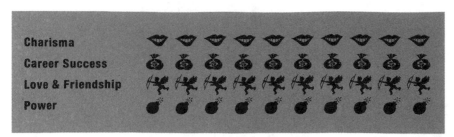

Charisma										
Career Success										
Love & Friendship										
Power										

Questing Unbiased Daring Temperamental Disconnected Puzzling

Q names are extremely rare and are represented by fewer than 100,000 individuals in the United States. It's an odd letter that is often used to describe unusual qualities: *queer, quackery, quagga, quaint, quirky* and *quandary*. Of all the *Q* names, *Quinn* and *Quentin* are the most common, accounting for almost 40% of its usage. People whose names begin with a *Q* are correspondingly unique, and place very few limits on themselves when it comes to living their *quixotic* lives.

Q people are pioneers at heart. They have to be. From an early age they were set apart from the rest of their friends by their unusual names, and were subtly conditioned into their atypical status. But this gave them an advantage over the rest of us. Because they were not expected to live up to any preset stereotypes, they were also encouraged to live out creative and original lives.

The *Q*'s strong right-brained tendencies result in a strange kind of logic that the conservatives among us would find downright creepy. But *Q*s thrive on confusion. It's not that they're anarchists or anything; it's just that they function best when they don't know what the future holds. They are surfers of life, who would rather

Queen
Quentin
Quiana
Quincy
Quinn
Quinten

ride a wave than try and control it. All they have to do is to concentrate on staying upright.

Tradition and fashion are an anathema to the *Q*'s flamboyant style. It's not that *Q*s consciously set out to make a statement with their clothing; they just seem to believe that vintage attire and mismatched colors are better suited to represent their quirky personalities. And true to this creative flair, *Q*s have a zest for the spotlight and relish all forms of public expression, whether it's singing, dancing or debating.

If curiosity killed the cat, it plays havoc on the *Q*'s social life as well, and maybe explains why *Q*s always seem to be hanging out with a new set of friends. It's true that many people can only take them in small doses, but their high turnover of friends is more than likely a reflection of the *Q*'s insatiable appetite for variety.

In spite of their eccentricities—or perhaps because of them—*Q*s have no real problem in negotiating dates or finding partners for their crimes against logic. Potential partners should be warned that *Q*s are creative in the bedroom too. If they're not the adventurous types, they're going to be surprised by the *Q*'s quirky carnal tastes.

Quentin Tarantino In one of the most riveting scenes in movie history, a helplessly bound policeman is imprisoned in a warehouse with the psychotic Mr. Blonde and Mr. Orange in *Reservoir Dogs*. For the next ten minutes the policeman is cruelly tortured in a musically accompanied, ear-slicing opus of violence. The ultraviolent film marked director/writer Quentin Tarantino's debut as a "director's director." ■ Quentin's next film, *Pulp Fiction*, rehabilitated the career of John Travolta and made Uma Thurman a bona fide star. Were it not for the fact that it was released the same year as *Forrest Gump*, *Pulp Fiction* would likely have won the Academy's Best Picture Award. ■ Quentin returned to his violent roots in 2003, with *Kill Bill*, a fanciful and lavishly choreographed tribute to martial-arts movies.

The Letter of Romance and Arousal

Most Popular Girl's Names

Ruth
Rebecca
Rose
Rachel
Ruby
Robin
Rita
Rosa
Rhonda
Regina

Most Popular Boy's Names

Robert
Richard
Ronald
Raymond
Ryan
Roger
Ralph
Roy
Randy
Russell

"The price of wisdom is above rubies."

—JOB 28:18,
King James Bible

Created by the gentle vibration of the tongue on the roof of the mouth, the red-blooded letter R gives birth to a low-throated grr as it rolls off the tongue, in impersonation of a human purr. This letter is relatively unusual in languages throughout the world, which may account for the fact that so many non-Europeans struggle to pronounce it. ■ This racy letter stands for Romeo, rapture, romance, risqué, reproductive, raunchy, rabbit, relish, rich, ripe, racy and randy. It also initializes rosy, ruby, rubiginous and ruddy, all of which have to do with red—the color traditionally associated with sexual arousal. Even in its darker manifestations, this passionate letter still clings to its sexual essence, as in ravished, raged, raped and ravage. ■ In addition to its indomitably carnal core, there's also the unmistakable element of the cheeky scoundrel found in the words rogue, raffish, rouge, rapscallion and ragamuffin. ■ The traditional meaning of names beginning with the red-blooded R tend to reflect its racy passion, as in Rena (reborn), Rhoda (roses), Ronald and Roy (royal), Russel (redhead) and Ryan (little king). ■ In general, people whose names begin with the letter R exhibit a high level of passion in their personal and professional lives. With their indomitable spirits, they embrace life with an animated zeal equal to those whose names begin with the other letter of passion, the V. Perhaps this is why people with an R name are the most likely to become millionaires and also the most likely to be involved in the medical professions. ■

THE ADAPTABLE

rb

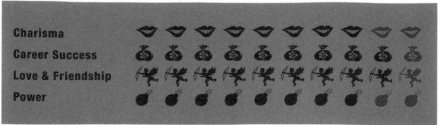

Charisma										
Career Success										
Love & Friendship										
Power										

Outgoing Sturdy Enthusiastic
Two-faced Variable Demanding

The letter *B's bullish* and *booming* resonance tends to infuse a sense of *brashness* and *belligerence* into words in which it appears. Its low-frequency tones are responsible for the words *bash, beat, break, battle, burly* and *beast,* and when it occurs in words initialized by the *racy, raunchy* and *randy* letter *R,* it takes on the brazen qualities found in the words *rebel, rugby, rabid, rebuke, rebuff* and *ribald.* These are people with a strong sense of self and show little interest in taking advice when it comes to forging their life paths.

Even though *RB*s have a firm grip on their own reins, they'll willingly submit to constraints in the workplace. One reason for accepting this trade-off is that money plays a big role in their lives and they are willing to swallow their pride if it helps them to succeed. It's also not unusual for *RB*s to move from place to place just to test whether the grass really *is* greener on the other side. So if you want your *RB* employee to stay put, make sure you offer them jobs with a great deal of upward mobility and a generous amount of green.

*RB*s are ideally suited for careers that involve travel, sales or outdoor work, but many *RB*s find success as small business owners or executives. Above all, *RB*s are restless people who enjoy testing their capabilities in various arenas and will tackle the most demanding jobs

Reba
Rob
Robby
Ruby

with nary a second thought. With their zeal and sense of purpose, *RB*s are among the highest earners in the *R* name category.

*RB*s are connoisseurs of the finer things in life, but although they appreciate art in all its forms, they are not the types to get their hands dirty in their creative pursuits: the concrete-minded *RB*s would rather buy artwork from people who know what they're doing. Likewise, *RB*s are picky about with whom they socialize, and they measure people against the same high standards that they apply to themselves.

If there's anything for which *RB*s can be faulted, it's their proclivity for concentrating too much on the things that *they* want to do, often at the expense of their personal relationships. Even though they have no problem (in principle) with accommodating their partners' needs, they prove less willing to compromise when it comes to issues of money and career. However, when matched with partners who are willing to put their *RB* mates on pedestals, marriages will function like well-oiled Rolls Royce engines. Children are not always first on the list of *RB*s' priorities—perhaps because they introduce a certain element of unpredictability to the *RB*'s otherwise orderly structure—but like most things *RB*s sink their teeth into, their kids will be efficiently raised and dutifully loved.

Rob Lowe Rob Lowe's acting career got off to an encouraging start when the Hollywood press dubbed him a member of "the Brat Pack," an amalgamation of up-and-coming actors that included Emilio Estevez, Sean Penn, Demi Moore and Ally Sheedy. ■ His appearance in his personally produced Sex and Videotape, in which he taped his own sex acts with a minor, created an avalanche of bad publicity in 1988 and sent his career into the doldrums. Some say that Rob owes the revival of his career to Mike Myers and company for hiring him for *Wayne's World* and *Austin Powers.* ■ In 2001, Rob received an Emmy Award nomination for his work on NBC's drama series *The West Wing,* but an unexpected salary dispute in 2002 triggered Rob's resignation from the show.

332

Charisma										
Career Success										
Love & Friendship										
Power										

Thoughtful Talented Multifaceted
Uptight Perfectionist Repressed

With its *brash* and *booming* resonance, the letter *B* reminds us of a *belligerent, bucking bronco,* while the cutting *K* sound (or hard *C*) evokes the images in the words *crack, crash, kick, king, kill, careen, clip* and *knuckle-sandwich*. Together, the *B* and *K* are so forcefully aggressive (*break, bonk, buck, block, brisk* and *bushwhack*) that it's clear that no one with an *RBK* name could ever be accused of being a milquetoast. Even when the *BK* combination appears in words softened by the *racy, romantic* and *randy* letter *R,* the ensuing words have an unmistakably assertive air: *rebuke, razorback, bark, bulwark, brisk, brick, break* and *berserk*. All told, it's not surprising that *RBK* people have reputations for being as unyielding as petrified oak and as reliable as gravity.

Making friends with such sanguine sprites can be a tricky mission at the best of times. The problem is that most *RBK*s show little interest in casual relationships, preferring the intimacy that comes with intense one-on-one relationships instead. The best approach to befriending these absorbed individuals is to remember that they distrust neediness in others and respond best when their friends affect attitudes of oblique interest. Even close personal friends find *RBK*s somewhat enigmatic, but would never question their strength of

Rebecca
Rebeka

character or their resolve to reach their full potential.

Despite their social reserve, *RBK*s can be quite emotional at times. They bond quite deeply and often find themselves entangled in darkly obsessive types of relationships from which they find it hard to emerge. Many *RBK*s have love adventures that could rival a soap opera, but since they are not ones to kiss and tell, you're not going to hear about these exploits firsthand.

The *RBK*'s feminine wiles combine with her masculine drive to make for an intimidating combination in the workplace, and her inner toughness is perfect for law, medicine or business. But there's still enough of the girl in the *RBK* to attract her to design, teaching and people-management. As workers, they have an abiding sense of responsibility toward their employers and would think little of working overtime if it meant getting the job done perfectly.

For all her impressive independence, at the end of the day, the *RBK* still needs companionship. A perfect union, from her point of view, is a working partnership with one part romance and one part down-and-dirty fun. And even when children are added to the equation, the *RBK*'s mate will remain her number-one priority. Her ideal mate is a man with the patience to unravel the thread of vulnerability running through her life.

Rebecca De Mornay Baby boomers will remember her as the icily alluring hooker who plucked Tom Cruise from boyhood in *Risky Business*. They may also remember her father, Wally George, incendiary patriarch of sensationalist talk shows, where guests were taunted until they leaped into the audience. Because Rebecca's connection to Wally wasn't deep, she took her stepfather's surname after being adopted at age five. ■ After making a splash in *Risky Business*, Rebecca followed up with *The Slugger's Wife* and *The Hand That Rocks the Cradle*, where her look of steely ruthlessness convinced audiences that sexy nannies were villainous home wreckers best to be avoided. ■ Tom Cruise fell for Rebecca off-screen as well, and lived with her for over two years before her brief marriage to fellow actor Bruce Wagner.

THE HELPFUL
rbn

Charisma										
Career Success										
Love & Friendship										
Power										

Willing Wide-eyed Driven
Irresponsible Immature Unfocused

If the letter *R* invariably connotes words with a cheeky sense of flirtatious fun, it's because it's the symbol for all things *racy, randy, romantic, ruddy, ripe* and *ribald*. The *brashly booming* tones of the letter *B*, on the other hand are commonly associated with *belligerence, beastly, blustery, bawdy* and *bully,* but are somewhat *blunted* when teamed up with the unassertive letter *N*, where it's transformed into *benign* words like *benevolent, bouncy, beneficial, bountiful* and *bunny*. All told, *RBN* people tend to be charming and strong, even if they lapse into the occasional bouts of gloom and immaturity.

These are people who could be described as romantics in the traditional sense: *RBN*s are often given to flights of fancy and love nothing better than indulging themselves in their imaginations. But don't make the mistake of characterizing them as wide-eyed innocents, because they're more than capable of fending for themselves and achieving great things. Still, it's not uncommon for *RBN*s to attach themselves to more decisive personalities who can inject them with a little motivation.

Sweet-natured though they may be, *RBN*s have decidedly feisty streaks that manifest when they sense

Reuben
Robena
Robin
Ruben

that someone is taking advantage of them. And while it's a little unfair to call them whiners, they're not above trying to make others feel guilty through a little teary-eyed manipulation. Friends and family soon learn that it's less of an effort to keep *RBN*s happy than it is to deal with their occasional spells of petulance.

Like most *R*-named people, *RBN*s know how to make money even if they're not particularly adept at hanging on to it. They are not natural savers, preferring to indulge themselves while the going's good . . . confident in their ability to make lots more in the future. Likewise, if they're going to invest, it'll probably be in the form of high-risk stocks rather than more conservative government bonds. When it comes to their careers, *RBN*s can certainly hold their own in competitive fields, but tend to excel when intellect and raw talent—rather than stamina and killer instinct—are the primary job requirements.

In their intimate unions, *RBN*s are generally upbeat and eager to please, but should avoid partnering with mates who are more pessimistic than they are. And because *RBN*s function best when the focus is taken off their own issues, marriages are far more likely to achieve stability when children are involved.

 **Ruben Studdard** When a teddy bear named Ruben Studdard auditioned for the chance to compete for the title of Fox Television's *American Idol* in 2003, all three judges—Simon Cowell, Randy Jackson and Paula Abdul—reported getting goose bumps during his performance. ■ Every week, over twenty million viewers watched and voted for the burly singer, eventually electing him the winner. Even though he survived a close call, Ruben, the early favorite in the competition, eventually edged out fellow Southerner Clay Aiken by a few thousand votes. For his efforts, Ruben was awarded a recording contract with J Records under the tutelage of industry legend Clive Davis. ■ Wearing his trademark oversized shirt emblazoned with the number 205, Ruben was responsible for bringing to national attention the area code of his hometown, Birmingham, Alabama.

334

THE ATTRACTIVE rbrt

Charisma	👄	👄	👄	👄	👄	👄	👄	👄	👄	👄
Career Success	💰	💰	💰	💰	💰	💰	💰	💰	💰	💰
Love & Friendship										
Power										

Agreeable Charismatic Balanced
Egotistical Morose Repressive

With its *brash* and *booming* resonance, the letter *B* imparts an aspect of *belligerence* to the words and names in which it appears. Its low-frequency tones are responsible for the words *bash, beat, break, battle, burly* and *beast,* and when combined with the *racy, randy* and *robust* letter *R* and the *triumphant, tremendous, terrific* and *talented* letter *T,* takes on all the *brilliant* qualities of the words *bright, bristling, vibrant, bratty, bravest* and *abrupt.* And because these names also *begin* with the letter *R, RBRTs* are usually those magnetic people who could charm the stripes off a sergeant.

It takes a great deal of energy to live up to the promise of an *RBRT* name and most of these people have had to deal with the expectations of parents and teachers from the time they were young. This explains why there are two kinds of *RBRTs* in the world: the overachievers, who are compelled to make an impression on the world, and the subdued *RBRTs,* who live life on their own terms, ignoring the expectations of society. But the one thing that all *RBRTs* have in common is the ability to knuckle down and do whatever it takes to excel in their careers and relationships.

If you've ever had the opportunity to date any *RBRTs,* you'll know that there's *something* about them that has a way of getting under your skin. Even if your

Robert
Roberta
Roberto

friends don't understand your attraction to your *RBRT* cohort, they'll have to concede that your *RBRT* lover is easygoing and companionable. Many *RBRTs* tend to be a little bookish at times, and even if they are not the most powerful public speakers, they will always have something interesting to say. And if you want to ingratiate yourself to an *RBRT,* just ask them for advice. They're always thrilled when people acknowledge their hard-won insights.

When it comes to love, *RBRTs* are fully aware of their sensual charms and won't hesitate to use them. When it comes to actually selecting their mates, no one has a clearer image of what constitutes the ideal relationship than they do. Many *RBRTs* have been working on their short-list of their mates' qualities since early childhood, and although it might take years to find *the one*, they're not going to give up until they do. And since *RBRTs* would *never* deign to lower their standards, if the perfect person doesn't materialize, they'll probably decide they're better off single. A word to the wise: if you're planning on courting one of these selective creatures, don't try to rush them by expecting too much after one or two dates. They'll know within the first five minutes if you are the right person; if you are, you'll get the message loud and clear.

Robert Downey, Jr. The irony of actor Robert Downey, Jr.'s breakout role as a strung-out drug user in the 1987 film *Less Than Zero* was not lost on the Hollywood press. They profited handsomely from his private-life exploits as an on-again off-again drug addict. But even though he's seen the inside of Betty Ford more than Gerald Ford ever did, Robert's career has flourished. ■ When working on the set of the Wesley Snipes film *U.S. Marshals,* Robert told director Mike Figgis, "I'd rather wake up in jail for a TB test than to have to wake up another morning knowing I'm going to the set of *U.S. Marshals.*" ■ In 1992, Robert delivered his tour de force as the title character in *Chaplin,* and his portrayal of the little tramp earned him an Oscar nomination for Best Actor.

Charisma										
Career Success										
Love & Friendship										
Power										

Versatile Contemplative Practical Closed Complex Stubborn

When a word contains the *CH* phoneme it invariably displays the benign sense of *cheeky cheerfulness* found in the words *cherub, cheeky, chocolate, chide, childhood, chummy, chamomile* and *chipmunk*. And since these names are initialized by the flagship letter of all things *racy, ribald, robust* and *romantic*, they tend to herald a personality of uncommon buoyant energy with a creative essence that's second to none.

*RCH*s may have a romantic streak to rival any Romeo or Juliet, but these are no wide-eyed dreamers. They may also flit in and out of relationships, but there's always a sense of purpose, like they have a plan and are sticking to it. And *RCH*s aren't going to let little things like tradition and society's expectations to get in their way either. They know what they want and are perfectly willing to break convention to get it. By the same token, *RCH*s aren't afraid of being judged. They are grounded by deep moral convictions and are supremely confident in the purity of their motives.

Versatility is the name of the game here, and these multifaceted folk are able to adapt to pretty much any situation; so if its Renaissance people you're after, look no further. When it comes to their careers, *RCH* people are willing to do just about anything—artwork, research, firefighting, waiting tables—as long as it doesn't distract them from their true purpose: exploring

Rachael
Rachel
Rich
Richard
Richelle
Richie
Rochelle

the universe. Monotony is the archenemy of the *RCH,* so if you find yourself in a relationship with one of these eager sprites, you'd better be able to keep the spices flowing.

In their professional lives, their streak of individualism means that they're far more likely to end up planting their own fields rather than tending someone else's. But whether or not they're in business for themselves, their lifestyles will always include plenty of time for self-expression and stimulation. Like most *R*-named people, *RCH*s are amongst the top wage earners in their peer group—even if they show a remarkable disinterest in accumulating wealth. Acting, music and dancing *do* hold their interest however, and even if *RCH*s aren't professionally involved in the arts, will likely be avid supporters of them.

Although these liberated spirits are often led to obscure and remote locales, they also have a strong desire to settle down and raise their families. Deciding which of these lifestyles to choose can cause considerable angst in *RCH*s' lives, but their urge to nest will *almost* always override their impulse to wander. Still, just because *RCH*s get married doesn't mean they're rejecting the joys of independence. This usually expresses itself in the way they raise their children, who are encouraged to follow in the *RCH*'s rambling footsteps.

Richard Gere Richard Gere has been the unfortunate recipient of more slander than any Hollywood actor in recent memory, but his on-screen persona remains compelling and unimpeachable. Despite rumors of homosexuality and even more hurtful stories, he continues to enjoy his heartthrob status and is one of the most consistently successful actors on the big screen. ■ International recognition came from his leading roles in movies showcasing his dramatic and comedic range: *American Gigolo, Pretty Woman, Mr. Jones* and *Internal Affairs.* ■ True to his Buddhist philosophy, Richard ignores rumors regarding his sexual orientation: "I know who I am; who cares what anyone thinks? If I were a leopard, and someone came up and started screaming, 'You're a cow!'—would a leopard be uptight about this?"

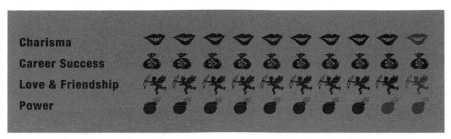

Charisma

Career Success

Love & Friendship

Power

**Determined Enthusiastic Spunky
Cranky Hot-tempered Volatile**

Because the letter *R* is the flagship letter of all things cheekily romantic (*racy, red-blooded, rosy, roguish, rapture* and *ripe*), its combination with the letter *D* tends to bring out its *darker* elements. For even though the *D* is often considered to be the icon of *discipline* and *dignity*, it can also be the harbinger of *doom, destruction* and *danger.* This is why, when the *R* and *D* are found in close proximity, they tend to form words with distinctly impudent tones: *rude, rowdy, ribald, randy, reprimand* and *ridiculous.*

It's hard to predict which *RD* you're going to encounter on any given day: the moody obsessive *RD*, or the easygoing dapper one. Either way, you won't be able to ignore these energized firebrands, who have personalities as hot as flames and just as dangerous. But don't let their explosive nature intimidate you, for *RD* people also have extraordinarily warm hearts that temper their extravagant dispositions, and would never dream of using their dominant natures for anything other than forming deeply intimate relationships.

Many people have love/hate relationships with the *RD*s in their lives, and this might be because *RD*s can be so uncommunicative about their intentions that it is hard to predict their next moves. Still, *RD*s are also deeply devoted to their loved ones and would go to any

Red
Reed
Rhoda
Ridge
Ridley
Rod
Roderick
Rodney
Rodrigo
Rudy
Ryder

lengths to ensure their happiness. *RD*s have their own high expectations of friendship as well and if they were to have a family crest, it would say something like, "Once a friend, always a friend. One betrayal and you're history."

*RD*s are drawn to jobs that promise them enough leeway to make their own decisions (and those that offer the most liberal vacation policies). And even though hard work is not *RD*s' cup of chai, it's a reflection of their natural intelligence that they invariably manage to succeed in the workplace. When *RD*s are lucky enough to find jobs that encompass one of their passions (science, philosophy, politics and money), odds are they're going to make their mark in a big way.

When it comes to their intimate relationships, their high emotional metabolism makes for extremely intense unions, and even if your *RD* sweetheart isn't the kind to shower you with roses and cards, chances are that they'll make up for it with surprises and romantic adventures. But don't expect *RD*s to throw themselves into relationships without a safety valve for their emotions—they are always poised to bail out if things don't go according to plan. Those who appreciate high drama in their lives will find the *RD* to be a perfect mate.

Rod Stewart Although he has been derisively called "Rod the Mod" for his flashy lifestyle, critics have lauded Rod Stewart's trademark fusion of rock, folk and blues. ■ Ever since his music career took off in the late sixties, Rod has lived the prototypical life of an eighties rocker: jet-setting across the world in search of parties, yet still finding time to put together quality songs, like "Some Guys Have All the Luck," "What Am I Gonna Do" and "Every Beat of My Heart." His 1995 album is considered by many to be his best. It came around his fiftieth birthday—a time when most singers are vying for center square on Hollywood Squares. ■ Rod's marriage to supermodel Rachel Hunter in 1990 produced two children and plenty of fodder for the tabloid press.

THE IRREPRESSIBLE rf

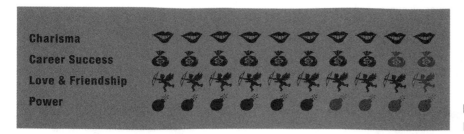

Charisma	
Career Success	
Love & Friendship	
Power	

Energetic Loving Openminded
Misunderstood Obtuse Frustrated

The letter *F* (and the sound created by the *PH* phoneme) is the icon for all things *fun, flamboyant, flirtatious, flighty, funky, flippant, fresh* and *friendly*. So when the sound combines with the *racy, randy, ravishing, romantic, restless* letter *R*, it takes on the cheeky and festive characteristics found in the words *raffish, artful, crafty, refreshing, cheerful* and *carefree*. No matter what people say about the *RF* personalities, it always includes something about their undaunted optimism. And even when this enthusiasm isn't always apparent on the surface, their imaginative natures can't help but show themselves in the *RFs*' unguarded moments.

When young, *RF* people were likely to have enjoyed popularity in their schools. But no matter how many friends *RFs* had, few people would have claimed to have truly known them. But don't make the mistake of thinking that *RFs* are stuck-up; it's just that most of them can't be bothered to take the time to explain their motivations.

RFs have excellent taste in people and a corresponding fondness for the finer things in life. They would rather have one good friend than a bunch of hangers-on, just as they will have a nice couch over a roomful of econo-furniture. Not that *RFs* aren't going to be able to

Rafaela
Ralph
Raphael
Rayford
Rodolfo
Rolf
Rudolph
Rufus

afford anything they want, mind you, for like most *R*-named people they know how to make money and are very capable with managing it. They pursue their careers with the same vigor as they do their relationships.

A well-developed reading habit makes them instant "experts" at just about any subject; a quality that evokes admiration and often jealousy. They spend an awful lot of time in their own heads—soaking up new ideas and testing them on friends and family—sometimes to the detriment of their relationships, but *RFs* usually manage to hide their know-it-all attitudes when they want to put others at ease.

Although *RFs* tend to settle down late in life, they really shine when it comes to matters of the heart. Unfailingly affectionate, these ebullient lovers will shower their mates with affection and support, even if it takes some effort to get them to completely open up. Those who bridge the gap will be rewarded with wonderfully optimistic and emotionally complex partners.

RFs may not be the most responsible parents in the world but they are among the most demonstrative. And because *RFs* are great believers in the advantages of education, they will often supplement their children's learning with some kind of hands-on home schooling.

Ralph Fiennes When Ralph (pronounced Rafe) Fiennes accepted a role in a remake of *Wuthering Heights*, it generated such withering criticism that his career seemed over before it began. Poor reviews notwithstanding, Ralph's brooding performance caught the eye of director Steven Spielberg, who cast him as a sadistic Nazi in *Schindler's List*. Ralph received an Oscar nomination for his dark portrayal and won a second nomination for his work as the romantic hero in *The English Patient*. ■ He revisited his villainous roots in the film *Red Dragon*, a prequel to *Silence of the Lambs*, bringing an element of sympathy to his otherwise noxious character. ■ Rumors abounded about his relationship with English actress Francesca Annis, but Ralph, seventeen years her junior, modestly denied rumors of a secret marriage.

rg

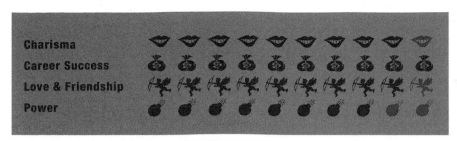

Charisma										
Career Success										
Love & Friendship										
Power										

Unique Self-directed Reassuring
Intimidating Uncommunicative Distant

Although most names that begin with the *red-blooded, racy* letter *R* tend to suggest individuals with cheekily irrepressible spirits, the sober aspects of the letter *G* tend to modulate this impudence and imbue these names with a touch of grace. For the *G* is the icon for all things *good, glorious, gentle, genuine* and *genial,* and it's hardly surprising to find, that when combined with the letter *R,* words take on a decidedly princely air: *regal, rightly, reign, regalia, regime, rugged, regulate* and *regimented.* This effect is somewhat subdued in the case of the *RGN* names (*Regan, Reagan* and *Reginald*) since the letter *N* is the essence of all things *negative* (*no, never, not, nyet, nada, nothing, null, none*) and gives these names their aspect of pessimism and self-doubt.

These people have well-deserved reputations for their strong sense of moral direction . . . and a superior attitude to boot. But *RG*s also have an unusual streak of humor that belies their aloofness and there's a touch of naïveté that makes them easy marks for conspiracy theories and practical jokes. It's not that they're dull-witted by any means; in fact, it's thanks to their extraordinary street smarts that they make the kind of money they do. Just don't tease the *RG*s about their gullibility. It is often said that *RG*s can laugh at anything except themselves.

Life is lived moment-to-moment with these individuals and it shows in their daily routine—or lack thereof. For *RG*s perform poorly in structured environments, and although they'll willing to bite their tongues when they sense sufficient financial rewards, they're far more interested in jobs that stimulate their minds than they are in jobs with high status. If *RG*s become doctors, you *know* they're not doing it for the money. However, like most *R*-named people, they're not the types to let hard work to keep them from having healthy social lives, and to cope with daily frustrations, they must find ways to blow them off—either in the gym or with a good stiff drink. Otherwise, as *RG*s well know, life's little problems can build up and threaten the balance of their finely tuned existence.

Having a partner is essential to *RG*s' well-being, but they place less emphasis on traditional romantic gestures than they do the practical issues of marriage. Since few things make an *RG* as uncomfortable as being emotionally vulnerable, they like to keep their spouses slightly off-balance with regards to their inner lives. But even though they may hide behind sarcasm or the occasional temper tantrum, *RG*s' motives are pretty transparent to those who know them well. That's why *RG*s can only relax and enjoy the ride once they've accepted the fact that their mates love them for better and worse.

Reagan
Regan
Reggie
Regina
Reginald
Regine
Regis
Rigoberto
Rogelio
Roger
Rogers

Reggie Jackson If baseball superstar Reggie Jackson had a motto, it would probably have something to do with talking loudly and carrying a big stick. Reggie certainly had a lot to say about his teammates, his fans, the owners, and especially his manager, Billy Martin, with whom he had a love/hate relationship. It wasn't always pretty. ■ But Reggie could be charming as well, and fans responded to his prowess with his big stick by bestowing on him the title, Mr. October, for his extraordinary successes in the post season. ■ Although criticized for his lack of defense, Reggie always rose to the occasion. He won the homerun title three times and was responsible for some of the most dramatic homeruns in the history of baseball. Reggie's teams played in seventeen post-season series, winning five World Series titles.

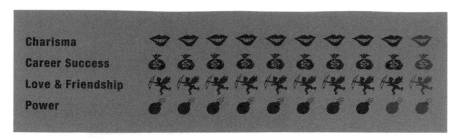

Charisma	👄	👄	👄	👄	👄	👄	👄	👄	👄	👄
Career Success	💰	💰	💰	💰	💰	💰		💰	💰	💰
Love & Friendship										
Power										

**Bold Intelligent Quick-thinking
Dramatic Impatient Distracted**

The sharply pronounced *K* sound imparts an aggressive sense of urgency to the words and names in which it appears, and its forceful nature can be discerned in the words *kick, kill, king, kidnap, knuckle, knife* and *knight.* And since the letter *R* is the symbol for the more defiant aspects of passion—*raunchy, racy, ribald, randy, rapture, ravish* and *relish*—its combination with the *K* sound tends to produce words with a dashing flair: *rakish, raconteur, prankster, remarkable, risky, rocket, perky* and *quirky. RK* people simply don't believe in holding anything back; on the contrary, they'll practically tear their hearts out and sew them to their sleeves.

*RK*s love being the center of attention, but aren't the types to leap onto center stage. They prefer, instead, standing apart from the crowd by either dressing a little better than most or driving the latest model car. And with a physical presence that matches their powerful desire for respect, *RK*s will let you know—in no uncertain terms—when you breach their zone of comfort by being too chummy. Even though they share the inherent playfulness of the *R* names, there's an added edge that puts some teeth into their smiles. *RK*s are typically active people who excel at a number of physical pastimes. But because of their strong competitive drives, they are more likely to choose activities that

Racquel
Raekwon
Ricardo
Rick
Ricky
Rico
Rieko
Rikki
Rocco
Rocio
Rocky
Roscoe

place the emphasis on individual achievement, rather than team sports in which their accomplishments may be diluted.

You'll never have to wonder where *RK*s stand on issues. In fact, with their unfiltered tell-it-like-it-is style of communication, you may wish that they *would* let you wonder a little more. But as tiresome as the drama in *RK*s' lives can be, one must admit that the world would be a much duller place without them. For *RK*s can be quite endearing when they choose to be, and there's plenty of room for rewarding friendships once you get used to their off-again on-again ways. If you're looking for a cheap way to befriend an *RK,* make sure you laugh at his or her jokes.

Mucking about in relationships is among *RK*s' favorite pastimes, and they usually devote a great deal of their energy to dating and mating. If falling in love is one of their specialties, it's because they have so much practice at it. But to be fair, *RK*s *will* give marriage a damn good shot once they've had a chance to sow their wild oats. Overall, marriage with an *RK* should be a rewarding affair mixed with moments that would try the patience of a saint, but if you love surprises and are up for adventures, you'll find your thrill with this urbane extrovert.

Ricky Martin Ricky Martin, the Puerto Rican prince of pop, took just eighteen years to reach his status as global heartthrob and sex symbol. ■ To date, Ricky has sold over fifteen million records worldwide, his extraordinary success a testament to the power of teenage lust. ■ Teens all over the world thrilled to Ricky's Latin rhythms, and for a while in the late nineties it seemed that every patron in nightclubs and bars was "Livin' la Vida Loca" and shaking their "Bon Bons." His concerts even evoked memories of the Elvis craze in the sixties, when breathless young beauties threw themselves (or sometimes just their panties) onto the stage. ■ Even though persistent rumors of homosexuality have plagued him for years, Ricky couldn't care less. To him, it's the rhythm that counts.

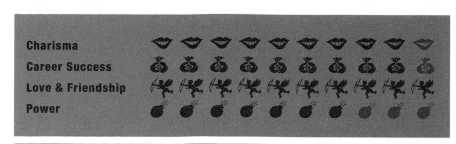

Charisma									
Career Success									
Love & Friendship									
Power									

Humorous Dignified Fashionable
Moody Cloying Manipulative

The letter *L* is the definitive symbol for all the things in life that can't be bought with money: *life, love, luck, liberty, learning* and *laughter*. Its languid articulation also categorizes it as a letter of romance, which explains why it is the initial letter of *lip-licking, leering, lascivious, libido, lacy* and *ladylike*. And because the *racy, ravishing, rapturous* letter *R* is another member of the romance group, it's hardly surprising that the *R* and *L* conspire to portray the sense of defiant passion found in the words *rascal, rebel, ribald, roll, rustler, revel, rumpled, brothel, harlot, swirl* and *arousal*. It's also true that both letters are associated with high levels of charm, warmth and intelligence, which is why *RL* people are typically bright, if not a little precocious. The name *Raylene* is the only one in this group to suffer from any kind of pessimistic downbeat, a result of the negative essence of the letter *N*—*no, not, never, nada, null* and *nothing*.

It has been said that the love of money is the root of all evil, but to the *RL* it's the *lack* of money, and no matter what they do for a living, you can be sure that they'll manage their money wisely. In both their careers and their personal lives, boredom is the *RL*'s archenemy, and it's unusual to find them in jobs that don't have some unique aspect to them. If they're going to be teachers, for example, they'll probably be involved in special edu-

Rael
Rahul
Raleigh
Raul
Raylene
Reilly
Rollin
Royal
Rylan

cation. And if they're working in an office, they're the ones who're in charge of the social planning. Still, most *RLs* find it difficult to stay with any one job for too long—unless of course the money's good—and it's not unusual for them to switch boats in midstream.

While this is obviously a drawback for some employers, it dovetails quite nicely into the *RL*'s nomadic philosophy.

Those who are turned on by the traditional notions of romance may not want to consider dating *RLs*, for these are men and women who don't go by the book when it comes to intimacy. You're likely to find yourself competing with a host of ex-lovers with whom they still have contact, or playing second fiddle to the *RL*'s career. Still, if you're not the jealous type and enjoy the challenges of dating someone as popular as the *RL*, then you're in for a wild ride. And if the *RL* isn't your first choice for a lifelong mate, you won't get any argument from them; they view their relationships as testing grounds for future marriage.

Only when the urge to raise a family overtakes them will they deign to restrict their lifestyles and concentrate on one partner. But *RLs* grow up pretty quickly when children enter the scene and will drop their party-animal façade to become a solid, grounded parent for whom family unity is a prime concern.

Raul Julia When he was only five years old, Raul Julia gave an intense performance as the devil in a red suit with little red horns. With his acting fire lit, the Puerto Rican native was poised to become one of the greatest stage actors of his generation. ■ Raul liked to portray deeply passionate characters, like the political prisoner in *Kiss of the Spider Woman* and the Brazilian activist Chico Mendes in *The Burning Season*. With his dark Latin looks and generous acting style, Raul could play anything from the flamboyant lawyer in *Presumed Innocent* to the macabre Gomez in the hit comedy *The Addams Family* opposite Anjelica Huston. ■ A connoisseur of wine and fine cigars, Raul died of throat cancer in the 1990s.

rmn

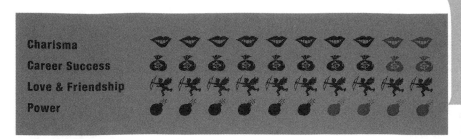

Charisma											
Career Success											
Love & Friendship											
Power											

Adventurous Personable Loving
Idealistic Vague Stubborn

The *R* is the symbol for all things *racy, randy, romantic, ruddy, ripe* and *ribald,* and the names it initializes are colored with a cheeky sense of defiant fun. The letter *M,* on the other hand, is the symbol for *maternal* love (*maiden, matron, mercy, mild* and *madam*) and is the key letter of the word *mother* in virtually every language on earth. It's not surprising, therefore, that the combination of the *M* and *R* creates words with a *warmly romantic* air: *harem, rhythm, romp, charm* and *Romeo.* But since the *RMN* names are also dominated by the letter *N*— the icon of all things *negative* (*no, not, never, nada, null, nothing, nada, nyet* and *naught*)—these are people who, for all their emotional intelligence, have a deeply rooted aspect of self-doubt that pervades their lives.

With their zest for stimulation, it's not likely that you'll find many *RMNs* who enjoy staying indoors. The universe is so irresistibly exciting to them that if they had their druthers, they would see it all. There's no question that *RMNs* are adventurers at heart, and even those who don't get the opportunity to tromp all over the place will have their share of adventures and engaging stories. And yet, even with their penchant for travel and exploration, *RMNs* never stray too far from their emotional nests: they are too tightly bound to their families and loved ones.

Ramon
Ramona
Ramonita
Raymond
Raymonde
Raymundo
Remington
Romaine
Roman
Romana

When it comes to their careers, *RMNs* are natural educators who are drawn to young people for their curiosity and love of learning. Children respond likewise to the *RMNs*' abilities to relate to them on their own level, and many *RMNs* make a good living in teaching and coaching. Their social skills are sophisticated enough to facilitate jobs in which they deal with the public, but very few *RMNs* actually enjoy the competitiveness of cutthroat sales and marketing careers.

Because *RMNs* are happiest when they're learning about the world and sharing it with others, their idea of a perfect evening is philosophizing with a group of friends over a bottle of wine. Most of their romantic matches materialize from situations like this, and if you're looking to spice up your love life with the equivalent of an Italian lover, then you might want to invite yourself to one of their soirées. Even if you're not in the mood for a romantic liaison, you'll certainly appreciate the *RMNs*' childlike sense of wonder.

When it comes intimate affairs, *RMNs* might be roamers but there is no greater goal in their lives than having their own families. As lovers they may be a little on the overeager side, but what they lack in finesse is more than made up for in sensitivity and affection.

Roman Polanski Roman Polanski is one of those rare people to achieve notoriety on three different fronts. ■ There's Roman Polanski the hero, an extraordinarily well-respected filmmaker with almost twenty feature films to his credit, including *Rosemary's Baby, Macbeth, The Tenant* and the Academy Award–winning *Chinatown.* ■ Then there's Roman Polanski the victim, whose wife, Sharon Tate, was carrying Roman's child when she was brutally murdered by Charles Manson's gang. ■ And then there's Roman the villain, who for over twenty-five years has been on the run from police for the statutory rape of a thirteen-year-old girl. ■ Still active as a director, Roman recently directed the critically acclaimed film *The Pianist,* which garnered its leading man, Adrien Brody, a Best Actor Academy Award.

rn

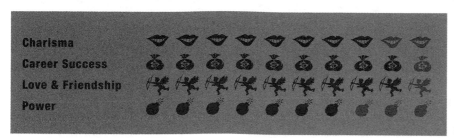

Charisma										
Career Success										
Love & Friendship										
Power										

Nurturing Reassuring Inspiring
Stubborn Pessimistic Emotional

The *nasally* pronounced letter *N* is associated with all things *negative* (*no, not, nyet, nada, null, nothing, nowhere, nitwit* and *naught*). Even the cheeky appeal of the *red-blooded* letter *R* does little to lift the *N* from its pessimistic funk, creating words like *runt, ruin, renege, rancid, rank, raunchy, rankle, repent, rodent* and *ruin.* Perhaps this is why most *RN* names either end with a vowel or with the infantilizing letters *I* and *Y.* (Words that end with these high-pitched letters, invariably connote things with a playful and less-serious air: *happy, silly, funny, dreamy, dizzy* and *goofy*). But even though most *RN*s are prone to occasional bouts of cynicism and self-doubt, these are people with extraordinarily high emotional IQs and a willingness to share their insights with those who need it.

In addition to their eager ability to nurture those around them, *RN*s have an unusually whimsical sense of humor that is often lost on those without an intimate understanding of what makes them tick. There's also a touch of impulsiveness in the way they conduct themselves, which ends up costing them in their professional lives, where they rarely make it to the top of their chosen careers. Always suckers for a sale (and online auctions), *RN*s have a tendency to medicate any emotional weaknesses with their somewhat out-of-control shopping habits. Still, like most people whose

Ron
Rona
Ronan
Raeann
Rahsaan
Ranee
Rayna
Rayshawn
Rena, Renee
Renna
Rhiannon
Rianna
Rohan
Roni, Ronna
Rowan
Rowena
Ryan

names begin with the letter *R*, money troubles are rare for *RN*s, who are likely to have tidy sums stashed away for those rainy days.

With an easy laugh that belies their earnest essence, *RN*s are careful to surround themselves with people they can trust. These aren't the kind of people to take unnecessary risks, and their politics, home lives and musical tastes all lean toward the right. The great thing about this is that you'll never have to worry about *RN*s' fidelity; their moral values are of the old-fashioned kind, which includes following through on *all* of their commitments.

RN individuals are particularly successful in relationships when paired with needy people who can really use their thoughtful advice. But theirs are going to be supportive roles (rather than those of leadership): born of intuitiveness and empathy. *RN*s are somewhat passive when it comes to the big decisions like marriage and having babies, and will rarely take the initial step in initiating the process. Even when *RN*s *think* they are doing the choosing, chances are their mates have subtly led them down the road. But once ensconced in a committed relationship, *RN*s will be as happy as a box of birds. And when they're able to unburden themselves with someone with whom they trust, their mates and children will experience that famous *RN* unconditional affection.

Renée Zellweger That old saw about hair color's relationship to intelligence doesn't seem to apply to Renée Zellweger. The strawberry blonde was a top student at the University of Texas and made the dean's list several times. ■ Her breakthrough role opposite Tom Cruise was in *Jerry* "You had me at 'hello'" *Maguire.* ■ Renée went on to display her acting versatility with her comedic performance in *Bridget Jones's Diary*, gaining forty pounds for the film and winning her first Oscar nomination. ■ In *Chicago*, Renée played Roxie Hart, an innocently sly ingénue whose on-screen chemistry with Catherine Zeta Jones helped land the film its Best Picture Oscar.

Charisma	💋	💋	💋	💋	💋	💋	💋	💋	💋	💋
Career Success	💰	💰	💰	💰	💰	💰	💰	💰	💰	💰
Love & Friendship	🏹	🏹	🏹	🏹	🏹	🏹	🏹	🏹	🏹	
Power	💣	💣	💣	💣	💣	💣	💣	💣	💣	💣

Energetic Kindhearted Spunky
Temperamental Unpredictable Intimidating

Whenever a name begins with the *red-blooded* letter *R*, we typically find a personality that contains heavy doses of passion and spunk. And in the case of the *RND* names, this high level of emotionality is often associated with an overly volatile nature. Perhaps this is because the letter *N* is the definitive symbol of all things *negative* (*no, not, never, nada, null, nothing, nada, nyet* and *naught*), while the *D*'s dark side is displayed in the words *doom, damnation, devil, demon, destroy, danger* and *dominate*. This is why many *RND* people terminate their names with a vowel or the youthful letter *Y* or *I*, as in *Randy* and *Randi*. Any time a name ends with a high-pitched letter, it has the diminutizing effects seen in *silly, funny, kitty, goofy, happy* and *dizzy*.

An *RND* can appear to be quite threatening to someone who doesn't know the difference between a bark and a bite. But if you've ever had one for a friend, you'll know that their feisty temperaments have their origins in hearts of gold. Unlike most people whose names begin with an *R*, *RND*s have a natural air of authority about them and a corresponding tendency to take control of situations. In part, this stems from the fact that *RND*s have a fear of rejection, but it's also a symptom of extraordinary talent and ability. Mind you, even though

Randall
Randolph
Randy
Reinaldo
Reynalda
Reynaldo
Rhonda
Roland
Rolanda
Rolande
Rolando
Ronald
Ronaldo

the *RND*s are softies deep down, they are not above capitalizing on their intimidating effect in the workplace where they often end up in positions of leadership and responsibility.

Like most people with a passion for life, *RND*s have a thirst for learning and discovery. This does not mean that they're necessarily going to do well in structured learning environments (formal education tends to retard their imaginations), but they are voracious readers and consumers of news and popular culture. And even if you wouldn't describe them as Renaissance men or women, they can hold their own on a surprising number of subjects: everything from computers to the arts to science and firefighting.

RND mates are good to have around when the chips are down. They will gladly hold the reins in difficult situations, and their calming presence will be welcome with the pressure is on. This isn't to say that they aren't going to have their down times, mind you, because for all their competent carriage, *RND*s can be somewhat obsessive and suffer from periodic bouts of depression and heavy soul-searching. In these melancholic moments, the normally sociable *RND*s prefer to lick their wounds in private: all the better to spin their angst into something creative.

Randy Quaid Randy Quaid has parlayed his distinctive joke's-on-me acting style into a career that has spanned thirty years. All this from a man who began his career as a clown at Houston's AstroWorld amusement park. ■ The brother of actor Dennis Quaid, Randy got his break when director Peter Bogdanovich cast him as the goofy guy who takes Cybill Shepherd to a nude party in *The Last Picture Show*. ■ Randy's biggest commercial success came from playing the goofball Cousin Eddie in *National Lampoon's* three *Family Vacation* movies, but it was his little-noticed dramatic roles that brought him critical acclaim; included among them, *Midnight Express*, *The Long Riders*, *The Missouri Breaks* and *Independence Day*. His role as a kleptomaniac sailor opposite Jack Nicholson in *The Last Detail* earned him an Oscar nomination in 1973.

THE RELIABLE

rp

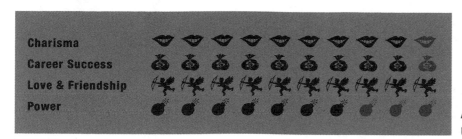

Charisma		
Career Success		
Love & Friendship		
Power		

Accepting Dignified Steady
Unemotional Misunderstood Smothering

As the initial letter of *patron, providence, Pope* and *paternal,* the *peaceful* letter *P* evokes an air of benign parental dependability. So when it occurs in names beginning with the *racy, ribald, red-blooded* letter *R*, it suggests an individual who manages to be both passionate and sober at the same time. The *RP* man is someone who—although he may have a high emotional metabolism—is unlikely to wear his heart on his sleeve. He carries himself with a quiet self-respecting air and reserves his passion for those moments when it will carry the most impact.

The *RP*'s natural affability lends itself well to dealing with all sorts of people and he can hold his own on pretty much any conversation topic. But if the *RP* personality is defined by gentility, it comes with a cheeky sense of humor that often goes over the head of his companions. It 's hard to get an *RP* stressed out, which is why he's so good at solving other people's problems, but then again, *RP*s don't expend too much physical energy on other people's issues. These are behind-the-scenes individuals who usually prefer to facilitate rather than direct.

And yet, *RP*s have a habit of getting involved in relationships with troubled individuals in an attempt to "fix them." Some would call this meddling, but it seems to help the *RP* feel useful. Loved ones get used to being

Rupert

the unwilling recipients of his insistent advice, and rolling their eyes isn't going to help either; he can be quite stubborn in getting his point across, even if his views on life are a little predictable at times.

The *RP*s' inclination to share their wisdom makes them terrific advisors and business partners, and they often choose sensible careers like accounting or banking in which their calm presence instills confidence in their customers. And even though they're not above the occasional foray into the more flamboyant, right-brained fields like acting and dancing, it's a rare *RP* that will be caught flaunting his feelings in public unless he's deeply outraged or deeply in love.

Talking of love, it usually comes relatively late in the lives of *RP*s for the simple reason that they don't put out their romantic welcome mats until they've achieved a certain level of success in their work. For like many people whose names begin with the letter *R*, they'll pursue their careers, their travels, and their hobbies with far more ardor than they pursue their love affairs. But if the magic moment finally arrives, *RP*s will blithely give up all these distractions for their new love. His mate can expect a well-feathered nest and all the benefits of being partnered to a stable and always dignified soul.

Rupert Everett He's been called a blend of Cary Grant and Joan Crawford, a title from which most red-blooded American male actors would shrink. Fortunately, Rupert Everett is quite at home with whatever title people suggest, thank you very much. ■ Rupert initially won rave reviews for his stage performances, but after some poor role choices, his career sank into virtual insignificance. Things took a turn for the better when he showed up in *My Best Friend's Wedding* as Julia Roberts' gay best friend. ■ If writers seem riveted by the subject of his sexuality, it might have something to do with the fact that Rupert openly admits to having supported himself through prostitution as a young man—an admission that would have certainly destroyed the careers of lesser men.

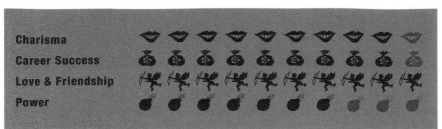

Charisma										
Career Success										
Love & Friendship										
Power										

Lighthearted Expressive Engaging
Immature Petty Changeable

Of all the names that begin with the *red-blooded, romantic* letter *R*, the *RS* group is perhaps the most irrepressible and outgoing. For when the *R* occurs in words alongside the *sexy, sassy, sensual, slippery* letter *S*, it typically creates the sense of vigorous sensuality found in the words: *rosy, robust, raffish, perverse, arouse* and *orgasm*. Consequently, most of us perceive the *RS* personalities to be extraordinarily physical and passionate people, with a yen for flirting and an impish sense of humor to boot.

If there's anything negative to say about these people, it's that they have a tendency to be somewhat immature. But while they are often accused of never really growing up, *RS*s consider this a compliment.

These may be generous and big-hearted people, but they can also be as stubborn as a '67 Buick on a winter's morning. And although many find their obstinacy somewhat off-putting, *RS*s are not aggressive by any measure, and possess a set of exceptional verbal skills that they use to gracefully defend themselves. The truth is, that while it may be easy to work yourself into the *RS*'s bad graces, it's unlikely that you'll remain there long. They're as temperamental as summer storms, and once the clouds have evaporated, you'll realize that your friend-

Risa
Raisa
Reece
Reese
Reyes
Rosaria
Rosario
Ramsey
Rashad
Rasheed
Rosia
Rosita
Ross
Rosy
Royce
Rush
Russ
Rusty
Rosie
Rose
Rosa

ship was never really in jeopardy. All this explains why *RS* people are so well known for their fiercely loyal cadres of friends.

If the *RS* could choose a dream job, it would probably involve something in show business: not because they're particularly talented, but because their egos require plenty of stroking. This may be why *RS* people so often draw attention to themselves in the way they dress or in the cars they drive, but it wouldn't be fair to label them as mere poseurs. Their hearts are clearly in the right place, and no matter how proud they may be, will always come down to earth when friends need their help.

*RS*s tend to be careful about making commitments, mainly because they are so determined to keep their word once it's been given. So if they take their time in tying the knot, it's usually a symptom of this fear—rather than a reflection of their lack of romantic feelings. Ultimately, *RS* mates will prove to be affectionate partners, even if their somewhat immature need for attention gets in the way of their relationships. But if you want to see *RS*s really shine, wait for them to become parents. Having children gives them the opportunity to relive the childhood they never wanted to leave behind.

Rosie O'Donnell Anyone who was homecoming queen, prom queen and class clown in the same high school year was certainly likely to succeed. ■ Rosie O'Donnell (born Roseann) had a successful stint as a stand-up comedienne around the same time that Jerry Seinfeld and Ellen DeGeneres were honing their crafts. ■ Rosie became the host of daytime's *The Rosie O'Donnell Show* and successfully competed for viewers against the likes of Oprah. Her show won a half-dozen Emmy awards and was still a moneymaker when it went off the air in 2001. ■ In 2003, Rosie was involved in a highly publicized lawsuit with the former publishers of her magazine, *Rosie*. The result was a draw. ■ Rosie, who has never been married, is the mother of three adopted children.

Charisma	😗😗😗😗😗😗😗😗😗
Career Success	💰💰💰💰💰💰💰💰💰
Love & Friendship	🏹🏹🏹🏹🏹🏹🏹🏹🏹
Power	💣💣💣💣💣💣💣💣💣

Innovative Sexual Compassionate Sarcastic Stubborn Uptight

When the *red-blooded* letter *R*—the symbol for all things *racy, randy, romantic, ruddy, ripe* and *ribald*—initializes a word, it usually instills it with a sense of mischievous fun. And as the initial letter of *sexy, sultry, sassy, sensuality* and *siren*, the letter *S* has a similar effect although it should be noted that when the *S* occurs in close proximity to the letter *L*, it creates the unmistakable sense of all things *slippery, sloppy, slick, slimy, slinky, slithery, slobber* and *slushy*. All told, *RSL* names suggest people who are hard to pin down and who have precocious senses of humor that can deliver unexpected bites.

Even though *RSLs* can come across as being rather sarcastic (and even a little aggressive) at times, it's really just a symptom of their inherent shyness in meeting new people. This isn't to say that they care much what others think of them, but *RSLs* aren't the kind to warm to people until they've had a chance to evaluate them fully. So even if your first encounter with the *RSL* didn't go as well as planned, consider that they have a lot to offer and certainly shouldn't be written off by first impressions.

Perhaps the most salient feature of the *RSL* personalities is that they have more talent than they know what to do with. These are exceptionally intelligent creatures—intellectually and emotionally—who have an ability to cruise through life without breaking a

Roosevelt
Rosalee
Rosalia
Rosalina
Rosalind
Rosalinda
Rosalyn
Roselia
Roseline
Rosella
Roselle
Roslyn
Russell

sweat. Those *RSLs* who put out just a *little* extra, are usually rewarded with just about everything they ever wanted. But even when *RSLs* are flush with cash, chances are that they aren't going to know what to do with it anyway. For like most people whose names begin with the letter *R*, *RSLs* only respect money because it gives them the freedom to do their own things.

RSLs aren't the type to call attention to themselves and aren't going to make much of an effort to ingratiate themselves with others. They're not exactly loners, but they have little need to go along with the crowd either. In fact, *RSLs* are free agents. They do what they want, the way they want to, when it damn well pleases them. While this can be somewhat grating to the *RSLs'* close companions, there's something refreshing about this kind of rugged individualism, which most people grudgingly respect.

Many *RSLs* have an interesting take on relationships. They simply won't go out of their way to please their partners. This may sound selfish, but to the *RSL's* way of thinking, it would be dishonest to behave in any other way. They'll do what comes naturally in the *hope* that it makes their partner happy, and if not, then they've simply chosen the wrong partner. This is why many *RSLs* take their time to settle down and why they have such a long history of failed relationships.

Russell Crowe Critics describe Russell Crowe as a mixture of Marlon Brando, James Dean and Dr. Jekyll, and bill him as the most intense actor on the Hollywood scene. ■ In the early nineties, Russell made a film called *Romper Stomper*, in which he portrayed a sadistic Nazi skinhead with such realism that Sharon Stone cast him in her film, *The Quick and the Dead*. ■ Russell's star went nova after the gritty crime film *L.A. Confidential*, and supernova after *Gladiator* and *Master and Commander*. ■ Russell disdains Hollywood and lives mostly in Australia. He says he would be willing to live in L.A. only "if Australia and New Zealand were swallowed up by a tidal wave, there was a bubonic plague in Europe, and Africa disappeared from some Martian attack."

THE MOTHERLY
rsmr

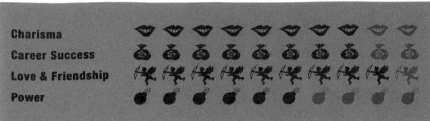

Charisma	
Career Success	
Love & Friendship	
Power	

Solicitous Genuine Spirited
Immature Narrow-minded Snobbish

Rosemarie
Rosemary

All the letters in the name *Rosemary* are characterized by a soft feminine gentility. The letter *M* is the icon of all things *maternal, motherly* and *matronly*, while the letter *S* is the icon of *sassy sensuality: sinful, sexy, sylph, slinky, sultry* and *sublime*. And since these names feature a double-dose of the cheeky *red-blooded romantic R (ravish, randy, raunchy, racy, rapture* and *relish),* they clearly evoke a woman of complex sensuality and emotional awareness. It's also noteworthy that names that end with the high-pitched letter *Y* or *IE* sound typically convey the youthful innocence found in the words: *frisky, happy, silly, funny, dreamy, dizzy* and *goofy*.

All told, there are no sharp edges in the *RSMR*'s name and no pointy bits in her personality either. But this doesn't mean that *RSMR*s are immune to occasional outbursts of passion: like most people whose names begin with an *R, RSMR*s are extraordinarily emotionally sensitive creatures. Fortunately, *RSMR*s have a sophisticated set of communication tools they use to express their ample feelings, so it's unlikely that anyone will be blindsided by an emotional outburst. On the rare occasions that some wayward person does manage to push their buttons, *RSMR*s can come up with a convincing show of anger—even though there's always the sense that it's more for theatrical effect than anything overtly aggressive.

There's something dignified about the way the *RSMR*s carry themselves that elicits respect, and this seems to immunize them from getting stepped on by the aggressive personalities with whom they often surround themselves. With their deep store of patience and goodwill, *RSMR*s are ideally suited for working with children or the general public, and because of their extraordinary abilities to adjust to any environment, they will succeed where others fail. But even though *RSMR*s are "people people," it's unlikely that you'd find them in jobs that require any kind of aggressive selling. They simply lack the killer instinct needed for competitive careers.

Her relatively cool dating style inhibits the *RSMR* from making the first advances to prospective partners. All the same, she's not shy about demonstrating affection once she's comfortable in her intimate relationships. It's also not uncommon for an *RSMR* to pair up with a domineering mate, and she certainly knows how to get her way without having to resort to a battle of wills. Once properly matched, it's only natural for such a nurturing personality to take on the duties of making a home and raising her kids: a happy occupation for her and a beneficial one for the children.

Rosemary Clooney Rosemary Clooney's deep and smoky voice earned her a place alongside America's premiere jazz musicians. ■ At twenty-one, Rosemary moved to New York, where she recorded the quirky song "Come On-A My House." Initially she thought the song cheesy—full of double entendres, it required a fake Italian accent—but the record proved to be such a success that it launched her career. ■ Rosemary went on to sing with Bing Crosby on a weekly radio show, and her appearance in the 1954 film *White Christmas* helped make it the year's box-office champion. ■ In 1968, Rosemary was only a few feet away when her long-time friend Bobby Kennedy was assassinated. Rosemary died after a long illness in June 2002.

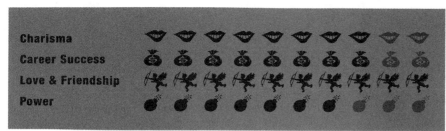

THE INSIGHTFUL

rsn

Charisma										
Career Success										
Love & Friendship										
Power										

Smart Loving Sexual
Impulsive Bullheaded Insensitive

Names that begin with the *red-blooded* letter *R* tend to evoke the saucily romantic characteristics found in the words: *raunchy, racy, randy, rapture, ravish* and *relish*. So when the *R* occurs in words in close proximity to the *sexy, sassy, sensual* and *slippery* letter *S*, it creates words with the decidedly vigorous sensuality found in *rosy, robust, raffish, perverse, arouse* and *orgasm*. But although the *RSN*s are undeniably flirtatious spirits, the letter *N*, which also dominates these names, is the flagship of *negativity* (*no, not, never, nada, null, nothing, nada, nyet* and *naught*). It could be said then, that *RSN*s' outward ebullience is simply an effort to cover up their inner doubts and fundamentally pessimistic views.

If you only know a *RSN* in superficial ways, you'll find her to be full of mischief and unpredictable feistiness. It seems that your *RSN* friend just can't pass up an opportunity to have fun (which explains her affinity for hanging around local watering holes), but if you've connected with an *RSN* on a more intimate level, you'll have discovered a reflective woman who cares deeply about life's little injustices.

Still, if you're in need of a pillow on which to cry, you may want give your *RSN* friend a miss. It's not that she doesn't care about your feelings: it's simply that she

Rashawn
Roseanna
Roseanne
Rosina

has her hands full coping with her own. But if you're in need of a laugh or a co-conspirator with whom to bemoan life's little complications, you'll be able to take advantage of the *RSN*'s avant-garde sense of humor. It could be said that what the *RSN* lacks in empathy, she makes up for with her whimsical world-view.

Perhaps as an expression of being commitment averse, *RSN*s often take their sweet time when it comes to choosing their careers. If you know an *RSN* who's in a go-nowhere job, chances are that she's just pondering her next move before she lands her dream job. Even if she's just waiting tables, the *RSN* has very little in the way of false modesty and will be relaxed in her faith that the future is going to take care of itself. And when she does sink her teeth into something substantial, her quick wits and keen survival instincts will pay off in a big way. It's not unusual to find *RSN*s in the arts, but they're also often found in people-oriented professions such as teaching, retail or public service.

*RSN*s aren't what you'd call the traditional family types but they do enjoy the security of a committed partner, and children too. The *RSN* has a nurturing instinct that runs deep, and nothing brings out her inherent (if well-hidden) soft side better than a little scrunched up face.

Roseanne Barr Brassy comedienne Roseanne Barr knew she had to take risks to remain in the public eye. Even though she was at the top of her game, she took a comedic chance while singing the national anthem at a San Diego baseball game in 1990. Her decision to act like a ballplayer—grabbing her crotch and spitting—was so misunderstood by the crowd that they jeered her off the field. ■ Her TV show, *Roseanne*, dealt with problems faced by real people and was able to be poignant and funny at the same time. Her tumultuous marriage to Tom Arnold became fodder for the show, and she proudly billed herself as Mrs. Roseanne Arnold. After an ugly public breakup, she resumed public life simply as "Roseanne."

349

Charisma										
Career Success										
Love & Friendship										
Power										

Bright Intriguing Witty
Temperamental Fickle Unpredictable

Because the vigorously pronounced letter *T* is the symbol for all things *talented, tremendous, terrific* and *triumphant*, its combination with the *red-blooded* letter *R* creates names that evoke passion and stick-to-itivenes. These are people who have a solid understanding of themselves and have no compunction about sharing their intricate philosophies of life with others. It's worth noting that, because the letter *N* is the symbol of negativity (*no, not, never, nada, null, nothing, nada, nyet* and *naught*) the names *Renita* and *Renato* tend to represent people with a streak of pessimism superimposed on their robust personalities.

The word *spicy* seems to crop up a lot when people describe the *RT*s, and this could either be a response to their restless natures, or their predilection for taking control of social situations. Either way, *RT*s are very much social creatures who, when left to their own devices, will quickly grow bored and restless. Torture for one of these active individuals is being forced to sit quietly for an hour, or having to wait in traffic.

No matter what the conversation is about, you can always expect a chipper (even a brusque) input from the *RT*s. These quick-witted people are usually two or three steps ahead in their thinking process and have little

Rita
Renata
Renate
Renato
Renita
Rhett
Ritchie
Rosetta
Retta
Reta

patience for beating around the bush. But despite their obvious intelligence, *RT*s function poorly in structured educational environments: they're much better off learning at their own pace and controlling the subject matter themselves. Maybe this is why most *RT*s don't achieve success until much later in their lives.

*RT*s are characterized by a can-do spirit that keeps them in the limelight. These socially adept people are equally comfortable in the company of both sexes and are drawn to careers that permit them to interact with the public. Still, they're not given to the "all work and no play" motif, and *RT*s will always find time for a gossip session with the girls, or a beer with the boys.

In their romantic lives, *RT*s may be affectionate, but they're definitely too feisty for some tastes. When beginning new relationships, they'll usually make it their business to "train" their significant other to their specifications (which can be a little intimidating to the uninitiated), and some *RT*s go so far as to undertake the task of honing their lovers' skills. So if you're the domineering type, there's a good chance you're going to knock heads with your *RT* mate, but if you have a sense of humor and an easygoing disposition, then you've got a decent shot at a long-lived and out-of-the-ordinary union.

Rita Hayworth Most Gen X'ers know Rita Hayworth from the line in Madonna's song "Rita Hayworth gave good face." What they may not know is that Rita was a pinup girl, dancer, actress and one of the first liberated women in Hollywood. ■ Margarita Carmen Cansino was born in Brooklyn and went on to become known as the Great American Love Goddess. Her frank sexuality, like her striptease in the film *Gilda*, led to problems with the censors, but when public mores loosened, she was able to star in *The Lady from Shanghai*, directed by her second husband, Orson Welles. ■ Rita began showing symptoms of Alzheimer's disease in her early forties and was only fully diagnosed decades later. She died in New York at the age of sixty-eight after a protracted illness.

Charisma	😊 😊 😊 😊 😊 😊 😊 😊 😊 😊
Career Success	💰 💰 💰 💰 💰 💰 💰 💰 💰 💰
Love & Friendship	🏹 🏹 🏹 🏹 🏹 🏹 🏹 🏹 🏹 🏹
Power	💣 💣 💣 💣 💣 💣 💣 💣 💣 💣

Gracious Hospitable Truthful
Moody Dry Narrow-minded

There's usually a little bit of the fuddy-duddy in people whose names contain a *TH* phoneme. But there's also the spiritually *thoughtful strength* that resonates in words like *theology, theory, thespian, thinker, thrifty, father, mother* and *thankful*. And because the *red-blooded* letter *R* initializes these names, it evokes an image of a woman with an impish sense of fun, a genteel charm and a willingness to please.

You may *think* that compliancy is their most defining trait, but let's get one thing straight: *RTH*s are extraordinarily self-assured and have titanium backbones that allow them to weather the most severe storms. This otherwise demure woman can be quite a pistol when the occasion arises, especially when she gets to defend her ideas. She doesn't exactly go looking for trouble, but she does seem to enjoy surprising people with her feisty outbursts. If people seem to instinctively trust *RTH*s, it's because they really don't seem to have hidden agendas. They are unfailingly up-front with their expectations and will rarely lose their composure—even in the face of aggression.

The *RTH*'s sense of balance serves her well in her career life, and like most people whose names begin with the letter *R*, she is likely to achieve her professional goals. She'll typically gravitate toward careers that involve working closely with people (like teaching,

Retha
Ruth
Rutha
Ruthann
Ruthie

medicine or legal work), and even if she has no great aspirations in the workplace, she'll probably make her mark as the best soccer mom in town. Her compassion often leads the *RTH* to play a central role in her community, acting as mother to a wide variety of individuals and opening her home to anyone who needs a little encouragement. These are comfortable and comforting people, and even when *RTH*s seem to lose their tempers, it's probably just calculated for effect.

An instinctive nurturer, the *RTH* dotes on her children but rears them with intractable discipline. She's the kind who pours chicken soup down sore throats in the same way as she forces advice into unwilling ears. But as much as her children may resent their mother's interference in their Internet and video-game lives, her maternal attentions will pay great dividends for them in later life.

The *RTH*'s mothering instincts extend to her spouse as well, and her partner can expect a well-regulated household and family routine. *RTH*s typically make wise choices when it comes to marriage partners, although the same can't be said for their casual relationships, in which they are often drawn to the bad-boy types. Once they've gotten it out of their systems though, they almost always snuggle up to someone with a little less testosterone.

Ruth Bader Ginsburg In 1981, Sandra Day O'Connor became the first woman ever to serve on the United States Supreme Court, and it was another twelve years before she was joined by a fellow female justice: Ruth Bader Ginsburg. ■ A longtime favorite of Democratic Presidents, Ruth was appointed to the U.S. Court of Appeals by President Carter in 1980, where she established a reputation for judicial restraint and gained her reputation as the "Thurgood Marshall of women's rights." ■ When the Supreme Court considered the issue of the hotly contested Gore/Bush Presidential election of 2000, Ruth strongly disagreed with the majority decision and rebuked the court with her dissent: ". . . the Court's conclusion that a constitutionally adequate recount is impractical . . . (and) should not decide the Presidency of the United States."

25000

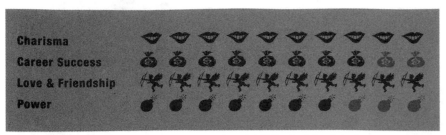

Charisma	
Career Success	
Love & Friendship	
Power	

Original Kindly Precocious
Clingy Distracting Unfocused

When the rarely used letter *X* occurs in words and names, it's usually a harbinger of something mysterious and extraordinary. And since *RX* people display the typically high level of brazenness common to people with names beginning with the *red-blooded, racy* and *robust* letter *R*, it could be said that they are enigmas wrapped in personalities of uncommon refinement.

*RX*s have no intention of following the mob, and you can often pick them out of a crowd without even knowing their names. They're the ones dressed in clothes that are consciously unconventional while somehow managing to remain stylish. They seem to relish the idea of marching to the beat of a different drummer, and even garnish their reputations by being deliberately contrary. Still, you could never accuse *RX*s of hiding their true intentions: they make no apologies for being precisely who they are.

If *RX*s are considered somewhat glamorous figures, it might have something to do with the fact that they are a little inaccessible, but it's also because they comport themselves with such dignity and self-confidence. In truth, they often do end up on the path to fame—given their flamboyant personalities and many talents—but they have no great desire to put themselves in the spotlight. *RX*s aren't much given to the dog-eat-

Rex
Roxanna
Roxanne
Roxy

dog world of competitive careers: if they had their druthers they would rather spend their days in the study of the aesthetic (art, drama or even other people). You could call them starry-eyed, but they're still practical enough to put making money near the top of their priority lists.

*RX*s are optimists at heart and choose to see the good in even the most difficult people and situations. But these are no goody two-shoes by any means, and it's obvious that the their idealistic outlooks are rooted in altruism, and not in a need for approval. *RX*s don't do anything halfway and they'll span the spectrum from ultra-success to ultra-failure. In typical *RX* fashion, failure is viewed not with alarm, but as an opportunity to learn and grow.

If you're a person in need of sloppy sentimentality, you're going to want to give your *RX* suitor a miss. But if you're looking for someone who's going to watch your back and support you with no strings attached, then a *RX* is definitely worth your consideration. All told, *RX*s are high on the list of desirable partners, and the only drawback (even if you're not the jealous type) is that you're going to have to share them with their wide circle of friends. You may even end up being one of those couples that have to make appointments for their romantic sessions.

Rex Harrison It was the role of a lifetime for journeyman actor Rex Harrison. Cast as Professor Higgins against Audrey Hepburn's Eliza Doolittle in *My Fair Lady*, Rex successfully transformed himself into a caustic linguistics professor—and won a Best Actor Oscar for his efforts. ■ Born Reginald Carey Harrison, Rex specialized in portraying roguish characters with impish charm. His nickname, Sexy Rexy, was as much a reflection of his professional career as it was of his private life, which included six marriages. ■ Rex published his autobiography in 1975, was knighted in 1989, and his final appearance was in the Broadway production of Somerset Maugham's *The Circle*. ■ When Rex died of pancreatic cancer in 1990, the world mourned its favorite black-tie comedian and gentleman actor.

THE MULTI-FACETED

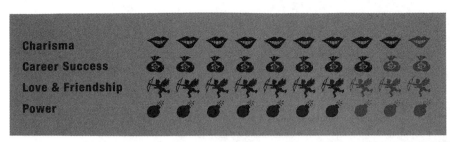

Charisma										
Career Success										
Love & Friendship										
Power										

Composed Observant Open-minded
Reserved Detached Complicated

RY names convey all the *robust, romantic, randy, ribald, racy* qualities that are typical of names beginning with the letter *R*, but because most of these names are terminated with a high-pitched *Y* or *IE*, this promise of passion remains largely unfulfilled. For when names end with a *Y* or *IE*, it's an indication of a happy-go-lucky— even childlike—personality that we find in the words *jolly, baby, kitty, goofy, funny, silly* and *doggy*. Still, these are people whose approach to life is characterized by a high level of optimism and a willingness to share this enthusiasm with their eclectic social groups.

Not known for overt bursts of temper, the self-contained *RY*s are somewhat of an anachronism among those with the passionate *R* names. Most *RY*s make decisions with their heads and not their hearts, giving them a restrained air unusual for this emotive group. Yet they are anything but cold fish; it's just that they've managed to find ways to discipline their emotions instead of indulging in them. Rather than letting it all hang out, they channel their feelings into their everyday work and lives, and often accomplish great things as a result. But because people mistakenly assume that *RY*s are all business and no romance, the downside is that they're often excluded from intimate relationships.

*RY*s seem to have an opinion on everything. This is less a reflection of the *RY*s need to win converts to their cause than it is a compulsion to rattle the cage to see what falls out. *RY*s subscribe to the dictum that if you're not making waves, you're not paddling, and they view life as one long opportunity to understand the universe. They pride themselves on their ability to listen, and seem eager to learn from the constant flow of new people in their lives. They'll pick up eclectic bits of information along the way, digest them, overlay them with their unique philosophies and dispense them to anyone who'll listen. It would be unusual for *RY*s to pass on opportunities to try something new—a trait that comes in handy in their professional lives—and even though they're not motivated by money alone, they always find a way to live comfortably.

For all their mental activity, *RY*s struggle with self-doubt when it comes to relationships. Perhaps this explains why the *RY* is a finicky sort when it comes to intimacy and is apt to test-drive a number of partners before finally settling on one. Relationships are optimistically pursued but with a lack of direction that leaves potential mates scratching their heads. Whether this stems from restlessness or it's simply an indication that *RY*s are slow learners (when it comes to matters of the heart) is a matter for debate.

Ray
Rhea
Rory
Roy

Roy Rogers Roy Rogers was one of the few movie stars who played himself and not a character. His name was synonymous with integrity, honesty and the homespun family values that embodied the American heartland in the 1950s. ■ Together with his wife, Dale, Roy made a controversial decision to include a religious song at each of their live concerts, and even though they were threatened with the cancellation of their contract at Madison Square Garden, the Rogers stuck to their guns. ■ In some ways Roy was the original Charlton Heston in his support of the second amendment, and was courted by Republicans to run for Congress. His reasons for refusing? "I have both Democrat and Republican fans, and I can't afford to lose any of them!"

**Most Popular
Girl's Names**

Susan

Sandra

Sharon

Sarah

Shirley

Stephanie

Sara

Sherry

Sylvia

Shannon

**Most Popular
Boy's Names**

Steven

Scott

Stephen

Samuel

Steve

Shawn

Sean

Stanley

Shane

Sam

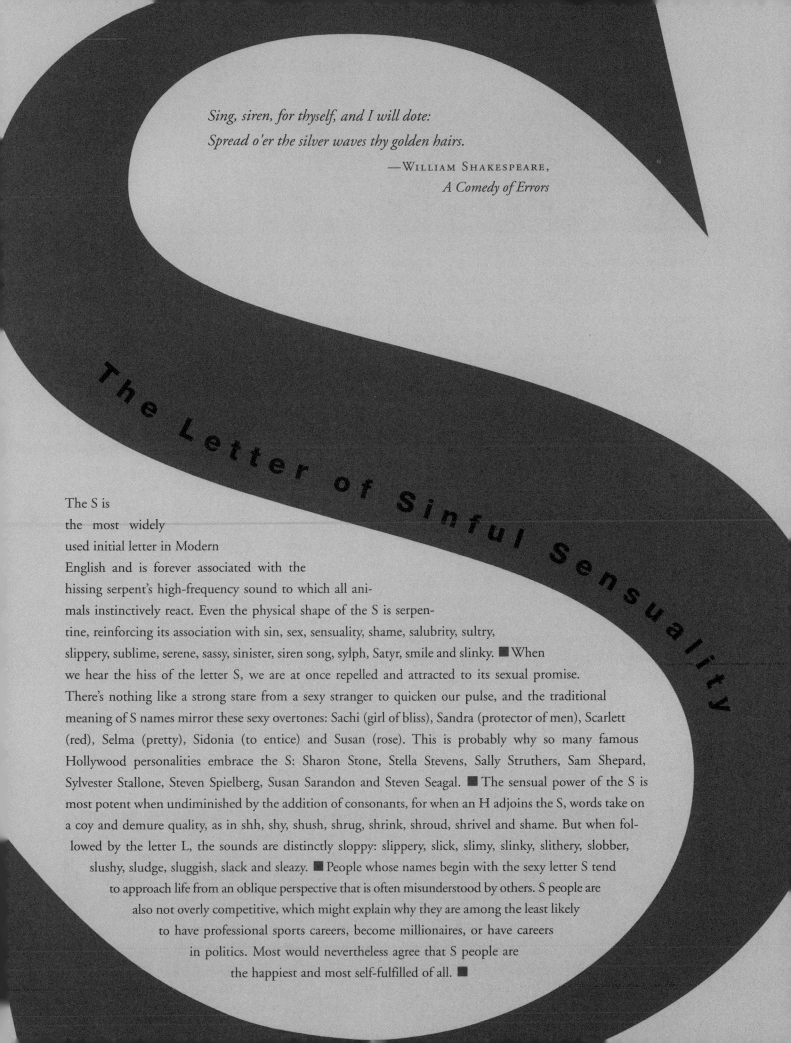

Sing, siren, for thyself, and I will dote:
Spread o'er the silver waves thy golden hairs.

—WILLIAM SHAKESPEARE,
A Comedy of Errors

The Letter of Sinful Sensuality

The S is the most widely used initial letter in Modern English and is forever associated with the hissing serpent's high-frequency sound to which all animals instinctively react. Even the physical shape of the S is serpentine, reinforcing its association with sin, sex, sensuality, shame, salubrity, sultry, slippery, sublime, serene, sassy, sinister, siren song, sylph, Satyr, smile and slinky. ■ When we hear the hiss of the letter S, we are at once repelled and attracted to its sexual promise. There's nothing like a strong stare from a sexy stranger to quicken our pulse, and the traditional meaning of S names mirror these sexy overtones: Sachi (girl of bliss), Sandra (protector of men), Scarlett (red), Selma (pretty), Sidonia (to entice) and Susan (rose). This is probably why so many famous Hollywood personalities embrace the S: Sharon Stone, Stella Stevens, Sally Struthers, Sam Shepard, Sylvester Stallone, Steven Spielberg, Susan Sarandon and Steven Seagal. ■ The sensual power of the S is most potent when undiminished by the addition of consonants, for when an H adjoins the S, words take on a coy and demure quality, as in shh, shy, shush, shrug, shrink, shroud, shrivel and shame. But when followed by the letter L, the sounds are distinctly sloppy: slippery, slick, slimy, slinky, slithery, slobber, slushy, sludge, sluggish, slack and sleazy. ■ People whose names begin with the sexy letter S tend to approach life from an oblique perspective that is often misunderstood by others. S people are also not overly competitive, which might explain why they are among the least likely to have professional sports careers, become millionaires, or have careers in politics. Most would nevertheless agree that S people are the happiest and most self-fulfilled of all. ■

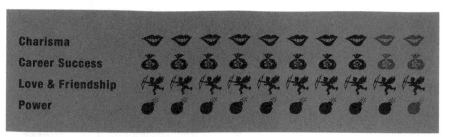

Charisma										
Career Success										
Love & Friendship										
Power										

Tenacious Capable Objective
Inconsistent Deceptive Reactionary

Because these names are so heavily dominated by the letter *S*—associated with all things *sexy, seductive, sublime, smiling, sultry, sylph-like, serene* and *sassy*—it's not surprising to find that these are women of uncommon allure, who are quite prepared to exploit their charms in achieving their goals. But all is not sweetness and light when it comes to the *S* personality, for the letter *S* also has its *saucy* side—declared by the words *sin, sneaky, slithering, snakelike, shame, Satyr, surreptitious* and *sinister*. So if you think that you know everything about your *S* friend, start asking around. You'll discover that opinions on the *S*s are more diverse than life in the rainforests used to be.

But there is one thing that everyone seems to agree on. And that is the *S*'s willingness to upset the status quo when they feel that some injustice has been committed. Soft-spoken and spotlight-averse, *S* people display an extraordinary passion for all living things; so expect them to be vocal (if somewhat strident) campaigners when it comes to their antiwar stance, distaste for animal cruelty, or as advocates for friends and loved ones.

Like many people whose names begin with the letter *S*, they're not particular fans of the 9–5 work routine and like to mix things up with regular changes of scenery by taking on new jobs. They're not particularly

Sau
Seth
Shu
So
Sue

fussy about the actual work they do, as long as it gives them some outlet for their strong right-brained creative tendencies. And speaking of right-brained people, *S* women are certainly more intuitive than most; relying almost wholly on their instincts when it comes to selecting friends and lovers. That's why it's difficult to ever get anything past an *S*, who always seems one step ahead of the game.

As potential mates, *S*s can be a complicated group. They may be able to reason logically, but this doesn't stop them from being as unpredictable as the Dow Jones. And with their network of finely woven emotional defenses, it's not uncommon for suitors to be left scratching their heads while trying to discern what their true motives are.

Your *S* mate will be the keeper of the social calendar so you'll never have to worry about remembering birthdays or party dates. But it should also be said that marriages to *S* women aren't known for their peace and quiet, and prospective mates should be prepared to parry wits and make compromises. Still, those who keep their eyes on the prize will inevitably end up with a wonderfully sensual and energetic mate whose attention to detail pervades the relationship and makes for a love-based and enduring marriage.

Sue Hawk It's not every day that a truck driver from Waukesha, Wisconsin, gets to co-host with Regis Philbin on *Live with Regis*. Sue Hawk did it the hard way by enduring discomfiting proximity to a naked fat guy on CBS's hit first season of *Survivor*. ■ More than forty million viewers tuned to watch Sue's struggle to win a million dollars, and most agree that the highlight of the series was when Sue told former friend, Kelly Wigglesworth, "If I ever pass you along in life again and you were lying there dying of thirst, I would let the vultures take you." ■ Sue made the most of her celebrity after the show, spending a week as a corner square on Hollywood Squares and playing a redneck waitress in the Disney movie, *Bubble Boy*.

THE PERSUASIVE sb

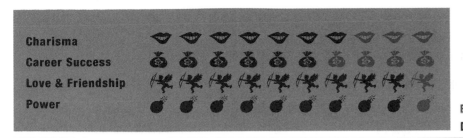

Charisma										
Career Success										
Love & Friendship										
Power										

Effervescent Nurturing Complex
Distracted Naïve Temperamental

The letter *B*—with its *brash* and *booming* resonance—brings a certain *belligerence* when it appears in words and names. Its low frequency tones are responsible for the words *bash, beat, break, battle, burly* and *beast*, and even when in occurs in words initialized by the *sassy* letter *S*, takes on the *somber* tones found in the words *saber, sable, scrub, scab, stab, stumble, subpoena, subversion* and *snub*. These names suggest people with intensely focused dispositions and a formidable desire to imprint their personalities onto the world.

*SB*s are determined not to rely on luck when it comes to their professional lives and actually seem to enjoy the kind of sweaty preparation that it takes to succeed. Even though most people whose names begin with the letter *S* aren't exactly overburdened by motivation, *SB*s always seem to be on a mission. Some people think that *SB*s are driven by financial rewards, while others just see their single-mindedness as a way for them to avoid intimacy. Either way, professions for *SB*s usually include plenty of routine and limited familiarity with people. If they happen to be the boss, then they're going to behave like one: dignified, knowledgeable and even a little rigid. And even when they're not leading the way, *SB*s chafe at being held to anyone else's schedule: they are trailblazers in the extreme and are confi-

Sabina
Sabine
Sabrina
Sebastian
Siobhan
Sybil

dent that they know their way around the universe.

Although *SB*s can be generous to a fault, it's unlikely that your *SB* friend would ever ask you for a loan. In most cases it's because they have a rainy-day approach to money, but it's also a symptom of their fierce internal pride. You'll have to give your *SB* friends some credit for their idealism, but be aware that it comes with a tendency for them to close their eyes to reality (particularly evident when one of their intimate relationships is souring). They are much more likely to judge people by their words than they are their actions, and even if everyone else can see the writing on the wall, *SB*s will act as if everything is hunky-dory.

In their intimate goings-on, *SB*s are active and sexually inquisitive people who will go to any lengths to keep their relationships exciting and fresh. Those *SB*s who apply their focused business techniques to their relationships are likely to get nowhere fast, but since most *SB*s are smarter than that, they usually scale back their intensity when it comes to wooing. Because these dynamic individuals make it their business to understand their lover's strengths and weaknesses, it can be hard to resist the lure of an *SB* courtship. So if an *SB* has you targeted for a marriage partner, you might as well call the caterer.

Sebastian Coe Following in the spike prints of the legendary British runner Roger Bannister (the first man to break the four-minute mile barrier), Sebastian Coe had the athletic world on its feet when he repeatedly smashed middle-distance records in the 1980s. ■ Unlike most international running stars, Sebastian had the same coach for his entire career (his father), but his total of eight world records and four Olympic medals was largely due to the help of fellow Briton Steve Ovett, who pushed Sebastian to his limits. Their ongoing duel produced many heart-stopping races in which the two men completely dominated the field. ■ Sebastian's elevation to international stardom was rewarded by a grateful British public, who elected him to Parliament as a member of the Conservative party in 1992.

THE STEADFAST

SD

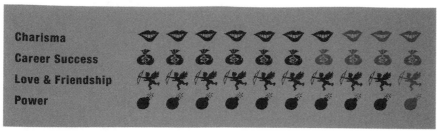

Charisma										
Career Success										
Love & Friendship										
Power										

Outgoing Life-loving Decisive
Demanding Moody Impulsive

Even though the letter *S* is the herald of all things *sexy, sassy, sylphlike* and *sweet,* its combination with the letter *D* tends to bring out its darker elements. The *D* is the icon of *discipline, destruction, dapper, dignity* and *danger,* and its combination with the *S* implies the aggressive sexuality found the words *seduce, scoundrel, soldier, stud, sturdy* and *sword.* It should be noted that *S* names ending in the letter *Y* or *IE* (for example, *Sydney* and *Sadie*) tend to have the relaxed air found in the words *sunny, spry, silly, sassy, sexy* and *snazzy.* Interestingly, most *SD* names also incorporate the *negative* letter *N* (*no, not, never, nada, null, nothing, nada, nyet* and *naught*), which implies a disposition toward moodiness and even the occasional emotional outburst.

SD people are not afraid to use a little flirting to achieve their goals, and there's nothing so serious in their lives that they cannot find something to laugh about. While it could be argued that their laid-back philosophy is the source from which they draw their social power, it might just be that people find *SD*s' simplicity and down-home bonhomie particularly attractive. Like most people whose names begin with the letter *S*, *SD*s don't understand why everyone around them seems to complicate their lives unduly. *SD*s construct

Sade
Sadie
Shad
Sid
Sidney
Sydney
Syed

their own lives with elegance, integrity and style.

Yet *SD*s aren't without their exhibitionist streaks, and once you get them in the spotlight, you'll need the marines to extract them. *SD*s are those talented, expressive individuals whose unconcerned affability can simultaneously charm and exasperate. With their penchant for drama and sly senses of humor, most people find them to be somewhat addicting.

*SD*s aren't likely to complicate things when it comes to their careers either. They certainly have enough energy to succeed in whatever field they enter, but they aren't going to sell their souls for a greenback. They'd much rather be on the dance floor, golf course or buying a round of drinks for their countless friends. This isn't to say that *SD*s don't have their downtimes, but when you catch them in their groove, you'll be surprised at their capacity for goofiness.

Mating with an *SD* is an adventure that's not for everyone . . . it takes a special kind of person to appreciate the *SD's* blend of excitability and demand for family structure. So if you don't mind the tradeoff that comes with living with a spouse who's not the most compassionate listener, but has old-fashioned principles instead, you aren't going to do much better than teaming up with an *SD.*

Sidney Poitier When Sidney Poitier was born, dangerously premature, in 1924, his father went looking for a container in which to bury the three-pound baby who seemed certain to die. ■ But young Sidney survived, to break Hollywood's race barrier and pave the way for modern black stars like Eddie Murphy, Denzel Washington and Samuel L. Jackson. Many of his movies dealt with issues involving blacks overcoming the corruption of white society, and he became the first black actor to be number one at the box office, with *Guess Who's Coming to Dinner* in 1967. ■ His 1958 film *The Defiant Ones* landed him the first Best Actor Academy Award nomination for a black man, and in 1963 he went on to win the award for *Lilies of the Field*. ■ Sidney was appointed Bahamian ambassador to Japan in 1997.

358

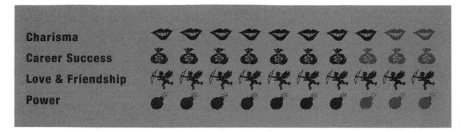

Charisma										
Career Success										
Love & Friendship										
Power										

Alive Spirited Magnetic
Self-indulgent Oversensitive Ditzy

It's remarkable how frequently words that describe the qualities of effervescence and liveliness contain the letter *F* or the *PH* sound. The *F* sound is responsible for the words *fun, frolic, flirtatious, flamboyant, fancy, friendly, flighty* and *flippant,* and when it occurs in words initialized by the *sexy, seductive* and *sassy* letter *S,* it takes on an even more unorthodox flair: *sylph, sophist, showoff, spoof, spitfire* and *suffragette.* Perhaps this is why so many people report that their *SF* friends' sparkle was on display when they were still small children. They were the ones singing away at their first-grade musical concert without a hint of self-consciousness. Talented? Not necessarily. Game? Undeniably.

Even though *SF*s are constantly on the go, they hardly ever seem to be in a hurry. These are women who know how to enjoy the finer things in life, such as languid shopping trips, fine dining and exotic vacations. This is not to say that *SF*s aren't prone to the same stresses endured by the rest of us, but it's as if they've negotiated a deal with themselves to work hard and play harder.

*SF*s are not only intellectual, but they're deeply spiritual as well (which may explain why they seem so well-adjusted). They have inordinately well-developed social skills, and if they cared to, could have a party with thirty of their closest friends on any given night. They *do* have

Sofia
Sophie

their favorites (maybe a girlfriend or two with whom they share absolutely everything), but true intimacy is solely reserved for their lovers. Despite their engaging charm, *SF*s are prone to moods of whimsy during which even close friends find themselves shut out for a while. Usually this is just an indication that the *SF* is recharging her batteries, but it can sometimes represent something more serious, like an upcoming change in her career or a new romantic partner.

*SF*s are spontaneous creatures who avoid putting themselves into situations that limit their options. They treasure their independence and, even when happily married, need to know that they can take off for a while without upsetting their mates. On the flipside, *SF*s' emotions can run away with them when it's least expected. And while some might think that this is a symptom of her immaturity, from the *SF*'s perspective, she's simply trying to communicate her feelings as honestly as possible.

There's nothing lethargic about the *SF* when it comes to mating and dating, and if you're hoping to have a successful relationship with one of these dynamos, you'd better have some oomph in your own life. Nowhere will this be more applicable than in the physical manifestations of your relationship, where the *SF* will need persistent reassurances of her desirability.

Sophie Tucker Known as the "Last of the Red-Hot Mamas," Sophie Tucker's singing career spanned almost six decades. ■ As an overweight child, Sophie didn't seem to mind being known as "the fat girl," and in later years actually turned her weight into an advantage, singing songs like "Don't Want to Be Thin" and "Nobody Loves a Fat Girl, But Oh How a Fat Girl Can Love." ■ When she first performed on the New York stage, Sophie was forced to wear blackface—perhaps, as one critic suggested, because "she was so big and ugly." ■ As vaudeville began to decline, Sophie began singing sophisticated jazz numbers, which she combined with her ragtime roots. Plying her craft to the day she died, she accumulated substantial capital with which she created the Sophie Tucker Foundation.

Charisma											
Career Success											
Love & Friendship											
Power											

Gentle Happy Self-aware
Thoughtless Distracted Compulsive

When the *sultry* letter *S* is paired with the *hushed* letter *H*, it takes on the reassuring tones of the words *shy, shame, shalom, sheepish, mushy, squishy, blush* and *bashful*. This is why, when soothing their crying children, mothers often use high-frequency words like *shh* or *hush*. And because the letter *L* is the icon for the most important things in life (*love, liberty, loyalty, learning* and *laughter*), *SHL*s universally exhibit a high internal happiness quotient (even if they tend to be on the reserved side).

While *SHL*s may come across as being a bit subdued, they are not people to drain energy from others. *SHL*s put more into their relationships than almost anyone you'll meet. And *SHL*s don't behave this way from some selfish need to be liked; they simply have immense hearts and ample emotional energy to spare.

If *SHL*s have a reputation for being a bit flighty, it doesn't seem to thwart their success in their chosen careers. It does, though, make for a lot of unanticipated adventures along the way, and it's sometimes impossible to predict what *SHL*s are going to do next. It's hard enough for *SHL*s to keep track of their own plans, let alone have someone else to pin them down. Still, *SHL*s seem to sense that people find their whimsical ways endearing and make little effort to curb their capricious ways.

Sasha
Shameka
Shamika
Shaquille
Shasta
Shayla
Shaylee
Sheila
Shelby
Sheldon
Shelly
Shelly
Shelton
Sherilyn
Sherryl

Like most people whose names begin with the letter *S*, *SHL*s have to work hard for their money. One reason they're not on the list of highest income earners has to do with the fact that *SHL*s put job satisfaction *way* ahead of everything else. Working in jobs that demand concentration or attention to detail just isn't the *SHL*'s schtick. They're much more likely to blossom when working in the public realm where they can take advantage of their uncommon social skills.

*SHL*s can be relied upon for solid friendship, even if it takes a long time coming. They're too smart to place their trust in just anyone, but once you've earned their respect, you'll have it for life. Loyalty is one of their highest ideals and they'll always be there for you in a pinch.

You can expect your courtship with your *SHL* to be a complicated business, mainly because you'll have to compete for his or her time. It's not that *SHL*s *play* hard to get, they *are* hard to get. But patience and persistence are held in high esteem, and chances are, the successful suitor will have these qualities in spades. Children are natural and welcome additions to *SHL*s' lives and these are the types of parents who make childrearing look so easy that everyone hates them for it.

Shelley Winters When a plump Shelley Winters starred in the 1972 epic *The Poseidon Adventure*, few people in the audience remembered how much of a sex symbol she once had been. In her heyday, Shelley was a highly sought-after ingénue, able to compete with the likes of Marilyn Monroe in films such as *A Double Life* and win an Oscar nomination for her role in *A Place in the Sun*. ■ Shelley's off-stage abrasiveness did little to endear her to fellow actors. After making *Winchester '73*, her normally soft-spoken co-star James Stewart was quoted as saying that she should have been spanked. She even poured water over Oliver Reed's head on *The Tonight Show*. ■ After a spell of bad movies and unhappy marriages, Shelley won her first Academy Award for playing the middle-aged Mrs. Van Daan in *The Diary of Anne Frank*.

Charisma	💋	💋	💋	💋	💋	💋	💋	💋	💋	💋
Career Success	💰	💰	💰	💰	💰	💰	💰	💰	💰	💰
Love & Friendship	🕊	🕊	🕊	🕊	🕊	🕊	🕊	🕊	🕊	🕊
Power	💣	💣	💣	💣	💣	💣	💣	💣	💣	💣

**Deliberate Protective Involved
Introverted Self-doubting Addictive**

It's quite remarkable how often words in which the letter *N* occurs denote some aspect of disagreeability. This is why the *N* is the symbol of all things negative (*no, not, never, nada, null, nothing, nada, nyet, naught*) and why it's a harbinger of some form of pessimism in names in which it appears. On the other hand, when the *sexy* letter *S* teams up with the gently whispered letter *H,* it creates the *hushed* tones of a mother soothing her child: *shh, shy, hush, shame, shalom, sheepish, mushy, squishy, blush* and *bashful.* Perhaps this is why the *SHN* names herald such gentle personalities with well-masked emotional brittleness.

*SHN*s have an unusual need for privacy, and you'll rarely catch them volunteering information about their intimate lives or behaving without considered restraint. This is not to say that the *SHN*s shun the spotlight, but even when they have occasion for celebrity, they retain their poise and jealously guard their inner lives. *SHN*s typically maintain a small group of intimates outside of which they don't expend their energies. This is why you should never take it personally if *SHN*s seem to snub you.

Shan
Shaina
Shana
Shane
Shanika
Shaniya
Shalonda
Shanae
Shanda
Shandra
Shania, Shanice
Shanna, Shannon
Shannen, Sheena
Shanta, Shante
Shawn, Shawna
Shayna, Shayne
Shantell
Shawana
Shawanda
Shawnee
Shonda
Shoshana
Shyanne
Shona

Nine times out of ten, it has absolutely nothing to do with you (and most times they weren't even aware that you were there in the first place).

*SHN*s have their ups and downs like everyone else, it's just that they occur with greater frequency than the rest of us. Perhaps this results from their tendency to separate their emotions from traumatic events, rather than dealing with them from the outset. But because they have the stamina to cope with emotionally draining situations, they are ideal for careers in emergency work and those high-stress jobs where others tend to burn out under pressure. This same trait typically keeps them away from the more touchy-feely professions such as counseling and teaching, which require one-on-one empathy and the ability to *really* listen.

Married to an *SHN*? Congratulations. Now, good luck holding on. These are people who appreciate (and expect) quality in all things and aren't shy about demanding the same from their partners. So unless you're the faithful type who's willing to keep their interest piqued with romance and intrigue, don't let the door hit you on the way out.

Shannen Doherty Shannen Doherty earned her reputation for being a brat while playing Brenda Walsh on Fox's huge television show, *Beverly Hills, 90210.* ■ Although Shannen was a huge hit with teen audiences, she left the show after only four years. The breakup was reportedly a result of arguments and differences with the show's creator, Aaron Spelling. But Shannen seemed determined to keep the tabloids in business. After a couple of failed engagements, she met Ashley Hamilton, the son of perennially tanned George Hamilton, married him within two weeks and divorced within one year. Shannen next dated, broke up with, got engaged to, and broke up with director Rob Weiss. ■ Quips Shannen: "If God wanted us to be naked, why did he invent sexy lingerie?"

shr

Charisma	💋	💋	💋	💋	💋	💋	💋	💋	💋	💋
Career Success										
Love & Friendship										
Power										

Giving Vigorous Spontaneous
Unstable Sexually overbearing Reckless

When the letter *S* is paired with the *hushed* letter *H*, it takes on the reassuring tones of the words *shy, shame, shalom, sheepish, mushy, squishy, blush* and *bashful.* This is why, when mothers soothe their crying children, they often use high-frequency words like *shh* or *hush.* And since the romantic letter *R* is the symbol for all things *raunchy, racy, randy, rapturous* and *ravishing, SHR* names are indicative of a somewhat easygoing individual whose puckish sense of fun emerges only after you've known them for a while.

Although *SHRs* can sometimes fall prey to feelings of inadequacy and self-doubt, these people radiate a positive energy and a can-do spirit. You'll usually find them surrounded by eclectic groups of friends, all of whom look to them as their emotional leaders.

Maybe it's because *SHRs* are nonjudgmental that they're as popular as they are, but it could also have something to do with their unflagging commitment to making their relationships work. In a way, *SHRs* make projects out of their friends by plying them with suggestions on how they might better their lives, and as annoying as this can be, the *SHR*'s sharp insights have to be respected.

Although *SHRs* enjoy the limelight, they're not the types to actively seek it out. They've learned that a demure and subtle approach will get them what they need—without them having to resort to showy behavior. From the *SHR*'s point of view, it's all about being emotionally honest: these are creatures with deeply spiritual and philosophical cores.

While people who bear an *SHR* name are not averse to intellectual pursuits, their endeavors tend to be of an artistic nature. Success and recognition are certainly among the things they would like to achieve, but they're hardly the most important things in their lives. It's more about what they can learn along their journey and how they can apply this knowledge to improve their relationships. Careers for *SHRs* usually include something besides the usual nine-to-five grind; like most curious people, *SHRs* don't have the patience for detail and repetition.

SHRs' emotional intelligence comes in handy when it comes to intimate applications, and they are superbly equipped for the give-and-take of exclusive partnerships. Their invigorating brand of sexuality makes them highly prized mates, but potential loves should tread lightly on sensitive emotional issues lest they become recipients of the *SHRs*' unexpected temper.

Shari
Sharla
Shakira
Shamar
Sharlene
Sharon
Sharonda
Sharyl
Shemar
Sherell
Sheridan
Sherill
Sherita
Sherman
Sherrell
Sherry
Sherwood
Sheryl
Shirlene
Shirley
Shreya

Shirley MacLaine Shirley MacLaine is one of the most intriguing stars of the twentieth century and—if we are to believe her best-selling book, *Out on a Limb*—of a few other centuries as well. The older sister of Hollywood bad-boy Warren Beatty, Shirley is an Oscar-winning actress, author, dancer and singer. ■ Shirley's first Oscar nomination was for her portrayal of a trampy waif opposite Frank Sinatra in *Some Came Running*. She next appeared in the original *Ocean's Eleven* with Frank Sinatra, Dean Martin, Sammy Davis Jr. and Peter Lawford. ■ Her other Oscar nominations came from her roles in *The Apartment* and *Irma La Douce*, but it was her role as an eccentric widow in *Terms of Endearment* that finally won her an Oscar for Best Actress.

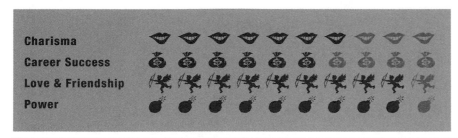

Charisma										
Career Success										
Love & Friendship										
Power										

When the letter *C* is pronounced with the sharp tone of the letter *K*, it takes on all the edgy aspects we associate with the words *crash, crime, cancer, caustic, crack, crunch, kill, kick* and *caffeine*. And when it occurs in words and names that begin with the *sassy* letter *S*, it tends to create the sense of youthful mischief found in *scamp, scallywag, scofflaw, scammer, scandalous, scantily, scapegoat, scold, scruffy* and *scrappy*. It's not surprising, therefore, that *SK* names reflect personalities with uncommon intelligence and finely honed senses of humor. The most popular name in this category (*Scott*), terminates in the *talented, triumphant* and *tough* letter *T,* implying a man with a crystal-clear vision for his life.

*SK*s are dynamic individuals with a lot to prove, who enjoy taking on the challenges that most others avoid. If they were a Starbucks's product, they'd be a triple-shot venti latte: bracing, motivating and with a just little creamy froth. But these somewhat Spartan personalities can be hard to warm up to without a little work. They aren't particularly snobbish, but there's a fine line between snobbishness and aloofness where *SK*s are concerned. Perhaps this is because they don't particularly care about what other people think—they're far too secure to be distracted by little things like that.

*SK*s seem to be constantly mulling something over.

Scarlett
Scott
Scotty
Skye
Skyla
Skyler
Socorro

It can be hard to tell exactly what's on their minds, but they'll often come out of left field with offbeat observations, which, upon further examination, prove deeply profound. But breaching *SK*s' emotional defenses is a bit like prying a clamshell open with a toothpick. The best strategy is to patiently wait (with a little bait) until their inquisitive natures entice them out in the open. The one thing you *can* count on about *SK*s is that they are going to have a rigid set of standards for their lives, which they cling to with almost religious zeal.

Because it's difficult to discern what *SK*s might really be feeling, they often make people a little uneasy. But their inscrutability can also be one of their greatest assets when it comes to their professional lives. Even if they're not professional poker players, they are highly effective salespeople who can hold their own in any negotiation.

As you might guess, *SK*s can present quite a puzzle in intimate relationships, and those who have *SK*s for mates are going to have to boost them with demonstrations of physical and emotional encouragement. They're certainly not the type to ask for this kind of reassurance, since what they really need is for you to be sensitive enough to *know* what they want. So if you're *not* the intuitive kind, then you have no business being in an *SK* relationship.

Scott Joplin The 1973 Academy Awarding–winning movie, *The Sting*, starring Paul Newman and Robert Redford, made the music of Scott Joplin an overnight sensation. A remarkable feat when you consider the man had been dead for almost seventy years. ■ Scott's father was a freed slave who encouraged his young son to practice on a piano belonging to a local white family. His musical style was commercially in tune to the tastes of the late nineteenth century, and Scott made his living by composing rags (ragtime melodies). His "Maple Leaf Rag" earned him $5,000 over ten years. ■ But it wasn't until Marvin Hamlisch, the music director of *The Sting*, decided to feature Scott's music that the world was reintroduced to the bouncy and witty rhythms of Scott's almost-hundred-year-old music.

Charisma	👄	👄	👄	👄	👄	👄	👄	👄	👄	👄
Career Success	💰	💰	💰	💰	💰	💰	💰	💰	💰	💰
Love & Friendship	🦅	🦅	🦅	🦅	🦅	🦅	🦅	🦅	🦅	🦅
Power	💣	💣	💣	💣	💣	💣	💣	💣	💣	💣

Energetic Observant Clever
Dogmatic Self-indulgent Superficial

The letter *L* is the symbol for all the things that money can't buy: *life, love, liberty, loyalty, learning* and *laughter.* So it's not surprising that names in which the *L* appears usually suggest *levelheaded* individuals with a *laidback* approach to life. But because these names begin with the *sassy, surreptitious* and *sexy* letter *S,* there's the suggestion of a person with a disquieting element of furtiveness that surrounds their intentions—a result of the *SL* phoneme's strong connection to all things: *sly, slick, slippery, sliding, slimy* and *slithery.*

SLs are those people that seem to have it all. Without much effort, they marry well, live apparently stress-free lives and have enough money to make it seem like they don't need any. But these resources don't come cheap, and the price is usually paid in *SLs'* close relationships where their natural inclination to maintain order in their own lives, translates into controlling the lives of others as well. *SLs* consider it their duty to confront people with their shortcomings and problems. And although they do this without malice, they are hardly overburdened with diplomatic skills and many people are put off by their somewhat pushy intrusions. Still, once sucked into the *SLs'* sphere of influence, many people find themselves becoming fans of the *SLs'* unswerving loyalty and systematic approach to friendship.

Sal
Salina
Sally
Salma
Saul
Schuyler
Solomon
Selena
Selina
Silas
Sol

Because *SL* people are so talented, it's not unusual to find them at the top of their chosen professions. And if you happen to work under one, you'd better have your ducks in a row because they are notoriously finicky when it comes to getting the job done right.

But to properly understand them, you should know that power for its own sake has very little appeal. What they're looking for (whether they know it or not) is simply social approval.

In light of the *SLs'* earnestly lived existence, you wouldn't expect much passion from them in the dating department. Fortunately, *SLs* also nurture a rather well hidden creative side that comes to the fore when they're sheltered in intimate relationships. And that's why they're so choosy about their intimate connections in which every nuance from potential suitors will have some significance. The *SLs'* mates will find it to their advantage to have well-developed communication skills if they expect to enjoy peaceful relationships with these finicky people.

Family life may come naturally, but it doesn't come without careful consideration. No matter what you say about *SL* personalities, they're anything but reckless when it comes to the important matters of marriage and children.

Sally Field When accepting her second Best Actress Oscar for her role in *Norma Rae* at the 1979 Academy Awards, an ebullient Sally Field sycophantically blurted out, "You like me; you really like me." The unfortunate turn of phrase made her a target for satirists for the next two decades. ■ It's not as if Sally hasn't had her fair share of acceptance speeches since—winning her next Oscar in 1984 for her performance in *Places in the Heart.* Her career began on TV as *Gidget,* and later as *The Flying Nun,* but she is probably best remembered by the over-thirty set for starring alongside Burt Reynolds in *Smokey and the Bandit.* ■ Sally's other film credits include *Steel Magnolias, Soapdish, Mrs. Doubtfire, Absence of Malice, Kiss Me Goodbye* and *Forrest Gump,* in which she played Tom Hanks's mother.

THE SMOOTH

sm

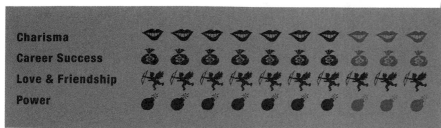

Charisma										
Career Success										
Love & Friendship										
Power										

Intelligent Quick-minded Well-spoken
Emotional Undependable Temperamental

The letter *M* is the symbol of maternal love and is the key letter in the word *mother* in virtually every language on earth. So it's not surprising that people whose names feature the letter *M,* are usually described as having gentle and nurturing cores. But when the *M* occurs in words beginning with the *sassy, sultry* letter *S,* it takes on an element of provocative affection—*smooch, smarmy, smack, smutty, smoky, smoldering, smirk* and *smoothie*—perhaps explaining why *SMs* so often display a high level of confidence and are universally well liked by the opposite sex.

SMs' high levels of physical and emotional energy enable them to seemingly cruise through life. With all this excess exuberance, these people are drawn to change and are always looking for new experiences to keep them on their toes. They could be considered high-maintenance in this regard, for friends are often left feeling that they're simply tools to keep the *SM* occupied. Fortunately, one of their defining characteristics is that *SMs* genuinely like people—and almost always, people genuinely like them back.

When choosing careers, *SMs* usually favor high-intensity jobs over those more sedate and predictable, but because they're famous for changing their minds,

Sam
Sammy
Samuel
Seamus
Seema
Selma
Semaj

it's not unusual for them to vacillate for years before making a commitment. The sharp-minded *SMs* are natural entrepreneurs, salespeople and marketers, and whatever they finally choose to do, they'll probably have a role in bringing up the level of enthusiasm within the company.

SMs have uniquely powerful powers of persuasion and it's hard to resist their charisma once they've set you in their sights. In light of these persuasive powers, it sometimes seems as if they could have anyone they wanted. So what explains all their vacillation when it comes to choosing mates? It could be that they secretly don't want to disappoint anyone by taking themselves off the market; but it's more likely that they are perfectionists who would rather spend quality time with themselves than making small talk with also-rans.

If you're married to an *SM,* you're likely familiar with the frustrations of living with a person who's in such high demand. As they're wont to remind you: just because they're wearing your ring doesn't mean that it's through their nose. Still, *SMs'* nurturing sides gets the better of them once children become involved, and they're always careful to reassure their mates that their families top their priority lists.

Samuel L. Jackson Raised by his mother and grandparents in Tennessee, a youthful Samuel Jackson was suspended from his Atlanta college after taking a number of the board's trustees hostage to protest the absence of black trustees and a black studies curriculum. ■ Although he originally made his mark as a character actor in films like *School Daze, Do the Right Thing, Mo' Better Blues, Jungle Fever* and *A Time to Kill,* Samuel's Oscar-nominated role as a proselytizing hit man in Quentin Tarantino's *Pulp Fiction* catapulted him to superstar status. The film, which narrowly missed winning an Oscar for Best Picture in 1994 (losing to *Forrest Gump*), featured John Travolta's comeback performance. ■ Samuel appealed to a new generation of movie fans as Mace Windu, the slick Jedi master in the prequel to George Lucas's *Star Wars.*

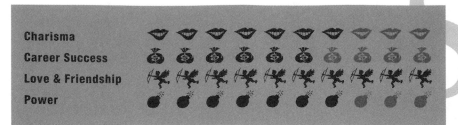

Charisma	💋	💋	💋	💋	💋	💋	💋	💋	💋	💋
Career Success	💰	💰	💰	💰	💰	💰	💰	💰	💰	💰
Love & Friendship	💘	💘	💘	💘	💘	💘	💘	💘	💘	💘
Power	💣	💣	💣	💣	💣	💣	💣	💣	💣	💣

**Discriminating Meticulous Prudent
Miserly Snappish Critical**

Although the letter *M* is the symbol of *maternal* and *motherly* love, when it occurs in close proximity to the *sassy, sexy* and *sultry* letter *S*, it takes on the provocatively seductive air found in the words *smooch, smack, smutty, smarmy, smoky, smoldering, smirk* and *smoothie*. But since the letter *N* is the symbol for most things *negative* (*no, not, never, nada, null, nothing, nada, nyet* and *naught*) there's usually some aspect to the *SMN* personality that involves pessimism, self-doubt and even a reputation for insensitivity.

These are quirky people who always manage to make a lasting impression, and even those who only know *SMN*s in superficial ways find their wry sense of humor quite charming. But when you get to know them on a deeper level they're going to reveal themselves to be sensible, wise and ultracomplex.

*SMN*s are more likely to be observers than doers, and it shows in the way they accumulate data about their surroundings and use this information to further their goals. Consequently, they often come up with insights about life and other people that prove to be quite astute. In fact, *SMN*s are so confident in their understanding of how the world works that they often come across as being a little smug. It may be true that *SMN*s are a little tactless at times, but they are really

Samantha
Samson
Simeon
Simon
Simona
Simone

softies beneath their thick skins and it wouldn't be fair to characterize them as being mean-spirited.

When it comes to choosing their careers, *SMN*s are usually very methodical and seem to have the ability to think ten moves ahead. One of their attributes is that they cope well with complexity, and when other people are cracking under the pressure, they're just warming up. That's why they are in such high demand for jobs calling for levelheadedness in time of crisis. So if you're looking for an employee to run your complaint department, handle pushy salespeople or just work on Christmas Eve with only minor grumbling, an *SMN* is an ideal choice.

In regards to their intimate lives, many people report that *SMN*s have quirky sexualities that have surprised many unsuspecting lovers. This might be a pleasant surprise if you're the adventurous type, but it obviously isn't for everyone. And don't think they're going to outgrow it either, for even when *SMN*s settle down, it's hardly ever in the traditional sense. These are people who secretly cherish their eccentric reputations and don't see marriage as a reason to give it up. *SMN*s' children will enjoy their confiding relationships with parents who handle problems with intelligence rather than selling out to conventional disciplinary techniques.

Simon Cowell Being a jerk takes a lot of work, and doing it well can make you a star—as Simon Cowell proved on the surprise hit TV show *American Idol*. ■ Basically a remake of the 1980s series *Star Search*, *Idol* featured hundreds of hopeful young singing stars from around the country and became a media sensation. But it soon became apparent that viewers were mainly tuning in to cringe at Simon's caustic and unflinching criticisms. With his instinct for what the American public really wanted, Simon supplied the voiceover for the agony of defeat. ■ When he's not acting as the dark destroyer of hope, Simon is a successful record producer in London and in the past ten years has achieved sales of over twenty-five million albums.

smr

Charisma — 🫦 🫦 🫦 🫦 🫦 🫦 🫦 🫦 🫦 🫦
Career Success — 💰 💰 💰 💰 💰 💰 💰 💰 💰
Love & Friendship — 🏹 🏹 🏹 🏹 🏹 🏹 🏹 🏹 🏹
Power — 💣 💣 💣 💣 💣 💣 💣 💣 💣

Meticulous Irreverent Positive
Self-deprecating Condescending Undisciplined

The one thing that the letters *S*, *M* and *R* all have in common is that they are all letters of passion and seduction. The letter *S* is the herald of all things *sexy, slinky, sassy* and *smilin*g, the *M* the symbol of *maternal* and *motherly* love, and the rolling letter *R* represents the cheeky sexuality found in the words *raunchy, racy, randy, rapture, ravish* and *relish*. Put them all together and you get words awash in the sensuality of *shimmer, summery, smolder, gossamer* and *mesmerize*. As such, *SMR* names are uniquely qualified to represent personalities that can brighten a Michigan winter.

But it would be a mistake to think of the happy-go-lucky *SMRs* as being one-dimensional. For as light-hearted as they can be, *SMRs'* philosophies of life are rooted in intellectuality-grounded spirituality. They're the kinds of people whose wisdom comes from a place few of us have visited. They also know how to make people laugh at just the right times, even if much of their humor goes right over the heads of their audience.

In terms of their careers, *SMRs* excel in jobs that require hand-eye coordination and the ability to solve short-range problems. But because these gregarious souls have such a hunger for human interaction, it would be rare to find *SMRs* in solo professions like writing or accounting. It's much more likely that they will be employed as teachers, managers, or in the restaurant industry . . . anything where large groups of people are involved. There's nothing lethargic about *SMRs* either, and it's common to find them falling in love with their work, or at least fixating on a problem until they've found the solution. If they're not the first people to show up at work in the morning, then they're going to be the last to leave.

Did we mention obsession? Well, watch out for the *SMR* in love. These expansive personalities can bowl anyone over with their grand expressions of affection—at least that's what *they* believe. The problem comes when they fail to capture the heart of their intended target and discover that *they* are the ones to have fallen in love. These are the times that *SMRs* are at their lowest ebb: for these kinds of philosophical failures are particularly traumatic for people with such secure attitudes on relationships. And because these sensitive individuals have such a hard time pulling out of downward emotional slides, their ideal spouses are the even-tempered types who will keep *SMRs'* upbeat attitudes on an even keel.

Samara
Samir
Samira
Seymour
Somer
Sommer
Summer

Summer Phoenix Born on December 10, 1978, Summer Joy Phoenix is the fifth and final child of a gifted performing family that includes her siblings Joaquin, Rain, Liberty and the late River Phoenix. ■ Summer's talents as an actress have landed her parts in the movies films include *The Believer, Russkies, SLC Punk!, The Laramie Project, Wasted* and *Suzie Gold*. She has also appeared on-stage, in London's Garrick Theatre, in *This is Our Youth*, alongside Matt Damon and Casey Affleck. ■ Summer is also a talented musician and played keyboards and sang in an alternative band called The Causey Way. She wrote and played piano on her sister Rain's CD. ■ Summer and actor Casey Affleck welcomed a son, Indiana, into the world on May 31, 2004.

Charisma	👄	👄	👄	👄	👄	👄	👄	👄	👄	👄
Career Success	💰	💰	💰	💰	💰	💰	💰	💰	💰	💰
Love & Friendship	💘	💘	💘	💘	💘	💘	💘	💘	💘	💘
Power	💣	💣	💣	💣	💣	💣	💣	💣	💣	💣

Shrewd Studious Talented Pessimistic Vain Caustic

Names that begin with the letter *S* imply a personality that is *sassy, sexy, slinky, sensual* and *stylish*. But when the letter *S* comes into close contact with the *negative* letter *N* (*no, not, never, nix, null, nothing, nada, nyet* and *naught*) it tends to create words that remind us of someone looking down their nose, as in *snooty, snobby, sneering, snotty, snippy, snappy* and *snub*. So if you know any *SN*s, there's a good chance that you've been charmed by their sharp intelligence and learned to be cautious of their biting tongues. It should be said that uppity behavior on the *SN*s' part doesn't stem from any sense of ego: it's more of a defensive reaction caused by their episodic forays into pessimism.

When you think of *SN*s, think of those no-frills types of people who need to know *exactly* where they stand with the people around them, and who will extend the same courtesy to others. This kind of direct approach gives *SN*s their reputation for being a little uptight, and while it's not completely unjustified, *SN*s are a lot more complicated than this. So you'd be underestimating them if you wrote them off as being single-minded snobs, for their motivations are typically the result of their unconventional minds and deeply

Son
Sana
Santana
Santiago
Santino
Santos
Sean
Sena
Sienna
Sina
Sonia
Sonja
Sonny
Sonya
Spencer
Spenser
Spring
Suanne
Suellen
Sunny
Sun

spiritual natures. In their personal lives, *SN*s tend to accumulate core groups of admirers who appreciate their unique brand of wisdom.

*SN*s prefer to avoid conflict, so careers in competitive or political environments like law and big business aren't going to be their cup of tea. They're much more comfortable in unstructured situations (like design, science or teaching) which allow them to articulate their creative talents. One could even call them nerdy, but it's not as if they don't like to unwind every now and then . . . perhaps it's just that mean perfectionist streak that makes them seem so prosaic. It's also best not to make any changes to *SN*s' routine, for they are creatures of habit who are ill-equipped to handle sudden changes in their personal and professional lives.

In matters of the heart, *SN* mates are equal parts idealistic, practical and irresponsible; they'd much rather remain single until they've found *the one*. Romance for romance's sake is lost on these sensible creatures, who view marriage as just another rite of passage. Because these are people who hate to fail, their contribution to the union may not come in the form of romantic gestures: it will show up in their terrierlike commitment to the partnership.

Sean Penn Hollywood bad boy Sean Penn has been a media magnet throughout his career. His relationship with Madonna was publicized for its tempestuousness (and alleged abusiveness) and collapsed after they co-starred in 1987's flop, *Shanghai Surprise*. ■ Sean's movie debut was in 1982's cult classic *Fast Times at Ridgemont High*, in which he stole every scene in which his surfer-dude character appeared. Although he could have had a great career in comedy, he opted for drama in movies like *Bad Boys* and *The Falcon and the Snowman*. ■ In 2002 Sean made a visit to Baghdad to gain a "deeper understanding" of the looming war. The move didn't win him many fans and suggested that (unless you're Ronald Reagan or Arnold Schwarzenegger), acting is acting and politics should be left to the politicians.

Charisma	💋	💋	💋	💋	💋	💋	💋	💋	💋	💋	
Career Success	💰	💰	💰	💰	💰	💰	💰	💰	💰	💰	
Love & Friendship	🏹	🏹	🏹	🏹	🏹	🏹	🏹	🏹	🏹	🏹	
Power	💣	💣	💣	💣	💣	💣	💣	💣	💣	💣	

**Discreet Capable Devoted
Careless Sentimental Dependent**

Names that begin with the *sensuous* letter *S* (or the sound of the soft letter *C*) are indicative of a personality rife with *sass* and *sauciness*. As a counterbalance to this free-spirited theme, the *ND* letter combination imparts the elements of benevolence and emotional generosity that can be discerned in the words *kindly, fondly, friend, lend, endear, slender, garland* and *Godsend*. It's also noteworthy that most *SND* names end with the *youthful* letter *Y*: words that end with high-pitched tones tend to advertise themselves as being distinctly accessible: *friendly, silly, goofy, zany* and *honey*.

Even though *SND*s can be as stubborn as two-year-olds on occasion, the majority of the time, the most annoying thing about them is their tendency to be so damned agreeable. It should be said that *SND*s aren't amenable because they fear confrontation: their brand of unpretentiousness is a reflection of their inner tranquility and spiritual relationship with life. And even when one *does* encounter their obstinate sides, it's likely to be rooted in a desire to see justice done and social equity restored. So if you're looking for a nonjudgmental friend who's capable of unconditional support, you won't do much better than an *SND*.

Like most people whose names begin with the letter *S*, *SND*s aren't motivated by power, authority or wealth.

Cinda
Cindy
Sandra
Sandy
Sanford
Sindy
Sondra
Sunday

These are people who derive satisfaction from a job well done—no matter how pedestrian it might be. Because they're so easily distracted by minutiae, *SND*s will need their work environments to be well organized, but once they've got all their ducks in a row, they're likely to be the most productive cogs in the machine. If there's a downside to *SND*s' meticulous approach to their professional lives, it's that they tend to vacillate when it comes to choosing their career paths, and some *SND*s will drift for years in meaningless jobs before deciding on a particular career. So if anyone accuses your *SND* friend of laziness, you can reassure him or her that they're simply taking time to ponder their future.

Things are very different when it comes to the *SND*s' emotional commitments, for they have no sense of fear when it comes to matters of the heart. And this isn't because they're overconfident or anything, it's just because they have a philosopher's faith in fate. These spiritual souls are at their best when teamed up with partners who connect with their unique outlooks on providence, and mates will appreciate the *SND*s' patient and accommodating ministrations. Their intrinsic calm will be welcome in touchy situations, their stubbornness invaluable when negotiating rent, and their social graces priceless in smoothing out conflict.

Cindy Crawford In the days before every model was a "supermodel," Cindy Crawford was a hypermodel. With her all-American beauty and Monroesque mole to boot, she was the highest-paid cover girl in the world. ■ A sad fact of the modeling business is that even a near-perfect body like Cindy's needed retouching before ending up on magazine covers. To emulate their role model, young girls desperately starved themselves to mold their bodies into what was literally an impossible shape. ■ Cindy's marriage to Richard Gere was dogged by rumors of homosexuality and reached such a crescendo that it prompted the couple to buy a full-page ad in the London Times that said: "We are heterosexual and monogamous and take our commitment to each other very seriously," ■ Three years later, Cindy filed for divorce.

Charisma										
Career Success										
Love & Friendship										
Power										

**Multi-talented Caring Strong-minded
Pessimistic Sarcastic Stubborn**

The letters *S* and *R* are two of the most provocatively passionate letters in the alphabet. The *S* is the symbol of all things *sassy, sexy, sensual, seductive* and *sinful,* while the rolling letter *R* conveys images of *romance, raunchiness, ribaldness, ripeness* and *raciness.* This isn't to imply that these women are unable to control their inner urges, but they certainly are strongly connected to their emotional and animalistic centers. *SR*s are those people who seem to glide through life, and even when things are running a little rough, you'd never know it by their outwardly *serene, sprightly* and *summery* dispositions.

Like most people who are tuned-in to their inner needs, *SR*s are cautious about making commitments in both their professional and personal lives, and it's not uncommon for them to vacillate for years before deciding on career tracks. And when they do finally decide to get their act going, they're able to handle pretty much any kind of work as long as it doesn't involve numbers. This is because *SR*s are creative types who aren't cut out for the humdrum logic of engineering and mathematics. So if you know an *SR* who's happy in his or her job, chances are it involves some form of design, medicine or teaching. It's also not unusual for *SR*s to suddenly switch careers even after they've found one that suits them, but this is less a symptom of instability than it is a reflection of their creative instincts: *SR*s need to know that they still have the ability to handle challenging situations.

Little things matter a lot to *SR*s in their personal lives; they have an eye for detail and a talent for discerning other people's motivations. At the same time, they aren't exactly well known for their bedside manners and unconditional sympathies. Their brand of social interaction has more to do with straightforward honesty, which is designed to motivate and not to commiserate. They might offend you with this candid approach, but at least you'll always know where you stand.

As potential life partners, *SR*s' blunt opinions understandably cause a few disruptions here and there, but you can expect them to blossom when mated with the right person. And the "right person" is someone who brings their own self-confidence to the game and who will curb the *SR*'s penchant for indecision.

Those married to an *SR* can expect an even-tempered mate who's quite happy to relinquish the reins if it's in the best interests of the relationship. *SR*s will certainly pull their own weight when it comes to bringing home the bacon and raising the children, and although they are low-maintenance in terms of material needs, they will function at maximum efficiency only when given large doses of love, support and encouragement.

Sara
Sarah
Sarahi
Sarai
Sarina
Serena
Serenity
Sergio
Sierra
Soraya

Sarah Jessica Parker One of four siblings and four half-siblings, Sarah Jessica Parker was born in a small Ohio town in 1965. After the young Sarah was cast in the Broadway production of *The Innocents,* her family relocated to New Jersey where she landed the lead in the Broadway run of *Annie.* ■ Although she turned up in a number of notable movies (like *Footloose* and *L.A. Story*), it took some time for Sarah to dominate the screen. ■ Most film actresses consider television to be a step down but Sarah's star turn as Manhattan sex-columnist Carrie Bradshaw in HBO's *Sex and the City* earned her international notoriety as well as a Golden Globe. Married to fellow actor Matthew Broderick, Sarah once lived with Robert Downey Jr. and dated the late John Kennedy Jr.

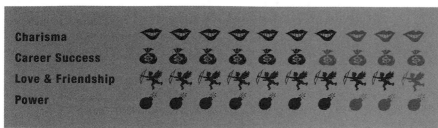

Charisma	
Career Success	
Love & Friendship	
Power	

ssn

Outgoing Physical Intelligent
Deceptive Unpredictable Dangerous

Names that begin with the letter *S* usually imply a personality that is *sassy, sexy, slinky, sensual* and *stylish*. And anyone with two *S*s in her name is bound to be able to beguile the socks off of a shoeless man. But it must also be said that when the letter *S* comes into close contact with the *negative* letter *N* (*no, not, never, nada, null, nothing, nyet* and *naught*) it creates words that remind us of someone looking down their nose: *snooty, snobby, sneering, snotty, snorting, snappy* and *snub*. So, if you know any *SSNs*, there's a pretty good chance that you've been charmed by their sharp intelligence but that you've also learned to be cautious of their snippy outbursts. To be fair, it should be recognized that their bouts of acerbic behavior are not a result of any egotistical expression but are simply defensive reactions designed to protect the *SSNs'* sensitive centers.

The sultry and smoldering undercurrent you sense in your *SSN* friend is real, but there's also a lightness to her that manifests in a touchy-feely approach. She'll wrap those close to her in a swath of physical affection, but like many people prone to emotional fragility, *SSNs* are experts at protecting their feelings (which is why penetrating their emotional cores can be quite tricky). While they're consistently friendly, they manage to project an air of untouchability that is sometimes perceived

Season
Sunshine
Susan
Susanna
Susanne

to be snobbishness. But given that these sensitive sprites have such an uncommon hunger for intimacy, they aren't going to risk their valuable emotional energies on anyone who hasn't given them some reliable indication of trustworthiness.

SSNs' appreciation for all things aesthetic makes them perfect for careers in design, food and music. Their job choices will usually include a good deal of people contact, and almost always in small and intimate settings, wherein they can construct meaningful bonds. If there's going to be a problem in their work lives, it'll probably have something to do with the *SSN's* disinterest in office politics, which often ends up costing them dearly when it comes to promotion and salary reviews.

In matters of the heart, the *SSN* will be as affectionate anyone could wish, but her partner must learn which buttons not to push—for an *SSN* in one of her sensitive moods is capable of biting sarcasm and obdurate stubbornness. *SSNs* also have that rare gift of being able to enforce discipline with a smile—perhaps because people fear what might happen if that smile ever went away. Still, if you are looking for a partner who understands the value of loyalty and the rewards of commitment, you would be hard pressed to find a more steadfast mate.

Susan B. Anthony Most people only know about Susan B. Anthony from her face on the dollar coin that was introduced in 1979. Susan was a nineteenth-century feminist who fought for women's suffrage long before "feminism" became a buzz word. ■ Susan was a lightning rod for negative public opinion generated by her cause and wrote strident, even racist comments about "ignorant" black men being able to vote. Still, her opinions largely reflected the prevailing attitude of the times, and though her speeches were unpopular, Susan eventually made headway. ■ No one knows why the Susan B. Anthony dollar failed to catch on, but the U.S. mint believed it had something to do with its similarity in size to the quarter. It has since been replaced by a new dollar coin with equally negative public acceptance.

THE POPULAR Stc

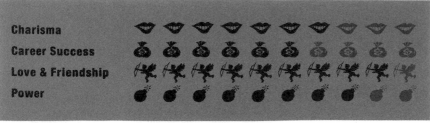

Charisma									
Career Success									
Love & Friendship									
Power									

**Gregarious Well-liked Capable
Snobbish Tense Demanding**

When the *sassy* letter *S* teams up with the *tightly* wound tones of the letter *T,* it evokes the *steadfast* and *strong* characteristics found in the words *stable, steely, stiff, stark, statue, stony, strict, stubborn* and *stoic.* Because these heavy-duty overtones are commonly associated with masculinity, most female *STC* names end with the high-pitched letters *I, Y* or *IE,* creating the diminutizing effect found in the words *sunny, funny, silly, goofy, happy, zany* and *preppie.*

STCs may not be known for their patience, but their determination and willingness to take risks are legendary. These are people who work and play hard, and have learned that you can't steal second when your foot is on first. *STCs* are straight shooters when it comes to their relationships too, and if there's something about you that rubs them the wrong way, chances are you'll know about it immediately. If you can't handle their heat, stay away from their friction.

Still, *STCs* have no trouble making friends and can afford to be choosy when it comes to selecting intimate partners. If at first they seem to be somewhat aloof or indifferent, this is simply symptomatic of being such hard-driven perfectionists. As assertive as they are about their choices, *STCs* don't see any great advantage to plunging into things without at least a little bit of

Stacey
Staci
Stacia
Stacie
Stacy

research. They are particularly prudent when it comes to spending money and don't live particularly flashy lives.

There are few careers for which *STCs* aren't suited, and their biggest challenge often comes in deciding which one to choose. But *STCs* are wary about committing to jobs that don't offer them long-term advancement, and many are found in design fields, legal maneuverings and medicine fields. But what suits them best are positions in which they're able to utilize their people skills. More than most, *STCs* thrive on the tumult of human contact and know that success, without someone to share it, is as hollow as a pumpkin on Halloween.

STCs take less of an emotional approach to their relationships than they do an intellectual one, and potential mates will be carefully vetted against their internal list of specifications. This is consistent with the *STCs'* need to maintain a high degree of control in their relationships, and—whether it's for financial or emotional reasons—the success of many *STC* marriages will be as a result of their capable stewardship. Their primary goal will be to create an environment in which they can feel completely open and relaxed, and will return the favor with unconditional love and support.

Stacy Keach Growing up with an irreparable harelip is difficult; overcoming this disability and becoming a successful actor is a virtual impossibility. Stacy Keach learned to ignore people who told him he would never be an actor and went on to become one of the most widely recognized faces on television. ■ Stacy is best known for his portrayal of the title character in the TV drama *Mike Hammer*, a show that ran for three years. Like many successful actors during the eighties, he fell prey to cocaine addiction and even spent some time in jail. But after shaking his habit, he successfully resumed his acting career.

stfn

Charisma	👄 👄 👄 👄 👄 👄 👄 👄 👄 👄
Career Success	💰 💰 💰 💰 💰 💰 💰 💰 💰 💰
Love & Friendship	🏹 🏹 🏹 🏹 🏹 🏹 🏹 🏹 🏹 🏹
Power	💣 💣 💣 💣 💣 💣 💣 💣 💣 💣

**Stable Trustworthy Entertaining
Skeptical Moody Cranky**

The enduring popularity of the *STFN* names may have something to do with the fact that the *ST* phoneme is the herald of all things *steadfast, strong, stable, stark, stony, strict, stubborn* and *stoic*. And even though these names are colored by the *negative* letter *N* (*no, not, nincompoop, nothing, nyet* and *never*), they lose much of their pessimism thanks to the *freeing* sounds of the *festive* letter *F* or *PH* sound: *fun, fancy, fanny, fawn, fantasy, friend, fine* and *fond*. Because the *ST* combination has a predominantly masculine flavor, *all* female *STFN* names end in the high-pitched tones of the *I, Y* or *IE,* which gives them the feminine resonance found in the words *sunny, cozy, fairy, happy, zany* and *honey*. *STFN*s are strong, funny, smart and warm, and by bringing a sense of balance to their environments, they can always be counted on to make an impact on the lives of those they touch.

With this wealth of self-assurance, *STFN*s believe that it's better doing something and regretting it, than *not* doing something and regretting it. This is why you'll never hear an *STFN* say, "if only I had . . ." and why many *STFN*s are willing to live out their dreams in unconventional ways. And if *STFN*s' avant-garde life choices generate criticism, it's certainly not going to put a damper on their behavior—after all, no one has ever put up a statue to a critic.

Stefan
Stefania
Stephane
Stephanie
Stephen
Stephon

Always ready with a joke, a shoulder to cry on, or sound advice when it's needed, people are irresistibly drawn to the *STFN*'s realm. But all this emotional energy can take its toll (especially on someone whose strengths don't include stamina) and *STFN*s will need regular episodes of downtime to recharge their social batteries.

If *STFN*s have reputations for being short-cut artists, you won't find them objecting to the characterization: *STFN*s hate doing anything the hard way if they suspect there might be a more efficient way. They're the kinds of people who justify not making the bed because they're just going to mess it up later in the evening. Even when they were in school, *STFN*s would do *just* enough to get by, which everyone agrees is a shame, considering their high potential.

*STFN*s are undoubtedly family types and, while they may not be the most romantic people on the planet, understand the value of commitment and the inevitable compromises that come with it. But because *STFN*s aren't likely to turn down any social invitations, prospective mates must be able to hack it with someone who's not going to abide by the family's appointment book. The ideal mates for the energetic *STFN*s are people with their *own* busy schedules and autonomous social domains.

Stephen Hawking The most widely recognized physicist since Albert Einstein, wheelchair-bound Stephen Hawking is a theoretical physicist, cosmologist, researcher and Cambridge professor. ■ Although Stephen suffers from a degenerative disease that has left him largely paralyzed, he has written two best-sellers on cosmology and has helped shed light on some of science's biggest mysteries. Stephen believes that his illness furthered his research by freeing his mind to dwell on the universe and its origins. ■ All of Stephen's work is done with the help of his colleagues and wife. His research has centered on general relativity, black holes, gravity and quantum theory—all subjects first postulated by Einstein. His life's dream is to create a new theory of the universe that combines all the current theories into the Theory of Everything.

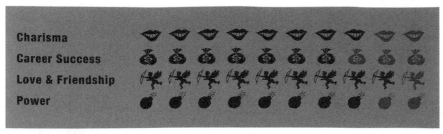

Charisma										
Career Success										
Love & Friendship										
Power										

Bright Humorous Buoyant
Abrasive Insensitive Judgmental

When the *sassy* letter *S* teams up with the *tightly* wound tones of the letter *T*, it evokes the *strong* and *steadfast* characteristics found in the words *stable, steely, stiff, stark, statue, stony, strict, stubborn* and *stoic*. But because the letter *L* is the symbol for all things *loving, laughing, light* and *learned*, it's not surprising that when people describe the *STL* personality, they invariably mention her strength and always cite her gentle, loving core. You could almost say the *STL* is the epitome of womanly confidence and strength—a Renaissance woman, in fact—with the *potential* to do anything, but dogged by the lack of focus to see it through.

Stella

No one has yet invented a problem that's too tough for an *STL* to tackle. This doesn't mean that she is able to solve everything that comes her way, mind you, but she'll certainly give it her best effort. That's why you definitely want to have an *STL* friend around when your life hits the rocks. Not only are these people blessed with a remarkable brand of street-intelligence, but they're also quite amenable to sharing their skills with anyone who asks. In another expression of their tender core, *STL*s always seem to be picking up human and animal strays.

There's an odd quirk to the *STL* personality: at times, nothing surprises her more than her own actions. She may resolve never to cross a certain line or commit a certain act, but before she knows what's happened, she's gone ahead and done it anyway. While this may not come as a huge revelation to her loved ones (who have long since gotten used to her impulsive moods), most *STL*s secretly wish they could be a little more stable at times.

Because of her changeable nature, the *STL* finds it impossible to stay in the same career for her whole life, and she will often switch horses in midstream to investigate new horizons. Because this is obviously a drawback for many employers, many *STL*s pay the price in terms of reduced income potential.

At heart, the *STL* is an explorer who feels driven to discover herself and can hold her own on pretty much any subject that doesn't involve math or war. And when it comes to settling down, she's going to be at her best when she lands a mate who shares her sense of adventure. If worst comes to worst, and she finds herself paired with some species of couch potato, she runs the risk of losing her chipper self and becoming the thing she fears most: complacent.

As mates, *STL*s are consistently upbeat and willing to please, and where children are involved, they take a stellar turn. Even though many *STL*s reported fearing that children would upset their intricately concocted dreams, without exception they discovered parenthood to be their ultimate calling.

Stella Stevens Stella Stevens was a medical student-turned-*Playboy* bunny who used her beauty to mask her intelligence and further her career in modeling. Considering that she was a seventeen-year-old divorced mother with few options, her stint with *Playboy* turned out to be the right move. ■ Stella proved to be an accomplished comedienne as well, playing Appassionata Von Climax in the 1959 movie *Li'l Abner*, Glenn Ford's girlfriend *in The Courtship of Eddie's Father* and the kooky heroine in *The Silencers*. She also survived a role in Elvis Presley's *Girls! Girls! Girls!* ■ Still, for the duration of her career Stella was unable to shake the public's view of her as a semi-naked bunny.

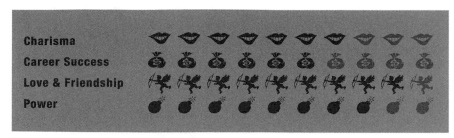

stn

Charisma	😊😊😊😊😊😊😊😊😊😊
Career Success	💰💰💰💰💰💰💰💰💰💰
Love & Friendship	🦅🦅🦅🦅🦅🦅🦅🦅🦅🦅
Power	💣💣💣💣💣💣💣💣💣💣

Creative Original Inspiring
Eccentric Misunderstood Indecisive

Names that begin with the letter *S* usually imply a *sassy, sexy, slinky, sensual* and *stylish* personality. But when the letter *S* comes into close contact with the *triumphant, talented* and *tightly wound* letter *T*, it creates the *steadfast* and *strong* masculine tones found in the words *stable, steely, stiff, stark, statue, stony, strict, stubborn* and *stoic.* The letter *N*, on the other hand, is the symbol of all things negative (*no, not, never, nyet, nada, naught, nix* and *nothing*) and usually intimates some aspect of pessimism. It could be said that the successes of *STN* people come not from any great inner drive, but from a pervasive (if unfounded) fear of failure.

When it comes to choosing between their heads or their gut instincts, *STN*s will almost always rely on their heads. It's not that they're not intuitive; it's just that when you have such a canny intelligence, it makes sense to trust it. And *STN*s have a work ethic that would put Jimmy Carter to shame; not only are they some of the most creative and intelligent individuals you could hope to meet, but they seem determined to make everyone take notice by taking on projects and problems that others consider to be intractable.

If there's a flaw in the *STN*'s old-fashioned work ethic, it's that he tends to take himself a little too seri-

Stan
Stanford
Stanley
Stanton
Stetson
Stone

ously. Even though he's not the controlling type, the *STN* isn't the kind of man who functions well under someone else's direction. If he's going to succeed, it'll be from the sweat of his *own* brow, and egged on by his refusal to accept the ignominy of broken commitments.

While many *STN*s make their mark as entrepreneurs, artists and scientists, most function well in careers that reward attention to detail. But if you have a project that demands immediate action, you might *not* want your *STN* employee to take control: he's simply too detail-oriented to do things in a hurry. Perhaps this is why *STN*s are so rarely found in positions of dynamic leadership.

Romantic life to the *STN* must sometimes seem like a mystery. For while no one would accuse them of being insensitive, they're not known for their powers of observation about human behavior. Emotions they understand; it's the nuances that get them tangled up. So while he might realize that his wife is upset, he'll need the reasons to be blown up to projector size before he's can do anything about it. If you're going to marry an *STN*, you've either got to be incredibly patient or really not care whether the toothpaste cap is on the tube. Still, the *STN* is one of the most reliable mates you're going to find (among people with *S* names) and his mate will never want for attention or affection.

Stanley Kubrick More often than not, Stanley Kubrick's work as a director was surrounded by criticism (and even outright revulsion) for its bold, unconventional content. Though widely regarded as a genius, many people felt uneasy around his controlling personality. ■ After a few failed marriages, Stanley moved to the UK, where he filmed his most controversial films, including *Lolita* (Nabakov's romance between an older man and a twelve-year-old girl), *Dr. Strangelove* and the ultraviolent *A Clockwork Orange*. Most critics agree that his defining work was the science-fiction cult classic, *2001: A Space Odyssey*. ■ Stanley died at the age of seventy after the top-secret filming of *Eyes Wide Shut*. His unfinished work, *AI*, was taken over by Steven Spielberg and resulted in a split-personality movie of unusual complexity and nuance.

Charisma	👄👄👄👄👄👄👄👄👄👄
Career Success	💰💰💰💰💰💰💰💰💰
Love & Friendship	🐦🐦🐦🐦🐦🐦🐦🐦🐦🐦
Power	💣💣💣💣💣💣💣💣💣💣

Sharp Attentive Quick learner
Careless Argumentative Arrogant

Names that begin with the letters *S* and *T* invariably denote individuals with an unmatched dose of *strength, stability, stubbornness* and *stoicism.* The *STR* root takes this robust theme a little further by creating words like *strident, strong, sterling, stormy, strive, streak, strike, zestier* and *rustler.* It's hardly a surprise then, that many people consider *STRs* to be highly motivated and earnest about their careers and loves. There's also no doubt that *STRs* are extraordinarily intelligent and are quick to rise to challenges. And if it sometimes seems that *everything* is a competition to the *STR* personalities (like discussing music, playing cards or hanging out), that's the price you pay for associating with those who believe they were meant to conquer the world.

Even when meddling in artistic pursuits, the concrete *STRs* prefer to keep things strictly businesslike, and they'll throw themselves so completely into their projects that they'll leave little room for fun. Their sharp minds serve them well in technological pursuits, and their inquisitive natures make them ideal for careers in journalism, science or computer programming. But if *STRs* have a tendency to go overboard on some of their projects, it doesn't mean that they're reckless in any way. Their single-minded approach to making money can be

Star
Starla
Starr
Sterling
Stewart
Stirling
Stormy
Stuart

as intense as a triple espresso on an empty stomach.

STRs love to entertain and will do so at the drop of a hat. Lack of a stage doesn't bother these sassy extroverts—they'll play to any audience, no matter how small or disinterested. If they don't get the response they're expecting, they might even initiate an argument just for the sake of a little mental exercise. You can understand why their friends get a little frazzled at times, but you can't deny that these are well-intentioned folks with an unusual combination of humor and stubbornness.

It won't be difficult to know what's going on with your *STR* friends: they're willing to let it all hang out—dirty laundry and all. It's not that they aren't mindful of how they're perceived by others; they're just so focused on meeting their goals, that if it's going to take a few raised eyebrows, so be it. With their natural good humor and easygoing attitudes, it's easy to forgive them for any shortcomings.

When rummaging around for a mate, *STRs* are more likely to pick someone with whom they can relate to intellectually. It's also an *STR* requirement that their partners have their *own* interests, for the egalitarian *STRs* would never expect anyone to sacrifice their dreams for their own personal needs.

Stirling Moss When you hear the term "auto racing" in the United States, the first person that comes to mind is Mario Andretti. In the United Kingdom, that name would be Stirling Moss. ■ Both of Stirling's parents were involved in motor sports: his father was an amateur racer and his mother competed in local rallies. Although he won an astonishing 194 of his 466 career races, the world championship eluded him, and he became known as the greatest driver to never win The Cup. ■ Stirling's career came to an end in 1962 with a horrifying head-on crash into an earthen bank. Although he narrowly survived, he retired soon afterward. ■ Posits Stirling: "It's hard to drive at the limit, but it's harder to know where the limits are."

Charisma										
Career Success										
Love & Friendship										
Power										

**Intelligent Enthusiastic Fun-loving
Reckless Controlling Fearful**

People whose names begin with the *sassy* and *sexy* letter *S* are usually described as having easygoing and expansive personalities. But when the *S* comes into close contact with the *talented, triumphant* and *tenacious* letter *T*, it exudes the uncommonly *strong* masculine qualities found in the words *steely, stiff, stability, stark, statue, stony, strict, stubborn* and *stoic*. The enduring popularity of the *STV* names may also have something to do with the fact that the letter *V* is the symbol of all that is *vigorous, virile, vibrant, vital, valiant* and *vivacious*. You'd be hard pressed to find someone with more spunky appeal and sheer determination.

You don't have to lead an *STV* into temptation—they'll find it for themselves, thank you very much. Boredom simply isn't an option for these curious personalities who are willing to try anything twice. Their taste in hobbies tends to lean toward more exotic activities like spelunking, skiing and rock climbing, but this doesn't mean that the *STV*s aren't able to entertain themselves. Their activities also include a great deal of solitary time dedicated to improving their knowledge of the universe: reading, music, chess and art.

*STV*s have a rather well-hidden sensitive side and they're the types of people who've learned to control their emotional output. Because they usually have their game faces on, it can be difficult to know how they feel about an issue unless you're prepared to press them. It's almost as if they have a self-imposed expectation to be strong silent types. So if any of your *STV* friends seem to be in a funk, chances are, they're just taking one of their periodic time-outs to brood over their next move. Given enough space, they'll soon resume their roles as stabilizing forces in their environments.

Given that *STV*s are self-starters (and quick learners) they can pretty much write their own tickets in the professional world. But before they settle into their niche, their job is going to have to offer them the kind of creative freedom and personal growth they'll need. *STV*s function best in environments with plenty of social interaction, but are by no means afraid to take on the lonely challenges of top management.

Certainly no one would accuse *STV*s of being hopeless romantics. These are practical-minded men and women who don't always understand that love is a game of nuance, and that it takes some time to bond intimately. Still, what they lack in subtlety is more than made up for with gusto and enthusiasm, and *STV* marriages are invariably long-lasting and stable.

**Steve
Steven
Stevie**

Steve McQueen Despite his intense competition with Paul Newman, nobody seriously doubted that Steve McQueen was the true hero of Hollywood. He didn't just play the role of the tough guy—he lived it. ■ As a boy, Steve was sent to the Boys' Republic, a home for troubled youths. As an actor, he gained a reputation as a hard-drinking, fast-living womanizer, and his lifestyle was reflected in many films: *The Great Escape, The Sand Pebbles, Bullitt, The Getaway* and *Papillion*. ■ Steve met Ali MacGraw while filming *The Getaway* and promptly ended his fifteen-year marriage to marry her. But in the midst of rumors of infidelity and cocaine addiction, the marriage collapsed. Shortly after making the decision to clean up his life at the age of fifty, Steve died of lung cancer.

Charisma										
Career Success										
Love & Friendship										
Power										

Creative Free-thinking Tender
Sullen Depressed Changeable

The letter *V* is the undisputed flagship of all that is *virile, vibrant, voluptuous, virtuous, vampish* and *valiant*, and tends to imbue words with a sense of *vim, vigor* and overt sexuality. And when names begin with the *sexy, sassy* letter *S*, it's quite understandable that they take on the provocative qualities found in the words *svelte, salivate, savor, salvo, slavish, strive, seductive* and *savvy*. These are people whose verve and humor dovetail quite nicely into a charmingly impulsive personality.

Their sleek physical appearance coupled with their calculating intelligence puts *SVs* in the power seat when it comes to their relationships. And because they're so competitive they'll use whatever they have—charm, sass or sex appeal—to get what they want. But don't expect *SVs* to throw tantrums when they lose: one of their defining aspects is their uncommon pride. So if you're going to see a burst of passion from them, it'll probably be a fit of pique over some trivial inconvenience like an overcooked steak or a poorly made movie. But, as everyone knows, it's better to put up with *SVs*' bark than it is their whining. No one takes their outbursts too seriously and *SVs*' easygoing baseline makes up for the occasional tantrums.

SVs certainly don't lack a sense of humor, but this

Salvador
Savannah
Savion
Silva
Sullivan
Sylvester
Sylvia

doesn't mean that they take their work or their relationships lightly. It's as if they feel destined to do something exceptional with their lives, and even if they may not know what it is, feel compelled to search under every rock for potential glory. There is one thing that *SVs* are extraordinarily good at, and that's communicating.

This inclination to express themselves often draws them to careers in the arts or education, but even when not actively engaged in direct conversation, *SVs* spend a great deal of time in their heads looking for new angles on their latest ideas. So be careful about giving your *SV* friend your email address—they'll put out more emails a week than most spammers do in a month.

These versatile individuals also enjoy family time and, surprising as it may seem, will enjoy settling down once they've had a chance to play the field. But no matter how hard *SVs* fall in love, they'll never be accused of smothering anyone. Their mates will enjoy the dubious freedom of having partners whose social engagements often take them out of the house, but whose warmth and open affections will always hold their interest. *SVs*' children will come to know them as smart, caring (if somewhat distracted) parents who will grant them the freedom to learn from their own mistakes.

Salvador Dali Considered by many to be the greatest surrealist artist of the twentieth century, Salvador Dali was also one of his era's most eccentric paranoids. Trained as an artist from the age of ten, his stint at the Royal Academy of Art in Madrid was marred by his failure to sit for his final exams. He simply refused to be judged by those he considered inferior. ■ Salvador specialized in the unconscious mind and, with his tremendous technical skills, created ultrarealistic and dreamlike visions, like his famous image of melting clocks. ■ Salvador deliberately cultivated his reputation as an eccentric and once showed up at a London exhibit dressed in a diving suit. ■ "The only difference between me and a madman," said Salvador, "is that I'm not mad."

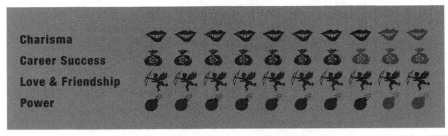

Charisma	
Career Success	
Love & Friendship	
Power	

Smart Fashionable Droll
Ditzy Unfocused Annoying

People whose names begin with the *sexy* and *sassy* letter S are usually described as outgoing and expressive. And since the letter *Z* is the symbol of all that is *zany, zealous, zippy* and *zesty*, it's not surprising that many people expect the *SZ* women to be particularly uninhibited . . . if not a little madcap on occasion.

*SZ*s are almost always a step ahead in their thinking and attitude. If this gives them their reputation for being eccentric, then that's just fine with the *SZ*s, who really can't be bothered about what other people say about them—as long as it's the truth. It's not that they're any more thick-skinned than the next guy; it's just that they'd much rather know who their enemies are.

SZ people seem to draw energy from new experiences and in meeting new people. And with their singular effervescence, an *SZ* thrown into a crowd of strangers will become an instant party. Even if you don't like her style you'll have to agree that your *SZ* friend is as blithe a spirit as you'll ever meet, and if you aren't going to take her seriously, she wouldn't have it any other way. Still, it would be a mistake to underestimate her sharp intelligence and worldly experience.

One salient trait of the *SZ* is her preference for the

Suzan
Suzanna
Suzanne
Suzette
Suzie

latest fashions and it's unlikely that you'd find one schlumping around without makeup unless she's just woken up. She may not be a model, but she certainly has no intention of being ignored, and because her fashion sense is a little ahead of the curve (playing into her quirky reputation) her ear-to-the-ground skill is often dovetailed into her professional life. This is why many *SZ*s end up being great journalists, designers and artists. But people contact remains her highest priority, and she'll gladly take a lower-paying job in a friendly office over a promotion to a cushier but lonelier cubicle.

People in general, and the opposite sex in particular, are drawn to the *SZ*'s winsome ways. Indeed, most *SZ*s make warmly caring mates when they finally get around to finding a partner, but they can be tough nuts to crack in the dating arena where they often find it difficult to shake off their footloose impulses.

Although *SZ*s are prone to playing the field, they also have strong instincts for settling down and raising families. And when their wanderlust finally falls prey to the joys of parenthood, their offspring will be induced to think for themselves and strongly encouraged to follow in their mother's unconventional footsteps.

Suzanne Somers Suzanne Somers must have felt she was born under an unlucky star. Born in 1946 to a family riddled by alcoholism, she lived in constant fear of a father whose physical abuse threatened the family. Diagnosed with dyslexia, Suzanne won a college music scholarship but six months later got pregnant, married the baby's father and divorced him two years later. In 1971 her son was hit by a car and badly injured. ■ Things came together after Suzanne landed a few film roles and hit it big as the ditzy blonde on the long-running series *Three's Company*. Even though she was arguably the reason for the show's huge success, she was fired after demanding higher pay. ■ Suzanne's autobiography, *Keeping Secrets*, was later turned into a TV movie.

**Most Popular
Girl's Names**

Teresa
Theresa
Tammy
Tina
Tracy
Tiffany
Thelma
Tara
Terri
Tonya

**Most Popular
Boy's Names**

Thomas
Timothy
Terry
Todd
Tony
Travis
Troy
Theodore
Tom
Tommy

The Triumphant and Upstanding

"This is the first truth that e'er thine own tongue was guilty of."
—WILLIAM SHAKESPEARE, *All's Well that Ends Well*

The letter T began its career as a symbol of a cattle brand in Egyptian hieroglyphics, and in the Cabala—the mystic writings of early Christians—T represents the union of groom and bride, which culminates in conception and the creation of three, the holy number of the Trinity. ■ With the lowercase t looking almost like a cross, its no wonder that it's so intimately associated with all things biblical. T is the first letter of the two tablets of the Ten Commandments, tradition, testament, truth, tabernacle, throne and Torah, and its biblical references reinforced by the Tetragrammaton, the symbol denoting the ineffable name of God. ■ When the T is united with the heavenly H, it assumes a deeply divine quality stemming from the Greek word for God, theos. These properties can be seen in the traditional meaning of the names Thaddeus (gift of god), Theo (divine gift), Dorothy (gift of God), Timothy (to honor God). ■ But when standing alone, the letter T's sharply pronounced form—generated by the abrupt release of air from the tip of the tongue off the top of the palate—imbues words with a sense of vigor and celebration, as in trumpet, triumphant, talented, twinkle, tremendous and terrific. And it is these decisive attributes that explain why T people are most likely to succeed in professional sports. ■

Charisma	
Career Success	
Love & Friendship	
Power	

Uncomplicated Gracious Insightful
Nervous Predictable Compulsive

Names that make use of the uncomplicated tones of the letter *T* (unadorned by other consonants) tend to be straightforward and to the point. These are people who know exactly where they're headed in life and won't appreciate you wasting their time with game-playing and dishonesty.

The *T* names represent the kind of people, who, when planning their vacations, know months in advance what they'll be doing every day. They've already worked the whole thing through in their heads, from which restaurants they'll be eating at, to where they'll go if their reservations are misplaced. If the *T* motto is "be prepared," it comes with the caveat that they're prone to getting caught up in internal monologues in order to anticipate every eventuality. So don't ever casually ask *T*s what they are thinking about unless you have the time to listen to a diatribe over the minutiae of their plans.

Fortunately, the flip side of the *T*'s methodical ways is an almost divine patience for the foibles of others—which is a good thing since they often find themselves in jobs involving a high degree of personal contact. If people enjoy interacting with these capable souls, it's not because they have a calming influence; it's because they're always so positive about everything. So there's no

Tate
Taya
Tia
Tito
Toya
Ty

need to pep talk *T*s into making something happen, and their lofty goals won't diminish with age. That's why, when planning their careers, *T*s gravitate toward professions that reward long-range vision and an eye for detail: accounting, banking or captains of industry. *T*s also have remarkable aptitudes for music and art that's surprising in such logic-based individuals.

Whether your particular *T* friends are stern taskmasters or egghead scholars, you've probably discovered that their lighter sides ignite on unexpected occasions. With their wicked sense of humor that asserts itself in all manner of unusual witticisms, it's not surprising that many people simply don't "get them," but *T*s really don't have the time to worry about what others think. They know that even if they're on the right track, they'll get run over if they just sit there.

When it comes to communication you'll find *T*s to be people of few words. Conversations tend to be curt and to the point, and one will be left in no doubt as to what they truly think. It's when accepting advice from their friends, however, that *T*s often prove reluctant. These self-contained characters prefer to solve problems in their own way and time. The best way to get their attention is through patience—*T*s respond better to a whisper than to a shout.

Ty Cobb Tyrus Raymond Cobb was born in a small town in Georgia in 1886 to a fifteen-year-old mother. In the modern era, Ty's father's relationship with such a young girl would raise a few eyebrows, but in those days the South was used to such uneven marriages (even if Ty's father was a principal at the schoolhouse where he met his young bride). ■ In his twenty-two years playing in the American League for Detroit, the "Georgia Peach" was easily the best hitter of his era, if not of all time. His career batting average was an amazing .367, and he batted over .400 in three different seasons. ■ A 1942 survey of baseball managers named Ty the greatest player to ever play the game.

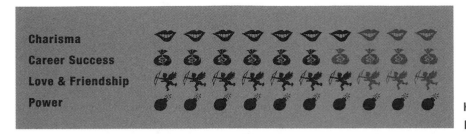

Charisma										
Career Success										
Love & Friendship										
Power										

Honorable Steady Moral
Boring Prissy Self-centered

When a name begins with the *triumphantly trumpeting* letter *T*, the *T*'s explosive energy heralds a person with a sharp mind and an easy laugh. But when the name also features the *brave* and *belligerent* letter *B*, it's going to take on a decidedly in-your-face tone. We see this forceful combination at work in words like *fastball, outburst, hotblooded, outback* and *football*. In fact, the *TB* is such an exceptionally masculine root that only the calming influence of the *TH* phoneme makes it appropriate for the feminine names (*Tabitha* and *Tabatha*). The *TH* is the symbol of all things *thankful, thoughtful, motherly, blithe* and *smooth*.

There's something vaguely dangerous about the *TB*'s combination of principle and steel, and people find themselves treading carefully around these potentially volatile people. Those who bear *TB* names need to be mindful of the effect that their powerful presence has on others. Perhaps it's their tendency to be overbearing, or their sometimes-annoying sense of self-satisfaction, that alienates prospective friends, but whatever the reason, *TB*s can be forgiven for their occasionally imperious flare-ups. It's hard to be humble when you've got the world at your feet.

*TB*s don't have much trouble with making friends

Tabitha
Tobias
Tobin
Toby

and can afford to be choosy when it comes to selecting their intimates. It's almost as if *TB*s feel the need to assert their superiority by shutting some people out while letting others in—"playing favorites" as it were. But this kind of behavior can be expected among hard-driven perfectionists, and once you get past their high-handed bent, you'll find they have a lot to offer in the way of friendship. Besides, if people realized the inner turmoil that results when *TB*s confront their own shortcomings, they wouldn't take this kind of behavior to heart. When all is said and done, *TB*s are far more judgmental of *themselves* than they are with any of their friends.

Since *TB*s aren't the sort to reach out for intimacy, love and marriage may be a long time coming. By taking a hands-off approach—and letting relationships come to *them*—they get the chance to evaluate their potential partners before committing themselves. Even when they do decide to mate, they're likely to treat the process with detached precision, instead of the emotional journey it should be. But *TB*s are not the kind to run out on their commitments; once they've jumped into the deep end, they will prove to be excellent swimmers.

Tabitha King It's helpful to have a little friendly professional rivalry with your husband. But when your husband happens to be Stephen King, juggernaut author of the macabre, you would be forgiven for hanging up your pen and taking up gardening. ■ But if you love writing as much as Tabitha King does, you'll deliver books at the rate of about one a year into the sweaty hands of eager fans. ■ Like her husband, Tabitha's writings deal with the themes of good and evil, even though they lack the sheer malevolence that characterizes his work. ■ Tabitha lives and works with her husband in Maine, along with their three children. Rumor has it that none of their children has ever asked their parents to read them bedtime stories.

Charisma										
Career Success										
Love & Friendship										
Power										

Open-minded Self-assured Outspoken Arrogant Dominant Inconstant

Short names that feature explosively pronounced consonants are invariably associated with doggedness and decisiveness. In the case of the *TD* root, the impressive combination of the *terrifically triumphant* letter *T* and the *dapper, dignified* letter *D* is responsible for the robust durability found in the words *tirade, tornado, torrid, trident, intrepid, matador* and *sturdy.* These undeniably masculine overtones explain why *all* female *TD*s (and politicians like *Teddy Roosevelt*) soften their names with the addition of the playful *I* or *IE.* (Names that end with a *Y* are indicative of people who don't take themselves very seriously, as in *silly, funny, preppy, witty* and *goofy.*)

TD people are forthright with their views and the possibility that they might be wrong doesn't faze them in the least. They've long since come to terms with their humanity and view any mistakes they've made as lessons well learned. Did we mention that they're forthright with their views? Debating with a *TD* can be like drinking from a firehose. They'll seize any opportunity to flaunt their first-rate verbal skills and relish the power that comes with having such a sharp intelligence. One might be tempted to accuse them of being intellectual bullies, but since they only pick battles with those of the same intellectual size, they're more like intellectual gladiators. Either way, it's better to

Tad
Ted
Teddy
Todd
Trudi
Trudie
Trudy

have them as your advocate than your adversary.

*TD*s may have smarts, but having emotional intelligence is another matter entirely, and no one would accuse them of being the most sensitive people in the world. This might explain their tendency for grandstanding when they aren't always aware how many people are being turned off by the self-centered monologues. But when *TD*s sense that someone else may actually be able to *teach* them something, then they'll be the most rapt listeners imaginable. If there's a lesson to be learned from all this, it's that the *TD*s must feel challenged by their relationships if there is to be any possibility of equilibrium.

With their high level of self-assurance, *TD*s usually have no trouble playing the dating game. The problem with having too much success, however, is that it makes one unaccustomed to failure, and rejection can knock them for such a loop that they have a hard time getting back on the horse, so when dating turns to mating, these heavy thinkers have a tendency to wallow in the muck of indecision. And even though *TD*s pride themselves on their reputation for loyalty and commitment, they'll readily exercise their option of swimming away when things get too rough. After all, why struggle with the rocky realities of life when there's a big, fish-filled ocean waiting to be explored?

Teddy Kennedy Teddy Kennedy served his country in the U.S. Senate for over forty years, but will forever be associated with an incident that took place in a matter of seconds on a Chappaquiddick bridge. ■ An admittedly drunk Teddy was driving home from a party with Mary Jo Kopechne when he drove the car into eight feet of water. The young woman never made it out. ■ Teddy left the scene and returned to the party. After a later unsuccessful attempt to rescue her, Teddy returned to his motel and fell asleep. In a testament to the strength of the Kennedy name, Teddy's popularity barely suffered.

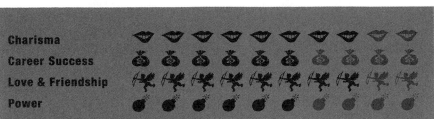

THE COY

tfny

Charisma										
Career Success										
Love & Friendship										
Power										

Fresh Amusing Active
Annoying Coquettish Frivolous

When a name begins with the *triumphant* and *trumpeting* letter *T*, it suggests an individual with a clear vision of the future *and* the self-confidence to make it happen. And when you consider that the *FNY* phoneme forms the basis for the words *funny, fanny, friendly, funky, affinity, fancy* and *fantasy*, it's easy to see why these names suggest people with enough infectious oomph to animate Al Gore.

The *TFNY* approaches life with a disarming demeanor that puts people at ease. You'll definitely want one of them around if you have a tense social situation on your hands and need someone to throw some light on it. But selling oneself as a gregarious extrovert sometimes takes more emotional energy that one can muster, and—even though they fancy themselves the life of the party—*TFNYs'* downtimes are marked by petty squabbles and bouts of antagonism.

Nervous about taking your girlfriend to meet your parents? If she's a *TFNY*, you won't have to sweat it: she'll have them under her spell in five minutes. And on those rare occasions where her charm fails to impress, the *TFNY's* streamlined personality allows her to slipstream any negative feelings directed her way. This tendency to sidestep the nitty-gritty in relationships may explain why it can be so difficult to fully connect with

Tiffany

an elusive *TFNY*, who often flits though life in a series of unsubstantial relationships.

Careers for *TFNY* personalities tend to revolve around jobs dealing with the public. Because she is the master of the instant connection, she is ideal for sales, marketing or any job involving animals. These are creative women as well, and their affinity for the limelight often leads them into the arts as singers, designers, musicians, dancers and songwriters. But whether she's a top-notch performer or a waitress at the local bar and grill, the *TFNY* can be quite churlish when she feels that she's being ignored. Friends and loved ones quickly learn to sidestep these little squalls and generally conclude they are a small price to pay for the affection she bestows when in her better moods.

Marriage can be a dicey proposition for the uncompromising *TFNY,* and fireworks are bound to ensue if her mate fails to meet her exacting standards. It's not that she isn't capable of feeling genuine love for her partner, but she will expect him to be dependable and financially sound. He who would marry this gregarious woman must learn to suspend his judgment and trust in his partner's desire—if not always the facility—for complete intimacy. Only then can both reap the rewards of a union that will most likely last forever.

Tiffany Darwish Everyone remembers Tiffany don't they? The hyper-teenaged singing sensation who set the trend for mall concerts in the 1980s? ■ Tiffany's fame seemed to come easily. Her very first album sold several million copies, while her second, *Hold an Old Friend's Hand*, went platinum in the United States with its featured top ten single, "All This Time." ■ But as Tiffany's professional life began to improve, things were deteriorating on the home front. Her mother divorced her stepfather in 1984 after he was accused of peeping into Tiffany's bedroom window at night. His claim that he was only making sure she was doing her breathing exercises fell on deaf ears. ■ After all was said and done, Tiffany began a comeback in 2002 to the delight of her core group of fans.

385

Charisma										
Career Success										
Love & Friendship										
Power										

Thoughtful Confident Motherly
Old-fashioned Overly protective Banal

Although the letter *T* is definitively associated with all things energetic and *triumphant*, its amalgamation with the *holy, humanistic, hallowed* letter *H* gives it the spiritual bent we find in the words *thankful, empathic, thoughtful, motherly, blithe* and *smooth. TH* people have a calming effect on others, much like a mother's firm voice to a wayward child. They are natural comforters with an innate understanding of other people's needs and a clear vision for solving problems.

With all this down-home goodness, you might think the *TH* is just too good to be true. Actually, this soft gentility can also be considered one of their greatest downfalls. They can be so agreeable that it's difficult not to take them for granted.

When *THs* think they're being flexible, others often see them being weak. But don't ever push them past their zone of integrity. Ever! All the pent-up annoyances from years of compliancy will spur them to tackle you head-on, and are liable to burst forth in a torrent of indignation. Think of the affable (if insipid) Thelma in the movie, *Thelma & Louise*, who had to endure a great deal of shoving before finding her assertive groove.

THs aren't ones to accumulate their resources through intimidation, and when it comes to choosing careers, instinctively look for jobs in which they are not required to do a lot of ladder-climbing. It rails against their altruistic natures to push others around for the sake of their own gain; they'd much rather spend their lives helping others to meet *their* goals. To this end, they are often found in the counseling or education professions, or any job that doesn't involve sales.

THs have remarkably expressive features, and when engaged in conversations, their faces will readily betray their emotions. They always manage to seem interested in what their partner is saying—perhaps cocking their heads to one side or adopting an adoring expression—and being one of their friends will require remarkably little work on your part.

Faith and idealism come with the territory when you're trying to court a *TH*, for when out on a date with one of these attentive individuals, you'll never have to worry about stolen glances toward members of the opposite sex. *THs* will often choose a strong personality to balance their natural reserve, and those lucky enough to be selected will discover that it's as a lover that the *TH's* star shines brightest. Marriage partners can expect plenty of affection (and a bit of smothering) from these naturally bonding spirits.

Thad
Thaddeus
Thalia
Thea
Theda
Thelma
Theo
Theodora
Theodore
Theron
Thurman

Theodore Roosevelt After President McKinley was killed by an assassin's bullet, the United State's Supreme Court Chief Justice swore in the youngest President ever. At the age of forty-three, Theodore Roosevelt brought a much-needed sense of vigor and enthusiasm to the nation's highest office. ■ More than any President in the modern era, Theodore is considered responsible for establishing the model of the assertive Presidency adopted by many of his successors. ■ To represent his "Big Stick," he built up the U.S. Navy to such a degree that America eventually became a world power, but many believe that his greatest legacy was his progressive attitude toward conservation. During his eight-year term, he created over two hundred National Forests, Bird Reservations and National Parks.

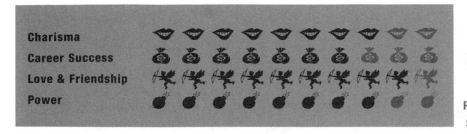

Charisma										
Career Success										
Love & Friendship										
Power										

THE CAPABLE tl

Reassuring Loving Understanding
Stubborn Codependent Uncooperative

Something interesting happens when the *trumpeting, triumphant* letter *T* comes into close contact with the letter of *love, life, laughter* and *learning*. The *TL* combination evokes the extraordinary sense of creative energy responsible for the words *vital, style, artful, astral, gentle, subtle, tactile* and *talent*. So it's not surprising that most *TL* personalities are noted for their gift of decisiveness, their air of relaxed flexibility and their talent for pulling off even the most outrageous dreams.

Rather than attempting to overtly control events and people (as many strong personalities are wont to do), *TLs* seem content to let things unfold naturally—only stepping in when things get too out of kilter. This method of benign manipulation requires a sharp brain and an acute understanding of human nature, a combination that makes them ideal for careers in management, medicine and psychology. Even when faced with failure, the confident *TLs* aren't likely to panic, they'll resolve the situation in typically methodical fashion. In light of such poise, it would be logical to expect there to be a *TL* on the top of every corporate pile. But this is almost never the case: these individuals value the health of their relationships far above personal gain, and measure their life success by the accumulated love given to them by friends and families.

Talia
Talon
Taylor
Telly
Twila
Tyler

Like most people whose names begin with a *T*, *TLs* are physically active and are drawn to sports that emphasize teamwork and cooperation. If they have a killer instinct, it only manifests itself in game play where no one is likely to get hurt. When there are problems, they're going to materialize when the *TL's* personal life gets thrown out of balance. For in the face of romantic turmoil, *TLs* tend to lose their sense of direction. Instead of throwing themselves into their work, *TLs* tend to wallow in the mud of their depleted emotional reservoirs. And if this seems to happen a little too often, it's because *TLs* aim so high in everything they do, they frequently find themselves in relationships that are way out of their leagues.

Dating and mating with *TLs* requires sensitive personalities who can match their subtle dictates with patience and tolerance. If they're not careful, *TLs* and their mates can fall into codependent unions, which end up draining the relationships' energy. But when things are clicking, *TLs* are fortified by the communal spirit that large families provide and place a high premium on togetherness and quality time. Their strong parental instincts explain why *TLs* tend to ply their children with so much babying well beyond the time they should have left the nest.

Talia Shire Although Talia Shire won critical applause for her role in the Academy's Best Picture of 1972, *The Godfather*, and was nominated for Best Actress in its sequel, it was her appearance in the *Rocky* series that cemented her in the minds of the American public. Her role as Adria-aan—the devoted waifish girlfriend of Sylvester Stallone's character—earned her yet another Oscar nomination. ■ Few actresses can boast a portfolio of four films grossing over one hundred million dollars. The five movies in the *Rocky* series grossed a total of over half a billion dollars and were mercifully shelved only after *Rocky V* took in less than $40,000,000. ■ Talia is the sister of Francis Ford Coppola and the aunt of Nicolas Cage.

387

THE EMOTIVE
tm

Charisma										

Charisma
Career Success
Love & Friendship
Power

Strong Sensitive Creative
Inconstant Nervous Impatient

The letter *T* is the icon for strength, commitment and spirituality, and when it comes into contact with the symbol of *maternal motherly* love (*mollycoddle, mammary, mediate, Mary Magdalene* and *Madonna*) it evokes the gently sensitive spirit we find in the words *altruism, esteem, tame, autumn, timid* and *optimal.* These desirable qualities may account for the fact that over one million Americans sport these names with no sign of declining popularity. Of particular interest is the fact that many *TM*s opt to infantilize their names by terminating them with the youthful sounds of the letters *Y* or *I*. This is why the *Tammy*s, *Tommy*s and *Timmy*s of the world convey a distinctly more engaging air than their abruptly named counterparts.

As a rule, *TM*s are sensitive and arty types who tend to gravitate toward music, writing and other forms of self-expression. Their spiritual outlook on life includes a priority on personal growth, and while they're not overly driven, they have an enviable way of coming out on top. Perhaps it's their relaxed attitude that encourages opportunities to *come to them*—rather than the other way round—but it also has something to do with *TM*s' steely side that (when the situation calls for it) has a surprisingly keen edge. This is especially true

Tam
Tama
Tameka
Tamela
Tami
Tamia
Tamika
Tamiko
Tammy
Tatum
Thomas
Timmy
Tommy
Tom
Tim

when *TM*s are put on the defensive where loved ones are concerned.

*TM*s' professional issues are conducted with the same panache that characterizes their personal dealings, and with their ability to brace themselves when necessary, they are ideal candidates for emotionally exhausting professions like medicine, relief work and teaching. These people are capable of tremendous empathy, but also know how to bury it when they sense themselves getting too personally involved. As long as they don't ply this technique in their relationships, *TM* mates will prove to be unswervingly communicative and reliable. But don't be surprised if they don't seem romantic: they believe that love should be expressed through loyalty and fidelity, and not through trinkets and platitudes.

*TM*s may be attractive and unafraid of flaunting their charms, but they often regard themselves as better lovers than their reputations warrant. And if you're considering dating a *TM*, you'd better get used to the fact that romance—the *traditional* kind of romance, that is—doesn't fit their notion of courtship. You won't get many evenings snuggling on the couch, but you will be kept on your toes by these unpredictable and alluring souls.

 Tom Cruise If you want to know why Tom Cruise divorced his wife of ten years (Nicole Kidman), "you'll have to ask Nick." The failure of his fairytale marriage had little effect on his career, and his asking price per movie is still more than any actor in the history of Hollywood. ■ Tom (a committed Scientologist) micromanages his career with an attention to detail that sets new standards. Every movie is carefully considered, its director vetted, and even movie posters have to have his OK before going to press. ■ This isn't to say that Tom is averse to creative risks. Most of his films have an element of controversy that could destabilize the career of many lesser stars, including *Vanilla Sky, Minority Report* and Stanley Kubrick's *Eyes Wide Shut.*

Charisma											
Career Success											
Love & Friendship											
Power											

**Feisty Energetic Positive
Immature Temperamental Stubborn**

When a name begins with the *triumphant* tones of the *titillating* letter *T*, we often expect to encounter a personality with supreme self-confidence and a high level of assertion. Nowhere is this truer than in the case of the *TMR* names, where the effects of the *maternal* letter *M* and the *randy, ravishing R* colors these people with the feminine hot-bloodedness found in the words *temper, temptress, tramp, tremble, extreme* and *nightmare*. If these women were animals, they would be wolves, with dark reputations attributable to jealousy of their consistent successes in life. It's noteworthy that these women forgo the option of calling themselves *Tammy* or *Tammi*, for names ending with the letter *Y* tend to indicate people who don't take themselves overly seriously (*silly, funny, preppy, witty* and *goofy*). *TMR*s most certainly do.

It may take a while for this fireball to get up a head of steam, but a *TMR* in full stride can be quite impressive. Firing orders at subordinates while on the phone to customers, few can get the job done quite as efficiently as she. And with an innate understanding of the value of teamwork, she's willing to take her place in the chain of command, whether it's as a leader or simply as a follower at the back of the pack. The only danger when it comes to her career is that the *TMR* sometimes puts so

Tamar
Tamara
Tamra

much energy into finding her ideal job that, due to exhaustion, she often ends up settling for less.

So what sort of career would attract a fun-loving extrovert like the *TMR*? Anything to do with the outdoors would be a good start. Hiking, biking, climbing, camping and beaching are some of the *TMR*'s favorite pastimes, and it makes sense that she'd succeed in any career with the promise of working *al fresco*. Still, job satisfaction alone isn't enough to complete the *TMR*'s image of the perfect life, and it will take plenty of close friendships and at least one solid romance to fit the bill. As tough and hard-bitten as she may appear, the *TMR*'s soft core always takes precedence in the affairs of the heart. But make no mistake; this wolf will devour anyone not strong enough to keep up with her vigorous lifestyle.

Perhaps the worst thing you could tell a *TMR* is "take my word for it." This is a woman who *has* to experiment on her own—success or failure be damned. But when a *TMR* is in love she's at her most vulnerable, for this is when her reliable instincts most often fail. That's why she's so committed to the truth and has learned not to take someone's word in matters of the heart. So if you're going to court her, make sure your words correspond to your actions.

Tamra Davis Tamra Davis may not be a household name, but she certainly is one of the most influential film directors in Hollywood today. When Britney Spear's handlers looked around for someone to introduce their cash cow to the movie-going public, it was in Tamra they put their trust. ■ Tamra's filmography dates back to 1990, when she directed the Indigo Girls in *Live at the Uptown Lounge*. From there she went on to direct Drew Barrymore in *Gun Crazy* and Dave Chappelle in *Half-Baked* in 1998. ■ It was the surprise success of the Adam Sandler vehicle *Billy Madison* that established her appeal with teen audiences. The film was responsible for launching Sandler's career as a billion-dollar box-office draw and put Tamra on the map as an A-list director.

Charisma										
Career Success										
Love & Friendship										
Power										

Careful Intelligent Altruistic
Finicky Overly cautious Preachy

Tamatha
Timothy

Names that sport more than two syllables often contain contradictory forces that result in personalities that exhibit a certain degree of complexity. In the *TMTH*'s case, the combination of the *trumpeting, triumphant* letter *T* and the *maternal motherly M* sets the tone of a wonderfully sensitive spirit that we see in words like *altruism, esteem, tame, autumn* and *optimal*. But the *TH* phoneme, with its spiritual associations of *thankful, thoughtful, motherly, blithe* and *smooth,* serve to define these people's unique brand of gentility. The addition of the high-pitched letter *Y* at the end of the name *Timothy,* injects an additional dose of playfulness and approachability.

TMTHs are renowned for their loyal and authentic friendships. They couldn't conceive of turning their backs on a loved one—no matter how strained the relationship became—and take great pride in their ability to forgive and forget. But somehow *TMTHs* seem drawn to controversy, and even if they don't actively create it, they always seem to be involved in a hullabaloo somewhere. Still, *TMs* aren't the sort to back down from these confrontations. They have extraordinary faith in their ability to negotiate their way out of anything.

On superficial examination, *TMTHs* seem to be rather reclusive souls. But make no mistake, even though they are not ones to volunteer opinions or make judgments regarding others, they're passionately committed to their ideals and will defend them vociferously. In a manifestation of their "I'll do it my way" philosophy, their views often run contrary to those of society, and if the word *visionary* seems to describe them perfectly, it's because *TMTHs* always seem to be ten years ahead in both attitude and fashion.

When choosing careers, *TMTHs'* major requirements are jobs that allow them to interact with other people. But when it comes to office politics, *TMTHs* are better off opting out completely. This is because *TMTHs* believe that it's better to be occasionally cheated than be perpetually suspicious and are often taken advantage of by more aggressive co-workers.

When it comes time to choose their mates, *TMTHs* are deliberate and calculating. Since they're patient souls in general, they'll delve quite deeply into the intimate details of their partners before jumping into the deepend and won't waste their time on frivolous relationships. But when it comes to revealing their *own* dark secrets, the *TMTHs* would do well to practice what they preach. It will take some persistent coaxing to lure them from behind their fortified walls.

Timothy Leary If you were to pick one man who embodied the heightened social consciousness of the sixties, it would have to be Timothy Leary. The philosopher/scientist risked his professional career in his attempt to understand the underlying motivations of the human mind. ■ It wasn't his introspective work that brought the negative publicity that dogged Timothy; it was his public promotion for the use of psychedelic drugs. Timothy believed that LSD and other hallucinogenic drugs held the key to the mind and believed in its potential as a therapeutic regimen. His personal motto: "Turn on, tune in, drop out." ■ Timothy also pursued the then-radical idea of group therapy, and it took forty years for the American Psychiatric Association to recognize his work. ■ Timothy on Timothy: "You get the Timothy Leary that you deserve."

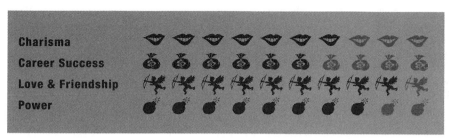

Charisma	
Career Success	
Love & Friendship	
Power	

Energetic Talented Warm
Self-important Pushy Demanding

Those whose names begin with the *triumphant* tones of the letter *T* are usually characterized by having a healthy dose of self-confidence and a gregarious nature. However, when the secondary letter in their name is the letter of *negative* influence (*no, not, never, nowhere, naught, none, nothing*), these names take on a sharply *tenacious* air. We see this effect in words like *tantrum, tarnish, taint taunt, torment, stern, taciturn* and *talon*. While these are individuals with a high level of drive and talent, they're not ones to suffer fools gladly. Some people even believe that *TN*s secretly consider themselves a little better than the rest of us.

Maintaining social status is important to the *TN* personalities who need to be seen as knowing the right people. To be fair, this is less an expression of ego than it has to with the practical problems of making money, because many *TN*s enter careers like law, real estate and finance, in which many of their clients come from their social spheres. There's certainly no questioning *TN*s' competence in their work-lives; they are take-charge people with long-range vision with little time for frivolity. But if you ever accuse a *TN* of being selfish or egotistical you'll find they are genuinely puzzled, for they really derive satisfaction from helping others. The *selfish* label proba-

Tana
Tien
Tina
Tania
Tanika
Tanisha
Taniya
Tanner
Tanya
Tanesha
Tangela
Tatiana
Tawana
Tawny
Tenisha
Tennille
Tiana
Tomika
Tonja
Tonio
Tony
Tonyo
Tien
Tina

bly arises from the *TN*'s ability to concentrate so exclusively on the task at hand that they don't give a second thought as to how their inattention can affect others. They are workaholics at worst, and at best, single-mindedly gifted.

As children they were probably bouncy, excitable and even hyperactive and, like most people whose names begin with a *T*, found release in their aptitudes for sports. And make no mistake: the *TN*'s talents include a highly competitive instinct and athletic ability to match. Though *TN*s have little time for those who can't pull their own weight, they will prove unfailingly generous to friends who want to get into the game. But even though money and comfort will be given freely, the price will sometimes be a condescending lecture on how to live your life.

Love and marriage with a *TN* can be a touchy affair, what with their soft bits buried beneath their tough-talking exteriors and argumentative visage. The *TN*s modus operandi for getting their own way is through prolonged sulks, which relegates intimacy to a sporadic affair. Still, marriages are successful when the *TN* is paired with an independently minded mate, and even with all their emotional oscillations, *TN*s prove to be extraordinarily dependable, punctual and organized partners.

Tina Turner Tina Turner's early career was characterized by the svengali-like control of her boyfriend/manager/co-star, whom she eventually married. ■ Ike Turner turned out to be an aggressive wife-beater, who convinced Tina that she could be nothing without him. His dominating style included physical and emotional abuse, and after a fearsome fight in Texas, Tina fled with only the clothes on her back. ■ She flourished on her own, and her album, *Private Dancer*, sold ten million copies and produced the number-one single "What's Love Got to Do With It?" Later the same year, Tina appeared in *Mad Max Beyond Thunderdome* and won three Grammys for the single, "We Don't Need Another Hero."

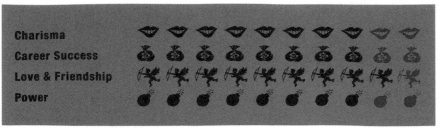

Charisma										
Career Success										
Love & Friendship										
Power										

Energetic Approachable Humorous
Supercilious Spoiled Arrogant

When the *titillating* and *triumphant* letter *T* comes into close contact with the *robustly romantic* letter *R*, it tends to create words with the combination of vigor and candidness found in *tremendous, trumpeting, Trojan, trustworthy, truth* and *trophy*. This unusual amalgam of strength and blunt sincerity may explain why this root has remained so popular over the last fifty years and why many people (particularly women) elect to add the high-pitched letter *Y* or *I* to the end of their names. Names that end with the *youthful* letter *Y* have the effect of making their owners more approachable and accessible.

With their down-home integrity and natural curiosity, *TR*s are drawn to careers in which they're able to express their original ideas. Their application of their strength/vulnerability trait allows them to take liberties that others find impossible: like befriending the company bully or waltzing into the CEO's office unannounced. An offbeat sense of humor contributes to their cheeky charms and they're among the first to defuse tense situations with witty observations. But once *TR*s get a bee in their bonnets, it's nigh on impossible to deflect them from their course. Sometimes we see this when they set their sights on a potential mate, but more likely it will be expressed in altruistic offerings like helping a friend move or working in a soup kitchen.

*TR*s learn quickly when they want to, but prefer to rely on their internal radars to warn them of danger. Still, even with their extraordinary powers of observation, *TR*s can get flustered when events catch them by surprise and seem poorly equipped to cope with crises. This is why, on the keyboard of life, *TR*s always have one finger on the escape key. This is particularly noticeable when it comes to the *TR*'s relationships, in which their unwillingness to tackle emotional issues can become a major barrier to intimacy. Relationships can also be tricky things for their partners, who can never quite sure as to what's *really* troubling their otherwise devoted mate. And yet, *TR*s are so confident of themselves that they really believe that they don't have issues. Maybe it's everyone else that has a perception problem.

The best marriage environments for these sensitive personalities are those that allow them to express their inner selves without fear of rejection. For like many people with hidden vulnerabilities, *TR*s prefer to operate on their own terms and from positions of emotional power. Dealing with children, on the other hand, presents no such problem, and *TR*s find their natural honesty to be refreshing and completely unthreatening.

Tara
Tari
Tariq
Tera
Terrell
Terry
Tiara
Tierra
Tor
Tory
Trey
Troy
Tyra
Tyree
Tyrell
Tora
Tori

Tori Spelling Tori Spelling was born Victoria Davey Spelling in 1973, to gazillionaire TV mogul Aaron Spelling and his wife, Candy. ■ Ironically, Aaron will probably be best remembered for his 1990s smash hit, *Beverly Hills, 90210*, in which his teenage daughter landed her recurring role. Tori was one of the few original cast members who stayed with the show for its duration. ■ Tori endured the biting tongues of critics, who labeled her a spoiled princess who only got her job because of her powerful father. Her performance in Miramax Films' *The House of Yes*, in which she played a college student meeting her fiancé's weird family, changed their minds.

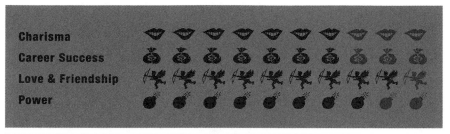

Charisma										
Career Success										
Love & Friendship										
Power										

Faithful Forward-thinking Steadfast
Arrogant Penny-pinching Quick tempered

The bright *trumpeting* sound created by the *TR* letter combination is responsible for the exultant sounds in the words *triumphant, Trojan, trophy, tremendous, truth, strumpet* and *trust,* and aptly defines the essence of the *TRN* personality. But because the letter *N* is the symbol for *negativity* (*no, not, never, nowhere, naught* and *nothing*), it injects an element of sober restraint to the *TRN* names depicted in the words *stern, tarnish, torment, thorny, truant, trying, tyranny* and *turnoff.*

Even with their occasional forays into cynicism, *TRN*s are the kind of people you can count on when you get yourself into a jam and need someone to bail you out— in fact their very sense of self-worth is based on playing the role of knight (or lady) in shining armor. It's important to note that the altruism of most *TRN*s originates from their belief in Karma. In other words, there's the expectation that you'd better do *your* part when they come calling on you.

While generous with their time and talents, *TRN*s are not known for their generosity when it comes to material resources, for the same protectiveness they feel toward their friends extends to their personal belongings as well. This may wear on intimate companions who often find it necessary to

Taryn
Taurean
Terence
Torrance
Tran
Tremaine
Trena
Trent
Trenton
Treyton
Trina
Trinity
Truman
Turner
Tyrone

sneak behind their suspicious backs when it comes to spending money. And if you have something to discuss with your *TRN* friend, you should think about asking him or her to dinner: there's nothing a *TRN* appreciates more than the promise of free food.

*TRN*s hate sitting on the fence when it comes to making decisions and, like many individuals whose names begin with a *T*, give their plans the benefit of some deep pondering before making up their (usually right of center) minds. But once the *TRN*s have found their obscure star, it will be unwaveringly followed.

Where their professional lives are concerned, *TRN*s prefer to carve their own routes rather than choosing well-trodden paths. It's not that they're particularly liberal or entrepreneurial; it's that they have well-developed senses of independence and hate being told what to do.

This same hardheadedness is apparent in *TRN*s' relationships. They hate the disorder that comes from unresolved issues and will invariably be the first to broach conversations regarding potential conflict. But even though they might prove unyielding at times, loved ones know that in the end, their *TRN* mates will put the interests of the relationship above their personal needs.

Tyrone Power Along with Douglas Fairbanks, Tyrone Power is regarded as one of the great swashbuckling romantic stars of the twentieth century. ■ Tyrone's acting roots stretched back to the eighteenth century, when his great-grandfather (Tyrone) was a famous Irish comedian. His father (Tyrone) was a theatrical star, who performed in classical roles. ■ Tyrone (the one we're discussing here) was born a sickly child in Cincinnati, and his parents moved to the warmer climes of California to help him recover. During World War II, he joined the Marines as a pilot and saw action against the Japanese. After returning home, he garnered critical notices for his performance in *Witness for the Prosecution* but collapsed and died of a heart attack halfway through shooting his next movie. ■ His son (Tyrone) followed in his acting footsteps.

Charisma	👄	👄	👄	👄	👄	👄	👄	👄	👄	👄
Career Success	💰	💰	💰	💰	💰	💰	💰	💰	💰	💰
Love & Friendship	🏹	🏹	🏹	🏹	🏹	🏹	🏹	🏹	🏹	🏹
Power	💣	💣	💣	💣	💣	💣	💣	💣	💣	💣

Determined Self-assured Committed Haughty Demanding Flighty

The letter *R* is the symbol for all things associated with *red-blooded* passion (*randy, romance, racy, ravish, raw, rigid, risqué* and *rouse*), while the *serpentine* letter *S* (and sibilant *C* as pronounced in *lace*) is the icon of *sensual, sybaritic sexuality*. And when the self-confident tones of the *triumphal* letter *T* come into close proximity with the *R* and *S*, it creates particularly feminine names that bespeak and enthusiasm. It's important to note that the *TRS*'s gusto isn't limited to romantic romping; sometimes it's expressed in a fierce drive to succeed.

*TRS*s become accustomed to success at an early age and, while this may have a healthy effect on their self-esteem, it means they don't always have the tools to deal with failure when it comes their way. *TRS*s who experience disappointment in their job hunts, for example, might give up too quickly and settle for something less than they really merit. But when *TRS*s are in their groove, they can be as tough as a three-dollar steak, and you can bet that they'll be formidable competitors in the workplace.

Still, if you're an employer of a *TRS* you're better off not turning your back. While your *TRS* employees will give you a fair day's work, they secretly believe that their jobs are simply means of supporting their social lives.

Teresa
Terese
Teresita
Teressa
Trace
Tracy
Tressa
Trista
Tristan
Tristian
Tyrese

So, when the workday is done, *TRS*s put their jobs behind them to live the life that matters most. It's not that they aren't blessed with her fair share of talent mind you, for when sufficiently motivated they'll display an uncommon aptitude for all things creative. Whether it's design, painting, playing music or just distractedly doodling, they have an eye-to-hand coordination that would make a fighter pilot proud.

If you're trying to court a *TRS,* make sure you're armed with gifts. It doesn't really matter *what* you give them; they just need to be shown that you're making an effort. You'll get extra points for creativity and style, and you'll find yourself in the bonus round if you spend a week's pay for something special. But under this materialistic crust the *TRS* can be quite mushy and romantic, and once you've successfully wooed this elusive sprite, you'll find her to be very protective of you and the relationship.

*TRS*s are anything but practical when it comes to matters of the heart, and their friends and families may as well kiss them good-bye when they're in the grip of a new relationship. This on-again off-again oscillation with their casual trysts can prove tiresome to *TRS*s' friends, who resent playing second fiddle to their primarily (albeit temporary) relationships.

Mother Teresa It's a cliché these days to use the term "Mother Teresa" to describe someone who performs unselfish acts. But even Mother Teresa was not always considered to be a "Mother Teresa," and during her lifetime she received criticism for taking donations without questioning their source. ■ Now well on her way to sainthood, Mother Teresa believed that suffering people were nothing other than "Christ in distressing disguise" and won the Nobel Peace Prize in 1979. During the award ceremony, she wore the same $1.00 sari she was wearing when she first founded her order, and dedicated her award to the "unwanted, unloved and uncared for." ■ "The other day I dreamed I was at the gates of heaven," she said, "and St. Peter said, 'Go back to Earth, there are no slums here.'"

THE ANACHRONISTIC
trsh

Charisma	👄	👄	👄	👄	👄	👄	👄	👄	👄	👄
Career Success	💰	💰	💰	💰	💰	💰	💰	💰	💰	💰
Love & Friendship	🏹	🏹	🏹	🏹	🏹	🏹	🏹	🏹	🏹	🏹
Power	💣	💣	💣	💣	💣	💣	💣	💣	💣	💣

**Soft-spoken Spiritual Gentle
Reticent Stubborn Complex**

There's a distinct duality to those who bear *TRSH* names. The *TR* phoneme is the symbol of impulsive action that we find in the words *triumphant, trespass, trick, troublemaker, trailblazer, tremendous, trumpeting, tripping* and *stripper,* while the high-pitched *SH* sound is almost exclusively reserved for words conveying softness and femininity: *hush, cashmere, shame, shiny, sheepish, sharing, shriek, she, blush* and *mushy.* Predicting which *TRSH* you're going encounter on any given day is like trying to forecast Maine weather.

In general, though, these are enigmatic spirits toward whom others naturally gravitate, and who are perceived to be non-threatening and approachable. *TRSH*s quietly relish their popularity and, although they never overtly seek the limelight, will sometimes create little dramas in their lives simply to attract attention. So don't be fooled by the *TRSH*'s demure show: they'll be as stubborn as two-year-olds at bedtime when they have to.

You'll have no chance of pushing her in a direction she doesn't want to go, which is all well and good if it happens to coincide with your plans, but if you're trying to get her to watch a football game, it's going to cost you an arm and a chick flick. She's probably smarter than most of her friends, too, but she's not the kind to lord it

Tarsha
Tricia
Trish

over anyone. The typical *TRSH* is always available to talk things over and will be so quick to forgive your little indiscretions that you might find it insulting.

A love of travel is one of the defining aspects of these footloose sprites, which is why they always seem to be on the move. This may not mean they'll actually change their address, but they will be constantly on the lookout for geographically challenging places to visit.

This yearning for frequent scenery changes carries over to the *TRSH*'s working life as well, and when regular promotions or transfers to new locations aren't forthcoming, they'll simply pack up and move on. It's not that they don't have a sense of obligation or a love of teamwork; it's simply that their first priority is to quench their thirst for new challenges.

The *TRSH* isn't in a big hurry to start her family, and until it's her turn to march down the aisle, her close friendships will more than fulfill her need for intimacy. But when she's ready, she's certainly not going to do it halfway. Her wedding will probably be big and chichi— and even a little ostentatious. Prospective mates will closely scrutinized and carefully chosen, and it's almost a given that *TRSH*'s marriage will work according to her plan.

Trisha Yearwood When a small-town schoolteacher from Georgia and her banker husband gave birth to a daughter, there was no way of knowing the little girl was destined to grow up to become one of country music's biggest recording stars, and earn a certified double-platinum album. ■ Trisha's debut single, "She's in Love with the Boy," struck a chord with country fans and spent two weeks at number-one on the charts. It was the first of a series of hits for the emerging country star, who went on to win Best New Artist at the American Music Awards. ■ "I just flat out love to sing," she says. "If you really feel it, other people will hopefully feel it too. Even if nobody's listening, I will do it forever."

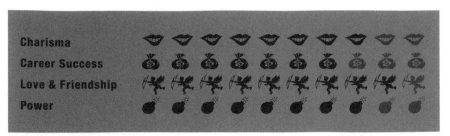

Charisma										
Career Success										
Love & Friendship										
Power										

Strong Independent Romantic
Stubborn Arrogant Selfish

When the letter *T* initializes a name, it is invariably associated with all things *triumphant, tremendous* and *trailblazing*. But the *TRV* names also enjoy the added benefit of the two most passionate letters in the alphabet: the *romantic R* and the *virile V*. The *R* is the symbol of all things *randy, ravishing, red* and *rosy,* while the *V* is *victorious, vanquishing* and very *volatile*. So when the *T, R* and *V* occur in the same words, it's not surprising to find them colored by their hot-blooded influence: *extrovert, strive, thrive, pervert, cavort, vibrator, virulent, fervent* and *verboten*.

If you're drawn to sensitive male types who'll treat you like a lady, chances are that you'll want to give *TRV*s a miss. They're handy with a beer bottle and always up for a football game, but don't expect them to ever reveal their feminine sides. These are hard-driven men who drive SUVs and aren't planning on winning any hearts with their tears, sighs or handmade cards.

Perhaps it's their healthy dose of testosterone that motivates them in their careers, but whatever the reason, these guys pile up the kind of achievements in their lifetimes that most people only dream about. Many will change careers several times in their working lives with each new attempt growing more grandiose. They may start out bagging groceries at the local supermarket, but they have a good shot at becoming CEOs of the grocery chain as well. The adolescent *TRV*s kicking footballs around with their friends may end up as high-school quarterbacks. Any way you look at it, these are overachievers in the extreme. But it should be said that many *TRV*s don't know their limitations, and their dreams often prove too grandiose for their talents.

Is it love or a deep animalistic lust that fuels the *TRV*'s secret hunger? The answer proves elusive even to the *TRV*s themselves, whose appetites for the hunt bedevil their romantic stability. *TRV*s are serial monogamists, preferring quality over quantity in their partners, but when it comes to *physical* expressions of love, many *TRV*s find it difficult to loosen up, so waiting for them to make the first move can prove maddening to those trying to win their hearts. Needless to say, this only tends to sweeten their desirability, and *TRV* boys must step carefully lest they trip over the girls that have thrown themselves at their feet. It's not that they're particularly good-looking, it's just they just exude the kind of inner confidence that proves irresistible to many women. Given all this, the *TRV* sometimes has trouble keeping his pumped-up ego under control. It's only life's harsh lessons that remind him that he's merely human.

Travis
Travon
Treva
Trevin
Trevion
Trevor
Treyvon

Travis Tritt It couldn't have been easy to get noticed on the country scene at the same time that Garth Brooks was hogging the spotlight, but as a leader of the new breed of country singers with roots in rock, Travis Triitt's Grammies began to pile up. ■ In spite of his growing successes, Nashville was uncertain of Travis's aggressive style of country. There was the way he dressed. To be a bona fide Country music singer, at the very least you had to wear an expensive cowboy hat. Travis not only refused to wear a hat but grew his hair long. Mercy! ■ But Travis let his singing do the talking, and garnered a string of platinum albums, three number-one country hits and a number of top ten crossover singles.

Charisma	👄👄👄👄👄👄👄👄👄👄
Career Success	💰💰💰💰💰💰💰💰💰💰
Love & Friendship	(cupids)
Power	💣💣💣💣💣💣💣💣💣💣

**Bright Good listener Mischievous
Procrastinating Unpredictable Sanctimonious**

The letter *T* is a symbol of decisiveness and resolve. And when it teams up with the *sexy, sensual, sylphlike* sound of the letter *S*, takes on the distinct air of sexual audacity found in the words *tryst, tasty, tipsy, trusty, cutesy, fetish* and *twisted*. These are people whose defiant charm seeps from every pore of their cheeky beings, even if you never actually know what's on their minds.

Trying to read the *TS*'s closely held cards can prove difficult at times, but it's always well worth the effort. Sure, they're not always the most open people at first, but once they've deemed someone worthy of friendship, they'll engage them enthusiastically and without reserve. *TS*s tend to base their relationships on intellectual terms rather than warm fuzzies, so be prepared to hold your own in political, religious and philosophical debates. Spirituality is also a big component of the *TS*'s personalities, and whether it expresses itself in quirky or mainstream principles, dominates their thoughts and values.

You'll never meet a *TS* whose house is decorated with fake plants, for like everything else in their lives, they insist on the genuine article. This holds true with their careers, their jewelry and their relationships, and since their career choices usually reflect their commit-ment to their inner ideals, it would be unusual to find them selling products in which they don't fully believe.

If people are drawn to the *TS*'s ethical temperaments, they are also likely to be attracted to their vivacious and outgoing styles. *TS*s are unabashedly hedonistic in their approach to their lives, and their open minds and youthful thinking has them involved in all manner of creative endeavors—particularly those oriented around right-brained pursuits like music, writing and art.

*TS*s are good for the long haul when it comes to their relationships and are particularly patient and playful with children, whom they treat as miniature adults. By acknowledging their individuality, *TS*s treat young people in the way that they themselves expect to be treated—teaching by example instead of from positions of authority.

But don't think you can relax just because you have a *TS* for a mate: they have a talent for spinning the most mundane subjects into philosophical debates. While these discussions might be provocative and engaging, they often prove to be barriers to true intimacy. Sometimes an old-fashioned hug would speak more eloquently than the *TS*'s verbosity ever could.

Tasha
Tess
Tessa
Tessie
Titus
Tyson

Tess Harper It's understandable that most people don't recall Tess Harper's role as Warren Beatty's girlfriend in *Ishtar*, or her forgettable performance in *Amityille 3D*. She's the strawberry blonde who everyone recognizes but whose name no one remembers. ■ And yet, this journeywoman actress managed to earn a nomination for an Academy Award for her work as Chick, in *Crimes of the Heart* in 1986. ■ Ultimately, it would be television that challenged Tess's range, and she has appeared in dozens of made-for-TV movies, including *The Turning* and *Dirty Laundry*. She also had an important role in the ABC TV movie *Starflight: The Plane That Couldn't Land* and played a lead role in *Willing to Kill: The Texas Cheerleader Story* (the account of a mother bumping off her daughter's cheerleading rival).

**Most Popular
Girl's Names**

Ursula
Una
Usha
Ute
Ula
Un

**Most Popular
Boy's Names**

Ulysses

Art upsets, science reassures.

—GEORGES BRAQUE

The Unexpected

The letter U owes its parentage to the letter V and is a relatively modern arrival in the English alphabet. Like all vowels, the letter U is frequently used to express emotions, but unlike the excited sounds of the E and O, the U is typically associated with unpleasantness: ugh, ugly, ulcer, uppity, usurp, urine, uh-oh and upset. ■ It's invariably a surprise when we encounter a U person, for only about one person in ten thousand has a name that begins with this unique, unusual, uncommon and unexpected letter. Because their names are such an uncommon commodity, they always manage to attract attention wherever they go. U people take this all in stride. ■ Ulysses and Ursula are the only names of any statistical significance. Ulysses is the Roman name for Odysseus, the mythical hero of Homer's epic poem *The Odyssey*, which recounts the arduous journey of Ulysses from the battlefields of Troy to his home in Ithaca. His name has since become synonymous with a long adventurous journey. ■ In most cases, people whose names begin with the letter U seem to enjoy defying societal conventions. They score higher on the scale of emotional intelligence and are more likely to be right-brained than left-brained. And while they're also able to think on their feet and have the uncommon ability to solve complex problems, all this comes at a price. For Us are big-picture people who are unable to pay close attention to the small details and are consequently more likely to be found in the arts than in the sciences. They will, however, almost always be remembered for their unusual approach to life and living. ■

Charisma										
Career Success										
Love & Friendship										
Power										

Charming Complex Elemental
Escapist Cynical Bored

When parents give their children names that begin with the *unusual* letter *U*, they set in motion a chain of events that results in a *uniquely* exceptional adult with *uncommon* flair. Those whose names include the *racy* and *ribald* letter *R* (*Uriel*, *Ursula* and *Uriah*) tend to be more sensually minded than the *Ulysses* of the world, but the one thing they all have in common is that anything smacking of "fitting in" repels them the way oil repels environmentalists. They will even go out of their way to cultivate their eccentric reputations.

While your first impression of a *U* person may be that of someone who needs to cheer down a little, these are intricate men and women with well directed compassion and a strong sense of destiny. But for all their complexity, *U*s are people people at heart, who find maintaining a wide range of social contacts essential to their peace of mind.

No matter what obstacles life happens to throw in their way, the quick-witted *U*s overcome them with style and elegance, doing little to hide their ebullience until someone tries to take advantage of their generosity. This is why *U*s are so often a surprise to casual acquain-

**Ulysses
Unique
Uriah
Uriel
Ursula**

tances; just when you think you know them, they'll become wholly different animals right before your eyes.

People with *U* names are not particularly successful when it comes to earning money, but these people are an exception. They can be found in nearly every career field—artistic, corporate and scientific—and almost always land up in positions of leadership. *U*s also have a knack of envisioning their goals and making them happen, which makes them ideal candidates for owning their own businesses.

It's arguable that many *U*s consider themselves to be somewhat superior, which might explain why they sometimes struggle to form deep emotional bonds. Friendships with them are multidimensional affairs which many people find to be above their comfort levels, and *really* getting to know them can be like navigating a maze. But like many difficult challenges, the rewards are directly proportional to the exertion.

Marriage for them isn't the end of their romantic explorations; it's a gateway through which they can indulge their boundless curiosities. Expect the relationship to take a myriad of twists and turns, but rest assured that the *U* is going to be there in the end.

Ursula Andress Born in Switzerland to German parents, Ursula Andress was originally billed in the U.S. as "the new Dietrich." But other than a magnificent pair of legs and a German accent, she had little in common with the great actress. ■ Those who saw the 1962 James Bond film *Dr. No* remember the bikini-clad Ursula emerging from the ocean like the Birth of Venus, and she was certainly a woman of her time—a not-so-wholesome symbol of the sixties sexual revolution. ■ But Hollywood can be cruel to an aging sex kitten, and in later years Ursula was relegated to exploiting her epidermis by showing up in a number of late-late-show movies like *Fun in Acapulco*, *The Sensuous Nurse* and *Slaves of the Cannibal God*.

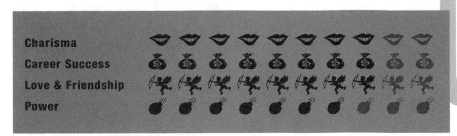

Charisma										
Career Success										
Love & Friendship										
Power										

Introspective Provocative Unique
Unstable Inconsistent Retiring

As with all names that begins with vowels, those who bear the *UGN* names tend to be emotionally expressive individuals whose behavior borders on the quirky. The sound of the *EU* in combination with the *gruff* letter *G* and the *negative* letter *N* (*no, not, never, nyet, nada, nothing, nix* and *naught*) tend to evoke the awkward images we find in the words *vulgarian, ungainly, impugn, unglued, ugliness, roughneck* and *mulligan* (the do-over in golf when your first shot goes awry). Ultimately, it's the *euphoric* sounds of the *EU* that defines these personalities as unpredictable and exciting types who are difficult to categorize.

If you're never quite sure what *UGNs* are going to do next, chances are that they don't know either, for these aren't people who fritter away their energies trying to plan for the future; they'd rather surf the wave of life as it arrives. But surfing requires a good sense of balance, which is something that no one would accuse them of having. Instead, they lurch through life in unconventional style, charming other people as they go. These aren't the kind of people you'd want to fly the plane after the pilot and autopilot have baled out, but they're not the type to leave you alone in a bind either. Their extraordinary sense of duty is derived from their philosophi-

Eugena
Eugene
Eugenia
Eugenie
Eugenio

cal take on Karma—and they'll expect the same from you.

There's a touch of the mad scientist in the *UGN*, who has to try everything at least once; success or failure be damned. They simply have to experience life for themselves. You're also never going to be bored in the *UGN*'s presence, for there's such an overflow of creativity emanating from these quirky folks that people hang around just to see what they're going to say next. It's not that they deliberately seek the spotlight, mind you, but the suspicion is that *UGNs* secretly enjoy their enigmatic reputations.

One of the paradoxes of being this unconventional is that people tend to give you wide latitude to make your mistakes. It usually starts in *UGNs*' youth, when they were the types of kids who kept a six-month-old ham sandwich in their lockers and noted its decay in their journals.

Things really get interesting when *UGNs* set out to choose their mates. Chances are the successful candidate will be someone who will shoulder the responsibilities of paying bills and keeping the car running. If this sounds like a lot of work, it is. But most spouses are willing to pay this price for the exhilaration of being married to such a fiercely loyal eccentric.

Eugene Levy Eugene Levy, a gangly, bushy-browed Canadian actor, got his start in the company of some of Canada's finest comedians on *Second City TV*. The comedy troupe starred John Candy, Joe Flaherty, Andrea Martin, Catherine O'Hara and Dave Thomas. ■ Success never came easily for Eugene. His 1972 B movie, *Cannibal Girls*, never even made it to video, but it did cement an important relationship with director Ivan Reitman, who went on to direct the enormously successful *Ghostbusters*. ■ The go-to-guy when it comes to eccentric cameos, Eugene stole the show as a demented scientist in Ron Howard's *Splash*. But his best known role, at least to Gen-X audiences, was his portrayal of an overly well-meaning father of a young man experimenting with sex in *American Pie*.

**Most Popular
Girl's Names**

Virginia
Victoria
Valerie
Veronica
Vivian
Vanessa
Vicki
Vera
Viola
Vickie

**Most Popular
Boy's Names**

Victor
Vincent
Vernon
Virgil
Van
Vicente
Vance
Vaughn
Vern
Vince

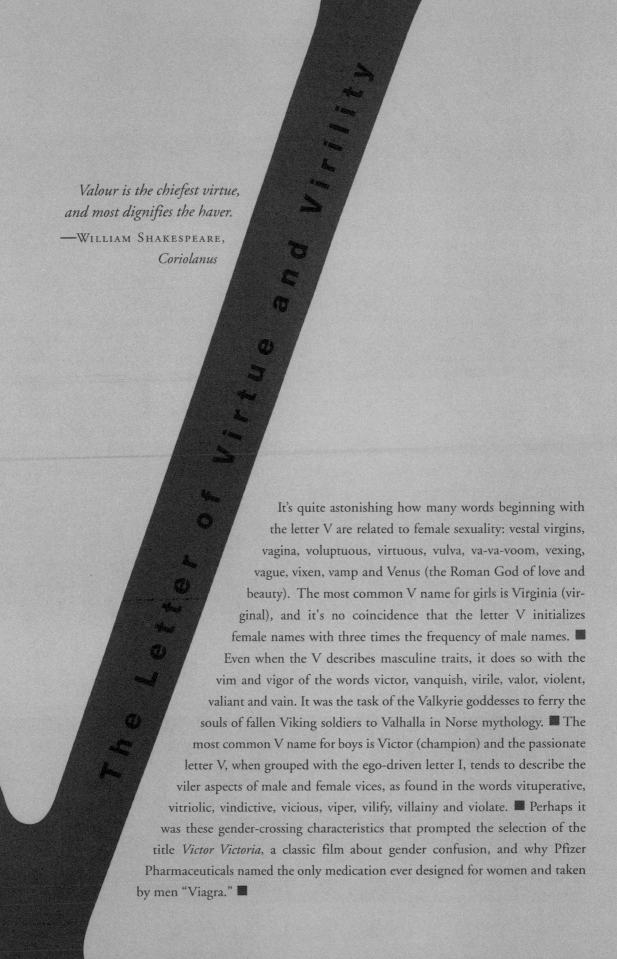

The Letter of Virtue and Virility

Valour is the chiefest virtue,
and most dignifies the haver.
—WILLIAM SHAKESPEARE,
Coriolanus

It's quite astonishing how many words beginning with the letter V are related to female sexuality: vestal virgins, vagina, voluptuous, virtuous, vulva, va-va-voom, vexing, vague, vixen, vamp and Venus (the Roman God of love and beauty). The most common V name for girls is Virginia (virginal), and it's no coincidence that the letter V initializes female names with three times the frequency of male names. ■ Even when the V describes masculine traits, it does so with the vim and vigor of the words victor, vanquish, virile, valor, violent, valiant and vain. It was the task of the Valkyrie goddesses to ferry the souls of fallen Viking soldiers to Valhalla in Norse mythology. ■ The most common V name for boys is Victor (champion) and the passionate letter V, when grouped with the ego-driven letter I, tends to describe the viler aspects of male and female vices, as found in the words vituperative, vitriolic, vindictive, vicious, viper, vilify, villainy and violate. ■ Perhaps it was these gender-crossing characteristics that prompted the selection of the title *Victor Victoria*, a classic film about gender confusion, and why Pfizer Pharmaceuticals named the only medication ever designed for women and taken by men "Viagra." ■

VK

Youthful Sensitive Devoted
Manipulative Conflicted Hypersensitive

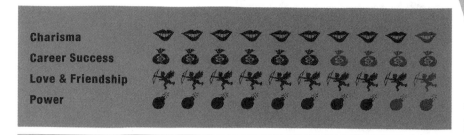

Charisma	
Career Success	
Love & Friendship	
Power	

Because the letter *V* is the icon of *virility* and *vitality* and the *K* (or hard *C* sound) is the symbol of forceful action we find in *king, kill, kick, Kaiser, kidnap* and *knock*, when these two letters are combined in a word the result is the dynamism found in the words *Viking, viscount, victory* and *Valkyries* (the battlefield maidens of Norse mythology). Typically, we find a strong contradiction embedded in the personalities of those who bear the *VK* names—their personalities are alternately alluring and slightly dangerous—depending on the mood of the moment. Those who choose to end their names with the feminizing, high-pitched *Y, I* or *IE* (*Vicky*) are signaling themselves to be somewhat more playful versions of the otherwise uncompromising *VK* names; creating a bit of uncertainty as to the *VK*'s true motives.

It could be said that the *VK*s have a simplistic view of the universe reminiscent of the fierce idealism of middle adolescence. *VK*s are the champions of right, the first to point out shortcomings in others but also the first to give support when it's needed. They seem born with the ability to manipulate their environments, a trait which stands them in good stead in their personal lives, but which doesn't win them many allies in the workplace.

Vic
Vicki
Vicky
Victor
Victoria

Although they're forceful at times, *VK*s also have a strangely powerful magnetic appeal—their playful sensuality and stunning smiles could disarm the NRA. But *VK*s aren't about to rely only on their charms for resources. Their recipe for success calls for finding other people's buttons and pushing them until they get what they want. *VK*s have the advantage here. Their control is subtle and their playful behavior distracts people while they're being outmaneuvered. Still, most of the time when a *VK* is being charming and friendly, it's no act. They have big hearts and even bigger hopes for you. In any event, it's not all bad if you find yourself succumbing to a *VK*'s will; they're quite generous in rewarding those who toe their line.

Marriage to a *VK* will be a treat for anyone who craves unconditional love and doesn't mind adhering to someone else's ideals. But make no mistake; if *VK*s believe that their partners aren't as committed as they are, they'll be out of there faster than a Taliban in Texas. But when their mates *are* dedicated to common ideals, *VK*s will do everything in their power to create a stable and loving environment in which both can reach their full potential.

Vicki Lawrence When Carol Burnett announced that she was looking for an actress to play her kid sister on her new variety television show, she received a invitation from a young Vicki Lawrence to attend a "Ms. Fireball" contest at a local fire station. ■ Carol was so amazed at how much Vicki looked like her; she made her an indispensable part of *The Carol Burnett Show*, which ran for more than a decade. ■ One of the skits on the show called for Vicki to play Carol's daughter, but at the last minute Carol switched the roles so that Vicki could play Mama. The decision proved to be a fortuitous for Vicki, who was offered her own sitcom featuring the character. The show, *Mama's Family*—featuring Carol as Eunice—was a huge success and enjoyed a profitable seven-year run.

Charisma	💋	💋	💋	💋	💋	💋	💋	💋	💋	💋
Career Success	💰	💰	💰	💰	💰	💰	💰	💰	💰	💰
Love & Friendship	🦅	🦅	🦅	🦅	🦅	🦅	🦅	🦅	🦅	🦅
Power	💣	💣	💣	💣	💣	💣	💣	💣	💣	

Passionate Vigorous Untraditional
Phobic Irresponsible Combative

The letter *L* is the iconic letter of the things that money can't buy: *life, love, liberty, laughter* and *learning*. And since the letter *V* is the symbol of *virility* and *voluptuousness*, it's no surprise that the *VL* combination gives rise to such *vital* words as *valor, viable, validity, voila* and *Vulcan* (the Roman god of fire). That's why people who bear *VL* names are usually perceived as having vigorous lives and smoldering sensualities to boot. These individuals are ready for anything and instinctively flex to fit every situation.

VLs are energetic people who can handle a variety of tasks at one time. They are drawn to physical activities, which highlight their extraordinary endurance, and even become edgy when they aren't juggling several projects at once. This quality makes them desirable as employees where *most* of the time *VLs*' co-workers appreciate their drive and flexibility. But *VLs* aren't corporate ladder-climbers by any means; they are lovers, not workers. Their penchant for socializing is, in fact, the one thing that impedes their rise to the top of their fields.

Oddly enough for such social extroverts, many *VLs* have quite a perfectionist streak. It seems as if they have a compulsive need to keep their environments neat and organized, and are easily distracted if their pens and

Val
Valance
Valence
Valeria
Valorie
Valrie
Velda
Velia
Vella
Velma
Veola
Vilma
Viola

paperclips aren't in their respective compartments. Once they've got all their ducks in a row though, they'll be as hardworking as Chinese farmers. Employers appreciate their precision and fanaticism for detail but sometimes their pickiness prolongs even the simplest tasks. Ideal jobs are those that can challenge the *VL* intellectually or give them a chance to flaunt their dogged energy. Like most people whose names begin with the letter *V*, *VLs* are consummate politicians who, even if they don't pursue politics professionally, will ply their people-charming skills to great effect in the workplace.

Few personalities can rival the *VLs* for passionate courtship—for *VLs* fall in love with as much consideration as they shampoo their hair (although with considerably more bounce). Since falling *out* of love comes just as easily, it takes a special someone to hold their attention beyond a few months. Marriage will have to be with someone who can stimulate more than their libidos—preferably with someone who can keep them intrigued.

Children will welcomed with open arms although *VL* parents are likely to start pushing them out of the nest almost as soon as they're born. These independent personalities see no reason why their children wouldn't share the same desire for freedom as they do.

Valerie Bertinelli Valerie Bertinelli was born in 1960, just a few months after her parents lost their young son to an accidental poisoning. ■ Valerie's first taste of national fame came when she starred as the squeaky-clean Barbara Royer in the long-running CBS TV sitcom, *One Day at a Time*, starting in 1975. The show was a huge success in a decade marked by a notable lack of quality programming, and spawned over two hundred episodes until it finally ran out of steam in 1984. It was never officially cancelled. ■ In 1981, Valerie wed Eddie Van Halen, the lead guitarist for the band Van Halen, to whom some people claim she bears a disquieting physical resemblance.

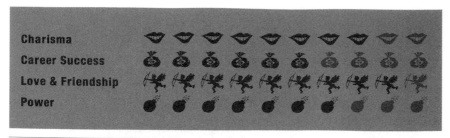

Charisma										
Career Success										
Love & Friendship										
Power										

Attractive Indomitable Magnetic
Silly Caustic Feckless

The letter *L* is the laconic symbol of the most valuable things in the universe: *life, love, law, laughter* and *learning,* and the *T* brings its essence to all things *triumphant, talented* and *tenacious.* And since the letter *V* is the symbol of all things *virile* and *virtuous,* it's no surprise that the *VLT* combination gives rise to the gallant and alluring words *valiant, validity, velocity, virility* and *svelte.* These are *vital* people who always seem to be up to something. To capture the essence of the *VLTs,* just take a look in their closet. Not only will it be full of eclectic fashions, but most of their clothes will be on the floor. *VLTs* just don't have time for life's minutiae like organizing and ironing.

The *VLT* personalities are an interesting mix of spice, mischief and magnanimity. And while it may be tough to get on *VLTs'* bad side, be warned that these sharp-tongued warriors can really pack a punch; if you hear an argument going on you can be sure they'll be in the thick of it. You'll never meet a fairer fighter, though; *VLTs* are always willing to forgive and forget. They don't go looking for trouble either; it's just that they truly believe that *their* brand of logic is the optimum method of solving problem. About the only time you'll encounter their aggressive side is if

Valentin
Valentina
Valentine
Valentino
Violet
Violeta
Violette

you happen to question their integrity: an unpardonable sin in the *VLTs'* book.

Friendship with a *VLT* is a special treat. They will staunchly stand by their friends, no matter what crimes they may have committed, even if it comes at the expense of a somewhat holier-than-thou reproach. In this spirit, they often assume parental roles with their friends and take it upon themselves to be responsible for their well-being. These nurturing characteristics make them ideal for professions that involve working with the public, and you'll often find *VLTs* in education, career counseling, or exercising their right-brained tendencies in art or interior design.

With their perfect meld of solicitude and zeal, *VLTs* make for great casual lovers, and their strong emotional constitutions come to full prominence once they've married. They take so readily to permanent partnerships that *VLTs* often choose their mates when in their early twenties, and by putting all their efforts into making their relationships work, their unions are more successful than most. But no *VLT* can be truly happy in a marriage without children. Some people even think they choose their partners based solely on how good they think their parenting skills will be.

Violet Cray London's east end at the turn of the twentieth century was a harsh, dirty, competitive Dickensian landscape, in which crime was one of the biggest employers. It was the place that Jack the Ripper once plied his trade, and where in the 1930s, Violet Kray raised her twin sons, Ronnie and Reggie. Nurtured and guided by their mother, the boys grew up to be leaders of one of England's most infamous (and violent) criminal empires. ■ Although the family was canny enough to avoid being charged or convicted of drug dealing, corruption, bribery, extortion or terrorism, their organization was so feared that when the law finally caught up with them in 1968, the boys received the heaviest prison sentence ever handed down by a British court.

Vn

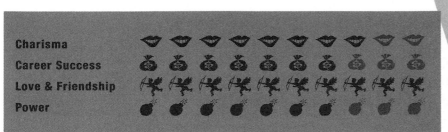

Charisma										
Career Success										
Love & Friendship										
Power										

**Considerate Affectionate Insightful
Thin-skinned Conservative Reserved**

As the initial letter of all things *negative* (*no, not, nyet, never, nada, naught, nothing* and *nix*), the letter *N* has a tendency to color names with pessimism and misgiving. And even when the *N* conjoins with the *vivacious* and *virile* letter *V*, it manages to infuse words with a sense of jaundiced passion: *vain, venal, vendetta, vent, violent, vixen, vengeance* and *Vulcan* (the Roman God of fire). Because the *VN* root is a melding of two very different elements (the enthusiastic and the cynical), *VN* people tend to struggle to find balance in their lives. But from this conflict emerges an extraordinarily energetic and artistic personality whose raison d'être has to do with uncovering of the secrets of universe as well their own convoluted impulses.

*VN*s are down-to-earth people who get a kick out of bantering with anyone willing to participate, and making friends with them will prove to be an uncomplicated business. There are few things that *VN*s enjoy more than hanging out with friends over a cup of coffee or a beer, but don't expect them to sit still for too long; life is too deliciously distracting.

*VN*s are usually in no hurry to discover their life's calling and often elect to put off college in lieu of traveling. Sometimes, they might go on job-hopping streaks and become Jacks-of-all-trades (which is why so many

Van
Vaughn
Venita
Vinnie
Von
Vonda
Vonnie

*VN*s are the go-to guys for fixing cranky computers or dripping taps). This inherent unwillingness to make up their minds often ends up costing them in their professional lives. *VN*s simply can't shake the notion that making *no* decision is better than making the wrong one.

*VN*s are emotionally and financially self-contained, and their extraordinary gregariousness stops well short of ever relying on others. They're methodical and considerate, and even if they'll admit to being a little on the conservative side, are the people most likely to organize the class reunion and manage small companies. With this kind of stability, *VN*s function well in careers that call for a high degree of mental and physical fitness. They're the first to respond when an emergency occurs and aren't ones to blame others for their mistakes. Supervisors of *VN*s would do well to watch out for their own jobs. These people are born to be upwardly mobile and will eventually percolate to the top ranks.

If you're hoping to pair up with a *VN* there's one thing to keep in mind: although they won't mind being criticized, they will not abide having their integrity questioned. Other than this, your *VN* mates will give you the same leeway to make mistakes as they do themselves.

Van Morrison Anyone who's done any soul searching over the meaning of life and love has probably come across the transcendent music of Van Morrison. ■ It was during a stint as a solo artist that "Brown-Eyed Girl" became a smash hit, and a year later he released an album that many consider to be one of the greatest of all time—*Astral Weeks*. In the seventies, he brought us more hits, such as "Moondance," "Domino," "Wild Night" and "Veedon Fleece." ■ Although his rendition of "Baby Please Don't Go" was a hit and "Gloria" stands as one of rock's enduring classics, Van was never one to cater to popular tastes. The artist, forever in transformation, sang about the joys of marriage one moment and filed for divorce the next. ■ But throughout his long and tumultuous career, Van remains, to many, The Man.

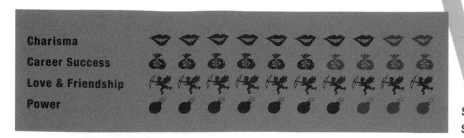

THE IRRESISTIBLE
Vns

Charisma	
Career Success	
Love & Friendship	
Power	

Sensual Connected Intense
Superior Impulsive Overly competitive

It's no surprise that the combination of the *voluptuous* letter *V*, the *nurturing* (if *negative*) letter *N* and the *sexy, slinky* letter *S* form the basis for the name *Venus* (the Roman god of love and beauty). But although these names fairly seethe with sexuality and verve, everything is not all fun and games. The *V, N* and *S* also form the root of the word *Vulcanism* (from the Roman God of fire), and aptly depicts their impulsive volatility. These are optimistic names that promise big things. And since it takes a special personality to pull off this fiery promise, prospective parents should be cautious about placing this burden on their children without carefully considering the consequences.

VNSs find it difficult to express themselves on a purely intellectual level but are adept at communicating with body language and facial expressions (they would rather act out a story than tell it). Since they are keenly aware of their charms and aren't shy about flaunting them, prospective lovers can never be quite sure whether their flirtations are serious expressions of intent or merely symptomatic of their playful dispositions.

VNSs also have an extraordinary understanding of the machinations of human interactions, and when it

Valencia
Vance
Vanessa
Venus
Vicente
Vince
Vincent
Vincenzo

comes to their careers they'll use their knowledge to full advantage. It's not like they're going to seduce their boss or anything, but they will certainly have no qualms about plying their magic on co-workers when it helps them get ahead. *VNSs* aren't particularly fussy about the kind of work they do but it doesn't mean that they don't expect recognition for their efforts. Like most *V*-named people, these are political creatures who recognize the value of being noticed in the workplace.

VNSs crave the physical side of romance and like to express themselves through all manner of corporeal adventures. But they're emotionally flexible as well, and when prospective partners are a little on the demure side, they'll tone down their approach and become masters of the subtle seduction. Those cool eyes and coy smiles could seduce a saint.

You don't have to be a saint to stay married to one of these hot-blooded souls, but it's not going to hurt. Unions with these volatile creatures are never without excitement (and even a bit of chaos), and the *VNSs'* partners will have to have to moderate their mates' emotional and physical appetites with consistent reassurances and utter fidelity.

Vanessa Williams Vanessa Williams is famous for three separate reasons. She became the first African-American woman to ever win a Miss America title, but after a short spell basking in the glory, *Penthouse* magazine published a set of racy nude pictures depicting her with another woman and Vanessa became the first Miss America to resign in disgrace. ■ Instead of slinking off to live in obscurity, Vanessa pursued a career in music and acting. Her album, *The Comfort Zone* featured the song, "Save the Best for Last" and went multi-platinum. ■ Vanessa has received two NAACP Image Awards and nine Grammy nominations, but her crowning glory was singing the Academy and Golden Globe award-winning single, "Colors of the Wind," from the soundtrack of the Disney film, *Pocahontas*.

Charisma										
Career Success										
Love & Friendship										
Power										

Appreciative Straightforward Progressive Earthbound Needy Rigid

When a name begins with the *vital, voluptuous* and *vivacious* letter *V*, it suggests a personality rife with sexual energy. And because the letter *R* is the emblem of *raw* carnal passion (*racy, randy, romantic, ruddy* and *ribald*), words dominated by *both* the *V* and *R* resonate with the unrestrained *vigor* found in *virile, virtue, voyeur, vibrant, verve* and *victory*. But notice how *VR* words that feature the *negative* letter *N* (*no, not, never, nix, nada, nyet, naught* and *nowhere*) take on the pessimistic qualities found in *vagrant, vermin, verboten, virginal, vulgarian* and *virulence*. These complex people are fully involved in life but struggle with emotional fluctuations that often prevent them from achieving their goals.

*VR*s love to talk (and have the verbal skill to back it up), but unlike other articulate people, aren't doing so because they're in love with the sound of their own voices. They talk because they have a powerful drive to communicate. So while you might have to listen to a detailed account of their Aunt Edna's problems with her spastic colon, the story is likely to be peppered with colorful and witty observations. Like most skillful communicators, *VR*s are also good listeners who won't just wait for a gap in your story to insert their own remarks.

Vera
Verena
Vern
Verna
Verne
Vernell
Vernia
Vernice
Vernie
Vernon
Verona
Veronica

For as much time as their heads spend in the clouds, their feet are firmly anchored in solid bedrock where their work is concerned and even close friends are surprised at how steely their spines are. These spunky self-starters excel in arenas that reward finesse and toughness, and have few equals legal professionals, salespeople or business executives. *VR*s have a taste for art, but as consumers—not producers. They'd rather make a lot of money and buy the best than putz around with their own handicrafts.

*VR*s will be tripping through life without a care in the world when love broadsides them out of nowhere. When this happens, marriage is in most cases inevitable. Their emotions, like their exceptional talking skills, are direct, well-communicated and never held back. The flipside to being so candid and upfront is that *VR*s tend to take people literally and get lost with subtexts and nuances. So if you want to keep your *VR* mate happy, you'll have to choose your words wisely.

*VR*s have high expectations for marriage and don't like to think of it as "settling down." The problem is, with so much energy to spare *VR*s can be quite high-maintenance as mates. So don't expect them to just be happy homemakers. If you do, your marriage will be as unstable as Microsoft Windows.

Veronica Lake Veronica Lake was born Constance Frances Marie Ockleman in 1922 and, after showing signs of schizophrenia as a teen, was given acting lessons as a form of therapy. ■ Veronica's poise caught the attention of Hollywood, where she set a trend with her trademark peek-a-boo hairstyle—the result of an ill-behaved lock of hair that fell over her eye during a photo session. ■ Veronica developed a reputation for being "difficult to work with" and was anointed "The Bitch" by co-star Eddie Bracken. As a result of her troubled personal life, she disappeared from view and showed up as a barmaid in Brooklyn in 1962. ■ "Hollywood gives a young girl the aura of one giant, self-contained orgy, its inhabitants dedicated to crawling into every pair of pants they can find," said Veronica.

vrg

Charisma										
Career Success										
Love & Friendship										
Power										

**Fashionable Observant Energetic
Childish Blunt Supercilious**

A strong theme of sexual magnetism runs through the *VRG* names. Not only is the letter *V* the symbol of all things *virile, vivacious, voluptuous, vexing* and *valiant,* but the letter *R* is the letter of raw carnal passion responsible for the words *racy, randy, ribald, ruddy* and *red* (the traditional color of love). Fortunately, the letter *G*—pronounced as in *gentle, genial* and *virgin*—takes the edge off and gives these names a nice meld of vigor and hospitality.

The nice thing about *VRG*s is that they aren't picky—at least when it comes to their friends. They form alliances easily and don't seem to mind if they're the ones giving more than they are receiving. This is usually a sign of people at peace with the universe and *VRG*s act like they're on a first-name basis with Karma. The other nice thing about them is their direct style of communication; a *VRG*'s conversation is like an arrow in flight. Not only do they have plenty of worldly experience, but they're also willing to put their ideas on the line. They're quite happy to demolish any poorly constructed ideas that you may have, too. Best solution? Don't provoke them.

When it comes to their professional lives, *VRG*s are constantly on the lookout for opportunities to test themselves. They are known for taking up great causes—human rights, the environment or social issues—and will defend their positions with passion. But like most projects, the *VRG*'s short attention span soon has them back on the move. These are great qualities if you need someone to help kick-start your new business venture, but it ultimately works against the *VRG*s, who rarely achieve their full potential in the workplace.

A powerful need to be around people propels the *VRG*s into careers that deal with the public. Prospective employers would be wise to put *VRG*s at the front desk, where their bubbling personalities have a way of making everybody feel they're the most important customers of the day. With their blend of physical energy, emotional intelligence and natural charm, *VRG*s can pull off almost any job as long as it doesn't involve repetition, attention to detail or reading maps.

What *VRG*s lack in the romance department they more than make up for in the bedroom, and if you're married to a *VRG,* you can count on having a well-rounded love life full of interesting surprises and intense encounters. And if your *VRG* disappears from time to time, there's probably nothing to worry about. It's just that like most intense people, *VRG*s need the occasion spell of solitude to top off their creative juices.

Virgie
Virgil
Virgilio
Virginia

Virgil Virgil was born in 70 B.C. and became the preeminent poet of antiquity. He was responsible for creating the idea of the wandering hero on a quest for self-discovery, and his influence reverberates in modern storytelling about everything from cowboys to bounty hunters to secret agents. ■ Commissioned by Augustus to glorify the founding of Rome, Virgil's *Aeneid* now stands as a monument of classical literature—even though it was never actually finished. ■ After ten years, as the Emperor was growing more frustrated that the work remained unfinished, Virgil took a trip to Greece, caught a fever and died. He had left instructions to have his unfinished manuscript burned, but Augustus overturned the dead man's wishes and had the manuscript published.

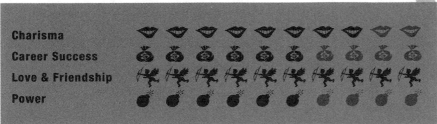

Charisma											
Career Success											
Love & Friendship											
Power											

Stylish Perceptive Bouncy
Contradictory Haughty Coy

Because the letter *V* is so overtly connected to the sexual aspects of human nature (*voluptuous, virile, vexatious, vibrant, vice, virgin* and *vulgarity*), names that contain a double dose of the *V* herald a personality with an unusually intense feminine mystique. But the letter *N*—the flagship of all things *negative* (*no, not, never, nix, nada, nyet* and *naught*)—suggests an underlying sense of melancholy to these otherwise *vivacious* and *convivial* individuals.

*VVN*s have that rare balance of right-brained and left-brained tendencies, which makes them versatile in creative arenas. Music particularly suits their analytical approach to art, and if the conductor of your local orchestra isn't a *VVN* then chances are one of the first violists is. *VVN*s are also people who always have their eyes out for something exciting. They might be soccer moms or dads, but they aren't going bury their passion for bungee jumping or frittering away nights in a karaoke bar. The point is, *VVN*s always have a surprise up their sleeves, and if you are interested in staying young, you'd do well to hang around them for pointers.

Like squirrels in winter, *VVN*s have a somewhat obsessive need to plan for the future. You would think

Vivian
Vivien
Viviana
Vivienne

this would make for well coordinated lives, but the downfall for these inveterate planners is their tendency to get bogged down in details—*VVN*s like to fuss over the little things and often lose track of the bigger picture. Perhaps this is because they aren't so much concerned with the *whys* of life as much as the *what, where* and *when*. If you're looking for a source on who's doing who, you have a veritable gossip encyclopedia at your disposal in your *VVN* friend.

*VVN*s are not known for their linear thinking processes and are rarely found in law or mathematically related fields. Instead, their native charms make them superbly equipped for careers in the public arena, where they are usually rewarded by being placed in positions of high responsibility. But even with their success in the workplace, it's unlikely that the even-keeled *VVN*s will ever become arrogant or self-centered.

*VVN*s approach their relationships with the same fastidiousness that they do their work. They become experts in their partners' needs and almost always prove to be obliging mates. *VVN*s also take pride in their ability to please but would hate to be thought of as compliant: they have too much self respect for that.

Vivien Leigh Vivien Leigh's performance as Blanche Dubois in Tennessee Williams's *A Streetcar Named Desire* was one of those rare moments when art and life merged. Anyone who watched her portrayal of a fallen Southern belle in the final stages of delusion would have been struck by the parallels to her own life. ■ After battling tuberculosis, manic depression and surviving the very public failure of her marriage to Laurence Olivier (who left her for a younger woman), Vivien was still able to go head-to-head with Marlon Brando in *Streetcar*. ■ But that wasn't the first time Vivien seemed to play herself—as Scarlett O'Hara in *Gone with the Wind*, she portrayed a determined, willful woman unafraid to pursue what she wanted. ■ She earned Best Actress Oscars for both of these, her most famous roles.

**Most Popular
Girl's Names**

Wanda
Wendy
Wilma
Willie
Whitney
Winifred
Willa
Winnie
Wendi
Wilda

**Most Popular
Boy's Names**

William
Walter
Willie
Wayne
Warren
Wesley
Wallace
Willard
Wade
Wendell

The Darkly Wise

*Wine is wicked, the king is wicked, women
are wicked, all the Children of men are
wicked, and such are all their wicked
works*

—THE FIRST BOOK OF ESDRAS,
The Apochrapha

Like the letter U, the W is a descendant of the letter V and only arrived on the scene after the Norman conquest of England in 1066. The mystics of these early times quickly embraced the authoritative W because of its association with the first warrior King of England—William the Conqueror. This explains the enormous popularity of the name William in Western society, which is the fifth most common first name for boys, and the third most common surname after Smith and Johnson. It also frequently appears in English literary circles, gracing the names of those with wit and a way with words: William Shakespeare, William Wordsworth, William Blake, Walt Whitman, William Barnes, William Cullen Bryant and Tennessee Williams. ■ Being a relatively new addition to the ever-increasing depository of English letters, the W is practically absent when it comes to names of biblical characters but makes its mark with its strong association to all that is mysterious and woeful: weird, wild, warlock, wicked, wispy, werewolf and the Wicked Witch of the West. Perhaps this is why the W has become such a workhorse for those questioning the mysteries of life as in who, where, when, why and what. ■ The W's enigmatic characteristics are also responsible for the darker elements of human endeavors; war, wreck, weapon, warning, wrong, and Wednesday (from Wodin, the god of war). Still, people whose names that begin with the wonderful, witty, wealthy and wise letter W are amongst the most likely to be millionaires. ■

THE IMPULSIVE
WD

Charisma
Career Success
Love & Friendship
Power

Enigmatic Athletic Street smart
Brusque Impatient Swaggering

When the mysterious forces of the letter *W* combine with the *dramatic* elements of the *dangerous* letter *D,* the result is a name infused with *wild* unpredictability. These effects are evident in the words *rowdy, bawdy, lewd* and *shrewd,* and if you deduce that the *WD*s are people with get-up-and-go and a tendency toward grandstanding; you wouldn't be far off. These are strong, masculine names that require equally strong personalities to pull them off. But these men are more than swashbucklers who like to attract attention; *WD*s' exploits are driven by a true sense of adventure and quest for knowledge. The name *Woody* tempers some of the *WD*'s assertiveness by ending in the *youthful* letter *Y,* signifying an individual who doesn't take himself quite so seriously.

*WD*s are those hearty and unconventional individuals who conduct their lives deliberately contrary to the flow of society . . . and pull it off with panache. It takes a strong sense of drama and natural intelligence to get away with being so defiant, and *WD*s have these in spades. You can always tell when a *WD* is in the room; the noise level drops, and the conversation turns to him and his recent escapades. No one would ever accuse *WD*s of having low self-esteem, but their social interactions stop well short of arrogance and condescension. In fact, these are generous men who love

Wade
Waldo
Ward
Wardell
Woodrow
Woody

nothing better than inspiring others to achieve great things.

*WD*s are always getting into some kind of adventure, whether they intend to or not, which is why you'll often find *WD*s filling roles as youth leaders, actors, or environmental activists; in short, anything requiring a high level of enthusiasm. When they curb their outspoken tendencies and accept that it's better to lead by example, they are unstoppable in business, and like most people whose names begin with the letter *W* are likely to be among the top wage earners in their peer groups. It's not that *WD*s don't make their share of missteps—when you're as productive as they are, you are going to overreach on occasion—but these are flexible fellows who, when things aren't working out, have no problems with taking ownership of their mistakes and going back to the drawing board.

When it comes to dating, *WD*s are usually drawn to the quieter timid types who will defer to their strong personalities. But like many alpha males, they may lose respect for partners who swallow their pride too readily. *WD*s are better people inside a marriage than they are outside; it brings them a measure of stability that they cannot achieve on their own. Partnering these men may be a tall order, but the rewards will be a mate who will show you the universe and give you the world.

Woodrow Wilson Not since Thomas Jefferson had the United States enjoyed a true intellectual as their President. Woodrow Wilson graduated from Princeton, received a law degree from the University of Virginia and received a doctorate from Johns Hopkins. ■ As President, Woodrow brought the then-isolationist United States onto the world stage (and into its first major international conflict) in 1917. But he was no warmonger: he had lived in Atlanta during the Civil War and had firsthand experience in the horrors of war. ■ After the war, Woodrow unsuccessfully pushed the United States to join the League of Nations and toured the country to rally support for the cause. But shouting at the top of his lungs from the caboose of a steam train took its toll, and in 1924, Woodrow suffered the stroke that took his life.

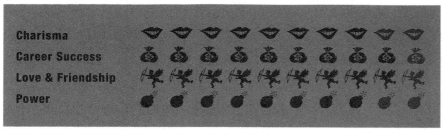

Charisma										
Career Success										
Love & Friendship										
Power										

**Generous Prudent Impartial
Elusive Vague Passive**

The letter *L* initializes the most important things in the universe: *life, love, laughter, liberty* and *learning*. And when it occurs in words initialized by the mysterious letter *W*, creates a sound that evokes a *howling wolf*: *wild, wily, wooly* and even a little bit *woeful*. Perhaps this is why some men (*Willy, Wally* and *Willie*) elect to add the high-pitched *Y* or *IE* and advertise their names as more approachable and friendly. The name *Willie Loman*—the hapless hero of Arthur Miller's *Death of a Salesman*—was carefully chosen to make this point. It's also noteworthy that the only female name in this group (*Wilfred*) uses the *friendly* and *feminine* letter *F* to distance itself from its wild counterparts. But *all WL* people are characterized by their determination to make their marks in life and share a common belief that tomorrow is going to be a better day.

WLs tend to be gracious and introspective types, who only feel at peace when there's balance between their careers and relationships. And because there's nothing *WLs* wouldn't do for their loved ones—and because it's a such an effort to say "no"—many end up giving more than they get. But this a trait that *WLs* hardly consider to be a weakness; their emotionally generous attitudes win them many friends and create a support system for when *they* are in need of help. (It's also great for attracting the opposite sex.)

Wally
Walker
Wallace
Waylon
Weldon
Wendell
Wilbert
Wilbur
Wilburn
Wilda, Wiley
Wilford
Wilfred
Wilfredo
Will, Willard
Williams
Willis
Willow
Willy
Wilson
Wilton

With their penchant for solving problems, many *WLs* are attracted to the computer, engineering and legal fields. Even if your *WL* friend doesn't have any outstanding talents, he or she will probably have a well-rounded skill set that comes in handy in their chosen career. In fact, the job market is like a giant candy store to *WLs* who often find themselves in the enviable position of having to select between many promising offers. *WLs* are opportunists when it comes to earning money, and even when they've committed themselves to a particular career, won't feel duty-bound to stay if another job has the potential of being more lucrative.

If *WLs* are lucky in love, it might have something to do with the peculiar energy they radiate when around the opposite sex. Some might call it *mojo,* but it might also be that *WLs* play so hard to get. Even when marriage becomes inevitable, they'll enter into it with a certain amount of trepidation. But once they've overcome the initial discomfort of their new environment, they'll rise to the challenge and become the best mates in the world (or at least, that's what they'll have you believe). By the time they're in their thirties, most are comfortably ensconced in permanent and gratifying relationships with (what they'll also tell you) their single life a distant dream.

Will Smith Will got his first dose of national exposure playing the lead role in *The Fresh Prince of Bel-Air*, but even before his appearance as an actor, he had achieved notoriety with his rap duo, *D.J. Jazzy Jeff and the Fresh Prince.* ■ His cross-cultural appeal and boyish charm helped him achieve one hit after another, including *Bad Boys, Independence Day, Men in Black I* and *II, Enemy of the State* and *Six Degrees of Separation.* Not that all his films were all successes, mind you; his remake of the Western television classic *Wild Wild West* was almost universally panned. ■ Will is currently married to actress Jada Pinkett.

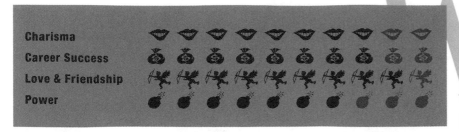

Charisma	💋	💋	💋	💋	💋	💋	💋	💋	💋
Career Success	💰	💰	💰	💰	💰	💰	💰	💰	💰
Love & Friendship									
Power	💣	💣	💣	💣	💣	💣	💣	💣	💣

Thoughtful Original Insightful
Perfectionist Brooding Scheming

The *WLM* group of names derives its sophistication from the influence of the *wise* and *weird* letter *W*. And when the *W* is combined with the letter *L*—the icon of *life, liberty, love, laughter* and *learning*—these names take on an exceptional air of dignity and poise. The appearance of the maternal letter *M* (*mother, mama* and *mammary*) contributes to their appeal by augmenting a warmly compassionate essence. So, if it's true that men whose names fall into the *WLM* category are in touch with their feminine sides, it's because they have so much confidence in their masculinity that they can afford to be a little sensitive. All this explains why the *WLM* names have retained their extraordinary popularity for over a thousand years. If there is anything negative to say, it's that these names are a little on the formal side since none of these people choose to use the more approachable contractions of *Will* or *Willy*.

WLMs are guided by their intellects and—even when they're relaxing—are usually the cause of heated debates from everything from politics to art and science. People quickly realize that their propensity for arguing is not a symptom of intellectual bullying; *WLM*s simply enjoy injecting fresh ideas that others may not have considered. It's only natural that this tendency leads them into the field of education where young minds seem to appreciate their frank delivery, and even if *WLM*s don't pursue careers in education, they'll probably end up in some kind of leadership position. These are not people happy with just being cogs in the machine.

A corollary to the *WLM*s' intellectual approach is their habit of placing impossibly high standards on themselves and those with whom they work: when goals can't be met, the resulting stresses do more harm than good. But *WLM*s are quick learners and have few ego issues when it comes to admitting their mistakes.

About the only time *WLM*s panic is when they have promised more than they can actually deliver. Breaking a commitment is an unpardonable sin.

You know that old trick for driving off unwanted boyfriends (or girlfriends) by telling him you're in love with them? Well this isn't going to work with *WLM*s, who are simply too receptive to intimacy to pass up opportunities like this. If you want to get rid of them, you're better off playing it cool. (*WLM*s get really uncomfortable when they don't know where they stand.) But unlike most people who see marriage as a gateway to stable home lives, *WLM*s are more likely to feather their nests *before* committing to marriage. All the better to control the relationship from ground zero.

Wilhelmina
Willem
William
Williemae
Wilma
Wilmer

Prince William On August 31, 1997, the heir to the British throne woke to the news that his mother had been fatally injured in a car accident. True to his stiff-upper-lip English breeding, he comported himself with dignity beyond his years. ■ The elder son of the Prince and Princess of Wales, William was christened William Arthur Philip Louis Windsor with water imported from the River Jordan. ■ With his mother's sparkling eyes and his father's decorum, the six-foot William became something of a sex symbol for teenage girls worldwide. But "The Family" was to carefully control William's social life—all potential girlfriends had to be carefully screened to exclude unsuitable elements. If Will showed any interest in a particular young lady, she and her mother were invited to tea and an interview.

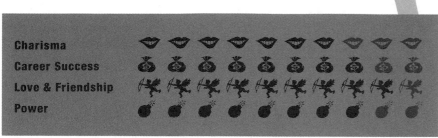

Charisma	
Career Success	
Love & Friendship	
Power	

Talented Adaptable Shrewd
Closed Suspicious Misunderstood

Like fine wines, *WN* names tend to evoke images of people who are complex, interesting and often misunderstood. Perhaps this stems from the *W*'s strong connection to the mysterious elements in life (*wild, wooly, wonderful* and *weird*) and the fact that the letter *N* is so often associated with cynicism and negativity (*nervous, nay-saying, no, not, nag, nix, ninny* and *naught*). When these two letters occur in close proximity to each other, they create the off-balance qualities found in *whine, winsome, winter, wind, wonky* and *wink*.

If it's true that *WN*s are somewhat isolated people, whose attempts at communication are often misconstrued, one can't deny that they also posses a creative streak second to none. But the thing that really defines the *WN*s' essence is their intelligence. It's not the conventional book-smartness that we find in more practical people, it's an odd combination of street smarts and emotional intelligence that is usually only found in artists and philosophers. *WN*s can be realistic when making important decisions, but if given their druthers, they'd live in a world in which there were no choices to be made.

Because they're so aware of themselves, it can be difficult to get a handle on what they think about *you*.

Wan
Wanda
Warner
Warren
Waymon
Wayne
Wen
Wendy
Werner
Windy
Winfred
Winifred
Winnie
Winona
Winston

Perhaps they enjoy the unease they create in people, but when they turn on the charm you'll wonder why you ever doubted their intentions in the first place. Somewhere deep down, the whimsical *WN*s know *exactly* why others misinterpret their motives.

*WN*s have so many levels of complexity that unraveling them all will provide more surprises than a Michael Jackson documentary. Their hot-and-cold oscillations make them perfect for careers that require oblique thinking—rather than analytical thought. Acting, for example, would be compatible with their rather elusive personalities, as would design, marketing and party planning. Although *WN*s will accept jobs requiring close social contact, most are not comfortable in situations where they have to act as role models to others and usually steer clear of the teaching and counseling professions.

With all their intricate machinations, *WN*s are not easy people to bond with, and it'll take a persistent suitor to win their confidence. Even once you've gained their trust, you'll find a familiar *WN* pattern: they'll dance nervously away from their emotions at first, then give themselves over to commitment with surprising abandon.

Winona Ryder It's a shame when an individual's body of work is overshadowed by a single dark incident in their lives. But the Hollywood press, being what it is, was determined to burn the image of Winona Ryder's shoplifting arrest into the minds of the public. Her 2002 trial featured witnesses who alleged that Winona had claimed to be preparing for a role in which the director had asked her to shoplift. Found guilty, Winona was sentenced to probation. ■ Winona first became a major celebrity after her role as Lydia, the morose teenager in the dark comedy *Beetlejuice*. Staying with the disaffected Gen-Xer theme, she followed up with *Heathers, Edward Scissorhands, Bram Stoker's Dracula* and *Reality Bites*. ■ Her roles in The *Age of Innocence* and *Little Woman* were both nominated for Oscars.

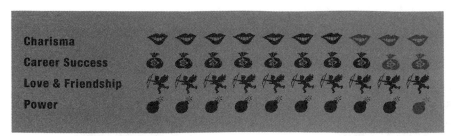

Charisma										
Career Success										
Love & Friendship										
Power										

Passionate Focused Idealistic
Moody Repressed Unreadable

When a name begins with the *wild* and *wonderful* letter *W*, we expect to encounter a certain level of moodiness from the individual who bears it. And since the letter *S* is the symbol for all things *sassy, sexy, sensual, saucy, scandalous* and *spirited*, its conjunction with the *W* tends to create words with the Zeitgeist of the tenth century: *whimsy, wise, winsome, wistful* and *whiskey*. These are smoldering people with a cryptic quality to them, and who are unafraid of striking out for what they want.

The universe to a *WS* is something to be experienced with all one's senses and not to be observed through the narrow lens of a telescope. It's unlikely, therefore, that you'd find one staying in one place or being with any one person for too long. It's not that he's particularly adverse to commitment, but it *is* a little suspicious that he's always either in the process of starting or ending a relationship.

*WS*s have reputations for being prolific flirters with strong libidos, but this is just a sample of their overall passion for life. With their mélange of physical energy, emotional intelligence and natural charm, *WS*s can pull off the role as a high-paid CEO, sports idol or a sales professional with equal ease. Most companies would jump at the chance to have a *WS* in their customer serv-

Wes
Wesley
Westley
Weston

ice or human resources department; their sharp wits and innate understanding of human nature enables them make other people feel important. *WS*s are easy to be around because they aren't worriers. On the other hand, they don't have a particularly well-developed sense of danger and often make poor choices in their professional lives.

Despite all that self-confident strutting, there's an unexpected reserve when *WS*s find themselves unsure of their standing in new relationships. This is about the only time you'll find them keeping a low profile, and just when you think you've learned all there is to know about them, they'll surprise you (pleasantly or otherwise) with an unexpected twist. It's just a symptom of their penchant for keeping people off balance. The best way for dealing with this is to drop all your expectations and allow them to blaze their own trails.

If you're thinking of tying the knot with a *WS*, you should make absolutely sure that *he's* absolutely sure that he's ready to commit to one person. Sometimes a *WS* will marry someone in order not to lose her—a decision that invariably ends in disappointment—but if he commits to you for the right reasons, hang onto your hat. It's going to be a wild and wonderful ride.

Wesley Snipes While he was working as a phone installer, a young Wesley Snipes won a bit part in the Warner Brothers film *Wildcats*, alongside Goldie Hawn. ■ Something about Wesley's brooding aura caught the eye of director Spike Lee, who offered him a part in his film *Do the Right Thing*. In an astonishing decision, Wesley turned the part down—something aspiring actors should never do to Spike Lee. Wesley later accepted Spike's offer to play a jazz saxophonist in *Mo' Better Blues* and the lead in his interracial-relationship drama *Jungle Fever*. ■ The movies *Blade* and *Blade II* were showcases for Wesley's physical talents. His dark portrayal of a super vampire battling legions of undead ghouls bent on eliminating the human race resulted in mega-million-dollar profits for the studio.

Wt

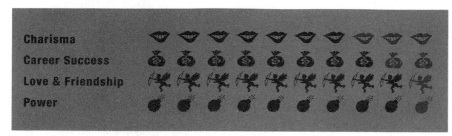

Charisma										
Career Success										
Love & Friendship										
Power										

Warm Multitalented Driven
Coy Judgmental Impatient

The letter *T* is the *triumphant* herald of *tenaciousness* we find in the words *trumpet, talent, twinkle, terrific* and *tremendous*. And when the *T* comes into close contact with the *wild, wooly* and *wily* letter *W*, it evokes the kind of unrestrained intensity we find in the words *wrath, wit, witch, winter, wildcat, watchful* and *thwart*. *WT* people exhibit a spontaneous energy and oblique thought process that comes to define their lives. If you're looking for something negative to say about them, it would include something about their exceptional stubbornness—but it also comes with an uncommon ability to concentrate on the task at hand. You'd also concede that they are guided by strong moral compasses and can be counted on to do the right thing.

Often found in leadership roles, *WTs* are respected for their sharp business instincts and even sharper senses of humor. They're quite comfortable taking the lead in business decisions by day, then joining their friends for a bunch of laughs by night, but are terribly serious when it comes to maintaining their relationships. Friends are important to *WTs* because they help keep a lid on their tendency for recklessness—*WTs* without friends are apt to run a little wild. But *WTs* are certainly not followers: they have big dreams and are not content with hitching rides on anyone else's star.

Walt
Walter
Walton
Whitley
Whitney
Wyatt

When there's a job to do, they'll happily accept responsibility for failure as long as they can take credit for its success.

WTs have unlimited potential in the workplace. They respond well to the pressures of the creative fields (design, software, and engineering), but their ability to think on their feet also makes them top-notch salespeople. When they're not working, *WTs* have to keep themselves busy. Whether they're puttering around the house and inventing new devices, partners must learn to curb their annoyance at the *WT*'s habit of constantly tinkering with things that are better left alone.

It's a good thing that *WTs* aren't shy. People from all social walks are drawn to them and find them to be wonderful conversationalists. It's not that they're particularly intellectual or anything, but they really seem able to hear what the other person is saying.

Potential mates find their rock-solid loyalty reassuring. Still, a *WT*'s spouse should have enough composure to deal with a colorful (and sometimes off-color) sense of humor. Even with their tendency to be a little fanciful in their personal lives, *WTs* prove to be down-to-earth parents and utterly dedicated to their children's well being.

Walt Disney Walt Disney's first attempts to create cute animated animals were rabbits, like the ones on his father's Missouri farm, and not mice as many people think. ■ After being turned down by the *Chicago Tribune* for a job as an artist, Walt tried his hand at advertising (the fall-back position of many frustrated writers and artists) and began dabbling in animation. His first ever full-length feature animation, *Snow White*, changed the genre forever, but his later films, including *Pinocchio*, *Fantasia* and *Bambi*, were less successful with American audiences, who didn't appreciate his sophisticated style of cartooning. ■ After Walt died of cancer in 1966 (a decade after founding Disneyland in California) rumors began to circulate that his corpse had been frozen for posterity. These reports were eventually proven unfounded.

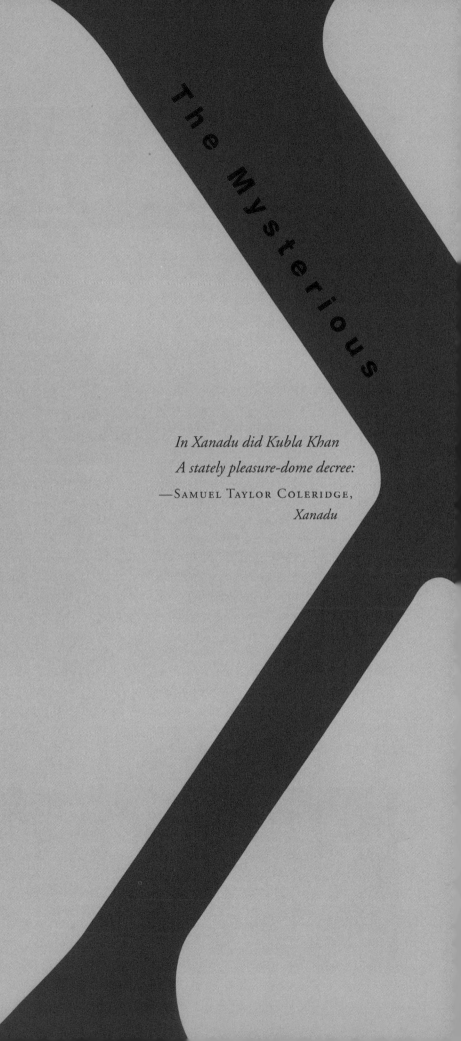

**Most Popular
Girl's Names**

Xiomara

Xena

Xuan

Xiao

**Most Popular
Boy's Names**

Xander

Xavier

In Xanadu did Kubla Khan
A stately pleasure-dome decree:
—SAMUEL TAYLOR COLERIDGE,
Xanadu

Perhaps because the KS sound makes a perfectly good substitute, the letter X remains the most underutilized letter in the entire alphabet—appearing in a less than 3% of all English words. So when we see the letter X in a word, it tends to stand out and force us to take notice. ■ But on the heels of the Generation-X, the X has recently experienced a surge in popularity. Microsoft named its videogame system the Xbox, Christine Aguilera has taken to calling herself Xtina, Nissan named their top-selling SUV the Xterra and the X-games are one of the most-watched sporting events on Fox. Along with the huge commercial successes of the films *X-Men* and *The X-Files*, the names Xander (short for Alexander) and Xavier even appeared on the list of the top one hundred baby names issued by the Social Security Administration in 2002. The name Xena is also rapidly growing in popularity due to the success of the television character made famous by Lucy Lawless. ■ X is the classic unknown variable in algebra, and its isolated disposition is well illustrated by the word xenophobia. When Wilhelm Roentgen discovered mysterious rays emanating from a piece of radioactive uranium, he named them X-rays because of elusive properties connoted by the letter. X also marks the spot, and is the name given to anything wishing to remain anonymous, as in Brand X, Mr. X and The X-Files. Movies you don't want your kids to see are labeled XXX, in the same way that beer is labeled in comic books. ■ Still, there are fewer people in the United States whose names begin with an X than any other letter (less than 1/100 of a percent), and it's clear that parents who give their child an X name are making a strong statement about the uniqueness of their offspring. ■

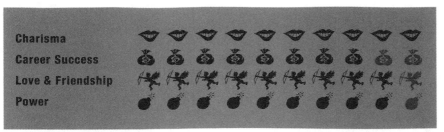

Charisma										
Career Success										
Love & Friendship										
Power										

**Charismatic Brilliant Independent
Arrogant Overbearing Presumptuous**

It's patently clear that parents who bestow their offspring names beginning with the letter *X* are trying to make a potent statement about their desire for their child to buck society's conventions. Not that there are any dire consequences to this deed, mind you, but chances are this act of free expression will produce a child with an independent spirit and a high level of self-esteem.

There's little doubt that *X* children will quickly learn how to cope with the vagaries of their names; for the *X* is like a bulls-eye in the playground. But after the taunts of adolescence mature into the teenage appreciation for the unusual, the young *X* will enjoy a sense of pride in standing out from the herd. If *X*s sometimes find themselves labeled as the black sheep of their families, it's a label they wear proudly. And it's this sense of "feeling special" that comes to define *X*s' lives.

There are usually few vulnerable edges to the *X*'s complex emotional makeup. These are people who have long since explored themselves from top to bottom and have made peace with their own idiosyncrasies. This gives them the ability to play counselor to their gener-

Xan
Xander
Xavier
Xaviera
Ximena
Xiomara

ally large set of friends and hangers-on, and even though they'll usually end up as a leader of their social pack, it isn't a role that they have to campaign for.

*X*s are drawn to things that fall outside the norm and seem determined to maintain their status as outsiders. They usually subscribe to unconventional philosophies, and although you could describe them as being amiable and attentive, they are difficult to emotionally pin down. *X*s' oddities inevitably lend them an irresistible charm and they know how to draw crowds at parties with their latest theories on yoga, spoon-bending or impressionistic paintings.

In the marriage department, *X* mates can be hard to fathom. In fact if you're a stickler for predictability, you might want to give the *X* a miss entirely (or join the queue of broken hearts in this charmer's wake). But if you do happen to be "the one," you can expect charming surprises and odd expressions of affection from your eccentric mate. But be aware that *X*s tends to suffer from disillusionment regarding marriage; for as much as they fantasize about the rewards of having a committed relationship, they often discover that marriage is too much like hard work.

Xaviera Hollander Xaviera Hollander, aka "The Happy Hooker" was, with the possible exception of tulips, the most famous of Holland's exports. ■ In her tell-all autobiography *A Child No More*, Xaviera detailed her early life when she and her mother were Japanese prisoners during World War II. Her father, a doctor imprisoned in a neighboring camp, was summoned to treat a young girl without realizing it was his own daughter. ■ After the war, Xaviera began to develop feelings that would later be diagnosed as full-fledged nymphomania and sought relief by turning to prostitution. Xaviera made a fortune, but her high-profile success also made her a target of both the police and the Mafia. ■ After seeking refuge in Canada, Xaviera finally found a measure of respectability when she married an antique dealer.

**Most Popular
Girl's Names**

Yvonne
Yolanda
Yvette
Yesenia
Young
Yon

**Most Popular
Boy's Names**

Young
Yong

Y

The Letter of Youthful Exuberance

Youth is wasted on the young.

—Anonymous

After the Romans extended their empire through-out the Mediterranean, they appropriated the Greek sign Upsilon to be the last letter of their alphabet, which until then had ended with X. Due to its recent arrival in the alphabet, the Y has had little time to develop its personality and has had virtually no impact on the historical record. With the unique distinction of not initializing any Greek or Roman deity, it is neither the initial letter of any first, middle, or last name of any American President or Vice President in history, nor is it the initial letter of any current member of the House of Representatives or Senate. ■ Given the lack of male role models, it's not surprising that girls are thirty times more likely to have a Y name than boys are. As the initial letter of the word yes, yep, yippee, yee-hah, yippee and yeah, Y names seem infused with a air of enthusiasm and zeal. Additionally, because of the human tendency to associate high-frequency sounds with friendly and reassuring situations, words that end with the high-pitched tones of the Y typically convey a feminizing or infantilizing tone: coy, play, baby, happy, downy, rosy, sunny, cozy, sassy, gay and shy. ■ The Y is used in algebra to denote an unknown variable (along with letters X and Z), and also initializes an unusually high number of words that pertain to the passing of time and measurement—yesterday, young, year, yardstick, yet, yonder and youthful. ■

THE CONTRARY Y

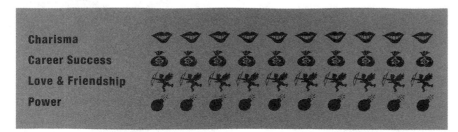

Charisma
Career Success
Love & Friendship
Power

Playful Precocious Unpredictable Immature Coy Clingy

Names that begin with the perennially *youthful* letter *Y* typically signify a personality full of defiance—particularly when it comes to following society's conventions. *Y*s tend to shy away from the realistic side of life and often engage in flights of fancy and castle-building in the sky. But giddy and undisciplined as *Y* people may appear to be, these people also possess an exceptionally high level of street-smartness and boast solid emotional cores that can be relied on in times of crisis.

These avant-garde personalities make lasting impressions. Leave it to a *Y* person to let fly with a funny comment at a funeral or collapse in a fit of giggles at a board meeting. It's not that they're trying to peeve anyone, mind you; it's just that to them, no aspect of life is so serious that it can't be laughed at. Their attitude is so infectious that it's hard to remain glum in their presence unless they're having one of their rare off days.

Y people are drawn to all sorts of odd professions, most of which involve working around other people. While their presence can liven up a serious workplace, supervisors may not always appreciate the disorder that tends to accompany these cheeky souls.

Yadira
Yahaira
Yahir
Yehuda
Yehudi
Yoko
Yolanda
Yolande
Yolando
Yong
Young
Yuliana

Still, they'll have to begrudgingly admit that productivity seems to go up when *Y* people are around.

Music and art play a large role in the lives of *Y* people and gives wings to their extraordinarily creative natures. And although these aren't people who *have* to be in the spotlight, the extroverted *Y*s have few qualms about performing in front of strangers.

Y people are keen observers of human nature—which shows in the way they mentally record every detail of their environment for later use—and explains why they so often come up with the oddest but truest statements about life and other people.

When the *Y* decides to settle down, it will hardly ever be in the traditional sense. But, if and when they decide to tie the knot, their partners can expect a string of surprises from their fun-loving mates. They can also be expected to be on the move at all times, for *Y*s get easily bored with routine and will descend into petty griping when stuck in a rut. Their spontaneous sense of adventure is guaranteed to keep their spouses and families on their toes, even if it comes at the cost of a somewhat unstable home life.

Yoko Ono Yoko Ono bore the heavy burden of being blamed for the breakup of The Beatles, the most popular band in history. She earned this status from her controlling relationship with John Lennon, whom she met at an avant-garde art show in London. ■ Yoko had already gone through two marriages, and her relationship with John was criticized from the start. Resentment grew over the way John made Yoko a priority over the band, but most historians disagree that Yoko was the key factor in The Beatle's breakup. ■ Yoko was an artist in her own right, holding degrees in philosophy and music. The two were inseparable throughout their marriage, which ended tragically the night Mark Chapman shot John three times in front of his Manhattan apartment building in 1980.

426

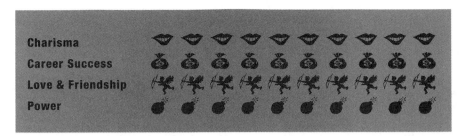

THE SPIRITED

YS

Charisma										
Career Success										
Love & Friendship										
Power										

Adaptable Expressive Outgoing
Escapist Inconsistent Opportunistic

When the youthful spunk of the letter *Y* combines in a name with the *sexy, sassy, smoky, savory* and *slinky* letter *S*, it's not surprising that we find it belonging to a someone fairly bursting with creative spunk . . . and a slyly charming spirit to boot. *YS*s are unusually bright individuals whose eccentric habits are usually the subject of conversation within their peer groups, and they are in particularly high demand whenever someone decides to throw a party. With their penchants for fine food, art and culture, *YS*s like to think of themselves as sophisticated, and most of the time manage to pull the illusion off perfectly.

Some people believe them to be high-maintenance personalities, for they often give the impression that they need to be the most important people in the room. And most of the time they are; with their stylishly cool social styles they usually end up dominating social gatherings in a subtle but very real sense.

In light of their somewhat controlling natures, recommended careers for the *YS* are those that involve organizing things—whether it's people, events or simply shuffling paperwork. If you're planning a wedding and your *YS* friend has some free time, be sure to rope him

Yaritza
Yasmine
Yesenia
Yosef
Yoselin
Yoshiko
Yusef

or her into helping you prepare. Chances are they'll be delighted and are sure to color the event with their signature flair. Just be aware that working under pressure seems to energize (rather than stress) these capable people, and they have a nasty habit of waiting till the last minute before getting anything done.

*YS*s aren't ones to put on a façade or pretend to be something they're not, and whatever else you may think of them, you can count on them to be unfailingly honest and upfront with you. As friends, *YS*s are tenaciously loyal, and it will be virtually impossible to shake their friendship once they've latched onto you. To those outside their inner circle, however, *YS*s seem to be a different story: somewhat cool personalities with a tendency to be standoffish. But it's not difficult to befriend these people-hungry souls and almost everyone's application for friendship will be accepted.

Being married to a *YS* is somewhat akin to being the groom to a champion thoroughbred. There may be plenty of work involved down in the stables, but if you're able to hold on, you're in for an interesting ride. Just remember that if you treat them with respect and dignity, they'll give you 100% in return.

Yasmine Bleeth At the age of only six months, Yasmine Bleeth was featured as the Johnson & Johnson baby, and six years later famous fashion photographer Francesco Scavullo asked her to pose for his photo-book *Scavullo's Women*. ■ All grown up and voted one of *People Magazine*'s 50 Most Beautiful, Yasmine secured her legacy by replacing Pamela Anderson Lee on the hugely popular nineties television series *Baywatch*. It wasn't easy to fill Pamela's high-cut red bathing suit, but Yasmine was up to the challenge. ■ After leaving what was billed as "the most watched show on earth," Yasmine continued her work in television movies and appeared in a number of little-watched feature films including, *Titans*; *Goodbye, Casanova* and *Coming Soon*.

427

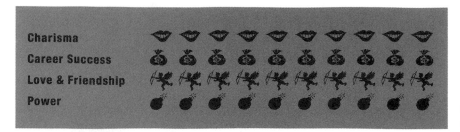

Charisma	👄👄👄👄👄👄👄👄👄👄
Career Success	💰💰💰💰💰💰💰💰💰💰
Love & Friendship	🦅🦅🦅🦅🦅🦅🦅🦅🦅🦅
Power	💣💣💣💣💣💣💣💣💣💣

Artistic Active Ambitious
Caustic Vengeful Miserly

When the letter *Y*—the symbol of playfulness and youth—teams up with the *vigorous, vampish* sexuality of the letter *V*, it evokes a well-defined air of lively femininity. *YV* names are almost always represented by vigorously outgoing women whose taste for adventure often gets the better of their high intelligence. It's worth noting that when the letter *V* combines with the negative letter *N* (as in the name *Yvonne*) it takes on the somewhat *vindictive* aspects seen in the words *venomous, vengeance, Calvinism, coven, evasion, vixen, vain* and *vandal*. Those whose names feature the *terrific* and *triumphant* letter *T (Yvette)*, tend to be a little more outspoken and definitely more approachable.

Yvette
Yvonne

Though all *YV* women are reasonably friendly, one should be on guard against their tendency for the occasional sarcastic remark, which usually manifests when they perceive rejection or some other slight. But it's not likely that you'll hear their tetchy comments firsthand, mind you, for *YV*s aren't the types to resort to overt aggression. Instead, they'll usually percolate their feelings through mutual friends or neutral parties, to give *you* the option of coming to *them* to apologize.

Like most people with *Y* names, these are active spirits who simply refuse to sit around doing nothing. Even when they're not working, there's always some project or other that needs their attention. Even their vacations are unlikely to be leisurely affairs and will involve some sort of exotic destination with plenty of gadding about.

Quick thinking and quite fearless, *YV*s can be your best friends or your worst enemies. They have extraordinarily keen intellects which enable them to outfox even the quickest minds . . . and there's always that acerbic wit should they ever need it for self-defense. So if you're looking for an advocate to fight your verbal battles, the *YV* is your woman. It's not that she's going to go looking for trouble, but you can be sure that she'll never back down from a confrontation. Lawyering and teaching are perfect careers for this persuasive talker, but she also excels in professions that require a certain amount of intellectual passion: fundraising, sales and the stock market.

Under the influence of family life and motherhood, the *YV*'s softer side becomes more pronounced. As a mother, her protective and nurturing instincts take such firm control that sometimes her children will have to fight for their independence. When it comes to negotiating the power balance in her relationship, the *YV* may be quite content to play a supporting role, but has too much self-esteem to ever accept a secondary one.

Yvonne de Carlo Best known for her role as Lily Munster in the 1960s long-running television hit *The Munsters*, Yvonne De Carlo originally had aspirations of being a dancer. ■ After a number of small bathing-beauty roles, Yvonne landed the title role in *Salome*, where she had an opportunity to show off her dancing skills. Unfortunately, Yvonne made little impact with the critics and was forced to accept low-grade projects like *Song of Scheherazade*, *Brute Force* and *Slave Girl*. ■ Still, Yvonne was beginning to accumulate a fan base, and her crowning glory came in 1956, when she played the wife of Moses in the box-office smash *The Ten Commandments*. ■ As film roles began to dry up, Yvonne turned her attention to the burgeoning television market and landed her wildly popular role on *The Munsters*.

Most Popular Girl's Names

Zelma

Zelda

Zella

Zoe

Zoila

Zenaida

Zoraida

Most Popular Boy's Names

Zachary

Zachery

Zane

Zachariah

Zack

Zackary

Father Zeus, whose hand
Doth wield the lightning brand,
Slay him beneath thy levin bold, we pray,
Slay him, O slay!
—SOPHOCLES

The Madcap, Zany

The letter Z dominated the lives of ancient Greeks in the form of the supreme ruler of heaven and earth, the rewarder of good and the punisher of evil: Zeus. Zeus was also the unpredictable creator of weather and amused himself by zapping miscreant Greeks with his random lightning thunderbolts. ■ Whereas people whose names begin with the letter A are first in roll call, Zs are consigned to wait their turn until the end. But don't expect them to get despondent about their place at the end of the line, for their personalities are zesty, zealous, zingy, zippy, zoom, zippidy-doo-dah and zany. These ebullient qualities can be seen in the traditional meaning of names like Zsa Zsa, Zoe (life), Zelia (eager) and Ziv (very bright). ■ Although Z names are rare, they still occur with ten times the frequency of the X and five times that of the U. They are conspicuously absent, however, from all of the lists of most successful people. ■

THE GIFTED

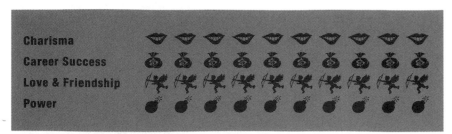

Charisma	😀😀😀😀😀😀😀😀😀😀
Career Success	💰💰💰💰💰💰💰💰💰💰
Love & Friendship	🐦🐦🐦🐦🐦🐦🐦🐦🐦🐦
Power	💣💣💣💣💣💣💣💣💣💣

**Dedicated Insightful Feminine
Volatile Jealous Combative**

When your name begins with the letter *Z*, you've long since come to terms with the fact that people react with surprise when they first hear it, and that they're unlikely to forget it. Chances are you've also had to come to terms with many things in your life, not the least having to deal with a set of parents with the chutzpah to name you *Zoe*, *Zane*, *Zena* or *Zandra* in the first place. All told, you're probably a very well-balanced individual with an extraordinary zest for life.

These pert little powerhouses are loaded with cuteness, and *Z* people tend to retain their childlike innocence throughout their lives—at least on the surface. But even though they may play the role of a coquettish ingénue, these are world-wise people with a high level of emotional and intellectual intelligence.

Nothing annoys *Z* people more than having someone talk when they're trying to interrupt. One could accuse them of being in love with the sound of their own voices, but it simply stems from an enthusiasm for all kinds of debate. And even though these are competitive people, they are not driven simply by a desire to win. They're mainly motivated by a desire to improve themselves, and even though winning is always better than losing, they're truly in it for the spirit of the game.

*Z*s love to dispense advice, whether it's solicited or not. From their perspective, it never hurts to have an extra mind working on a problem, and they're also the first to seek help when struggling with *their* issues. If people get a little snappish with their sometimes-intrusive style, *Z*s take it all in stride. They recognize that people only get cranky when they need a little tender care. So when it comes to their careers, their natural inclination to motivate others makes them ideal for any work requiring upbeat, positive attitudes. Preferring the role as a co-conspirator, rather than actually taking the lead, they certainly know how to pull a team together.

Dating or mating with such outgoing people would seem like a cinch . . . except that it's not. For the more intimate you get with them, the more you'll encounter their need to control the minutiae of their relationships. What starts out as an irresistible attraction can easily turn into frustration unless the *Z*'s partner is willing to relinquish a certain level of control. But once the power-balance has been established, these playful and sexy extroverts will charm you into submission every time.

Zaida
Zain
Zaire
Zander
Zandra
Zane
Zaria
Zavier
Zelda
Zella
Zelma
Zena
Zion
Zoe
Zola
Zoraida

Zola Budd The most dramatic incident of the 1984 L.A. Olympic Games came in the woman's 3,000-meter when a barefooted South African teenager collided with Mary Decker, the American favorite. The impact left Decker facedown on the track while the seventeen-year-old Zola, near tears, was left to dispiritedly complete the race without a victory. ■ The match-up between the slightly built Zola and the powerful Decker had been the talk of every sport magazine in the country. The running phenomenon from South Africa had recently set a world record in this distance, but Decker was the reigning U.S. champion. ■ In an embarrassingly unsportswomanly fit of pique, Decker blamed Zola for the accident and refused to accept her apology.

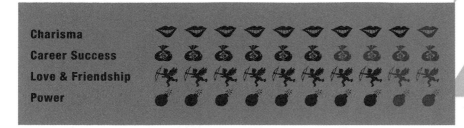

Charisma	👄👄👄👄👄👄👄👄👄👄
Career Success	💰💰💰💰💰💰💰💰💰💰
Love & Friendship	🏹🏹🏹🏹🏹🏹🏹🏹🏹🏹
Power	💣💣💣💣💣💣💣💣💣💣

**Artistic Imaginative Zany
Unpredictable Moody Conceited**

Most people whose names begin with the letter *Z* have gotten used to the fact that others react with surprise when hearing their name. And because *Z* people have had to come to terms with standing out in a crowd, they are almost universally comfortable in their own skins. But what separates the *ZK* names from the other *Z* names is the powerful influence of the aggressive letter *K*—the symbol of forceful action (*kick, kill, king, knight, keen* and *knuckle*). This is why—even though *Z* names almost all belong to women—the *ZK* combination creates names that are exclusively masculine. So if your *ZK* friend perceives himself to be special, there's probably an element of truth to it.

It's hard not to be impressed by a *ZK* when he's in full swing. In his "up" mode he'll work harder than a sharecropper's mule, and even with his nose on the grindstone will manage to have a great time. These are people who march to a different drummer, so you can expect the *ZK* never to do the expected. He's the first in his peer group to adopt new trends, and last to ridicule someone else for coloring outside the lines.

The flipside of the unconventional *ZK* personality is that when he's plumbing the depths of his convoluted nature, it can be nearly impossible to communicate with him. There will also be times when he locks himself inside himself, to journey even deeper into his analytical nature. When this happens, the worst thing you can do is tell him to snap out of it—from his perspective, it's simply another form of self-expression. Left to his own devices he'll soon snap back into his fun-loving mode to reap the fruits of his creative introspection.

Love and marriage in the *ZK*'s world are characterized by passion and even obsession. It seems he can't help pouring his dynamic and moody nature into his relationships—a prospect that can prove alarming to uninitiated partners. But overall, *ZK*s are friendly fellows who like to make the rounds with their tight circle of friends (which invariably includes members of the opposite sex). That's why the best mate for *ZK*s are those incapable of feeling jealousy, and when paired with the right person, *ZK*s will prove loyal, loving and somewhat eccentric lovers. At heart, they are hopeless romantics who are delighted at the prospect of raising children and having families of their own.

**Zachariah
Zachary
Zack
Zechariah**

Zachary Taylor Zachary Taylor, the twelfth President of the United States, was born in 1784. A career soldier with little formal education, Zachary served as President for less than five hundred days and died in office before he could resolve any of the great issues of his day. ■ In the 1840s, there was a great deal of talk about a looming civil war, and Zachary, a slaveholder himself, was firmly on the side of preserving the Union. ■ There was also fear that the Texas militia would chase the U.S. army out of Santa Fe, but since Zachary was a man with an intimate knowledge of war, people respected his threat to use maximum force, and an uneasy peace reigned. ■ After Zachary's death in 1850, the country plunged into its bloody civil war.

NAMES
INDEX

Alvie *see*	AV	Andree *see*	AND	Antione *see*	ANT	Armani *see*	ARN	Augustus *see*	AG
Alvin *see*	AV	Andrei *see*	AND	Antionette *see*	ANT	Armanti *see*	ARN	Aundrea *see*	AND
Alvina *see*	AV	Andrej *see*	AND	Antoine *see*	ANT	Arminda *see*	AMD	Aurea *see*	AR
Alvis *see*	AV	Andres *see*	AND	Antoinette *see*	ANT	Armon *see*	ARN	Aurelio *see*	AR
Alwin *see*	AL	Andrew *see*	AND	Anton *see*	ANT	Armondo *see*	ARN	Aurelius *see*	AR
Alyce *see*	ALS	Andria *see*	AND	Antone *see*	ANT	Arnaldo *see*	ARN	Aurora *see*	AR
Alycia *see*	ALS	Andy *see*	AND	Antonetta *see*	ANT	Arne *see*	ARN	Austen *see*	AN
Alyn *see*	ALN	Anestes *see*	AN	Antonette *see*	ANT	Arnie *see*	ARN	Austin *see*	AN
Alysa *see*	ALS	Anette *see*	ANT	Antonia *see*	ANT	Arno *see*	ARN	Auston *see*	AN
Alyse *see*	ALS	Aneurin *see*	AN	Antonietta *see*	ANT	Arnold *see*	ARN	Austyn *see*	AN
Alysha *see*	ALS	Angel *see*	ANG	Antonina *see*	ANT	Arnoldo *see*	ARN	Ava *see*	AV
Alysia *see*	ALS	Angela *see*	ANG	Antonio *see*	ANT	Arnulfo *see*	ARN	Avedig *see*	AV
Alyson *see*	ALS	Angele *see*	ANG	Antony *see*	ANT	Aro *see*	AR	Avel *see*	AV
Alyssa *see*	ALS	Angelena *see*	ANG	Antwan *see*	ANT	Aron *see*	ARN	Averil *see*	AV
Amadeus *see*	AMD	Angelia *see*	ANG	Antwon *see*	ANT	Arri *see*	AR	Avery *see*	AV
Amadis *see*	AMD	Angelica *see*	ANG	Anurag *see*	AN	Arron *see*	ARN	Avi *see*	AV
Amado *see*	AMD	Angelina *see*	ANG	Anya *see*	AN	Arslan *see*	ARN	Avis *see*	AV
Amal *see*	AML	Angeline *see*	ANG	Anzhel *see*	AN	Art *see*	AR	Avraham *see*	AV
Amalia *see*	AML	Angelique *see*	ANG	Aodh *see*	AD	Arte *see*	AR	Avril *see*	AV
Amanda *see*	AMD	Angelita *see*	ANG	April *see*	AL	Artemis *see*	AR	Axel *see*	AL
Amani *see*	AM	Angella *see*	ANG	Apryl *see*	AL	Arther *see*	ARTH	Ayana *see*	AN
Amar *see*	AM	Angelo *see*	ANG	Ar *see*	AR	Arthur *see*	ARTH	Ayanna *see*	AN
Amara *see*	AM	Angelyn *see*	ANG	Araceli *see*	AR	Arthuro *see*	ARTH	Ayden *see*	AD
Amari *see*	AM	Anghared *see*	ANG	Aracely *see*	AR	Artie *see*	AR	Ayla *see*	AL
Amarion *see*	AM	Angie *see*	ANG	Archer *see*	ARCH	Artin *see*	AR	Aylin *see*	ALN
Amaya *see*	AM	Angila *see*	ANG	Archibald *see*	ARCH	Artis *see*	AR	Aylwin *see*	ALN
Amber *see*	AMBR	Angla *see*	ANG	Archie *see*	ARCH	Artur *see*	AR		
Ambrose *see*	AMBR	Angle *see*	ANG	Archy *see*	ARCH	Arturo *see*	AR	Baby *see*	BB
Ameer *see*	AM	Anglea *see*	ANG	Arcy *see*	AR	Arun *see*	ARN	Bailee *see*	BL
Amela *see*	AML	Angus *see*	ANG	Arden *see*	AR	Arvid *see*	AV	Bailey *see*	BL
Amelia *see*	AML	Anh *see*	AN	Ardon *see*	AR	Aryana *see*	ARN	Bal *see*	BL
Ameni *see*	AM	Anibal *see*	ANBL	Are *see*	AR	Aryanna *see*	ARN	Baldric *see*	BL
America *see*	AM	Anika *see*	AN	Aref *see*	AR	Ash *see*	ASH	Baldwin *see*	BL
Ami *see*	AM	Aniol *see*	AN	Areli *see*	AR	Ashanti *see*	ASH	Balthazar *see*	BL
Amie *see*	AM	Anissa *see*	AN	Arely *see*	AR	Ashely *see*	ASH	Balto *see*	BL
Amiel *see*	AM	Anita *see*	ANT	Aren *see*	ARN	Asher *see*	ASH	Bambi *see*	BB
Amin *see*	AM	Anitra *see*	ANT	Arend *see*	ARN	Ashish *see*	ASH	Bane *see*	BN
Amina *see*	AM	Aniya *see*	AN	Ares *see*	AR	Ashlee *see*	ASH	Barabara *see*	BRBR
Amir *see*	AM	Aniyah *see*	AN	Aretha *see*	ARTH	Ashleigh *see*	ASH	Barb *see*	BB
Amira *see*	AM	Anjali *see*	AN	Ari *see*	AR	Ashley *see*	ASH	Barbar *see*	BRBR
Amit *see*	AM	Anjanette *see*	ANG	Aria *see*	AR	Ashli *see*	ASH	Barbara *see*	BRBR
Amlan *see*	AML	Anjelica *see*	ANG	Arian *see*	ARN	Ashlie *see*	ASH	Barbera *see*	BRBR
Ammar *see*	AM	Anka *see*	AN	Ariana *see*	ARN	Ashlin *see*	ASH	Barbie *see*	BB
Ammie *see*	AM	Ann *see*	AN	Ariane *see*	ARN	Ashly *see*	ASH	Barbra *see*	BRBR
Amon *see*	AM	Anna *see*	AN	Arianna *see*	ARN	Ashlyn *see*	ASH	Bard *see*	BRD
Amos *see*	AM	Annabel *see*	ANBL	Arianne *see*	ARN	Ashlynn *see*	ASH	Bardo *see*	BRD
Amy *see*	AM	Annabella *see*	ANBL	Aric *see*	AR	Ashton *see*	ASH	Bardon *see*	BRD
Amya *see*	AM	Annabelle *see*	ANBL	Ariel *see*	AR	Ashtyn *see*	ASH	Bari *see*	BR
An *see*	AN	Annalise *see*	AN	Arielle *see*	AR	Ashur *see*	ASH	Barn *see*	BRN
Ana *see*	AN	Annamarie *see*	AM	Aries *see*	AR	Aubert *see*	ABR	Barnabas *see*	BRN
Anabel *see*	ANBL	Annan *see*	AN	Arjun *see*	AR	Aubree *see*	ABR	Barnaby *see*	BRN
Anahi *see*	AN	Anne *see*	AN	Arkin *see*	AR	Aubrey *see*	ABR	Barnard *see*	BRN
Anais *see*	AN	Anneliese *see*	AN	Arlean *see*	ARN	Aubrie *see*	ABR	Barney *see*	BRN
Anand *see*	AND	Annemarie *see*	AN	Arleen *see*	ARN	Audie *see*	AD	Barnie *see*	BRN
Anastasia *see*	ANT	Annett *see*	ANT	Arleigh *see*	AR	Audra *see*	ADR	Baron *see*	BRN
Anatole *see*	ANT	Annetta *see*	ANT	Arlen *see*	ARN	Audrey *see*	ADR	Barrett *see*	BRT
Anaya *see*	AN	Annette *see*	ANT	Arlena *see*	ARN	Audric *see*	ADR	Barrie *see*	BR
Andera *see*	AND	Annie *see*	AN	Arlene *see*	ARN	Audrie *see*	ADR	Barron *see*	BRN
Anders *see*	AND	Annika *see*	AN	Arley *see*	AR	Audry *see*	ADR	Barry *see*	BR
Anderson *see*	AND	Annita *see*	ANT	Arline *see*	ARN	Audvard *see*	ADR	Bart *see*	BRT
Andie *see*	AND	Annmarie *see*	AN	Arlyne *see*	ARN	Augie *see*	AG	Bartek *see*	BRT
Andra *see*	AND	Anouk *see*	AN	Arman *see*	ARN	August *see*	AG	Bartholo *see*	BRT
Andre *see*	AND	Anselm *see*	AN	Armand *see*	AMD	Augusta *see*	AG	Bartholomew *see*	BRT
Andrea *see*	AND	Ansley *see*	AN	Armanda *see*	AMD	Augustin *see*	AG	Bartholomieu *see*	BRT
Andreas *see*	AND	Anthony *see*	ANT	Armando *see*	AMD	Augustine *see*	AG	Bartolomiy *see*	BRT

438

Name	See	Name	See	Name	See	Name	See	Name	See
Barton see	BRT	Bertok see	BRT	Bond see	BN	Brennon see	BRN	Bryson see	BRS
Bartram see	BRT	Bertram see	BRT	Bondi see	BN	Brent see	BRT	Bubba see	BB
Basham see	BS	Bertrand see	BRT	Bonita see	BN	Brenton see	BRT	Buck see	BK
Basil see	BS	Beryl see	BR	Bonito see	BN	Breonna see	BRN	Buckminster see	BK
Basilio see	BS	Bess see	BS	Bonnie see	BN	Bret see	BRT	Bucky see	BK
Bastian see	BS	Bessie see	BS	Bonny see	BN	Brett see	BRT	Bud see	BD
Bastien see	BS	Beth see	BTH	Booker see	BK	Bria see	BR	Buddy see	BD
Baudouin see	BD	Bethany see	BTH	Bor see	BR	Brian see	BRN	Buena see	BN
Baul see	BL	Betsey see	BT	Borg see	BR	Briana see	BRN	Buffy see	BF
Bavol see	BV	Betsy see	BT	Boria see	BR	Brianna see	BRN	Buford see	BF
Bay see	B	Bette see	BT	Boris see	BRS	Brianne see	BRN	Bula see	BL
Baylee see	BL	Bettie see	BT	Botan see	BT	Briar see	BR	Bunny see	BN
Bayley see	BL	Bettina see	BT	Bour see	BR	Brice see	BRS	Burian see	BRN
Bea see	B	Betty see	BT	Bowle see	BL	Bridget see	BRD	Burl see	BL
Beatrice see	BT	Bettye see	BT	Boyce see	BS	Bridgett see	BRD	Burne see	BRN
Beatriz see	BT	Beula see	BL	Boyd see	BD	Bridgette see	BRD	Burr see	BR
Beau see	B	Beulah see	BL	Boyu see	B	Brielle see	BR	Burt see	BRT
Bebe see	BB	Bev see	BV	Brad see	BRD	Brigette see	BRD	Burton see	BRT
Beck see	BK	Beverley see	BV	Bradburn see	BRD	Brigid see	BRD	Buster see	BT
Becki see	BK	Beverly see	BV	Braden see	BRD	Brigitte see	BRD	Butch see	BT
Beckie see	BK	Bevis see	BV	Bradford see	BRD	Brinda see	BRND	Byrn see	BRN
Becky see	BK	Beyonce see	BN	Bradlee see	BRD	Brionna see	BRN	Byron see	BRN
Beldon see	BL	Bhanu see	BN	Bradley see	BRD	Brisa see	BRS		
Belen see	BL	Bhaven see	BV	Bradly see	BRD	Britany see	BRT	Caddy see	CD
Belia see	BL	Bheki see	BK	Bradshaw see	BRD	Britney see	BRT	Cade see	CD
Belinda see	BD	Bialy see	BL	Brady see	BRD	Britni see	BRT	Cadel see	CD
Bell see	BL	Bianca see	BN	Bradyn see	BRD	Britt see	BRT	Caden see	CD
Bella see	BL	Bibi see	BB	Braeden see	BRD	Britta see	BRT	Cadence see	CD
Belle see	BL	Bienvenido see	BV	Braedon see	BRD	Brittaney see	BRT	Cadfael see	CD
Bello see	BL	Bilal see	BL	Braiden see	BRD	Brittani see	BRT	Cadwallader see	CD
Beltran see	BL	Bildad see	BL	Brain see	BRN	Brittanie see	BRT	Cael see	CL
Ben see	BN	Bill see	BL	Branda see	BRND	Brittany see	BRT	Caesar see	CS
Benedict see	BN	Billi see	BL	Brandan see	BRND	Brittney see	BRT	Caiden see	CD
Benita see	BN	Billie see	BL	Brande see	BRND	Brittni see	BRT	Cain see	CN
Benito see	BN	Billy see	BL	Brandee see	BRND	Brittny see	BRT	Caitlin see	KTLN
Benjamin see	BN	Bily see	BL	Brandeis see	BRND	Broc see	BRK	Caitlyn see	KTLN
Benji see	BN	Bing see	BN	Branden see	BRND	Brock see	BRK	Caitlynn see	KTLN
Bennett see	BN	Binyong see	BN	Brandi see	BRND	Broderick see	BRD	Caius see	CS
Bennie see	BN	Birdie see	BRD	Brandie see	BRND	Brodie see	BRD	Cal see	CL
Benny see	BN	Bjorn see	BN	Brandon see	BRND	Brodney see	BRD	Calder see	CLD
Benoit see	BN	Blaine see	BL	Brandt see	BRNT	Brody see	BRD	Cale see	CL
Bent see	BN	Blair see	BL	Brandy see	BRND	Bronson see	BRN	Caleb see	CB
Bentley see	BN	Blaise see	BL	Brandyn see	BRND	Brook see	BRK	Caleigh see	CL
Benton see	BN	Blake see	BL	Brannible see	BRN	Brooke see	BRK	Cali see	CL
Berenice see	BRN	Blanca see	BL	Brannon see	BRN	Brooklyn see	BRK	Calista see	CLT
Berna see	BRN	Blanch see	BL	Branson see	BRN	Brooklynn see	BRK	Callen see	CLN
Bernabe see	BRN	Blanche see	BL	Brant see	BRT	Brooks see	BRK	Callie see	CL
Bernadette see	BRND	Blane see	BN	Braulio see	BR	Brown see	BRN	Callum see	CL
Bernadine see	BRND	Blaze see	BL	Braxton see	BT	Browning see	BRN	Calo see	CL
Bernal see	BRN	Bo see	B	Brayan see	BRN	Bruce see	BRS	Calum see	CL
Bernard see	BRND	Bob see	BB	Brayden see	BRD	Bruin see	BRN	Calut see	CLT
Bernarda see	BRND	Boba see	BB	Braydon see	BRD	Bruna see	BRN	Calv see	CL
Bernardo see	BRND	Bobbi see	BB	Breana see	BRN	Brunilda see	BRND	Calvin see	CLN
Bernetta see	BRT	Bobbie see	BB	Breann see	BRN	Bruno see	BRN	Camelia see	CML
Bernhard see	BRND	Bobby see	BB	Breanna see	BRN	Bruns see	BRN	Camellia see	CML
Bernice see	BRN	Bobbye see	BB	Breanne see	BRN	Bryan see	BRN	Camerino see	CMRN
Bernie see	BRN	Bobush see	BB	Bree see	BR	Bryana see	BRN	Cameron see	CMRN
Berniece see	BRN	Bodaway see	BD	Brencis see	BRS	Bryanna see	BRN	Camila see	CML
Bernita see	BRT	Boddu see	BD	Brenda see	BRND	Bryant see	BRT	Camilla see	CML
Berry see	BR	Bodi see	BD	Brendan see	BRND	Bryce see	BRS	Camille see	CML
Bert see	BRT	Bodie see	BD	Brenden see	BRND	Brycen see	BRS	Camren see	CMRN
Berta see	BRT	Bodog see	BD	Brendon see	BRND	Bryne see	BRN	Camron see	CMRN
Bertha see	BTH	Bogdan see	BD	Brenna see	BRN	Brynn see	BRN	Camryn see	CMRN
Bertie see	BRT	Bohdan see	BD	Brennan see	BRN	Bryon see	BRN	Can see	CN
Bertin see	BRT	Bolie see	BL	Brennen see	BRN	Bryrony see	BRN	Candace see	CND

Cole *see*	CL
Coleen *see*	CLN
Coleman *see*	CLN
Colene *see*	CLN
Colette *see*	CLT
Colin *see*	CLN
Colleen *see*	CLN
Collen *see*	CLN
Collene *see*	CLN
Collette *see*	CLT
Collin *see*	CLN
Collins *see*	CLN
Colman *see*	CLN
Colon *see*	CLN
Colt *see*	CLT
Colten *see*	CLT
Colter *see*	CLT
Colton *see*	CLT
Columbus *see*	CL
Conan *see*	CN
Conley *see*	CN
Connaire *see*	CN
Conner *see*	CN
Connie *see*	CN
Connor *see*	CN
Conor *see*	CN
Conrad *see*	CD
Constance *see*	CN
Constantin *see*	CN
Constantinos *see*	CN
Consuelo *see*	CN
Cora *see*	CR
Coral *see*	CRL
Coralee *see*	CRL
Corbin *see*	CRN
Cordelia *see*	CD
Cordell *see*	CD
Coreen *see*	CRN
Corene *see*	CRN
Corey *see*	CR
Cori *see*	CR
Corie *see*	CR
Corina *see*	CRN
Corine *see*	CRN
Corinna *see*	CRN
Corinne *see*	CRN
Corky *see*	CK
Corliss *see*	CRL
Cornelia *see*	CN
Cornelius *see*	CN
Cornell *see*	CN
Corrie *see*	CR
Corrin *see*	CRN
Corrina *see*	CRN
Corrine *see*	CRN
Corrinne *see*	CRN
Cort *see*	CRT
Cortez *see*	CRT
Cortney *see*	CRT
Corwin *see*	CRN
Cory *see*	CR
Court *see*	CRT
Courtney *see*	CRT
Craig *see*	CRG
Creighton *see*	CRT
Creola *see*	CRL
Cris *see*	CHRS
Crispin *see*	CR
Crispus *see*	CR
Crissy *see*	CHRS
Cristal *see*	CRT
Cristi *see*	CHRS
Cristian *see*	CHRS
Cristie *see*	CHRS
Cristin *see*	CHRS
Cristina *see*	CHRS
Cristine *see*	CHRS
Cristobal *see*	CHRS
Cristopher *see*	CHRS
Cristy *see*	CHRS
Crystal *see*	CRT
Crystle *see*	CRT
Cullen *see*	CLN
Curly *see*	CRL
Curran *see*	CRN
Curt *see*	CRT
Curtis *see*	CRT
Curtiss *see*	CRT
Cuthbert *see*	CTH
Cyndi *see*	SND
Cyndy *see*	SND
Cynthia *see*	CNTH
Cyrek *see*	CK
Cyril *see*	CRL
Cyrill *see*	CRL
Cyrus *see*	CR
D'arcy *see*	DRS
Dabid *see*	DB
Dabney *see*	DB
Dacey *see*	DS
Dafne *see*	DN
Dain *see*	DN
Daina *see*	DN
Daisey *see*	DS
Daisuke *see*	DS
Daisy *see*	DS
Dak *see*	DK
Dakota *see*	DK
Dakotah *see*	DK
Dal *see*	DL
Dalal *see*	DL
Dale *see*	DL
Dalene *see*	DLN
Daley *see*	DL
Dali *see*	DL
Dalia *see*	DL
Dalila *see*	DL
Dallas *see*	DL
Dallin *see*	DLN
Dalton *see*	DLN
Damaris *see*	DM
Dame *see*	DM
Damek *see*	DM
Dameon *see*	DMN
Damian *see*	DMN
Damien *see*	DMN
Damion *see*	DMN
Damon *see*	DMN
Damondraos *see*	DMN
Dan *see*	DN
Dana *see*	DN
Danae *see*	DN
Dandre *see*	DN
Dandy *see*	DN
Dane *see*	DN
Danelle *see*	DNL
Danette *see*	DN
Dangelo *see*	DNL
Dani *see*	DN
Dania *see*	DN
Danial *see*	DNL
Danica *see*	DK
Daniel *see*	DNL
Daniela *see*	DNL
Daniele *see*	DNL
Danielek *see*	DNL
Daniell *see*	DNL
Daniella *see*	DNL
Danielle *see*	DNL
Daniil *see*	DNL
Danille *see*	DNL
Danilo *see*	DNL
Danita *see*	DN
Danko *see*	DN
Danne *see*	DN
Dannie *see*	DNL
Dannielle *see*	DNL
Danny *see*	DN
Dante *see*	DN
Danyaal *see*	DNL
Danyel *see*	DNL
Danyell *see*	DNL
Danyelle *see*	DNL
Danylko *see*	DNL
Danyon *see*	DN
Daphne *see*	DN
Daquan *see*	DK
Dara *see*	DR
Darby *see*	DB
Darci *see*	DRS
Darcie *see*	DRS
Darcy *see*	DRS
Darell *see*	DRL
Daren *see*	DRN
Daria *see*	DR
Darian *see*	DRN
Darien *see*	DRN
Darin *see*	DRN
Dario *see*	DR
Darion *see*	DRN
Darius *see*	DRS
Darl *see*	DRL
Darla *see*	DRL
Darleen *see*	DRN
Darlena *see*	DRN
Darlene *see*	DRN
Darlin *see*	DRL
Darline *see*	DRN
Darling *see*	DRL
Darnell *see*	DRN
Darold *see*	DRL
Daron *see*	DRN
Darr *see*	DR
Darrel *see*	DRL
Darrell *see*	DRL
Darren *see*	DRN
Darrian *see*	DRN
Darrick *see*	DK
Darrien *see*	DRN
Darrin *see*	DRN
Darrion *see*	DRN
Darrius *see*	DRS
Darron *see*	DRN
Darryl *see*	DRL
Darwin *see*	DRN
Daryl *see*	DRL
Daryle *see*	DRL
Dashawn *see*	DS
Dasia *see*	DS
Dave *see*	DV
Davey *see*	DV
David *see*	DV
Davida *see*	DV
Davidde *see*	DV
Davidek *see*	DV
Davin *see*	DV
Davina *see*	DV
Davion *see*	DV
Davis *see*	DV
Davon *see*	DV
Davonte *see*	DV
Davy *see*	DV
Dawayne *see*	DN
Dawid *see*	DW
Dawn *see*	DW
Dawna *see*	DW
Dawne *see*	DW
Dawson *see*	DW
Dayana *see*	DN
Dayle *see*	DL
Dayna *see*	DN
Daysi *see*	DS
Dean *see*	DN
Deana *see*	DN
Deandre *see*	DD
Deane *see*	DN
Deangelo *see*	DN
Deann *see*	DN
Deanna *see*	DN
Deanne *see*	DN
Deasia *see*	DS
Deb *see*	DB
Debbi *see*	DB
Debbie *see*	DB
Debbra *see*	DB
Debby *see*	DB
Debi *see*	DB
Debora *see*	DB
Deborah *see*	DB
Debra *see*	DB
Debrah *see*	DB
Debroah *see*	DB
Decker *see*	DK
Declan *see*	DK
Dede *see*	DD
Dederick *see*	DK
Dedra *see*	DD
Dedric *see*	DK
Dedrick *see*	DK
Dee *see*	DD
Dee Dee *see*	DD
Deeann *see*	DN
Deena *see*	DN
Deepak *see*	DK
Deidra *see*	DD
Deidre *see*	DD
Deion *see*	DN
Deirdre *see*	DD
Del *see*	DL
Del-Mar *see*	DM
Delaine *see*	DLN
Delana *see*	DLN
Delaney *see*	DLN
Delano *see*	DLN
Delbert *see*	DB
Delena *see*	DLN
Delfina *see*	DLN
Delia *see*	DL
Delila *see*	DL
Delilah *see*	DL
Dell *see*	DL
Della *see*	DL
Delma *see*	DM
Delmar *see*	DM
Delmore *see*	DM
Delois *see*	DL
Deloras *see*	DL
Delores *see*	DL
Deloris *see*	DL
Delorse *see*	DL
Delphine *see*	DLN
Delton *see*	DL
Delvin *see*	DV
Demarco *see*	DM
Demarcus *see*	DM
Demario *see*	DM
Demetria *see*	DM
Demetris *see*	DM
Demetrius *see*	DM
Demi *see*	DM
Demond *see*	DMN
Demothi *see*	DM
Demyan *see*	DM
Den *see*	DN
Dena *see*	DN
Dene *see*	DN
Deneen *see*	DN
Denes *see*	DNS
Denese *see*	DNS
Denholm *see*	DN
Denice *see*	DNS
Denis *see*	DNS
Denise *see*	DNS
Denisse *see*	DNS
Deniz *see*	DNS
Denna *see*	DN
Dennie *see*	DN
Dennis *see*	DNS
Dennise *see*	DNS
Denny *see*	DN
Denton *see*	DN
Denver *see*	DN
Denys *see*	DNS
Denyse *see*	DNS

Denzel *see*	DNS	Dillon *see*	DLN	Donte *see*	DN	Dylan *see*	DLN	Eleanora *see*	ELN
Denzil *see*	DNS	Dillwyn *see*	DLN	Donya *see*	DN	Dylanne *see*	DLN	Eleanore *see*	ELN
Deon *see*	DN	Dilwyn *see*	DLN	Dora *see*	DR	Dyllan *see*	DLN	Elease *see*	ELS
Deondre *see*	DN	Dimitri *see*	DM	Doreen *see*	DRN	Dylon *see*	DLN	Elena *see*	ELN
Deonte *see*	DN	Dimitrius *see*	DM	Dorene *see*	DRN	Dyre *see*	DR	Elene *see*	ELN
Dequan *see*	DK	Dimo *see*	DM	Doretha *see*	DTH			Elenor *see*	ELN
Dereck *see*	DK	Dina *see*	DN	Doria *see*	DR	Eamon *see*	EM	Elenora *see*	ELN
Derek *see*	DK	Dinah *see*	DN	Dorian *see*	DRN	Eamonn *see*	EM	Elenore *see*	ELN
Derick *see*	DK	Dino *see*	DN	Dorinda *see*	DRN	Ean *see*	EN	Eleonor *see*	ELN
Derik *see*	DK	Dion *see*	DN	Dorine *see*	DRN	Earl *see*	ERL	Eleonora *see*	ELN
Deron *see*	DRN	Dione *see*	DN	Doris *see*	DRS	Earle *see*	ERL	Eleonore *see*	ELN
Derrek *see*	DK	Dionna *see*	DN	Dorla *see*	DRL	Earlene *see*	ERL	Eli *see*	EL
Derrell *see*	DRL	Dionne *see*	DN	Dorotha *see*	DTH	Earline *see*	ERL	Elia *see*	EL
Derrick *see*	DK	Dionte *see*	DN	Dorothea *see*	DTH	Earnest *see*	ERN	Elian *see*	ELN
Derwin *see*	DW	Dionys *see*	DN	Dorothy *see*	DTH	Earnestine *see*	ERN	Eliana *see*	ELN
Derya *see*	DR	Direk *see*	DK	Dorrell *see*	DRL	Eartha *see*	ETH	Elias *see*	ELS
Deryck *see*	DK	Dirk *see*	DK	Dorris *see*	DRS	Ed *see*	ED	Eliezer *see*	ELZ
Deshaun *see*	DS	Divinia *see*	DV	Dorsey *see*	DRS	Eda *see*	ED	Elijah *see*	EL
Deshawn *see*	DS	Dmitriy *see*	DM	Dortha *see*	DTH	Edda *see*	ED	Elin *see*	ELN
Desirae *see*	DS	Dob *see*	DB	Dorthea *see*	DTH	Eddie *see*	ED	Elina *see*	ELN
Desire *see*	DS	Dobbs *see*	DB	Dorthey *see*	DTH	Eddy *see*	ED	Elinor *see*	ELN
Desiree *see*	DS	Dobie *see*	DB	Dorthy *see*	DTH	Eden *see*	EDN	Elinore *see*	ELN
Desmond *see*	DMN	Dobry *see*	DB	Doug *see*	DG	Edgar *see*	ED	Elisa *see*	ELS
Dessie *see*	DS	Doby *see*	DB	Dougie *see*	DG	Edgardo *see*	ED	Elisabeth *see*	ELZ
Destin *see*	DST	Dodge *see*	DD	Douglas *see*	DG	Edgars *see*	ED	Elise *see*	ELS
Destinee *see*	DST	Dolan *see*	DLN	Douglass *see*	DG	Edie *see*	ED	Eliseo *see*	ELS
Destiney *see*	DST	Dollie *see*	DL	Dovie *see*	DV	Edison *see*	EDN	Elisha *see*	ELS
Destini *see*	DST	Dolly *see*	DL	Doyle *see*	DL	Edith *see*	ED	Elissa *see*	ELS
Destiny *see*	DST	Dolores *see*	DL	Drake *see*	DK	Edko *see*	ED	Eliza *see*	ELZ
Devan *see*	DV	Doloris *see*	DL	Draven *see*	DV	Edlin *see*	EDN	Elizabeth *see*	ELZ
Devante *see*	DV	Dom *see*	DM	Drew *see*	DR	Edmon *see*	EDN	Elizbeth *see*	ELZ
Deven *see*	DV	Domenic *see*	DMN	Dru *see*	DR	Edmond *see*	EDN	Elizebeth *see*	ELZ
Devin *see*	DV	Domenica *see*	DMN	Dryden *see*	DD	Edmund *see*	EDN	Ella *see*	EL
Devon *see*	DV	Dominga *see*	DMN	Duane *see*	DN	Edmundo *see*	EDN	Ellan *see*	ELN
Devona *see*	DV	Domingo *see*	DMN	Dud *see*	DD	Edmundson *see*	EDN	Elle *see*	EL
Devonta *see*	DV	Dominic *see*	DMN	Duddley *see*	DD	Edna *see*	EDN	Ellen *see*	ELN
Devontae *see*	DV	Dominica *see*	DMN	Dude *see*	DD	Edo *see*	ED	Ellena *see*	ELN
Devonte *see*	DV	Dominick *see*	DMN	Dudley *see*	DD	Eduard *see*	ED	Ellie *see*	EL
Devora *see*	DV	Dominik *see*	DMN	Dug *see*	DG	Eduardo *see*	ED	Elliot *see*	ELT
Devyn *see*	DV	Dominique *see*	DMN	Duig *see*	DG	Edward *see*	EDW	Elliott *see*	ELT
Dewayne *see*	DW	Dominque *see*	DMN	Dukarai *see*	DK	Edwardo *see*	EDW	Ellis *see*	ELS
Dewey *see*	DW	Domonique *see*	DMN	Duke *see*	DK	Edwin *see*	EDW	Ellwood *see*	EL
Dewitt *see*	DW	Domuel *see*	DM	Dulce *see*	DL	Edwina *see*	EDW	Ellyn *see*	ELN
Diamond *see*	DMN	Don *see*	DN	Dumaka *see*	DK	Edyth *see*	ED	Elma *see*	EL
Dian *see*	DN	Dona *see*	DN	Duman *see*	DMN	Edythe *see*	ED	Elmar *see*	EL
Diana *see*	DN	Donahue *see*	DN	Dunc *see*	DK	Eileen *see*	ELN	Elmer *see*	EL
Diane *see*	DN	Donald *see*	DNL	Duncan *see*	DK	Eilene *see*	ELN	Elmien *see*	ELN
Diann *see*	DN	Donaldo *see*	DNL	Dunk *see*	DK	Einar *see*	EN	Elmira *see*	EL
Dianna *see*	DN	Donalt *see*	DNL	Duran *see*	DRN	Eiran *see*	ERN	Elmo *see*	EL
Dianne *see*	DN	Donavan *see*	DV	Durand *see*	DRN	Ela *see*	EL	Elna *see*	ELN
Dick *see*	DK	Donavon *see*	DV	Durriken *see*	DK	Eladio *see*	EL	Elnora *see*	ELN
Dickens *see*	DK	Donella *see*	DNL	Durril *see*	DRL	Elaina *see*	ELN	Elof *see*	EL
Dickie *see*	DK	Donita *see*	DN	Dusten *see*	DST	Elaine *see*	ELN	Elois *see*	ELS
Dickson *see*	DK	Donley *see*	DNL	Dustin *see*	DST	Elan *see*	ELN	Eloisa *see*	ELS
Dicky *see*	DK	Donn *see*	DN	Dusty *see*	DST	Elana *see*	ELN	Eloise *see*	ELS
Dicta *see*	DK	Donna *see*	DN	Duwayne *see*	DN	Elane *see*	ELN	Elouise *see*	ELS
Diederich *see*	DD	Donnell *see*	DNL	Dwain *see*	DW	Elanor *see*	ELN	Eloy *see*	EL
Diego *see*	DG	Donnelly *see*	DNL	Dwaine *see*	DN	Elayne *see*	ELN	Elrad *see*	EL
Digby *see*	DG	Donnie *see*	DN	Dwana *see*	DW	Elba *see*	EL	Elroy *see*	EL
Diggory *see*	DG	Donny *see*	DN	Dwane *see*	DW	Elbert *see*	ELT	Elsa *see*	ELS
Diglio *see*	DG	Donohue *see*	DN	Dwayne *see*	DW	Eldad *see*	EL	Else *see*	ELS
Dilbert *see*	DB	Donovan *see*	DV	Dwight *see*	DW	Elden *see*	ELN	Elsie *see*	ELS
Dillan *see*	DLN	Donovon *see*	DV	Dyami *see*	DM	Eldon *see*	ELN	Elsu *see*	EL
Dillard *see*	DL	Donta *see*	DN	Dyan *see*	DN	Eldridge *see*	ED	Elton *see*	ELT
Dillion *see*	DLN	Dontae *see*	DN	Dyl *see*	DL	Eleanor *see*	ELN	Elva *see*	EV

Elvera *see*	EV	Erskin *see*	ERK	Fabio *see*	FB	Flip *see*	FL	Freida *see*	FRD
Elvia *see*	EV	Ervin *see*	ERN	Fabiola *see*	FB	Flo *see*	FL	Frida *see*	FRD
Elvin *see*	EV	Erwin *see*	ERN	Fairleigh *see*	FL	Flora *see*	FL	Frieda *see*	FRD
Elvira *see*	EV	Eryn *see*	ERN	Faith *see*	FTH	Florance *see*	FL	Frits *see*	FR
Elvis *see*	EV	Esmeralda *see*	EML	Fallon *see*	FL	Florence *see*	FL	Fritz *see*	FR
Elwood *see*	EL	Esra *see*	EZ	Fan *see*	FN	Florencia *see*	FL	Fulton *see*	FL
Ely *see*	EL	Esteban *see*	EST	Fannie *see*	FN	Florencio *see*	FL	Fynn *see*	FL
Elyse *see*	ELS	Estefania *see*	EST	Fanny *see*	FN	Florene *see*	FL		
Elyssa *see*	ELS	Estefany *see*	EST	Fareed *see*	FRD	Florentino *see*	FL	Gabby *see*	GB
Ema *see*	EM	Estela *see*	EST	Farhad *see*	FRD	Florian *see*	FL	Gabe *see*	GB
Eman *see*	EM	Estell *see*	EST	Faron *see*	FRN	Florida *see*	FL	Gabriel *see*	GB
Emanuel *see*	EML	Estella *see*	EST	Farrah *see*	FR	Florine *see*	FL	Gabriela *see*	GB
Emelia *see*	EML	Estelle *see*	EST	Farrell *see*	FR	Flossie *see*	FL	Gabriele *see*	GB
Emely *see*	EML	Ester *see*	EST	Farris *see*	FR	Floyd *see*	FL	Gabriella *see*	GB
Emerald *see*	EML	Estevan *see*	EST	Faruk *see*	FR	Flynn *see*	FL	Gabrielle *see*	GB
Emerson *see*	EM	Esther *see*	ETH	Fawn *see*	FN	Ford *see*	FRD	Gage *see*	G
Emery *see*	EM	Estifano *see*	EST	Fay *see*	FY	Forest *see*	FR	Gaige *see*	G
Emil *see*	EML	Estivido *see*	EST	Faye *see*	FY	Forester *see*	FR	Gail *see*	GL
Emile *see*	EML	Estrella *see*	EST	Federico *see*	FRD	Forrest *see*	FR	Gala *see*	GL
Emilee *see*	EML	Ethan *see*	ETH	Felecia *see*	FL	Forrester *see*	FR	Gale *see*	GL
Emilia *see*	EML	Ethel *see*	ETH	Felica *see*	FL	Fran *see*	FRN	Galen *see*	GLN
Emiliano *see*	EML	Ethelyn *see*	ETH	Felice *see*	FL	Franc *see*	FRN	Galilea *see*	GL
Emilie *see*	EML	Ethen *see*	ETH	Felicia *see*	FL	Frances *see*	FRN	Galina *see*	GLN
Emilio *see*	EML	Ethyl *see*	ETH	Feliciano *see*	FL	Francesca *see*	FRNK	Gallard *see*	GL
Emils *see*	EML	Eugena *see*	UGN	Felicidad *see*	FL	Francesco *see*	FRNK	Galloway *see*	GL
Emily *see*	EML	Eugene *see*	UGN	Felicita *see*	FL	Franchesca *see*	FRN	Galt *see*	GL
Emlyn *see*	EML	Eugenia *see*	UGN	Felicity *see*	FL	Francheska *see*	FRN	Galway *see*	GL
Emma *see*	EM	Eugenie *see*	UGN	Felike *see*	FL	Franchot *see*	FRN	Gamaliel *see*	GL
Emmalee *see*	EML	Eugenio *see*	UGN	Feliks *see*	FL	Francine *see*	FRN	Gannon *see*	GN
Emmanuel *see*	EML	Eula *see*	EL	Felino *see*	FL	Francis *see*	FRN	Gar *see*	GR
Emmeline *see*	EML	Eunice *see*	EN	Felip *see*	FL	Francisca *see*	FRNK	Gardner *see*	GRD
Emmet *see*	EM	Ev *see*	EV	Felipa *see*	FL	Francisco *see*	FRNK	Garek *see*	GR
Emmett *see*	EM	Eva *see*	EV	Felipe *see*	FL	Franco *see*	FRNK	Garemy *see*	GR
Emmitt *see*	EM	Evalyn *see*	EVN	Felippe *see*	FL	Francois *see*	FRN	Garen *see*	GR
Emok *see*	EM	Evan *see*	EVN	Felisa *see*	FL	Francoise *see*	FRN	Gareth *see*	GR
Emory *see*	EM	Evander *see*	EVN	Felisha *see*	FL	Franjo *see*	FRN	Garett *see*	GRT
Eneas *see*	EN	Evangelina *see*	EVN	Felix *see*	FL	Frank *see*	FRNK	Garfield *see*	GR
Enid *see*	ED	Evangeline *see*	EVN	Felton *see*	FL	Frankie *see*	FRNK	Garland *see*	GR
Enli *see*	EN	Eve *see*	EV	Ferdinand *see*	FRD	Franklin *see*	FRNK	Garner *see*	GR
Ennis *see*	EN	Evelia *see*	EV	Ferghus *see*	FR	Franklyn *see*	FRNK	Garnet *see*	GRT
Enoch *see*	EN	Evelin *see*	EVN	Fergus *see*	FR	Franko *see*	FRNK	Garnett *see*	GRT
Enos *see*	EN	Evelina *see*	EVN	Ferguson *see*	FR	Franky *see*	FRNK	Garold *see*	GRD
Enrico *see*	ERK	Eveline *see*	EVN	Feris *see*	FR	Frans *see*	FRN	Garret *see*	GRT
Enrique *see*	ERK	Evelyn *see*	EVN	Fermi *see*	FR	Fransisc *see*	FRN	Garreth *see*	GR
Enyeto *see*	EN	Evelyne *see*	EVN	Fermin *see*	FR	Franz *see*	FRN	Garrett *see*	GRT
Erek *see*	ERK	Evelynn *see*	EVN	Fern *see*	FRN	Fraser *see*	FR	Garrick *see*	GR
Eric *see*	ERK	Everardo *see*	EV	Fernanda *see*	FRD	Frasier *see*	FR	Garrison *see*	GRS
Erica *see*	ERK	Everett *see*	EV	Fernande *see*	FRD	Fred *see*	FRD	Garry *see*	GR
Erich *see*	ERK	Everette *see*	EV	Fernando *see*	FRD	Freda *see*	FRD	Garth *see*	GRT
Erick *see*	ERK	Everhard *see*	EV	Ferris *see*	FR	Fredda *see*	FRD	Gary *see*	GR
Ericka *see*	ERK	Evert *see*	EV	Fidel *see*	FL	Freddie *see*	FRD	Gaston *see*	GS
Erico *see*	ERK	Evette *see*	EV	Filip *see*	FL	Freddy *see*	FRD	Gaurav *see*	GR
Erik *see*	ERK	Evia *see*	EV	Filippo *see*	FL	Frederic *see*	FRD	Gav *see*	GV
Erika *see*	ERK	Evie *see*	EV	Fin *see*	FN	Frederich *see*	FRD	Gaven *see*	GV
Erin *see*	ERN	Evon *see*	EVN	Finbar *see*	FN	Frederick *see*	FRD	Gavin *see*	GV
Erinn *see*	ERN	Evonne *see*	EVN	Fineas *see*	FN	Fredericka *see*	FRD	Gavyn *see*	GV
Erle *see*	ERL	Ewan *see*	EN	Finlay *see*	FN	Fredi *see*	FRD	Gawain *see*	GWN
Erna *see*	ERN	Ezekiel *see*	EZ	Finley *see*	FN	Fredia *see*	FRD	Gawayne *see*	GWN
Ernest *see*	ERN	Ezequiel *see*	EZ	Finn *see*	FN	Fredric *see*	FRD	Gay *see*	G
Ernestina *see*	ERN	Ezer *see*	EZ	Finnegan *see*	FN	Fredrick *see*	FRD	Gaye *see*	G
Ernestine *see*	ERN	Ezhno *see*	EZ	Fiona *see*	FN	Fredricka *see*	FRD	Gayla *see*	GL
Ernesto *see*	ERN	Ezra *see*	EZ	Firth *see*	FTH	Fredrik *see*	FRD	Gayle *see*	GL
Ernie *see*	ERN			Fletch *see*	FL	Fredy *see*	FRD	Gaylene *see*	GLN
Ernst *see*	ERN	Faber *see*	FB	Fletcher *see*	FL	Freeda *see*	FRD	Gayler *see*	GLR
Errol *see*	ERL	Fabian *see*	FB	Flint *see*	FL	Freeman *see*	FRN	Gaylon *see*	GLN

444

Name		Code
Herby	see	HB
Heremias	see	HR
Heri	see	HR
Heriberto	see	HB
Herm	see	HM
Herman	see	HM
Hermann	see	HM
Hermina	see	HM
Hermine	see	HM
Herminia	see	HM
Herminio	see	HM
Hermoine	see	HM
Hermon	see	HM
Hernan	see	HN
Hernando	see	HN
Hero	see	HR
Heronim	see	HR
Herriberto	see	HR
Hersch	see	HR
Herschel	see	HR
Hersh	see	HR
Hershel	see	HR
Herta	see	HT
Hertz	see	HR
Herve	see	HR
Hervey	see	HR
Hester	see	HT
Hettie	see	HT
Hew	see	HW
Hewart	see	HW
Hewes	see	HW
Hewett	see	HW
Hewie	see	HW
Heywood	see	HW
Hiedi	see	HD
Hiermo	see	HR
Hieronym	see	HR
Hieronymos	see	HR
Hilary	see	HL
Hilda	see	HD
Hildegard	see	HG
Hilfredo	see	HL
Hillary	see	HL
Hillel	see	HL
Hilmar	see	HL
Hilton	see	HT
Himanshu	see	HM
Hinko	see	HN
Hinun	see	HN
Hiram	see	HM
Hiromi	see	HR
Hiroshi	see	HR
Hirsch	see	HR
Hirsh	see	HR
Hirus	see	HR
Hob	see	HB
Hobard	see	HB
Hobart	see	HB
Hobbes	see	HB
Hobert	see	HB
Hodge	see	HG
Hodges	see	HG
Hodgkins	see	HG
Hohan	see	HN
Hoibeard	see	HB
Holden	see	HLN
Holic	see	HL
Holleb	see	HL
Holles	see	HL
Holley	see	HL
Holli	see	HL
Hollie	see	HL
Hollings	see	HL
Hollins	see	HL
Hollis	see	HL
Holly	see	HL
Holt	see	HL
Homer	see	HM
Honey	see	HN
Hong	see	HN
Honor	see	HN
Hood	see	HD
Hope	see	HP
Horace	see	HR
Horacio	see	HR
Horatio	see	HR
Horentio	see	HR
Horis	see	HR
Hortense	see	HT
Houman	see	HM
Houston	see	HT
Howard	see	HW
Howel	see	HW
Howell	see	HW
Howi	see	HW
Howie	see	HW
Hoyle	see	HL
Hoyt	see	HT
Hub	see	HB
Hubbard	see	HB
Hubert	see	HB
Huberto	see	HB
Hudson	see	HD
Hugh	see	HG
Hughes	see	HG
Hughie	see	HG
Hugibert	see	HG
Hugo	see	HG
Hulin	see	HLN
Humberto	see	HM
Humfrey	see	HM
Humphrey	see	HM
Hung	see	HN
Hunter	see	HT
Hurley	see	HR
Husain	see	H
Hyman	see	HM
Hywel	see	HW
Ian	see	IN
Ibrahim	see	IM
Iesha	see	IS
Ignacio	see	IN
Ilan	see	IL
Ildefonso	see	IL
Ileana	see	IL
Ilene	see	IL
Iliana	see	IL
Iliia	see	IL
Ilona	see	IL
Ilse	see	IL
Ilya	see	IL
Ima	see	IM
Imani	see	IM
Imanol	see	IM
Imelda	see	IM
Immanuel	see	IM
Immauel	see	IM
Imogene	see	IM
Ina	see	IN
Inderpreet	see	IN
India	see	IN
Indu	see	IN
Inermo	see	IN
Ines	see	IN
Inez	see	IN
Infant	see	IN
Inga	see	IN
Inge	see	IN
Ingemar	see	IN
Ingmar	see	IN
Ingrid	see	IN
Inigo	see	IN
Iniko	see	IN
Inriques	see	IN
Inteus	see	IN
Ioan	see	IN
Ioannes	see	IN
Ioel	see	IL
Iola	see	IL
Iona	see	IN
Ione	see	IN
Ira	see	IR
Ireland	see	IR
Irena	see	IR
Irene	see	IR
Irina	see	IR
Iris	see	IR
Irma	see	IR
Irv	see	IV
Irvin	see	IV
Irvine	see	IV
Irving	see	IV
Irwin	see	IN
Irwyn	see	IN
Isaac	see	ISK
Isaak	see	ISK
Isabel	see	ISBL
Isabela	see	ISBL
Isabell	see	ISBL
Isabella	see	ISBL
Isabelle	see	ISBL
Isac	see	ISK
Isacc	see	ISK
Isai	see	IS
Isaia	see	IS
Isaiah	see	IS
Isaias	see	IS
Isamar	see	IS
Ishmael	see	IS
Isiah	see	IS
Isidro	see	IS
Isis	see	IS
Ismael	see	IS
Isobel	see	ISBL
Israel	see	IS
Isreal	see	IS
Issa	see	IS
Issac	see	ISK
Istran	see	IS
Istu	see	IS
Itzhak	see	ISK
Iva	see	IV
Ivan	see	IV
Ivana	see	IV
Ivanovitch	see	IV
Ivar	see	IV
Ivelisse	see	IV
Ives	see	IV
Ivette	see	IV
Ivon	see	IV
Ivonne	see	IV
Ivory	see	IV
Ivy	see	IV
Iyana	see	IN
Iyanna	see	IN
Izaak	see	ISK
Izabella	see	ISBL
Izraelius	see	ISK
Izrail	see	ISK
Izzie	see	IS
Izzy	see	IS
Jaafar	see	JF
Jaan	see	JN
Jabari	see	JR
Jacalyn	see	JCLN
Jace	see	JS
Jacelyn	see	JCLN
Jacey	see	JS
Jacinta	see	JS
Jacinto	see	JS
Jack	see	JK
Jackeline	see	JK
Jacki	see	JK
Jackie	see	JK
Jacklyn	see	JK
Jackson	see	JK
Jacky	see	JK
Jaclyn	see	JCLN
Jacob	see	JK
Jacoby	see	JK
Jacqualine	see	JCLN
Jacque	see	JK
Jacquelin	see	JCLN
Jacqueline	see	JCLN
Jacquelyn	see	JCLN
Jacquelyne	see	JCLN
Jacquelynn	see	JCLN
Jacques	see	JK
Jacquez	see	JK
Jacquiline	see	JCLN
Jacquline	see	JCLN
Jacqulyn	see	JCLN
Jada	see	JD
Jade	see	JD
Jaden	see	JD
Jadon	see	JD
Jadyn	see	JD
Jae	see	J
Jaeden	see	JD
Jael	see	JL
Jaelyn	see	JLN
Jaheem	see	JM
Jaheim	see	JM
Jahiem	see	JM
Jai	see	J
Jaida	see	JD
Jaiden	see	JD
Jaidyn	see	JD
Jailyn	see	JLN
Jaime	see	JM
Jaimee	see	JM
Jaimie	see	JM
Jairo	see	JR
Jairy	see	JR
Jakayla	see	JK
Jake	see	JK
Jakob	see	JK
Jakobe	see	JK
Jal	see	JL
Jaleel	see	JL
Jalen	see	JLN
Jalisa	see	JL
Jaliyah	see	JL
Jalon	see	JLN
Jalyn	see	JLN
Jalynn	see	JLN
Jama	see	JM
Jamaal	see	JM
Jamal	see	JM
Jamar	see	JM
Jamarcus	see	JM
Jamari	see	JM
Jame	see	JM
Jamee	see	JM
Jamel	see	JM
James	see	JM
Jameson	see	JM
Jamey	see	JM
Jami	see	JM
Jamie	see	JM
Jamil	see	JM
Jamila	see	JM
Jamir	see	JM
Jamison	see	JM
Jammie	see	JM
Jamya	see	JM
Jan	see	JN
Jana	see	JN
Janae	see	JN
Janay	see	JN
Jane	see	JN
Janeen	see	JNN
Janek	see	JK
Janel	see	JN
Janell	see	JN
Janelle	see	JN
Janene	see	JNN
Janessa	see	JNS
Janet	see	JNT
Janett	see	JNT
Janetta	see	JNT
Janette	see	JNT
Janey	see	JN

Janice *see* JNS	Jaylan *see* JLN	Jens *see* JN	Jimena *see* JM	Jones *see* JNS
Janick *see* JK	Jaylen *see* JLN	Jensen *see* JNS	Jimi *see* JM	Joni *see* JN
Janie *see* JN	Jaylene *see* JLN	Jeoffroi *see* JF	Jimmie *see* JM	Jonna *see* JNN
Janiece *see* JNS	Jaylin *see* JLN	Jer *see* JR	Jimmy *see* JM	Jonnie *see* JNN
Janina *see* JNN	Jaylon *see* JLN	Jerad *see* JRD	Jin *see* JN	Jonson *see* JNS
Janine *see* JNN	Jaylyn *see* JLN	Jerald *see* JRD	Jina *see* JN	Jonty *see* JNT
Janis *see* JNS	Jaylynn *see* JLN	Jeraldine *see* JRD	Jiro *see* JR	Joquin *see* JK
Janita *see* JNT	Jayme *see* JM	Jeramie *see* JRM	Jivin *see* JV	Joran *see* JR
Janiya *see* JN	Jaymie *see* JM	Jeramy *see* JRM	Jo *see* J	Jordan *see* JRD
Jann *see* JNN	Jayne *see* JN	Jered *see* JRD	Joan *see* JN	Jorden *see* JRD
Janna *see* JNN	Jayson *see* JSN	Jerel *see* JR	Joana *see* JN	Jordi *see* JRD
Janne *see* JN	Jazlyn *see* JSN	Jereme *see* JRM	Joanie *see* JN	Jordon *see* JRD
Jannet *see* JNT	Jazmin *see* JSN	Jeremey *see* JRM	Joann *see* JNN	Jordy *see* JRD
Jannette *see* JNT	Jazmine *see* JSN	Jeremiah *see* JRM	Joanna *see* JNN	Jordyn *see* JRD
Jannie *see* JN	Jazmyn *see* JSN	Jeremiahm *see* JRM	Joanne *see* JNN	Jorge *see* GRG
Janos *see* JN	Jazmyne *see* JSN	Jeremie *see* JRM	Joaquim *see* JK	Jorgy *see* GRG
Jansen *see* JN	Jean *see* JN	Jeremy *see* JRM	Joaquin *see* JK	Jori *see* JR
Janyce *see* JNS	Jean-Paul *see* JN	Jeri *see* JR	Jocelyn *see* JLN	Jorji *see* GRG
Jaquan *see* JK	Jeana *see* JN	Jerilyn *see* JR	Jodi *see* JD	Jory *see* JR
Jaquelin *see* JK	Jeane *see* JN	Jerm *see* JRM	Jodie *see* JD	Jose *see* JS
Jaqueline *see* JK	Jeanene *see* JNN	Jermaine *see* JRM	Jody *see* JD	Joseef *see* JSF
Jaquez *see* JK	Jeanett *see* JNT	Jermey *see* JRM	Joe *see* J	Josef *see* JSF
Jared *see* JRD	Jeanetta *see* JNT	Jerod *see* JRD	Joeann *see* JNN	Josefa *see* JSF
Jarek *see* JK	Jeanette *see* JNT	Jeroen *see* JR	Joel *see* JL	Josefeno *see* JSF
Jaren *see* JN	Jeanice *see* JNS	Jerold *see* JRD	Joella *see* JL	Josefina *see* JSF
Jaret *see* JR	Jeanie *see* JN	Jerome *see* JRM	Joelle *see* JL	Josefine *see* JSF
Jarett *see* JR	Jeanine *see* JNN	Jeromy *see* JRM	Joellen *see* JLN	Joselyn *see* JSN
Jari *see* JR	Jeanna *see* JNN	Jeronimo *see* JRM	Joerg *see* GRG	Joseph *see* JSF
Jarod *see* JRD	Jeanne *see* JNN	Jerrell *see* JR	Joesph *see* JSF	Josephina *see* JSF
Jaron *see* JN	Jeannetta *see* JNT	Jerri *see* JR	Joey *see* J	Josephine *see* JSF
Jarred *see* JRD	Jeannette *see* JNT	Jerrica *see* JR	Johan *see* JN	Josette *see* JST
Jarrell *see* JR	Jeannie *see* JNN	Jerrie *see* JR	Johana *see* JN	Josh *see* JSH
Jarren *see* JR	Jeannine *see* JNN	Jerrod *see* JRD	Johanan *see* JN	Joshua *see* JSH
Jarrett *see* JRD	Jed *see* JD	Jerrold *see* JRD	Johann *see* JN	Joshuah *see* JSH
Jarrod *see* JRD	Jedediah *see* JD	Jerrome *see* JRM	Johanna *see* JN	Josia *see* JS
Jarvis *see* JV	Jedidiah *see* JD	Jerry *see* JR	Johanne *see* JN	Josiah *see* JSH
Jas *see* JS	Jedrek *see* JK	Jervis *see* JV	Johannes *see* JNS	Josie *see* JS
Jascha *see* JS	Jeeves *see* JV	Jesenia *see* JSN	John *see* JN	Joslyn *see* JSN
Jasen *see* JSN	Jeff *see* JF	Jesica *see* JSK	Johna *see* JN	Josphine *see* JSF
Jasmin *see* JSN	Jefferey *see* JF	Jesito *see* JST	Johnathan *see* JTH	Josue *see* JS
Jasmine *see* JSN	Jeffers *see* JF	Jess *see* JS	Johnathon *see* JTH	Jotham *see* JTH
Jasmyn *see* JSN	Jefferson *see* JF	Jessamie *see* JS	Johnie *see* JN	Jourdan *see* JRD
Jason *see* JSN	Jeffery *see* JF	Jesse *see* JS	Johnna *see* JN	Journey *see* JR
Jasper *see* JS	Jeffrey *see* JF	Jessenia *see* JSN	Johnnie *see* JNN	Jov *see* JV
Jaunita *see* JNT	Jeffry *see* JF	Jessi *see* JS	Johnny *see* JNN	Jovan *see* JV
Javas *see* JV	Jehan *see* JN	Jessia *see* JS	Johnpaul *see* JN	Jovani *see* JV
Javen *see* JV	Jelani *see* JLN	Jessica *see* JSK	Johns *see* JNS	Jovanny *see* JV
Javier *see* JV	Jellow *see* JL	Jessie *see* JS	Johnson *see* JNS	Jovany *see* JV
Javin *see* JV	Jem *see* JM	Jessika *see* JSK	Joi *see* J	Joy *see* J
Javion *see* JV	Jen *see* JN	Jessy *see* JS	Joleen *see* JLN	Joya *see* J
Javis *see* JV	Jena *see* JN	Jestin *see* JST	Jolene *see* JLN	Joyce *see* JS
Javon *see* JV	Jenelle *see* JL	Jestine *see* JST	Jolie *see* JL	Joycelyn *see* JLN
Javonte *see* JV	Jenette *see* JNT	Jesu *see* JS	Joline *see* JLN	Joye *see* J
Jaxon *see* JK	Jenice *see* JNS	Jesus *see* JS	Jolon *see* JLN	Ju *see* J
Jaxson *see* JK	Jenifer *see* JNFR	Jesusa *see* JS	Jolyn *see* JLN	Juan *see* JN
Jay *see* J	Jeniffer *see* JNFR	Jethro *see* JTH	Jolynn *see* JLN	Juana *see* JN
Jayant *see* JNT	Jenine *see* JNN	Jevon *see* JV	Jomar *see* JM	Juanita *see* JNT
Jayce *see* JS	Jenna *see* JNN	Jewel *see* JL	Jon *see* JN	Judah *see* JD
Jaycee *see* JS	Jennefer *see* JNFR	Jewell *see* JL	Jona *see* JN	Judas *see* JD
Jayda *see* JD	Jennette *see* JNT	Ji *see* J	Jonah *see* JN	Judd *see* JD
Jayde *see* JD	Jenni *see* JNN	Jian *see* JN	Jonam *see* JN	Jude *see* JD
Jayden *see* JD	Jennie *see* JNN	Jie *see* J	Jonas *see* JNS	Judi *see* JD
Jaydon *see* JD	Jennifer *see* JNFR	Jill *see* JL	Jonatan *see* JTH	Judie *see* JD
Jaye *see* J	Jenniffer *see* JNFR	Jillian *see* JLN	Jonathan *see* JTH	Judith *see* JD
Jayla *see* JL	Jenny *see* JNN	Jim *see* JM	Jonathon *see* JTH	Judson *see* JD

Judy *see* JD
Jule *see* JL
Julee *see* JL
Julene *see* JLN
Jules *see* JL
Juli *see* JL
Julia *see* JL
Julian *see* JLN
Juliana *see* JLN
Juliane *see* JLN
Juliann *see* JLN
Julianna *see* JLN
Julianne *see* JLN
Julie *see* JL
Julieann *see* JLN
Julien *see* JLN
Julienne *see* JLN
Juliet *see* JLT
Julieta *see* JLT
Julietta *see* JLT
Juliette *see* JLT
Julio *see* JL
Julissa *see* JL
Julius *see* JL
June *see* JN
Junior *see* JN
Junita *see* JNT
Junko *see* JK
Juno *see* JN
Jurgen *see* GRG
Juri *see* JR
Just *see* JST
Justen *see* JST
Justice *see* JST
Justin *see* JST
Justina *see* JST
Justine *see* JST
Justinian *see* JST
Justino *see* JST
Justivo *see* JST
Justo *see* JST
Juston *see* JST
Justus *see* JST
Justyn *see* JST
Juwan *see* JN

KB *see* KB
Kabil *see* KB
Kacey *see* CS
Kaci *see* CS
Kacie *see* CS
Kacy *see* K
Kadin *see* CD
Kadir *see* CD
Kaela *see* KL
Kaelyn *see* KL
Kaenan *see* KN
Kai *see* K
Kaia *see* K
Kaila *see* KL
Kailee *see* KL
Kailey *see* KL
Kailyn *see* KL
Kain *see* KN
Kaine *see* KN
Kait *see* KT
Kaitlin *see* KTLN
Kaitlyn *see* KTLN
Kaitlynn *see* KTLN
Kaiya *see* K
Kala *see* KL
Kalb *see* KL
Kale *see* KL
Kaleb *see* KB
Kaleigh *see* KL
Kalen *see* KL
Kaley *see* KL
Kali *see* KL
Kalie *see* KL
Kalin *see* KL
Kaliyah *see* KL
Kalle *see* KL
Kallie *see* KL
Kalman *see* KL
Kaloosh *see* KL
Kalus *see* KL
Kalvin *see* KVN
Kalyn *see* KL
Kamali *see* KM
Kameron *see* CMRN
Kami *see* KM
Kamil *see* KM
Kamron *see* CMRN
Kamryn *see* CMRN
Kandace *see* KND
Kandi *see* KND
Kandice *see* KND
Kandra *see* KND
Kandy *see* CND
Kane *see* KN
Kanishka *see* KN
Kantu *see* KN
Kara *see* KR
Karan *see* KRN
Kareem *see* KM
Kareen *see* KRN
Karel *see* KRL
Karen *see* KRN
Karena *see* KRN
Karey *see* KR
Kari *see* KR
Karie *see* KR
Karim *see* KR
Karime *see* KR
Karin *see* KRN
Karina *see* KRN
Karine *see* KRN
Karisa *see* KRS
Karissa *see* KRS
Karl *see* KRL
Karla *see* KRL
Karlee *see* KRL
Karley *see* KRL
Karli *see* KRL
Karlie *see* KRL
Karlik *see* KRL
Karly *see* KRL
Karmel *see* KRL
Karol *see* KRL
Karole *see* KRL
Karolek *see* KRL
Karolis *see* KRL
Karoly *see* KRL
Karon *see* KRN
Karren *see* KRN
Karri *see* KR
Karrie *see* KR
Karry *see* KR
Karson *see* KRS
Kary *see* KR
Karyl *see* KRL
Karyn *see* KRN
Kasandra *see* CSNDR
Kasey *see* CS
Kasim *see* CS
Kason *see* CS
Kaspar *see* CS
Kasper *see* CS
Kassandra *see* CSNDR
Kassidy *see* CS
Kassie *see* CS
Kat *see* KT
Katarina *see* KT
Kate *see* KT
Katelin *see* KTLN
Katelyn *see* KTLN
Katelynn *see* KTLN
Katerina *see* KT
Kathaleen *see* KTH
Katharina *see* KTH
Katharine *see* KTH
Katharyn *see* KTH
Kathe *see* KTH
Katheleen *see* KTH
Katherin *see* KTH
Katherina *see* KTH
Katherine *see* KTH
Kathern *see* KTH
Katheryn *see* KTH
Kathey *see* KTH
Kathi *see* KTH
Kathie *see* KTH
Kathleen *see* KTH
Kathlene *see* KTH
Kathline *see* KTH
Kathlyn *see* KTH
Kathrin *see* KTH
Kathrine *see* KTH
Kathryn *see* KTH
Kathryne *see* KTH
Kathy *see* KTH
Kathyrn *see* KTH
Kati *see* KT
Katia *see* KT
Katie *see* KT
Katina *see* KT
Katlin *see* KTLN
Katlyn *see* KTLN
Katlynn *see* KTLN
Katrick *see* KT
Katrina *see* KT
Katsuji *see* KT
Katy *see* KT
Kau *see* K
Kay *see* K
Kaya *see* K
Kaycee *see* K
Kayden *see* CD
Kaye *see* K
Kayin *see* KN
Kayla *see* KL
Kaylah *see* KL
Kaylee *see* KL
Kayleigh *see* KL
Kayley *see* KL
Kayli *see* KL
Kaylie *see* KL
Kaylin *see* KL
Kaylyn *see* KL
Kaylynn *see* KL
Kayne *see* KN
Keagan *see* KN
Kean *see* KN
Keanu *see* KN
Keara *see* KR
Keaton *see* KT
Keegan *see* KN
Keeley *see* KL
Keely *see* KL
Keena *see* KN
Keenan *see* KN
Kegan *see* KN
Keighry *see* KR
Keiko *see* K
Keila *see* KL
Keir *see* KR
Keira *see* KR
Keith *see* KTH
Keitha *see* KTH
Kelash *see* KL
Kelby *see* KB
Kelcey *see* KL
Kelcie *see* KL
Kele *see* KL
Kelemen *see* KL
Keli *see* KL
Kelle *see* KL
Kellee *see* KL
Kellen *see* KL
Kelley *see* KL
Kelli *see* KL
Kellie *see* KL
Kelly *see* KL
Kellye *see* KL
Kelsay *see* KL
Kelsea *see* KL
Kelsey *see* KL
Kelsi *see* KL
Kelsie *see* KL
Kelton *see* KT
Kelvin *see* KVN
Kemberly *see* KMBL
Ken *see* KN
Kena *see* KN
Kenan *see* KN
Kendall *see* KND
Kendra *see* KND
Kendric *see* KND
Kendrick *see* KND
Keneth *see* KTH
Kenia *see* KN
Kenichi *see* KN
Kenji *see* KN
Kenn *see* KN
Kenna *see* KN
Kennedi *see* KND
Kennedy *see* KND
Kenneth *see* KTH
Kenney *see* KN
Kennie *see* KN
Kennith *see* KTH
Kenny *see* KN
Kent *see* KN
Kenton *see* KN
Kenya *see* KN
Kenyatta *see* KN
Kenyon *see* KN
Kenzie *see* KN
Keon *see* KN
Kerby *see* KB
Kerel *see* KR
Kerem *see* KR
Keren *see* KRN
Kerey *see* KR
Keri *see* KR
Kerk *see* KR
Kermit *see* KT
Kern *see* KRN
Kerri *see* KR
Kerrie *see* KR
Kerry *see* KR
Kers *see* KR
Kersen *see* KRS
Kerstin *see* KRST
Kerwin *see* KR
Kesar *see* KS
Keshaun *see* KN
Keshawn *see* KN
Kesin *see* KS
Kesse *see* KS
Kester *see* KS
Keven *see* KVN
Kevin *see* KVN
Kevon *see* KVN
Kevyn *see* KVN
Keyla *see* KL
Keyon *see* KN
Keyshawn *see* KN
Khaled *see* KL
Khalid *see* KL
Khalil *see* KL
Khallil *see* KL
Khari *see* KR
Khristian *see* KRST
Khristoforos *see* KRST
Khrystiyiyan *see* KRST
Khrystofor *see* KRST
Kian *see* KN
Kiana *see* KN
Kianna *see* KN
Kiara *see* KR
Kibbe *see* KB
Kiel *see* KL
Kiera *see* KR
Kieran *see* KRN

Kierra *see*	KR	Kris *see*	KRS	Lad *see*	LD	Latrice *see*	LT	Lee *see*	L
Kiersten *see*	KRST	Krishna *see*	KRS	Ladarius *see*	LD	Latricia *see*	LT	Leeann *see*	LN
Kieth *see*	KTH	Krispin *see*	KRS	Ladd *see*	LD	Lauento *see*	LNT	Leeanna *see*	LN
Kiko *see*	K	Kriss *see*	KRS	Lado *see*	LD	Launa *see*	LN	Leeanne *see*	LN
Kil *see*	KL	Krista *see*	KRST	Ladonna *see*	LD	Launce *see*	LN	Leeland *see*	LND
Kiley *see*	KL	Kristal *see*	KRST	Lael *see*	LL	Launcelot *see*	LN	Leesa *see*	LS
Kilian *see*	KL	Kristan *see*	KRST	Lai *see*	L	Laura *see*	LR	Leia *see*	L
Killian *see*	KL	Kristeen *see*	KRST	Laila *see*	LL	Lauran *see*	LRN	Leida *see*	LD
Kim *see*	KM	Kristel *see*	KRST	Laine *see*	LN	Laure *see*	LR	Leigh *see*	LH
Kimber *see*	KM	Kristen *see*	KRST	Laird *see*	LD	Laureen *see*	LRN	Leigh-Ann *see*	LH
Kimberely *see*	KMBL	Krister *see*	KRST	Lakeisha *see*	LK	Laurel *see*	LR	Leigh-Anne *see*	LH
Kimberlee *see*	KMBL	Kristi *see*	KRST	Lakesha *see*	LK	Lauren *see*	LRN	Leigha *see*	LH
Kimberley *see*	KMBL	Kristian *see*	KRST	Lakeshia *see*	LK	Laurena *see*	LRN	Leighann *see*	LH
Kimberli *see*	KMBL	Kristianna *see*	KRST	Lakia *see*	LK	Laurence *see*	LRN	Leighanne *see*	LH
Kimberlie *see*	KMBL	Kristie *see*	KRST	Lakisha *see*	LK	Laurene *see*	LRN	Leila *see*	LL
Kimberly *see*	KMBL	Kristin *see*	KRST	Lal *see*	LL	Laurens *see*	LRN	Leilani *see*	LL
Kimmi *see*	KM	Kristina *see*	KRST	Lala *see*	LL	Laurent *see*	LRN	Leisa *see*	LS
Kin *see*	KN	Kristine *see*	KRST	Lamar *see*	LR	Laurentius *see*	LRN	Leit *see*	LT
Kina *see*	KN	Kristle *see*	KRST	Lambert *see*	LB	Laurenz *see*	LRN	Lela *see*	LL
Kindra *see*	KND	Kristo *see*	KRST	Lamont *see*	LNT	Lauretta *see*	LRT	Leland *see*	LND
King *see*	KN	Kristof *see*	KRST	Lan *see*	LN	Laurette *see*	LRT	Lelia *see*	LL
Kingsley *see*	KN	Kristofer *see*	KRST	Lana *see*	LN	Lauri *see*	LR	Lemuel *see*	LL
Kinsey *see*	KN	Kristoffer *see*	KRST	Lance *see*	LN	Laurie *see*	LR	Len *see*	LN
Kinyon *see*	KN	Kristopher *see*	KRST	Landen *see*	LND	Laurine *see*	LRN	Lena *see*	LN
Kira *see*	KR	Kristy *see*	KRST	Landon *see*	LND	Lauryn *see*	LRN	Lenard *see*	LNR
Kiral *see*	KRL	Kristyn *see*	KRST	Lane *see*	LN	Lavada *see*	LV	Lenci *see*	LN
Kirby *see*	KB	Kronos *see*	KRN	Lanell *see*	LNL	Lavern *see*	LV	Lenhart *see*	LN
Kiril *see*	KRL	Kruin *see*	KRN	Lanelle *see*	LNL	Laverna *see*	LV	Lenita *see*	LNT
Kirill *see*	KRL	Krys *see*	KRS	Lanette *see*	LNT	Laverne *see*	LV	Lenka *see*	LK
Kirk *see*	K	Krysta *see*	KRST	Laney *see*	LN	Lavi *see*	LV	Lenn *see*	LN
Kirsten *see*	KRST	Krystal *see*	KRST	Lang *see*	LN	Lavina *see*	LV	Lenna *see*	LN
Kirstie *see*	KRST	Krysten *see*	KRST	Lani *see*	LN	Lavinia *see*	LV	Lennard *see*	LN
Kirstin *see*	KRST	Krystin *see*	KRST	Lanita *see*	LNT	Lavon *see*	LV	Lennie *see*	LN
Kirt *see*	KT	Krystina *see*	KRST	Lannie *see*	LN	Lavonda *see*	LV	Lenno *see*	LN
Kit *see*	KT	Krystle *see*	KRST	Lanny *see*	LN	Lavonne *see*	LV	Lennor *see*	LNR
Kito *see*	KT	Krystyna *see*	KRST	Lanora *see*	LNR	Law *see*	LW	Lennox *see*	LN
Kittie *see*	KT	Kulen *see*	KL	Lanu *see*	LN	Lawanda *see*	LW	Lenny *see*	LN
Kitty *see*	KT	Kumar *see*	KM	Laquita *see*	LK	Lawerence *see*	LW	Lenora *see*	LNR
Kiya *see*	K	Kurt *see*	CRT	Lara *see*	LR	Lawren *see*	LW	Lenore *see*	LNR
Klaus *see*	KL	Kurtis *see*	CRT	Larae *see*	LR	Lawrence *see*	LW	Lenox *see*	LN
Klemens *see*	KL	Kwam *see*	KM	Laraine *see*	LRN	Lawry *see*	LW	Lensar *see*	LN
Klement *see*	KL	Kwame *see*	KM	Laree *see*	LR	Laws *see*	LW	Lenz *see*	LN
Klemo *see*	KL	Kya *see*	K	Laren *see*	LRN	Lawson *see*	LW	Leo *see*	L
Klimek *see*	KL	Kyla *see*	KL	Larissa *see*	LS	Layla *see*	LL	Leola *see*	LL
Kliment *see*	KL	Kylan *see*	KL	Larita *see*	LRT	Layne *see*	LN	Leon *see*	LN
Klyne *see*	KL	Kyle *see*	KL	Larkin *see*	LRN	Layton *see*	LT	Leona *see*	LN
Knoton *see*	KT	Kylee *see*	KL	Laron *see*	LRN	Lazaro *see*	LZ	Leonard *see*	LNR
Kobe *see*	KB	Kyleigh *see*	KL	Larraine *see*	LRN	Lazarus *see*	LZ	Leonarda *see*	LNR
Koby *see*	KB	Kyler *see*	KL	Larrance *see*	LRN	Le *see*	L	Leonardo *see*	LNR
Kody *see*	CD	Kylie *see*	KL	Larrie *see*	LR	Lea *see*	L	Leonardus *see*	LNR
Kolby *see*	KB	Kym *see*	KM	Larry *see*	LR	Leah *see*	LH	Leone *see*	LN
Kole *see*	KL	Kymberly *see*	KMBL	Lars *see*	LR	Lealand *see*	LL	Leonel *see*	LNL
Kolton *see*	KL	Kyra *see*	KR	Larson *see*	LR	Leana *see*	LN	Leonia *see*	LN
Kolya *see*	KL	Kyree *see*	KR	Larue *see*	LR	Leanardo *see*	LND	Leonid *see*	LN
Konane *see*	KN	Kyril *see*	KRL	Lashanda *see*	LS	Leander *see*	LND	Leonida *see*	LND
Konnor *see*	KN	Kyrillos *see*	KRL	Lashawn *see*	LS	Leandra *see*	LND	Leonie *see*	LN
Kontar *see*	KN			Lashonda *see*	LS	Leandro *see*	LND	Leonila *see*	LNL
Korb *see*	KB	LaMarr *see*	LR	Latanya *see*	LT	Leann *see*	LN	Leonor *see*	LNR
Korbin *see*	KR	LaVelle *see*	LV	Latasha *see*	LT	Leanna *see*	LN	Leonora *see*	LNR
Korey *see*	KR	Laban *see*	LB	Latisha *see*	LT	Leanne *see*	LN	Leonore *see*	LNR
Kori *see*	KR	Labid *see*	LB	Latonia *see*	LT	Leanora *see*	LNR	Leora *see*	LR
Kortney *see*	CRT	Lacey *see*	LS	Latonya *see*	LT	Leatha *see*	LTH	Lera *see*	LR
Kory *see*	KR	Laci *see*	LS	Latosha *see*	LT	Leben *see*	LB	Leron *see*	LRN
Kourtney *see*	CRT	Lacie *see*	LS	Latoya *see*	LT	Leda *see*	LD	Leroy *see*	LR
Kraig *see*	CRG	Lacy *see*	LS	Latrell *see*	LT	Ledama *see*	LD	Les *see*	LS

Name		Code
Lesa	*see*	LS
Lesia	*see*	LS
Leslee	*see*	LS
Lesley	*see*	LS
Lesli	*see*	LS
Leslie	*see*	LS
Lesly	*see*	LS
Lessie	*see*	LS
Lester	*see*	LT
Leta	*see*	LT
Letha	*see*	LTH
Leticia	*see*	LT
Letitia	*see*	LT
Lettie	*see*	LT
Levan	*see*	LV
Levar	*see*	LV
Levi	*see*	LV
Levy	*see*	LV
Lew	*see*	LW
Lewie	*see*	LW
Lewis	*see*	LW
Lex	*see*	LX
Lexi	*see*	LX
Lexie	*see*	LX
Lexus	*see*	LX
Lexy	*see*	LX
Leyland	*see*	LND
Li	*see*	L
Lia	*see*	L
Liana	*see*	LN
Liane	*see*	LN
Lianne	*see*	LN
Libby	*see*	LB
Liberty	*see*	LB
Lida	*see*	LD
Lidia	*see*	LD
Liko	*see*	LK
Lila	*see*	LL
Lili	*see*	LL
Lilia	*see*	LL
Lilian	*see*	LL
Liliana	*see*	LL
Lilla	*see*	LL
Lilli	*see*	LL
Lillia	*see*	LL
Lillian	*see*	LL
Lilliana	*see*	LL
Lillie	*see*	LL
Lilly	*see*	LL
Lily	*see*	LL
Lilyan	*see*	LL
Lin	*see*	LN
Lina	*see*	LN
Lincoln	*see*	LK
Linda	*see*	LND
Linden	*see*	LND
Lindon	*see*	LND
Lindsay	*see*	LND
Lindsey	*see*	LND
Lindsy	*see*	LND
Lindy	*see*	LND
Linette	*see*	LNT
Ling	*see*	LN
Link	*see*	LN
Linn	*see*	LN
Linnea	*see*	LN
Linnie	*see*	LN
Linsey	*see*	LN
Linus	*see*	LN
Linwood	*see*	LW
Lio	*see*	L
Lionardo	*see*	LND
Lionel	*see*	LNL
Lionello	*see*	LNL
Lisa	*see*	LS
Lisandro	*see*	LS
Lisbeth	*see*	LS
Lise	*see*	LS
Lisette	*see*	LT
Lissa	*see*	LS
Lissette	*see*	LT
Lita	*see*	LT
Lito	*see*	LT
Litzy	*see*	LZ
Liu	*see*	L
Liv	*see*	LV
Livia	*see*	LV
Liwanu	*see*	LW
Liz	*see*	LZ
Liza	*see*	LZ
Lizabeth	*see*	LZ
Lizbeth	*see*	LZ
Lizeth	*see*	LZ
Lizette	*see*	LZ
Lizzie	*see*	LZ
Llewellyn	*see*	LW
Lloyd	*see*	LD
Lodewick	*see*	LD
Lodewijk	*see*	LD
Lodovico	*see*	LD
Loe	*see*	L
Loew	*see*	LW
Logan	*see*	LN
Loida	*see*	LD
Lois	*see*	LS
Loise	*see*	LS
Lola	*see*	LL
Lolita	*see*	LL
Lon	*see*	LN
Lona	*see*	LN
Lonato	*see*	LN
Londa	*see*	LND
London	*see*	LND
Loni	*see*	LN
Lonna	*see*	LN
Lonnie	*see*	LN
Lonny	*see*	LN
Lora	*see*	LR
Loraine	*see*	LRN
Loran	*see*	LRN
Lorant	*see*	LRN
Loranzio	*see*	LRN
Lord	*see*	LD
Lore	*see*	LR
Lorean	*see*	LRN
Loree	*see*	LR
Loreen	*see*	LRN
Lorelei	*see*	LL
Loren	*see*	LRN
Lorena	*see*	LRN
Lorene	*see*	LRN
Lorens	*see*	LRN
Lorenza	*see*	LRN
Lorenzo	*see*	LRN
Loreta	*see*	LRT
Loretta	*see*	LRT
Lorette	*see*	LRT
Lori	*see*	LR
Loria	*see*	LR
Loriann	*see*	LRN
Lorie	*see*	LR
Lorina	*see*	LRN
Lorine	*see*	LRN
Lorita	*see*	LRT
Lorna	*see*	LRN
Lorne	*see*	LRN
Lorraine	*see*	LRN
Lorretta	*see*	LRT
Lorri	*see*	LR
Lorriane	*see*	LRN
Lorrie	*see*	LR
Lorrine	*see*	LRN
Lory	*see*	LR
Lothar	*see*	LTH
Lottie	*see*	LT
Lotus	*see*	LT
Lou	*see*	L
Louann	*see*	LN
Louanne	*see*	LN
Loudon	*see*	LD
Louella	*see*	LL
Louie	*see*	L
Louis	*see*	LS
Louisa	*see*	LS
Louise	*see*	LS
Loura	*see*	LR
Lourdes	*see*	LD
Lourie	*see*	LR
Lovell	*see*	LV
Lovie	*see*	LV
Lovre	*see*	LV
Lowe	*see*	LW
Lowell	*see*	LW
Lowenhard	*see*	LW
Lowther	*see*	LW
Loyd	*see*	LD
Lu	*see*	L
Luana	*see*	LN
Luann	*see*	LN
Luanne	*see*	LN
Luca	*see*	LK
Lucas	*see*	LK
Lucero	*see*	LS
Luci	*see*	LS
Lucia	*see*	LS
Lucian	*see*	LS
Luciano	*see*	LS
Lucie	*see*	LS
Lucien	*see*	LS
Lucienne	*see*	LS
Lucila	*see*	LS
Lucile	*see*	LS
Lucilla	*see*	LS
Lucille	*see*	LS
Lucinda	*see*	LS
Lucius	*see*	LS
Lucretia	*see*	LK
Lucy	*see*	LS
Ludovic	*see*	LD
Ludvig	*see*	LD
Lue	*see*	L
Luella	*see*	LL
Luis	*see*	LS
Luisa	*see*	LS
Luise	*see*	LS
Luister	*see*	LS
Luiz	*see*	LZ
Lukas	*see*	LK
Luke	*see*	LK
Lukyan	*see*	LK
Lula	*see*	LL
Lulu	*see*	LL
Luna	*see*	LN
Lura	*see*	LR
Luteris	*see*	LT
Luther	*see*	LTH
Lutherio	*see*	LTH
Luz	*see*	LZ
Lyda	*see*	LD
Lydia	*see*	LD
Lyel	*see*	LL
Lyell	*see*	LL
Lyla	*see*	LL
Lyle	*see*	LL
Lyn	*see*	LN
Lynda	*see*	LND
Lyndia	*see*	LND
Lyndon	*see*	LND
Lyndsay	*see*	LND
Lyndsey	*see*	LND
Lynell	*see*	LNL
Lynelle	*see*	LNL
Lynetta	*see*	LNT
Lynette	*see*	LNT
Lynn	*see*	LN
Lynne	*see*	LN
Lynnette	*see*	LNT
Lynsey	*see*	LN
Lynwood	*see*	LN
Lyric	*see*	LR
Lyron	*see*	LRN
Mabel	*see*	MB
Mabelle	*see*	MB
Mable	*see*	MB
Mac	*see*	MK
MacKeefry	*see*	MK
MacKeighry	*see*	MK
Macaliano	*see*	MK
Mace	*see*	MS
Macey	*see*	MS
Machelle	*see*	MSH
Maci	*see*	MS
Macie	*see*	MS
Mack	*see*	MK
Mackenzie	*see*	MK
Macy	*see*	MS
Madalene	*see*	MDN
Madaline	*see*	MDN
Madalyn	*see*	MDN
Madalynn	*see*	MDN
Maddie	*see*	MD
Maddison	*see*	MDN
Maddy	*see*	MD
Madelaine	*see*	MDN
Madeleine	*see*	MDN
Madelene	*see*	MDN
Madeline	*see*	MDN
Madelyn	*see*	MDN
Madelynn	*see*	MDN
Madge	*see*	MG
Madhu	*see*	MD
Madhujit	*see*	MD
Madilyn	*see*	MDN
Madisen	*see*	MDN
Madison	*see*	MDN
Madisyn	*see*	MDN
Madlyn	*see*	MDN
Madoc	*see*	MD
Madog	*see*	MD
Madonna	*see*	MDN
Madyson	*see*	MDN
Mae	*see*	M
Maegan	*see*	MG
Maeve	*see*	MV
Magan	*see*	MG
Magda	*see*	MG
Magdalena	*see*	MG
Magdalene	*see*	MG
Magen	*see*	MG
Maggie	*see*	MG
Maggio	*see*	MG
Maggy	*see*	MG
Magnolia	*see*	MG
Magnus	*see*	MG
Maher	*see*	MR
Maia	*see*	M
Maik	*see*	MK
Maira	*see*	MR
Mairav	*see*	MV
Maire	*see*	MR
Majorie	*see*	MRJ
Makaila	*see*	MKL
Makan	*see*	MK
Makayla	*see*	MKL
Makena	*see*	MK
Makenna	*see*	MK
Makenzie	*see*	MK
Makis	*see*	MK
Maksim	*see*	MK
Mal	*see*	ML
Malachi	*see*	MK
Malachy	*see*	MK
Malakai	*see*	MK
Malcolm	*see*	MK
Malcom	*see*	MK
Maleah	*see*	ML
Malek	*see*	ML
Malia	*see*	ML
Malik	*see*	MK
Malinda	*see*	MLD
Malique	*see*	ML
Malisa	*see*	MLS
Malissa	*see*	MLS
Maliya	*see*	ML

Mallie *see*	ML	Mari *see*	MR	Marquita *see*	MRK	Matt *see*	MT	McCullouch *see*	MK
Mallory *see*	ML	Maria *see*	MR	Marquitos *see*	MRK	Matte *see*	MT	McCullough *see*	MK
Malon *see*	ML	Mariah *see*	MR	Marr *see*	MR	Matteo *see*	MT	McKay *see*	MK
Malvina *see*	MV	Mariam *see*	MRM	Marrim *see*	MR	Matthaeus *see*	MTH	Mckayla *see*	MKL
Mamie *see*	M	Marian *see*	MRN	Marsh *see*	MRS	Matthaus *see*	MTH	Mckenna *see*	MK
Mandi *see*	MND	Mariana *see*	MRN	Marsha *see*	MSH	Mattheo *see*	MTH	Mckenzie *see*	MK
Mandie *see*	MND	Mariann *see*	MRN	Marshal *see*	MRS	Matthes *see*	MTH	Mckinley *see*	MKL
Mandrill *see*	MND	Marianna *see*	MRN	Marshall *see*	MRS	Mattheus *see*	MTH	Meadow *see*	MD
Mandy *see*	MND	Marianne *see*	MRN	Marshalll *see*	MSH	Matthew *see*	MTH	Meagan *see*	MG
Manie *see*	MN	Mariano *see*	MRN	Marsilio *see*	MRS	Matthia *see*	MTH	Meaghan *see*	MG
Manny *see*	MN	Maribel *see*	MB	Mart *see*	MRT	Matthias *see*	MTH	Mechelle *see*	MSH
Manoj *see*	MN	Maribeth *see*	MB	Marta *see*	MRT	Mattie *see*	MT	Meg *see*	MG
Manual *see*	MN	Marica *see*	MRS	Martainn *see*	MRT	Mattieu *see*	MT	Megan *see*	MG
Manuel *see*	MN	Maricela *see*	MRS	Martel *see*	MRT	Matty *see*	MT	Meggan *see*	MG
Manuela *see*	MN	Marie *see*	MR	Marten *see*	MRT	Matyas *see*	MT	Meghan *see*	MG
Manus *see*	MN	Mariel *see*	MRL	Marth *see*	MTH	Maud *see*	MD	Meghann *see*	MG
Many *see*	MN	Mariela *see*	MRL	Martha *see*	MTH	Maude *see*	MD	Mehdi *see*	MD
Mara *see*	MR	Mariella *see*	MRL	Marti *see*	MRT	Mauli *see*	ML	Mehtar *see*	MT
Maragaret *see*	MGR	Marietta *see*	MRT	Martie *see*	MRT	Maur *see*	MR	Meir *see*	MR
Maragret *see*	MGR	Mariette *see*	MRT	Martijn *see*	MRT	Maura *see*	MR	Mekhi *see*	MK
Maranda *see*	MND	Mariko *see*	MRK	Martin *see*	MRT	Maureen *see*	MRN	Mel *see*	ML
Marc *see*	MRK	Marilee *see*	MRL	Martina *see*	MRT	Maureo *see*	MR	Melani *see*	MLN
Marcel *see*	MRS	Marilou *see*	MRL	Martine *see*	MRT	Maurice *see*	MRS	Melanie *see*	MLN
Marcela *see*	MRS	Marilu *see*	MRL	Martinicino *see*	MRT	Mauricio *see*	MRS	Melany *see*	MLN
Marcelino *see*	MRS	Marilyn *see*	MRLN	Marton *see*	MRT	Maurie *see*	MR	Melba *see*	MB
Marcell *see*	MRS	Marilynn *see*	MRLN	Marty *see*	MRT	Maurine *see*	MRN	Melina *see*	MLN
Marcella *see*	MRS	Marin *see*	MRN	Marut *see*	MRT	Maurita *see*	MRT	Melinda *see*	MLD
Marcelle *see*	MRS	Marina *see*	MRN	Marv *see*	MV	Maurits *see*	MRT	Melisa *see*	MLS
Marcellus *see*	MRS	Marine *see*	MRN	Marva *see*	MV	Mauro *see*	MR	Melissa *see*	MLS
Marcelo *see*	MRS	Mario *see*	MR	Marve *see*	MV	Maurosio *see*	MRS	Melissia *see*	MLS
Marci *see*	MRS	Marion *see*	MRN	Marven *see*	MV	Maursio *see*	MRS	Mellie *see*	ML
Marcia *see*	MRS	Maris *see*	MRS	Marvin *see*	MV	Maury *see*	MR	Mellisa *see*	MLS
Marcial *see*	MRS	Marisa *see*	MRS	Mary *see*	MR	Maverick *see*	MV	Mellissa *see*	MLS
Marcie *see*	MRS	Marisela *see*	MRS	Marya *see*	MR	Mavis *see*	MV	Melodi *see*	MLD
Marciela *see*	MRS	Marisha *see*	MSH	Maryam *see*	MRM	Max *see*	MX	Melodie *see*	MLD
Marcius *see*	MRS	Marisol *see*	MRS	Maryann *see*	MRN	Maxie *see*	MX	Melody *see*	MLD
Marco *see*	MRK	Marissa *see*	MRS	Maryanna *see*	MRN	Maxim *see*	MX	Melonie *see*	MLN
Marcos *see*	MRK	Marita *see*	MRT	Maryanne *see*	MRN	Maxime *see*	MX	Melony *see*	MLN
Marcus *see*	MRK	Maritza *see*	MRS	Marybeth *see*	MB	Maximilian *see*	MX	Melton *see*	MLN
Marcy *see*	MRS	Marjorie *see*	MRJ	Maryellen *see*	MRLN	Maximiliano *see*	MX	Melva *see*	MV
Marek *see*	MRK	Marjory *see*	MRJ	Maryetta *see*	MRT	Maximilianus *see*	MX	Melvern *see*	MV
Maren *see*	MRN	Mark *see*	MRK	Maryjane *see*	MRJ	Maximilien *see*	MX	Melvin *see*	MV
Margaret *see*	MGR	Markel *see*	MRK	Maryjo *see*	MRJ	Maximillia *see*	MX	Melvina *see*	MV
Margareta *see*	MGR	Markell *see*	MRK	Marylee *see*	MRL	Maximillian *see*	MX	Melvyn *see*	MV
Margarete *see*	MGR	Markie *see*	MRK	Marylin *see*	MRLN	Maximino *see*	MX	Melynda *see*	MLD
Margarett *see*	MGR	Markos *see*	MRK	Marylou *see*	MRL	Maximo *see*	MX	Mendeley *see*	MND
Margaretta *see*	MGR	Markus *see*	MRK	Marylyn *see*	MRLN	Maximus *see*	MX	Mendy *see*	MND
Margarette *see*	MGR	Marla *see*	MRL	Maryrose *see*	MRS	Maxine *see*	MX	Menker *see*	MK
Margarita *see*	MGR	Marlee *see*	MRL	Mason *see*	MS	Maxino *see*	MX	Meranda *see*	MRN
Margarite *see*	MGR	Marlena *see*	MRLN	Masou *see*	MS	Maxio *see*	MX	Mercedes *see*	MRS
Margarito *see*	MGR	Marlene *see*	MRLN	Massey *see*	MS	Maxwell *see*	MX	Mercy *see*	MRS
Margart *see*	MGR	Marley *see*	MRL	Massimilano *see*	MS	Maxy *see*	MX	Meredith *see*	MTH
Marge *see*	MRJ	Marlin *see*	MRLN	Masud *see*	MS	May *see*	M	Meri *see*	MR
Margene *see*	MG	Marlo *see*	MRL	Mat *see*	MT	Maya *see*	M	Merideth *see*	MTH
Margeret *see*	MGR	Marlon *see*	MRLN	Mata *see*	MT	Maybell *see*	MB	Meridith *see*	MTH
Margert *see*	MGR	Marlyn *see*	MRLN	Matejo *see*	MT	Maybelle *see*	MB	Merissa *see*	MRS
Margery *see*	MRJ	Marlys *see*	MRS	Mateo *see*	MT	Mayer *see*	MR	Merle *see*	MRL
Margie *see*	MGR	Marna *see*	MRN	Matheo *see*	MTH	Mayme *see*	M	Merlin *see*	MRLN
Margo *see*	MG	Marnie *see*	MRN	Mathew *see*	MTH	Maynard *see*	MND	Merna *see*	MRN
Margot *see*	MG	Maron *see*	MRN	Mathias *see*	MTH	Mayo *see*	M	Merri *see*	MR
Margret *see*	MGR	Marquerite *see*	MRK	Mathieu *see*	MTH	Mayon *see*	MN	Merrie *see*	MR
Margrett *see*	MGR	Marques *see*	MRK	Matilda *see*	MT	Mayra *see*	MR	Merrilee *see*	MRL
Marguerita *see*	MGR	Marquez *see*	MRK	Matilde *see*	MT	McCain *see*	MK	Merrill *see*	MRL
Marguerite *see*	MGR	Marquis *see*	MRK	Mato *see*	MT	McCullagh *see*	MK	Merry *see*	MR
Margurite *see*	MGR	Marquise *see*	MRK	Matope *see*	MT	McCullock *see*	MK	Mertie *see*	MRT

Mertin *see*	MRT	Millicent *see*	MLS	Morgan *see*	MG	Nado *see*	ND	Nayati *see*	NT
Mervin *see*	MV	Millie *see*	ML	Moriah *see*	MR	Nahele *see*	NL	Nayeli *see*	NL
Mervyn *see*	MV	Mills *see*	ML	Moricz *see*	MR	Nahma *see*	NM	Nayely *see*	NL
Meryl *see*	MRL	Milly *see*	ML	Moritz *see*	MR	Nahum *see*	NM	Neal *see*	NL
Meson *see*	MS	Milo *see*	ML	Morley *see*	MRL	Naida *see*	ND	Neale *see*	NL
Messimo *see*	MS	Milos *see*	MLS	Morrel *see*	MRL	Nakia *see*	NK	Nealey *see*	NL
Mestipen *see*	MS	Milt *see*	MT	Morrell *see*	MRL	Nalin *see*	NL	Neall *see*	NL
Meta *see*	MT	Milton *see*	MLN	Morrice *see*	MRS	Nallely *see*	NL	Nealson *see*	NL
Meyer *see*	MR	Milun *see*	MLN	Morris *see*	MRS	Nalren *see*	NL	Necolas *see*	NK
Mi *see*	M	Mimi *see*	M	Morrison *see*	MRS	Namid *see*	NM	Necole *see*	NK
Mia *see*	M	Mina *see*	MN	Morriss *see*	MRS	Namir *see*	NM	Ned *see*	ND
Miah *see*	M	Mindi *see*	MND	Morse *see*	MRS	Nan *see*	NN	Neda *see*	ND
Mic *see*	MK	Mindy *see*	MND	Mort *see*	MRT	Nana *see*	NN	Neddie *see*	ND
Micaela *see*	MKL	Minerva *see*	MV	Mortie *see*	MRT	Nance *see*	NN	Neddy *see*	ND
Micah *see*	MK	Minky *see*	MK	Mortimer *see*	MRT	Nancela *see*	NN	Nedra *see*	ND
Micalao *see*	MK	Minnie *see*	MN	Morton *see*	MRT	Nancey *see*	NN	Neel *see*	NL
Michael *see*	MKL	Mira *see*	MR	Morven *see*	MV	Nanci *see*	NN	Neely *see*	NL
Michaela *see*	MKL	Miracle *see*	MKL	Mose *see*	MS	Nancie *see*	NN	Neeraj *see*	NR
Michaele *see*	MK	Miranda *see*	MRN	Moses *see*	MS	Nancy *see*	NN	Nehemiah *see*	NM
Michail *see*	MKL	Mireille *see*	MRL	Moshe *see*	MSH	Nanda *see*	NN	Nehru *see*	NR
Michal *see*	MKL	Mirella *see*	MRL	Mosheh *see*	MSH	Nandin *see*	NN	Neida *see*	ND
Michale *see*	MKL	Mireya *see*	MR	Mosi *see*	MS	Nando *see*	NN	Neil *see*	NL
Micheal *see*	MKL	Miriam *see*	MRM	Mosie *see*	MS	Nandor *see*	NN	Neill *see*	NL
Micheil *see*	MKL	Mirian *see*	MRN	Moss *see*	MS	Nanette *see*	NN	Neirin *see*	NR
Michel *see*	MSH	Mirit *see*	MRT	Mossimo *see*	MS	Nannette *see*	NN	Neith *see*	NTH
Michele *see*	MSH	Mirna *see*	MRN	Mostyn *see*	MS	Nannie *see*	NN	Nelda *see*	ND
Michell *see*	MSH	Mirta *see*	MRT	Moswen *see*	MS	Nano *see*	NN	Nelek *see*	NL
Michelle *see*	MSH	Mirtha *see*	MTH	Motega *see*	MT	Naomi *see*	NM	Nelia *see*	NL
Michiel *see*	MKL	Misael *see*	MS	Moy *see*	M	Napoleon *see*	NL	Nelida *see*	NL
Mick *see*	MK	Misha *see*	MSH	Moyes *see*	MS	Narain *see*	NR	Nell *see*	NL
Mickel *see*	MKL	Missy *see*	MS	Moze *see*	MS	Nard *see*	NR	Nella *see*	NL
Mickey *see*	MK	Misti *see*	MT	Mozes *see*	MS	Narinder *see*	NR	Nelle *see*	NL
Micki *see*	MK	Mistie *see*	MT	Muhammad *see*	MHMD	Nash *see*	NSH	Nellie *see*	NL
Mickie *see*	MK	Misty *see*	MT	Mull *see*	ML	Nasir *see*	NR	Nelly *see*	NL
Micky *see*	MK	Misu *see*	MS	Munda *see*	MND	Nat *see*	NT	Nelo *see*	NL
Migael *see*	MG	Mitch *see*	MT	Mundek *see*	MND	Natal *see*	NTL	Nels *see*	NL
Migdalia *see*	MG	Mitchel *see*	MT	Mundy *see*	MND	Natale *see*	NTL	Nelson *see*	NL
Mignon *see*	MG	Mitchell *see*	MT	Munroe *see*	MN	Natalia *see*	NTL	Nen *see*	NN
Miguel *see*	MG	Mitzi *see*	MT	Munrow *see*	MN	Natalie *see*	NTL	Nena *see*	NN
Miguelangel *see*	MG	Miya *see*	M	Murdoch *see*	MRK	Nataly *see*	NTL	Neomi *see*	NM
Miguelito *see*	MG	Miyoko *see*	MK	Muriel *see*	MRL	Natalya *see*	NTL	Nereida *see*	ND
Mika *see*	MK	Modesto *see*	MD	Murphy *see*	MR	Natan *see*	NT	Nermin *see*	NR
Mikael *see*	MKL	Moe *see*	M	Murray *see*	MR	Nataneal *see*	NTL	Neron *see*	NR
Mikaela *see*	MKL	Mohamed *see*	MHMD	Murry *see*	MR	Nataniel *see*	NTL	Nestor *see*	NT
Mikaila *see*	MKL	Mohammad *see*	MHMD	Murthy *see*	MTH	Natascha *see*	NSH	Neto *see*	NT
Mikala *see*	MKL	Mohammed *see*	MHMD	Mustafa *see*	MT	Natasha *see*	NSH	Nettie *see*	NT
Mikayla *see*	MKL	Moira *see*	MR	Mya *see*	M	Natashia *see*	NSH	Nev *see*	NV
Mike *see*	MK	Moises *see*	MS	Myah *see*	M	Nate *see*	NT	Neva *see*	NV
Mikel *see*	MKL	Mollie *see*	ML	Mykel *see*	MKL	Nathalia *see*	NTL	Nevaeh *see*	NV
Mikhael *see*	MKL	Molly *see*	ML	Myles *see*	MLS	Nathalie *see*	NTL	Nevil *see*	NV
Mikhail *see*	MKL	Mona *see*	MN	Myra *see*	MR	Nathaly *see*	NTL	Nevile *see*	NV
Miki *see*	MK	Monica *see*	MN	Myranda *see*	MRN	Nathan *see*	NTH	Neville *see*	NV
Mikkel *see*	MKL	Monika *see*	MK	Myriam *see*	MRM	Nathanael *see*	NTH	Nevin *see*	NV
Mikki *see*	MK	Monique *see*	MK	Myrl *see*	MRL	Nathanial *see*	NTH	Newlin *see*	NL
Miklos *see*	MKL	Monnie *see*	MN	Myrle *see*	MRL	Nathaniel *see*	NTH	Newt *see*	NT
Mil *see*	ML	Monroe *see*	MR	Myrna *see*	MRN	Nathen *see*	NTH	Newton *see*	NT
Mila *see*	ML	Monserrat *see*	MT	Myron *see*	MRN	Natilio *see*	NTL	Nia *see*	N
Milagros *see*	MLS	Montana *see*	MT	Myrta *see*	MRT	Natisha *see*	NSH	Nial *see*	NL
Milan *see*	MLN	Monte *see*	MT	Myrtie *see*	MRT	Natividad *see*	NT	Niall *see*	NL
Milap *see*	ML	Montgomery *see*	MT	Myrtle *see*	MRT	Natosha *see*	NSH	Nicabar *see*	NK
Mildred *see*	MLD	Monty *see*	MT			Natty *see*	NT	Nicanor *see*	NK
Miles *see*	MLS	Moore *see*	MR	Nada *see*	ND	Nav *see*	NV	Niccolini *see*	NK
Milford *see*	MLD	Mora *see*	MR	Nader *see*	ND	Naveed *see*	NV	Niccolo *see*	NK
Milissa *see*	MLS	Morel *see*	MRL	Nadia *see*	ND	Navin *see*	NV	Nichol *see*	NK
Millard *see*	MLD	Morey *see*	MR	Nadine *see*	ND	Nawat *see*	NT	Nicholas *see*	NK

Nicholaus *see*	NK	Noelia *see*	NL	Ohannes *see*	ON	Osbaldo *see*	OS	Parsifal *see*	PR
Nichole *see*	NK	Noella *see*	NL	Ohin *see*	ON	Osbert *see*	OS	Parzival *see*	PR
Nicholle *see*	NK	Noelle *see*	NL	Ola *see*	OL	Osborn *see*	OS	Pascal *see*	PK
Nick *see*	NK	Noemi *see*	NM	Olaf *see*	OL	Osborne *see*	OS	Paschall *see*	PK
Nicki *see*	NK	Nola *see*	NL	Olav *see*	OL	Oscar *see*	OS	Pascoe *see*	PK
Nickie *see*	NK	Nolan *see*	NL	Oleg *see*	OL	Oseep *see*	OS	Pasqual *see*	PK
Nicklas *see*	NK	Noland *see*	NL	Olen *see*	OL	Oskar *see*	OS	Pasquale *see*	PK
Nicklaus *see*	NK	Noldy *see*	NL	Olery *see*	OL	Osman *see*	OS	Pat *see*	PT
Nickolas *see*	NK	Noll *see*	NL	Oles *see*	OL	Osmans *see*	OS	Patamon *see*	PT
Nicky *see*	NK	Nona *see*	NN	Oleta *see*	OL	Osmin *see*	OS	Patience *see*	PT
Nico *see*	NK	Nora *see*	NR	Olevia *see*	OV	Osric *see*	OS	Patric *see*	PTR
Nicol *see*	NK	Norbert *see*	NR	Olga *see*	OL	Ossian *see*	OS	Patrica *see*	PTR
Nicola *see*	NK	Norberto *see*	NR	Olin *see*	OL	Ossie *see*	OS	Patrice *see*	PTR
Nicolaas *see*	NK	Noreen *see*	NR	Oliva *see*	OV	Osmin *see*	OS	Patricia *see*	PTR
Nicolai *see*	NK	Norene *see*	NR	Olive *see*	OV	Osvaldo *see*	OS	Patriciano *see*	PTR
Nicolao *see*	NK	Norine *see*	NR	Oliver *see*	OV	Oswald *see*	OS	Patricio *see*	PTR
Nicolas *see*	NK	Norm *see*	NR	Oliverio *see*	OV	Oswaldo *see*	OS	Patrick *see*	PTR
Nicolasa *see*	NK	Norma *see*	NR	Olivia *see*	OV	Oswell *see*	OS	Patrin *see*	PTR
Nicolaus *see*	NK	Norman *see*	NR	Olivier *see*	OV	Oswin *see*	OS	Patritio *see*	PTR
Nicole *see*	NK	Normand *see*	NR	Olivo *see*	OV	Ovid *see*	OV	Patrizius *see*	PTR
Nicolette *see*	NK	Normie *see*	NR	Olley *see*	OL	Owain *see*	OW	Patsy *see*	PT
Nicolle *see*	NK	Normy *see*	NR	Ollie *see*	OL	Owayne *see*	OW	Patti *see*	PT
Nicolum *see*	NK	Norris *see*	NR	Olly *see*	OL	Owen *see*	OW	Pattie *see*	PT
Nida *see*	ND	Nort *see*	NR	Olo *see*	OL	Owudunni *see*	OW	Pattin *see*	PT
Nidia *see*	ND	Norton *see*	NR	Olorun *see*	OL	Oz *see*	OS	Pattison *see*	PT
Niel *see*	NL	Nowel *see*	NL	Olwen *see*	OL	Ozzie *see*	OS	Patty *see*	PT
Niels *see*	NL	Nowell *see*	NL	Oma *see*	OM			Patwin *see*	PT
Nielson *see*	NL	Nowles *see*	NL	Omar *see*	OM	Pablino *see*	PL	Paul *see*	PL
Nigan *see*	NN	Noy *see*	N	Omari *see*	OM	Pablo *see*	PL	Paula *see*	PL
Nigel *see*	NL	Numair *see*	NM	Omarion *see*	OM	Pabolo *see*	PL	Paulene *see*	PL
Nihat *see*	NT	Numps *see*	NM	Omayra *see*	OM	Paco *see*	PK	Pauletta *see*	PL
Nik *see*	NK	Nuri *see*	NR	Omer *see*	OM	Paddington *see*	PD	Paulette *see*	PL
Nike *see*	NK	Nuru *see*	NR	Omero *see*	OM	Paddy *see*	PD	Paulico *see*	PL
Nikhil *see*	NK	Nya *see*	N	Onan *see*	ON	Padraic *see*	PD	Paulie *see*	PL
Niki *see*	NK	Nyah *see*	N	Onani *see*	ON	Padraig *see*	PD	Paulina *see*	PL
Nikia *see*	NK	Nydia *see*	ND	Ondro *see*	ON	Padrig *see*	PD	Pauline *see*	PL
Nikita *see*	NK	Nykia *see*	NK	Ora *see*	OR	Padruig *see*	PD	Paulino *see*	PL
Nikki *see*	NK	Nyla *see*	NL	Oral *see*	OR	Page *see*	PG	Paulita *see*	PL
Nikky *see*	NK	Nyle *see*	NL	Oralia *see*	OR	Pahl *see*	PL	Paulius *see*	PL
Niklas *see*	NK			Oran *see*	OR	Paige *see*	PG	Paullin *see*	PL
Niko *see*	NK	O'Neil *see*	ON	Orasio *see*	OR	Paki *see*	PK	Paulo *see*	PL
Nikolai *see*	NK	Octavia *see*	OV	Orazio *see*	OR	Pal *see*	PL	Paulos *see*	PL
Nikolaos *see*	NK	Octavio *see*	OV	Orban *see*	OR	Palacido *see*	PL	Paulot *see*	PL
Nikolas *see*	NK	Octavius *see*	OV	Ordando *see*	OR	Paladin *see*	PL	Paultje *see*	PL
Nikolaus *see*	NK	Odalys *see*	OD	Orel *see*	OR	Pall *see*	PL	Paulum *see*	PL
Nikole *see*	NK	Oday *see*	OD	Oren *see*	OR	Pallaton *see*	PL	Paulus *see*	PL
Nikolos *see*	NK	Odell *see*	OD	Oriel *see*	OR	Paloma *see*	PL	Pauly *see*	PL
Nila *see*	NL	Odessa *see*	OD	Orien *see*	OR	Pam *see*	PM	Pavek *see*	PK
Nilda *see*	ND	Odette *see*	OD	Orin *see*	OR	Pamala *see*	PM	Pavlo *see*	PL
Niles *see*	NL	Odile *see*	OD	Oriole *see*	OR	Pamela *see*	PM	Pawley *see*	PL
Nilo *see*	NL	Odin *see*	OD	Orion *see*	OR	Pamelia *see*	PM	Paxton *see*	PT
Nils *see*	NL	Odinan *see*	OD	Orito *see*	OR	Pamella *see*	PM	Payat *see*	PT
Nilsa *see*	NL	Odinum *see*	OD	Orji *see*	OR	Pamila *see*	PM	Payton *see*	PT
Nilson *see*	NL	Odion *see*	OD	Orland *see*	OR	Pamula *see*	PM	Pearce *see*	PRS
Nina *see*	NN	Odis *see*	OD	Orlando *see*	OR	Paola *see*	PL	Pearl *see*	PRL
Nionios *see*	NN	Odissan *see*	OD	Orlondo *see*	OR	Paoli *see*	PL	Pearle *see*	PRL
Nishu *see*	NSH	Odo *see*	OD	Orpha *see*	OR	Paolino *see*	PL	Pearlie *see*	PRL
Nita *see*	NT	Odoardo *see*	OD	Orren *see*	OR	Paolo *see*	PL	Pearson *see*	PRS
Nitin *see*	NT	Odom *see*	OD	Orsino *see*	OR	Paquin *see*	PK	Peddy *see*	PD
Nitis *see*	NT	Odon *see*	OD	Orson *see*	OR	Paris *see*	PR	Peder *see*	PD
Noah *see*	N	Odysseus *see*	OD	Orunjan *see*	OR	Park *see*	PK	Pedr *see*	PD
Nod *see*	ND	Ofelia *see*	OL	Orv *see*	OV	Parker *see*	PK	Pedran *see*	PD
Nodin *see*	ND	Ogden *see*	OD	Orvie *see*	OV	Parnell *see*	PR	Pedro *see*	PD
Noe *see*	N	Ogdon *see*	OD	Orville *see*	OR	Parris *see*	PR	Peers *see*	PR
Noel *see*	NL	Ogdun *see*	OD	Osamu *see*	OS	Parrish *see*	PR	Peg *see*	PG
						Parsefal *see*	PR		

Name	Code
Peggie see	PG
Peggy see	PG
Pelo see	PL
Pelota see	PL
Penelope see	PN
Penney see	PN
Penni see	PN
Pennie see	PN
Penny see	PN
Per see	PR
Perce see	PRS
Perceval see	PRS
Percifull see	PRS
Percival see	PRS
Percy see	PRS
Perico see	PR
Periquin see	PR
Perkin see	PK
Perla see	PRL
Pernel see	PR
Pernell see	PR
Pero see	PR
Perrin see	PR
Perry see	PR
Perseus see	PRS
Pershing see	PRS
Pete see	PT
Peter see	PTR
Peters see	PTR
Petey see	PT
Petie see	PT
Petr see	PTR
Petra see	PTR
Petrick see	PTR
Petrie see	PTR
Petronio see	PTR
Petronius see	PTR
Petros see	PTR
Petruccio see	PTR
Petrus see	PTR
Petruscha see	PTR
Peyton see	PT
Phelis see	PHL
Phil see	PHL
Philip see	PHL
Philipa see	PHL
Philippe see	PHL
Philippos see	PHL
Philips see	PHL
Phillip see	PHL
Phillipa see	PHL
Phillips see	PHL
Phillis see	PHL
Phoebe see	FB
Phylis see	PHL
Phyliss see	PHL
Phyllis see	PHL
Pico see	PK
Piedro see	PD
Pierce see	PRS
Pierin see	PR
Piero see	PR
Pierre see	PR
Pierrot see	PR
Piers see	PR
Piet see	PT
Pieter see	PTR
Pietro see	PTR
Pilan see	PL
Pilar see	PL
Pili see	PL
Pilib see	PL
Pillan see	PL
Pinkie see	PK
Pinon see	PN
Piper see	PR
Piquin see	PK
Pirro see	PR
Piter see	PTR
Pito see	PT
Pitricio see	PTR
Pjotr see	PTR
Plato see	PL
Platon see	PL
Plesido see	PL
Pol see	PL
Polin see	PL
Polly see	PL
Porsha see	PRS
Porter see	PTR
Portia see	PT
Pranav see	PR
Precious see	PRS
Presley see	PRS
Preston see	PRS
Pricilla see	PRS
Prince see	PRS
Princess see	PRS
Priscila see	PRS
Priscilla see	PRS
Prudence see	PD
Puck see	PK
Purdy see	PR
Pursey see	PR
Purvis see	PR
Pyotr see	PTR
Qiang see	Q
Quaashie see	Q
Quan see	Q
Queen see	Q
Quentin see	Q
Quiana see	Q
Quico see	Q
Quill see	Q
Quillan see	Q
Quillermo see	Q
Quina see	Q
Quincy see	Q
Quinitus see	Q
Quinlan see	Q
Quinn see	Q
Quint see	Q
Quinten see	Q
Quintin see	Q
Quinton see	Q
Quinzell see	Q
Quirin see	Q
Quito see	Q
Rab see	RB
Rabbie see	RB
Rabi see	RB
Rabin see	RB
Rachael see	RCH
Rachal see	RCH
Racheal see	RCH
Rachel see	RCH
Rachele see	RCH
Rachell see	RCH
Rachelle see	RCH
Racho see	RCH
Racquel see	RK
Radames see	RD
Radman see	RD
Radomil see	RD
Radoslav see	RD
Rae see	RY
Raeann see	RN
Raegan see	RG
Raekwon see	RK
Rael see	RL
Rafael see	RF
Rafaela see	RF
Rafal see	RF
Rafalek see	RF
Rafayil see	RF
Rafe see	RF
Raff see	RF
Raffael see	RF
Raffaello see	RF
Rafi see	RF
Rafiq see	RF
Rafiuddin see	RF
Rag see	RG
Raghnall see	RG
Ragnar see	RG
Rahsaan see	RN
Rahul see	RL
Raiden see	RD
Raimondo see	RMN
Raimont see	RMN
Raimund see	RMN
Raimundo see	RMN
Raina see	RN
Rainer see	RN
Raini see	RN
Raisa see	RS
Raleigh see	RL
Ralf see	RF
Ralph see	RF
Ralphie see	RF
Ramadan see	RMN
Ramman see	RMN
Ramon see	RMN
Ramona see	RMN
Ramonita see	RMN
Ramsay see	RS
Ramsden see	RMN
Ramsey see	RS
Rana see	RN
Ranae see	RN
Rand see	RN
Randal see	RND
Randall see	RND
Randell see	RND
Randey see	RND
Randi see	RND
Randie see	RND
Randle see	RND
Randolf see	RND
Randolph see	RND
Randy see	RND
Ranee see	RN
Ranon see	RN
Raoul see	RL
Raphael see	RF
Raquel see	RK
Rashad see	RS
Rashadi see	RS
Rashawn see	RSN
Rasheed see	RS
Rashid see	RS
Rashmi see	RS
Rasmus see	RS
Rastus see	RS
Raul see	RL
Raulio see	RL
Raulo see	RL
Ray see	RY
Rayford see	RF
Rayke see	RK
Raylene see	RL
Raymon see	RMN
Raymond see	RMN
Raymonde see	RMN
Raymundo see	RMN
Rayna see	RN
Rayshawn see	RN
Read see	RD
Reade see	RD
Reagan see	RG
Reamonn see	RMN
Reanna see	RN
Reatha see	RTH
Reba see	RB
Rebbeca see	RBK
Rebbecca see	RBK
Rebeca see	RBK
Rebecca see	RBK
Rebekah see	RBK
Red see	RD
Redbert see	RD
Redd see	RD
Reddy see	RD
Rede see	RD
Redmond see	RMN
Redmund see	RMN
Redolfo see	RD
Redvers see	RD
Reece see	RS
Reed see	RD
Reena see	RN
Rees see	RS
Reese see	RS
Reg see	RG
Regan see	RG
Regena see	RG
Regenia see	RG
Reges see	RG
Reggie see	RG
Reggy see	RG
Regina see	RG
Reginald see	RG
Regine see	RG
Reginia see	RG
Reginmunt see	RG
Regis see	RG
Regnauld see	RG
Regnault see	RG
Regulo see	RG
Reico see	RK
Reid see	RD
Reilly see	RL
Reina see	RN
Reinald see	RND
Reinaldo see	RND
Reinaldos see	RND
Reinhart see	RN
Reinhold see	RND
Reinold see	RND
Reinwald see	RND
Reiss see	RS
Reita see	RT
Remington see	RMN
Remona see	RMN
Rena see	RN
Renae see	RN
Renaldo see	RND
Renata see	RT
Renate see	RT
Renato see	RT
Renaud see	RND
Renault see	RN
Renaut see	RN
Rendor see	RND
Rene see	RN
Renea see	RN
Renee see	RN
Renenet see	RN
Renetta see	RT
Renita see	RT
Renna see	RN
Renny see	RN
Renouf see	RN
Renzo see	RN
Ressie see	RS
Reta see	RT
Retha see	RTH
Retta see	RT
Reuben see	RBN
Reubin see	RBN
Reuven see	RV
Rex see	RX
Rexford see	RX
Rey see	RY
Reyes see	RS
Reyhan see	RY
Reymond see	RMN
Reymundo see	RMN
Reyna see	RN
Reynalda see	RND
Reynaldo see	RND
Reynaldos see	RND

Name		Code
Reynold	see	RND
Reynolds	see	RND
Rhea	see	RY
Rhett	see	RT
Rhiannon	see	RN
Rhoda	see	RD
Rhodri	see	RD
Rhonda	see	RND
Rhydderch	see	RD
Rhys	see	RS
Riana	see	RN
Ric	see	RK
Ricardo	see	RK
Riccardo	see	RK
Ricciardo	see	RK
Rich	see	RCH
Richard	see	RCH
Richardson	see	RCH
Richart	see	RCH
Richelle	see	RCH
Richerd	see	RCH
Richi	see	RCH
Richie	see	RCH
Rick	see	RK
Rickert	see	RK
Rickey	see	RK
Ricki	see	RK
Rickie	see	RK
Ricky	see	RK
Rico	see	RK
Ricordio	see	RK
Ridge	see	RD
Ridley	see	RD
Riduan	see	RD
Rie	see	RY
Rieko	see	RK
Rigoberto	see	RG
Riik	see	RK
Rikard	see	RK
Rikki	see	RK
Riks	see	RK
Riley	see	RL
Rimington	see	RMN
Rimon	see	RMN
Rina	see	RN
Rinaldo	see	RND
Ringo	see	RN
Riobard	see	RB
Rion	see	RN
Riquerto	see	RK
Riqui	see	RK
Risa	see	RS
Risto	see	RS
Rita	see	RT
Ritchie	see	RT
Riya	see	RY
Roald	see	RD
Roan	see	RN
Rob	see	RB
Robar	see	RB
Robb	see	RB
Robbi	see	RB
Robbie	see	RB
Robbin	see	RBN
Robby	see	RB
Robbyn	see	RBN
Robena	see	RBN
Robert	see	RBRT
Roberta	see	RBRT
Roberto	see	RBRT
Robertson	see	RBRT
Robi	see	RB
Robin	see	RBN
Robinson	see	RBN
Robson	see	RBN
Robyn	see	RBN
Rocco	see	RK
Rochel	see	RCH
Rochell	see	RCH
Rochelle	see	RCH
Rocio	see	RK
Rock	see	RK
Rockwell	see	RK
Rocky	see	RK
Rod	see	RD
Rodalfo	see	RD
Rodas	see	RD
Roddie	see	RD
Roddy	see	RD
Roderic	see	RD
Roderich	see	RD
Roderick	see	RD
Rodge	see	RD
Rodger	see	RG
Rodgers	see	RG
Rodhlann	see	RD
Rodin	see	RD
Rodman	see	RD
Rodney	see	RD
Rodolfo	see	RF
Rodrego	see	RD
Rodrick	see	RD
Rodrigo	see	RD
Roel	see	RL
Roeland	see	RL
Rog	see	RG
Rogelio	see	RG
Roger	see	RG
Rogerio	see	RG
Rogero	see	RG
Rogers	see	RG
Roguerio	see	RG
Rohan	see	RN
Rohin	see	RN
Rohit	see	RT
Roi	see	RY
Roland	see	RND
Rolanda	see	RND
Rolande	see	RND
Rolando	see	RND
Rolf	see	RF
Rolfe	see	RF
Rollan	see	RL
Rolland	see	RND
Rollie	see	RL
Rollin	see	RL
Rollins	see	RL
Rollo	see	RL
Rollon	see	RL
Rolly	see	RL
Rolo	see	RL
Rolon	see	RL
Rolph	see	RF
Romain	see	RMN
Romaine	see	RMN
Roman	see	RMN
Romana	see	RMN
Romance	see	RMN
Romano	see	RMN
Romino	see	RMN
Romney	see	RMN
Romona	see	RMN
Ron	see	RN
Rona	see	RN
Ronald	see	RND
Ronaldo	see	RND
Ronan	see	RN
Ronda	see	RD
Roni	see	RN
Ronin	see	RN
Ronna	see	RN
Ronni	see	RN
Ronnie	see	RN
Ronny	see	RN
Roosevelt	see	RSL
Rorie	see	RY
Rory	see	RY
Rosa	see	RS
Rosalee	see	RSL
Rosalia	see	RSL
Rosalie	see	RSL
Rosalina	see	RSL
Rosalind	see	RSL
Rosalinda	see	RSL
Rosaline	see	RSL
Rosalyn	see	RSL
Rosana	see	RSN
Rosann	see	RSN
Rosanna	see	RSN
Rosanne	see	RSN
Rosaria	see	RS
Rosario	see	RS
Roscoe	see	RK
Rose	see	RS
Roseann	see	RSN
Roseanna	see	RSN
Roseanne	see	RSN
Roselee	see	RSL
Roselia	see	RSL
Roseline	see	RSL
Rosella	see	RSL
Roselle	see	RSL
Roselyn	see	RSL
Rosemarie	see	RSMR
Rosemary	see	RSMR
Rosena	see	RSN
Rosetta	see	RT
Rosia	see	RS
Rosie	see	RS
Rosina	see	RSN
Rosio	see	RS
Rosita	see	RS
Roslyn	see	RSL
Rosmer	see	RSMR
Ross	see	RS
Rossana	see	RSN
Rossie	see	RS
Rosy	see	RS
Roth	see	RTH
Rowan	see	RN
Rowena	see	RN
Rowland	see	RND
Roxana	see	RX
Roxane	see	RX
Roxann	see	RX
Roxanna	see	RX
Roxanne	see	RX
Roxie	see	RX
Roxy	see	RX
Roy	see	RY
Royal	see	RL
Royce	see	RS
Royd	see	RD
Rubben	see	RBN
Rube	see	RB
Ruben	see	RBN
Ruberto	see	RBRT
Rubi	see	RB
Rubie	see	RB
Rubin	see	RBN
Ruby	see	RB
Rubye	see	RB
Rudd	see	RD
Ruddy	see	RD
Rudgerd	see	RD
Rudiger	see	RD
Rudo	see	RD
Rudolf	see	RF
Rudolph	see	RF
Rudolpho	see	RF
Rudolphus	see	RF
Rudro	see	RD
Rudy	see	RD
Rudyard	see	RD
Rueben	see	RBN
Rufe	see	RF
Rufeo	see	RF
Ruferto	see	RF
Ruffo	see	RF
Rufino	see	RF
Rufinus	see	RF
Rufio	see	RF
Rufo	see	RF
Rufus	see	RF
Ruggero	see	RG
Ruggiero	see	RG
Rugino	see	RG
Rulf	see	RF
Runako	see	RN
Rune	see	RN
Rupert	see	RP
Ruperto	see	RP
Rupo	see	RP
Ruprecht	see	RP
Rurich	see	RCH
Rurik	see	RK
Rush	see	RS
Russ	see	RS
Russel	see	RSL
Russell	see	RSL
Rusty	see	RS
Rutger	see	RG
Ruth	see	RTH
Rutha	see	RTH
Ruthann	see	RTH
Ruthe	see	RTH
Ruthie	see	RTH
Rutty	see	RT
Ruy	see	RY
Ruyen	see	RY
Ryan	see	RN
Ryann	see	RN
Rydell	see	RD
Ryder	see	RD
Rylan	see	RN
Ryland	see	RL
Rylee	see	RL
Ryleigh	see	RL
Ryley	see	RL
Rylie	see	RL
Ryne	see	RN
Saad	see	SD
Sabarain	see	SB
Sabastian	see	SB
Sabin	see	SB
Sabina	see	SB
Sabine	see	SB
Sabino	see	SB
Sabriam	see	SB
Sabrina	see	SB
Saburo	see	SB
Sacarias	see	SK
Sacco	see	SK
Sade	see	SD
Sadie	see	SD
Saffron	see	SF
Sakima	see	SK
Sal	see	SL
Salih	see	SL
Salim	see	SL
Salina	see	SL
Salley	see	SL
Salli	see	SL
Sallie	see	SL
Sally	see	SL
Salma	see	SL
Salmalin	see	SL
Salman	see	SL
Salome	see	SL
Salomon	see	SL
Salos	see	SL
Salud	see	SL
Salustiano	see	SL
Salvador	see	SV
Salvadore	see	SV
Salvatore	see	SV
Sam	see	SM
Samantha	see	SMN
Samara	see	SMR
Samaresh	see	SMR
Sameer	see	SMR
Samein	see	SMN
Samella	see	SM
Sami	see	SM

Name	Code	Name	Code	Name	Code	Name	Code	Name	Code
Samir *see*	SMR	Seamus *see*	SM	Shannon *see*	SHN	Sherie *see*	SHR	Silvia *see*	SV
Samira *see*	SMR	Sean *see*	SN	Shanon *see*	SHN	Sherill *see*	SHR	Sim *see*	SM
Sammie *see*	SM	Seann *see*	SN	Shanta *see*	SHN	Sherilyn *see*	SH(L)	Sima *see*	SM
Sammon *see*	SMN	Season *see*	SSN	Shante *see*	SHN	Sherita *see*	SHR	Simao *see*	SM
Sammy *see*	SM	Seaton *see*	ST	Shantel *see*	SHN	Sherley *see*	SHR	Simen *see*	SMN
Samouel *see*	SM	Sebastian *see*	SB	Shantell *see*	SHN	Sherm *see*	SHR	Simeon *see*	SMN
Samson *see*	SMN	Sebastiano *see*	SB	Shanti *see*	SHN	Sherman *see*	SHR	Simon *see*	SMN
Samual *see*	SM	Sebastianos *see*	SB	Shaquille *see*	SH(L)	Sheron *see*	SHR	Simona *see*	SMN
Samuel *see*	SM	Sebastien *see*	SB	Sharan *see*	SHR	Sherrell *see*	SHR	Simone *see*	SMN
Samuele *see*	SM	Sebastiene *see*	SB	Sharell *see*	SHR	Sherri *see*	SHR	Simonne *see*	SMN
Samuelo *see*	SM	Sebrina *see*	SB	Sharen *see*	SHR	Sherrie *see*	SHR	Simpkins *see*	SMN
Samuru *see*	SM	Seema *see*	SM	Shari *see*	SHR	Sherril *see*	SH(L)	Simpson *see*	SMN
Sana *see*	SN	Seker *see*	SK	Sharie *see*	SHR	Sherrill *see*	SH(L)	Sina *see*	SN
Sanat *see*	SN	Selbastiano *see*	SB	Sharla *see*	SHR	Sherron *see*	SHR	Sincere *see*	SN
Sandeep *see*	SND	Selena *see*	SL	Sharlene *see*	SHR	Sherry *see*	SHR	Sinclair *see*	SN
Sander *see*	SND	Selim *see*	SL	Sharon *see*	SHR	Sherryl *see*	SH(L)	Sindy *see*	SND
Sanders *see*	SND	Selina *see*	SL	Sharonda *see*	SHR	Sherwin *see*	SHR	Singh *see*	SN
Sandi *see*	SND	Selma *see*	SM	Sharri *see*	SHR	Sherwood *see*	SHR	Siobhan *see*	SB
Sandie *see*	SND	Selmar *see*	SL	Sharron *see*	SHR	Shery *see*	SHR	Siomonn *see*	SMN
Sandip *see*	SND	Selvestre *see*	SV	Sharyl *see*	SHR	Sheryl *see*	SHR	Sirilio *see*	SR
Sandon *see*	SND	Sem *see*	SM	Sharyn *see*	SHR	Sheryll *see*	SHR	Sirol *see*	SR
Sandor *see*	SND	Semaj *see*	SM	Shasta *see*	SH(L)	Sheyla *see*	SH(L)	Siva *see*	SV
Sandra *see*	SND	Sena *see*	SN	Shaun *see*	SHN	Shiela *see*	SH(L)	Sivan *see*	SV
Sandy *see*	SND	Senon *see*	SN	Shauna *see*	SHN	Shila *see*	SH(L)	Sky *see*	SK
Sanford *see*	SND	Senwe *see*	SN	Shaunna *see*	SHN	Shiloh *see*	SH(L)	Skye *see*	SK
Sangdrax *see*	SND	Serena *see*	SR	Shawana *see*	SHN	Shimon *see*	SHN	Skyla *see*	SK
Sani *see*	SN	Serenity *see*	SR	Shawanda *see*	SHN	Shing *see*	SHN	Skylar *see*	SK
Sanjay *see*	SN	Sergio *see*	SR	Shawanna *see*	SHN	Shino *see*	SHN	Skyler *see*	SK
Sanjeev *see*	SN	Sesha *see*	SH(L)	Shawn *see*	SHN	Shirely *see*	SHR	Slade *see*	SL
Santa *see*	SN	Seth *see*	S	Shawna *see*	SHN	Shirl *see*	SHR	Slane *see*	SL
Santana *see*	SN	Seton *see*	STN	Shawnee *see*	SHN	Shirlee *see*	SHR	Slava *see*	SV
Santiago *see*	SN	Seumas *see*	SM	Shawnna *see*	SHN	Shirlene *see*	SHR	Slavik *see*	SV
Santino *see*	SN	Seumus *see*	SM	Shayla *see*	SH(L)	Shirley *see*	SHR	Slevin *see*	SV
Santos *see*	SN	Sevastian *see*	SV	Shaylee *see*	SH(L)	Shirly *see*	SHR	Sly *see*	SL
Santosh *see*	SN	Sevilen *see*	SV	Shayna *see*	SHN	Shiro *see*	SHR	Slyvia *see*	SV
Sara *see*	SR	Seymore *see*	SMR	Shayne *see*	SHN	Sholom *see*	SH(L)	Snehal *see*	SN
Sarah *see*	SR	Seymour *see*	SMR	Shea *see*	SH	Sholto *see*	SH(L)	So *see*	S
Sarahi *see*	SR	Shad *see*	SD	Sheehan *see*	SHN	Shona *see*	SHN	Socorro *see*	SK
Sarai *see*	SR	Shahriyar *see*	SHR	Sheena *see*	SHN	Shonda *see*	SHN	Sofia *see*	SF
Sarina *see*	SR	Shaina *see*	SHN	Sheila *see*	SH(L)	Shonna *see*	SHN	Sofian *see*	SF
Sasha *see*	SH(L)	Shakira *see*	SHR	Shela *see*	SH(L)	Shoshana *see*	SHN	Sol *see*	SL
Sau *see*	S	Shala *see*	SH(L)	Shelbi *see*	SH(L)	Shreya *see*	SHR	Solaman *see*	SL
Saul *see*	SL	Shalom *see*	SH(L)	Shelbie *see*	SH(L)	Shrihas *see*	SHR	Solamh *see*	SL
Saulo *see*	SL	Shalonda *see*	SHN	Shelby *see*	SH(L)	Shrijay *see*	SHR	Solia *see*	SL
Saundra *see*	SND	Shamar *see*	SHR	Sheldon *see*	SH(L)	Shul *see*	SH(L)	Sollie *see*	SL
Saurav *see*	SV	Shameel *see*	SH(L)	Shelia *see*	SH(L)	Shyann *see*	SHN	Solly *see*	SL
Sauveur *see*	SV	Shameka *see*	SH(L)	Shella *see*	SH(L)	Shyanne *see*	SHN	Solomon *see*	SL
Savana *see*	SV	Shamika *see*	SH(L)	Shelley *see*	SH(L)	Shyenti *see*	SHN	Somer *see*	SMR
Savanah *see*	SV	Shamir *see*	SHR	Shelli *see*	SH(L)	Shyla *see*	SH(L)	Sommer *see*	SMR
Savanna *see*	SV	Shan *see*	SHN	Shellie *see*	SH(L)	Sibian *see*	SB	Son *see*	SN
Savannah *see*	SV	Shana *see*	SHN	Shelly *see*	SH(L)	Sicilio *see*	SK	Sona *see*	SN
Savion *see*	SV	Shanae *see*	SHN	Shelomoh *see*	SH(L)	Sid *see*	SD	Sondra *see*	SND
Savvas *see*	SV	Shanda *see*	SHN	Shelton *see*	SH(L)	Sidath *see*	SD	Sonia *see*	SN
Sayre *see*	SR	Shandra *see*	SHN	Shemar *see*	SHR	Siddharth *see*	SD	Sonja *see*	SN
Scarlett *see*	SK	Shane *see*	SHN	Shemuel *see*	SH(L)	Sidney *see*	SD	Sonny *see*	SN
Schroeder *see*	SD	Shania *see*	SHN	Shen *see*	SHN	Sienna *see*	SN	Sonya *see*	SN
Schuyler *see*	SL	Shanice *see*	SHN	Shena *see*	SHN	Sierra *see*	SR	Soo *see*	S
Scot *see*	SK	Shanika *see*	SHN	Shengdar *see*	SHN	Silas *see*	SL	Sopharith *see*	SF
Scotie *see*	SK	Shaniqua *see*	SHN	Shenna *see*	SHN	Silva *see*	SV	Sophia *see*	SF
Scott *see*	SK	Shanita *see*	SHN	Sheratan *see*	SHN	Silvain *see*	SV	Sophie *see*	SF
Scotti *see*	SK	Shaniya *see*	SHN	Sherborn *see*	SHN	Silvano *see*	SV	Soraya *see*	SR
Scottie *see*	SK	Shankar *see*	SHN	Sheree *see*	SHR	Silverio *see*	SV	Sorley *see*	SL
Scotty *see*	SK	Shanna *see*	SHN	Sherell *see*	SHR	Silvester *see*	SV	Spencer *see*	SN
Scuit *see*	SK	Shannan *see*	SHN	Sheri *see*	SHR	Silvestre *see*	SV	Spenser *see*	SN
Seaian *see*	SN	Shannen *see*	SHN	Sheridan *see*	SHR	Silvestro *see*	SV	Spring *see*	SN

Sreko *see* SK	Subir *see* SB	Talis *see* TL	Tau *see* T	Terumi *see* TR
Stacey *see* STC	Sudi *see* SD	Taliyah *see* TL	Tauno *see* TN	Tess *see* TS
Staci *see* STC	Sue *see* S	Talli *see* TL	Taunya *see* TN	Tessa *see* TS
Stacia *see* STC	Sueann *see* SN	Talman *see* TL	Taurean *see* TRN	Tessie *see* TS
Stacie *see* STC	Suellen *see* SN	Talon *see* TL	Taurin *see* TRN	Thad *see* TH
Stacy *see* STC	Sullivan *see* SV	Tam *see* TM	Tawana *see* TN	Thaddaus *see* TH
Stan *see* STN	Sultan *see* SL	Tama *see* TM	Tawanda *see* TN	Thaddeo *see* TH
Stancio *see* STN	Sumit *see* SM	Taman *see* TM	Tawanna *see* TN	Thaddeus *see* TH
Stane *see* STN	Summer *see* SMR	Tamar *see* TMR	Tawny *see* TN	Thaddy *see* TH
Stanford *see* STN	Sun *see* SN	Tamara *see* TMR	Tawnya *see* TN	Thady *see* TH
Stanislaus *see* STN	Sunday *see* SND	Tamas *see* TM	Taya *see* T	Thaine *see* TH
Stanislav *see* STN	Sunnie *see* SN	Tamatha *see* TMTH	Tayler *see* TL	Thales *see* TH
Stanlee *see* STN	Sunny *see* SN	Tameka *see* TM	Taylor *see* TL	Thalia *see* TH
Stanleigh *see* STN	Sunshine *see* SSN	Tamela *see* TM	Tayna *see* TN	Thanh *see* TH
Stanley *see* STN	Susan *see* SSN	Tamera *see* TMR	Tayor *see* TR	Thanos *see* TH
Stanly *see* STN	Susana *see* SSN	Tami *see* TM	Te *see* T	Thayne *see* TH
Stannard *see* STN	Susann *see* SSN	Tamia *see* TM	Ted *see* TD	Thea *see* TH
Stanton *see* STN	Susanna *see* SSN	Tamie *see* TM	Teddy *see* TD	Theador *see* TH
Star *see* STR	Susannah *see* SSN	Tamika *see* TM	Tedi *see* TD	Theadore *see* TH
Starla *see* STR	Susanne *see* SSN	Tamiko *see* TM	Teemofe *see* TM	Theda *see* TH
Starling *see* STL	Susie *see* SZ	Tammara *see* TMR	Teena *see* TN	Thelma *see* TH
Starr *see* STR	Susy *see* SZ	Tammera *see* TMR	Telek *see* TL	Thematheo *see* TH
Steaphan *see* STFN	Suzan *see* SZ	Tammi *see* TM	Telem *see* TL	Theo *see* TH
Stefan *see* STFN	Suzann *see* SZ	Tammie *see* TM	Tellis *see* TL	Theoderic *see* TH
Stefani *see* STFN	Suzanna *see* SZ	Tammy *see* TM	Telly *see* TL	Theodor *see* TH
Stefania *see* STFN	Suzanne *see* SZ	Tamra *see* TMR	Tem *see* TM	Theodora *see* TH
Stefanie *see* STFN	Suzette *see* SZ	Tana *see* TN	Teman *see* TM	Theodore *see* TH
Stefano *see* STFN	Suzie *see* SZ	Tandy *see* TN	Temotio *see* TM	Theodoric *see* TH
Stefany *see* STFN	Suzy *see* SZ	Tanek *see* TN	Tena *see* TN	Theodorus *see* TH
Steffanie *see* STFN	Sven *see* SV	Taner *see* TN	Tenisha *see* TN	Theresa *see* TRS
Steffen *see* STFN	Sy *see* S	Tanesha *see* TN	Tennie *see* TN	Therese *see* TRS
Stella *see* STL	Sybil *see* SB	Tangela *see* TN	Tennille *see* TN	Theresia *see* TRS
Stephaine *see* STFN	Syble *see* SB	Tani *see* TN	Tente *see* TN	Theressa *see* TRS
Stephan *see* STFN	Syd *see* SD	Tania *see* TN	Teodero *see* TD	Theron *see* TH
Stephane *see* STFN	Sydnee *see* SD	Tanika *see* TN	Teodocio *see* TD	Thersa *see* TRS
Stephani *see* STFN	Sydney *see* SD	Tanisha *see* TN	Teodoro *see* TD	Thiago *see* TH
Stephania *see* STFN	Sydni *see* SD	Taniya *see* TN	Tera *see* TR	Thierry *see* TH
Stephanie *see* STFN	Sydnie *see* SD	Tanna *see* TN	Terance *see* TRN	Thom *see* TM
Stephanos *see* STFN	Syed *see* SD	Tanner *see* TN	Tereasa *see* TRS	Thoma *see* TM
Stephanus *see* STFN	Sylvesdre *see* SV	Tano *see* TN	Terence *see* TRN	Thomas *see* TM
Stephany *see* STFN	Sylvester *see* SV	Tanya *see* TN	Terenciano *see* TRN	Thomasina *see* TH
Stephen *see* STFN	Sylvia *see* SV	Tao *see* T	Terencio *see* TRN	Thomesito *see* TM
Stephenie *see* STFN	Syril *see* SR	Tara *see* TR	Terentilo *see* TRN	Thompson *see* TM
Stephine *see* STFN	Syrus *see* SR	Tarah *see* TR	Tererso *see* TRS	Thor *see* TH
Stephnie *see* STFN		Taren *see* TRN	Teres *see* TRS	Thorsten *see* TH
Stephon *see* STFN	Tabatha *see* TB	Tari *see* TR	Teresa *see* TRS	Thresa *see* TRS
Sterling *see* STR	Tabetha *see* TB	Tarik *see* TR	Terese *see* TRS	Thurman *see* TH
Stetson *see* STN	Tabib *see* TB	Tarintino *see* TR	Teresia *see* TRS	Tia *see* T
Steuart *see* STR	Tabitha *see* TB	Tariq *see* TR	Teresita *see* TRS	Tiana *see* TN
Stevan *see* STV	Tabo *see* TB	Tarn *see* TRN	Teressa *see* TRS	Tianna *see* TN
Steve *see* STV	Tabor *see* TB	Taro *see* TR	Teri *see* TR	Tiara *see* TR
Steven *see* STV	Tad *see* TD	Tarquin *see* TRN	Terina *see* TRN	Tibs *see* TB
Stevie *see* STV	Tadanobu *see* TD	Tarra *see* TR	Terisa *see* TRS	Tielman *see* TL
Stevin *see* STV	Tadeo *see* TD	Tarrus *see* TR	Terra *see* TR	Tien *see* TN
Steward *see* STR	Tadhg *see* TD	Tarsha *see* TRSH	Terrance *see* TRN	Tiennot *see* TN
Stewart *see* STR	Tadi *see* TD	Taryn *see* TRN	Terrel *see* TR	Tieodoro *see* TD
Stirling *see* STR	Tadzi *see* TD	Tas *see* TS	Terrell *see* TR	Tiera *see* TR
Stone *see* STN	Tahir *see* TR	Tasha *see* TS	Terrence *see* TRN	Tierra *see* TR
Stori *see* STR	Taina *see* TN	Tate *see* T	Terresa *see* TRS	Tifany *see* TFNY
Stormy *see* STR	Taison *see* TS	Tatiana *see* TN	Terri *see* TR	Tiffaney *see* TFNY
Strom *see* STR	Tal *see* TL	Tatianna *see* TN	Terrie *see* TR	Tiffani *see* TFNY
Stuart *see* STR	Talal *see* TL	Tatsu *see* TS	Terrill *see* TR	Tiffanie *see* TFNY
Su *see* S	Tales *see* TL	Tatsuya *see* TS	Terrin *see* TRN	Tiffany *see* TFNY
Suanne *see* SN	Talia *see* TL	Tatum *see* TM	Terris *see* TRS	Tiffiny *see* TFNY
Subhani *see* SB	Taliesin *see* TL	Tatyana *see* TN	Terry *see* TR	Tilden *see* TL

Tilo *see* TL
Tim *see* TM
Timateo *see* TM
Timeen *see* TM
Times *see* TM
Timeto *see* TM
Timex *see* TM
Timin *see* TM
Timiro *see* TM
Timiteo *see* TM
Timmie *see* TM
Timmothy *see* TMTH
Timmy *see* TM
Timofei *see* TM
Timoteo *see* TM
Timothee *see* TMTH
Timotheos *see* TMTH
Timotheus *see* TMTH
Timothy *see* TMTH
Timoty *see* TM
Timour *see* TM
Timur *see* TM
Tina *see* TN
Tino *see* TN
Tiny *see* TN
Tiomoid *see* TM
Tito *see* T
Titus *see* TS
Tivon *see* TV
Tobal *see* TB
Tobalito *see* TB
Tobbar *see* TB
Tobias *see* TB
Tobin *see* TB
Toby *see* TB
Tod *see* TD
Todd *see* TD
Todor *see* TD
Todorko *see* TD
Todoro *see* TD
Tohon *see* TN
Tola *see* TL
Tolek *see* TL
Toli *see* TL
Tom *see* TM
Toma *see* TM
Toman *see* TM
Tomas *see* TM
Tomasens *see* TM
Tomash *see* TM
Tomaso *see* TM
Tomaz *see* TM
Tomeka *see* TM
Tomi *see* TM
Tomika *see* TN
Tomito *see* TM
Tomlin *see* TM
Tommie *see* TM
Tommy *see* TM
Tommye *see* TM
Tomoaki *see* TM
Tomoichiro *see* TM
Tomotaka *see* TM
Tona *see* TN
Toncho *see* TN

Tonek *see* TN
Toney *see* TN
Tong *see* TN
Toni *see* TN
Tonia *see* TN
Tonico *see* TN
Tonie *see* TN
Tonio *see* TN
Tonja *see* TN
Tony *see* TN
Tonya *see* TN
Tonyo *see* TN
Tor *see* TR
Tora *see* TR
Tord *see* TR
Tore *see* TR
Torey *see* TR
Tori *see* TR
Torrance *see* TRN
Torrence *see* TRN
Torrey *see* TR
Torri *see* TR
Torrie *see* TR
Tory *see* TR
Toya *see* T
Trace *see* TRS
Tracee *see* TRS
Tracey *see* TRS
Traci *see* TRS
Tracie *see* TRS
Tracy *see* TRS
Trae *see* TR
Tran *see* TRN
Trav *see* TRV
Travis *see* TRV
Travon *see* TRV
Tre *see* TR
Treasa *see* TRS
Treena *see* TRN
Tremaine *see* TRN
Tremayne *see* TRN
Trena *see* TRN
Trent *see* TRN
Trenton *see* TRN
Tresa *see* TRS
Tressa *see* TRS
Trev *see* TRV
Treva *see* TRV
Trevalyn *see* TRV
Trever *see* TRV
Trevin *see* TRV
Trevion *see* TRV
Trevon *see* TRV
Trevor *see* TRV
Trevorlan *see* TRV
Trey *see* TR
Treyton *see* TRN
Treyvon *see* TRV
Tricia *see* TRSH
Trina *see* TRN
Trinity *see* TRN
Trish *see* TRSH
Trisha *see* TRSH
Trista *see* TRS
Tristam *see* TRS

Tristan *see* TRS
Tristem *see* TRS
Tristen *see* TRS
Tristian *see* TRS
Tristin *see* TRS
Triston *see* TRS
Tristram *see* TRS
Troy *see* TR
Trudi *see* TD
Trudie *see* TD
Trudy *see* TD
Truman *see* TRN
Trystan *see* TRS
Tu *see* T
Tuan *see* TN
Tudor *see* TD
Tudur *see* TD
Tudyr *see* TD
Tunu *see* TN
Turner *see* TRN
Tuta *see* T
Tuto *see* T
Twila *see* TL
Twyla *see* TL
Ty *see* T
Tyler *see* TL
Tylor *see* TL
Tymon *see* TM
Tyne *see* TN
Tyra *see* TR
Tyree *see* TR
Tyreek *see* TR
Tyrek *see* TR
Tyrell *see* TR
Tyrese *see* TRS
Tyrik *see* TR
Tyriq *see* TR
Tyrique *see* TR
Tyrome *see* TR
Tyron *see* TRN
Tyrone *see* TRN
Tyson *see* TS

Uberto *see* U
Ude *see* U
Ugo *see* U
Ugolino *see* U
Ugon *see* U
Uilleam *see* U
Uilliam *see* U
Uillioe *see* U
Uinsionn *see* U
Ulick *see* U
Ulises *see* U
Ulmar *see* U
Ulric *see* U
Ulrike *see* U
Ulysses *see* U
Umesh *see* U
Unique *see* U
Urbaine *see* U
Urban *see* U
Urbano *see* U
Urbanus *see* U
Uriah *see* U

Uriel *see* U
Urien *see* U
Urlando *see* U
Urso *see* U
Urson *see* U
Ursuelo *see* U
Ursul *see* U
Ursula *see* U
Urvan *see* U
Usman *see* U
Ussulo *see* U
Uval *see* U
Uzomas *see* U

Vaclav *see* VK
Val *see* VL
Valance *see* VL
Valarie *see* VL
Valen *see* VL
Valence *see* VL
Valencia *see* VNS
Valente *see* VLT
Valentijn *see* VLT
Valentin *see* VLT
Valentina *see* VLT
Valentine *see* VLT
Valentino *see* VLT
Valeri *see* VL
Valeria *see* VL
Valerie *see* VL
Valery *see* VL
Valiant *see* VLT
Valin *see* VL
Valmy *see* VL
Valorie *see* VL
Valrie *see* VL
Van *see* VN
Vance *see* VNS
Vanesa *see* VNS
Vanessa *see* VNS
Vanka *see* VN
Vann *see* VN
Vannesa *see* VNS
Vannessa *see* VNS
Vanni *see* VN
Vanny *see* VN
Varden *see* VR(N)
Vartan *see* VR(N)
Vaughan *see* VN
Vaughn *see* VN
Velda *see* VL
Velden *see* VL
Velia *see* VL
Vella *see* VL
Velma *see* VL
Vencel *see* VNS
Venessa *see* VNS
Venita *see* VN
Venu *see* VN
Venudhar *see* VN
Venus *see* VNS
Venya *see* VN
Veola *see* VL
Vera *see* VR(N)
Verena *see* VR(N)

Vergil *see* VRG
Vern *see* VR(N)
Verna *see* VR(N)
Vernaldo *see* VR(N)
Vernaldos *see* VR(N)
Vernavela *see* VR(N)
Verne *see* VR(N)
Vernell *see* VR(N)
Verney *see* VR(N)
Vernia *see* VR(N)
Vernice *see* VR(N)
Vernie *see* VR(N)
Vernon *see* VR(N)
Verona *see* VR(N)
Veronica *see* VR(N)
Verrie *see* VR
Vic *see* VK
Vicencio *see* VNS
Vicente *see* VNS
Vick *see* VK
Vickey *see* VK
Vicki *see* VK
Vickie *see* VK
Vicky *see* VK
Vico *see* VK
Victo *see* VK
Victoir *see* VK
Victor *see* VK
Victoria *see* VK
Victorianas *see* VK
Victro *see* VK
Viki *see* VK
Vikki *see* VK
Vila *see* VL
Vildor *see* VL
Vilhelm *see* VL
Vili *see* VL
Viljo *see* VL
Vilma *see* VL
Viltoriano *see* VL
Vin *see* VN
Vinai *see* VN
Vince *see* VNS
Vincent *see* VNS
Vincenzo *see* VNS
Vincze *see* VNS
Vinn *see* VN
Vinnie *see* VN
Vinny *see* VN
Vinod *see* VN
Viola *see* VL
Violet *see* VLT
Violeta *see* VLT
Violette *see* VLT
Viren *see* VR(N)
Virge *see* VRG
Virgen *see* VRG
Virgie *see* VRG
Virgil *see* VRG
Virgilio *see* VRG
Virgina *see* VRG
Virginia *see* VRG
Vivan *see* VVN
Vivian *see* VVN
Viviana *see* VVN

Name		Code
Vivien	see	VVN
Vivienne	see	VVN
Von	see	VN
Vonda	see	VN
Vonnie	see	VN
Vuk	see	VK
Wade	see	WD
Wald	see	WD
Walden	see	WD
Waldo	see	WD
Waleed	see	WD
Waleska	see	WL
Walker	see	WL
Wallace	see	WL
Wallache	see	WL
Wallie	see	WL
Wallis	see	WL
Wally	see	WL
Walsh	see	WL
Walt	see	WT
Walter	see	WT
Walters	see	WT
Walton	see	WT
Wan	see	WN
Wanda	see	WN
Ward	see	WD
Wardell	see	WD
Warden	see	WD
Warder	see	WD
Warner	see	WN
Warren	see	WN
Wasi	see	WS
Wasif	see	WS
Wasseem	see	WS
Wat	see	WT
Wataru	see	WT
Waterio	see	WT
Watkin	see	WT
Watson	see	WT
Watty	see	WT
Wayland	see	WL
Waylen	see	WL
Waylon	see	WL
Waymon	see	WN
Wayne	see	WN
Weed	see	WD
Weldon	see	WL
Wen	see	WN
Wenceslas	see	WN
Wende	see	WN
Wendell	see	WL
Wendi	see	WN
Wendie	see	WN
Wendy	see	WN
Wenona	see	WN
Wenzel	see	WL
Werner	see	WN
Wes	see	WS
Wesh	see	WS
Wesley	see	WS
Wessel	see	WS
West	see	WS
Westleigh	see	WS
Westley	see	WS
Weston	see	WS
Whitley	see	WT
Whitney	see	WT
Wicent	see	WS
Wilber	see	WL
Wilbert	see	WL
Wilbur	see	WL
Wilburn	see	WL
Wilda	see	WL
Wilder	see	WL
Wildon	see	WL
Wiley	see	WL
Wilford	see	WL
Wilfred	see	WL
Wilfredo	see	WL
Wilfrid	see	WL
Wilfried	see	WL
Wilhelm	see	WL
Wilhelmina	see	WLM
Wilkes	see	WL
Will	see	WL
Willard	see	WL
Willem	see	WLM
Willet	see	WL
Willi	see	WL
William	see	WLM
Williams	see	WL
Williamson	see	WLM
Willie	see	WL
Williemae	see	WLM
Willis	see	WL
Willow	see	WL
Willy	see	WL
Wilma	see	WLM
Wilmer	see	WLM
Wilmot	see	WLM
Wilny	see	WL
Wilson	see	WL
Wilton	see	WL
Wilu	see	WL
Win	see	WN
Windy	see	WN
Winfield	see	WN
Winfred	see	WN
Wingi	see	WN
Winifred	see	WN
Winn	see	WN
Winnie	see	WN
Winnifred	see	WN
Winny	see	WN
Winona	see	WN
Winston	see	WN
Winter	see	WN
Winthrop	see	WN
Winton	see	WN
Winward	see	WN
Witold	see	WT
Wonda	see	WN
Wood	see	WD
Woodie	see	WD
Woodrow	see	WD
Woody	see	WD
Wuliton	see	WL
Wullie	see	WL
Wunand	see	WN
Wyatt	see	WT
Wylie	see	WL
Wynona	see	WN
Wynono	see	WN
Wynton	see	WN
Xabiel	see	X
Xabier	see	X
Xan	see	X
Xanatos	see	X
Xander	see	X
Xavier	see	X
Xayvion	see	X
Xeno	see	X
Xenos	see	X
Xerex	see	X
Xerxes	see	X
Xever	see	X
Xiaobing	see	X
Xietian	see	X
Ximena	see	X
Ximon	see	X
Xiomara	see	X
Xun	see	X
Xzavier	see	X
Yaar	see	Y
Yadid	see	Y
Yadiel	see	Y
Yadin	see	Y
Yadira	see	Y
Yafeu	see	Y
Yahaira	see	Y
Yahir	see	Y
Yajaira	see	Y
Yakar	see	Y
Yale	see	Y
Yan	see	Y
Yanai	see	Y
Yancy	see	YS
Yang	see	Y
Yanira	see	Y
Yann	see	Y
Yannis	see	YS
Yao	see	Y
Yaritza	see	YS
Yasin	see	YS
Yasir	see	YS
Yasmeen	see	YS
Yasmin	see	YS
Yasmine	see	YS
Yassen	see	YS
Yasuo	see	YS
Yayo	see	Y
Yazmin	see	YS
Yehuda	see	Y
Yen	see	Y
Yered	see	Y
Yesenia	see	YS
Yessenia	see	YS
Yevette	see	YV
Yitzchak	see	Y
Yoko	see	Y
Yolanda	see	Y
Yolande	see	Y
Yolando	see	Y
Yolonda	see	Y
Yonah	see	Y
Yonas	see	YS
Yong	see	Y
Yoni	see	Y
Yosef	see	YS
Yoselin	see	YS
Yoseph	see	YS
Yosha	see	YS
Yoshiko	see	YS
Youlanda	see	Y
Young	see	Y
Ysaac	see	YS
Ysaax	see	YS
Ysaye	see	YS
Yssach	see	YS
Yulanda	see	Y
Yuliana	see	Y
Yunis	see	YS
Yuri	see	Y
Yusef	see	YS
Yushua	see	YS
Yussuf	see	YS
Yusuf	see	YS
Yuval	see	YV
Yuyo	see	Y
Yvaine	see	YV
Yves	see	Y
Yvette	see	YV
Yvon	see	YV
Yvone	see	YV
Yvonne	see	YV
Zac	see	ZK
Zacarias	see	ZK
Zacariaz	see	ZK
Zacario	see	ZK
Zacaris	see	ZK
Zaccaria	see	ZK
Zacchaeus	see	ZK
Zach	see	ZK
Zachaios	see	ZK
Zachariah	see	ZK
Zacharias	see	ZK
Zacharie	see	ZK
Zacharjasz	see	ZK
Zachary	see	ZK
Zachery	see	ZK
Zack	see	ZK
Zackary	see	ZK
Zackery	see	ZK
Zackry	see	ZK
Zaed	see	Z
Zafar	see	Z
Zaida	see	Z
Zain	see	Z
Zaire	see	Z
Zak	see	ZK
Zakai	see	ZK
Zakarias	see	ZK
Zakarij	see	ZK
Zakariyya	see	ZK
Zakary	see	ZK
Zaki	see	ZK
Zakur	see	ZK
Zamir	see	Z
Zan	see	Z
Zander	see	Z
Zandra	see	Z
Zane	see	Z
Zaria	see	Z
Zavier	see	Z
Zayne	see	Z
Zeb	see	Z
Zebadiah	see	Z
Zebedee	see	Z
Zechariah	see	ZK
Zed	see	Z
Zeke	see	Z
Zelda	see	Z
Zella	see	Z
Zelma	see	Z
Zena	see	Z
Zenon	see	Z
Zerach	see	ZK
Zerachia	see	ZK
Zerika	see	ZK
Zev	see	Z
Zig	see	Z
Ziggy	see	Z
Zikomo	see	ZK
Zina	see	Z
Zion	see	Z
Zoe	see	Z
Zoey	see	Z
Zoie	see	Z
Zola	see	Z
Zollie	see	Z
Zolly	see	Z
Zoraida	see	Z
Zubin	see	Z

Abigail van Buren (Courtesy of Photofest), Abraham Lincoln (Courtesy of Photofest), Ada Lovelace (Photo courtesy of Getty Images), Adam West (The Kobal Collection), Adelaide Hall (Photo courtesy of Getty Images), Alfred Nobel (Photo courtesy of Getty Images), Agnes Moorehead (The Kobal Collection/Columbia), Al Franken (Courtesy of Photofest), Alanis Morrisette (Courtesy of Photofest), Albert Einstein (Courtesy of Photofest), Alec Baldwin (The Kobal Collection/20th Century Fox), Alexander Graham Bell (Courtesy of Photofest), Alicia Silverstone (The Kobal Collection/Paramount), Alvin Ailey (Courtesy of Photofest), Amber Benson (Courtesy of Photofest), Amelia Earheart (Courtesy of Photofest), Amy Irving (The Kobal Collection/Sony Pictures Classics/Hernandez, Ana), Anastasia Romanov (Courtesy of Photofest), Andrew Jackson (Courtesy of Photofest), Angelina Jolie (The Kobal Collection/Mandalay Ent/Paramount/Duhamel, Francois), Anne Heche (The Kobal Collection/20th Century Fox/Sebastian, Lorey), Archibald Macleish (Photo courtesy of Getty Images), Armand Hammer (Courtesy of Photofest), Arnold Schwarzenegger (The Kobal Collection), Art Garfunkle (Courtesy of Photofest), Arthur Ashe (Courtesy of Photofest), Ashley Judd (The Kobal Collection/Fox 2000 Pictures), Audrey Hepburn (The Kobal Collection), Barbra Streisand (The Kobal Collection/Columbia), Barry Bonds (Courtesy of Photofest), Beck (Courtesy of Photofest), Ben Affleck (The Kobal Collection/Columbia/Revolution Studios/Caruso, Phillip), Bess Truman (Courtesy of Photofest), Beth Henley (Photo courtesy of Getty Images), Bette Davis (The Kobal Collection/Fryer/Elmer), Beverly D'Angelo (The Kobal Collection), Bill Clinton (Courtesy of Photofest), Bo Jackson (Courtesy of Photofest), Bob Crane (The Kobal Collection/CBS-TV), Brandi Chastain (Courtesy of Photofest), Brian Dennehy (The Kobal Collection/Mondial/Tangram), Brigitte Bardot (The Kobal Collection/Films Ege/Hoche/Limot), Britney Spears (The Kobal Collection/Wong, Roger), Brooke Shields (The Kobal Collection/NBC-TV/Ragel, Jon), Bruce Willis (The Kobal Collection), Buddy Holly (Courtesy of Photofest), Buffy/Sarah Michelle Gellar (The Kobal Collection/20th Century Fox Television/MacPherson, Andrew), Camilla Parker-Bowles (Ken Goff Photos/WireImage.com), Candice Bergen (The Kobal Collection/Touchstone/Iovino, Peter), Carl Sagan (Courtesy of Photofest), Cameron Diaz (The Kobal Collection/Columbia/Michaels, Darren), Carmine Galante (Photo courtesy of Getty Images), Carolyn Bessette Kennedy (Photo courtesy of Getty Images), Carrie Fisher (The Kobal Collection/20th Century Fox), Casey Stengel (Photo courtesy of Getty Images), Cassandra Peterson (Courtesy of Photofest), Catherine Zeta-Jones (The Kobal Collection/Fefer, Stephane), Cecil B. Demille (The Kobal Collection/Paramount), Celine Dion (Courtesy of Photofest), Charlie Chaplin (The Kobal Collection), Chelsea Clinton (Jim Spellman/WireImage.com), Cher (The Kobal Collection), Chet Baker (Photo courtesy of Getty Images), Christiane Amanpour (Courtesy of Photofest), Chuck Norris (The Kobal Collection/CBS/Redin, Van), Chyna (Kevin Mazur/WireImage.com), Cindy Crawford (The Kobal Collection/Warner Bros/Silver Pictures), Claire Danes (The Kobal Collection/MFM/Morton, Merrick), Clarke Gable (The Kobal Collection/Willinger, Laszlo), Claudia Schiffer (Courtesy of Photofest), Clifford Irving (Courtesy of Photofest), Clint Eastwood (The Kobal Collection), Cobi Jones (Essy Ghavameddini/MLS/WireImage.com), Connie Chung (The Kobal Collection/ABC News-TV/Fenn, Steve), Conrad Hilton (Courtesy of Photofest), Corbin Bernsen (The Kobal Collection/20th Century Fox), Courteney Cox (The Kobal Collection/Franchise/Morgan Creek/WB/Markfield, Alan), Craig T. Nelson (The Kobal Collection), Cynthia Rothrock (Courtesy of Photofest), Daisy Fuentes (The Kobal Collection/Women's Entertainment), Dale Earnhardt (Allen Kee/WireImage.com), Dame Edna (The Kobal Collection), Daryll Hannah (The Kobal Collection/Touchstone), David Geffen (Courtesy of Photofest), Debbie Harry (The Kobal Collection/United Artists), Demi Moore (The Kobal Collection/Warner Bros/Baltimore/Constant/Hamill, Brian), Dennis Rodman (The Kobal Collection/Columbia/Mandalay), Diana Ross (The Kobal Collection / Costa, Tony), Dick Butkus (Courtesy of Photofest), Dominick Dunne (Courtesy of Photofest), Donald Trump (Jim Spellman/WireImage.com), Dorian Harewood (Courtesy of Photofest), Doris Day (The Kobal Collection), Dorothea Lange (Library of Congress), Douglas Fairbanks (The Kobal Collection), Drew Carey (The Kobal Collection/Warner Bros TV/Mohawk Prod), Dudley Moore (The Kobal Collection), Dustin Hoffman (The Kobal Collection), Dwight D. Eisenhower (Courtesy of Photofest), Dylan McDermott (The Kobal Collection/Warner Bros/Village Roadshow/Little, Blake), Ed Harris (The Kobal Collection/Dreamworks/Universal/Reed, Eli), Edwin Moses (Jean-Paul Aussenard/WireImage.com), Elisa Donovan (Courtesy of Photofest) Elizabeth Taylor (The Kobal Collection), Ella Fitzgerald (Courtesy of Photofest), Ellen Degeneres (The Kobal Collection/HBO/Brusso, Andrew), Elton John (Courtesy of Photofest), Emma Thompson (The Kobal Collection/Universal/Duhamel, Francois), Emmeline Pankhurst (Photo courtesy of Getty Images), Erica Jong (Courtesy of Photofest), Ernest Hemingway (Courtesy of Photofest), Errol Flynn (The Kobal Collection/Hurrell, George), Esther Williams (The Kobal Collection/MGM/Apger, Virgil), Ethel Merman (The Kobal Collection/Paramount), Eugene Levy (The Kobal Collection/Touchstone/Emerson, Sam), Eunice Shriver (Photo courtesy of Getty Images), Eva Gabor (The Kobal Collection), Evelyn Waugh (Photo courtesy of Getty Images), Ezra Pound (Photo courtesy of Getty Images), Fabio (Courtesy of Photofest), Faith Hill (Courtesy of Photofest), Farrah Fawcett (The Kobal Collection), Faye Dunaway (The Kobal Collection/Warner Bros), Federico Fellini (The Kobal Collection), Fiona Apple (Courtesy of Photofest), Florence Nighingale (Photo courtesy of Getty Images), Frances McDormand (The Kobal Collection/Working Title/Polygram/Tackett, Michael), Frank Sinatra (The Kobal Collection), Gabriel Byrne (The Kobal Collection/Beacon Communications/Rosenthal, Zade), Gail Devers (Photo courtesy of Getty Images), Gary Oldman (The Kobal Collection/Handmade Films), Geena Davis (The Kobal Collection/Touchstone TV/D'Amico. Bob), Genevieve Bujold (Courtesy of Photofest), George Clooney (The Kobal Collection), Gerard Depardieu (The Kobal Collection/Touchstone), Ginger Rogers (The Kobal Collection/MGM/Apger, Virgil), Glenn Close (The Kobal Collection), Gloria Swanson (The Kobal Collection/Gray, Eric), Goldie Hawn (The Kobal Collection), Grace Kelly (The Kobal Collection), Greta Garbo (Courtesy of Photofest), Gus Grissom (Courtesy of Photofest), Guy Pearce (The Kobal Collection/Monarchy/Regency), Gwen Stefani (Courtesy of Photofest), Halle Berry (The Kobal Collection/MGM/EON/Hamshere, Keith), Harry Belafonte (The Kobal Collection), Hazel Wightman (Photo courtesy of Getty Images), Heather Locklear (The Kobal Collection/ABC-TV), Heidi Fleiss (Courtesy of Photofest), Helen Hunt (The Kobal Collection/WB/Universal/Amblin), Henry Fonda (The Kobal Collection/Coburn, Bob), Herman Melville (Courtesy of Photofest), Hope Davis (The Kobal Collection/Holedigger Films Inc), Howard Stern (The Kobal Collection/Paramount/Rysher/Bailey, K C), Hubert Humphrey (Courtesy of Photofest), Hugo Black (Photo courtesy of Getty Images), Ilene Graff (Courtesy of Photofest), Imelda Marcos (Courtesy of Photofest), Ingrid Bergman (The Kobal Collection), Ira Gershwin (Courtesy of Photofest), Iris Murdoch (Courtesy of Photofest), Isaac Newton (Photo courtesy of Getty Images), Isabella Rosselini (The Kobal Collection), Ivana Trump (Courtesy of Photofest), Jack Nicholson (The Kobal Collection/Warner Bros.), Jacqueline Bisset (The Kobal Collection), James Dean (The Kobal Collection), Janet Jackson (Courtesy of Photofest), Janis Joplin (Courtesy of Photofest), Jared Leto (The Kobal Collection/Paramount/Moseley, Melissa), Jason Priestley (The Kobal Collection/Spelling), Javier Perez de Cuellar (Courtesy of Photofest), Jay Leno (The Kobal Collection / Costa, Tony), Jeff Goldblum (The Kobal Collection/Bel-Air Ent/Lord-Weaver/Markfield, Alan), Jennifer Aniston (The Kobal Collection/20th Century Fox/Laurence Mark/Wetcher, Barry), Jeremy Irons (The Kobal Collection/Pressman/Shochiku Fuji/Sovereign), Jerry Seinfeld (The Kobal Collection), Jesse Jackson (Photo courtesy of Getty Images), Jessica Lange (The Kobal Collection), John F. Kennedy, Jr. (Courtesy of Photofest), Jodie Foster (The Kobal Collection/Columbia/Morton, Merrick), Johnny Depp (The Kobal Collection), Jonathan Winters (The Kobal

Collection), Josephine Baker (Courtesy of Photofest), Josh Hartnett (The Kobal Collection/20th Century Fox/Fox 2000 Pics/Emerson, Sam), Julia Roberts (The Kobal Collection/20th Century Fox), Julianne Moore (The Kobal Collection/Scott Rudin Productions/Coote, Clive), Juliette Lewis (The Kobal Collection/Blum Israel/HBO/Karuna Dream/Riley, Larry), Justin Timberlake (Courtesy of Photofest), Karen Carpenter (Courtesy of Photofest) , Karl Marx (Photo courtesy of Getty Images), Kate Hepburn (The Kobal Collection/Coburn, Bob), Kathleen Turner (The Kobal Collection/20th Century Fox), Kelsey Grammer (The Kobal Collection/NBC-TV), Ken Starr (Photo courtesy of Getty Images), Kennedy (Jim Smeal/WireImage.com), Kevin Bacon (The Kobal Collection/Turman-Foster), Kim Basinger (The Kobal Collection), Kimberley Locke (Jeffrey Mayer/ WireImage.com), Kiri te Kanawa (Photo courtesy of Getty Images), Kirk Douglas (The Kobal Collection/MGM), Kobe Bryant (Pool Photographer/WireImage.com), Kris Kristofferson (The Kobal Collection), Kristen Scott Thomas (The Kobal Collection/Tiger Moth/Miramax/Bray, Phil), Lara Flynn Boyle (The Kobal Collection/Wong, Roger), Latoya Jackson (Gregg DeGuire/WireImage.com), Lauren Bacall (The Kobal Collection), Leah Remini (Courtesy of Photofest), LeAnn Rimes (Photo courtesy of Getty Images), Leonardo DiCaprio (The Kobal Collection/20th Century Fox/Paramount), Lewis Carrol (Courtesy of Photofest), Lex Barker (Photo courtesy of Getty Images), Libby Larsen (Photo by Ann Marsden), Linda Hamilton (The Kobal Collection), Lionel Richie (Courtesy of Photofest), Liv Tyler (The Kobal Collection/Touchstone/Masi, Frank), Liza Minelli (The Kobal Collection/Warner Bros), Lloyd Bridges (The Kobal Collection / Costa, Tony), Loretta Lynn (Courtesy of Photofest), Louis Armstrong (The Kobal Collection), Lucille Ball (The Kobal Collection), Luke Perry (The Kobal Collection/Spellling), Luther Vandross (Courtesy of Photofest), Lyle Lovett (Courtesy of Photofest), Lynette Jennings (Courtesy of Photofest), Mabel Normand (Courtesy of Photofest), Macy Gray (The Kobal Collection), Madeline Albright (Courtesy of Photofest), Mae West (The Kobal Collection), Margaret Thatcher (Courtesy of Photofest), Mariah Carey (Courtesy of Photofest), Marilyn Monroe (The Kobal Collection), Marion Ross (The Kobal Collection), Marisa Tomei (The Kobal Collection/MGM), Marjorie Tallchief (Photo courtesy of Getty Images), Mark Hamill (The Kobal Collection/LucasFilm/20th Century Fox), Marshall McLuhan (Courtesy of Photofest), Martina Navratilova (Courtesy of Photofest), Marvin Gaye (Courtesy of Photofest), Matthew Broderick (The Kobal Collection/20th Century Fox), Matt Damon (The Kobal Collection/Paramount/Caruso, Phillip), Maude Adams (Courtesy of Photofest), Max von Sydow (The Kobal Collection/MGM/UA), Meg Ryan (The Kobal Collection/Warner Bros/Hamill, Brian), Mel Gibson (The Kobal Collection/Touchstone/Perry, Nigel), Melanie Griffith (The Kobal Collection), Melissa Etheridge (Courtesy of Photofest), Meryl Streep (The Kobal Collection/Columbia), Michael Jordan (Courtesy of Photofest), Mickey Rourke (The Kobal Collection/MGM/UA), Millard Fillmore (Photo courtesy of Getty Images), Mindy Sterling (Courtesy of Photofest), Minnie Driver (The Kobal Collection/Buena Vista/Touchstone Pictures), Miriam Makeba (Courtesy of Photofest), Mother Teresa (Courtesy of Photofest), Muhammad Ali (The Kobal Collection), Nadia Comaneci (Courtesy of Photofest), Naomi Campbell (The Kobal Collection/40 Acres & a Mule/20th Century Fox), Nastassja Kinski (The Kobal Collection/Universal/Zenk, James), Natalie Portman (The Kobal Collection / Fox 2000 Pics / Sebastian, Lorey), Nathan Lane (Courtesy of Photofest), Neil Armstrong (Courtesy of Photofest), Neve Campbell (The Kobal Collection/Warner Bros/Village Roadshow/Little, Blake), Newt Gingrich (Courtesy of Photofest), Nia Vardalos (The Kobal Collection/Universal/Schroter, Eike), Nick Nolte (The Kobal Collection), Nina Simone (Courtesy of Photofest), Norman Schwarzkopf (Courtesy of Photofest), Odette Hallowes (Photo courtesy of Getty Images), Olga Korbut (Courtesy of Photofest), Oliver Stone (The Kobal Collection/Universal), Omar Sharif (The Kobal Collection/MGM), Orville Wright (Courtesy of Photofest), Oscar Wilde (Photo courtesy of Getty Images), Owen Hart (Courtesy of Photofest), Pam Dawber (The Kobal Collection), Parker Posey (The Kobal Collection/Warner Bros/Hamill, Brian), Pat Boone (The Kobal Collection), Paul Newman (The Kobal Collection), Pearl Bailey (The Kobal Collection), Pedro Almodovar (The Kobal Collection/Fefer, Stephane), Peggy Fleming (Courtesy of Photofest), Penny Marshall (The Kobal Collection/Paramount Television), Peter Jennings (The Kobal Collection/Edwards, Charlene), Pierre Curie (Photo courtesy of Getty Images), Prince Philip (Courtesy of Photofest), Priscilla Presley (The Kobal Collection/Paramount/Phillips, Ron), Quentin Tarantino (The Kobal Collection/Colubia/Torres, Rico), Ralph Fiennes (The Kobal Collection/Hollywood/Wiildwood/Baltimore), Randy Quaid (Courtesy of Photofest), Raul Julia (Courtesy of Photofest), Rebecca De Mornay (The Kobal Collection/Tri-Star/Tolot, Alberto), Reggie Jackson (Photo courtesy of Getty Images), Renee Zellweger (The Kobal Collection/Universal/Reed, Eli), Rex Harrison (The Kobal Collection), Richard Gere (The Kobal Collection/Paramount/Wynne, Luke), Ricky Martin (Courtesy of Photofest), Rita Hayworth (The Kobal Collection/Columbia/Coburn, Bob), Rob Lowe (The Kobal Collection), Robert Downey Jr. (The Kobal Collection/20th Century Fox/Stambler, Wayne), Rod Stewart (Courtesy of Photofest), Roman Polanski (The Kobal Collection), Roseanne Barr (The Kobal Collection), Rosemary Clooney (The Kobal Collection), Rosie O'Donnell (The Kobal Collection/NBC-TV/Matthews, Mary E), Roy Rogers (Courtesy of Photofest), Ruben Studdard (Courtesy of Photofest), Rupert Everett (The Kobal Collection/Tri-Star), Russell Crowe (The Kobal Collection/Dreamworks/Universal/Buitendijk, Jaap), Ruth Bader Ginsburg (Courtesy of Photofest), Sally Field (The Kobal Collection/Warner Bros TV/Amblin TV), Salvador Dali (The Kobal Collection/Selznick/United Artists), Samuel L. Jackson (Courtesy of Photofest), Sarah Jessica Parker (The Kobal Collection/Darren Starr Productions/Blankenhorn, Craig), Scott Joplin (Photo courtesy of Getty Images), Sean Penn (The Kobal Collection/Crosslight/MDP Worldwide), Sebastian Coe (Photo courtesy of Getty Images), Shannon Doherty (The Kobal Collection/Spelling/Ockenfels, Frank), Shelley Winters (The Kobal Collection), Shirley Maclaine (The Kobal Collection), Sidney Poitier (The Kobal Collection), Simon Cowell (Courtesy of Photofest), Sophie Tucker (Courtesy of Photofest), Stacy Keach (The Kobal Collection), Stanley Kubrick (The Kobal Collection), Stella Stephens (The Kobal Collection/Paramount), Stephen Hawking (The Kobal Collection/Triton), Steve McQueen (The Kobal Collection), Stirling Moss (Ferdaus Shamim/WireImage.com), Sue Hawk (Mychal Watts/WireImage.com), Summer Phoenix (Photo courtesy of Getty Images), Susan B. Anthony (Courtesy of Photofest), Suzanne Somers (The Kobal Collection), Tabitha King (Photo courtesy of Getty Images), Talia Shire (The Kobal Collection/Paramount), Tamra Davis (Courtesy of Photofest), Teddy Kennedy (Courtesy of Photofest), Tess Harper (Courtesy of Photofest), Theodore Roosevelt (Photo courtesy of Getty Images), Tiffany Darwish (Kathryn Indiek/WireImage.com), Timothy Leary (Courtesy of Photofest), Tina Turner (The Kobal Collection/Walt Disney Pictures/Mc Claren, Richard), Tom Cruise (The Kobal Collection/Coumbia Tri Star), Tori Spelling (The Kobal Collection/Spelling), Travis Tritt (Courtesy of Photofest), Trisha Yearwood (Courtesy of Photofest), Ty Cobb (Courtesy of Photofest), Tyrone Power (The Kobal Collection), Ursula Andress (The Kobal Collection/Hammer), Valerie Bertinelli (The Kobal Collection), Van Morrison (Photo courtesy of Getty Images), Vanessa Williams (The Kobal Collection/Mandalay Ent/Rosenthal, Zade), Veronica Lake (The Kobal Collection/Richee, E.R.), Vicki Lawrence (The Kobal Collection/Punkin/Whacko Inc), Violet Kray (Photo courtesy of Getty Images), Vivien Leigh (The Kobal Collection), Walt Disney (The Kobal Collection/Walt Disney), Wesley Snipes (The Kobal Collection/20th Century Fox), Will Smith (The Kobal Collection/20th Century Fox/Barius, Claudette), Winona Rider (The Kobal Collection/Columbia Tristar/Tenner, Suzanne), Woodrow Wilson (Courtesy of Photofest), Xaviera Hollander (Courtesy of Photofest), Yasmine Bleeth (The Kobal Collection/Baywatch Co/Tower 12 Prods), Yoko Ono (Courtesy of Photofest), Yvonne DeCarlo (The Kobal Collection/CBS/MCA/Universal), Zachary Taylor (Photo courtesy of Getty Images), Zola Budd (Photo courtesy of Getty Images)